GOALS	SUPPORT IN *REAL WRITING*	SUPPORT IN STUDENT ANCILLARIES	SUPPORT IN INSTRUCTOR ANCILLARIES
Reading closely and critically	■ "Reading Basics" in Chapter 1 (with advice on reading in college and more) ■ Critical reading questions with model readings in Part Two and at the end of *Real Writing with Readings* ■ Appendix B, "Building Your Vocabulary"	■ *Real Writing* companion Web site: Additional model readings, annotated for important features (**bedfordstmartins .com/realwriting**)	■ *Instructor's Annotated Edition:* Tips for teaching with the selections in *Real Writing with Readings*
Thinking critically	■ Critical reading questions with model readings in Part Two and at the end of *Real Writing with Readings* ■ Checklists encouraging students to think critically about their own writing and writing process	■ Quick reference card: Checklist for writing and editing	■ *Instructor's Annotated Edition:* Tips for encouraging critical thinking and class discussion ■ *Additional Resources:* Reproducible writing checklists for students ■ *Practical Suggestions:* Advice on integrating critical thinking into the course
Preparing for — and passing — tests	■ Advice on reading tests in Chapter 1 ■ Practice tests at the end of chapters and parts ■ Appendix A, "Succeeding on Tests"	■ *Real Writing* companion Web site: Grammar exercises, with instant scoring and feedback advice (**bedfordstmartins.com/ realwriting**) ■ Supplemental Exercises: Editing exercises in print ■ *Exercise Central to Go* CD-ROM: Editing exercises on CD. For even more exercises, visit **bedfordstmartins.com/ exercisecentral.** ■ *From Practice to Mastery:* Study guide for the Florida Basic Skills Exit Test	■ *Additional Resources:* General diagnostic tests as well as tests on specific grammar topics ■ *Practical Suggestions:* Advice on assessing student writing, with model rubrics, advice on marking difficult papers, and more ■ *Testing Tool Kit* CD-ROM: Tests on every writing and grammar issue covered in *Real Writing*
Addressing issues of ESL and Generation 1.5 students, and speakers of nonstandard English	■ "Language notes" throughout the grammar instruction ■ Thorough ESL chapter, with special attention to verb usage	■ *Real Writing* companion Web site: ESL exercises with instant scoring and feedback (**bedfordstmartins.com/ realwriting**) ■ *The Bedford/St. Martin's ESL Workbook:* Special instruction and abundant exercises ■ *Exercise Central to Go* CD-ROM: Includes ESL exercises on CD. For even more exercises, visit **bedfordstmartins .com/exercisecentral.**	■ *Instructor's Annotated Edition:* Tips for teaching ESL students ■ *Practical Suggestions:* Advice on teaching ESL students and speakers of nonstandard English ■ *Testing Tool Kit* CD-ROM: Test items on ESL issues

To order any of the ancillaries for *Real Writing,* please contact your Bedford/St. Martin's sales representative, e-mail sales support at **sales_support@bfwpub.com**, or visit our Web site at **bedfordstmartins.com**.

Real Writing

with Readings

*Paragraphs and Essays for College,
Work, and Everyday Life*

Susan Anker

Bedford / St. Martin's   *Boston* ◆ *New York*

For Bedford/St. Martin's

Senior Developmental Editor: Beth Castrodale
Developmental Editor: Karin Halbert
Production Editor: Kerri A. Cardone
Senior Production Supervisor: Joe Ford
Senior Marketing Manager: Rachel Falk
Copyeditor: Lisa Wehrle
Text Design: Claire Seng-Niemoeller
Cover Design: Donna Lee Dennison, Billy Boardman
Composition: Stratford Publishing Services, Inc.
Printing and Binding: R. R. Donnelley & Sons Company

President: Joan E. Feinberg
Editorial Director: Denise B. Wydra
Editor in Chief: Karen S. Henry
Director of Marketing: Karen Melton Soeltz
Director of Editing, Design, and Production: Marcia Cohen
Managing Editor: Elizabeth M. Schaaf

Library of Congress Control Number: 2006926012

Manufactured in the United States of America.

1   0   9   8

f   e   d   c   b

For information, write: Bedford/St. Martin's, 75 Arlington Street, Boston, MA 02116
(617-399-4000)

ISBN-10: 0–312–45637–9 (*Real Writing*)   ISBN-13: 978–0–312–45637–5
        0–312–44883–X (*Real Writing with Readings*)   978–0–312–44883–7
        0–312–43162–7 (Instructor's Annotated Edition)   978–0–312–43162–4

Acknowledgments

Richard Campbell, Christopher R. Martin, Bettina Fabos. Excerpt from "Sounds and Images" in Chapter 3, pp. 98–99, from *Media and Culture: An Introduction to Mass Communication,* Fifth Edition. Copyright © 2006 by Bedford/St. Martin's. Reprinted with permission of Bedford/St. Martin's.

Janice E. Castro with Dan Cook and Cristina Garcia. "Spanglish." From *Time,* July 11, 1988. Copyright © 1988 Time, Inc. Reprinted with permission.

Linda Chavez. "Everything Isn't Racial Profiling." Reprinted by permission of Linda Chavez and Creator's Syndicate, Inc.

Patrick Conroy. "Chili Cheese Dogs, My Father, and Me." From *Parade* magazine, November 14, 2004, pp. 4–5. Copyright © 2004 Pat Conroy. Reprinted by permission of the author. All rights reserved.

Damon Darlin. "Some Ways to Prepare for the Absolute Worst." From the *New York Times,* September 10, 2005. Copyright © 2005 the New York Times Company. Reprinted by permission.

Firoozeh Dumas. "Bernice." From *Funny in Farsi: A Memoir of Growing Up Iranian in America.* Copyright © 2003 Villard/Random House. Reprinted by permission.

Daryn Eller. "Move Your Body, Free Your Mind." From *Health* magazine, May 2002. Copyright © 2002. Reprinted by permission of the author.

Stephanie Ericsson. "The Ways We Lie." Originally published by the *Utne Reader.* Copyright © 1992 by Stephanie Ericsson. Reprinted by the permission of Dunham Literary as agents for the author. Also published in *Companion into Dawn: Inner Dialogues on Loving* by Stephanie Ericsson. Published by HarperCollins, 1997.

Gabrielle Glaser. "Scents." From *Health* magazine, July–August 2001. Copyright © 2001. Reprinted by permission of Writers' Representatives, Inc. on behalf of the author.

Carol Glazer. "Obesity Is Not Just about Food." From the *Boston Globe,* December 5, 2005. Reprinted by permission of the author.

Joey Green. "Beauty and the Beef." Copyright © 1987 by Joey Green. Reprinted by permission of the author.

Dianne Hales. "Why Are We So Angry?" From *Parade* magazine, September 2, 2001. Copyright © 2001 Dianne Hales. Reprinted by permission of *Parade* magazine and the author.

Adora Houghton. "My Indian." Originally published in *Multitude: Cross-Cultural Readings for Writers* (McGraw-Hill, Inc.), edited by Chitra Banerjee Divakaruni. Copyright © 1993 by Adora Houghton. Reprinted by permission of the author.

Nancy Huehnergarth. "Sugar High." From the *New York Times,* July 17, 2005, section 14WC, column 1. Copyright © 2005 the New York Times Company. Reprinted by permission.

Barbara Kingsolver. "Creation Stories." From *High Tide in Tucson: Essays from Now or Never* by Barbara Kingsolver. Copyright © 1995 by Barbara Kingsolver. Reprinted by permission of HarperCollins Publishers.

David Myers. Excerpted text from page 347 in *Psychology.* Seventh Edition, by David Myers. Copyright © 2004 by Worth Publishers. Used with permission.

Jeffrey S. Nevid, Spencer A. Rathus, Hannah R. Rubenstein. Excerpted text from pp. 33, 80–81, and 171 in *Health in the New Millennium.* Copyright © 1998 by Worth Publishers. Used with permission.

William Raspberry. "Why Profiling Won't Work." From the *Washington Post,* August 22, 2005, p. A17. Copyright © 2005, the Washington Post Writers Group. Reprinted with permission.

Walter Scanlon. "It's Time I Shed My Ex-Convict Status." From *Newsweek,* February 21, 2000. Copyright © 2000 Newsweek, Inc. Reprinted by permission. All rights reserved.

Preface for Instructors

More than ever, students aren't only students: They are also workers, parents, people with diverse responsibilities for whom "student" is just one of many demanding roles. If what they learn is not directly related to the rest of what they do, it is easily lost among other pressing concerns. When their textbooks fail to make the connection, it is not surprising that writing remains for students something that is done only in college, or even only in the writing class.

The success of *Real Writing,* along with the many endorsements of this approach that I have received from students and instructors, has confirmed the absolute necessity of making this connection between writing and students' lives. It remains the primary goal of each edition of *Real Writing.* In each chapter, students can see people like themselves—students, workers, and parents—who have struggled with writing, who have wondered why it is important, and who are learning that good writing is not a mysterious, divinely inspired gift but a skill that can be learned by any person who is willing to pay attention and practice. Throughout *Real Writing,* photos, quotes, profiles, and advice from real students help to emphasize both the hard work involved in becoming a competent writer and the absolute necessity of learning this skill.

Features

Many of the features of the third edition of *Real Writing* have been carried over to the fourth edition, with significant revisions based on suggestions from a large number of instructors. Several new features have also been added as a result of my observations of students using *Real Writing* in class, discussions with both faculty and students who use the text, and other extensive comments from users and reviewers (these new features are described in the box on pp. viii–ix).

Provides Clear, Detailed Writing Guidance with a Focus on the Basics

Real Writing teaches writing strategies as practical, essential processes. It first takes students step-by-step—with plenty of examples and models—through every stage of the writing process. It then shows them how to write effective paragraphs and essays using all the major modes of development. The modes coverage focuses on the four basic elements students need to understand about a rhetorical strategy before they can use it successfully in academic, professional, or personal settings. Chapters on writing summaries, reports, and the research essay provide concrete strategies for succeeding in these writing situations. Additionally, step-by-step writing checklists walk students through the process of writing each type of essay. Throughout, the instruction is infused with appealing real-world examples and writing assignments.

Motivates Students As No Other Text Does

That's quite a claim, but that's what users — professors and students alike — tell us. They point to the following features:

The Real-World Context

Throughout, *Real Writing* shows students how they will actually use writing and editing skills in other college courses, in their work, and in their everyday lives. All the assignment topics, exercises, and models in the book are drawn from real-world situations that are relevant to students.

Voices of Current and Former Students

In Chapter 1, students who had recently completed their first college writing course offer candid, practical advice on how to succeed in the course and in college. Additionally, all Part Two chapters (covering the methods of development) include Profile of Success — interviews with, and photos of, former students who have overcome significant challenges to succeed in the real world. These profiles show students that success is within reach, but more important, they demonstrate very explicitly how writing is used in the workplace. For example, in the Profile of Success in Chapter 9 (Narration), a nurse describes how writing good narration is important in her job. Her comments are followed by an actual narrative that she wrote on the job.

The "Can Do" Attitude

Students who have used and reviewed *Real Writing* have responded enthusiastically to the "can do" tone and to the examples and activities that are relevant to their lives. For the first time, many students have told us, they are motivated to read and use a textbook. One of the many features they single out is the "You Know This" boxes that begin many of the chapters. With concrete, specific examples, these boxes link the content of the chapter to activities that students are already familiar with.

Makes Grammar Less Overwhelming

Real Writing gives special emphasis to the four most serious errors. In a survey conducted for the first edition, instructors throughout the country identified four errors as the most serious: **fragments, run-ons and comma splices, subject-verb agreement problems**, and **verb-tense problems**. These errors are each covered in a separate chapter in Part Four, which opens the "Editing" section of the book. By concentrating on a limited number of major sentence problems as they begin to edit their papers, students feel they have a shot at mastering these problems and are more likely to remember strategies for avoiding them. Other important grammar concepts and problems are covered thoroughly in Part Five, "Other Grammar Concerns," after students have gained confidence by focusing on the most troublesome errors. Throughout the grammar coverage, Find-and-Edit charts and review charts help students find and correct grammar errors in their own work.

Real Writing gives students **practice, practice**, and **more practice** with grammar and editing. Each exercise is on a high-interest topic with language that is neither too simple nor too difficult for students. Every chapter in Parts Four through Seven ends with paragraph-editing practices and new review tests. Also new are part tests. (See p. vi for a fuller description.)

Is Easy for Students to Use

The consistent, three-part format of most chapters (either Understand/Practice/Write, or Understand/Practice/Edit) helps students successfully navigate the information. Most chapters end with a chapter review that can be used as a review quiz. In addition, chapters in the Editing section end with flowcharts that help students, especially visual learners, find and correct errors.

An Introduction for Students helps students find information they need and introduces the important features of the book.

Provides a Reader that Connects Reading and Writing

The "Readings" section at the end of the longer edition of *Real Writing* is a collection of twenty-four high-interest selections in the areas of college, work, and everyday life, all of which have been reviewed and approved by students. The selections are organized according to rhetorical mode, which parallels the arrangement of the writing chapters, making it easier for students to see the connection to their own writing and for instructors to link the readings to the writing instruction.

New to This Edition

- **More support for active, critical reading throughout the book.** New "Reading Basics" coverage in Chapter 1 helps students read and understand essential course materials, such as textbooks and test directions, and apply critical-thinking strategies to a variety of documents in college, work, and everyday life. The model essays in the assignment chapters are accompanied by new questions that help students read more closely and critically, and by new writing assignments that ask students to apply the insights from their reading in writing.

- **A stronger collection of readings,** offering better preparation for college composition. First, model selections from textbooks have been added to the assignment chapters to help prepare students for college reading. Also, a thoroughly updated reader ("Readings for Writers" in *Real Writing with Readings*) covers engaging new topics such as Spanglish, racial profiling, and the "supersizing" of all kinds of products to accommodate overweight Americans. In all, two-thirds of the selections are new. Finally, a new casebook on the theme of cultural stereotypes concludes the reader. Writing assignments in the casebook encourage students to think critically while drawing on multiple selections — an important skill for college.

- **A stronger emphasis on how to organize writing.** In addition to covering how to develop and support a main idea, each assignment chapter includes a new section on how to organize paragraphs and essays — one of the most pressing problems for students. Graphic organizers in these sections help students visualize how to structure effective writing.

- **More to help students understand and use the conventions of academic English,** emphasizing the importance of using standard, formal English in college and at work. New exercises (in the book and online) give students practice with translating informal writing (like that in e-mails and text messages) into writing that is appropriate for addressing instructors, employers, and other formal audiences. Also, new "Language notes" throughout the grammar coverage highlight issues that can be especially challenging for ESL students, Generation 1.5 students, and other speakers of nonstandard English. Additionally, a completely revised ESL chapter, written with the help of ESL experts, gives advice, examples, and practices in areas — like verb usage — that are particularly difficult for nonnative speakers and not fully covered in other books.

- **New help with preparing for tests.** New tests at the end of each grammar chapter and part help instructors check students' knowledge of grammar concepts. These tests include questions like those on major standardized tests, such as the Florida College Basic Skills Exit Test and the Texas Higher Education As-

sessment (THEA), helping students to prepare for such exams.
Also, a new appendix of test-taking advice and strategies provides
further test preparation.

- **Better vocabulary support.** Expanded glossaries and a new
  appendix on building vocabulary skills help students become
  better readers—and writers.

Ancillaries

Print Resources for Instructors and Students

- **Instructor's Annotated Edition of *Real Writing*, Fourth Edition.**
  Gives practical page-by-page advice on teaching with *Real Writing* and
  contains answers to all exercises and suggestions for using the other
  ancillaries.

- **Practical Suggestions for Teaching *Real Writing*, Fourth Edition.** An ideal resource for teachers new to teaching or to *Real Writing*.
  Contains information and advice on bringing the real world into the
  classroom, using computers, teaching ESL students, and more. Includes new advice for responding to the most difficult student papers.

- **Additional Resources to Accompany *Real Writing*, Fourth Edition.** Supplements the instructional materials in the text with a variety
  of transparency masters, planning forms, handouts, and other reproducibles for classroom use.

- ***Teaching Developmental Writing: Background Readings*, Third
  Edition.** This professional resource, edited by Susan Naomi Bernstein, co-chair of the Conference on Basic Writing, offers essays on
  topics of interest to basic writing instructors, along with editorial apparatus pointing out practical applications for the classroom.

- **Supplemental Exercises to Accompany *Real Writing*, Fourth
  Edition.** Supplements the exercises in the editing and research chapters of *Real Writing* with more than one hundred additional practices.

- **Quick Reference Card on writing, editing, word processing, and
  Internet research.** Students can prop this handy three-panel card up
  next to their computers for easy reference while they're writing and researching.

- ***The Bedford/St. Martin's ESL Workbook.*** Covers grammar issues
  for multilingual students with varying English-language skills and cultural backgrounds. Instructional introductions are followed by illustrative examples and exercises.

- ***From Practice to Mastery*** (study guide for the Florida Basic Skills
  Exit Tests in reading and writing). Gives students all the resources they
  need to practice for—and pass—the Florida tests in reading and
  writing. It includes pre- and post-tests, abundant practices, and clear instruction in all the skills covered on the exams.

New Media Resources for Instructors and Students

- *Make-a-Paragraph Kit.* This fun, interactive CD-ROM coming Spring 2007, includes an "Extreme Paragraph Makeover" animation teaching students about paragraph development as well as exercises that get students to build their own paragraphs. It also includes a set of audiovisual tutorials on the four most serious errors and additional grammar practices.

- **Book Companion Site at bedfordstmartins.com/realwriting.** Provides additional resources for instructors as well as resources that help students with writing and grammar. New practices on Exercise Central for *Real Writing* help students learn to translate informal language to formal English.

- **bedfordstmartins.com/susananker.** Includes a videotaped message from Susan Anker that tells the story of her series, tools for finding the right Anker text, helpful instructional resources, and more.

- *Exercise Central to Go: Writing and Grammar Practices for Basic Writers.* This student CD-ROM includes hundreds of practice items to help basic writers build their writing and editing skills and provides audio instructions and instant feedback. Drawn from the popular online Exercise Central resource, the practices have been extensively class-tested. No Internet connection is necessary.

- *Testing Tool Kit: A Writing and Grammar Test Bank.* This CD-ROM allows instructors to create secure, customized tests and quizzes from nearly two thousand questions covering forty-seven topics. It also includes ten pre-built diagnostic tests. Charts on the inside front covers of the *Practical Suggestions* and *Additional Resources* print ancillaries correlate topics from *Testing Tool Kit* with chapters in *Real Writing* so that you can use the CD to support your teaching with the text.

- *Re: Writing* at **bedfordstmartins.com/rewriting.** Collects the most popular and widely used free online resources from Bedford/ St. Martin's in an easy-to-navigate Web site. Offerings include writing and grammar exercises, research and documentation advice, model documents, and instructor resources.

- **Course management software content for *Real Writing.*** Content includes tests and quizzes from the *Testing Tool Kit* CD-ROM; writing, grammar, and research resources from Bedford/St. Martin's popular *Re: Writing* Web site; and topics for online chats and discussion boards.

- *Comment.* This Web-based peer-review tool allows instructors to respond to student writing quickly and easily. Students can also use *Comment* to respond to each other's work. For more information, visit **comment.bedfordstmartins.com.**

Ordering Information

To order any of the ancillaries for *Real Writing,* please contact your Bedford/St. Martin's sales representative, e-mail sales support at **sales _support@bfwpub.com**, or visit our Web site at **bedfordstmartins .com**.

Use these ISBNs when ordering the following supplements packaged with your students' books:

Real Writing with Readings and

- *Supplemental Exercises:* ISBN-10: 0–312–46102–X / ISBN-13: 978–0–312–46102–7
- Quick Reference Card: ISBN-10: 0–312–46101–1 / ISBN-13: 978–0–312–46101–0
- *Exercise Central to Go* CD-ROM: ISBN-10: 0–312–46261–1 / ISBN-13: 978–0–312–46261–1
- *Make-a-Paragraph Kit* CD-ROM: ISBN-10: 0–312–46105–4 / ISBN-13: 978–0–312–46105–8
- *From Practice to Mastery* (for Florida): ISBN-10: 0–312–46104–6 / ISBN-13: 978–0–312–46104–1
- *The Bedford/St. Martin's ESL Workbook:* ISBN-10: 0–312–46103–8 / ISBN-13: 978–0–312–46103–4

Real Writing and

- *Supplemental Exercises:* ISBN-10: 0–312–46125–9 / ISBN-13: 978–0–312–46125–6
- Quick Reference Card: ISBN-10: 0–312–46124–0 / ISBN-13: 978–0–312–46124–9
- *Exercise Central to Go* CD-ROM: ISBN-10: 0–312–46262–X / ISBN-13: 978–0–312–46262–8
- *Make-a-Paragraph Kit* CD-ROM: ISBN-10: 0–312–46128–3 / ISBN-13: 978–0–312–46128–7
- *From Practice to Mastery* (for Florida): ISBN-10: 0–312–46127–5 / ISBN-13: 978–0–312–46127–0
- *The Bedford/St. Martin's ESL Workbook:* ISBN-10: 0–312–46126–7 / ISBN-13: 978–0–312–46126–3

Acknowledgments

While my name is the only one that appears on the cover of this book, this revision of *Real Writing* was anything but a solo enterprise: The supporting cast was both immense and instrumental in conceiving and implementing new ideas, in refining existing ones, and in making the book happen. To those whose names follow, I am deeply grateful.

Editorial Advisory Board

Instructors on our Editorial Advisory Board have graciously offered insigh.-
ful suggestions that are reflected on each page of *Real Writing*. This is their
book as much as mine, and I am beholden to each of them. Members of the
Editorial Advisory Board, several of whom have special expertise in teaching ESL and Generation 1.5 students, are Erick J. Alburez, SUNY Farm-
ingdale; Karen Eisenhauer, Brevard Community College; Sally Gearhart,
Santa Rosa Junior College; Shelly Hedstrom, Palm Beach Community College; Catherine Hutcheson, Troy University; Luli Lopez-Merino, Palm
Beach Community College; Timothy L. Roach, St. Louis Community College, Forest Park; Sandra Roy, San Antonio College; Valerie Russell, Valen-
cia Community College; Tamara Shue, Georgia Perimeter College; William
Shute, San Antonio College; and Rose Yesu, Massasoit Community College.

I want to single out those advisers who have been with me through three
revisions because our lives have become intertwined: Karen Eisenhauer,
Tim Roach, Tamara Shue, and Bill Shute. I have consulted with Tamara
from the start of the first edition of *Real Writing*, and I started consulting
with Bill Shute while the first edition was just a twinkle in our eyes.

I also want to thank Eddye Gallagher, whose work remains an important
part of *Practical Suggestions*.

Student Advisory Board

Although we always have students review certain parts of *Real Writing*, we
wanted to work with some conscientious students who had just taken the
course using the book. We found just such students through recommendations from trusted editorial advisers and reviewers. They are Mark Balderas,
San Antonio College; Michelle Bassett, Quinsigamond Community College; Michelle Bostick, Brevard Community College; Nicole Day, Brevard
Community College; and Katilya Labidou, Brevard Community College.

Beyond their behind-the-scenes suggestions about things that worked or
didn't work in *Real Writing*, we wanted these students to speak—student-to-
student—to those who are just beginning the course. The result is the
"Course Basics" section of Chapter 1, which includes candid, practical advice
from the students about how to succeed in this and other college courses.

I'm honored to have been able to work with these student advisers, who
gave us lots of time, thought, and careful suggestions.

Other Student Contributors

Aside from the student advisers, many current and former students have
contributed to this book. The nine former students featured in the "Profiles
of Success" have been an inspiration, and I have been honored to talk with
them. I thank them all for their hard work, their writing, and their well-
deserved successes. The "Profiles of Success" are Rosalind Baker (Human
Services Director); Mary LaCue Booker (Singer and Actress); Celia Hyde
(Police Chief); Kelly Layland (Nurse); Brad Leibov (Company President);

Rocío Murillo (Teacher); Sandro Polo (Architect); Walter Scanlon (Consultant); and Alan Whitehead (Builder).

Other current and former students contributed model paragraphs and essays to the book, or provided quotes and other helpful suggestions: Jesse Calsado, Jeanette Castro, Sophie Fleck, Dale Hill, Joyce Kenneally, Carol Parola, Marcus Shanks, and Cathy Vittoria.

Reviewers

In addition to the Editorial Advisory Board, a large group of reviewers helped to develop the fourth edition of *Real Writing*. I would like to thank Tricia Amiel-Pugh, Indian River Community College; NaKeya Bazemore, Georgia Perimeter College, Dunwoody Campus; Kay Blue, Owens Community College; Sandra Chumchal, Blinn College; Lillian Dailey, Cuyahoga Community College; Kristen di Gennaro, Pace University; Heather Elko, Brevard Community College; Merrill Glustrom, Front Range Community College; Andrea Hammock, Mt. San Jacinto Community College; Gail Hardaway, Mesa Community College; Levia Hayes, Community College of Southern Nevada; Marion Hernandez, Bunker Hill and MassBay community colleges; Peggy Hopper, Walters State Community College; Lorena Horton, San Jacinto College North; Jennifer Jett, Bakersfield College; Charles N. Johnson, Tyler Junior College; Edwina Jordan, Illinois Central College; Patsy Krech, University of Memphis; Sharon Ladin, Minneapolis Community and Technical College; Catherine Lally, Brevard Community College; Nickie Medina, Aims Community College; Theresa Mohamed, Onondaga Community College; Paula L. Parks, Bakersfield College; Jarrod E. Patterson, Alabama A&M University; Lonnie Pidel, Bunker Hill Community College; Sarah Risdahl, Walters State Community College; Linda Robinett, Oklahoma City Community College; Karen Roth, formerly of Garden City Community College; Nancy Johnson Squair, Sheridan College, Gillette Campus; Mary Srougi, Owens Community College; Cheli J. Turner, Greenville Technical College; and Margaret Waguespack, Amarillo College.

The following instructors reviewed previous editions: Althea Allard, Community College of Rhode Island; Marla Allegre, Allan Hancock College; Norman Asmar, Miami-Dade College; Sandra Barnhill, South Plains Community College; Kathleen Beauchene, Community College of Rhode Island; Andre Belyi, Brevard Community College; William Boggs, Slippery Rock University; Denise Bostic, Nicholls State University; Kathleen Briton, Florence-Darlington Technical College; Mike Chu, College of DuPage; Joseph Colavito, Northwestern State University; Dawn Copeland, Motlow State Community College; Judy D. Covington, Trident Technical College; Norma Cruz-Gonzales, San Antonio College; Linda Elaine, College of DuPage; Steven A. Garcia, Riverside Community College; Julie Hanwell, Tri-County Community College; Sarah Harris, Southern Mississippi Planning and Development District; Robin Havenick, Linn-Benton Community College; Earl Hawley, College of DuPage; Deanna S. Highe, Central Piedmont Community College; Claudia House, Nashville State Technical Institute; Michael Hricik, Westmoreland County Community College; Gloria Isles, Greenville Technical College; Yvonne Robinson Jones, Southwest Tennessee

Community College; Kevin Kelly, Andover College; Melissa Knous, Angelina College; Carol A. Kontos, University of Maine at Augusta; Reginald F. Lockett, San Jose City College; Susan Lockwood, Chattahoochee Valley Community College; Catherine A. Lutz, Texas A&M University, Kingsville; Patricia Malinowski, Finger Lakes Community College; Eric Meyer, St. Louis Community College-Meramec; Dan Moody, Southwestern College; Mercy Moore, Broward Community College; Heather L. Morgan, Bakersfield College; Patricia Pallis, Naugatuck Valley Community-Technical College; Diane Payne, University of Arkansas-Monticello; Betty Peterson, Somerset Community College; Verlene Pierre, Southeastern Louisiana University; Diane L. Polcha, Tulsa Community College; Melissa Price, Piedmont Technical College; Dee Pruitt, Florence-Darlington Technical College; Sharon Race, South Plains College; Linda Rollins, Motlow State Community College; David Rollinson, College of Marin; Renee Santos, Piedmont Technical College; Shaheen Sayeed, Moraine Valley Community College; Richard A. Schmitt, Nunez Community College; Ingrid Schreck, Chaffey College; Kimberly Shuckra, Harrisburg Area Community College; William E. Smith, Western Washington University; Lerah A. Spikes, Georgia Perimeter College; Debbie Stallings, Hinds Community College; Geraldine Stiles, Andover College; Sandra A. Torrez, Texas A&M University, Kingsville; James E. Twining, Community College of Rhode Island; Gregory J. Underwood, Pearl River Community College; Paul Vantine, Cameron University; Linda Van Vickle, St. Louis Community College–Meramec; Kenneth R. Vorndran, Pima Community College; Barbara Schwarz Wachal, St. Louis Community College–Forest Park; Susan Waugh, St. Louis Community College, Meramec; and Linda Whisnant, Guilford Technical Community College.

Contributors

Many talented people contributed to this edition of *Real Writing*. Bruce Thaler helped to write grammar exercises, and Mark Gallaher created wonderful pedagogical apparatus for the reader. Sally Gearhart guided the revision of the ESL chapter, synthesizing multiple expert reviews and contributing many of her own valuable suggestions. She also helped with the "Language notes" that appear throughout the book. Adam Moss of DeVry South Florida helped to develop Appendix A on taking tests, and Patti Levine-Brown of Florida Community College, Jacksonville, wrote Appendix B on building vocabulary. Lynette Ledoux helped to create online editing exercises and contributed a valuable section on responding to the most challenging student papers to *Practical Suggestions*. Warren Drabek cleared text permissions under the guidance of Sandy Schechter, and Linda Finigan researched and cleared permission for photographs and other art.

Bedford/St. Martin's

Bedford/St. Martin's richly deserves its reputation as the premier publisher of English texts. It devotes inordinate time, brainpower, money, and plain old blood, sweat, and tears to each of its books. Each project is a messy, collaborative, draining, and finally rewarding effort. Everyone at Bedford/St. Martin's demands much and gives much more.

Karin Halbert, editor, did her usual fine job of helping to find readings that are both engaging and useful models for writing. Christina Gerogiannis, editorial assistant, also helped find readings, and she coordinated extensive review programs, helped with permissions, and oversaw numerous other editorial details. Martha Friedman helped coordinate the art research program. Kerri Cardone ably guided the book through production, and Lisa Wehrle copyedited the manuscript with a keen eye.

The energy and enthusiasm of Rachel Falk, senior marketing manager, never flagged. Others who helped keep me tuned in to the market were Karen Melton Soeltz, director of marketing; Jane Helms, associate director of marketing; Jimmy Fleming, senior humanities specialist; and Ed Tiefenthaler, senior sales representative. Also, David Mogolov, editor, traveled the country, absorbing and communicating ideas and news about emerging trends. Humanities specialist Brian Donnellan's market research and suggestions based on reviews provided plenty of good direction. Many other suggestions from members of the sales force made their way into the book, and I apologize to contributors I haven't formally thanked here.

On the artistic side, Claire Seng-Niemoeller once again fit the diverse pieces of the book's interior design into a unified and lovely whole, while Donna Dennison and Billy Boardman created yet another great cover. Tom Macy and Brian Fraley produced a colorful and informative brochure.

The new media group always amazes me with its knowledge, creativity, and humor. I thank Nick Carbone, Katie Schooling, Tari Fanderclai, and Harriet Wald for their patience, instruction, and ability to produce high-quality technology products. Coleen O'Hanley deserves special thanks for producing the Web site to accompany *Real Writing,* and Daniel Cole also aided in the production process. Cate Kashem oversaw the production of an informative Web site on all of my books, at **<bedfordstmartins.com/susananker>**.

As always, I am grateful to Joan Feinberg, Denise Wydra, and Karen Henry for their expertise, wisdom, and superior insight, as well as their friendship.

Finally, I am truly blessed to work with Beth Castrodale as an editor. She can accomplish more brilliant work in a day than anyone I've ever known: I've accused her of having magical powers that give her forty-eight hours to a single day. Beth and I referred to this past year as "Mission Impossible," and it would have remained impossible without her Herculean powers of prose, thought, and productivity. Thank you, Beth.

My husband, Jim Anker, provides assurance and confidence when I worry that I have too much to do and won't do it well. He reminds me that I am very lucky.

—Susan Anker

Contents

Thematic Table of Contents

Introduction for Students

How to Use This Book

Why Use *Real Writing*?

As the title suggests, *Real Writing: Paragraphs and Essays for College, Work, and Everyday Life* isn't just an academic text. Its purpose is to improve your writing so that you can succeed not only in this course but in other courses, on the job, and in your everyday life. Writing is a skill that you'll use throughout college, but it is also a skill that you will need for most jobs. In fact, employers usually cite good communication skills as the number-one ability they look for in job candidates. Mastering basic writing skills may turn out to be your most significant college achievement.

How will *Real Writing* help? It focuses on the practical: It zeroes in on the most important writing and editing skills you need to succeed. It gives you simple explanations, reality-based assignments, concrete steps for completing tasks, and tips for moving ahead if you get stuck. *Real Writing* isn't removed from your life; it starts where you are and helps you get to where you want to go.

Make sure to read Chapters 1 and 2 carefully. In Chapter 1, students who have completed the writing course you are taking offer practical advice on how to succeed in the course. Both Chapters 1 and 2 give you a quick head start on the basics of reading and writing in college.

How to Find Information in *Real Writing*

There are many ways to find information in this book.

To Find a Chapter or Section

TABLE OF CONTENTS This tool, after the title page of the book, gives you chapter titles and specific sections of each chapter with page numbers. A thematic table of contents after the main table of contents helps you find readings related to particular themes.

INDEX   At the end of *Real Writing* is a complete index that lists the topics covered in the book, in alphabetical order, and indicates what page each topic is on. Using the index will almost always get you to the right place. For example, to find information on how to write a topic sentence, you would look up *topic sentence*. There you would find the page number not only for the section that deals with topic sentences in general but for other sections that cover topic sentences in specific types of writing. The index includes many of the terms you might use to look up a particular concept or topic, so you won't have to look in several places.

To Find Help with Writing or Grammar Problems

CHART OF CORRECTION SYMBOLS   At the back of the book is a chart of the symbols that your instructors may use to indicate writing or grammar problems in your work.

LIST OF USEFUL CHARTS AND QUICK REFERENCES   On the inside of the back cover is a list of charts, checklists, and other quick reference tools that you will find helpful as you write and edit.

To Find the Page You Need

HEADINGS AT THE TOPS OF PAGES   Next to the page number at the top of each page is a heading that will tell you exactly where you are in the book. The first line of the heading is the part title—the name of the part of the book you're in. On each left-hand page under the part title are the chapter number and title. On each right-hand page under the part title is the name of the major section you're in. The following sample, for instance, shows that you are in the part "How to Write Paragraphs and Essays," in Chapter 1, "Course and Reading Basics." Within that chapter, you are in the major section "Reading Basics."

HOW TO WRITE PARAGRAPHS AND ESSAYS	**HOW TO WRITE PARAGRAPHS AND ESSAYS**
12 Chapter 1 • Course and Reading Basics	Reading Basics **13**

XXX   Introduction for Students

How to Use *Real Writing* When You Write

Real Writing is filled with charts, checklists, and other aids to help you complete your writing assignments successfully and become a better writer. Here are descriptions of a few of these aids with samples from the book.

■ **TIP:** If you find that talking about your ideas with someone is a good way to get going, you might want to ask another student to be your regular partner and discuss ideas before beginning any paragraph or essay assignment.

■ **IDEA JOURNAL:** What are your strongest communication skills? What other skills or talents do you have?

MARGINAL NOTES   Throughout the book you will see two kinds of notes in the margins. Tips provide hints on how to do a particular writing task, remind you of information you may have forgotten, refer you to other pages where you can review material, and offer other kinds of advice. Idea journal and learning journal notes suggest topics for you to write about in your journal.

MODELS   Each chapter includes examples that provide good models for writing. For example, there are many models of the various stages of the writing process showing you examples of topic sentences, thesis statements, and support. Also, model paragraphs illustrate the "four basics" of writing various types of paragraphs and essays.

■■
■■   **FOUR BASICS OF GOOD NARRATION**

1.   It reveals something of importance to you (your main point).
2.   It includes all of the major events of the story (primary support).
3.   It brings the story to life with details about the major events (secondary support).
4.   It presents the events in a clear order, usually according to when they happened.

In the following paragraph, each number corresponds to one of the Basics of Good Narration.

   1 Last night, my husband saved my life. We were sitting out on the porch with a couple of friends, enjoying the cool breeze of the evening. **2** While eating a piece of melon for dessert, I laughed at something my friend said, and suddenly the fruit stuck in my windpipe, entirely blocking any air. **3** I tried to swallow hard and dislodge it, but it didn't move. When I tried taking a deep breath, I couldn't get one. **2** Fortunately, my husband, seated across the table from me, saw that something was wrong and asked me if I needed help. Close to panic, I nodded yes. **3** My eyes were filled with tears, and I could hear the blood pounding in my ears. I thought, briefly, *I could die.* **2** My husband ran in behind me,

CHECKLISTS FOR WRITING Each chapter on writing paragraphs and essays has checklists that will help you complete the assignment. These checklists contain specific steps for writing either a paragraph or an essay.

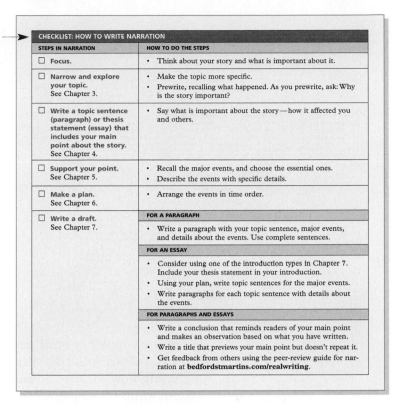

STEPS IN NARRATION	HOW TO DO THE STEPS
☐ Focus.	• Think about your story and what is important about it.
☐ Narrow and explore your topic. See Chapter 3.	• Make the topic more specific. • Prewrite, recalling what happened. As you prewrite, ask: Why is the story important?
☐ Write a topic sentence (paragraph) or thesis statement (essay) that includes your main point about the story. See Chapter 4.	• Say what is important about the story—how it affected you and others.
☐ Support your point. See Chapter 5.	• Recall the major events, and choose the essential ones. • Describe the events with specific details.
☐ Make a plan. See Chapter 6.	• Arrange the events in time order.
☐ Write a draft. See Chapter 7.	**FOR A PARAGRAPH** • Write a paragraph with your topic sentence, major events, and details about the events. Use complete sentences. **FOR AN ESSAY** • Consider using one of the introduction types in Chapter 7. Include your thesis statement in your introduction. • Using your plan, write topic sentences for the major events. • Write paragraphs for each topic sentence with details about the events. **FOR PARAGRAPHS AND ESSAYS** • Write a conclusion that reminds readers of your main point and makes an observation based on what you have written. • Write a title that previews your main point but doesn't repeat it. • Get feedback from others using the peer-review guide for narration at **bedfordstmartins.com/realwriting**.

Checklist heading: **CHECKLIST: HOW TO WRITE NARRATION**

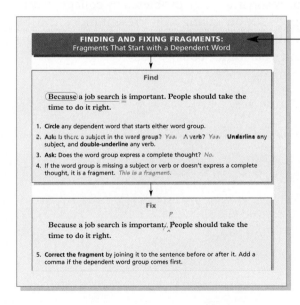

CHARTS THAT SHOW HOW TO FIND AND FIX ERRORS The chapters on grammar, word use, and punctuation include charts that take you through the steps of finding and correcting specific types of sentence errors. Each chart includes a sentence with an error that is corrected according to the steps. The example is followed immediately by practices with the same type of error, making it easy for you to refer to the example as you complete the exercises. You can also use these examples to check your work.

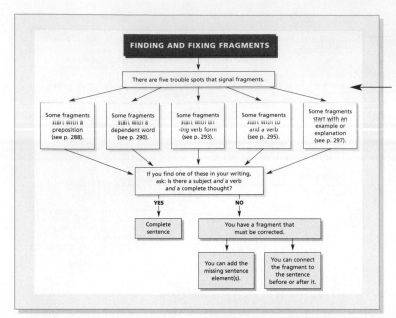

CHAPTER REVIEWS AND QUICK REVIEW CHARTS

Each chapter ends with a review and test that check your understanding of key concepts. Additionally, most of the chapters on editing end with quick review charts, which present all the types of errors covered in the Find-and-Fix charts (described on the preceding page) and help you decide what type of error you have and how to fix it. You can use the charts to troubleshoot for problems in your writing.

Helpful Appendices

Real Writing has five appendices that will aid you in college, work, and everyday life. The first appendix gives you advice on how to succeed on tests. The second appendix is a guide to building your vocabulary, which will help you read, write, and speak better. A third appendix is a step-by-step guide to getting a job, including how to write a résumé and a cover letter. The fourth appendix presents simple steps to solving problems that you can use for certain writing assignments in this book and for resolving other problems in college, work, or your everyday life. A final appendix on giving oral presentations can be found online at **bedfordstmartins.com/realwriting**. I hope *Real Writing* helps you — good luck in this and your other college courses!

Part One
How to Write Paragraphs and Essays

1
Course and Reading Basics
What You Need to Know to Get Started

This chapter reviews basic information you will need to get off to a good start in your writing class.

Course Basics

The students pictured in this chapter recently completed the course you are now taking. For this section, we asked them to tell you "things they wish they'd known." In the margins, you'll find their best tips for succeeding in the course.

Have a Positive Attitude

A few of you may think that you don't belong in this class because you always got good grades in writing when you were in high school. If you were given a test that determined you should be here, accept this and think of this course as an opportunity. Get everything you can from the class: You will need to write in every other course you will take and in any job you will want.

MARK BALDERAS: "If you really want to learn to write, and you follow the clear and simple steps in this Course Basics and in the book, you will get a good grade."

NICOLE DAY: "It is very important to have a positive attitude when starting the class and going through it. This way, you can open your mind to a variety of lifetime learning experiences. Having a positive attitude lets your teacher know that you are willing to try."

NICOLE DAY: "Doing the assignments is crucial to your grade in the class and to your future. By doing the assignments, you might learn something that you never knew before."

KATILYA LABIDOU: "I'm not one who grasps things easily. I had to go to my instructor's office every chance I had, both before class and also on days when I didn't have to be at school. I finally understand my writing better as well as my speech."

Also remember that you get from this course only what you give. Your instructor doesn't decide what grade to give you: He or she evaluates and grades the work that *you* do—or don't do.

Do the Assignments

Take the course and the course work seriously. Do not make the mistake of thinking that you can do nothing and still manage to pass. Although no one will make life difficult or uncomfortable for you if you choose not to do the work, you risk failing the course. More important, you will not learn to be a better writer, and that will affect your future plans.

Make Sure You Understand, and Get Help if You Don't

If you don't understand a concept during class, the quickest way to clear up your confusion is to ask the instructor to go over it again or to give another example. If you don't understand, probably others don't either, so don't feel foolish asking for clarification. Or, ask your question after class.

Don't be embarrassed to ask for help. See your instructor during office hours, or make an appointment for another time if you have a conflict. In addition to your instructor, you have other possible sources of help, such as the library, computer lab, writing center, tutors, and your adviser. Your tuition pays for these resources, so find out how they can help you and use them. Whatever you do, don't remain confused or give up.

Manage Your Time

Passing this course requires—at the very least—that you attend class and that you complete the homework and writing assignments. To do so, you need to manage your time effectively. Here is some advice about time management that our student advisers wanted to pass on to you.

Get to Class (on Time) and Stay until the End

Make a commitment to go to every class. Things do come up in life that may conflict with your class, but if you are going to miss a session, be late, or leave early, let your instructor know in advance, if possible, and ask what you should do on your own.

Make a Calendar

With all the demands on your time, it can be hard to remember what is due when. Using the syllabus that your instructor gives you, make a calendar that covers the whole course, listing due dates for papers, tests, and other assignments. Papers take more than one night to write, so make sure to schedule in the various steps, as shown in the partial course calendar that follows.

If you use a computer, you can download free online calendars (for example, try <**www.calendar.yahoo.com**>) that cover months, a week at a time, or a day at a time. Keep the electronic calendar on your hard drive in a folder with the course title. You can put papers and other course documents in this folder too. Or, you can print out or draw a calendar and staple it to the front of a paper folder for the course. This way, you can look at the calendar without going through the whole folder.

TRADITIONAL COURSE CALENDAR

<table>
<tr><td colspan="7" align="center">**English 098, Tuesday/Thursday, 8:30–10**
Professor Murphy
Office hours: T/Th, 11–12:30 and by appointment</td></tr>
<tr><td></td><td></td><td>**1**
Prewriting for illustration paper due</td><td>**2**</td><td>**3**</td><td>**4**</td><td>**5**</td></tr>
<tr><td>**6**</td><td>**7**</td><td>**8**
Draft of illustration paper due</td><td>**9**</td><td>**10**
Test, fragments</td><td>**11**</td><td>**12**</td></tr>
<tr><td>**13**</td><td>**14**</td><td>**15**
Final illustration paper due</td><td>**16**</td><td>**17**</td><td>**18**</td><td>**19**</td></tr>
<tr><td>**20**</td><td>**21**</td><td>**22**
Review, test on subject-verb agreement</td><td>**23**</td><td>**24**
Test, subject-verb agreement
11—Appt. with Prof. Murphy</td><td>**25**</td><td>**26**</td></tr>
<tr><td>**27**</td><td>**28**</td><td>**29**
Prewriting for description paper due</td><td>**30**</td><td>**31**</td><td></td><td></td></tr>
</table>

If you don't like calendars, there are lots of other formats you can use. Here is a weekly calendar that is more visual and allows you to write notes or reminders to yourself.

CLUSTER CALENDAR (FOR A WEEK)

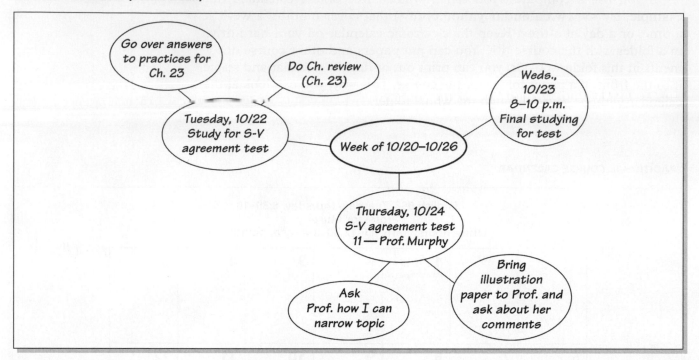

Go over answers to practices for Ch. 23

Do Ch. review (Ch. 23)

Tuesday, 10/22 Study for S-V agreement test

Week of 10/20–10/26

Weds., 10/23 8–10 p.m. Final studying for test

Thursday, 10/24 S-V agreement test 11 — Prof. Murphy

Ask Prof. how I can narrow topic

Bring illustration paper to Prof. and ask about her comments

■ **TIP:** For lots of good tips on time management, reading and study skills, and more, visit <**www.sarc.sdes.ucf.edu/learningskills.html**> or <**www.howtostudy.org**>.

Whatever format you choose, you should review your calendar at the start of every month or week. Make it a habit.

MICHELLE BASSETT: "You'd be surprised at how much you miss when you're absent for just one class. As for getting there on time, two things: Many instructors give out important information right at the start of class. Also, many consider coming in late an absence."

MICHELLE BASSETT: "Make sure you begin writing assignments long before they're due. Then, you have time to revise and edit before handing in something that you know isn't as good as it could be."

■ **TEACHING TIP:** Devote a few minutes of class time to allowing students to get to know their neighbors and to exchange contact information if they wish.

Be a Part of the Class

As we all know, it's possible to go to every class and still not be part of it. Decide that you will be an active part of the class; you are more likely to do well. Our student advisers offer these suggestions, as a start.

Make a Friend

In most classes, students sit in about the same place in each session. Take advantage of this, and get to know at least one other person in the class. Exchange names, phone numbers, and e-mail addresses with students who sit near you. That way, if for some reason you can't make it to a class, you'll know someone who can tell you what you missed. Also, if you find you don't understand an assignment, you can double-check with another student. You might also want to study with other students.

Get to Know Your Instructor

Your instructor wants you to succeed in the class as much as you want to. It helps him or her to know you a little bit: who you are, what you do, what you need help with. Make an appointment to visit your instructor during his or her office hours. When you go, ask questions about material you are not sure you understood in class or problems you have with writing. You and your instructor will get the most out of these sessions if you bring examples of your writing or specific assignments you're having trouble with.

MICHELLE BOSTICK: "Going to see your instructor in her office allows you to identify areas where your writing is weak, and you can get help that might embarrass you if you had to ask in class. It helps you become a more confident student. It also shows the instructor that you are concerned about your writing and will take initiative."

Using e-mail is not quite as good as talking face-to-face, which allows for more personal interaction. You may need to use e-mail if, for some reason, you can't see your instructor during office hours.

If you do e-mail your instructor, remember this: Whenever you communicate, you create an impression of yourself. Even though e-mail is less formal than, for example, a writing assignment, what you say and how you say it are still important. Reread your e-mail messages before sending them.

Sit Near the Front

Don't hide in the back of the class and hope that no one will notice that you're there. Instead, when you go to the first class, sit in one of the first few rows. It really is easier to learn when you're closer to the instructor.

Speak Up

For many students, speaking in class is difficult: You're not sure you have the right answer, or you think your question might be stupid. But speaking up in class is important. School is exactly the right place for getting over the fear of talking in a group, and the ability to speak to people in a group will help you at work and in your everyday life. Speaking up also allows you to get answers to questions and to take part in class discussions. If you wait until later, you may forget your questions or the points you wanted to make.

NICOLE DAY: "Knowing your instructor is important because then she knows who you are and what you need help with. When you're having trouble with something, you feel more comfortable going to your instructor when you know her."

NICOLE DAY: "Sitting in front is very beneficial to your learning. You can see everything, and it lets your teacher know that you want to learn and not just hide in the back."

■ **RESOURCES:** *Practical Suggestions* includes more advice on fostering class participation.

Once you get used to speaking in class, you'll find that it's not hard. Challenge yourself, early on, to participate orally: Volunteer to answer a question or to ask a question. Here are some tips that might help you:

- Don't be afraid to make a mistake. No one in the class, including your instructor, will make fun of you. As teachers are fond of saying, "There's no such thing as a dumb question."
- When you speak, look at your instructor (or whomever you're speaking to).
- Speak loudly enough for people to hear; otherwise, you'll have to repeat yourself.

Identify Your Goals and Needs

MARK BALDERAS: "Be sure to set your *own* goals. They will help you succeed."

What do you, personally, want from this course? Once you have a good idea of what you want, you will be more able to focus on what you need and to get specific help from your instructor.

First, what are some of your real-world goals, both small and large, right now and in the future? Some short-term goals might be persuading your boss to give you a raise, getting a bank loan, or getting a promotion. Longer-term goals might include deciding what kind of job or career you hope to have or what degree you want to finish. Do some thinking and list at least five short-term and longer-term goals, the more concrete and specific the better (for example, "be happy" is too general and abstract).

Once you have some real-world goals in mind, try to link those goals to the writing skills you want to learn or improve in this course. For example, if one of your real-world goals is to convince your boss that you deserve a raise, you might want help with making a good argument for that. You can use the worksheet on page 9 to fill in these goals.

Hang in There

Don't give up on yourself if things get hard. You can get help, and you can become a better writer and pass this course. If you drop out, you'll either have to take the same course next term or have the same writing problems that you had coming in. This course is the time and place to improve your writing, and better writing skills will give you more control over your life and how you communicate with others.

Believe in your ability to pass this course and stay focused; don't panic and run away. If you want some inspiration, check out the former students highlighted in the Profiles of Success at the beginning of Chapters 9–17. All of these people are successful, yet all of them had to overcome some major obstacles, often their own fear of writing.

KATILYA LABIDOU: "Acknowledging your faults is the first step. I was really surprised when I first got a failing grade. Wanting to be better than average is what got me through. Sometimes, I wasn't sure I could do it, but I stuck with it and spent time learning about writing and grammar."

NAME: _____

COURSE: _____ **DATE:** _____

REAL-WORLD GOALS

_____
_____
_____
_____
_____
_____

COURSE GOALS

Think about your writing and comments you have received about it in the past. What do you think your major problems with writing are? What should you work on improving? Jot down a few ideas and then, based on your answers to these questions, list three specific skills you want to improve during this course. Keep your real-world goals in mind as you decide on your course goals because what you learn in this class should be related to what you want to do with what you have learned.

_____
_____
_____
_____
_____
_____
_____

Reading Basics

Reading carefully can boost your chances of success not only in college but also on the job and in everyday life. Good readers can find good, practical information about anything they are interested in: starting a business, finding a job, investing, treating an illness, protecting themselves from unfairness, buying a car at the best price, and so on.

In college, you read for many reasons: to understand assignments and test instructions, to understand the information in your textbooks, to participate in class discussions based on reading assignments. This section previews

■ **DISCUSSION:** Ask students to think of other reasons they need to read in college.

■ **BASIC READING QUESTIONS:**
• What is the author's main point?
• What are the supporting points?

the reading skills you need in this course and others, with a particular focus on reading the course syllabus, textbooks, and test directions. Whatever you read, you need to be able to identify the main point — the author's main message — and the support for that point.

Find the Main Point

The main point is usually introduced early in a selection, so read the first few sentences or paragraphs with special care. If the writer has stated the main point in a single sentence or a couple of sentences, highlight or underline these words.

PRACTICE 1   FINDING THE MAIN POINT . . . .

Underline the main point in the following paragraphs. Then, write the main point in your own words in the space provided.

1. <u>Psychologists have for some time noted the difference in problem-solving styles of Americans and Chinese, and new research underscores that difference.</u> Psychologists say that Americans are specific problem solvers, focusing on one problem at a time. In contrast, Chinese consider the broader context of a problem before acting. Researchers at the University of Michigan recently charted the eye movements of two groups of people when they were shown photographs. Americans focused on the foreground with only brief sweeps of the background. Chinese people focused on the background, with many eye movements back and forth and limited stops at a particular object. It appears that eye movements parallel problem-solving styles.

MAIN POINT: *Answers will vary.*

2. Many people look at me blankly when I say I am a vegan. They think maybe it is a religion or some unusual ethnic background. <u>But a vegan is a normal person, a vegetarian who eats only plant products.</u> Vegans do not eat meat (including fowl), fish, eggs, or milk products. That means I don't eat cheese, yogurt, or ice cream, among many other milk products. I don't eat anything that comes from a living creature. But that doesn't make me weird, or even a difficult dinner guest. I eat all kinds of vegetables, fruits, and beans. And I'm one of a growing number of people who believe that it is healthier and more humane to eat only plant products. Because my diet does have restrictions, I have learned a lot about nutrition, and I eat no junk food. I am healthy, and I am a vegan.

MAIN POINT: *Answers will vary.*

PRACTICE 2   STATING THE MAIN POINT . . . .

The following paragraph does not have a main point that is stated in a single sentence. Read the paragraph and write the main point in the space provided.

The woman stopped in traffic holds her hand down on the horn. The man in back of her makes an obscene gesture. The people in the car in front of them swear at the two others, screaming. When traffic starts moving, everyone jostles for position, no one giving an inch, so the traffic remains jammed. A fight breaks out, at first just loud exchanges of anger. But it gets worse until two people are standing nose to nose screaming, the veins in their necks swollen, their eyes wide and flaming. Their body language is scary. Soon, one hits the other, and someone calls the police. This causes yet another jam and delay. By this point, everyone is late and at least irritated if not downright furious. The next day, the same kind of thing happens, and I ask myself what these sick people are thinking.

MAIN POINT: _Answers will vary but should have something to do with the negative effects of road rage or commuting by car in congested areas._

■ **TIP:** For more information on the main idea in writing, see Chapter 4.

. . . .

Find the Support for the Main Point

Support—the details that show, explain, or prove the main point—comes in different forms, depending on what you're reading:

- In instructions, the support is the steps of the process of doing, using, or making something.
- In memos, reports, or e-mails at work, the support provides reasons for, or details about, the topic of your writing.
- In textbooks, the support explains topics or concepts.
- In essays or literature, the support describes or details the characters and events so that you understand them.

In tests and writing assignments, you are often asked to respond to reading selections. For example, you may be asked to agree or disagree with the author and to explain why. Whether you agree or disagree, you can explain _why_ only by referring to the author's support.

■ PRACTICE 3   **FINDING THE MAIN POINT AND SUPPORT** . . . .

The following excerpt is taken from an introduction to business textbook for college. Double-underline the main idea and underline the support.

NEW SKILLS NEEDED

The active participation of employees adds new responsibilities and opportunities to jobs at all levels. For starters, employees need new skills. The employee training budgets of U.S. businesses show the kinds of

■ **TIP:** For more practice identifying the main point and support, visit **bedfordstmartins.com/realwriting**.

skills companies stress. The most common type of employee training is, and always has been, employee orientation, training that brings new employees up to speed on how the business and its industry work. Nine out of ten large and midsized businesses provide new-employee orientation.

Beyond employee orientation, several new kinds of training are increasingly common. Six out of ten large and midsized businesses now train employees in quality improvement. Three-fourths provide training in leadership skills. More participative approaches to business require managers and supervisors to make the shift from giving orders to coaching teams of employees, and some employee teams are now expected to manage themselves. Seven out of ten large and midsized companies now provide employee training in teamwork because new approaches to business require more cooperation and less personal competition.

■ **TIP:** For basic advice on problem solving and teamwork, see Appendix D.

Also new is the emphasis on problem-solving skills and creativity—two-thirds of midsized and large companies now train employees in problem solving and well over one-third stress creativity. They recognize that these thinking skills are important for employees at all levels of business.

■ **TIP:** For more information on support in writing, see Chapter 5. If you are using *Real Writing with Readings*, see Chapter 41 for more on reading.

Finally, more than half of these businesses are now giving employees training in how to deal with change. You are the first generation of students to receive training in how to cope with and lead change in business.

—K. Blanchard, C. Schewe, R. Nelson, and A. Hiam,
from *Exploring the World of Business* (1996) p. 26

Understand Your Syllabus

It is important to understand your syllabus so that you know what your instructor expects from you. Read it on the first day of class, and ask your instructor about any questions you have. Check it regularly to make sure you're on course. Syllabi often include headers to help you find important information. The following example notes some critical features.

English 098 — Tuesday/Thursday, 8:30–10

Professor Murphy

Phone: 708-555-1113/E-mail: murphy@sssc.edu

Office hours: T/Th, 11–12:30 and by appointment

COURSE DESCRIPTION: This course focuses on writing paragraphs and essays. Students will use the writing process and will read, write, and edit effectively as well as use and document online and library sources.

COURSE OBJECTIVES:

- Use a variety of writing strategies.
- Recognize and correct grammar errors.
- Read and think critically and apply information.
- Develop ideas in paragraphs and essays with clear theses.
- Etc.

COURSE MATERIALS: Susan Anker, *Real Writing with Readings,* Fourth Edition

GRADING POLICIES (PERCENTAGE OF GRADE):

Papers	60%
Tests	25%
Homework	10%
Class participation	5%

GRADING SCALE FOR TESTS AND PAPERS:

A   90–100%

B   80–89%

Etc.

COURSE POLICIES:

- **Attendance:** Class attendance is required. Students who miss more than one week, . . . etc.
- **Classroom rules:** Arrive on time, turn off cell phones, . . . etc.
- **Late or missed work:** No late work is accepted without my consent . . . etc.
- **Academic integrity:** This course adheres to the college handbook . . . etc.

Read carefully: Your grade will depend on how well you achieve these objectives.

Explanation of grading policies

Explanation of grading criteria

Explanation of course policies

PRACTICE 4   REVIEWING YOUR SYLLABUS . . . .

Read the syllabus for this course and answer these questions: (1) Describe the goals of the course in your own words. (2) What is the policy for absences?

■ **TEACHING TIP:** You might ask students to check off tasks on the syllabus as they complete them.

Understand Textbook Features

Textbooks often have special features to help you understand their content, such as headings, words in **boldface**, charts and boxes, definitions, and chapter reviews and summaries.

Following is an excerpt from a college psychology textbook explaining the ways in which we encode, or take in, information. The notes in the margin indicate what each feature is and what purpose it serves.

Chapter number and title

Major heading introduces main concept: encoding

Encoding: Getting Information In

Preview: How does sensory information, once registered, get encoded and transferred into the memory system? What types of information do we absorb incidentally? What types require intentional effort?

Diagram shows and illustrates types of encoding

Minor heading introduces two types of encoding

How We Encode

Some encoding occurs automatically, freeing your attention to simultaneously process information that requires effort. Thus, your memory for the route you walked to your last class is handled by **automatic processing**. Your learning of this chapter's concepts requires **effortful processing** (FIGURE 9.2).

Boldface type highlights key terms

Subheading 1: Introduces one way of encoding

Automatic Processing

Often with little or no effort, you encode an enormous amount of information about *space*, *time*, and *frequency*: During an exam, you may recall the place on the textbook page where forgotten material appears. To guess where you left your coat, you can re-create a sequence of the day's events. Passing a classmate, you may realize that "this is the third time I've run into you this afternoon." Effort may help us retain such memories, yet they form almost automatically. Not only does *automatic processing* occur effortlessly, it is difficult to shut off. When you hear or read a familiar word in your native language, whether an insult or a compliment, it is virtually impossible not to register its meaning automatically.

Some types of automatic processing we learn. For example, learning to read reversed sentences at first requires effort:

.citamotua emoceb nac gnissecorp luftroffE

After practice, some *effortful processing* becomes more automatic, much as reading from right to left becomes easy for students of Hebrew (Kolers, 1975).

Automatic processing occurs with little or no effort, without our awareness, and without interfering with our thinking about other things. (This is another example of our brain's capacity for parallel processing of multiple information streams.) What then would happen if we asked people to attend to information they encode automatically, such as judging the frequency of words presented during an experiment? Lynn Hasher and Rose Zacks (1979, 1984) found that this extra attention is of little benefit. Although memory for such material may be modestly boosted by effort, our encoding is mostly automatic: We cannot switch it on and off at will.

Subheading 2: Introduces another way of encoding

Effortful Processing

We encode and retain vast amounts of information automatically, but we remember other types of information only with effort and attention. When learning novel information such as names, we can boost our memory through **rehearsal**, or conscious repetition. This was shown long ago by the pioneering researcher of verbal memory, German philosopher Hermann Ebbinghaus (1850-1909). Ebbinghaus was to the study of memory what Ivan Pavlov was to the study of conditioning. Ebbinghaus became impatient with philosophical speculations about memory and decided to study it scientifically. To do so, he chose to study his own learning and forgetting of novel verbal materials.

FIGURE 9.2
Automatic versus effortful processing Some information, such as this chapter's concepts, requires effort to encode and remember. Other information, such as where you ate dinner yesterday, you process automatically.

Caption explains diagrams and illustrations

Definitions explain key terms

- **automatic processing** unconscious encoding of incidental information, such as space, time, and frequency, and of well-learned information, such as word meanings.

- **effortful processing** encoding that requires attention and conscious effort.

- **rehearsal** the conscious repetition of information, either to maintain it in consciousness or to encode it for storage.

■ **PRACTICE 5   REVIEWING THIS TEXTBOOK** . . . .

Working by yourself or with another student, find the special features in one chapter of this book: Chapter 21 (on sentence fragments). Use the following questions to guide you:

1. If you wanted to remember the five fragment trouble spots, what headings would you highlight? *the headings on the five kinds of fragments*

2. What kind of information is in the green boxes in the chapter? *lists or* *important words*

3. What kinds of reviews do you find in the chapter? *A chapter review.*

   Students may cite other reviews as well, such as practices and "Finding and *Fixing" charts.*

■ **TEACHING TIP:** You may want to refer students to the answers to odd-numbered practices on pages AK–1–AK–10.

■ **TIP:** For advice on using this book, see the Introduction for Students.

Highlighting a Textbook Chapter

As you read a textbook chapter, use a brightly colored highlighter to mark important headings and information that explains the headings and that will help you review information later. For example, the first two pages from Chapter 5 follow. Look at the information that is highlighted.

Understand What Support Is

Support is the collection of examples, facts, or evidence that show, explain, or prove your main point. **Primary support** points are the major ideas that back up your main point, and **secondary support** gives details to back up your primary support.

Without support, you *state* the main point, but you don't *make* the main point. Consider these unsupported statements:

The amount shown on my bill is incorrect.

I deserve a raise.

I am innocent of the crime.

The statements may be true, but without good support, they are not convincing. If you sometimes get papers back with the comment "You need to support/develop your ideas," the suggestions in this chapter will help you.

Writers sometimes confuse repetition with support. The same point repeated several times is not support. It is just repetition.

REPETITION, **NOT SUPPORT**	The amount shown on my bill is incorrect. You overcharged me. It didn't cost that much. The total is wrong.
SUPPORT	The amount shown on my bill is incorrect. I ordered the bacon-cheeseburger plate, which is $6.99 on the menu. On the bill, the order is correct, but the amount is $16.99.

As you develop support for your main point, make sure that it has these three features.

BASICS OF GOOD SUPPORT

- **It relates to your main point.** The purpose of support is to show, explain, or prove your main point, so the support you use must be directly related to that main point.
- **It considers your readers.** Create support that will show your readers what you mean.
- **It is detailed and specific.** Give readers enough detail, particularly through examples, so that they can see what you mean.

Heading: Indicates important topic

Definition of topic: Support

Examples of what is *not* support

Important information about support

If you do not want to mark up your book, write the important information in a review notebook. Following is a possible setup for the information:

Important Chapter Information

Chapter # and title

Important headings

Headings and page numbers

Locations of important definitions

Terms and page numbers

Locations of boxes and other key extras

Titles and page numbers

Review items

Page numbers

■ **PRACTICE 6   HIGHLIGHTING THIS TEXTBOOK** . . . .

Look at Chapter 22 (on run-ons and comma splices) or one that your instructor chooses, and highlight the important information. Or, record key information on a separate piece of paper as shown in the previous example.

After you have read and highlighted a textbook chapter, go back and review your highlighting. In the margin or in your review notebook, write a few notes, in your own words, that will remind you of what is important. Also, note what you do not understand so that you can ask your instructor about it. This kind of reading and reviewing takes a little time, but it will save you time later when you are studying for a test. Also, highlighting and making notes will definitely improve your test results, making information "stick" in your memory better than reading alone will.

. . . .

Reviewing for a Test on a Textbook Chapter

To study for a test on a textbook chapter or chapters, try to set aside at least two different study sessions (more if it's a test on a whole unit). Also, allow extra review time the night before the test if you can, and also on the day of the test.

In addition to reviewing what you highlighted and made notes about, try one or more of the following techniques to firmly store the information in your brain:

- Read your highlighting and notes aloud, especially standing up. Repeat this technique several times, in both study sessions.

- Rewrite your notes and the information you highlighted several times, in both study sessions.

- Create a study guide for each chapter. To make a study guide, think about what will probably be on the test based on the course syllabus and on what your instructor has emphasized in class.

Study Guide

Chapter _____

1. The most important information in this chapter is _____.
2. The test is likely to have questions about _____.
3. The most important thing(s) to know about the topics I listed in question 2 are

   Topic

      What I need to know

   Topic

      What I need to know

   Topic

      What I need to know

   Etc.
4. What are some specific questions the instructor might ask?
5. Is the test likely to be multiple choice or essay?
6. The pages I want to review right before the test are

   _____.

Instructors might answer some of the previous questions. For instance, they might tell you whether a test will be multiple choice or essay. However, do not expect them to tell you exactly what will be on a test. In college, you will be expected to know the material well enough to be prepared.

PRACTICE 7   MAKING A STUDY GUIDE . . . .

Working with another student or a group of students, assume that you are going to be tested on Chapter 23 (on subject-verb agreement) or on a chapter that your instructor assigns. Create a study guide that you could use to study for the test.

. . . .

Understand Test Directions

Have you ever answered test questions incorrectly because you didn't follow the directions? If you're like most people, the answer is "yes." Probably, you were nervous about taking the test and wanted to get started so that you didn't run out of time or forget what you studied. But if you don't understand what the test requires, you might make mistakes, wasting the time you spent preparing. To get off to a good start, follow these steps:

1. Listen to Oral Directions.   It's tempting to start flipping through the exam as soon as you get it, but resist the temptation. Your instructor may be giving you key advice or information that's not written anywhere else. For example, you may have only thirty minutes for the test, not the whole class period. Listen carefully.

2. Survey the Whole Test before Starting.   Look at each part of the test to see what type of questions it has and the points each item is worth. Also, look for questions that you can answer quickly and easily. Decide what section you will start with, and write down how much time you can spend on each part of the test.

■ **TIP:** For more advice on taking tests, see Appendix A.

3. Read the Written Directions.   The rest of this section gives advice for the most common types of directions.

Directions for Multiple-Choice and Short-Answer Questions

Underline or highlight the important instructions, as shown in the example that follows. Important details include the step(s) you take to answer the question completely.

Typically, each part of a test has its own set of directions. The example that follows is for one part of a history test, which has multiple-choice and short-answer questions.

Two parts to each question

PART 2: Each of the numbered items below consists of two parts: (A) a multiple-choice question and (B) a short-answer question. For each item, circle the correct choice for A and answer question B.— Two steps to each question

1A. The Eighteenth Amendment to the U.S. Constitution was passed in

    a. **1917**

    b. 1864

    c. 1945

    d. 1900

B. What did the Eighteenth Amendment do? *It began Prohibition, making the producing, selling, and transporting of liquor illegal.*

Make sure you understand what a multiple-choice question is asking you to select, looking out for words like *not*.

1. Which of the following is not a symptom of shock?

    a. changes in body temperature

    b. fast heart rate

    c. **tongue swelling**

    d. changes in blood pressure

The answer is what's *not* a shock symptom.

■ **PRACTICE 8   UNDERSTANDING TEST DIRECTIONS** . . . .

Turn to page 367 (the review test for Part Four) and read the directions for Part One. What are the steps to answering the test questions?

Directions for Essay Questions

Underlining or highlighting directions for essay questions is essential because these instructions often have many parts. The first example that follows is the instructions for the essay part of an introduction to business test. The second example is an actual essay question from the test. In both examples, key words are underlined.

INSTRUCTIONS FOR ESSAY PART OF EXAM

PART 4. ESSAY QUESTIONS. Choose two of the following questions and write a well-developed essay that demonstrates that you understand the subject thoroughly. Use at least two specific examples from what we have discussed in class or from the textbook.

INSTRUCTIONS FOR ESSAY QUESTION

12. Identify and discuss three factors that influence consumer buying behavior.

. . . .

The chart on page 20 will help you recognize and understand key words that are often used in essay questions. They may also be used in short-answer questions.

■ **PRACTICE 9   FINDING KEY WORDS** . . . .

Read each of the following essay questions and circle the key words. In the space below each question, explain what the question asks you to do.
Answers may vary. Possible answers shown.

EXAMPLE: Discuss the effects of Prohibition on drinking practices in the United States.

List and explain the effects of Prohibition on drinking practices.

1. Discuss the effects of alcohol.

List and explain the effects of alcohol.

2. What are the main differences between the U.S. Senate and the House of Representatives?

Contrast the Senate and the House of Representatives.

■ **TIP:** Regular course assignments often have directions like those of essay exams. Follow the advice here when completing any assignment.

Common Key Words in Essay Exam Questions

KEY WORD	WHAT IT MEANS
Analyze	Break into parts (classify) and discuss
Define	State the meaning and give examples
Describe the **stages** of	List and explain steps in a process
Discuss the **causes** of	List and explain the causes
Discuss the **concept** of	Define and give examples
Discuss the **differences between**	Contrast and give examples
Discuss the **effects/results** of	List and explain the effects
Discuss the **meaning** of	Define and give examples
Discuss the **similarities between**	Compare and give examples
Discuss the **stages/steps** of	Explain a process
Explain the **term**	Define and give examples
Follow/Trace the **development** of	Give the history; narrate the story
Follow/Trace the **process** of	Explain the sequence of steps or stages in the process
Identify	Define and give examples
Should	Argue for or against
Summarize	Give a brief overview of narrative

3. (Discuss) the (four) main (stages of collective bargaining.)

   Explain the four main stages of collective bargaining, with examples.

4. (Identify and discuss) (three) major (learning styles.)

   Define and give examples of three learning styles.

5. (Agree or disagree:) Downloading music from the Internet should be free.

   State your opinion and give reasons to support it.

6. (Trace the development) of (cell phone technology.)

   Tell what happened and when.

Think Critically Whenever You Read

Many people tend to believe what they see, read, and hear without thinking, particularly if it seems real. For example, people often believe advertisements in print, on the TV or radio, or online. Diet pills that work while you sleep? Prescription drugs without a prescription? Great pay for ten hours of work a week? People fall for these lines over and over. However, to be successful in college, at work, and in your everyday life, you need to think critically about everything you see, read, and hear. This means learning to examine ideas, information, rules, and so on before accepting them as the truth.

Learning to think critically is a habit that you can start by asking some basic questions. The following questions address things you read, but you can also apply them to nonprint information, like televised advertisements.

Critical Reading Questions

NEWSPAPER/MAGAZINE ARTICLES/ESSAYS

Typical purpose: To inform or entertain

QUESTIONS TO ASK:

- Who wrote this? What are his or her qualifications to write on the subject? (Look for an "about the author" note, or look up his or her name on the Internet or a library database.)
- What is the main point?
- Does the writer provide enough evidence (such as facts and examples) for the main point? If he or she presents an opinion, is that supported with enough evidence?
- Does the writer favor one angle of an issue over others? If so, what points seem to be missing?
- Do I agree with the main point as the author has presented and supported it?
- Does anything seem odd, or unrealistic, based on what I know?
- Does the writing achieve its purpose?
- What questions, if any, remain unanswered by the article or essay?

ADVERTISEMENTS/OFFERS

Typical purpose: To get you to do something (usually buy something)

QUESTIONS TO ASK:

- What are the main claims? (Look for words in headlines especially.)
- Does anything seem odd or unrealistic—"too good to be true"? If you have doubts about an advertising claim, you might check with the Federal Trade Commission at **<www.ftc.gov>** or at 1-877-382-4357 (toll-free).
- If there is fine print, what's in it?

continued

■ **TIP:** See Part Two for questions that help you think critically as you read and write about essays.

> • What, if any, guarantee is made? Is it realistic? If so, will the sponsor of the ad or offer put the guarantee in writing?
>
> • If I accept the offer, what are my obligations—financial or otherwise?
>
> ### TEXTBOOKS
>
> **Typical purpose:** To inform or to explain concepts, events, or processes
>
> **QUESTIONS TO ASK (ABOUT AN ASSIGNED CHAPTER OR SECTION):**
>
> • Who wrote the textbook or chapter? What are his or her qualifications to write on the subject? (Look for an "about the author" note, or look up his or her name on the Internet or a library database.)
>
> • What is the main point?
>
> • If the writer cites and lists sources of the information, are the sources recent?
>
> • Do I understand what I've read?
>
> • Does the writing achieve its purpose?
>
> • What questions, if any, remain unanswered? (These are good questions to ask your instructor.)

And *always* ask this question: **WHAT DO I THINK? WHY?**

■ **PRACTICE 10**   **READING CRITICALLY** . . . .

■ **TEACHING TIP:** You might also have students apply the critical reading questions to essays or articles that you bring in (or ones from this book) or to textbooks for this or other classes.

Working by yourself or with other students, read the following documents from college, work, and everyday life and answer the critical reading questions.   *Answers may vary. Possible answers shown.*

1. What is the writer's purpose? *With the exception of the drug label, the purpose of all of documents is to make money for the people who created them.*

2. What are the key words or major claims? *Answers could include any words in headlines or bold type.*

3. What's in the fine print? *See "for those who qualify" in the e-mailed advertisement and "Some supply purchases may be required" in the telephone pole posting.*

4. Does anything seem odd, unrealistic, or unreliable? *None of the information is reliable. The college and work documents make claims that can't possibly be true. The everyday life documents contain errors or misleading information. (Note the excessively high dosage on the drug label.)*

COLLEGE

AN E-MAILED ADVERTISEMENT:

GET A COLLEGE DEGREE IN *TWO* WEEKS!

Are a few letters after your name the only thing that's keeping you from your dream job? Degree Services International will grant you a B.A., M.A., M.S., M.B.A., or Ph.D. from a prestigious nonaccredited institution based on what you already know!

NO CLASSES, EXAMS, OR TEXTBOOKS ARE REQUIRED
for those who qualify

If you order now, you'll receive your degree within two weeks.

CALL 1-800-555-0021

HURRY! **Qualified institutions can grant these diplomas only because of a legal loophole that may be closed within weeks.**

WORK

A POSTING ON A TELEPHONE POLE:

Earn Thousands of Dollars a Week Working at Home!

Flexible Hours ◆ No Experience Needed

The health-care system is in crisis because of the millions of medical claims that have to be processed each day. You can benefit from this situation now by becoming an at-home medical claims processor. Work as much or as little as you like for great pay!

CALL 1-800-555-5831

for your starter kit

Some supply purchases may be required.

EVERYDAY LIFE

ADVERTISEMENTS:

Gift Certificate
Redeem this Certificate for a
FREE
GENUINE faux 9 CARAT SAPPHIRE PENDANT
...ow you the quality
...king this o... and low prices of our merchandise.
...pphire pendant: Print your name and address below, and
...te, along with $9.95 cash, check, or money order to cover

New beautiful 4 BR home on oversized lot. Huge with separated bedrooms, large area upstairs unfinished. The pictured home is next door. On Hilton Head for only $239,000.

■ **TIP:** Pay attention to the dosage for adults.

PART OF A DRUG LABEL:

Drug Facts	
Directions	
■ Do not take more than directed.	
Adults and children 12 years and over	■ Take 4 to 6 caplets every 2 hours as needed. ■ Do not take more than 8 caplets in 24 hours.
Children under 12 years	Do not use this product in children under 12 years of age. This could cause serious health problems.

The examples in Practice 10 all have impossible claims or errors that you can detect, saving yourself a lot of wasted time and money and—in the case of the last item—preventing a health problem. You should do this same kind of questioning as you read and learn in your college classes. Question new information, and try to verify it whenever it seems unrealistic.

· ·

Chapter Review

Before doing this review, go back over this chapter using the techniques described in "Understand Textbook Features," including highlighting key terms.

1. Make your own list of important terms with the page numbers on which they appear. This will help you refer to them later.

2. What are the five "course basics" that can help you succeed in this course and others? *have a positive attitude, manage your time, be a part of the class, identify your goals and needs, and hang in there*

3. As you read a textbook, what features should you pay attention to? *Answers may vary but could include words in boldface, headings, charts and boxes, definitions, chapter reviews, and summaries.*

4. What should you pay attention to when you receive a test? *oral and written directions*

5. Without looking back at the page that lists them, what are some questions you should ask yourself as you read critically? *Answers could include any of the "Critical Reading Questions" (p. 21).*

6. What questions should you always ask about what you read, see, or hear? *What do I think? Why?*

7. Which of the "basics" in this chapter were new to you? Which ones do you need to practice the most? Which course and reading basics apply to work and everyday life as well as to your college courses? Write for one minute about what you learned and what you think you need practice in. If you don't understand something in the chapter, write about that.

2

Writing Basics

Audience, Purpose, and Process

Four elements are key to good writing. Keep them in mind whenever you write.

▪▪ FOUR BASICS OF GOOD WRITING

1. It considers the needs and knowledge of the audience.
2. It fulfills the writer's purpose.
3. It includes a clear, definite point.
4. It provides support that explains or proves the main point.

This chapter discusses audience and purpose first because they are key to effective writing; purpose determines a writer's main point, and audience determines how that point is made.

The chapter then discusses how to structure writing to meet the four basics. Finally, it outlines the writing process, previewing steps that will be covered in more detail in the next six chapters.

Understand Audience and Purpose

Your **audience** is the person or people who will read what you write. In college, your audience is usually your instructors. Whenever you write, always have at least one real person in mind as a reader. Think about what that person already knows and what he or she will need to know to understand your main point. In most cases, assume that readers know only what you write about your topic. Your **purpose** is your reason for writing. Often in college, your purpose for writing will be to show, explain, or argue.

Your writing may be very different for two different audiences or purposes. Read the following two notes, which describe the same situation but are written for different audiences. Notice the tone and content of each note.

SITUATION: Marta woke up one morning with a fever. When she went into the bathroom, she saw in the mirror that her face was swollen and red. Then, she was hit with a violent attack of nausea. Marta immediately called her doctor, who said she could come right in. Marta's mother was coming to stay with her children in a few minutes, so Marta asked a neighbor to watch her children until her mother got there. Marta then left a note for her mother telling her why she had already left. When she got to the doctor's office, the nurse asked her to write a brief description of her symptoms for the doctor.

MARTA'S NOTE TO HER MOTHER

> Ma,
>
> Not feeling very well this morning. Stopping by doctor's office before work. Don't worry, I'm okay, just checking it out. Can't miss any more work. See you after.

MARTA'S NOTE TO THE DOCTOR

> When I woke up this morning, I had a fever. When I looked in the mirror, my face was very swollen, especially around the eyes, which were almost shut. My lips and skin were red and dry, and my face was very itchy. Within a few minutes, I vomited several times.

PRACTICE 1   COMPARING MARTA'S NOTES . . . .

Read Marta's two notes and answer the following questions. *Answers will vary but should be similar to those supplied.*

1. How does Marta's note to her mother differ from the one to the doctor?

   The note to the doctor is more specific and more formal.

2. How do the different audiences and purposes affect what the notes say (the content) and how they say it (the tone)? *Marta doesn't want to worry her mother, so she is very general, and she is also very informal. Marta wants the doctor to know exactly what happened, so she provides more specifics. She also writes more formally.*

3. Which note has more detail, and why? *the one to the doctor because Marta wants the doctor to know the symptoms she had.*

. . . .

As these examples show, we speak to family members and friends differently than we speak to people in authority (like employers, instructors, or other professionals) — or we should. Marta's note to her mother uses informal English, like incomplete sentences, because the two women know each other well and are used to speaking casually to one another. Also, Marta's purpose is to get quick information to her mother and to reassure her; she doesn't need to provide a lot of details. On the other hand, Marta's note to her doctor is more formal, with complete sentences, because the relationship is more formal. Also, the note to the doctor is more detailed because the doctor will be making treatment decisions based on it.

In college, at work, and in your everyday life, when you are speaking or writing to someone in authority for a serious purpose, use formal English. Otherwise, you won't achieve your purpose, whether that is to pass a course, to get and keep a good job, to get good medical care, or to solve a personal problem (like being billed on your credit card for a purchase you didn't make). Formal English makes sure you are taken seriously in these situations, so it is important to know how to use it.

■ **TIP:** For more practice with writing for a formal audience, see some of the problem-solving assignments in Part Two and the "Using Formal English" practices in Chapters 21–24. Or, visit Exercise Central at **bedfordstmartins.com/ realwriting.**

■ **PRACTICE 2   WRITING FOR A FORMAL AUDIENCE** . . . .

A student, Terri Travers, sent the following e-mail to a friend to complain about not getting into a criminal justice course. Rewrite the e-mail as if you were Terri and address Professor Widener. The purpose is to ask whether the professor would consider allowing you into the class given that you signed up early and have the necessary grades.

To:	Miles Rona
Fr:	Terri Travers
Subject:	Bummin'

Seriously bummin' that I didn't get into Prof. Widener's CJ class. U and Luis said it's the best—so interesting. Wonder Y I didn't. I signed up early and I have the grades. I mean, what's the deal?

See U,
TT

Understand Paragraph and Essay Form

In this course (and in the rest of college), you will write paragraphs and essays. Each of these has a basic structure.

Paragraph Form

A **paragraph** has three necessary parts—the topic sentence, the body, and the concluding sentence.

PARAGRAPH PART	PURPOSE OF THE PARAGRAPH PART
1. The **topic sentence**	states the **main point**. The topic sentence is often the first sentence of the paragraph.
2. The **body**	supports (shows, explains, or proves) the main point. It is usually made up of about three to six **support sentences**, which contain facts and details supporting the main point.

3.   The **concluding sentence**   reminds readers of the main point and often makes an observation.

Topic sentence

Read the paragraph that follows with the paragraph parts labeled.

Body
(with support sentences)

Concluding sentence

Gambling is a growing addiction in this country. As more casinos open, more people have the opportunity to try gambling. For most people, a casino is simply a fun place to visit, filled with people, lights, noise, food, and a feeling of excitement as patrons try to beat the odds and win. Most people set a limit on how much money they are willing to lose, and when they reach that amount, they stop. Addicts, however, can't stop. They always want to play just one more game to get back what they lost. If they do make up for their losses, they feel lucky and don't want to end their winning streak. Win or lose, they keep playing, and the vast majority lose, returning repeatedly to the cash machine to replenish their funds, or getting cash advances on their credit cards. People have been known to spend their entire savings because they are caught up in the frenzy of trying to win. Because casinos and gambling games like keno are now more widespread, more addicts are surfacing, and the casinos encourage the addiction: It means more money for them. The gamblers' support group,[1] Gamblers Anonymous, based on the principles of Alcoholics Anonymous, has seen vastly increased membership in the last few years as more potential addicts are introduced to gambling, fall into its clutches, and struggle to get free. Clearly, gambling needs to be taken as seriously as any other addiction.

Essay Form

An **essay** is a piece of writing with more than one paragraph. A short essay may have four or five paragraphs, totaling three hundred to six hundred words. A long essay is six paragraphs or more, depending on what the essay needs to accomplish—persuading someone to do something, using research to make a point, or explaining a complex concept.

An essay has three necessary parts: an introduction, a body, and a conclusion.

■ **TEACHING TIP:** Have students interview a second- or third-year student in their major to find out what kind of writing that person does for his or her classes.

■ **TEACHING TIP:** For some students, it helps to present visual analogies. Explain that just as a skyscraper needs more substantial support than a three-story apartment building, an essay needs more detailed support than a paragraph.

ESSAY PART	PURPOSE OF THE ESSAY PART
1. The **introduction**	states the **main point,** or **thesis,** generally in a single strong statement. The introduction may be a single paragraph or multiple paragraphs.
2. The **body**	supports (shows, explains, or proves) the main point. It generally has at least three **support paragraphs,** each containing facts and details that develop the main

[1] **Support group:** A group of people who meet regularly to talk about, and try to overcome, a difficulty.

point. Each support paragraph begins with a **topic sentence** that supports the thesis statement.

3. The **conclusion**   reminds readers of the main point. It may summarize and reinforce the support in the body paragraphs, or it may make an observation based on that support. Whether it is a single paragraph or more, the conclusion should relate back to the main point of the essay.

The parts of an essay correspond to the parts of a paragraph:

- The **thesis** of an essay is like the **topic sentence** of a paragraph.
- The **support paragraphs** in the body of an essay are like the **support sentences** of a paragraph.
- The **conclusion** of an essay is like the **concluding sentence** of a paragraph.

For a diagram showing how the parts of an essay correspond to the parts of a paragraph, see below.

■ **RESOURCES:** *Additional Resources* contains reproducible forms that students can use to plan their paragraphs and essays.

RELATIONSHIP BETWEEN PARAGRAPHS AND ESSAYS

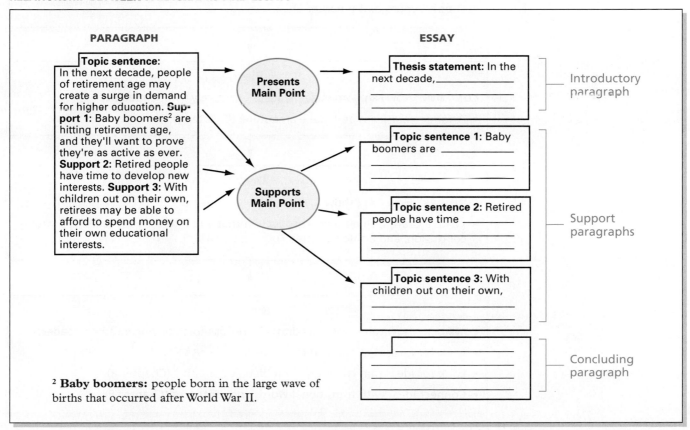

PARAGRAPH

Topic sentence: In the next decade, people of retirement age may create a surge in demand for higher education. **Support 1:** Baby boomers[2] are hitting retirement age, and they'll want to prove they're as active as ever. **Support 2:** Retired people have time to develop new interests. **Support 3:** With children out on their own, retirees may be able to afford to spend money on their own educational interests.

Presents Main Point

Supports Main Point

ESSAY

Thesis statement: In the next decade,_____ _____ _____   Introductory paragraph

Topic sentence 1: Baby boomers are _____ _____ _____   Support paragraphs

Topic sentence 2: Retired people have time _____ _____ _____

Topic sentence 3: With children out on their own, _____ _____

_____ _____ _____   Concluding paragraph

[2] **Baby boomers:** people born in the large wave of births that occurred after World War II.

Understand the Writing Process

■ **TEACHING TIP:** Ask students to describe a process related to their college experience, such as registering for classes, buying books, or applying for financial aid.

With writing, like something as simple as tying a shoe, there are many steps that you have to learn. But once you know the steps, you do them automatically, and they seem to blend together.

The chart that follows shows the five stages of the **writing process**: the steps you will follow to write well, especially in college. The rest of the chapters in Part One cover every stage except editing, which is detailed later in the book. You will practice each stage, see how another student completed it, and write your own paragraph or essay.

THE WRITING PROCESS

Generate Ideas

CONSIDER: What is my purpose in writing? Given this purpose, what interests me? Who will read this? What do they need to know?

- Find and explore your topic (Chapter 3).
- Make your point (Chapter 4).
- Support your point (Chapter 5).

Plan

CONSIDER: How can I organize my ideas effectively for my readers?

- Arrange your ideas and make an outline (Chapter 6).

Draft

CONSIDER: How can I show my readers what I mean?

- Write a draft, including an introduction that will interest your readers, a strong conclusion, and a title (Chapter 7).

Revise

CONSIDER: How can I make my draft clearer or more convincing to my readers?

- Look for ideas that don't fit (Chapter 8).
- Look for ideas that could use more detailed support (Chapter 8).
- Connect ideas with transitional words and sentences (Chapter 8).

> ### Edit
>
> **CONSIDER:** What errors could confuse my readers and weaken my point?
>
> • Find and correct errors in grammar (Chapters 21–32).
>
> • Look for errors in word use (Chapters 33–34), spelling (Chapter 35), and punctuation and capitalization (Chapters 36–40).

A Final Note: Avoiding Plagiarism

In all the writing you do, it is important to avoid plagiarism—handing in information you gather from another source as your own. Writers who plagiarize, either on purpose or by accident, risk failing a course, being expelled from school, or losing their jobs and damaging their reputations. Your instructors are very aware of plagiarism and know how to look for it; so if you plagiarize, you have a good chance of getting caught.

■ **TIP:** For more information on avoiding plagiarism, and citing and documenting outside sources, see Chapter 19.

To avoid plagiarism, take careful notes on every source (books, interviews, television shows, Web sites, and so on) you might use in your writing. When recording information from sources, take notes in your own words, unless you plan to use direct quotations. In that case, make sure to record the quotation word for word and include quotation marks around it, both in your notes and in your paper.

■ **RESOURCES:** Visit the Bedford/St. Martin's Workshop on Plagiarism at **bedfordstmartins.com/ plagiarism/** for online resources on avoiding plagiarism.

When you use material from other sources—whether you directly quote or paraphrase—you must name these sources in your paper. Therefore, as you take notes from sources, record the author's name, the title of the work, the date and place of publication, the publisher and its location, page numbers of the referenced material, and volume numbers (if relevant). With Web sites, be sure to also record the URL (the "address" where the Web site is located), the date you accessed the site, the date of publication or latest update, and the name of the sponsoring organization.

Chapter Review

1. Go back and highlight important terms in this chapter. Make a list of them, noting what page they appear on.

2. In your own words, define audience. *the person or people who will read what you write*

3. In college, who is your audience likely to be? *my instructors*

4. What are the stages of the writing process? *generating ideas, planning, drafting, revising, editing*

5. Think of other courses in which you have written papers or taken tests. What purposes has that writing had? *Answers could include showing knowledge of the material, giving examples, and so on.*

6. Did you know the stages of the writing process before you read this chapter? Do you understand how audience and purpose affect how you write? *Answers will vary.*

You Know This

You already know what a topic is:

- What was the topic of a movie you saw recently?
- What topic is in the headlines this week?
- What was the topic of a conversation you had recently?

3

Finding, Narrowing, and Exploring Your Topic

Choosing Something to Write About

Understand What a Topic Is

A **topic** is who or what you are writing about. A good topic is one that interests you, that you can say something about, and that you can get involved in.

QUESTIONS FOR FINDING A GOOD TOPIC

- Does this topic interest me? If so, why do I care about it?
- Do I know something about the topic? Do I want to know more?
- Can I get involved with some part of the topic? Is it relevant to my life in some way?
- Is the topic specific enough for the assignment (a paragraph or a short essay)?

Choose one of the following topics or one of your own and focus on one part of it with which you are familiar. (For example, focus on one personal goal or a specific aspect of romantic relationships that interests you.)

- Music/band I like
- Problems of working students
- An activity/group I'm involved in
- Something I'm really good at
- Reality television
- Relationships
- Sports
- An essential survival skill
- A personal goal
- A time I took a big risk
- A time I was really lucky/unlucky

■ **PRACTICE 1   FINDING A GOOD TOPIC** . . . .

Ask the "Questions for Finding a Good Topic" about the topic you have chosen. If you answer "no" to any of them, keep looking for another topic or modify the topic.

MY TOPIC: *Answers will vary.*

. . . .

With the general topic you have chosen in mind, read this chapter and complete all the practices. When you finish the chapter, you will have found a good topic to write about and explored ideas related to that topic.

If your instructor assigns a general topic, it may at first seem uninteresting, unfamiliar, or very general. It is up to you to find a good, specific topic based on the general one. Whether the topic is your own or assigned, you next need to narrow and explore it.

Practice Narrowing a Topic

To **narrow** a general topic, focus on the smaller parts of it until you find one that is interesting and specific.

There are many ways to narrow a topic. For example, you can try dividing a general category into smaller subcategories. Or you can think of specific examples from your life or from current events.

■ **TEACHING TIP:** To give students an example of what narrowing a topic is like, use a camera analogy. The general topic is similar to using a wide-angle lens. Narrowing it is like zooming in closer so that you can examine or focus on smaller elements of your subject.

Divide it into smaller categories

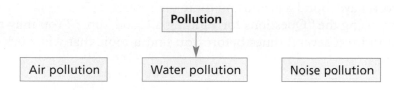

Think of specific examples

GENERAL TOPIC   Crime
Stolen identities (how does it happen?)
When I had my wallet stolen by two kids (how? what happened?)
The telemarketing scheme that my grandmother lost money in (how did it work?)

GENERAL TOPIC   Web sites
Shopping online (for what, and where?)
Music (what kind? what can I get?)
My favorite sites (why do I like them?)

Think of something related to the topic that happened in the last two weeks (or past month or year)

GENERAL TOPIC   **Energy problems**
High gas prices
Hot weather causing the state to run out of power

GENERAL TOPIC   **Heroism**
The guy who pulled a perfect stranger from a
    burning car
The people who stopped the robbery downtown

A topic for an essay can be a little broader than one for a paragraph, because essays are longer than paragraphs and allow you to develop more ideas. But be careful: Most of the extra length in an essay should come from developing ideas in more depth (giving more examples and details, explaining what you mean), not from covering a broader topic.

Read these examples of how a general topic was narrowed to a more specific topic for an essay, and an even more specific topic for a paragraph.

GENERAL TOPIC	NARROWED ESSAY TOPIC	NARROWED PARAGRAPH TOPIC
Drug abuse	How alcoholism affects family life	How alcoholism affects a family's budget
Public service opportunities	Volunteering at a homeless shelter	My first impression of the homeless shelter
A personal goal	Getting healthy	Eating the right foods
A great vacation	A family camping trip	What I learned on our family camping trip

When you have found a promising topic for a paragraph or essay, be sure to test it by using the "Questions for Finding a Good Topic." You may need to narrow and test several times before you find a topic that will work for the assignment.

■ **TEACHING TIP:** Give students examples of questions they might be asked that are too "big" to answer in a paragraph or essay. Have them figure out how to narrow the question or assignment.

■ **PRACTICE 2   NARROWING A GENERAL TOPIC** . . . .

Use one of the three methods above to narrow your topic. Then, ask yourself the "Questions for Finding a Good Topic." Write your narrowed topic below.

MY NARROWED TOPIC: *Answers will vary.* _____

C: If I were telling you how depressed I was or something and then found out you weren't listening, I'd think you didn't care about me and weren't my friend. My feelings would really be hurt, and I might not want to be friends anymore. Sometimes I wonder if even stuff like wars could be avoided if people just really listened and focused on what the other person was saying and tried to understand that other person's point of view. I mean really get inside the person's head.

T: Do you think you're a good listener?

C: No, not really. I'm always in a hurry and thinking about a million different things and not concentrating on any one thing. But I want to change that. Listening's important.

Clustering/Mapping

Clustering, also called mapping, is like listing except that you arrange your ideas visually. Start by writing your narrowed topic in the center. Then, write the questions Why? What interests me? What do I know? and What do I want to say? around the narrowed topic. Circle these questions and draw lines to connect them to the narrowed topic. Next, write three things in response to each of these questions. Circle these ideas and connect them to the questions. Keep branching out from the ideas you have added until you feel that you have fully explored your topic. Below is an example of Carol's clustering.

■ **RESOURCES:** It is helpful to provide students with a form they can use for clustering. A form is provided in *Additional Resources.*

■ **PRACTICE 3   EXPLORING YOUR NARROWED TOPIC** . . . .

Choose two or three prewriting techniques, and use them to explore your narrowed topic.

. . . .

Using the Internet

Go to a search engine such as Google, at **<www.google.com>**, and type in key words about your topic, being as specific as possible. The search will probably result in many more results than you can use, but it will give you lots of possible ideas. For example, Carol typed in "the importance of listening skills" and got lots of information about aspects of her topic that she didn't know much about, such as why people have trouble listening. Make notes about the most important or useful ideas you get from the Internet.

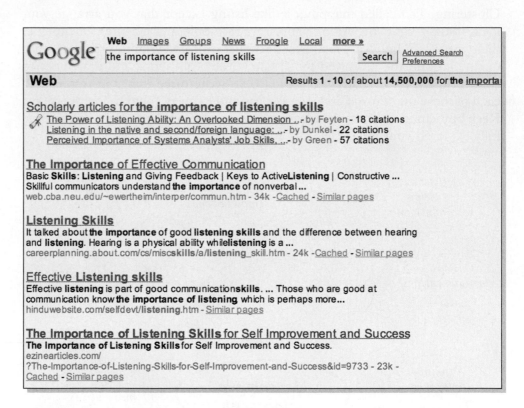

Keeping a Journal

■ **RESOURCES:** For tips on helping students keep journals, see *Practical Suggestions.*

Setting aside a few minutes on a regular schedule to write in a journal will give you a great source of ideas when you need them. What you write doesn't need to be long or formal.

You can use a journal in many ways:

- To record and explore your personal thoughts and feelings
- To comment on things that happen, either to you, or in politics, in your neighborhood, at work, in college, and so on

- To explore situations you don't understand (as you write, you may figure them out)

Jack was assigned to write in his journal, and at first he didn't like the idea: It seemed too much like a girl keeping a diary. But as he got used to writing in one, he found that it not only gave him ideas he could use in writing assignments but also helped him understand his own behaviors.

> *12/13/05—I've been doing some kinda weird things, like worse than usual road rage (yelling at other drivers, hitting the steering wheel, tailgating) and getting really mad at my girlfriend. At first I thought other people were just doing stupid things, but it's happening so often I'm starting to wonder if it's me. But I don't know why I'd be mad except everyone's all whipped up about Christmas. I hate this season. Everyone's got this fake cheery stuff going and buying like crazy and pretending the world is like a fairy tale. It's not and I hate Christmas, always have. Might want to think about when I started hating it and what happened to start it.*

■ **TEACHING TIP:** Some students may feel uncomfortable with journal writing. Emphasize that journal entries will not be graded, are confidential, and don't have to be written in polished prose.

This book contains two kinds of journal assignments.

IDEA JOURNAL: These prompts ask you to think about and comment on your experience with a topic or idea. They can provide interesting possibilities for future writing.

LEARNING JOURNAL: These end-of-chapter prompts help you see what you have learned.

Write Your Own Topic and Ideas

If you have worked through this chapter, you should have both your narrowed topic (recorded in Practice 2) and ideas from your prewriting. Now is the time to make sure your topic and ideas about it are clear. Use the checklist that follows to make sure that you have completed this step of the writing process.

CHECKLIST: EVALUATING YOUR NARROWED TOPIC
☐   This topic interests me.
☐   My narrowed topic is specific.
☐   I can write about it in a paragraph or an essay (whichever you have been assigned).
☐   I have generated some things to say about this topic.

Now that you know what you're going to write about, you're ready to move on to the next chapter, which shows you how to express what's important to you about your narrowed topic.

Chapter Review

1. Highlight important terms from this chapter (for example, *topic, narrow,* and *prewriting techniques*), and make a list of them with their page numbers.

2. The four questions for good topics are

   Does It Interest me?

   Do I know something about it?

   Can I get involved with some part of it?

   Is it specific enough for the assignment?

3. What are some prewriting techniques?

   freewriting

   listing/brainstorming

   discussing

   clustering/mapping

   using the Internet

   keeping a journal

4. What are two kinds of journals?

   idea journal

   learning journal

5. Write for one minute about "What questions I should ask my professor."

4

Writing Your Topic Sentence or Thesis Statement

Making Your Point

You Know This

You already have experience in making your point:

- You explain the point of a movie to someone who hasn't seen it.
- When a friend asks you, "What's your point?" you explain it.
- When you persuade someone to do something you want, you make your point about why they should.

Understand What a Topic Sentence and a Thesis Statement Are

Every good piece of writing has a **main point**—what the writer wants to get across to the readers about the topic, or the writer's position on that topic. A **topic sentence** (for a paragraph) and a **thesis statement** (for an essay) express the writer's main point. To see the relationship between the thesis statement of an essay and the topic sentences of paragraphs that support this thesis statement, see the diagram on page 45.

In many paragraphs, the main point is expressed in either the first or last sentence. In essays, the thesis statement is usually one sentence (often the first or last) in an introductory paragraph that contains several other sentences related to the main point.

A good topic sentence or thesis statement has several basic features.

BASICS OF A GOOD TOPIC SENTENCE OR THESIS STATEMENT

- It fits the size of the assignment.
- It states a single main point or position about the topic.
- It is specific.
- It is something you can show, explain, or prove.
- It is a forceful statement.

> **WEAK** Bill Gates, chairman of Microsoft,[1] started programming computers when he was thirteen, and I think he does a lot of good.
> [This statement doesn't follow the basics for three reasons: It has more than one point (Gates's age and his doing good), it is not specific (what is the good that he does?), and it is not forceful (the writer says, "I think").]

---

[1] **Microsoft:** the largest software company in the world.

■ **ESL:** Some cultures (particularly Asian ones) avoid making direct points in writing. You may need to explain that in English the rhetorical convention is that the writer make a clear, direct point. Ask students if writing conventions in their countries approach the main point differently.

■ **IDEA JOURNAL:** What are your strongest communication skills? What other skills or talents do you have?

GOOD   Bill Gates, chairman of Microsoft, is a computing genius who showed his talents early.

Bill Gates, chairman of Microsoft, uses his vast wealth for the good of society.

One way to write a topic sentence for a paragraph or a thesis statement for an essay is to use this basic formula as a start:

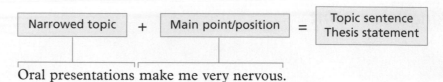

Oral presentations make me very nervous.

If you have trouble coming up with a main point or position, look back over the prewriting you did. For example, when Carol Parola looked over her prewriting about the importance of listening (see pp. 35–37), she realized that she'd mentioned several times how not listening had caused problems for her in college, at work, and in her personal life. Here's how she stated her main point:

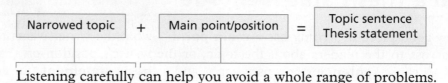

Listening carefully can help you avoid a whole range of problems.

■ **TEACHING TIP:** Ask students to bring in newspaper or magazine articles in which they've highlighted thesis statements or topic sentences. They should also label the topic and main point or position about that topic. Read and discuss some of these examples in class.

PRACTICE 1   **FINDING THE TOPIC SENTENCE AND MAIN POINT** . . . . .

Read the paragraph that follows and underline the topic sentence. In the spaces below the paragraph, identify the narrowed topic and the main point.

<u>A recent survey reported that employers consider communication skills more critical to success than technical skills.</u> Employees can learn technical skills on the job and practice them every day. But they need to bring well-developed communication skills to the job. They need to be able to make themselves understood to colleagues, both in speech and in writing. They need to be able to work cooperatively as part of a team. Employers can't take time to teach communication skills, but without them an employee will have a hard time.

NARROWED TOPIC: *communication skills*

MAIN POINT: *Employers consider communication skills more*

critical to success than technical skills.

Writing Your Topic Sentence or Thesis Statement

Making Your Point

Understand What a Topic Sentence and a Thesis Statement Are

Every good piece of writing has a **main point**—what the writer wants to get across to the readers about the topic, or the writer's position on that topic. A **topic sentence** (for a paragraph) and a **thesis statement** (for an essay) express the writer's main point. To see the relationship between the thesis statement of an essay and the topic sentences of paragraphs that support this thesis statement, see the diagram on page 45.

In many paragraphs, the main point is expressed in either the first or last sentence. In essays, the thesis statement is usually one sentence (often the first or last) in an introductory paragraph that contains several other sentences related to the main point.

A good topic sentence or thesis statement has several basic features.

BASICS OF A GOOD TOPIC SENTENCE OR THESIS STATEMENT

- It fits the size of the assignment.
- It states a single main point or position about the topic.
- It is specific.
- It is something you can show, explain, or prove.
- It is a forceful statement.

> **WEAK**   Bill Gates, chairman of Microsoft,[1] started programming computers when he was thirteen, and I think he does a lot of good.
> [This statement doesn't follow the basics for three reasons: It has more than one point (Gates's age and his doing good), it is not specific (what is the good that he does?), and it is not forceful (the writer says, "I think").]

---

[1] **Microsoft:** the largest software company in the world.

■ **IDEA JOURNAL:** What are your strongest communication skills? What other skills or talents do you have?

GOOD   Bill Gates, chairman of Microsoft, is a computing genius who showed his talents early.

Bill Gates, chairman of Microsoft, uses his vast wealth for the good of society.

One way to write a topic sentence for a paragraph or a thesis statement for an essay is to use this basic formula as a start:

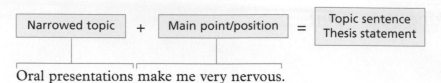

Oral presentations make me very nervous.

If you have trouble coming up with a main point or position, look back over the prewriting you did. For example, when Carol Parola looked over her prewriting about the importance of listening (see pp. 35–37), she realized that she'd mentioned several times how not listening had caused problems for her in college, at work, and in her personal life. Here's how she stated her main point:

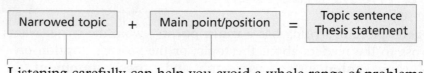

Listening carefully can help you avoid a whole range of problems.

■ **TEACHING TIP:** Ask students to bring in newspaper or magazine articles in which they've highlighted thesis statements or topic sentences. They should also label the topic and main point or position about that topic. Read and discuss some of these examples in class.

■ **PRACTICE 1   FINDING THE TOPIC SENTENCE AND MAIN POINT** . . . .

Read the paragraph that follows and underline the topic sentence. In the spaces below the paragraph, identify the narrowed topic and the main point.

A recent survey reported that employers consider communication skills more critical to success than technical skills. Employees can learn technical skills on the job and practice them every day. But they need to bring well-developed communication skills to the job. They need to be able to make themselves understood to colleagues, both in speech and in writing. They need to be able to work cooperatively as part of a team. Employers can't take time to teach communication skills, but without them an employee will have a hard time.

NARROWED TOPIC: *communication skills*

MAIN POINT: *Employers consider communication skills more*

critical to success than technical skills.

■   **PRACTICE 2   IDENTIFYING TOPICS AND MAIN POINTS** . . . .

In each of the following sentences, underline the topic and double-underline the main point about the topic.

> **EXAMPLE:** Rosie the Riveter was the symbol of working women during World War II.

1. Discrimination in the workplace is alive and well.

2. The oldest child in the family is often the most independent and ambitious child.

3. Gadgets created for left-handed people are sometimes poorly designed.

4. Presidential campaigns are dirty politics at their worst.

5. Companies that default on their employees' pensions should be taken to court.

6. The magazine *Consumer Reports* can help you decide which brands or models are the best value.

7. Of all the fast-food burgers, Burger King's Whopper is the best buy.

8. Status symbols are for insecure people.

9. Some song lyrics have serious messages about important social issues.

10. The Puritans came to America to escape religious intolerance, but they were very intolerant themselves.

Your first try at your topic sentence or thesis statement will probably need some changes to make it better. As you get further along in your writing, you may go back several times to revise the topic sentence or thesis statement, based on what you learn as you develop your ideas. Look at how one student revised the example sentence on page 42 to make it more detailed:

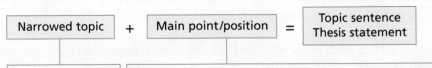

| Narrowed topic | + | Main point/position | = | Topic sentence / Thesis statement |

Oral presentations make me so nervous that I freeze and forget what I want to say.

Although a topic sentence or thesis statement states a single main point or position, this main point or position may include more than one idea; however, the ideas should be closely related. For example:

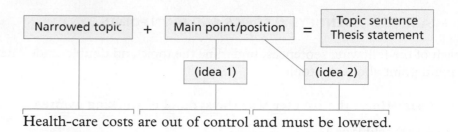

Health-care costs are out of control and must be lowered.

Practice Developing a Good Topic Sentence or Thesis Statement

The explanations and practices in this section, organized according to the "basics" described previously, will help you write good topic sentences and thesis statements.

It Fits the Size of the Assignment

As you develop a topic sentence or thesis statement, think carefully about the length of the assignment.

Sometimes, a main-point statement can be the same for a paragraph or essay.

                          Topic   Main point

In the next decade, people of retirement age may create a surge in the demand for higher education.

If the writer had been assigned a paragraph, she might write sentences that included the following support points:

SUPPORT 1: Baby boomers are hitting retirement age, and they'll want to prove they're as active as ever.

SUPPORT 2: Retired people have time to develop new interests.

SUPPORT 3: With children out on their own, retirees may be able to afford to spend money on their own educational interests.

If the writer had been assigned an essay, she might develop the same support, but instead of writing single sentences to support her main idea, she would develop each support point into a paragraph. The support sentences she wrote in a paragraph might be topic sentences for support paragraphs. (For more on providing support, see Chapter 5.)

Other times, however, a topic sentence for a paragraph is much narrower than a thesis statement for an essay, simply because a paragraph is shorter and allows less development of ideas.

RELATIONSHIP BETWEEN PARAGRAPHS AND ESSAYS

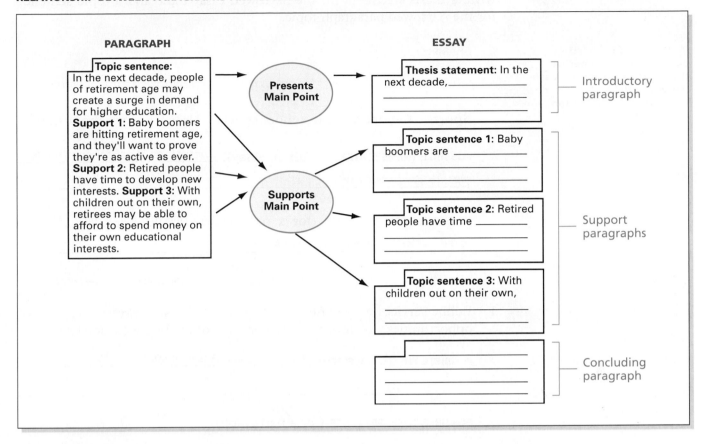

Consider how one general topic could be narrowed into an essay topic, and into an even more specific paragraph topic.

GENERAL TOPIC	NARROWED ESSAY TOPIC	NARROWED PARAGRAPH TOPIC
Drug abuse ———→	How alcoholism affects family life ———→	How alcoholism affects a family's budget

POSSIBLE THESIS STATEMENT (FOR THE ESSAY): Alcoholism can destroy family life.

[The essay might go on to give several ways in which alcoholism negatively affects the family.]

POSSIBLE TOPIC SENTENCE (FOR THE PARAGRAPH): Alcoholism quickly destroys a family's budget.

[The paragraph focuses on one way alcoholism affects family life—its budget—and might go on to give examples of how the budget gets destroyed.]

PRACTICE 3   WRITING SENTENCES TO FIT THE ASSIGNMENT . . . . .

For each of the three items in this practice, read how the topic has been narrowed for an essay or a paragraph. Using the following example as a guide, write a thesis statement for the narrowed essay topic and a topic sentence for the narrowed paragraph topic.

■ **RESOURCES:** To test students on choosing effective thesis statements and topic sentences, see the *Testing Tool Kit* CD-ROM available with this book.

EXAMPLE:

Topic	Narrowed for an essay	Narrowed for a paragraph
Sports	Competition in school sports	User fees for school sports

POSSIBLE THESIS STATEMENT (for an essay): *Competition in school sports has reached dangerous levels.*

POSSIBLE TOPIC SENTENCE (for a paragraph): *This year's user fees for participation in school sports are too high.*

Topic	Narrowed for an essay	Narrowed for a paragraph
1. Public service opportunities	Volunteering at a homeless shelter	My first impression of the homeless shelter

POSSIBLE THESIS STATEMENT (for an essay): *Answers will vary.*

_____

POSSIBLE TOPIC SENTENCE (for a paragraph): _____

_____

Topic	Narrowed for an essay	Narrowed for a paragraph
2. A personal goal	Getting healthy	Eating the right foods

POSSIBLE THESIS STATEMENT (for an essay): _____

_____

POSSIBLE TOPIC SENTENCE (for a paragraph): _____

_____

■ **COMPUTER:** When students write on the computer, have them use bold type for their topic sentence or thesis statement. This helps you see what they consider their main point and helps them stay focused as they provide support.

Topic	Narrowed for an essay	Narrowed for a paragraph
3. A great vacation	A family camping trip	A lesson I learned on our family camping trip

POSSIBLE THESIS STATEMENT (for an essay):

_____

POSSIBLE TOPIC SENTENCE (for a paragraph):

_____

Some topic sentences or thesis statements are too broad for either a short essay or a paragraph. A main idea that is too broad is impossible to show, explain, or prove within the space of a paragraph or short essay.

TOO BROAD   Art is important.

[How could a writer possibly support such a broad concept in a paragraph or essay?]

NARROWER   Art instruction for young children has surprising benefits.

A topic sentence or thesis that is too narrow leaves the writer with little to write about. There is little to show, explain, or prove.

TOO NARROW   Buy rechargeable batteries.

[Okay, so now what?]

BROADER   Choosing rechargeable batteries over conventional batteries is just one thing you can do to save the environment.

■ **PRACTICE 4   WRITING TOPIC SENTENCES THAT ARE NEITHER TOO BROAD NOR TOO NARROW** . . . .

In the following five practice items, three of the topic sentences are either too broad or too narrow, and two of them are OK. In the space to the left of the item, write either "B" for too broad, "N" for too narrow, or "OK" for just right. Rewrite the three weak sentences to make them broader or narrower as needed.

EXAMPLE: *B* Life is tough for soldiers in Iraq.

We are not providing our soldiers in Iraq with the equipment they need to fight

the war.

1. *N* Take public transportation.

   Answers will vary.

2. *OK* Because of state and national education budget cuts, schools are

   having to lay off teachers and cut important programs.

   _____

   _____

3. *B* College is challenging.

   _____

   _____

4. _B_ I would like to be successful in life.

_____

_____

5. _OK_ Having a positive attitude improves people's ability to function, improves their interactions with others, and reduces stress.

_____

_____

. . . .

It Contains a Single Main Point

Your topic sentence or thesis statement should focus on only one main point. Two main points can split and weaken the focus of the writing.

Main Idea with Two Main Points

High schools <u>should sell healthy food instead of junk food</u>, and they <u>should start later in the morning</u>.

The two main points are underlined. Although both are good main points, together they split both the writer's and the readers' focus. The writer would need to give reasons to support each point, and they are very different ideas.

Main Idea with a Single Main Point

High schools <u>should sell healthy food instead of junk food</u>.

OR

High schools <u>should start later in the morning</u>.

The main point may contain more than one idea, but these ideas should be closely related and serve an overall main point you want to make. For example, some writers use a three-point topic sentence (for a paragraph) or thesis statement (for an essay) that includes the main point and previews three support points that will be explored in the body paragraphs.

Three-Point Thesis

High schools should sell healthy food instead of junk food because (1) it is better for students, (2) it is often less expensive, and (3) it can boost levels of energy and attention.

■ **PRACTICE 5   WRITING SENTENCES WITH A SINGLE MAIN POINT** . . .

In each of the following sentences, underline the main point(s). Identify the sentences that have more than a single main point by marking an X in the space provided to the left of that item. Put a check (✓) next to sentences that have a single main point.

EXAMPLE: _X_ Shopping at second-hand stores is a fun way to save money, and you can meet all kinds of interesting people as you shop.

_✓_   1.   My younger sister, the baby of the family, was the most adventurous of us.

_X_   2.   Political campaigns are often nasty, and the voting ballots are difficult to understand.

_X_   3.   My brother, Bobby, is incredibly creative, and he takes in stray animals.

_X_   4.   Pets can actually bring families together, and they require lots of care.

_✓_   5.   Unless people conserve voluntarily, we will deplete our supply of water.

It Is Specific

A good topic sentence or thesis statement gives readers specific information so that they know exactly what the writer's main point is.

GENERAL   Students are often overwhelmed.
[How are students overwhelmed?]

SPECIFIC   Working college students have to learn how to successfully juggle many responsibilities.

One way to make sure that your topic sentence or thesis statement is specific is to make it a preview of what you are planning to say in the rest of the paragraph or essay.

PREVIEW: Working college students have to learn how to juggle many responsibilities: doing a good job at work, getting to class regularly and on time, being alert in class, and doing the homework assignments.

PREVIEW: I have a set routine every Saturday morning that includes sleeping late, going to the gym, and shopping for food.

■   **PRACTICE 6   WRITING SENTENCES THAT ARE SPECIFIC** . . . .

In the space below each item, revise the sentence to make it more specific. There is no one correct answer. As you read the sentences, think about what would make them more understandable to you if you were about to read a paragraph or essay on the topic.

EXAMPLE: Marriage can be a wonderful thing.

Marriage to the right person can add love, companionship, and support to life.

1. My job is horrible.

   Answers will vary.

2. Working with others is very rewarding.

   _____

3. I am a good worker.

   _____

4. This place could use a lot of improvement.

   _____

5. Getting my driver's license was challenging.

   _____

It Is an Idea That You Can Show, Explain, or Prove

If a main point is so obvious that it doesn't need support, or if it states a simple fact, you won't have much to say about it.

OBVIOUS   Models are very thin.

The Honda Accord is a popular car model.

Many people like to take vacations in the summer.

REVISED   In order to be thin, many models have to starve themselves.

Japanese cars became popular because they appealed to customer wishes that American car makers had missed.

The vast and incredible beauty of the Grand Canyon[2] draws crowds of visitors each summer.

FACT   Guns can kill people.

Violent crime was up 10 percent this summer.

More than 60 percent of Americans aged twenty and older are overweight.

REVISED   More than twenty thousand youths under age twenty are killed or injured by firearms each year in the United States.

Summer, a time of vacations, is also a time of increased violent crime.

The obesity rate in the United States is so high that reduction of it is now a national priority.

PRACTICE 7   WRITING SENTENCES THAT YOU CAN SHOW, EXPLAIN, OR PROVE . . . .

Revise the following sentences so that they contain an idea that you could show, explain, or prove.

EXAMPLE: Leasing a car is popular.

Leasing a car has many advantages over buying one.

1. I wear my hair long.

   Answers will vary.

2. My monthly rent is $750.

   _____

3. Health insurance rates rise every year.

   _____

4. Many people in this country work for minimum wage.

   _____

5. Technology is becoming increasingly important.

   _____

. . . .

[2] **Grand Canyon** (in Arizona): one of the most popular tourist attractions in the United States.

It Is Forceful

A good topic sentence or thesis is forceful. Don't say you *will* make a point. Just make it. Don't say "I think." Just state your point.

WEAK	In this paragraph I will talk about why people go to college.
FORCEFUL	People have many complex reasons for going to college.
WEAK	In my opinion, everyone should exercise.
FORCEFUL	Everyone should exercise to reduce stress, maintain a healthy weight, and feel better overall.
WEAK	I think student fees are much too high.
FORCEFUL	Student fees need to be explained and justified.

■ PRACTICE 8   WRITING FORCEFUL SENTENCES . . . .

Rewrite each of the following sentences to make them more forceful. Also, try to make up details to make the sentences more specific.

EXAMPLE: Jason's Supermarket is the best.

Jason's Supermarket is clean, well organized, and filled with top-quality

products.

1. I will prove that drug testing in the workplace is an invasion of privacy.

   Answers will vary. Possible answer: Drug testing in the workplace is an invasion

   of privacy.

2. This school should consider banning cell phones from classrooms.

   Possible answer: Because ringing cell phones are disruptive to class, this

   school should ban their classroom use.

3. I strongly think that I deserve a raise.

   Possible answer: I deserve a raise based on my strong performance over the

   past year.

4. Nancy should be the head of the Students' Association.

   Possible answer: Because she is hard-working, dedicated, and concerned

   about campus issues, Nancy should be the head of the Students' Association.

5. I think my neighborhood is really nice.

Possible answer: My neighborhood is safe, close to stores, and diverse.

Write Your Own Topic Sentence or Thesis Statement

If you have worked through this chapter, you should have a good sense of how to write a topic sentence or thesis statement that includes the five features of a good one (see p. 41).

Before writing your own topic sentence or thesis, consider the process that one student, Jeanette Castro, used. First, she narrowed her general topic.

GENERAL TOPIC: _an activity that you are very involved in_

NARROWED TOPIC (FOR A PARAGRAPH): _training to run a marathon_

NARROWED TOPIC (FOR AN ESSAY): _running a marathon_

Then, she did some prewriting (see Chapter 3) to get some ideas about her narrowed topic.

FOR A PARAGRAPH: _training to run a marathon_

Start six months before

Get good shoes

Work up to distance

Use a schedule (can find one on the Web)

FOR AN ESSAY: _running a marathon_

Training (schedule, shoes, routine, the final practice run)

The day before a marathon (what to eat and drink, whether to practice, how much sleep to get)

The morning of the marathon (how much time to leave before the race, what to eat and drink, how to dress, how to get psyched)

During the run (how often to drink, what to watch out for — physical symptoms, how to pace yourself, how to stay motivated and focused on your goal)

Next, she decided on the point she wanted to make about her topic — in other words, her position on it:

FOR A PARAGRAPH: _Training for a marathon is essential._

FOR AN ESSAY: _Running a marathon requires lots of planning and thought._

Then, she was ready to write the statement of her main point.

> **TOPIC SENTENCE (FOR A PARAGRAPH):** *Training is important if you want to run a marathon.*
>
> **THESIS STATEMENT (FOR AN ESSAY):** *Running a marathon is a process, not just something that happens on one day.*

Finally, Jeanette revised this statement to make it more forceful:

> **TOPIC SENTENCE:** *Training for success in a marathon involves several important steps.*
>
> **THESIS STATEMENT:** *Successfully running a marathon demands careful planning from start to finish.*

You may want to change the wording of your topic sentence or thesis statement later, but following a sequence like Jeanette's should start you off with a good basic statement of your main point.

■ **WRITING ASSIGNMENT** . . . .

■ **TEACHING TIP:** Even if you aren't reading a student's entire first draft, it always helps to check the topic sentence or thesis statement, because you can clear up numerous potential problems before you have to give a grade.

Write a topic sentence or thesis statement using the narrowed topic and ideas you developed in Chapter 3, your response to the idea journal prompt on page 42, or one of the following topics (which you will have to narrow).

Community service	Music	Exciting experiences
A controversial issue	Holiday traditions	Juggling many responsibilities
Dressing for success	A strong belief	
Movies	Medical marijuana use	Friendship
Good/bad neighbors	Parenting	Fast food
Interviewing for jobs		

. . . .

After writing your topic sentence or thesis statement, complete the checklist that follows.

CHECKLIST: EVALUATING YOUR MAIN POINT
☐   It is a complete sentence.
☐   It fits the assignment.
☐   It includes my topic and the main point I want to make about it.
☐   It states a single main point.
☐   It is specific.
☐   It is something I can show, explain, or prove.
☐   It is forceful.

Coming up with a good working topic sentence or thesis statement is the foundation of the writing you will do. Now that you know what you want to say, you're ready to learn more about how to show, explain, or prove it to others. That is covered in the next chapter: Supporting Your Point.

■ **LEARNING JOURNAL:**
How would you help someone who said, "I have some ideas about my topic, but how do I write a good topic sentence or thesis statement?"

Chapter Review

1. Highlight important terms from this chapter (for example, *topic sentence*, *thesis statement*, and *main point*), and make a list of them with their page numbers.

2. The **main point** of a piece of writing is *what the writer wants to get across to the readers about the topic.*

3. One way to write a **topic sentence** or a **thesis statement** is to include the narrowed topic and *the main point/position about the topic.*

4. The basics of a good topic sentence or thesis statement are

   It fits the size of the assignment.

   It states a single main point or position about the narrowed topic.

   It is specific.

   It is something you can show, explain, or prove.

   It is a forceful statement.

5. Write for one minute about "What questions I should ask my professor."

You Know This

You have lots of experience in supporting your point:

- You explain why you think a movie was boring.
- You explain to a child why locking the door is important.
- You give reasons to persuade someone of your opinion.

5

Supporting Your Point

Finding Details, Examples, and Facts

Understand What Support Is

Support is the collection of examples, facts, or evidence that show, explain, or prove your main point. **Primary support points** are the major ideas that back up your main point, and **secondary support** gives details to back up your primary support.

Without support, you *state* the main point, but you don't *make* the main point. Consider these unsupported statements:

The amount shown on my bill is incorrect.
I deserve a raise.
I am innocent of the crime.

The statements may be true, but without good support, they are not convincing. If you sometimes get papers back with the comment "You need to support/develop your ideas," the suggestions in this chapter will help you.

Writers sometimes confuse repetition with support. The same point repeated several times is not support. It is just repetition.

■ **IDEA JOURNAL:** Write about a time that you were overcharged for something. How did you handle it?

REPETITION, NOT SUPPORT	The amount shown on my bill is incorrect. You overcharged me. It didn't cost that much. The total is wrong.
SUPPORT	The amount shown on my bill is incorrect. I ordered the bacon-cheeseburger plate, which is $6.99 on the menu. On the bill, the order is correct, but the amount is $16.99.

As you develop support for your main point, make sure that it has these three features.

BASICS OF GOOD SUPPORT

- **It relates to your main point.** The purpose of support is to show, explain, or prove your main point, so the support you use must be directly related to that main point.

- **It considers your readers.** Create support that will show your readers what you mean.

- **It is detailed and specific.** Give readers enough detail, particularly through examples, so that they can see what you mean.

■ **TIP:** Showing involves providing visual details or other supporting observations. Explaining involves offering specific examples or illustrating aspects of the main point. Proving involves providing specific evidence, sometimes from outside sources.

Read the following two paragraphs, both written by Jeanette Castro, whose topic sentence you saw at the end of Chapter 4. In the first paragraph, she provides some support for her main point but does not give many details about it. In the second paragraph, she has added details (secondary support) to help her reader see the main point the way she does. The supporting details are in **bold;** in both paragraphs, the topic sentence is underlined.

PARAGRAPH WITH PRIMARY SUPPORT

Training for success in a marathon demands several important steps. Runners should first get a schedule developed by a professional running organization. They should commit to carefully following the schedule. On the night before and the morning of the big day, runners should take special steps to make sure they are prepared for the race.

PARAGRAPH WITH SECONDARY SUPPORT ADDED

Training for success in a marathon demands several important steps. Runners should first get a schedule developed by a professional running organization. **These schedules are available in bookstores or on the Web. A good one is available at <www.runnersworld .com>. All of the training schedules suggest starting training three to six months before the marathon.** Runners should commit to carefully following the schedule. **If they cannot stick to it exactly, they need to come as close as they possibly can. The schedules include a mixture of long and short runs at specified intervals. Carefully following the training schedule builds up endurance a little at a time so that by the time of the race, runners are less likely to hurt themselves. The training continues right up until the start of the marathon.** On the night before and the morning of the big day, runners should take special steps to make sure they are prepared for the race. **The night before the race, they should eat carbohydrates, drink plenty of water, and get a good night's sleep. On the day of the marathon, runners should eat a light breakfast, dress for the weather, and consider doing a brief warm-up before the race's start. Before and during the race, they should drink plenty of water.** Running a marathon without completing the essential steps will not bring success; instead it may bring pain and injury.

■ **TIP:** To see how the author of this paragraph provided support for a full essay on this topic, see Chapter 7, pages 73–88.

Practice Supporting a Main Point

Generate Support

To generate support for the main point of a paragraph or essay, try one or more of these three strategies:

THREE QUICK STRATEGIES FOR GENERATING SUPPORT

1. **Circle an important word or phrase** in your topic sentence (for a paragraph) or thesis statement (for an essay) and write about it for a minute or two. Reread your main point to make sure you're on the right track. Keep writing about the word or phrase.

2. **Reread your topic sentence or thesis statement and write down the first thought you have.** Then, write down your next thought. Keep going.

3. **Use a prewriting technique** (freewriting, listing, discussing, clustering, and so on) while thinking about your main point and your audience. Write for three to five minutes without stopping.

■ **TEACHING TIP:** Emphasize to students that prewriting can help them at every stage of the writing process, whenever they need to develop ideas further or provide more detail.

■ PRACTICE 1 **GENERATING SUPPORTING IDEAS** . . . .

Choose one of the following sentences, or your own topic sentence or thesis, and use one of the three strategies just mentioned to generate support. Because you will need a good supply of ideas to support your main point, try to find at least a dozen possible supporting ideas. Keep your answers because you will use them in later practices in this chapter.   *Answers will vary.*

1. This year's new TV programs are worse than ever.

2. Today there is no such thing as a "typical" college student.

3. Learning happens not only in school but throughout a person's life.

4. Practical intelligence can't be measured by grades.

5. I deserve a raise.

■ **IDEA JOURNAL:** Write about any of the sentences you don't choose for Practice 1.

. . . .

Select the Best Primary Support

After you have generated possible support, review your ideas and select the best ones to use as primary support. This is where you get to take control of your topic, because by choosing the support you give your readers, you are shaping the way they will see your topic and main point. These are *your* ideas, and you need to sell them to your readers.

The following steps can help:

1. Carefully read the ideas you have generated.

2. Select three to five primary support points that will best get your main point across to readers. If you are writing a paragraph, these will become the primary support for your topic sentence. If you are writing an essay, they will become topic sentences of paragraphs that support your thesis statement.

3. Choose the support that will be clearest and most convincing to your readers, providing the best examples, facts, and observations to support your main point.

4. Cross out ideas that are not closely related to your main point.

5. If you find that you have crossed out most of your ideas and do not have enough left to support your main point, use a prewriting technique to find more.

As you review your ideas, you may also come up with new ones that would be good support. If you come up with a new idea, jot it down.

■ **TIP:** To see the relationship between topic sentences and support in paragraphs, and thesis statements and support in essays, see the diagram on page 45 of Chapter 4.

■ **TEACHING TIP:** Remind students that just because they find a point interesting doesn't necessarily mean they should include it in their writing. It must support their main point.

▇ PRACTICE 2   SELECTING THE BEST PRIMARY SUPPORT . . . .

For each of the following two topic sentences, put a check mark (✓) next to the three points you would choose to support it. Be ready to explain your choices.

EXAMPLE:

TOPIC SENTENCE OR THESIS STATEMENT: Keeping a journal is the best thing I can do for myself.

POSSIBLE PRIMARY SUPPORT:

Can get out the anger and hurt

✓ Forces me to think

✓ Helps me understand my thoughts and feelings

Helps me decide what to do

Gives me good and bad memories

No one judges what I do there

No stress, just letting go

✓ Helps me decide what I want and what I should do to get there

1. **TOPIC SENTENCE OR THESIS STATEMENT:** Most Americans are not good listeners.

   POSSIBLE PRIMARY SUPPORT: *Answers may vary. Possible answers shown.*

   People talk more than they listen

   ✓ Competitive streak—everyone wants to say the most

   ✓ Even when quiet, thinking about what to say next, not listening

   ✓ Good listening is hard work

   Preparing a good "comeback"

   Good listening is active, not passive

   If you can't talk most of the time, talk faster

   Talk louder

2. **TOPIC SENTENCE OR THESIS STATEMENT:** Instead of being afraid of those who are different, people should learn to appreciate and learn from those differences.

   POSSIBLE PRIMARY SUPPORT:

   They're interesting

   ✓ Different ideas and perspectives

   Friendly

   Shouldn't teach your children to be afraid or hateful

   Gifted in other ways even if physically challenged

   ✓ Builds sensitivity

   ✓ Helps you to learn how to see and do things differently

   Shouldn't make fun of others

■ **PRACTICE 3   SELECTING THE BEST SUPPORT** . . . .

Refer to your response to Practice 1 (p. 58). Of your possible primary support points, choose three to five that you think will best show, explain, or prove your main point to your readers. Write your three to five points in the space provided here.

Answers will vary.

_____

_____

_____

_____

_____

Add Secondary Support

Once you have selected your best primary support points, you need to flesh them out for your readers. Do this by adding **secondary support**, specific examples, facts, and observations to back up your primary support points.

■ **PRACTICE 4   ADDING SECONDARY SUPPORT** . . . .

Using your answers to Practice 3, choose three primary support points and write them in the spaces indicated. Then, read each of them carefully and write down at least three supporting details (secondary support) for each one. For examples of secondary support, see the example paragraph on page 57. *Answers will vary.*

PRIMARY SUPPORT POINT 1:

_____

    SUPPORTING DETAILS: _____

_____

PRIMARY SUPPORT POINT 2:

_____

    SUPPORTING DETAILS: _____

_____

PRIMARY SUPPORT POINT 3:

_____

    SUPPORTING DETAILS: _____

_____

Write Your Own Support

Before developing your own support for a main point, look at how one student, Jesse Calsado, developed support for his.

> **TOPIC SENTENCE:** *Cheating comes in many forms, not just students cheating on tests.*

First, he did some prewriting and selected the best primary support points, while eliminating ones that he didn't think he would use:

> ~~Being paid under the table/not reporting income~~
>
> ✓ Not telling cashiers when they've undercharged you, or getting too much money back
>
> ✓ Doctors and dentists who tell patients they need stuff that's not really necessary because the insurance company will pay
>
> Not reporting stuff you find
>
> ~~Trying to sneak in free~~
>
> Even perfect Martha Stewart[1]
>
> ~~Cheating on a partner~~
>
> ~~Cheating at games~~
>
> ✓ Cheating on company time by using computers to e-mail friends or surf the Web
>
> ~~Scam artists~~
>
> ✓ Then there are the big cheaters: CEOs[2]

■ **COMPUTER:** Have students first type in possible support and then cut and paste to group it. They can easily move the points around to try new groupings.

Then, Jesse added supporting details for his possible primary support points. Before thinking of new supporting details, he reread his list of prewriting ideas to see if any of them would work. As he added detail, he wrote down other things that he thought of, too.

> **PRIMARY SUPPORT POINT:** Not telling a cashier you've been undercharged, or getting too much money back
>
> **SUPPORTING DETAIL:** A report in last week's paper: During a one-month period, reporters noted each instance of a customer being undercharged or getting too much change, and not once did the customer report it.
>
> **PRIMARY SUPPORT POINT:** Professionals recommend treatments that may not be necessary, just because the insurance company will reimburse the patient.
>
> **SUPPORTING DETAIL:** My dentist recommended that I get crowns for two teeth, for $1,400, and said my insurance would cover it. After I told him I didn't have insurance, he said that fillings would probably be fine.
>
> **PRIMARY SUPPORT POINT:** Cheating on company time
>
> **SUPPORTING DETAIL:** Using computers to write e-mails to friends and spending lots of time surfing the Web. Not as easy for supervisors to see as personal phone calls.
>
> **PRIMARY SUPPORT POINT:** Speaking of cheating, CEOs who mislead investors, spend company money on personal stuff, and cheat employees

---

[1] **Martha Stewart:** television and magazine personality who was convicted of lying to investigators about a stock-trading deal.

[2] **CEOs:** chief executive officers—leaders of corporations.

> **SUPPORTING DETAIL:** *The creative accounting of the former energy company Enron hid debt and inflated profits, and bosses sold stock off but wouldn't let employees. Former telecommunications giant WorldCom also used accounting to hide losses. Executives at Adelphia Communications used shareholder money to purchase the Buffalo Sabres, and for other stuff. Employees left with no jobs or savings plans or pensions. Even Martha Stewart was accused of getting "insider information"[3] that allowed her to sell stock before it dropped in value.*

Writing Assignment

Develop primary support points and supporting details using your topic sentence or thesis statement from Chapter 4, your response to the idea journal prompt on page 58, or one of the following topic sentences/thesis statements.

Same-sex marriages hurt the institution of marriage. *Or* Same-sex marriages should be legal.

Companies expect too much of their employees.

All families have some unique family traditions.

People who don't speak "proper" English are discriminated against.

Many movies have important messages for viewers.

After developing your support, complete the following checklist:

CHECKLIST: EVALUATING YOUR SUPPORT
☐ It is related to my main point.
☐ It uses examples, facts, and observations that will make sense to my readers.
☐ It includes enough specific details to show my readers exactly what I mean.

■ **LEARNING JOURNAL:** In your own words, explain what good support points are and why they are important.

Once you've pulled together your primary support points and secondary supporting details, you're ready for the next step: arranging them into a plan for a draft of a paragraph or essay. For information on making a plan, go on to the next chapter.

---

[3] **insider information**: Secret information about a company whose stocks are publicly traded.

Chapter Review

1. Highlight important terms from this chapter (for example, *support, primary support,* and *secondary support*), and make a list of them with their page numbers.

2. Support points are examples, facts, or evidence that _____*show*_____, _____*explain*_____, or _____*prove*_____ your main point.

3. Three basics of good support points are:

    It relates to your main point.

    It considers your readers.

    It is detailed and specific.

4. To generate support, try these three strategies:

    Circle an important word or phrase in your topic sentence or thesis statement and write about it.

    Reread your topic sentence or thesis statement and write down the first thought you have, then your second, and so on.

    Use a prewriting technique.

5. When you have selected your primary support points, what should you then add?

    secondary support (or supporting details)

6. Write for one minute about "What questions I should ask my professor."

6

Making a Plan

Arranging Your Ideas

Understand What a Logical Order Is

In writing, **order** means the sequence in which you present your ideas: what comes first, what comes next, and so on. There are three common ways of ordering—arranging—your ideas: **time order** (also called chronological order), **space order**, and **order of importance**.

Read the paragraph examples that follow. In each paragraph, the primary support points are underlined, and the secondary support is in italics.

■ **IDEA JOURNAL:** Write about a plan you came up with recently. How well did it work?

Use Time Order to Write about Events

Use **time order** (chronological order) to arrange points according to when they happened. Time order works best when you are writing about events. You can go from

- First to last/last to first
- Most recent to least recent/least recent to most recent

EXAMPLE USING TIME ORDER

Because I'm not a morning person, I have to follow the same routine every morning or I'll just go back to bed. First, I allow myself three "snooze" cycles on the alarm. *That gives me an extra fifteen minutes to sleep.* Then, I count to three and haul myself out of bed. *I have to do this quickly, or I may just sink back onto the welcoming mattress.* Next, I head to the shower. *I run the water for a minute so it will be warm when I step in. While waiting for it to warm up, I wash my face with cold water. It's a shock, but it jolts me awake.* After showering and dressing, I'm ready for the two cups of coffee *that are necessary to get me moving out of the house.*

What kind of time order does the author use? first to last

65

Use Space Order to Describe Objects, Places, or People

Use **space order** to arrange ideas so that your readers picture your topic the way you see it. Space order usually works best when you are writing about a physical object or place, or a person's appearance. You can move from

- Top to bottom/bottom to top
- Near to far/far to near
- Left to right/right to left
- Back to front/front to back

EXAMPLE USING SPACE ORDER

■ **IDEA JOURNAL:** What would you wear to look professional?

Donna looked very professional for her interview. Her long, dark, curly hair was held back with a gold clip. *No stray wisps escaped. Normally wild and unruly, her hair was smooth, shiny, and neat.* She wore a white silk blouse with *just the top button open at her throat. Donna had made sure to leave time to iron it so it wouldn't be wrinkled. The blouse was neatly tucked in to her* black A-line skirt, *which came just to the top of her knee.* She wore black stockings that she had *checked for runs* and black low-heeled shoes. Altogether, her appearance marked her as serious and professional, and she was sure to make a good first impression.

What type of space order does the example use? *top to bottom*

Use Order of Importance to Emphasize a Particular Point

Use **order of importance** to arrange points according to their importance, interest, or surprise value. Usually, save the most important for last.

EXAMPLE USING ORDER OF IMPORTANCE

■ **IDEA JOURNAL:** What do you think about keeping guns in your house? Does it guard against robberies? Is there risk involved?

People who keep guns in their houses risk endangering both themselves and others. Many accidental injuries occur when a weapon is improperly stored or handled. *For example, someone cleaning a closet where a loaded gun is stored may handle the gun in a way that causes it to go off and injure him or her.* There have also been many reports of "crimes of passion" with guns. *A couple with a violent history has a fight, and in a fit of rage one gets the gun and shoots the other, wounding or killing the other person.* Most common and most tragic are incidents in which children find loaded guns and play with them, accidentally killing themselves or their playmates.

What is the writer's most important point? *that children sometimes find loaded guns and accidentally kill themselves or their playmates*

Practice Arranging Ideas in a Logical Order

Choose an Order

After you have chosen support for your main point, you need to decide how to arrange your ideas. You might not always want to use one of the orders of time, space, or importance, but they help you to begin organizing your ideas.

■ **PRACTICE 1   CHOOSING AN ORDER** . . . .

Read each of the three topic sentences and the support points that follow them, and decide what order you would use to arrange the support in a paragraph. Indicate which point would come first, second, and so on by writing the number in the blank at the left. Then, indicate the type of order you used (time, space, or importance).

EXAMPLE: Many grocery stores share the same basic layout so that shoppers will have a sense of where to find what they want. *Answers may vary. Possible answers shown.*

_2_ juices and teas to the left of the produce

_3_ medicines and home goods in the middle

_1_ produce section (fruits and vegetables) on the far right

_4_ refrigerated foods on the far left

Type of order: *space: right to left or left to right*

1. It was one of those days when everything went wrong.

   _4_ My boss was waiting for me.

   _2_ I had no hot water for a shower.

   _6_ I got sick at lunch and had to go home.

   _3_ I missed the regular bus to work.

   _1_ My alarm didn't go off.

   _5_ I forgot to save work on my computer and lost it.

Type of order: *time: first to last*

2. For his fiftieth birthday, Elton John threw himself a huge party and dressed like a king from the eighteenth century.

   _4_ a powdered white wig of long curls

   _2_ tight white satin pants that came only to the knee

■ **RESOURCES:** To test students on ordering support effectively, see the *Testing Tool Kit* CD-ROM available with this book.

___5___ a headdress made of feathers and long plumes

___3___ a blue satin jacket with a high neck and diamonds sewn into it

___1___ blue satin high-heeled shoes studded with diamonds

Type of order: *space: bottom to top*

3. Properly extinguishing a campfire is every camper's duty.

___3___ You can even get a fine.

___1___ It cuts down on the smell of smoke, which can bother other campers.

___2___ If you don't extinguish well, you can get a citation.

___4___ Partially doused fires can ignite and burn wild.

Type of order: *importance*

■ **TIP:** Try using the cut-and-paste function on your computer to experiment with different ways to order support for your main point. Doing so will give you a good sense of how your final paragraph or final essay will look.

Make a Written Plan

When you have decided how to order your primary support points, it's time to make a more detailed plan for your paragraph or essay. A good, visual way to plan a draft is to arrange your ideas in an outline. An **outline** lists the topic sentence (for a paragraph) or thesis statement (for an essay), the primary support points for the topic sentence or thesis statement, and secondary supporting details for each of the support points. It provides a map of your ideas that you can follow as you write. Below are sample outlines for a paragraph and for an essay.

Outlining Paragraphs

SAMPLE OUTLINE FOR A PARAGRAPH

Topic sentence

    Primary support point 1

        Supporting detail for point 1

    Primary support point 2

        Supporting detail for point 2

    Primary support point 3

        Supporting detail for point 3

    Concluding sentence

Outlining Essays

If you are writing an essay, the primary support points for your thesis statement will become topic sentences for paragraphs that will make up the body of the essay. These paragraphs will consist of details that support the topic sentences. To remind yourself of the differences between paragraph and essay structure, see the diagram on page 45.

The outline below is for a typical five-paragraph essay, in which three body paragraphs support a thesis statement, which is included in an introductory paragraph; the fifth paragraph is the conclusion. However, essays may include more or fewer than five paragraphs, depending on the scope of the topic.

SAMPLE OUTLINE FOR A FIVE-PARAGRAPH ESSAY

This example is a "formal" outline form, with letters and numbers to distinguish between primary supporting and secondary supporting details. Some instructors prefer this format. If you are making an outline just for yourself, you don't have to use the formal system—but you do need a plan to order the points you want to make. In an informal outline, you might want to simply indent the secondary supporting details under each primary support.

■ **TIP:** For an example of a five-paragraph essay, see Chapter 7, pages 73–88.

Thesis statement (part of introductory paragraph 1)

    A. Topic sentence for support point 1 (paragraph 2)

        1. **Supporting detail 1 for support point 1**

        2. **Supporting detail 2 for support point 1** (and so on)

    B. Topic sentence for support point 2 (paragraph 3)

        1. **Supporting detail 1 for support point 2**

        2. **Supporting detail 2 for support point 2** (and so on)

    C. Topic sentence for support point 3 (paragraph 4)

        1. **Supporting detail 1 for support point 3**

        2. **Supporting detail 2 for support point 3** (and so on)

Concluding paragraph (paragraph 5)

■ **PRACTICE 2   MAKING AN OUTLINE** . . . .

The paragraph in this practice appeared earlier in this chapter to illustrate time order of organization. Read it and make an outline for it in the space provided.

    Because I'm not a morning person, I have to follow the same routine every morning or I'll just go back to bed. First, I allow myself three "snooze" cycles on the alarm. That gives me an extra fifteen minutes to sleep. Then, I count to three and haul myself out of bed. I have to do this quickly, or I may just sink back onto the welcoming mattress. Next, I head to the shower. I run the water for a minute so it will be warm when I step in. While waiting for it to warm up, I wash my face with cold water. It's a shock, but it jolts me awake. After showering and dressing, I'm ready for the two cups of coffee that are necessary to get me moving out of the house.

TOPIC SENTENCE: *Because I'm not a morning person, I have to follow the same routine every morning or I'll just go back to bed.*

    A. PRIMARY SUPPORT 1: *First, I allow myself three "snooze" cycles on the alarm.*

        1. SUPPORTING DETAIL: *That gives me an extra fifteen minutes to sleep.*

    B. PRIMARY SUPPORT 2: *Then, I count to three and haul myself out of bed.*

        1. SUPPORTING DETAIL: *I have to do this quickly, or I may just sink back onto the welcoming mattress.*

    C. PRIMARY SUPPORT 3: *Next, I head to the shower.*

        1. SUPPORTING DETAIL: *I run the water for a minute so it will be warm when I step in.*

        2. SUPPORTING DETAIL: *While waiting for it to warm up, I wash my face with cold water. It's a shock, but it jolts me awake.*

    D. PRIMARY SUPPORT 4: *After showering and dressing, I'm ready for the two cups of coffee*

        1. SUPPORTING DETAIL: *that are necessary to get me moving out of the house.*

Make Your Own Plan

■ RESOURCES: A reproducible blank outline for essays is in *Additional Resources.*

Before making your own plan, consider the process that another student used. In Chapter 3, you saw Carol Parola's prewriting on the importance of listening. After reviewing her prewriting, she saw that she'd mentioned the importance of listening in several different contexts. She grouped her support according to the importance of listening in school, at work, and in her everyday life. When she considered various ways in which to order her points (time, space, importance), she decided to present her ideas in the order of their importance to her, with the personal context last.

    Here is Carol's outline for a paragraph or an essay on the importance of listening.

TOPIC SENTENCE/THESIS STATEMENT: *Taking the time to listen carefully can help you avoid a whole range of problems.*

　PRIMARY SUPPORT POINT 1: *In school: Listening can help you prevent stupid mistakes that cause low grades.*

　　SUPPORTING DETAILS: *doing wrong assignment, getting due date wrong, getting test date wrong*

　PRIMARY SUPPORT POINT 2: *At work: Listening can help you avoid mistakes that can get you in trouble.*

　　SUPPORTING DETAILS: *shipping the wrong order, causing an accident with machinery*

　PRIMARY SUPPORT POINT 3: *Personal level: Listening can help you avoid misunderstandings.*

　　SUPPORTING DETAILS: *once hurt a good friend by not listening to something that was important to her; can avoid lots of misunderstandings with family; not miss important appointments*

CONCLUSION: *don't know yet; maybe review the importance of listening in so many areas*

■　**WRITING ASSIGNMENT** . . . .

Make a plan for a paragraph or an essay using the support you generated in Chapter 5, your responses to the idea journal prompts, or one of the following topic sentences/thesis statements.

The teacher I remember best is ＿＿＿＿＿＿＿＿＿＿＿＿＿＿＿＿＿ .

This school would make students happier/more successful if ＿＿＿＿＿ .

Work to live, don't live to work.

If I could make one change in my life, it would be ＿＿＿＿＿＿＿＿＿

＿＿＿＿＿＿＿＿＿＿＿＿＿＿＿＿＿＿＿＿＿＿＿＿＿＿＿＿＿＿＿ .

Most people are very poor listeners.

. . . .

After writing your plan, complete the following checklist.

CHECKLIST: EVALUATING YOUR PLAN
☐　It follows a logical order of organization.
☐　It includes all of my ideas, arranged in the order I want to present them.

■ **LEARNING JOURNAL:** In your own words, explain why making a written plan for your writing is helpful.

　　Now that you have a plan, you're ready to write a complete draft of your paragraph or essay, so move on to the next chapter.

Chapter Review

1. Highlight the important terms from this chapter (for example, *time order, space order,* and *order of importance*), and make a list of them with their page numbers.

2. In writing, what does order mean? *the sequence in which you present your ideas.*

3. Three ways to order ideas are ____*time*____, ____*space*____, and ____*importance*____.

4. Making ____*an outline*____ is a useful way to plan your draft.

5. Write for one minute about "What questions I should ask my professor."

7

Drafting

Putting Your Ideas Together

Understand What a Draft Is

A **draft** is the first whole version of all your ideas put together in a piece of writing. Do the best job you can in drafting, but know that you can make changes later.

■ **IDEA JOURNAL:** Write about a time when you had a trial run before doing something.

Practice Writing a Draft Paragraph

The draft of a paragraph needs to have the following characteristics:

BASICS OF A GOOD DRAFT PARAGRAPH

- It has a topic sentence that makes a clear main point.
- It has primary and secondary support that shows, explains, or proves the main point.
- It has ideas arranged in a logical order.
- It has a concluding sentence that makes an observation about the main point.
- It follows standard paragraph form (see pp. 77–78).

■ **TEACHING TIP:** Students can refer to these characteristics of a good draft in evaluating one another's papers in peer review.

Write a Draft Using Complete Sentences

When you begin to write a draft, work with your outline in front of you. Be sure to include your topic sentence, and express each point in a complete sentence. As you write, you may want to add support or change the order. It's okay to make changes from your outline as you write—an outline is only a plan.

Read the following paragraph, annotated to show the various parts of the paragraph.

Title

Topic sentence

Support

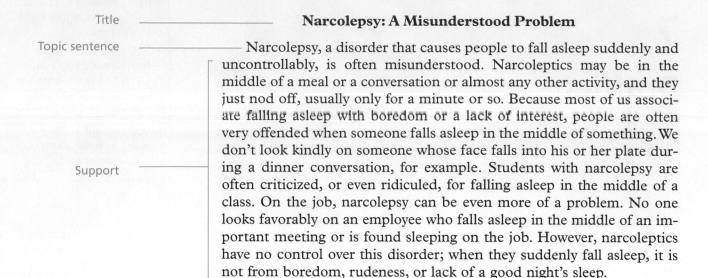

Narcolepsy: A Misunderstood Problem

Narcolepsy, a disorder that causes people to fall asleep suddenly and uncontrollably, is often misunderstood. Narcoleptics may be in the middle of a meal or a conversation or almost any other activity, and they just nod off, usually only for a minute or so. Because most of us associate falling asleep with boredom or a lack of interest, people are often very offended when someone falls asleep in the middle of something. We don't look kindly on someone whose face falls into his or her plate during a dinner conversation, for example. Students with narcolepsy are often criticized, or even ridiculed, for falling asleep in the middle of a class. On the job, narcolepsy can be even more of a problem. No one looks favorably on an employee who falls asleep in the middle of an important meeting or is found sleeping on the job. However, narcoleptics have no control over this disorder; when they suddenly fall asleep, it is not from boredom, rudeness, or lack of a good night's sleep.

■ **TIP:** For more on topic sentences, see Chapter 4.

Although paragraphs typically begin with topic sentences, they may also begin with a quote, an example, or a surprising fact or idea. The topic sentence is then presented later in the paragraph. For examples of various introductory techniques, see page 80.

Write a Concluding Sentence

■ **TEACHING TIP** Tell students that the concluding sentence gives them an opportunity to express a personal opinion based on the support they have provided, but they should not use it to introduce new, unrelated ideas.

A **concluding sentence** refers back to the main point and makes an observation based on what you have written. The concluding sentence does not just repeat the topic sentence.

In the paragraph above, the main point, expressed in the topic sentence, is "Narcolepsy, a disorder that causes people to fall asleep suddenly and uncontrollably, is often misunderstood."

A good concluding sentence might be "Narcolepsy is a legitimate physical disorder, and narcoleptics do not deserve the harsh reactions they often receive." This sentence **refers back to the main point** by repeating the word *narcolepsy* and by restating that it is a real disorder. It **makes an observation** by stating, ". . . narcoleptics do not deserve the harsh reactions they often receive."

■ **TIP:** In some cases, a paragraph is better off without a concluding sentence. If you want to omit a concluding sentence, be sure your instructor does not require one.

Concluding paragraphs for essays are discussed on pages 82–83.

■ **PRACTICE 1   CHOOSING A CONCLUDING SENTENCE** . . . .

Each of the following paragraphs has three possible concluding sentences. Circle the letter of the one you prefer, and be prepared to say why you chose it.

1. Have you ever noticed that people often obey minor rules while they ignore major ones? For example, most people cringe at the thought of ripping off the "Do not remove under penalty of law" tag from a new pillow. This rule is meant for the seller so that the buyer knows what the pillow is made of. The owner of the pillow is allowed to remove the tag, but people hesitate to do so. Another minor rule that people obey is the

waiting-line procedure in a bank. Ropes often mark off where a line should form, and a sign says "enter here." Customers then zigzag through the rope lines even when there is no one in line. The same people who tremble at the thought of removing a tag or ignoring the rope lines may think nothing of exceeding the speed limit, even at the risk of a possible accident.

    a. This doesn't make sense to me.

    b. What is it about those minor rules that makes people follow them?

    ⓒ Apparently "under penalty of law" is a greater deterrent than "endangering your life."

2. Student fees should not be increased without explanation. These fees are a mystery to most students. Are the fees for campus improvements? Do they support student activities and, if so, which ones? What exactly do we get for these mysterious fees? We are taught in classes to think critically, to look for answers, and to challenge accepted wisdom. We are encouraged to be responsible citizens. As responsible citizens and consumers, we should not blindly accept increases until we know what they are for.

    ⓐ We should let the administration know that we have learned our lessons well.

    b. Student fees should be abolished.

    c. Only fees that go directly to education should be approved.

> ■ **TEACHING TIP:** Warn students about two common problems in endings of paragraphs: (1) stopping abruptly so it seems that the paragraph is unfinished or that the writer ran out of time; (2) changing focus so readers are left wondering what the point is.

■ **PRACTICE 2 WRITING CONCLUDING SENTENCES** . . . .

Read the following paragraphs and write a concluding sentence for each one.

    1. One of the most valuable ways that parents can help children is to read to them. Reading together is a good way for parents and children to relax, and it is sometimes the only "quality" time they spend together during a busy day. Reading develops children's vocabulary. They understand more words and are likely to learn new words more easily. Also, hearing the words aloud helps children's pronunciation and makes them more confident with oral language. Additionally, reading at home increases children's chances of success in school because reading is required in every course in every grade.

Possible Concluding Sentence: _Answers will vary but should include the idea_

that reading helps children in many ways and/or that it is an important activity

for parents and children to share.

    2. There are certain memory devices, called *mnemonics,* that almost everyone uses. One of them is the alphabet song. If you want to remember what letter comes after *j,* you will probably sing the alphabet song in your head. Another is the "Thirty days hath September" rhyme that people use when they want to know how many days are in a certain

■ **TEACHING TIP:** If students
are required to write paragraphs for a standardized
test, tell them how many sentences are ideal for those paragraphs. Some test graders
penalize students for writing
short paragraphs

month. Another mnemonic device is the rhyme "In 1492, Columbus
sailed the ocean blue."

Possible Concluding Sentence: <u>Answers will vary but should refer to the</u>
<u>memory devices and how commonly they are used.</u>

Title Your Paragraph

The title is the first thing readers see, so it should give them a good idea of
what your paragraph is about. Decide on a title by rereading your draft, especially your topic sentence. A paragraph title should not repeat your topic
sentence.

Look at the title of the paragraph on page 74. It includes the topic (narcolepsy) and the main point (that this condition is misunderstood). It lets readers know what the paragraph is about, but does not repeat the topic sentence.

Titles for essays are discussed on pages 84–85.

■ **DISCUSSION:** Ask students
to name favorite TV shows,
movies, or songs, and write
them on the board. Then, in-
vite students to discuss what
makes these titles interesting
or dull, topic-appropriate or ir-
relevant. Can they think of better alternatives?

■ **PRACTICE 3**   **WRITING TITLES** . . . .

Write possible titles for the paragraphs in Practice 2.

1. <u>Answers will vary.</u>

2. _____

Write Your Own Draft Paragraph

Before you draft your own paragraph, read Jeanette Castro's annotated draft
below. (You saw her developing her main point in Chapter 4 and supporting it in Chapter 5.)

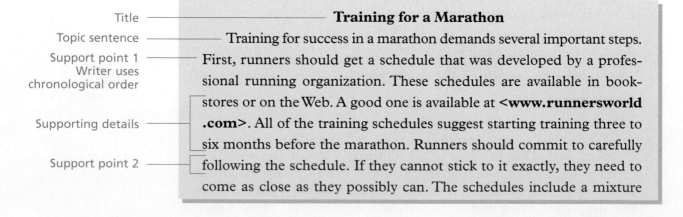

Title — **Training for a Marathon**

Topic sentence — Training for success in a marathon demands several important steps.

Support point 1 — First, runners should get a schedule that was developed by a profes-
Writer uses sional running organization. These schedules are available in book-
chronological order stores or on the Web. A good one is available at **<www.runnersworld**
.com>. All of the training schedules suggest starting training three to
Supporting details — six months before the marathon. Runners should commit to carefully

Support point 2 — following the schedule. If they cannot stick to it exactly, they need to
come as close as they possibly can. The schedules include a mixture

of long and short runs at specified intervals. Carefully following the training schedule builds up endurance a little at a time so that by the time of the race, runners are less likely to hurt themselves. The training continues right up until the start of the marathon. Closer to the time of the marathon, runners should make sure they are prepared for the big day. The night before the race, they should eat carbohydrates, drink plenty of water, and get a good night's sleep. On the day of the marathon, runners should eat a light breakfast, dress for the weather, and consider doing a brief warm-up before the race's start. Before and during the race, they should drink plenty of water. Running a marathon without completing the essential steps will not bring success; instead it may bring pain and injury.

Supporting details

Support point 3

Supporting details

Concluding sentence: refers back to main point and makes an observation

■ **WRITING ASSIGNMENT: PARAGRAPH** . . . .

Write a draft paragraph, using what you have developed in previous chapters, your response to the idea journal prompt on page 73, or one of the following topic sentences. If you use one of the topic sentences below, you may want to revise it to fit what you want to say.

Being a good ———————————— requires ————————————.

I can find any number of ways to waste my time.

People tell me I'm ————————————, and I guess I have to agree.

So many decisions are involved in going to college.

The most important thing to me in life is ————————————.

■ **COMPUTER:** Suggest to students that they highlight (using boldface or underlining) the support points in their drafts. This keeps them on track and also helps peer editors focus on the support points.

. . . .

After writing your draft, complete the following checklist.

CHECKLIST: EVALUATING YOUR DRAFT PARAGRAPH

- ☐ There is a clear, confident topic sentence that states my main point.
- ☐ Each primary support point is backed up with supporting details, examples, or facts.
- ☐ The support is arranged in a logical order.
- ☐ The concluding sentence reminds readers of my main point and makes an observation.

---

continued

☐   The title reinforces the main point.

☐   All of the sentences are complete, consisting of a subject and verb, and expressing a complete thought.

☐   The draft is properly formatted:

• My name, my instructor's name, the course, and the date appear in the upper left corner.

• The first sentence of the paragraph is indented, and the text is double-spaced (for easier revision).

• I have followed any other formatting guidelines provided by my instructor.

Practice Writing a Draft Essay

The draft of an essay needs to have the following characteristics:

BASICS OF A GOOD DRAFT ESSAY

• It has a thesis statement that makes a clear main point.

• It has primary and secondary support that shows, explains, or proves the main point.

• Each of its primary support points is a topic sentence for a paragraph.

• It has ideas arranged in a logical order.

• It has an introductory paragraph that draws readers in.

• It has a concluding paragraph that reminds readers of the main point and makes an observation about this point.

• It follows standard essay form (see p. 87).

Write Topic Sentences and Draft the Body of the Essay

When you start to draft your essay, use your outline to write complete sentences for your primary support points. These will serve as the topic sentences for the body paragraphs of your essay.

■   **PRACTICE 4   WRITING TOPIC SENTENCES** . . . .

Each thesis statement that follows has support points that could be topic sentences for the body paragraphs of an essay. For each support point, write a topic sentence.

EXAMPLE:

THESIS STATEMENT: My daughter is showing definite signs of becoming a teenager.

SUPPORT POINT: talking on the phone with friends

> **TOPIC SENTENCE:** *She talks on the phone for as long as she possibly can.*

SUPPORT POINT: a new style of clothes

> **TOPIC SENTENCE:** *She used to like really cute clothing, but now she has a new style.*

SUPPORT POINT: doesn't want me to know what's going on

> **TOPIC SENTENCE:** *While she used to tell me everything, she is now very secretive and private.*

SUPPORT POINT: developing an "attitude"

> **TOPIC SENTENCE:** *The surest and most annoying sign that she's becoming a teenager is that she's developed a definite "attitude."*

1. **THESIS STATEMENT:** Rhonda acts as if she is trying to fail this course.

   SUPPORT POINT: misses most classes

   > **TOPIC SENTENCE:** *Answers will vary.* _____

   SUPPORT POINT: is always late whenever she does come

   > **TOPIC SENTENCE:** _____

   SUPPORT POINT: never has her book or does any homework

   > **TOPIC SENTENCE:** _____

2. **THESIS STATEMENT:** The Latin American influence is evident in many areas of U.S. culture.

   SUPPORT POINT: Spanish language used in lots of places

   > **TOPIC SENTENCE:** _____

   SUPPORT POINT: lots of different kinds of foods

   > **TOPIC SENTENCE:** _____

   SUPPORT POINT: new kinds of music and popular musicians

   > **TOPIC SENTENCE:** _____

Drafting topic sentences for your essay is a good way to start drafting the body of the essay (the paragraphs that support each of these topic sentences). As you write support for your topic sentences, refer back to your outline, where you listed supporting details. (For an example, see Carol Parola's outline on page 71 of Chapter 6.) Turn these supporting details into complete sentences, and add additional support if necessary. (Prewriting techniques can help here; see Chapter 3.) Don't let yourself get stalled if you're having trouble with one word or sentence. Just keep writing. If you are writing by hand, use every other line to leave space for changes. Remember, a draft is a first try; you will have time later to improve it.

Write an Introduction for Your Essay

The introduction to your essay captures your readers' interest and presents the main point. Ask yourself: How can I sell my essay to readers? You need to market your main point.

The thesis statement is usually either the first or the last sentence in an introductory paragraph.

BASICS OF A GOOD INTRODUCTION

- It should catch readers' attention.
- It should present the thesis statement of the essay.
- It should give readers a clear idea of what the essay will cover.

Here are some common kinds of introductions that spark readers' interest. In each one, the introductory technique is in boldface. These are not the only ways to start essays, but they should give you some useful models.

Open with a Quote

A good short quote definitely gets people interested. It must lead naturally into your main point, however, and not be there just for effect. If you start with a quote, make sure that you tell the reader who the speaker is.

> 1. **George Farquhar once said that necessity was the mother of invention, but we know that to be nonsense, really:** Who needs an iPod that holds 10,000 songs? There is, however, one area of life in which technology keeps step with nature—the size of things. As we Americans are getting bigger (the Centers for Disease Control and Prevention in Atlanta estimate that roughly a third of Americans are overweight, with 20 percent of us qualifying as obese), so, too, is our stuff.
>
> —James Verini, "Supersize It"

Give an Example or Tell a Story

People like stories, so opening an essay with a brief story or example often draws them in.

> 2. **This is a true story: I was sitting at my desk, facing the challenge of how to begin a piece about the power of exercise to enhance creative thinking.** Naturally, I wanted this beginning to engage you, but nothing all that engaging was coming to mind. Zilch, in fact. So I did what I often do: I went to the pool and swam for an hour. Now here I am, back at my desk typing away, my writer's block well behind me.
>
> —Daryn Eller, "Move Your Body, Free Your Mind"

Start with a Surprising Fact or Idea

Surprises capture people's interest. The more unexpected and surprising something is, the more likely people are to take notice of it.

3. Now here is something to bear in mind should you ever find yourself using a changing room in a department store or retail establishment. **It is perfectly legal—indeed, it is evidently routine—for the store to spy on you while you are trying on their clothes.**

—Bill Bryson, "Snoopers at Work"

Offer a Strong Opinion or Position

The stronger the opinion, the more likely it is that people will pay attention. Don't write wimpy introductions! Make your point and shout it!

4. **Racial profiling is an ugly business—and I have been on record opposing it for years.** But I'm not opposed to allowing—no, requiring—airlines to pay closer attention to passengers [who] fit a terrorist profile, which includes national origin. The problem is distinguishing between what is permissible, indeed prudent, behavior and what is merely bigotry. As the Christmas day incident involving an Arab American Secret Service agent who was denied passage on American Airlines makes clear, it's not always easy to tell the difference.

—Linda Chavez, "Everything Isn't Racial Profiling"

Ask a Question

A question needs an answer, so if you start your introduction with a question, your readers will need to read on to get the answer.

5. **What is intelligence, anyway?** When I was in the Army, I received a kind of aptitude test that all soldiers took and, against a normal of 100, scored 160. No one at the base had ever seen a figure like that, and for two hours they made a big fuss over me. (It didn't mean anything. The next day I was still a buck private with KP[1] as my highest duty.)

—Isaac Asimov, "What Is Intelligence, Anyway?"

■ PRACTICE 5   MARKETING YOUR MAIN POINT . . . .

As you know from advertisements, a good writer can make just about anything sound interesting. For each of the following topics, write an introductory statement using the technique indicated. Some of these topics are purposely dull to show you that you can make an interesting statement about almost any subject if you put your mind to it.

EXAMPLE:

TOPIC: Reality TV

TECHNIQUE: Question

How many worms have contestants on Fear Factor eaten exactly?

---

[1] **KP:** kitchen patrol; kitchen duties in the military

■ **TEACHING TIP:** In the inverted-pyramid strategy, the introductory paragraph starts with a general statement and narrows to a thesis statement.

■ **TIP:** If you get stuck while writing your introductory statement, try one or more of the prewriting techniques described in Chapter 3, pages 32–40.

■ **TEACHING TIP:** Remind students that since the introduction should catch readers' attention, they should consider who their readers are and what they would find interesting.

1. **TOPIC:** Smoking cigarettes

   TECHNIQUE: Strong opinion

   Answers will vary.

2. **TOPIC:** Food in the cafeteria

   TECHNIQUE: Example or story

3. **TOPIC:** Credit cards

   TECHNIQUE: Surprising fact or idea

4. **TOPIC:** Role of the elderly in society

   TECHNIQUE: Question

5. **TOPIC:** Stress

   TECHNIQUE: Quote (You can make up a good one.)

■ **PRACTICE 6   IDENTIFYING STRONG INTRODUCTIONS** . . . .

In a newspaper, a magazine, an advertising flier—anything written—find a strong introduction. Bring it to class and be prepared to explain why you chose it as an example of a strong introduction.

. . . .

Write a Conclusion

Conclusions too often just fade out because writers feel they're near the end and think the task is over—but it isn't *quite* over. Remember, people usually remember best what they see, hear, or read last. Use your conclusion to drive your main point home one final time. Make sure your conclusion has the same energy as the rest of the essay, if not more.

BASICS OF A GOOD ESSAY CONCLUSION

- It should refer back to the main point.
- It should sum up what has been covered in the essay.
- It should make a further observation or point.

In general, a good conclusion creates a sense of completion: It brings readers back to where they started, but it also shows them how far they have come.

One of the best ways to end an essay is to refer directly to something in the introduction. If you asked a question, re-ask it and answer it. If you started a story, finish it. If you used a quote, use another one—maybe a quote by the same person or maybe one by another person on the same topic. Look again at two of the introductions you read earlier, and note how the writers conclude their essays. Pay special attention to the text in bold.

1. INTRODUCTION

This is a true story: I was sitting at my desk, facing the challenge of how to begin a piece about the power of exercise to enhance creative thinking. Naturally, I wanted this beginning to engage you, but nothing all that engaging was coming to mind. Zilch, in fact. So I did what I often do: I went to the pool and swam for an hour. Now here I am, back at my desk typing away, my writer's block well behind me.

> —Daryn Eller, "Move Your Body, Free Your Mind"

CONCLUSION

You may have to experiment a little to find out what works for you. For me, a moderate workout is best—that is, one long enough to help me get an "empty mind," but not so hard that it tires me out. **Once I get to that quiet state, so many ideas start percolating in my head that when I get home I often go straight to my desk to capitalize on the momentum. Need proof that it works? I finished this article, didn't I?**

> —Daryn Eller, "Move Your Body, Free Your Mind"

2. INTRODUCTION

Racial profiling is an ugly business—and I have been on record opposing it for years. But I'm not opposed to allowing—no, requiring—airlines to pay closer attention to passengers that fit a terrorist profile, which includes national origin. The problem is distinguishing between what is permissible, indeed prudent, behavior and what is merely bigotry. As the Christmas day incident involving an Arab American Secret Service agent who was denied passage on American Airlines makes clear, it's not always easy to tell the difference.

> —Linda Chavez, "Everything Isn't Racial Profiling"

CONCLUSION

Sure it's unpleasant to be a suspect when you're innocent. But it's worse to overlook terrorists because we ignored their pertinent characteristics. I sometimes felt annoyed when I was singled out, but I also felt safer because the airlines were doing their job.

> —Linda Chavez, "Everything Isn't Racial Profiling"

■ **PRACTICE 7   ANALYZING CONCLUSIONS** . . . .

How is the conclusion to the essay "Move Your Body, Free Your Mind" linked to the introduction (example 1 on p. 83)? How does it refer back to the introduction? Make some notes about these questions and be prepared to discuss your answers in class.

> *Answers will vary, but students might point out that the writer concludes the*
>
> *"story" begun in the introduction by showing how exercise helps free her mind.*

■ **PRACTICE 8   FINDING GOOD INTRODUCTIONS AND CONCLUSIONS** . .

> ■ **TEAMWORK:** Cut out the introductions and conclusions that students bring in, scramble them, and have the students work in small groups to match introductions and conclusions.

In a newspaper or magazine or anything written, find a piece of writing that has a strong introduction and conclusion. (You may want to use what you found for Practice 6.) Answer the questions that follow.

1. What method of introduction is used? *Answers will vary.*

2. What does the conclusion do? Restate the main idea? Sum up the support? Make a further observation? _____

3. How are the introduction and the conclusion linked? _____

> ■ **RESOURCES:** To test students on choosing effective introductions and conclusions, see the *Testing Tool Kit* CD-ROM available with this book.

Title Your Essay

Even if your title is the *last* part of the essay you write, it is the *first* thing readers read. Use your title to get your readers' attention and to tell them, in a brief way, what your paper is about. Use vivid, strong, specific words.

BASICS OF A GOOD ESSAY TITLE

• It makes people want to read the essay.
• It does not merely repeat the thesis statement.
• It may hint at the main point but does not state it outright.

One way to find a good title is to consider the type of essay you are writing. If you are writing an argument (as you will in Chapter 17), state your position in your title. If you are telling your readers how to do something (as you will in Chapter 12), try using the term *steps* or *how to* in the title. This way, your readers will know immediately not only what you are writing about but how you will discuss it.

> ■ **TIP:** Center your title at the top of the page before the first paragraph. Do not put quotation marks around it or underline it.

■ **PRACTICE 9   TITLING AN ESSAY** . . . .

Reread the paired paragraphs on page 83, and write alternate titles for the essays that they belong to.

Introduction/conclusion 1: _Answers will vary._ _____

Introduction/conclusion 2: _____

. . . .

Write Your Own Draft Essay

Before you draft your own essay, read Jeanette Castro's annotated draft below. (You saw her developing her main point in Chapter 4 and supporting it in Chapter 5.)

A Plan to Cross the Finish Line

——— Title indicates main point

"I want to run a marathon by the time I'm forty," I announced to my family last year. Little did I know what that would mean for a slightly lumpy, out-of-shape thirty-nine-year-old. I soon found out and now have some important information to pass on to any of you who are interested in running a marathon. Successfully running a marathon requires careful planning from start to finish.

Introductory paragraph: Writer opens with a quote. Writer uses chronological order.

Thesis statement

The whole process begins three to four months before the race. The first step is to get a good training schedule from a reliable source. I used the Web to find one at <**www.runnersworld.com**>, which has a variety of useful information in addition to schedules. The schedule is detailed and easy to understand, though quite rigorous. Around the time you get the schedule, buy a good pair of shoes. The *Runner's World* Web site has lots of advice about these, too. Go to a real runner's shoe store rather than a discount store where clerks don't know anything about shoes. Without good shoes, you will hurt your feet and run the risk of injury, so even if they're expensive, they are worth every penny.

Topic sentence
Support point 1

Supporting details

Next comes the actual training. Understanding the schedule is easy; following it isn't. Training takes a good deal of time, which I didn't have, and you probably don't either. Try to stick closely to the schedule, though. Finding a training partner can keep you on track: You can help each other make the time and go out in the bad

Topic sentence
Support point 2

Supporting details

Supporting details —

weather, deal with aching muscles, and face other unpleasantness along the way. If possible, try to run part of the actual course. Vary short and long runs as recommended to develop muscles and endurance and to avoid injury. A final practice run before the race will set you up physically and mentally. You might do this practice run two or three days before the marathon, leaving yourself some resting time before the race.

Topic sentence
Support point 3 —

Finally, the night before the marathon arrives, eat a nutritious, carbohydrate-rich meal and get a good night's sleep. Avoid coffee, alcohol, or sleep remedies. When you get up on the morning of the race, eat a light breakfast. Then, make sure to dress appropriately for the weather. If it's a cool day, you might want to bring layers that you can strip off. Allow plenty of time to get to the start of the race. In the minutes before the start cue, breathe deeply, relax, and psych yourself up. During the run, pace yourself and drink plenty of fluids at rest stops. If this is your first marathon, you probably aren't in it to win, so don't push yourself to the point of injury. After the race, drink more water if you need it, and cover up to keep your body temperature from dropping too low. You will need a lot of rest and recovery time in the hours and days that follow.

Supporting details —

Concluding paragraph:
First sentence relates
back to thesis statement. —

Refers back to
opening quote —

Anyone who is in reasonably good shape can run a marathon by carefully following several important steps. All that is required are patience, persistence, and determination. I should know, because, guess what? I ran a marathon before I turned forty, and you can run one, too.

■ **WRITING ASSIGNMENT: ESSAY** . . . .

Write a draft essay using what you have developed in previous chapters, your response to the idea journal prompt on page 73, or one of the following thesis statements. If you choose one of the thesis statements below, you may want to modify it some to fit what you want to say.

Taking care of a sick (child/parent/spouse/friend) can test even the most patient person.

Being a good ———————————— requires ————————————.

Doing ———————————— gave me a great deal of pride in myself.

A good long-term relationship involves flexibility and compromise.

Some of the differences between men and women create misunderstandings.

. . . .

After you have finished writing your draft, complete the following checklist.

CHECKLIST: EVALUATING YOUR DRAFT ESSAY

☐ There is a clear, confident thesis statement that states my main point.

☐ The primary support points are now topic sentences that support the main point.

☐ Each topic sentence is part of a paragraph, and the other sentences in the paragraph support the topic sentence.

☐ The support is arranged in a logical order.

☐ The introduction will interest readers.

☐ The conclusion reinforces my main point and makes an additional observation.

☐ The title reinforces the main point.

☐ All of the sentences are complete, consisting of a subject and verb, and expressing a complete thought.

☐ The draft is properly formatted:

- My name, my instructor's name, the course, and the date appear in the upper left corner.
- The first sentence of each paragraph is indented, and the text is double-spaced (for easier revision).
- The pages are numbered.
- I have followed any other formatting guidelines provided by my instructor.

Don't think about your draft anymore—for the moment. Give yourself some time away from it—at least a few hours and preferably a day. Taking a break will allow you to return to your writing later with a fresher eye and more energy for revision, resulting in a better piece of writing—and a better grade. After your break, you'll be ready to take the next step: revising your draft.

■ **LEARNING JOURNAL:** In your own words, explain how you write a draft.

Chapter Review

1. Highlight important terms from this chapter (for example, *draft*, *concluding sentence,* and *title*), and make a list of them with their page numbers.

2. A draft is _the first whole version of all your ideas put together in a piece of writing_

3. List the basic features of a good draft paragraph *or* essay: <u>*(Lists should include features on page 73*</u>

    <u>*or page 78.)*</u>

    _____

    _____

    _____

    _____

FOR AN ESSAY:

4. Five ways to start an essay are

    Open with a quote. _____

    Give an example or tell a story. _____

    Start with a surprising fact or idea. _____

    Offer a strong opinion or position. _____

    Ask a question. _____

5. Three features of a good conclusion are

    It refers back to the main point. _____

    It sums up what has been covered in the essay. _____

    It makes a further observation or point. _____

6. Three basic features of a good essay title are

    It makes people want to read the essay. _____

    It does not merely repeat the thesis statement. _____

    It may hint at the main point but does not state it outright. _____

7. Write for one minute about "What questions I should ask my professor."

8

Revising

Improving Your Paragraph or Essay

You Know This

You often make changes to improve things:

- You dress for an important occasion and then decide to try other clothes you think will be more suitable.
- You go to a store to buy a specific model of something (such as a CD player or a computer) and then, based on the information the salesperson gives you, you rethink your decision.
- You arrange furniture one way and then rearrange it a couple of times until it's right.

Understand What Revision Is

Revising and editing are two different ways to improve a paper.

Revising is taking another look at your ideas and making them clearer, stronger, and more convincing. When revising, you might add, cut, or change whole sentences or groups of sentences.

Editing is finding and correcting problems with grammar, style, word choice and usage, and punctuation. While editing, you usually add, cut, or change words and phrases.

Most writers find it difficult to revise and edit well if they try to do both at once. It is easier to solve idea-level problems first (by revising) and then to correct smaller, word-level ones (by editing).

REVISION STRATEGIES

- Search for ideas that do not fit.
- Search for ideas that are not as specific or complete as they could be.
- Search for ways to connect ideas so that they flow smoothly from one to the next.
- Search for ways to improve your overall paper.

No one gets everything right in one draft, so do not skip the revising stage. Commit yourself to making changes in any draft. Revising isn't optional: It is a critical part of any kind of writing you do, whether it is for college, for work, or for everyday life.

REVISION TIPS

- Give yourself a break from your draft (a few hours or a day).
- Read your draft aloud and listen to your words.

- Imagine yourself as your reader.
- Get feedback from a friend, classmate, or colleague (see the next section).
- Get help from a tutor at your college writing center or lab.

Understand What Peer Review Is

Peer review—exchanging drafts with other students and commenting on the drafts—is one of the best ways to get help with revising your writing. Other students can often see things that you might not—parts that are good and parts that need to be strengthened or clarified.

If you are working with one other student, read one another's papers and write down a few comments. If you are working in a small group, you may want to have writers take turns reading their papers aloud. Group members can make notes while listening and then offer comments to the writer that will help improve the paper. The first time someone comments on what you have written, you may feel a little awkward or embarrassed, but you'll get over it.

BASICS OF USEFUL FEEDBACK

- It is given in a positive way.
- It is specific.
- It offers suggestions.
- It may be given in writing or orally.

Often, it is useful for the writer to give the person or people providing feedback a few questions to focus on as they read or listen.

QUESTIONS FOR PEER REVIEWERS

1. What is the main point?
2. Can I do anything to make the introduction more interesting?
3. Do I have enough support for my main point? Where could I use more support?
4. Where could I use more details?
5. Are there places where you have to stop and reread something to understand it? If so, where?
6. What about the conclusion? Does it just fade out? How could I make my point more forcefully?
7. Where could the paper be better? What would you do if it were your paper?
8. If you were getting a grade on this paper, would you turn it in as is?
9. What other comments or suggestions do you have?

■ **TIP:** Among the useful Internet resources for writers revising a draft, two good online writing labs are found at the University of Missouri, <**www.missouri.edu/~writery**> and Purdue University, <**owl.english.purdue.edu**>. Other writers' resources are available at <**bedfordstmartins.com/rewriting**>.

■ **TEAMWORK:** Try modeling peer review. Bring in a short paragraph or essay, and have students answer the Questions for Peer Reviewers in small groups, with one person acting as a recorder. You can join each group for a few minutes to make sure students understand the process. Then, discuss the comments as a class.

■ **RESOURCES:** *Practical Suggestions* contains a discussion of peer feedback. Also, Comment, a Web-based peer review tool, is available with this book.

Practice Revising for Unity, Detail, and Coherence

You may need to read what you have written several times before deciding what changes would improve it. Remember to consider your audience and your purpose and focus on three areas: unity, detail, and coherence.

Revise for Unity

Unity in writing means that all the points you make are related to your main point; they are *unified* in support of your main point. As you draft a paragraph or an essay, you may detour from your main point without even being aware of it, as the writer of the following paragraph did with the underlined sentence. The diagram after the paragraph shows what happens when readers read the paragraph.

First, double-underline the main point in the paragraph that follows. This will help you see where the writer got off-track.

If you want to drive like an elderly person, use a cell phone while driving. A group of researchers from the University of Utah tested the reaction times of two groups of people—those between the ages of sixty-five to seventy-four and those who were eighteen to twenty-five—in a variety of driving tasks. All tasks were done with hands-free cell phones. That part of the study surprised me because I thought the main problem was using only one hand to drive. Among other results, braking time for both groups slowed by 18 percent. A related result is that the number of rear-end collisions doubled. The study determined that the younger drivers were paying as much—or more—attention to their phone conversations as they were to what was going on around them on the road. The elderly drivers also experienced longer reaction times and more accidents, pushing most of them into the category of dangerous driver. This study makes a good case for turning off the phone when you buckle up.

■ **TEACHING TIP** Read the paragraph aloud to the class, and ask students to stop you as soon as they hear it detouring from the main point.

■ **IDEA JOURNAL:** Write about your reactions to this study, including your own experiences with cell phones and driving.

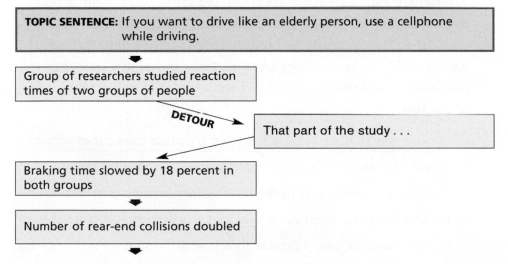

continued

■ **COMPUTER:** If you can send material to students' computers, type in a short paragraph or essay and have students add a sentence to the paragraph (or to each paragraph in the essay) that doesn't support the main point. Then, have students move to another computer and find the unrelated sentence or sentences that other students have input. They should put the detouring sentences in italics. Have them return to the original computer and see if the correct sentences are italicized.

Younger drivers paid too much attention to talking on the phone

↓

Elderly drivers also got worse

↓

CONCLUDING SENTENCE: This study makes a good case for turning off the cell phone when you buckle up.

Detours weaken your writing because readers' focus is shifted from your main point. As you revise, check to make sure that your paragraph or essay has unity.

 PRACTICE 1   REVISING FOR UNITY . . . .

Each of the following paragraphs contains a sentence that detours from the main point. First double-underline the main point, and then underline the detour in each paragraph.

■ **IDEA JOURNAL:** Write about the statement "Education is one of the few things people are willing to pay for and not get." Do you agree? How does this statement apply to you?

EXAMPLE:

<u><u>"Education is one of the few things people are willing to pay for and not get."</u></u> When we buy something expensive, we make sure we take it home and use it. For example, we wouldn't think of spending a couple of hundred dollars on a new coat and shoes only to hide them away in a closet never to be worn. And we certainly wouldn't pay for those items and then decide to leave them at the store. <u>I once left a bag with three new shirts in it at the cash register, and I never got it back.</u> People pay a lot for education, but sometimes look for ways to leave the "purchase" behind. They cheat themselves by not attending class, not paying attention, not studying, or not doing assignments. At the end of the term, they have a grade, but didn't get what they paid for: education and knowledge. They have wasted money, just as if they had bought an expensive sound system and had never taken it out of the box.

1. <u><u>One way to manage time is to keep a written calendar or schedule.</u></u> It should have an hour-by-hour breakdown of the day and evening, with space for you to write next to the time. As appointments or responsibilities come up, write them in on the right day and time. Before the end of the day, consult your calendar to see what's going on the next day.

Using a calendar saves you trouble, because once you write down the appointment or activity, you don't have to think about it anymore. Calendars come in all sizes, colors, and shapes. Once you are in the habit of using a calendar, you will see that it frees your mind because you are not always trying to think about what you're supposed to do, where you're supposed to be, or what you might have forgotten.

2. As you use a calendar to manage your time, think about how long certain activities will take. A common mistake is to underestimate the time needed to do something, even something simple. For example, when you are planning the time needed to get cash from the cash machine, remember that there may be a line of people. Last week in the line I met a woman I went to high school with. When you are estimating time for a more complex activity, such as reading a chapter in a textbook, block out more time than you think you will need. If you finish in less time than you have allotted, so much the better. Allow for interruptions. It is better to allow too much time than too little.

■ **TIP:** For more advice on managing your time, see Chapter 1, pages 4–6.

3. Effective time management means allowing time for various "life" activities. For example, it is important to budget time for chores, like paying bills, buying food, picking up a child, or going to the doctor. It seems as if my dentist is always a half hour behind schedule. A daily schedule should also account for communication with other people, such as family members, friends, service people, and others. It is important to allow time for relaxation. Do not schedule an activity for every minute; give yourself some "down" time. Finally, leave time for unexpected events that are a huge part of life, like last-minute phone calls, a car that won't start, or a bus that is late.

. . . .

Revise for Detail and Support

When you revise a paper, look carefully at the support you have developed, and imagine yourself as your reader: Do you have enough information to understand the main point? Are you convinced of the main point?

■ **TIP:** One advantage of writing on a computer is that revision is easier. You can even try out different versions and then decide later which one you like best.

In the margin of your draft (or between the lines), note ideas that seem weak or unclear. (As we noted in Chapter 7, you should double-space your drafts to allow room for revisions.) As you revise, build up your support by adding more details.

 PRACTICE 2   REVISING FOR DETAIL AND SUPPORT . . . .

Read the following paragraph, double-underline the main point, and add at least three additional support points or supporting details to it. Write them in the spaces provided under the paragraph, and indicate where they should go in the paragraph by writing in a caret (^) and the number.

EXAMPLE:

<u><u>Sojourner Truth was a brave woman who helped educate people about the evils of slavery.</u></u> She was a slave herself in New York₁. ₂After she had a religious vision, she traveled from place to place giving speeches about how terrible it was to be a slave. ₃But even after the Emancipation Proclamation was signed in 1863, slave owners did not follow the laws. Sojourner was active in the Civil War, nursing soldiers and continuing to give speeches. She was active in the fight for racial equality until her death in 1883.

1. *and was not allowed to learn to read or write.*

2. *Sojourner ran away from her owner because of his cruelty.*

3. *Although she was beaten for her beliefs, she continued her work and was part of the force that caused Abraham Lincoln to sign the Emancipation Proclamation freeing the slaves.*

<u>1. Sports fans can turn from normal people into maniacs.</u> After big wins, fans sometimes riot. Police have to be brought in. Even in school sports, parents of the players can become violent. People get so involved that they lose control of themselves and are dangerous.

1. *Answers will vary.*

2. _____

3. _____

<u>2. If you make your own pizza, you can add all the toppings you want.</u> Just start with dough you buy in the supermarket. Then, think about what toppings you want to use and put lots on. You can add dif-

ferent toppings to each half, making it the most delicious pizza you can imagine.

1. _____

2. _____

3. _____

. . . .

Revise for Coherence

Coherence in writing means that all of your support connects to form a whole. In other words, even when the points and details are assembled in an order that makes sense, they still need "glue" to connect them.

Coherence in writing helps readers see how one point leads to another. Individual ideas should be connected to make a clear overall impression. A good way to improve coherence is to use transitions.

Transitions are words, phrases, and sentences that connect your ideas so that your writing moves smoothly from one point to the next. Use transitions when moving from one main support point to another. Also use them wherever you want to improve the flow of your writing. The table on page 96 shows some common transitionals and what they are used for.

Here are two paragraphs, one that does not use transitions and one that does. Read them and notice how much easier the second paragraph is to follow. Both paragraphs make the same points, but the transitions (underlined) in the second paragraph help "hold it together."

■ **DISCUSSION:** Ask students who they think revises more—new writers or experienced writers. Students will often say that new writers do. Point out that experienced writers typically revise a great deal.

NO TRANSITIONS

It is not difficult to get organized—it takes discipline to stay organized. All you need to do is follow a few simple ideas. You must decide what your priorities are and do these tasks first. You should ask yourself every day: What is the most important goal I have to accomplish? Make the time to do it. To be organized, you need a personal system for keeping track of things. Making lists, keeping records, and using a schedule help you remember what tasks you need to do. It's a good idea not to let belongings and obligations stack up. Get rid of possessions you don't need, put items away every time you use them, and don't take on more responsibilities than you can handle. It isn't a mystery; it's just good sense.

TRANSITIONS ADDED

It is not difficult to get organized—<u>even though</u> it takes discipline to stay organized. All you need to do is follow a few simple ideas. You must decide what your priorities are and do these tasks first. <u>For example,</u> you should ask yourself every day: What is the most important task I have to accomplish? <u>Then,</u> make the time to do it. To be organized, you <u>also</u> need a personal system for keeping track of things. Making lists, keeping records, and using a schedule help you remember what tasks you

■ **TEACHING TIP:** Ask students to bring in a newspaper or magazine article with all transitions underlined.

need to do. <u>Finally</u>, it's a good idea not to let belongings and obligations stack up. <u>Get rid</u> of possessions you don't need, put items away every time you use them, and don't take on more responsibilities than you can handle. Organization isn't a mystery; it's just good sense.

Common Transitional Words and Phrases

INDICATING SPACE

above	below	near	to the right
across	beside	next to	to the side
at the bottom	beyond	opposite	under
at the top	farther/further	over	where
behind	inside	to the left	

INDICATING TIME

after	eventually	meanwhile	soon
as	finally	next	then
at last	first	now	when
before	last	second	while
during	later	since	

INDICATING IMPORTANCE

above all	in fact	more important	most
best	in particular	most important	worst
especially			

SIGNALING EXAMPLES

for example	for instance	for one thing	one reason

SIGNALING ADDITIONS

additionally	and	as well as	in addition
also	another	furthermore	moreover

SIGNALING CONTRAST

although	in contrast	nevertheless	still
but	instead	on the other hand	yet
however			

SIGNALING CAUSES OR RESULTS

as a result	finally	so	therefore
because			

■ **TIP:** More help with editing (and writing) is offered in the Writing Guide Software included with this book. For online editing exercises, visit Exercise Central at **bedfordstmartins.com/ realwriting**. To test students on transitions and other writing and grammar topics, use the *Testing Tool Kit* CD-ROM available with this book.

■ **PRACTICE 3   ADDING TRANSITIONS** . . . .

Read the following paragraphs. In each blank, add a transition that would smoothly connect the ideas. In each case, there is more than one right answer.

EXAMPLE:

Life Gem, a Chicago company, has announced that it can turn cremated human ashes into high-quality diamonds. _____After_____ cremation, the ashes are heated to convert their carbon to graphite. _____Then_____, a lab wraps the graphite around a tiny diamond piece and again heats it and pressurizes it. _____After_____ about a week of crystallizing, the result is a diamond. _____Because of_____ the time and labor involved, this process costs about $20,000. _____Although_____ the idea is very creative, many people will think it is also very weird.   *Answers will vary.*

1. Selena Quintanilla's story is both inspiring and tragic. _____When_____ she was very young, Selena sang in English in her father's band. _____As_____ a teenager, she started singing Tejano music in Spanish. Tejano literally means "Texan," but it has come to represent a culture of Mexican Americans. Selena's new Tejano music became very popular and successful, and she was ready to release an album in English. _____However_____, she was murdered right before the album's release. _____After_____ it was released, her album sold 175,000 copies in a single day, becoming one of the best-selling albums in history. Selena's death and stardom occurred almost simultaneously, when she was only twenty-four.

2. Many fast-food restaurants are adding healthier foods to their menus. _____For example_____, several kinds of salads are now on most menus. These salads offer fresh vegetables and roasted, rather than fried, chicken. _____However_____, be careful of the dressings, which can be very high in calories. _____Also_____, avoid the huge soft drinks that have large amounts of sugar. _____Finally_____, avoid the french fries. They are high in fat and calories and do not have much nutritional value.

■ **LEARNING JOURNAL:**
How would you explain the terms *unity, support,* and *coherence* to someone who had never heard them?

One other way to give your writing coherence is to repeat a **key word**, a word that is directly related to your main point. For example, look back at the paragraph on pages 95–96, the example with transitions added. The main point of the paragraph is that it's not difficult to get organized. Note that the writer repeats the word *organized* several times throughout the paragraph. Repetition of a key word is a good way to keep your readers focused on your main point, but make sure that you don't overdo the repetition.

Revise Your Own Paragraph

In Chapter 5, you saw Jesse Calsado developing support for his main point. Before you revise your own paragraph, read Jesse Calsado's paragraphs below. The first is his draft with his notes for revision. The second shows the revisions he made to his draft to make sure that it has unity, that it provides enough support and detail for his topic sentence, and that it is coherent.

Is affect the right word? Work on this topic sentence.

Add some kind of transition.

Add some kind of transition? This seems jumpy.

Add a transition.

Does this sentence really belong?

Be more specific about article.

Give more detail about experience.

This last sentence sounds weird.

Something seems wrong with the support. Rearrange points? Save worst or most common for last?

Cheating: It's Not Just a Classroom Concern

Cheating is not just a classroom concern: It affects nearly every aspect of life. Probably the most widespread and costly kind of cheating occurs in the workplace. Employees use computers to write e-mails to friends on company time. Speaking of corporate cheating, let us not forget CEOs who spend company money on personal stuff and cheat employees out of pensions and benefits when the company goes bankrupt. People usually do not speak up when being undercharged or getting too much money back. Cashiers really should be paying better attention; that's a real problem I've noticed lately. An article in last week's paper had information about that. Another example of cheating outside the classroom occurs when health-care providers recommend treatments that may not be necessary, just because the insurance company will reimburse the patient. I have had that experience with my dentist. When people hear the word *cheating,* they often think of students and tests, but there are lots of ways of cheating and lots of people doing it.

Cheating: It's Not Just a Classroom Concern

Topic sentence

Support point 1

Supporting detail

Support point 2

Supporting detail

Support point 3

Cheating isn't limited to the classroom; it occurs in nearly every aspect of life. One example of cheating is when people do not speak up when being undercharged or getting too much money back. ~~Cashiers really should be paying better attention; that's a real problem I've noticed lately.~~ An article in last week's *Sacramento Bee* indicated that during a one-month period, reporters stationed at certain stores noted each instance of a customer being undercharged or getting too much change, and not once did the customer report it. Another example of cheating outside the classroom occurs when health-care providers recommend treatments that may not be necessary, just because the insurance company will reimburse the patient. For instance, my dentist recommended that I get two very expensive crowns for two of my teeth and said my insurance would cover it. After I told him I didn't have insurance, he said that fillings would probably be fine. The most widespread and

Revised topic sentence

Added transition

Changed order to build up to the most costly cheating

Deleted a "detour"

Added detail

Added detail

Support point 3

Supporting detail

Conclusion

> costly kind of cheating occurs in the workplace. Employees use computers to write e-mails to friends and spend lots of time surfing the Web. The worst kind of corporate cheating is when CEOs spend company money on personal items and rob employees of pensions and benefits when the company goes bankrupt. As a student, I do not approve of academic cheating, but I do not believe that students are alone in this problem.

Transition added

Changed concluding sentence

WRITING ASSIGNMENT: PARAGRAPH

Revise the draft paragraph you wrote in Chapter 7. After revising your draft, complete the following checklist.

CHECKLIST: EVALUATING YOUR REVISED PARAGRAPH

- ☐ My topic sentence is confident, and my main point is clear.
- ☐ My ideas are detailed, specific, and organized logically.
- ☐ My ideas flow smoothly from one to the next.
- ☐ This paragraph fulfills the original assignment.
- ☐ I am ready to turn in this paragraph for a grade.
- ☐ This is the best I can do.

After you have finished revising your paragraph, you are ready to edit it. See the Important Note about this on page 102.

Revise Your Own Essay

In Chapter 5, you saw Jesse Calsado developing support for his main point. Before you revise your own essay, read Jesse Calsado's essays below. The first is his draft with his notes for revision. The second shows the revisions he made to his draft to ensure that it has unity, that it provides enough support and detail for his topic sentence, and that it is coherent.

Is "affects" the right word? Work on this thesis statement.

Cheating: It's Not Just a Classroom Concern

Cheating is not just a classroom concern: It affects nearly every aspect of life. By making that claim, I am not defending student cheating. I am saying, however, that our society has problems with all kinds of cheating, and we should recognize, admit to, and deal with those, too.

Add some kind of transi-
tion? This seems jumpy.

This one does, too. Do I
know enough to be more
specific? If not, maybe cut.

Add a transition.

Does this sentence really
belong?

Be more specific
about article.

Give more detail
about experience.

Rearrange support
points? Save worst
or most common for last?

This last sentence
sounds weird.

Probably the most widespread and costly kind of cheating occurs in the workplace. Employees use computers to write e-mails to friends on company time. Speaking of corporate cheating, let us not forget CEOs who spend company money on personal stuff and cheat employees out of pensions and benefits when the company goes bankrupt. Enron and WorldCom used creative accounting, and even Martha Stewart isn't perfect. Long-time employees were left with no jobs or savings plans or pensions.

People usually do not speak up when being undercharged or getting too much money back. Cashiers really should be paying better attention; that's a real problem I've noticed lately. An article in last week's paper indicated that during a one-month period, reporters stationed at certain stores noted each instance of a customer being undercharged or getting too much change, and not once did the customer report it.

Another example of cheating outside the classroom occurs when health-care providers recommend treatments that may not be necessary, just because the insurance company will reimburse the patient. I have had that experience with my dentist. He recommended that I get two very expensive crowns for two of my teeth and said my insurance would cover it.

When people hear the word *cheating*, they often think of students and tests, but there are lots of ways of cheating and lots of people doing it. Student cheating is not right. Neither is cheating by anybody else.

Cheating: It's Not Just a Classroom Concern

Introduction: Thesis statement is first sentence

Cheating is not just a classroom concern: It is all around us. By making that claim, I am not defending student cheating. I am saying, however, that our society has problems with all kinds of cheating, and we should recognize, admit to, and deal with those, too. Cheating isn't just for students.

Topic sentence: support point 1

One common example of cheating happens when people are undercharged or get too much money back. They never report it. ~~Cashiers really should be paying better attention; that's a real problem I've noticed lately.~~ An article in last week's *Sacramento Bee* indicated that during a one-month period, reporters stationed at certain stores noted each instance of a customer being undercharged or getting too much

Supporting detail

Changed thesis statement

Added transition sentence

Changed order of support.

Added transition

Deleted a "detour"

Supporting detail — change, and not once did the customer report it. When customers were overcharged or did not get enough change, they were very quick to speak up. However, they were quite comfortable cheating when the error was to their benefit.

Topic sentence: support point 2 —   Another example of cheating outside the classroom occurs when health-care providers recommend treatments that may not be necessary, just because the insurance company will reimburse the patient.

Supporting detail — I have had that experience with my dentist. He recommended that I get two very expensive crowns for two of my teeth and said my insurance would cover it. After I told him I didn't have insurance, he said that fillings would probably be fine. I had another experience like that, too. When my father was in the hospital with what turned out to be the flu, doctors ordered the most expensive and complicated tests available. They said they wanted to rule out serious problems, but I'm not convinced that they thought he really needed the tests. The more tests, the more money for the hospital.

Added detail

Transitional sentence added

Topic sentence: support point 3 —   The most widespread and costly kind of cheating occurs in the workplace. Employees use computers to write e-mails to friends on company time and to amuse themselves by surfing the Web. The worst kind of corporate cheating happens when CEOs spend company money on personal items and cheat employees out of pensions and benefits when the company goes bankrupt. For example, executives at Adelphia Communications used shareholder money to purchase the

Supporting detail — Buffalo Sabres and to buy personal items. Also, Enron used creative accounting to hide debt and inflate profits, misleading investors. Then, when the company got in trouble, top executives sold off stock but wouldn't let employees do the same. This kind of cheating robs long-time employees of jobs and savings, and it robs the public of trust in corporations.

Transition added

Word change

Added information about CEOs spending money on personal items and dropped WorldCom and Martha Stewart; not enough information

Conclusion —   When people hear the word *cheating*, they often zero in on students and tests, but cheating really is all around us. Student cheating is not right and should not be practiced or tolerated. But we are surrounded by even more damaging cheating practices, and we should be aware of that as well. Cheating, whoever is doing it, is harmful to our society.

Added to conclusion

■ **WRITING ASSIGNMENT: ESSAY** . . . .

Revise the draft essay you wrote in Chapter 7. After revising your draft, complete the following checklist.

- -

CHECKLIST: EVALUATING YOUR REVISED ESSAY

☐ My thesis statement is confident, and my main point is clear.

☐ My ideas are detailed, specific, and organized logically.

☐ My ideas flow smoothly from one to the next.

☐ This essay fulfills the original assignment.

☐ I am ready to turn in this essay for a grade.

☐ This is the best I can do.

IMPORTANT NOTE: Editing—making changes in grammar, word use, punctuation, and capitalization—follows revising and is the final stage in the writing process. After you have revised your writing to make the ideas clear and strong, you need to edit it to be sure there are no errors or distractions that could prevent readers from understanding your message. When you are ready to edit your writing, turn to Part Four, the beginning of the editing chapters.

Chapter Review

1. Highlight the important terms from this chapter (for example, *revising* and *editing*) and make a list of them with their page numbers.

2. Revising is _taking another look at your ideas and making them clearer, stronger, and more convincing_.

3. Why is revision important? (See p. 89.)
   No one gets everything right in one draft. Revision is critical to good writing.

4. Four basic features of useful feedback are
   It is given in a positive way.

   It is specific.

   It offers suggestions.

   It may be given in writing or orally.

5. As you revise, make sure that your paragraph or essay has these three things: _unity_, _detail/support_, and _coherence_.

6. _____*Unity*_____ means that all the points you make are related to your main point.

7. Coherence means *that all of your points and details connect to form a whole.*

8. An important way to ensure coherence in your writing is to *use transitions.*

9. Transitions are *words, phrases, and sentences that connect your ideas so that your writing moves smoothly from one point to the next.*

10. Write for one minute about "What questions I should ask my instructor."

Part Two

Writing Different Kinds of Paragraphs and Essays

9

Narration

Writing That Tells Stories

You Know This

You often use narration:

- You tell a friend what you did or where you went over the weekend.
- You explain the plot of a movie you saw to people who haven't seen it.
- You say, "You won't believe what happened the other day." Then you tell the story.

Understand What Narration Is

Narration is writing that tells the story of an event or an experience.

■■ FOUR BASICS OF GOOD NARRATION
■■■

1. It reveals something of importance to you (your main point).
2. It includes all of the major events of the story (primary support).
3. It brings the story to life with details about the major events (secondary support).
4. It presents the events in a clear order, usually according to when they happened.

In the following paragraph, each number corresponds to one of the Basics of Good Narration.

> **1** Last night, my husband saved my life. We were sitting out on the porch with a couple of friends, enjoying the cool breeze of the evening. **2** While eating a piece of melon for dessert, I laughed at something my friend said, and suddenly the fruit stuck in my windpipe, entirely blocking any air. **3** I tried to swallow hard and dislodge it, but it didn't move. When I tried taking a deep breath, I couldn't get one. **2** Fortunately, my husband, seated across the table from me, saw that something was wrong and asked me if I needed help. Close to panic, I nodded yes. **3** My eyes were filled with tears, and I could hear the blood pounding in my ears. I thought, briefly, *I could die.* **2** My husband ran in behind me, pulled me up, and placed his arms around me. My heart was really beating hard by this time, and I was panicky. He jerked his fists firmly into my body, under my rib cage. The melon flew out of my mouth. I breathed in precious air and hugged my husband for a long time, half laughing, half crying. For a while, at least, I'll try to remember that I owe him my life and not get irritated when he forgets to do something.

4 Events in chronological order

■ **IDEA JOURNAL:** Write about something that happened to you this week.

You can use narration in many practical situations:

COLLEGE	In a reading or English course, you are asked to tell, in your own words, the basic story of a piece of literature.
WORK	Something goes wrong at work, and you are asked to explain to your boss—in writing—what happened.
EVERYDAY LIFE	In a letter of complaint about service you received, you need to tell what happened that upset you.

Profile of Success: Narration in the Real World

Kelly Layland
Registered Nurse

■ **RESOURCES:** For a discussion of how to use the profiles in Part Two, see *Practical Suggestions.*

The following profile shows how a nurse uses narration on the job.

BACKGROUND: In high school, I wasn't a good student. I had a lot of other things to do, like having fun. I'm a very social person; I loved my friends, and we had a great time. But when I decided I wanted to go to college, I had to pay the price. I had to take lots of noncredit courses to get my skills up to college level because I'd fooled around during high school. The noncredit English course I took was very beneficial to me. After I passed it, I took English 101 and felt prepared for it.

COLLEGE(S)/DEGREES: A.S., Monroe Community College; L.P.N., Isabella Graham Hart School of Nursing; R.N., Monroe Community College

EMPLOYER: Rochester General Hospital

WRITING AT WORK: I don't write long pieces at work, but I write every day, mostly patient notes, summaries, and reports. The accuracy of my writing affects patient treatment.

HOW KELLY USES NARRATION: Every day I write brief narratives that recount all that went on with the patient during the day: things that went wrong and things about his or her treatment that need to be changed.

KELLY'S NARRATION

The following paragraph is an example of the daily reports that Kelly writes on each patient.

<u>Karella Lehmanoff, a two-month-old female infant, is improving steadily.</u> When she was born, her birth weight was 1.3 pounds, but <u>it has increased to 3.1 pounds.</u> <u>Her jaundice has completely disappeared,</u> and her skin has begun to look rosy. Karella's pulse rate is normal for her development, and <u>her resting heart rate has stabilized at about 150 beats per minute.</u> Lung development was a big concern because of Karella's premature birth, but <u>her lungs are now fully developed and largely functional.</u> <u>Dr. Lansing saw Karella at 1 P.M. and pronounced her in good condition.</u> The parents were encouraged, and so am I. The prognosis for little Karella gets better with each day.

1. Double-underline the **main point** of the narration.

2. Underline the **major events**.

3. What order of organization does Kelly use? _____ *time order* _____

Main Point in Narration

In narration, the **main point** is what is important about the story—to you (and to your readers). To help you discover the main point for your own narration, complete the following sentence:

What's important to me about the experience is . . .

Doing so can help you avoid the "So what?" response from readers. Notice the difference between the following two opening sentences in a narration:

IMPORTANCE NOT CLEAR   My child plays soccer. [So what?]

IMPORTANCE CLEAR   Soccer takes up all of my child's free time.

The topic sentence (paragraph) or thesis statement (essay) usually includes the topic and the main point the writer wants to make about it.

My first day at my new job was nearly a disaster.

My first date with Pat was full of surprises.

Although writers usually reveal the main point either at the beginning or at the end of their narration, here we suggest that you start off with your main point and remind readers of that main point at the end of your paragraph or essay.

▮ PRACTICE 1   DECIDING ON A MAIN POINT . . . .

For each of the following topics, write what main point you might make in a narration. Then, write a sentence that includes your topic and your main point. This is your topic sentence (paragraph) or thesis statement (essay). There is no one correct answer; you are practicing how to decide on a main point about a topic. Before writing your answer, you may need to make some notes about the topic.

EXAMPLE:

TOPIC: A fight I had with my sister

MAIN POINT: _learned it's better to stay cool_

TOPIC SENTENCE/THESIS: _After a horrible fight with my sister, I learned the_
value of staying calm.

1. **TOPIC:** A commute to work or school

   MAIN POINT: _Answers will vary._

   TOPIC SENTENCE/THESIS: _Answers will vary._

2. **TOPIC:** An embarrassing experience

   MAIN POINT: _____

   TOPIC SENTENCE/THESIS: _____

3. **TOPIC:** A funny incident that you witnessed

   MAIN POINT: _____

   TOPIC SENTENCE/THESIS: _____

4. **TOPIC:** A typical evening at home

   MAIN POINT: _____

   TOPIC SENTENCE/THESIS: _____

5. **TOPIC:** A funny or frightening dream

   MAIN POINT: _____

   TOPIC SENTENCE/THESIS: _____

. . . .

Support in Narration

■ **TIP:** In an essay, the major events may form the topic sentences of paragraphs. The details supporting the major events then make up the body of these paragraphs.

In a narration, the **support** consists of the major events you include (primary support) and the details (secondary support) you give the reader about those events. Your support should demonstrate your main point—what's important to you about the story.

The way you describe events creates a story with a certain point of view. For example, two people who witness or participate in the same series of events may give very different accounts of it because they either focused on different events or saw those events differently. The stories Charlene and Daryl tell in the following two paragraphs reflect different points of view. Read these two accounts of the same experience.

CHARLENE'S STORY

■ **TIP:** In writing a narration, you may use direct quotations (as this writer did) or indirect quotations. For more information on how to incorporate and punctuate quotations, see Chapter 19, pages 248–271.

This morning, I could have killed my husband. While I was running around yelling at the kids, trying to get them fed and off to school, he sat there reading the newspaper. When I finally sat down, he just kept on reading that newspaper, even though I needed to talk with him. After several attempts to get through to him, I finally barked out, "Daryl! I have a few things I need to say!" He looked up, smiled, got another cup of coffee, and said, "What?" But as I began talking, he resumed reading the paper. Does he live in another world?

DARYL'S STORY

> This morning my family enjoyed some "quality time" together. The children were all in the kitchen eating and talking with each other. After they left for school, my wife and I were able to sit and share some quiet time at the table. We chatted about various things while drinking coffee and looking at the newspaper. It really started the day out right.

As you can see, the events are the same, but the stories aren't; they are told from two different points of view. Be careful to describe events in a way that will tell the story you want to tell.

Choosing Major Events

When you tell a story to a friend in person or on the phone, you have the luxury of including events that aren't essential to the story or of going back and filling in events that you've forgotten. When you are writing a narration, however, you need to make choices about which events to include, selecting only those that most clearly demonstrate your main point. If you find later that you've left out an important event, you can add it when you are revising.

■ **ESL:** Ask students if they have seen certain events differently than other people because of language or cultural differences.

■ **TEACHING TIP:** Ask students to write a narrative joke they've heard—then, examine the structure of one or two of these jokes.

■ PRACTICE 2   **CHOOSING MAJOR EVENTS** . . . .

This practice uses three items from Practice 1, where you wrote topic sentences/thesis statements. Using three sentences from that practice, write three events for each that would help you make your main point. Remember, there is no one correct answer: What you want to do is think logically about three essential events that will demonstrate your main point to readers.

EXAMPLE:

TOPIC: A fight I had with my sister

TOPIC SENTENCE/THESIS: _After a horrible fight with my sister, I learned the value of staying calm._

EVENTS: _We disagreed about who was going to have the family party. She made me so mad I started yelling at her, and I got nasty. I hung up on her, and now we're not talking._

1. **TOPIC:** A commute to work or school

   TOPIC SENTENCE/THESIS: _Answers will vary._

   EVENTS: _Answers will vary._

2. **TOPIC:** An embarrassing experience

   TOPIC SENTENCE/THESIS: _____

   EVENTS: _____

3.   TOPIC: A typical evening at home

TOPIC SENTENCE/THESIS: _____

EVENTS: _____

. . . .

Giving Details about the Events

When you write a narration, look for examples and details that will make each event more realistic and specific. Remember that you want your readers to share your point of view and see the same message in the story that you do. One way to give readers more information is to add at least one or two details that explain each event.

■ **PRACTICE 3   GIVING DETAILS ABOUT THE EVENTS** . . . .

Choose two of the items in Practice 2 and write your topic sentence or thesis statement for each. Then, write the major events in the spaces provided. Give a detail about each event.

EXAMPLE:

TOPIC SENTENCE/THESIS: *After a horrible fight with my sister, I learned the value of staying calm.*

EVENT: *We disagreed about who was going to have the family party.*

DETAIL: *Even though we both work, she said she was too busy and that I would have to do it.*

EVENT: *She made me so mad I started yelling at her, and I got nasty.*

DETAIL: *I brought up times in the past when she'd tried to pass responsibilities off on me and told her I was sick of being the one who did everything.*

EVENT: *I hung up on her, and now we're not talking.*

DETAIL: *I feel bad, and I know I'll have to call her sooner or later because she is my sister. I do love her even though she's a pain sometimes.*

1.   TOPIC SENTENCE/THESIS: *Answers will vary.*

EVENT: *Answers will vary.*

DETAIL: *Answers will vary.*

EVENT: _____

DETAIL: _____

EVENT: _____

    DETAIL: _____

2. **TOPIC SENTENCE/THESIS:**

EVENT: _____

    DETAIL: _____

EVENT: _____

    DETAIL: _____

EVENT: _____

    DETAIL: _____

Organization in Narration

Narration usually uses **time (chronological) order** to organize ideas. Start at the beginning of the story, and describe the events in the order in which they happened.

When using time order to organize your writing, include **time transitions** to signal when events occurred and to move readers from one event to the next.

■ **TIP:** For more on time order, see page 66.

Common Time Transitions

after	eventually	meanwhile	soon
as	finally	next	then
at last	first	now	when
before	last	second	while
during	later	since	

PRACTICE 4   USING TRANSITIONS IN NARRATION

Read the paragraph that follows and fill in the blanks with time transitions.
Answers may vary. Possible answers shown.

_____*After*_____ a horrible fight with my sister, I learned the value of staying calm. The fight started over who was going to have the family party. _____*First*_____, she said that she was too busy, even though we both work. _____*Then*_____, I got mad and started yelling at her. I brought up times in the past when she'd tried to pass responsibilities off on me and told her I was sick of being the one who did everything. _____*Finally*_____, I hung up on her, and _____*now*_____ we're not talking.

I feel bad because she's my sister, and I do love her. *Eventually*, I know that I will have to call her.

Read and Understand Narration

■ **READING SELECTIONS:**
For further examples of and activities for narration, see Chapter 42.

Reading examples of narration to understand their structure and content will help you write your own. The first example, a paragraph, is followed by questions about the structure of narration. The second example, an essay, has questions in the margin to help you read closely. It is followed by questions about both structure and content, along with writing assignments. These activities will help you practice your critical reading and thinking skills.

Narration Paragraph: Professional

VOCABULARY DEVELOPMENT
Underline these words as you read the narration paragraph.

gawky: *awkward*

transformed: *changed*

transplanted: *moved from one place to another*

stutter: *speech problem involving repeated sounds*

recite: *speak*

astonishment: *surprise*

salvation: *something that saves someone*

At age fourteen, a gawky and shy James Earl Jones was transformed. Transplanted from rural Mississippi, he felt out of place at Dickson High School in Brethren, Michigan. His stutter was so pronounced that he never spoke out in class. Understandably, he often felt alone. Jones found refuge in writing poetry. One day in class, he wrote a poem and submitted it to his English teacher. The teacher, surprised at how good it was, wondered whether Jones had copied it and challenged Jones, "The best way for you to prove that you wrote this poem yourself is for you to recite it by heart to the class." Jones then walked to the front of the room, thinking it would be better to be laughed at for stuttering than to be disgraced. He was scared, but he opened his mouth and began to speak. To the astonishment of everyone in the class, the words flowed smoothly. The stutter disappeared. He had stumbled upon what speech therapists would one day discover: that the written page can be a stutterer's salvation. He went on to become a high school public-speaking champion and won a scholarship to the University of Michigan. Today, fifty years later, the voice of James Earl Jones is among the most familiar in the world.

—Wallace Terry, "When His Sound Was Silenced"

■ **TIP:** For advice on building your vocabulary, see Appendix B.

■ **TEACHING TIP:** You might check to see if there is any contest in your community, county, or state similar to the one Hill entered; you could then work with students who are interested in entering.

1. Double-underline the **topic sentence**.

2. What is important about the story? *A fourteen-year-old boy with a stutter became a man with one of the most recognizable voices in the world.*

3. Underline the **major events** in the paragraph.

4. Circle the **time transitions**.

5. Does the paragraph have the Four Basics of Good Narration (see p. 107)? Why or why not?

Yes. Specific answers will vary, but students should be able to give examples of

the Four Basics.

Narration Essay: Student

Dale Hill, a student at Kaskaskia College in Illinois, wrote the following essay, which received an honorable mention in the Paul Simon Student Essay Contest sponsored by the Illinois Community College Trustees Association.

How Community College Has Changed My Life
Dale Hill

Grandpa was a sharecropper. With only a second-grade education, he planted his seeds and raised his family of seven sons and three daughters. My father, third eldest of the sons, broke new ground when he became the first person ever in the family to graduate from high school. Although Dad was very bright, it never occurred to him to go on to college. He and Grandpa shared the attitude that college was only for rich people and that you cannot change a sow's ear into a silk purse. Dad was expected to work to help support his younger brothers and sisters, and that is what he did. And that is what I did, too, for a long while. Now, however, my attitude has changed, and I have learned that there are other ways to seed future growth. The change did not happen overnight.

While I was growing up in the same small farming town and attending Dad's same high school, people still thought that college was only for the rich. College was my dream deferred. Like my father before me, I was expected to work after graduation to help support the family, and like my father before me, that is what I did. What followed was twenty wasted and fruitless years of unfulfilling factory and retail jobs. Only last year, faced with the prospect of starting over again with a son of my own to set an example for, did I return to my dream.

The prospect of attending college, leaving old attitudes and beliefs behind, was daunting. The world I knew was greatly different from the academic world, and I was unsure that I would fit in. I was twenty years older than traditional students and was not confident that I could compete. Going to a university full-time would require a commitment of time and money that would cause hardship for my family. My wife suggested that I enroll at my local community college first, which I did.

VOCABULARY DEVELOPMENT
Underline these words as you read the narration essay.

deferred: *to put off until later*

fruitless: *not successful*

unfulfilling: *not satisfying*

prospect: *something expected*

daunting: *discouraging*

mundane: *ordinary*

proximity: *closeness*

What do you think "change a sow's ear into a silk purse" (para. 1) means?

1 **PREDICT:** Read the title and the first paragraph. How do you think the writer's attitude might have changed?

2 **REFLECT:** How does your family feel about your going to college?

3 **REFLECT:** Do you share any of Dale's feelings?

I discovered that community college acts as the perfect stepping   4
stone between the mundane life that I wished to leave behind and
the new one I wished to begin. The proximity, affordability, and flexibility offered by my local community college lessen the sacrifices my
family is called upon to make. Community college allows me to test
the waters of an academic environment without fear of plunging in
over my head. It encourages me to challenge myself and build my
confidence even as it expands my horizons. My community college
nourishes me and helps me to grow.

I have discovered that my father's and grandfather's attitudes   5
about college were right. College education *is* for the rich: the rich in
mind and spirit, the rich in wonder and curiosity. How has community college changed my life? It has shown me how rich I am. I am
planting a new seed for my family now, a crop that will bear fruit for
generations to come.

■ **TIP:** For reading advice, see Chapter 1.

CRITICAL THINKING: READING

1. What is Dale's purpose for writing? *Answers will vary. Possible answers:*

   to explain how his attitude about college changed; to win the essay contest

   Does he achieve it? *Answers will vary.*

2. In your own words, state his main point.

   Answers will vary. Possible answer: that breaking with family tradition is

   sometimes important

3. Double-underline the **thesis statement**, and underline the **topic sentences** that support the thesis.

4. How has Dale organized his essay? _____*time order*_____ Circle the **transitional words and phrases** that indicate this order.

5. Double-underline the sentence in the last paragraph that reminds
   readers of the main point and makes an observation.

6. What do you think of this essay? Why?
   Answers will vary.

CRITICAL THINKING: WRITING

Choose one of the following questions and respond in a paragraph or essay.

1. Have you broken with family tradition in some way? How, and why?
2. What are your dreams for your life?

3. What expectations docs your family have for you? Are they the same as or different from those you have for yourself?

4. What changes in your life did becoming a parent make?

5. Dale writes, "College education *is* for the rich: the rich in mind and spirit, the rich in wonder and curiosity." In what ways is your life rich?

Write Your Own Narration

In this section, you will write your own narration paragraph or essay based on your (or your instructor's) choice among three assignments below.

To complete your narration, follow this sequence:

1. Review the Four Basics of Good Narration (p. 107).
2. Choose your assignment (see below).
3. If you are asked to complete Assignment 3, read Solving Problems, Appendix D.
4. Write your narration using the Checklist: How to Write Narration on pages 119–20.

■ **TIP:** Look back at your idea-journal entry (p. 107) for ideas.

NARRATION AT A GLANCE

Topic sentence (paragraph) or thesis statement (essay) Says what's important about the experience

↓

First major event Details about the event

↓

Second major event Details about the event

↓

Third major event Details about the event

↓

Conclusion Reminds readers of the main point and makes an observation based on it

■ **ASSIGNMENT 1   WRITING ABOUT COLLEGE, WORK, AND EVERYDAY LIFE** . . . .

Write a narration on one of the following topics.

COLLEGE

PARAGRAPH	ESSAY
• A time you succeeded	• How a teacher made a difference
• Your best school year	• Your most challenging college experience

WORK

PARAGRAPH	ESSAY
• A funny work story	• A work day that you'd rather forget
• A conflict at work	• A work achievement you are proud of
• A work achievement you are proud of	• Your first day at your first (or most recent) job

EVERYDAY LIFE

PARAGRAPH	ESSAY
• A childhood memory	• A day when everything went right (or wrong)
• A mistake you made that helped you learn a lesson	• Your biography
• A difficult decision	• An experience that triggered a strong emotion in you: happiness, sadness, relief, fear, regret, nervousness

■ **RESOURCES:** Reproducible peer-review guides for different kinds of papers are available in *Additional Resources*.

■   **ASSIGNMENT 2**   **WRITING ABOUT IMAGES** . . . .

Look carefully at the photograph below. In a paragraph or essay, either tell the story of what might have happened to bring the couple to this point or tell a story about a time when you felt the same way as one of the people in this photograph.

■   **LEARNING JOURNAL:**
Reread your idea-journal entry from page 107. Write another entry on the same topic, using what you have learned about narration.

■   **RESOURCES:** All chapters in Part Two have writing checklists, which have been reproduced in *Additional Resources.* Photocopy and distribute them if you want students to hand in the checklists with their assignments.

■   **TEAMWORK:** For more detailed guidance on group work, see *Practical Suggestions.*

■   **ASSIGNMENT 3**   **WRITING IN THE REAL WORLD/SOLVING A PROBLEM** . . . .

PROBLEM: You are driving at 40 miles per hour on a wide, straight stretch of road on which you have never driven before. You see a police car on the side of the road ahead and automatically slow down because you don't know the speed limit. As soon as you pass the police car, it pulls out behind you and signals for you to stop. Although you didn't notice the blinking yellow light or see the school, you were in a school zone, where the speed limit is 20 miles per hour. The officer writes you a ticket for $275. When you see the amount, you explain that you have a good driving record and had never driven on this road before. The officer says he has to give the ticket but that you can argue it in court, where the judge might either cancel the ticket or reduce the fine. All you have to do is tell the judge exactly what happened and why you believe that you don't deserve such a high fine.

ASSIGNMENT: Working in a small group or on your own, write what you would say to the judge, telling him or her what happened. If you are writing an essay instead of a paragraph, add details about the events that occurred and your good driving record.

CHECKLIST: HOW TO WRITE NARRATION	
STEPS IN NARRATION	**HOW TO DO THE STEPS**
☐ **Focus.**	• Think about your story and what is important about it.
☐ **Narrow and explore your topic.** See Chapter 3.	• Make the topic more specific. • Prewrite, recalling what happened. As you prewrite, ask: Why is the story important?
☐ **Write a topic sentence (paragraph) or thesis statement (essay) that includes your main point about the story.** See Chapter 4.	• Say what is important about the story—how it affected you and others.
☐ **Support your point.** See Chapter 5.	• Recall the major events, and choose the essential ones. • Describe the events with specific details.
☐ **Make a plan.** See Chapter 6.	• Arrange the events in time order.
☐ **Write a draft.** See Chapter 7.	**FOR A PARAGRAPH** • Write a paragraph with your topic sentence, major events, and details about the events. Use complete sentences. **FOR AN ESSAY** • Consider using one of the introduction types in Chapter 7. Include your thesis statement in your introduction. • Using your plan, write topic sentences for the major events. • Write paragraphs for each topic sentence with details about the events. **FOR PARAGRAPHS AND ESSAYS** • Write a conclusion that reminds readers of your main point and makes an observation based on what you have written. • Write a title that previews your main point but doesn't repeat it. • Get feedback from others using the peer-review guide for narration at **bedfordstmartins.com/realwriting**.
☐ **Revise your draft, making at least four improvements.** See Chapter 8.	• Read to make sure that all events and details about them show, explain, or prove your main point. • Add events and/or details that help make your point about the story. • Add time transitions to move your readers from one event to another.

continued

CHECKLIST: HOW TO WRITE NARRATION	
STEPS IN NARRATION	**HOW TO DO THE STEPS**
☐ **Edit your revised draft.** See Parts Four through Seven.	• Correct errors in grammar, spelling, word use, and punctuation.
☐ **Ask yourself:**	• Does my paper have the Four Basics of Good Narration (p. 107)? • Is this the best I can do?

Chapter Review

1. Narration is writing that _tells the story of an event or experience_ .

2. List the Four Basics of Good Narration.

    It reveals something of importance to you.

    It includes all of the major events of the story.

    It brings the story to life with details about the major events.

    It presents the events in a clear order, usually according to when they happen.

3. The topic sentence in a narration paragraph or the thesis statement in a narration essay usually includes what two things?

    your narrowed topic

    your main point

4. What type of organization do writers of narration usually use?

    time order

5. List five common transitions for this type of organization.

    Answers will vary.

6. Choose five of the vocabulary words on pages 114–15 and use each in a sentence.

10

Illustration

Writing That Gives Examples

You Know This

You use examples to illustrate your point in daily communication:

- You answer the question "Like what?"
- You tell a friend that she's been acting weird, and she asks, "How?" You remind her of something she did.

Understand What Illustration Is

Illustration is writing that uses examples to show, explain, or prove a point. Giving examples is the basis of all good writing and speaking: You make a statement, and then you give an example that shows (illustrates) what you mean.

■■ FOUR BASICS OF GOOD ILLUSTRATION
1. It has a point to illustrate.
2. It gives specific examples that show, explain, or prove the point.
3. It gives details to support these examples.
4. It uses enough examples to get the writer's point across.

In the following paragraph, each number corresponds to one of the Four Basics of Good Illustration. Notice that the writer also uses narration (see Chapter 9).

■ IDEA JOURNAL: Give some examples of things that annoy you.

1 Working full time while going to college requires good time management skills, and planning ahead is essential. **2** Because mornings are hectic around my house, I try to collect what I need for work and school the night before. **3** For example, before bedtime I make sure to put the books and papers I'll need the next day into my backpack. **2** At work, I always try to stay in control of my time. **3** I limit socializing and breaks, because if I don't leave by 5:05 P.M. I'll have a hard time finding a parking space, and I'll also miss the beginning of class. **2** The biggest time management challenge is finding time to do homework. **3** When I'm home, everyone in my family wants a piece of me, and it's really easy to respond to their requests and put off my work. Therefore, I try to set aside a specific time slot to do my school work, and to stay focused on it until it's done. Before I started school, I thought my life was pretty busy already. Now that I'm combining work, school, and family, time management is a must.

4 Enough examples to make the writer's point

121

It is hard to explain anything without using examples, so you use illustration in almost every communication situation:

COLLEGE   An exam question asks you to explain and give examples of a concept.

WORK   Your boss asks you to tell her what office furniture or equipment needs to be replaced and why.

EVERYDAY LIFE   You complain to your landlord that the building superintendent is not doing his job. The landlord asks for examples.

Profile of Success: Illustration in the Real World

Alan Whitehead
Home Development Company
Vice President

The following profile shows how a home development company vice president uses illustration on the job.

BACKGROUND: I grew up in Maryville, Tennessee, and after graduating from high school worked in a store. After my wife and I had our first child, I decided that I would like to be a better provider for them, so I enrolled in a local community college, where I developed computer-aided design skills. Upon graduation, I was offered a job using those skills at Richmond American Homes. Since then, I have risen steadily in the company.

COLLEGE(S)/DEGREES: A.A.S. in computer-aided design and drafting, Pellissippi State Technical College

EMPLOYER: Richmond American Homes

WRITING AT WORK: Memos describing changes or additions to blueprints, detailed letters to architects about products in order to bid for design services, letters to developers or city-government officials requesting architectural approval, e-mail to employees and subcontractors

HOW ALAN USES ILLUSTRATION: In nearly every type of writing I do, I have to give examples to explain what is being done or needs to be done.

ALAN'S ILLUSTRATION

Alan wrote the following memo to keep his coworkers in the company informed about a project he was working on.

To: President, Richmond American Homes

    Vice President of Construction

    Vice President of Purchasing

Fr: Alan Whitehead

Re: Replacement plans, the "Aspen" (model 2180)

We are making some changes to improve ease of access to our Aspen home, one of our most popular designs. This memo is a follow-up to our walk-through of the framed home last week. The first change is in the master bedroom, where we are enlarging the door space. The new plan calls for a pair of 2668 double-doors. The second change is in the kitchen, where the island will shift 12 inches to the right, toward the family room.

The last change to the Aspen model is in the width of the curved stairs leading from the first to the second floor. The width of the stairs has increased to 4 feet, 6 inches. The revised drawings are available for the subcontractors working in the new development. The changes will make the Aspen even more attractive to our prospective buyers. Please see that the changes and the revised drawings are distributed to appropriate workers.

1. Double-underline the **main point**.
2. Number the **major examples** that explain the main point.
3. Underline the **specific details** about the examples.

Main Point in Illustration

In illustration, the **main point** is the message you want your readers to receive and understand. To help you discover your main point, complete the following sentence:

What I want readers to know about this topic is . . .

The topic sentence (paragraph) or thesis statement (essay) usually include the topic and the main point the writer wants to make about it.

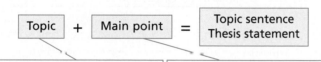

The bus drivers in my city have no sense of courtesy.

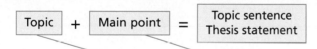

This year, the city council has passed four unpopular regulations.

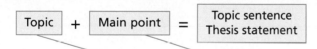 **PRACTICE 1   MAKING A MAIN POINT** . . . .

Each of the items in this practice is a narrowed topic. Think about each of them, and in the space provided, write a main point about each topic.

EXAMPLE: Early morning walks (or runs) *give me energy and a positive outlook.*

1. A few moments alone *Answers will vary.* _____

2. A course I'm taking _____

3. The busiest time at work _____

■ **TEACHING TIP:** It might help to tell students that with illustration, examples often come to mind before the main point does. For example, in work situations someone might notice several examples of a problem, and then to write an e-mail or memo summing up the problem and listing examples.

4. Being a parent of a newborn baby _____

5. Working with other people _____

Support in Illustration

In illustration, the **support** consists of examples and details that explain your main point to readers.

The best way to generate good detailed examples (if you don't already have some in mind) is to use one or more prewriting techniques discussed in Chapter 3. First, write down all of the examples you can think of. Then, review your examples and choose the ones that will best communicate your point to your readers.

■ PRACTICE 2 SUPPORTING YOUR MAIN POINT WITH EXAMPLES . . .

Read the following main points and give three examples you might use to support each one.

EXAMPLE: My boss is very cheap.

makes us reuse envelopes _____

has a lock on the phone _____

gives us only a certain amount of paper each week _____

1. My (friend, sister, brother, husband, wife—choose one) has some very admirable traits.

   Answers will vary. _____

   _____

   _____

2. My boss is fair (unfair). [Choose one or the other.]

   _____

   _____

   _____

3. This weekend is particularly busy.

   _____

   _____

   _____

■ **ESL:** Tell students that if they are writing about something from their native country's culture, they have to think about what their readers may not be familiar with. They may need to give more details than they would need to provide for people from their native culture.

■ **PRACTICE 3   GIVING DETAILS ABOUT THE EXAMPLES** . . . .

Choose two of the items from Practice 2, where you wrote specific examples to support main points. In the spaces provided, first copy the main point you are using and your examples from Practice 2. Then, write a detail that further shows, explains, or proves what you mean.

EXAMPLE: My boss is very cheap.

EXAMPLE: _makes us reuse envelopes_

    DETAIL: _have to tape them shut_

EXAMPLE: _has a lock on the phone_

    DETAIL: _have to find him and get him to unlock the phone for business calls_

EXAMPLE: _gives us only a certain amount of paper each week_

    DETAIL: _have to cut up into pieces to make sure we don't run out_

1. **MAIN POINT:** _Answers will vary._

    EXAMPLE: _Answers will vary._

        DETAIL: _Answers will vary._

    EXAMPLE: _____

        DETAIL: _____

    EXAMPLE: _____

        DETAIL: _____

2. **MAIN POINT:** _____

    EXAMPLE: _____

        DETAIL: _____

    EXAMPLE: _____

        DETAIL: _____

    EXAMPLE: _____

        DETAIL: _____

■ **TIP:** For more on order of importance and time order, see page 66.

Organization in Illustration

Illustration often uses **order of importance**, saving the most powerful example for last. Or it might be organized by **time order** if the examples are given according to when they happened.

Transitions in illustration let readers know that you are introducing an example or moving from one example to another.

Common Illustration Transitions			
also	finally	for example	in addition
another	first, second, and so on	for instance	one example/another example
		for one thing/ for another	

PRACTICE 4   USING TRANSITIONS IN ILLUSTRATION

Read the paragraph that follows and fill in the blanks with transitions.
Answers may vary. Possible answers shown.

My computer was working against me today. _____First_____, I had to try several times just to get it turned on. _____Second_____, after I finally got it turned on, it froze. I turned the computer off and on again, and it worked for a few minutes, but then it crashed yet again. When I restarted the computer, the work I'd done was lost. _____Another_____ problem with my computer today was that it wouldn't accept a disk to save my work. _____For example_____, when I inserted the disk into the disk drive, the computer froze. I think I need a new computer. _____For one thing_____, a new computer should work just fine. _____For another_____, it will make life much less stressful for me.

Read and Understand Illustration

■ **READING SELECTIONS:** For further examples of and activities for illustration, see Chapter 43.

Reading examples of illustration to understand their structure and content will help you write your own. The first example, a paragraph, is followed by questions about the structure of illustration. The second example, an essay, has questions in the margin to help you read closely. It is followed by questions about both structure and content, along with writing assignments. These activities will help you practice your critical reading and thinking skills.

Illustration Paragraph: Student

<u><u>Although they don't consider it stealing, many people regularly take things from their companies.</u></u> The most common items to disappear are <u>pens and pencils that employees almost unconsciously stuff into their purses, knapsacks, or briefcases.</u> (Over time), they may accumulate quite a stash of them. Another big item is all kinds of paper: <u>pads of lined paper, handy little notepads that can be used for shopping lists and phone messages, and file folders to organize home records.</u> (Yet another) "innocent" theft is the long-distance personal phone call. Those calls cost the company in two ways: They use company time for personal business, and the company has to pay for the calls. <u>Even though companies may have special discounted telephone rates, no call is free.</u> (Finally), one of the more significant ways people steal is by taking home <u>samples of the products the company makes: food, clothing, supplies, and so on.</u> Employees seem to think they are entitled to these products and even give them to friends. By doing so, they hurt the company by robbing it of a product it depends on for revenue. These examples may not seem like stealing, but the results are the same: extra costs to the company, which may result in lower pay raises.

VOCABULARY DEVELOPMENT
Underline these words as you read the illustration paragraph.

unconsciously: *without thinking*

knapsacks: *packs for carrying items*

accumulate: *gather*

stash: *collection*

revenue: *income; sales*

■ **TIP:** For advice on building your vocabulary, see Appendix B.

1. Double-underline the **topic sentence**.

2. Underline the **examples** that support the main point.

3. Circle the **transitions**.

4. Does the paragraph have the Four Basics of Good Illustration (p. 121)? Why or why not? *Yes. Specific answers will vary, but students should be able to give examples of the Four Basics.*

5. What kind of organization does the writer use in the paragraph? *order of importance*

Illustration Essay: Professional

Scents
Gabrielle Glaser

People have been using fragrance to cure what ails them for thousands of years. Yet until recently, scientists have viewed aromatherapy as hocus-pocus. <u>Now researchers are finding that some scents really can give you a psychological lift.</u>

1   **PREDICT:** What do you expect this essay will be about?

_____

_____

VOCABULARY DEVELOPMENT
Underline these words as
you read the illustration
essay.

fragrance: *a scent or smell;
same as* aroma

aromatherapy: *influencing
moods with aromas or fra-
grances*

hocus-pocus: *nonsense*

pungent: *strong*

jasmine: *a flowering plant
with a pleasant smell*

enhancement: *improvement*

petrified: *very frightened*

jeering: *shouting abusively*

lavender: *a plant whose
flowers are used for per-
fumes*

insomniacs: *people who
have trouble sleeping*

sedatives: *drugs that relax*

What do you think "Take
time to stop and smell the
roses" (para. 5) means?

REFLECT: Are there any aromas that have a positive effect on you?

Some scents seem to have the ability to boost one's confidence. In a recent study, the pungent aroma of peppermint helped college athletes perform better with less effort, or at least it made them *feel* like superstars. In fact, according to measurements such as heart rate and blood pressure, the athletes got just as much benefit from the scent of jasmine and a stinky chemical called dimethyl sulfite. But in sports, believing you have a mental edge can translate into the real thing—and that's all that matters, right?

Other scents have the effect of calming one down. When you're anxious, sniff something that you associate with a more relaxed time in your life, suggests Will A. Wiener, Ph.D., a psychologist and di-rector of the Institute for Performance Enhancement in Manhattan. This strategy has helped one of Wiener's clients, a professional bas-ketball player who gets petrified at the free-throw line. Just before he shoots a basket, the player buries his nose in a handkerchief scented with a loved one's favorite cologne. The smell allows him to block out the jeering crowd and concentrate.

Still other scents appear to improve one's focus. Researchers in Miami found that adults who sniffed lavender before and after tack-ling simple math problems worked faster, felt more relaxed, and made fewer mistakes. The fragrant herb can also improve your nights: In a small study, a British doctor found that lavender helped elderly insomniacs fall asleep sooner—and slumber longer—than sedatives did.

Researchers continue to study the effects of other herbs on people's moods. Because herbs are natural substances, they are less expensive to produce, and do not require Federal Department of Agriculture (FDA) approval. The old saying, "Take time to stop and smell the roses" may, after all, be good advice for us all.

—From *Health* magazine, July/August, 2001

TIP: For reading advice, see Chapter 1.

CRITICAL THINKING: READING

1. Double-underline the **thesis statement**. In your own words, what is Glaser's main point? *Answers will vary.*
   Possible answer: Scents really do affect people.

2. Underline the three **major examples** of how scents affect people.

3. Does the author provide enough evidence for her thesis?
   Opinions will vary but should discuss whether the examples are sufficient.

4. In the last paragraph, what observation does Glaser make, based on what she has written? *that maybe the old saying is true*

5. This article appeared in *Health* magazine, which is written for non-experts. How might the article be different if it were written for scientists? *Answers will vary. Possible answer: It would contain more scientific facts and details on the research described.*

CRITICAL THINKING: WRITING

Choose one of the following topics and respond in a paragraph or essay.

1. Write about scents that remind you of particular people, events, or places.
2. Choose one of the following places (or another place that interests you) and write about how it affects you.

   a restaurant   a movie theater   a place you like

3. Agree or disagree with Glaser's statement in paragraph 2 that in sports, "believing you have a mental edge can translate into the real thing—and that's all that matters, right?"
4. Agree or disagree with scientists who think that aromatherapy is hocus-pocus.
5. Agree or disagree with this statement: "Experts aren't always right." Give examples from your own experience.

Write Your Own Illustration

In this section, you will write your own illustration paragraph or essay based on your (or your instructor's) choice among three assignments.

To complete your illustration, follow this sequence:

■ **TIP:** Look back at your idea-journal entry (p. 121) for ideas.

1. Review the Four Basics of Good Illustration (p. 121).
2. Choose your assignment.
3. If you are asked to complete Assignment 3, read Solving Problems, Appendix D.
4. Write your illustration using the Checklist: How to Write Illustration (pp. 131–132).

■ **ASSIGNMENT 1   WRITING ABOUT COLLEGE, WORK, AND EVERYDAY LIFE** . . . .

Write an illustration on one of the following topics.

COLLEGE

PARAGRAPH	ESSAY
• Your goals for taking this course	• Obstacles to coming to college
• Students in your class	• Today's students

ILLUSTRATION AT A GLANCE

Topic sentence (paragraph) or thesis statement (essay)
Says what you want readers to know about the topic

↓

First major example
Details about the example

↓

Second major example
Details about the example

↓

Third major example (often the most powerful)
Details about the example

↓

Conclusion
Reminds readers of the main point and makes an observation based on it

WORK

PARAGRAPH	ESSAY
• Skills you have • Information to include on a résumé	• Jobs you've had • Odd things about your job or the place you work

EVERDAY LIFE

PARAGRAPH	ESSAY
• Stresses in your life • Something that annoys you	• Stresses in your life • Three things that annoy you

■ **ASSIGNMENT 2   WRITING ABOUT IMAGES** . . . .

Look at the photograph below, and write a paragraph or essay giving examples of how people are discriminated against. You can use your own experiences or current or historical events.

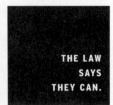

DISCRIMINATION SAYS THEY CAN'T BE NEIGHBORS.

THE LAW SAYS THEY CAN.

■ **ASSIGNMENT 3   WRITING IN THE REAL WORLD/SOLVING A PROBLEM**

PROBLEM: Your college is increasing its tuition by $500 next year, and you don't think that you can continue. You have done well so far, and you really want to get a college degree.

ASSIGNMENT: Rather than just giving up and dropping out next year, as many students do, make a list of resources you could consult to help you, and explain how they might help. You might want to start with the following sentence:

Before dropping out of school for financial reasons, students should

consult ＿＿＿＿＿＿ because ＿＿＿＿＿＿.

Work in a small group or on your own.

For a paragraph: Name your best resource and give examples of how this person or office might help you.

For an essay: Name your three best resources and give examples of how they might help you.

■ **RESOURCES:** Reproducible peer-review guides for different kinds of papers are available in *Additional Resources*.

■ **RESOURCES:** All chapters in Part Two have writing checklists, which are also reproduced in *Additional Resources*. You can photocopy and distribute them if you want students to hand in the checklists with their assignments.

■ **LEARNING JOURNAL:** Reread your idea-journal entry from page 121. Write another entry on the same topic, using what you have learned about illustration.

CHECKLIST: HOW TO WRITE ILLUSTRATION	
STEPS IN ILLUSTRATION	**HOW TO DO THE STEPS**
☐ **Focus.**	• Think about your topic and what point you want to make about it.
☐ **Narrow and explore your topic.** See Chapter 3.	• Make the topic more specific. • Prewrite to get ideas about that narrowed topic.
☐ **Write a topic sentence (paragraph) or thesis statement (essay) that includes your main point about the topic.** See Chapter 4.	• Decide what is most important to you about the topic and what you want your readers to understand.
☐ **Support your point.** See Chapter 5.	• Choose examples to show, explain, or prove what is important about your topic. • Give specific details that will make your examples clear to your readers.
☐ **Make a plan.** See Chapter 6.	• Put the examples in a logical order.

continued

STEPS IN ILLUSTRATION	HOW TO DO THE STEPS
☐ **Write a draft.** See Chapter 7.	**FOR A PARAGRAPH**
	• Write a paragraph with your topic sentence, major examples, and details about the examples. Use complete sentences.
	FOR AN ESSAY
	• Consider using one of the introduction types in Chapter 7. Include your thesis statement in your introduction.
	• Using your plan, write topic sentences for the major examples.
	• Write paragraphs for each topic sentence with details about the examples.
☐ **Write a draft.** See Chapter 7.	**FOR PARAGRAPHS AND ESSAYS**
	• Write a conclusion that reminds readers of your main point and makes an observation based on what you have written.
	• Write a title that previews your main point but doesn't repeat it.
☐ **Revise your draft, making at least four improvements.** See Chapter 8.	• Get feedback from others using the peer-review guide for illustration at **bedfordstmartins.com/realwriting**.
	• Read to make sure that all examples show, explain, or prove your main point.
	• Add examples and/or details that help make your point.
	• Add transitions to move your readers from one example to another.
☐ **Edit your revised draft.** See Parts Four through Seven.	• Correct errors in grammar, spelling, word use, and punctuation.
☐ **Ask yourself:**	• Does my paper have the Four Basics of Good Illustration (p. 121)?
	• Is this the best I can do?

Chapter Review

1. Illustration is writing that _uses examples to show, explain, or prove a point._

2. What are the Four Basics of Good Illustration?

   It has a point to illustrate.

   It gives specific examples that show, explain, or prove the point.

   It gives details to support these examples.

   It uses enough examples to get the writer's point across.

3. Choose five of the vocabulary words on pages 127–128 and use each in a sentence.

You Know This

You use description every day:

- You describe what someone looks like.
- You describe an item you want to buy.
- You describe a place you visited to a friend.

11

Description

Writing That Creates Pictures In Words

Understand What Description Is

Description is writing that creates a clear and vivid impression of the topic. Description translates your experience of a person, place, or thing into words, often by appealing to the physical senses: sight, hearing, smell, taste, and touch.

▓▓ FOUR BASICS OF GOOD DESCRIPTION

1. It creates a main impression—an overall effect, feeling, or image—about the topic.
2. It uses specific examples to support the main impression.
3. It supports those examples with details that appeal to the five senses: sight, hearing, smell, taste, and touch.
4. It brings a person, place, or physical object to life for the reader.

In the following paragraph, each number corresponds to one of the Four Basics of Good Description.

4 Examples and details bring the subject to life.

1 A tour of Robinson Hall, a historic home in an early stage of renovation, feels like entering a scene out of a horror movie. **2** Just inside the arched entrance is a small foyer with a stairwell set in the corner. **3** The paint is peeling, some of the floorboards are missing, and there is trash on the floor. With many of the windows broken, the cold, damp air from outside comes right in. To the left is a door that leads to the front room, or living room. **2** From here, one can see through a wide doorway into the dining room and then into the kitchen, which is recognizable only by the **3** old farm sink, knocked onto the floor. **2** To the left of the kitchen are two small rooms, one of which will become a bathroom. The entire floor on the first level looks as if it is about to fall out of the house. But the restorer, John Carroll, is enthusiastic about the prospects for the renovation. While he admits the restoration will take a long time, he has already made progress with the shell, which was filled with knee-deep debris when he first saw it. He hopes that Robinson Hall will be transformed within a year from a scary wreck to an elegant historic building.

—Sophie Fleck

Being able to describe something or someone accurately and in detail is important in many situations:

COLLEGE   On a nursing test, you describe the symptoms you observed in a patient.

WORK   You write a memo to your boss describing how the office could be arranged for increased efficiency.

EVERYDAY LIFE   You have to describe something you lost to the lost-and-found clerk at a store.

Profile of Success: Description in the Real World

Celia Hyde
Chief of Police

■ **RESOURCES:** For a discussion of how to use the profiles in Part Two, see *Practical Suggestions.*

The following profile shows how a chief of police in a small town uses description on the job.

BACKGROUND: When I graduated from high school, I wasn't interested in academics. I took some courses at a community college, then dropped out to travel. After traveling and trying several different colleges, I returned home. The police chief in town was a friend of the family's and encouraged me to think about law enforcement. I entered that field and have been there since.

COLLEGE(S)/DEGREES: Greenfield Community College, Mt. Wachusett Community College, Fort Lauderdale Community College

EMPLOYER: Town of Bolton, Massachusetts

WRITING AT WORK: As chief of police, I do many kinds of writing: policies and procedures for the officers to follow; responses to attorneys' requests for information; letters, reports, and budgets; interviews with witnesses; statements from victims and criminals; accident reports. In all of the writing I do, detail, clarity, and precision are essential. I have to choose my words carefully to avoid any confusion or misunderstanding.

HOW CELIA USES DESCRIPTION: When I am called to a crime scene, I have to write a report that describes precisely and in detail what the scene looks like.

CELIA'S DESCRIPTION

The following report is one example of the descriptive reports Celia writes every day. The name of the homeowner has been changed.

Report, breaking and entering scene

Response to burglar alarm, November 15, 2003, 17:00 hours

The house at 123 Main Street is situated off the road with a long, narrow driveway and no visible neighbors. The dense fir trees along the drive block natural light, though it was almost dusk and getting dark. There was snow on the driveway from a recent storm. I observed one set of fresh tire marks entering the driveway and a set of foot-prints exiting it.

The homeowner, Mr. Smith, had been awakened by the sounds of smashing glass and the squeaking of the door as it opened. He felt a cold draft from the stairway and heard a soft shuffle of feet crossing the dining room. Smith descended the stairs to investigate and was met at the bottom by the intruder, who shoved him against the wall and ran out the front door.

While awaiting backup, I obtained a description of the intruder from Mr. Smith. The subject was a white male, approximately 25–30 years of age and 5'9"–5'11" in height. He had jet-black hair of medium length, and it was worn slicked back from his forehead. He wore a salt-and-pepper, closely shaved beard and had a birthmark on his neck the size of a dime. The subject was wearing a black nylon jacket with some logo on it in large white letters, a blue plaid shirt, and blue jeans.

1. What is your **main impression** of the scene and of the intruder?
   a dark, isolated crime scene/an ordinary-looking man

2. Underline the **details** that support the main impression.

3. What senses do the details appeal to? *sight, hearing, touch*

4. How is the description organized? *time order*

Main Point in Description

In description, the **main point** is the main impression you want to create for your readers. If you do not have a main impression about your topic, it usually helps to think about how it smells, sounds, looks, tastes, or feels. To help you discover the main point for your description, complete the following sentence:

What's most vivid and important to me about this topic is . . .

 PRACTICE 1   FINDING A MAIN IMPRESSION . . . .

For the following general topics, jot down four impressions that appeal to you, and circle the one you would use as a main impression. Base your choice on what is most interesting, vivid, and important to you.

EXAMPLE:

TOPIC: A vandalized car

IMPRESSIONS: *wrecked, smashed, damaged*

1. **TOPIC:** A movie-theater lobby

   IMPRESSIONS: _Answers will vary._ _____

2. **TOPIC:** A fireworks display

   IMPRESSIONS: _____

3. **TOPIC:** A pizza place

   IMPRESSIONS: _____

4. **TOPIC:** An old person

   IMPRESSIONS: _____

5. **TOPIC:** The room you're in

   IMPRESSIONS: _____

The topic sentence (paragraph) or thesis statement (essay) in description usually contains both your narrowed topic and your main impression.

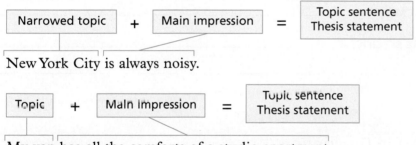

| Narrowed topic | + | Main impression | = | Topic sentence / Thesis statement |

New York City is always noisy.

| Topic | + | Main Impression | = | Topic sentence / Thesis statement |

My van has all the comforts of a studio apartment.

To be effective, your topic sentence or thesis statement should be specific. You can make it specific by adding details and using descriptive words that appeal to the senses. Here is a more specific version of the preceding statement about New York City.

MORE SPECIFIC: Even in the middle of the night, New York City is alive with the noises of people at work and at play.

■ **PRACTICE 2 WRITING A STATEMENT OF YOUR MAIN IMPRESSION**

Choose three of the items from Practice 1 to use in this practice. In the spaces below, write the topic and the main impression you chose. Then, write a statement of your main impression. Finally, revise the sentence to make the main impression sharper and more specific.

EXAMPLE:

TOPIC/MAIN IMPRESSION: *A vandalized car/battered*

STATEMENT: *The vandalized car on the side of the highway was battered.*

MORE SPECIFIC: *The shell of a car on the side of the road was dented all over, apparently from a bat or club, and surrounded by broken glass.*

1.   **TOPIC/MAIN IMPRESSION:** *Answers will vary.*

     STATEMENT: _____

     MORE SPECIFIC: _____

     _____

2.   **TOPIC/MAIN IMPRESSION:** _____

     STATEMENT: _____

     MORE SPECIFIC: _____

     _____

3.   **TOPIC/MAIN IMPRESSION:** _____

     STATEMENT: _____

     MORE SPECIFIC: _____

     _____

Support in Description

■ **TEAMWORK:** Put students in small groups, and give each group an object to describe using the questions in the text.

In description, **support** is the specific, concrete details that show the sights, sounds, smells, tastes, and textures of your topic. Your description should show your readers what you mean, not just tell them. Sensory details can bring your description to life. Here are some qualities to consider.

SIGHT	SOUND	SMELL
Colors?	Loud/soft?	Sweet/sour?
Shapes?	Piercing/soothing?	Sharp/mild?
Sizes?	Continuous/off and on?	Good? (Like what?)
Patterns?		Bad? (Rotten?)
Shiny/dull?	Pleasant/unpleasant? (How?)	New? (New what? Leather? Plastic?)
Does it look like anything else?	Does it sound like anything else?	Old?
		Does it smell like anything else?

TASTE	TOUCH
Good? (What does "good" taste like?)	Hard/soft?
Bad? (What does "bad" taste like?)	Liquid/solid?
Bitter/sugary? Metallic?	Rough/smooth?
Burning? Spicy?	Hot/cold?
Does it taste like anything else?	Dry/oily?
	Textures?
	Does it feel like anything else?

PRACTICE 3   FINDING DETAILS TO SUPPORT A MAIN IMPRESSION . . . .

Read the statements below and write four sensory details you migh e to support the main impression.

EXAMPLE:

Even at night, New York City echoes with noise.

a. *police and fire sirens*

b. *people on the street*

c. *sounds of music from clubs*

d. *car horns*

1. My favorite meal smells as good as it tastes.

a. *Possible answers: sweetness of sweet potatoes*

b. *sage in stuffing*

c. *buttery roasting turkey*

d. *apple pie with cinnamon*

2. The new office building has a very contemporary look.

a. *Possible answers: lots of glass*

b. *concrete*

c. *steel*

d. *tall*

3. A classroom during an exam echoes with the "sounds of silence."

a. *Possible answers: people coughing*

b. *rustle of papers*

c. *radiator hissing*

d. *sounds of pens scratching paper*

Organization in Description

■ **TIP:** For more on these orders of organization, see pages 65–66.

Description can use any of the orders of organization—**time**, **space**, or **importance**—depending on the purpose of the description. If you are writing to create a main impression of an event (for example, a description of fireworks, an explosion, or a storm), you might use time order. If you are describing what someone or something looks like, you might use space order, the most common way to organize description. If there is one detail about your topic that is the strongest and most likely to cement the impression you want to create, you could use order of importance and leave that detail for last.

ORDER	SEQUENCE
Time	first to last/last to first, most recent to least recent/least recent to most recent
Space	top to bottom/bottom to top, right to left/left to right, near to far/far to near
Importance	end with detail that will make the strongest impression

Use **transitions** to move your readers from one sensory detail to the next. Usually, use transitions that match your order of organization.

Common Description Transitions

TIME

as	finally	next	then
at last	first	now	when
before/after	last	second	while
during	later	since	
eventually	meanwhile	soon	

SPACE

above	below	inside	to the left/right
beneath/underneath	beside	near	to the side
across	beyond	next to	under
at the bottom/top	farther/further	opposite	where
behind	in front of	over	

IMPORTANCE		
especially	more/even more	most vivid
in particular	most	strongest

■ PRACTICE 4   USING TRANSITIONS IN DESCRIPTION . . . .
Answers may vary. Possible answers shown.
Read the paragraph that follows and fill in the blanks with transitions.

As I walked into the airport terminal, I knew something had to be wrong. Just __inside, beyond__ the doors, people were packed about forty deep. There was a loud, harsh buzzing that was actually the noise of people's voices. The room was steamy, the result of many people in winter clothing jammed into an overheated space. Looking ____over____ the heads of the crowd, I could see the ticket counter far in the distance. A young woman spoke quickly as a man waved his arms angrily, punching air. __Behind, In front of__ her, two armed guards stood solemnly, eyes straight ahead, stony. ____Over____ their heads, the flight board read, "All flights canceled." Unable to do anything else, I joined the helpless mob, waiting for someone to give us information.

Read and Understand Description

Reading examples of description to understand their structure and content will help you write your own. The first example, a paragraph, is followed by questions about the structure of description. The second example, an essay, has questions in the margin to help you read closely. It is followed by questions about both structure and content, along with writing assignments. These activities will help you practice your critical reading and thinking skills.

■ **READING SELECTIONS:**
For further examples of and activities for description, see Chapter 44.

Description Paragraph: Student

The Peach Tree
Cathy Vittoria

When I reminisce about my childhood, the fondest memories I have revolve around food. Our family often went on picnics to the beach. There at the water's edge, my father would struggle to light the charcoal

VOCABULARY DEVELOPMENT
Underline these words as you read the description paragraph.

reminisce: *recall past experiences*

anise: *an herb that tastes like licorice*

succulent: *juicy*

integral: *essential; necessary*

in the gusty wind. My mother's anise-flavored bread was the perfect match for ham on Easter morning and the days that followed. On my birthday we always had gnocchi, fluffy pillows of pasta that melted in my mouth, tossed with a heavenly tomato sauce. In August we had peaches, not just any peaches, but the peaches from our own peach tree. I loved our peach tree, it produced the sweetest, most succulent peaches I've ever eaten. When I think about my past, that peach tree plays an integral part in my childhood memories.

> —From Cathy Vittoria, "The Peach Tree," Diablo Valley Community College Web site (Brian McKinney, instructor)

■ **TIP:** For advice on building your vocabulary, see Appendix B.

1. Double-underline the **topic sentence**.

2. What main impression does Vittoria create?

3. Underline the **sensory details** (sight, taste, smell, sound, texture) that create the main impression.

4. What order of organization does Vittoria use? _time order_
   Circle the **transitions**.

5. Does the paragraph have the Four Basics of Good Description (p. 134)? Why or why not?

   Yes. Specific answers will vary, but students should be able to give examples of the

   Four Basics.

Description Essay: Student

The Peach Tree
Cathy Vittoria

PREDICT: What do you think this essay will be about?

Although it may seem an odd childhood memory, a peach tree was an important part of my childhood. The peach tree was special to my sisters and me. It was, in fact, the only tree in our small yard. We grew through the seasons with it. Every February the first bits of pink showed through the tightly closed flower buds. By March it was covered in pink, like overgrown cotton candy. In April little flecks of green accented the pink blossoms and slowly pushed out the pink until a fresh, vibrant green blanketed the crown of the tree. During this transition, the lawn became a carpet of pink. Then slowly the fruit came, growing from little nubs like pumpkin seeds to the size of walnuts. In June, the tree dropped its excesses, and green fruit, hard as golf balls, would bomb us as we played in the yard. After

IDENTIFY: Circle details that appeal to the senses.

1

that, it was just a matter of waiting. Being children, we put the time to good use. We climbed and swung on the tree's branches. We played house and frontier fort in the tree. We were pirates, Tarzan,[1] Jane,[2] and George of the Jungle.[3]

By mid-August the fragrance perfumed the air. The fruit, the size of softballs, bent the branches. Not heeding our parents' advice, we would sneak a peach, unable to resist. We were usually greeted by a tasteless, crunchy disappointment. One day, Mom and Dad would summon us to tell us it was time. We picked baskets full of peaches, more than we could eat. We stood on the lawn eating while leaning forward to keep the juice from dripping onto our clothing. The juice still ran down our faces and arms onto everything. We were sticky but satisfied. Mom would make the best peach pies, but my father's favorite dessert was peaches and red wine. We would have peaches on pancakes, peaches on ice cream, peaches on cereal, and peaches on peaches. After that, the canning began. Mom would peel, slice, and carefully cut away any of the bad parts of the peach before canning. The jars would be lined up on the kitchen counter under the open window, waiting to cool before being stored in the basement. Knowing that there would be peaches for us during the other eleven months of the year was always great comfort.

The peach tree declined in health as we grew up. Peach leaf curl was a chronic problem. Winter storms caused some damage; limbs cracked and broke off. Eventually, the old tree was producing only a few runt-sized fruit. One winter my parents cut down the tree. It left a scar on the lawn and a barren space in the yard. I hadn't thought much about that old tree for some time, even though it was the peach tree that planted the seed, so to speak, of my passion for gardening. The first fruit trees I planted in my own back yard were peaches. When I told my sisters that I was writing about the peach tree, they both smiled a familiar smile. For a moment, they were transported to another place and time. And I knew that it wasn't simply nostalgia; it was real. In the years that have followed, I have never found a peach as large, juicy, and luscious as the ones from our tree.

—Diablo Valley Community College Web site
(Brian McKinney, instructor)

2

3

VOCABULARY DEVELOPMENT
Underline these words as you read the description essay.

flecks: *small marks; dots*

vibrant: *bright*

excesses: *extra amounts*

summon: *call*

runt: *small (refers to an undersize animal)*

barren: *empty*

nostalgia: *longing for the past*

luscious: *delicious*

REFLECT: How do you think the author felt when the peach tree was cut down?

_____

_____

---

[1] **Tarzan:** a fictional man who lived in the jungle.

[2] **Jane:** Tarzan's mate.

[3] **George of the Jungle:** a Tarzan-like cartoon character.

■ **TIP:** For reading advice, see Chapter 1.

CRITICAL THINKING: READING

1. The paragraph on page 141, also written by Vittoria, is another part of this essay. Where do you think the paragraph would fit in the essay? *It is the introductory paragraph.*

2. Double-underline the **thesis statement**.

3. Underline the **transitions**.

4. Why do you think the peach tree was an important part of Vittoria's life? *Answers will vary. Possible answer: The tree was part of a family tradition.*

5. Why do you think that Vittoria has never found a peach that was as good as the ones from her family's tree? *Answers will vary.*

6. Do you think Vittoria's description of the peach tree would be different if she were writing about a tree she had never seen before? Why or why not? *Answers will vary.*

   Possible answer: The new tree would not have the fond memories attached to it.

CRITICAL THINKING: WRITING

Choose one of the following topics and respond in a paragraph or essay.

1. Describe a tradition, family or otherwise, that is important to you.
2. Describe an object or a place that was important to you or your family when you were a child.
3. How did you and your sisters, brothers, or friends play as children?
4. Think about your childhood. What experiences did you have that you hope your own children could have?

Write Your Own Description

■ **TIP:** Look back at your idea-journal entry (p. 134) for ideas.

In this section, you will write your own description paragraph or essay based on your (or your instructor's) choice among three assignments.

To complete your description, follow this sequence:

1. Review the Four Basics of Good Description (p. 134).
2. Choose your assignment.

3. If you are asked to complete Assignment 3, read Solving Problems, Appendix D.

4. Write your description using the Checklist: How to Write Description (pp. 147–48).

ASSIGNMENT 1   WRITING ABOUT COLLEGE, WORK, AND EVERYDAY LIFE ·

Write a description on one of the topics.

> **TIP:** If you use the Writing Guide Software with this book, you'll find step-by-step guidance for writing description paragraphs and essays.

COLLEGE

PARAGRAPH	ESSAY
• A classroom just before the start of class	• Your first school
• Sounds in the cafeteria	• An art display on campus
• The entrance to the student center	• The college library

WORK

PARAGRAPH	ESSAY
• The physical sensations you experience as you work	• The sounds and smells of your workplace
• A coworker or a boss	• Your favorite (or least favorite) coworker
• Your own work space	• The products your workplace produces

EVERYDAY LIFE

PARAGRAPH	ESSAY
• A favorite photograph	• A busy store
• A season	• Music you like or a concert you attended
• Your favorite piece of clothing	• A favorite photograph

ASSIGNMENT 2   WRITING ABOUT IMAGES · · · · · · · · · · · · · · ·

The picture on the next page is from a book that shows families' possessions in various places in the world. In either a paragraph or an essay, describe the photograph, including what certain possessions tell you about the particular family and their world.

> **DESCRIPTION AT A GLANCE**
>
> **Topic sentence (paragraph) or thesis statement (essay)**
> Gives a main impression
>
> ↓
>
> **First example to support main impression**
> Details to create picture of first example
>
> ↓
>
> **Second example to support main impression**
> Details to create picture of second example
>
> ↓
>
> **Third example to support main impression**
> Details to create picture of third example
>
> ↓
>
> **Conclusion**
> Reminds readers of the main impression

> **ESL:** Have students describe a famous place or popular meal in their native countries.

ASSIGNMENT 3   WRITING IN THE REAL WORLD/SOLVING A PROBLEM

■ **RESOURCES:** All chapters in Part Two have writing checklists, which are reproduced in *Additional Resources.* You can photocopy and distribute them if you want students to hand in the checklists with their assignments.

■ **TIP:** For more on using formal English, see Chapter 2. For related exercises, visit Exercise Central at **bedfordstmartins .com/realwriting**.

PROBLEM: You are the chair of a committee that has been appointed to report on the safety of the classrooms in an old section of your child's school. Your committee has consulted many experts and found that the school has numerous safety issues that threaten children's health. A member of the committee volunteered to draft a summary of the findings, which will go to the city council next week. This is what he gave you to review:

Our committee founded many threat to childin safty. The paint is led-basted for one thing. It poison childrin, not be safe. Hanging it in strips on wall. Exposed nail culd hurt peple. Another ting the carpit have mould, big time. It let off dangers organisms and a bad smell. Be buckled and people maybe trip. Classrooms have the bad ventilation so fumes not got out.

ASSIGNMENT: Working in a small group or on your own, rewrite the summary in formal English, correcting errors first and then adding details that make the room's safety problems more vivid. **Hint:** The problems your committee found were peeling, lead-based paint; exposed nails; molding carpets; and a nonfunctioning ventilation system.

■ **RESOURCES:** Reproducible peer-review guides for different kinds of papers are available in *Additional Resources*.

■ **LEARNING JOURNAL:** Reread your idea-journal entry from page 134. Write another entry on the same topic, using what you have learned about good description.

CHECKLIST: HOW TO WRITE DESCRIPTION	
STEPS IN DESCRIPTION	**HOW TO DO THE STEPS**
☐ **Focus.**	• Think about what you want to describe and what picture you want to create for your readers.
☐ **Narrow and explore your topic.** See Chapter 3.	• Prewrite, thinking of the senses you could use to describe your topic.
☐ **Write a topic sentence (paragraph) or a thesis statement (essay) that includes your narrowed topic and the main impression you want to give your reader.** See Chapter 4.	• Review your prewriting. Then, close your eyes and try to experience your topic as you first did. • Decide what is most important to you about the experience.
☐ **Support your main impression.** See Chapter 5.	• Prewrite for details and images that bring your topic to life. • Read the details and add more to fill in the picture.
☐ **Make a plan.** See Chapter 6.	• Arrange your details in a logical order (time, space, or importance).
☐ **Write a draft.** See Chapter 7.	**FOR A PARAGRAPH** • Write a paragraph with your topic sentence, major examples/images, and supporting sensory details. Use complete sentences. **FOR AN ESSAY** • Consider using one of the introduction types in Chapter 7. Include your thesis statement in your introduction. • Using your plan, write topic sentences for the major examples/images. In each paragraph, include sensory details that bring the examples/images to life.

continued

STEPS IN DESCRIPTION	HOW TO DO THE STEPS
	FOR PARAGRAPHS AND ESSAYS
☐ **Write a draft.** See Chapter 7.	• Write a conclusion that reminds your readers of the topic and main impression and makes an observation based on what you have written. • Write a title that previews your main point but doesn't repeat it.
☐ **Revise your draft, making at least four improvements.** See Chapter 8.	• Get feedback from others using the peer-review guide for description at **bedfordstmartins.com/realwriting**. • Read to make sure that all examples and details serve to create your main impression. • Add more sensory details that make the description stronger. • Add transitions to move your readers from one detail to another.
☐ **Edit your revised draft.** See Parts Four through Seven.	• Correct errors in grammar, spelling, word use, and punctuation.
☐ **Ask yourself:**	• Does my paper have the Four Basics of Good Description (p. 134)? • Is this the best I can do?

Chapter Review

1. Description is writing that _creates a clear and vivid impression of the topic._

2. What are the Four Basics of Good Description?

   It creates a main impression about the topic.

   It uses specific examples to support the main impression.

   It supports those examples with details that appeal to the five senses.

   It brings a person, place, or physical object to life for the reader.

3. The topic sentence in a description paragraph or the thesis statement in a description essay includes what two elements? _a narrowed topic and main impression about that topic_

4. Choose five of the vocabulary words on pages 141 or 143 and use each in a sentence.

12

Process Analysis

Writing That Explains How Things Happen

Understand What Process Analysis Is

Process analysis either explains how to do something (so your readers can do it) or explains how something works (so your readers can understand it). Both types of process analysis present the steps involved in the process.

■■ FOUR BASICS OF GOOD PROCESS ANALYSIS
■■

1. It tells readers what process you want them to know about and makes a point about it.
2. It presents the essential steps in the process.
3. It explains the steps in detail.
4. It presents the steps in a logical order (usually time order).

■ **IDEA JOURNAL:** Write about something you recently learned how to do—and how you do it.

In the following paragraph, each number corresponds to one of the Four Basics of Good Process Analysis.

4 Time order used.

    1 Making microwave popcorn is a snap. **2** First, read the box to find out how many minutes the popcorn should cook in the microwave oven. Next, place the popcorn bag in the microwave oven, **3** making sure that the correct side is facing up, as written in big letters on the bag. **2** Then, close the door **3** firmly and **2** push the "cook" button, if your microwave oven has this feature. Press the number buttons to indicate the amount of time that you want the popcorn to pop. Next, push the "start" button. Stay close by and **3** listen for when the popping slows down to two or three seconds between pops. **2** When that happens, even if the time isn't yet up, push the "stop" button. Take the bag out and **3** open it just a little bit at first to let the burst of hot steam escape. **2** Then, rip the rest of the top off, pour the popcorn into a big bowl, and top it with whatever you like: **3** salt, butter, cheese, chili powder—use your imagination. The whole process takes well under five minutes, and you're then ready to enjoy that great popcorn.

You use process analysis in many situations:

COLLEGE	In a science course, you explain how photosynthesis works.
WORK	You write instructions to explain how to operate something (the copier, the fax machine).
EVERYDAY LIFE	You write out a recipe for an aunt.

Profile of Success: Process Analysis in the Real World

Rocío Murillo
Teacher

■ **RESOURCES:** For a discussion of how to use the profiles in Part Two, see *Practical Suggestions.*

The following profile shows how a teacher uses process analysis on the job.

BACKGROUND: I grew up speaking only Spanish because my father didn't want us to forget our native language. My high school counselor insisted that I did not have what it takes to go to college. Fortunately, I didn't listen to him, but I wasn't confident about my abilities.

After high school, I went to El Camino College and found out about the Puente Project. In this specialized program, I was blessed with a caring Latino counselor, a gifted English teacher, and an inspiring mentor. I blossomed in this program and realized that I was good enough to be accepted as a University of California, Irvine, student.

My first quarter at UC Irvine was incredibly difficult. I was working three jobs, and I received a letter of probation that stated that if I did not better my grades by the next quarter I would be kicked out. I remember sitting on the outside steps of a building one lonely afternoon and crying. But I was determined to go on and did better the next quarter.

Now I have a master's degree, a job I love, and a wonderful husband; also, I am expecting twins. I am a survivor.

COLLEGE(S)/DEGREES: A.A., El Camino College; B.A., University of California, Irvine; M.Ed., Pepperdine University

EMPLOYER: Lennox (California) School District

WRITING AT WORK: Regular lesson plans; materials for classroom use; letters to parents, administrators, and businesses; memos to other teachers; grant proposals.

HOW ROCÍO USES PROCESS ANALYSIS: I give students directions for assignments and activities, explaining, step-by-step, how to do something.

ROCÍO'S PROCESS ANALYSIS

Rocío gave her students the following instructions for responding to a fire alarm.

When you hear the fire alarm, please follow these directions exactly to make sure that we exit the building safely.^First, stop what you are doing immediately.^Then, pick up your backpack, but do not stop to fill it up with materials you have out.^Make a single line in front of the door, quickly but without pushing or talking.^When I tell you to, proceed out of the classroom and into the hall, staying in line.^We

will turn right and walk directly to the first stairway on our right. Do
₆not stop to talk with friends or to use the water fountain or restroom.
^₇Walk, don't run, down the two flights of stairs, and exit the building.
^Walk over to the left of the basketball hoop and stop.^⁸When I get there,
I will take attendance to make sure that everyone has exited safely.

1. What **process** is being analyzed? _a fire drill_

2. Is this a paragraph that tells how to do something or a paragraph that
   explains how something works?

   It tells how to do something.

3. Number the **major steps**.

4. What order of organization does the writer use? _time order_

Main Point in Process Analysis

In process analysis your **purpose** is to explain how to do something or how
something works by presenting the steps in the process. Your **main point**
should tell readers what about the process you want them to know. Your
topic sentence (paragraph) or thesis statement (essay) should not simply
state the process: It should make a point about it.

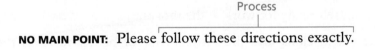

Process

NO MAIN POINT: Please follow these directions exactly.

Process   Main point

WITH A MAIN POINT: Please follow these directions exactly to make sure
that we exit the building safely.

To help you discover the main point for your process analysis, complete the
following sentence:

What I want readers to know about this process is that . . .

Here are more examples of effective topic sentences/thesis statements:

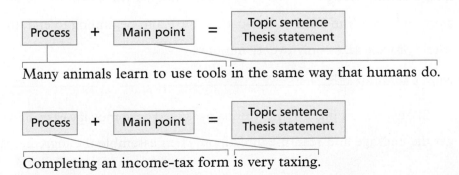

| Process | + | Main point | = | Topic sentence / Thesis statement |

Many animals learn to use tools in the same way that humans do.

| Process | + | Main point | = | Topic sentence / Thesis statement |

Completing an income-tax form is very taxing.

Support in Process Analysis

To perform or understand a process, your readers must know all of its essential steps; those steps are the **support** for your main point in a process analysis.

Because you are describing a process that you are familiar with, you may not think about each individual step. For example, as you tie your shoes, you probably aren't aware of the steps involved; you just do them. But when you explain a process in writing, you need to think carefully about what the individual steps are so that you do not leave out any essential ones.

Your readers may also need to know details, facts, or examples that will help them understand each step. As you describe the process, think about what you would need to know about each step in order to understand it or perform it.

■ PRACTICE 1   **FINDING THE MAIN POINT AND SUPPLYING MISSING STEPS** . . . .

In each of the following process analysis paragraphs, an essential step is missing. In real life, the writer would naturally do that essential step, but he or she left it out of the paragraph.

Either by yourself, with a partner, or in a small group, first identify the main point, and then underline it. Next, supply the missing step in each paragraph. Indicate with a caret sign (^) where it should appear in the paragraph. *Placement of carets may vary.*

1. <u>Getting myself ready for work in the morning is a mad dash.</u> First, I shut off the alarm clock and drag myself out of bed. I turn on the shower and splash cold water on my face while waiting for the shower to get hot. Then, I jump into the shower for a quick shampoo and lather up with soap. After rinsing myself off and shutting off the water, I grab the towel and dry myself off.^Blow-drying my hair takes just two minutes. Then, I go down to the kitchen for coffee that my roommate has already made. I gulp down one cup at the table and then walk around with a second one, gathering up what I need to take with me to work. After running a comb through my hair, I'm out the door. I run down to the bus stop, and I'm off to another fast-paced day. From beginning to end, the whole process takes only twenty minutes.

WHAT'S MISSING? *getting dressed*

2. <u>Anyone can make a cake from a packaged cake mix; it's easy.</u> First, get the package and read the directions.^Then assemble the ingredients

you will need to add. These usually include water, eggs, and sometimes oil. If the instructions say so, grease and flour the cake pan or pans you will use to bake the cake. Next, mix the ingredients together in a bowl and stir or beat as directed. Then, transfer the batter into the right-sized cake pans. Put the pans into the oven and set the timer for the baking time indicated. It's hard to go wrong.

WHAT'S MISSING? *turning on the oven*

■ **PRACTICE 2   FINDING AND CHOOSING THE ESSENTIAL STEPS** . . . . .

For each of the following topics, write the essential steps in the order you would perform them.

1. Making (your favorite food) is simple.

    Answers will vary.

    _____

2. I think I could teach anyone how to _____.

    _____

3. Operating a _____ is _____.

    _____

    _____

■ **PRACTICE 3   ADDING DETAILS TO ESSENTIAL STEPS** . . . .

Choose one of the topics from Practice 2. In the spaces that follow, first copy down that topic and the steps you wrote for it in Practice 2. Then, add a detail to each of the steps. If the process has more than four steps, you might want to use a separate sheet of paper.

TOPIC: *Answers will vary.* _____

STEP 1: _____

   DETAIL: _____

STEP 2: _____

   DETAIL: _____

■ **TIP:** If you have written a narration paragraph already, you will notice that narration and process analysis are alike in that they both usually present events or steps in time order—the order in which they occur. The difference is that narration reports what happened, whereas process analysis describes how to do something or how something works.

■ **TIP:** For more on time order, see page 66.

STEP 3: _____

DETAIL: _____

STEP 4: _____

DETAIL: _____

Organization in Process Analysis

Process analysis is usually organized by **time (chronological) order** because it explains the steps of the process in the order in which they occur, starting with the first step.

Process analysis uses **time transitions** to move readers smoothly from one step to the next.

Common Transitions in Process Analysis			
after	eventually	meanwhile	soon
as	finally	next	then
at last	first	now	when
before	last	second	while
during	later	since	

■ **PRACTICE 4   USING TRANSITIONS IN PROCESS ANALYSIS** . . . .

Read the paragraph that follows and fill in the blanks with transitions.
Answers may vary. Possible answers shown.

Recording a television show is simple, but it involves a few steps. _____First_____, turn on the VCR and insert a videotape. _Then, Next, Second_, turn on the television set and press the VCR button on the remote control. _Next, Then, Third_, turn the television to the station showing the program you want to record. Use the up and down arrows at the bottom of the remote to turn the VCR to the same channel as the television. _Finally, Last, Third_, press Record on the remote or the VCR when the show begins, and the VCR will start recording. You can _then, now_ turn off the television and do whatever else you want. Your show will be on the videotape whenever you want to watch it.

Read and Understand Process Analysis

Reading examples of process analysis to understand their structure and content will help you write your own. The first example, a paragraph, is followed by questions about the structure of process analysis. The second example, an essay, has questions in the margin to help you read closely. It is followed by questions about both structure and content, along with writing assignments. These activities will help you practice your critical reading and thinking skills.

■ **READING SELECTIONS:** For further examples of and activities for other process analysis paragraphs and essays, see Chapter 45.

Process Analysis Paragraph: Professional

A Workout for Your Brain
Daryn Eller

Brain gym movements, created in the 1970s by educator Paul E. Dennison, Ph.D., are short, easy exercises that are designed to enhance neural connections and reduce stress. Most of the brain gym movements are designed to help shuttle information between the left and right sides of your brain. (When) you don't have time to squeeze in a longer workout, try this simple brain gym movement: [1]Stand with your arms at your sides. [2](At the same time), bend your right knee and left elbow at a 90-degree angle and [3]move them toward each other (don't crouch to make them meet; it's not necessary that they touch). [4]Return to the starting position, [5](then) repeat with your left knee and right elbow. [6]Continue at a moderate pace for about one minute. You can find this move and others at <**www.braingym.org**>. Using the brain gym regularly will keep your brain in good shape and help you deal with daily stress more efficiently.

—Daryn Eller, sidebar from "Move Your Body, Free Your Mind,"
Health magazine, May 2002

VOCABULARY DEVELOPMENT
Underline these words as you read the process analysis paragraph.
enhance: *improve*
neural: *related to the brain or nervous system*
shuttle: *carry*
moderate: *neither too fast nor too slow*

■ **TIP:** For advice on building your vocabulary, see Appendix B.

1. Double-underline the **topic sentence**.

2. Is this a paragraph that tells how to do something or a paragraph that explains how something works?

   It tells how to do something.

3. Number the **steps** in the sample paragraph.

4. Underline the **details** the writer includes for each step.

5. Circle the **transitions**.

VOCABULARY DEVELOPMENT
Underline these words as
you read the process analysis essay.

digitally: *referring to the
conversion of sound waves
into numbers*

tracks: *separate sound
recordings that are com-
bined into one musical piece*

flaws: *defects or imperfec-
tions*

synthesizers: *instruments
that can produce sounds of
other instruments*

enhanced: *improved*

IDENTIFY: Number the steps
of producing a CD.

REFLECT: Does all this work
make CDs sound even bet-
ter than live music?

Process Analysis Essay: Textbook

Making a Recording

A typical recording session is a complex process that involves   1
musicians and audio technicians and is directed by a session engineer and a producer. George Martin, for example, served as both
chief engineer and producer for the Beatles' sessions in the 1960s.

Today, the engineer and producer roles usually fall to different   2
people. A chief engineer oversees the technical parts of the recording session, everything from choosing recording equipment to arranging microphone placement. In charge of the overall recording
process, the producer handles most nontechnical elements of the
session, including reserving studio space and hiring musicians.
During recording, the producer takes command and, in most cases,
decides whether certain vocal or instrumental parts work well or
need to be rerecorded.

Most popular CDs and tapes are now produced part by part.   3
[1]Using separate microphones, the vocalists, guitarists, drummers,
and other musical sections are digitally recorded onto audio tracks.
To produce one song, as many as two or three dozen tracks might be
recorded, often at different times and in different studios.[2]Control-
ling the overall sound quality, the chief engineer mixes the parts onto
a two-track stereo master tape.[3]Then, mixing engineers specialize in
other postproduction editing; they mix the multiple tracks after the
recording sessions.[4]After that, mastering engineers prepare the song
for transfer to a final version on audiotape and CD.[5]Finally, remix
engineers work with tapes that are already mastered, removing flaws
or adding new instrumental or vocal parts. Because digital keyboard
synthesizers are able to reproduce most instrumental sounds, engineers can now duplicate many instrumental parts without recalling
the studio musicians. Over the years, the recording process has been
both enhanced and made more complex by technological advances.
When people listen to a CD, the various parts of the process produce a seamless blend of music and voices.

—Adapted from Richard Campbell, Christopher R. Martin,
and Bettina Fabos, *Media and Culture: An Introduction to
Mass Communication,* 5th ed. (Bedford/St. Martin's, 2006)

CRITICAL THINKING: READING

1. Double-underline the **thesis statement**. In your own words, what is
   the main point that the authors make about the process?

   Possible answer: Recording requires a series of efforts by various experts.

2. What is the basic difference in the jobs of chief engineer and producer?

   The chief engineer handles technical parts of recording, and the producer

   handles nontechnical parts.

■ **DISCUSSION:** Ask students about the likely effects of illegal music downloads on the recording industry. Do they think that such downloading is acceptable? Why or why not?

3. Circle the **transitions** that the authors use to move readers from one step in the process to the next.

4. What kinds of engineers work to produce a CD? *chief engineers, mixing*

   engineers, mastering engineers, remix engineers

   Why do you think so many different engineers are needed?

   Possible answer: Each step of the process calls for specialized skills.

5. Write down a question about the recording process that remains unanswered by this excerpt. *Answers will vary. Possible answer: How much of a*

   say do singers and musicians have in what is changed or kept in a recording?

■ **TIP:** For reading advice, see Chapter 1.

6. Highlight this textbook excerpt as you might if you were reading it for a mass communications class. (For guidance, see Chapter 1, pp. 15–16.)

CRITICAL THINKING: WRITING

Choose one of the following topics and respond in a paragraph or essay.

1. Discuss how technology (for example, automated telephone responses) can make an everyday process more difficult or complicated.
2. Describe a process you participated in that required several different people (for example, moving or doing a job at work). What were the advantages and disadvantages of working in a group?
3. Describe a recording you like, focusing on parts that you especially enjoy—for instance, the singing, the guitars or drums, a rap. Name at least three qualities that make the recording special.

Write Your Own Process Analysis

In this section, you will write your own process analysis paragraph or essay based on your (or your instructor's) choice among three assignments.

To complete your process analysis, follow this sequence:

1. Review the Four Basics of Good Process Analysis (p. 149).
2. Choose your assignment.

■ **TIP:** Look back at your idea-journal entry (p. 149) for ideas.

3. If you are asked to complete Assignment 3, read Solving Problems, Appendix D.

4. Write your process analysis using the Checklist: How to Write Process Analysis (pp. 160–161).

PROCESS ANALYSIS AT A GLANCE

Topic sentence (paragraph) or thesis statement (essay)
Includes the process you are describing

↓

First step in process
Details about the first step (how to do it or how it works)

↓

Second step in process
Details about the second step (how to do it or how it works)

↓

Third step in process
Details about the third step (how to do it or how it works)

↓

Conclusion
Reminds readers of the process and makes an observation related to your main point

 ESL: Suggest that students write about a process that they used in their native country or culture but don't use where they live now.

 ASSIGNMENT 1   WRITING ABOUT COLLEGE, WORK, AND EVERYDAY LIFE . . . .

Write a process analysis on one of the following topics.

COLLEGE

PARAGRAPH	ESSAY
How to	How to
• Register for a course	• Find a book in the library
• Use a spell-checker	• Apply for admission to the college
• Get a parking permit	• Study for an exam

WORK

PARAGRAPH	ESSAY
How to	How to
• Get information about a company you want to work for	• Get a job
• Perform a specific task at work	• Make a product that your company produces

EVERYDAY LIFE

PARAGRAPH	ESSAY
How to	How to
• Quickly clean up your home or room	• Convince someone to help you (for example, lend you money or a car; help you at work)
• Do something that you do every day	
• Politely get rid of a telephone sales call	• Do something that you are good at (dance, cook, play video games, etc.)

 ASSIGNMENT 2   WRITING ABOUT IMAGES . . . .

In either a paragraph or an essay, describe a process (humorous or otherwise) for breaking a bad habit. Make sure to include details about the steps.

"One patch makes me stop smoking, one makes me eat less, one makes me put my clothes in the hamper instead of leaving them on the floor, one makes me put the toilet seat back down..."

ASSIGNMENT 3   WRITING IN THE REAL WORLD/SOLVING A PROBLEM

PROBLEM: Midway through a course you are taking, your instructor asks the class to tell her how she could improve the course. You haven't been happy with the class because the instructor is always late and comes in seeming rushed and tense. She then lectures for most of the class before giving you an assignment that you start on while she sits at her desk, busily grading papers. You are afraid to ask questions about the lecture or assignment. You want to tell the instructor how the course could be better, but you don't want to offend her.

ASSIGNMENT: Working in a small group or on your own, write to your instructor about how she could improve the course. Think of how the class could be structured differently so that you could learn more. Begin with how the class could start and then describe how the rest of the class period could go, suggesting specific activities if you can. State your suggestions in positive terms. For example, instead of telling the instructor what *not* to do, make suggestions using phrases like *you could, we could,* or *the class could.* Make sure to use formal English.

You might start in this way:

Several simple changes might improve our learning. At the start of each

class, ———————————————————————.

At the end, remember to thank your instructor for asking for students' suggestions.

■ **TEAMWORK:** For more detailed guidance on group work, see *Practical Suggestions.*

■ **RESOURCES:** All chapters in Part Two have writing checklists, which are reproduced in *Additional Resources.* You can photocopy and distribute them if you want students to hand in the checklists with their assignments.

■ **RESOURCES:** Reproducible peer-review guides for different kinds of papers are available in *Additional Resources.*

CHECKLIST: HOW TO WRITE PROCESS ANALYSIS	
STEPS IN PROCESS	**HOW TO DO THE STEPS**
☐ **Focus.**	• Think about a process that interests you or that you need to describe for others.
☐ **Narrow and explore your topic.** See Chapter 3.	• Make sure the process is specific/narrow enough to write a paragraph or essay about. • Prewrite to get ideas about the narrowed topic.
☐ **Write a topic sentence (paragraph) or thesis statement (essay) that includes your main point about the process.** See Chapter 4.	• Ask: What do you want your readers to know about the process, other than how to do it or how it works?
☐ **Support your point.** See Chapter 5.	• Include all of the steps in the process. • Give specific details about how to do the steps or about how they work so that your readers will understand them.
☐ **Make a plan.** See Chapter 6.	• Arrange the steps in time order.
☐ **Write a draft.** See Chapter 7.	**FOR A PARAGRAPH** • Write a paragraph with your topic sentence, essential steps, and details about the steps. Use complete sentences. **FOR AN ESSAY** • Consider using one of the introduction types in Chapter 7. Include your thesis statement in your introduction. • Using your plan, write topic sentences for the essential steps. • For each topic sentence, write paragraphs with details about the steps.
☐ **Write a draft.** See Chapter 7.	**FOR PARAGRAPHS AND ESSAYS** • Write a conclusion that reminds your readers of your main point and makes an observation based on what you have written. • Write a title that previews your main point but doesn't repeat it. • Get feedback from others using the peer-review guide for process analysis at **bedfordstmartins.com/realwriting**.
☐ **Revise your draft, making at least four improvements.** See Chapter 8.	• Read to make sure that you have included all of the essential steps in the process. • Add more details about the steps. • Add time transitions to move your readers from one step to another.

STEPS IN PROCESS	HOW TO DO THE STEPS
☐ **Revise your draft, making at least four improvements.** See Chapter 8.	• Read to make sure that you have included all of the essential steps in the process. • Add more details about the steps. • Add time transitions to move your readers from one step to another.
☐ **Edit your revised draft.** See Parts Four through Seven.	• Correct errors in grammar, spelling, word use, and punctuation.
☐ **Ask yourself:**	• Does my paper have the Four Basics of Good Process Analysis (see p. 149)? • Is this the best I can do?

Chapter Review

1. Process analysis is writing that _either explains how to do something or explains how something works._

2. What are the Four Basics of Good Process Analysis?

   It tells readers what process you want them to know about and makes a point about it.

   It presents the essential steps in the process.

   It explains the steps in detail.

   It presents the steps in a logical order (usually time order).

3. Choose five of the vocabulary words on pages 155 or 156 and use each in a sentence.

■ **LEARNING JOURNAL:**
Reread your idea-journal entry on how to do something you recently learned (p. 149). Make another entry on the same process, using what you have learned about process analysis. Assume you are teaching someone else this process.

You Know This

You have had experience classifying various items:

- You see how movies in a video store are arranged.
- You group items into boxes when you move.
- You sort laundry by color before washing it.

13

Classification

Writing That Sorts Things into Groups

Understand What Classification Is

Classification is writing that organizes, or sorts, people or items into categories. It uses an **organizing principle**: *how* the people or items are sorted. The organizing principle is directly related to the purpose for classifying. For example, you might sort clean laundry (your purpose) using one of the following organizing principles: by ownership (yours, your roommate's) or by where it goes (the bedroom, the bathroom).

▪▪ FOUR BASICS OF GOOD CLASSIFICATION

1. It makes sense of a group of people or items by organizing them into categories.
2. It has a purpose for sorting the people or items.
3. It categorizes using a single organizing principle.
4. It gives detailed examples or explanations of what fits into each category.

In the following paragraph, each number corresponds to one of the Four Basics of Good Classification.

▪ **IDEA JOURNAL:** Write about the different kinds of students in this class or the different kinds of friends you have.

> **1** Since I've been working as a cashier at Wal-Mart, I've discovered there are several kinds of customers **2** who drive me crazy. **3** First are the openly rude ones. **4** They frown and make loud, sarcastic remarks about how long the line is and how long they've been waiting. They throw their money on the counter and never say hello or acknowledge me as anything but human scum. I'm embarrassed for myself, but I'm also embarrassed for them. **3** Second are the silent but obviously impatient customers. **4** Although they don't say anything, you've been aware of them since the time they got in line. They make faces, roll their eyes,

and look at their watches every ten seconds. What do they expect? This is Wal-Mart; there are always lines. **3** The third kind is really my least favorite: suspicious customers who watch my every move as if my goal in life is to overcharge them. **4** They turn the monitor so they can see every price, but that's not enough. After looking at the price there, they lean over the counter toward me and look at what price comes up on the register. Then their heads snap back to look at the monitor. They clearly don't trust me and are just waiting for me to make a mistake, at which point they will jump all over me. This kind of customer makes me nervous and a lot more likely to mess up. If you are one of these three kinds of customers, remember me next time you're at Wal-Mart; I'm the one just trying to do my job, and you're driving me crazy!

—Joyce Kenneally

Sometimes, it helps to think of classification in diagram form. Here is a diagram of the previous paragraph:

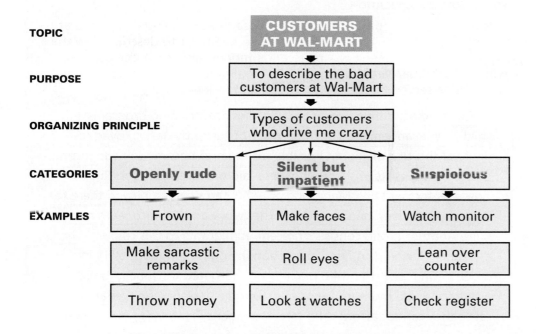

TOPIC		CUSTOMERS AT WAL-MART	
PURPOSE		To describe the bad customers at Wal-Mart	
ORGANIZING PRINCIPLE		Types of customers who drive me crazy	
CATEGORIES	Openly rude	Silent but impatient	Suspicious
EXAMPLES	Frown	Make faces	Watch monitor
	Make sarcastic remarks	Roll eyes	Lean over counter
	Throw money	Look at watches	Check register

You use classification any time you want to organize people or items.

COLLEGE   In a criminal justice course, you are asked to discuss the most common types of chronic offenders.

WORK   For a sales presentation, your boss asks you to classify the kinds of products your company produces.

EVERYDAY LIFE   You classify your typical monthly expenses to make a budget.

Profile of Success: Classification in the Real World

Rosalind Baker
Director of Human Services

■ **RESOURCES:** For a discussion of how to use the profiles in Part Two, see *Practical Suggestions.*

The following profile shows how a director of human services uses classification on the job.

BACKGROUND: At eighteen, I was a homeless single mother living in a shelter for abused women and children. I realized that things weren't going to get any better unless I helped myself, so I enrolled in a community college, where I met some teachers who encouraged me. Going to school was hard, but once I'd taken a few courses, I got the hang of it and started to do better. I knew it was the only good way out for me.

COLLEGE(S)/DEGREES: A.A., Massachusetts Bay Community College; B.S. in history from Suffolk University, with a minor in public policy

EMPLOYER: City of Marlborough, Massachusetts

WRITING AT WORK: Reports, proposals, summaries, letters, requests for proposals, memos

HOW ROSALIND USES CLASSIFICATION: Many of the grants and proposals I write classify people, projects, or funding into different categories. Breaking things down into categories helps other people understand the whole project and who it benefits.

ROSALIND'S CLASSIFICATION

This paragraph was part of a grant proposal that Rosalind completed at her job. The grant application requires the applicant to describe how the funds will be spent, who will receive the money, and what the outcome will be. In the paragraph that follows, Rosalind classifies the population that will be served by the grant program.

The funding from this grant would subsidize training programs and child-care arrangements for three types of currently unemployed residents of this city, making it possible for them to become self-supporting. One group consists of those who were laid off when Johnson Rubber closed its factory here. Many workers who had been employed there for decades have been unable to find other work and need to learn new skills. Another group consists of recent immigrants to this country who are eager to work but need instruction in English-language skills in order to find jobs. The third major group targeted for funds from the grant are single mothers, many of whom are presently on welfare because they cannot afford child care. Our agency has already identified and interviewed many people from each of these three groups, and they are very eager to do whatever they can to find suitable jobs in our area.

1. Double-underline the **topic sentence**.

2. What is the **main point**? *that the grant would help unemployed residents become self-supporting*

3. How many **categories** are there? *three* What are they?
   unemployed factory workers, recent immigrants, single mothers

4. Underline the **explanations of people or items** in each category.

Main Point in Classification

The **main point** in classification uses a single **organizing principle** to sort items in a way that serves the writer's purpose. The categories should help to achieve the purpose.

To help you discover the organizing principle for your classification, complete the following sentences:

> **My purpose for classifying my topic is . . .**
> **It would make most sense to my readers if I sorted this topic by . . .**

Imagine the following situation in your college bookstore. The purpose of sorting textbooks is to help students find them. The best way to organize the books is by subject area or course number. But not in this bookstore . . .

> You walk into the bookstore looking for an algebra text and expect to find it in the math textbook area, classified according to its subject area. Instead, the books on the shelves aren't classified in any way you can make sense of.
>
> When you ask the sales clerk how to find the book, he says, "What color is it? The right half of the store has books arranged by color: blue over there, green in the middle, and so on. The left half of the store has them arranged by author."

This new arrangement is confusing for three reasons:

1. It doesn't serve the purpose of helping students to find textbooks.
2. It doesn't sort the books into useful categories. (You probably don't know what color the book is.)
3. It doesn't have a single organizing principle. (There are two: color and author.)

The following diagram shows how you would expect textbooks to be classified.

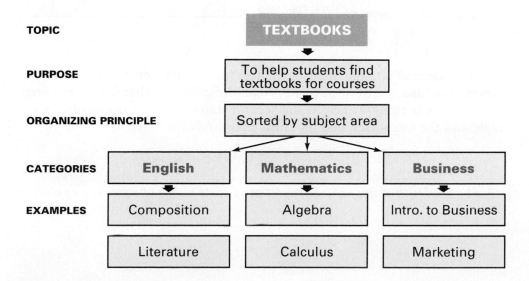

■   **PRACTICE 1   USING A SINGLE ORGANIZING PRINCIPLE** . . . .

For each topic that follows, one of the categories does not fit the same organizing principle as the rest. Circle the letter of the category that does not fit, and write the organizing principle the rest follow in the space provided. *Answers may vary. Possible answers shown.*

EXAMPLE:

TOPIC: Shoes

CATEGORIES:

a.   Running   c.   Golf

ⓑ   Leather   d.   Bowling

ORGANIZING PRINCIPLE: *by type of activity*

1.   **TOPIC:** Relatives

CATEGORIES:

a.   Aunts   c.   Sisters

ⓑ   Uncles   d.   Nieces

ORGANIZING PRINCIPLE: *female relatives*

2.   **TOPIC:** Jobs

CATEGORIES:

a.   Weekly   c.   Monthly

b.   Hourly   ⓓ   Summer

ORGANIZING PRINCIPLE: *pay period*

3.   **TOPIC:** Animals

CATEGORIES:

a.   Dogs   c.   Rabbits

b.   Cats   ⓓ   Whales

ORGANIZING PRINCIPLE: *pets; four legs*

. . . .

In classification, the topic sentence (paragraph) or thesis statement (essay) can take one of three forms. Read the examples that follow: the first states the organizing principle, the second states both the organizing principle and the categories, and the third states only the categories.

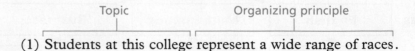

Topic   Organizing principle

(1) Students at this college represent a wide range of races.

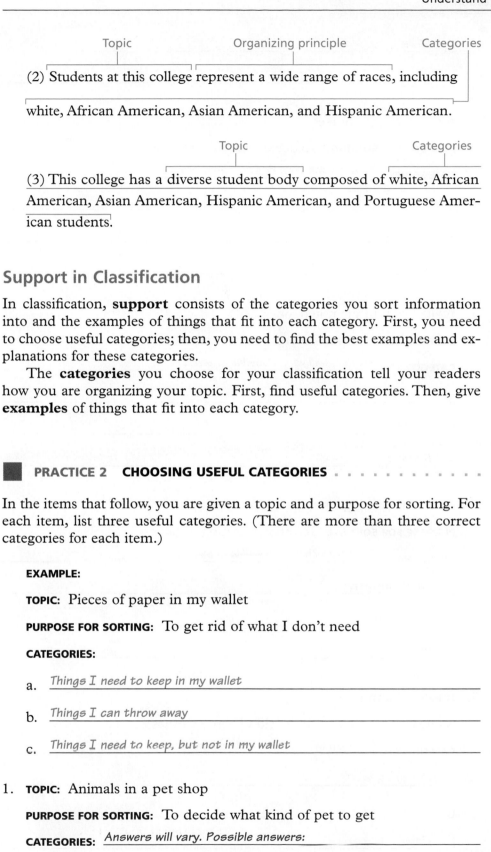

Topic Organizing principle Categories

(2) Students at this college represent a wide range of races, including white, African American, Asian American, and Hispanic American.

Topic Categories

(3) This college has a diverse student body composed of white, African American, Asian American, Hispanic American, and Portuguese American students.

Support in Classification

In classification, **support** consists of the categories you sort information into and the examples of things that fit into each category. First, you need to choose useful categories; then, you need to find the best examples and explanations for these categories.

The **categories** you choose for your classification tell your readers how you are organizing your topic. First, find useful categories. Then, give **examples** of things that fit into each category.

■ **PRACTICE 2   CHOOSING USEFUL CATEGORIES** . . . .

In the items that follow, you are given a topic and a purpose for sorting. For each item, list three useful categories. (There are more than three correct categories for each item.)

EXAMPLE:

TOPIC: Pieces of paper in my wallet

PURPOSE FOR SORTING: To get rid of what I don't need

CATEGORIES:

a. *Things I need to keep in my wallet*

b. *Things I can throw away*

c. *Things I need to keep, but not in my wallet*

1. **TOPIC:** Animals in a pet shop

PURPOSE FOR SORTING: To decide what kind of pet to get

CATEGORIES: *Answers will vary. Possible answers:*

a. *Dogs*

b. *Birds*

c. *Fish*

? **TOPIC:** College courses

   PURPOSE FOR SORTING: To decide what I'll register for

   CATEGORIES: *Answers will vary. Possible answers:*

   a. *English*

   b. *Accounting*

   c. *Math*

3. **TOPIC:** Stuff in my notebook

   PURPOSE FOR SORTING: To organize my schoolwork

   CATEGORIES: *Answers will vary. Possible answers:*

   a. *Homework*

   b. *Notes*

   c. *Doodles*

4. **TOPIC:** Wedding guests

   PURPOSE FOR SORTING: To arrange seating at tables

   CATEGORIES: *Answers will vary. Possible answers:*

   a. *Family members*

   b. *Neighbors*

   c. *Friends*

5. **TOPIC:** Clothing

   PURPOSE FOR SORTING: To get rid of some clothes

   CATEGORIES: *Answers will vary. Possible answers:*

   a. *Out of style*

   b. *Don't fit*

   c. *Good*

Organization in Classification

Classification can be organized in different ways (**time order**, **space order**, or **order of importance**) depending on its purpose.

PURPOSE	LIKELY ORGANIZATION
to explain changes or events over time	time
to describe the arrangement of people/items in physical space	space
to discuss parts of an issue or problem	importance

PRACTICE 3   ORGANIZING CLASSIFICATION . . . .

For each of the three items, read the topic sentence/thesis statement and purpose. Then, fill in the likely type of organization.

■ **TIP:** For more on the orders of organization, see pages 65–66.

EXAMPLE:

TOPIC SENTENCE/THESIS: Richmond Forest attracts three colorful types of campers, each one preferring a particular camp site.

PURPOSE: To describe the different types of campers and where they like to camp

LIKELY ORGANIZATION: *space order*

1. **TOPIC SENTENCE/THESIS:** There are three kinds of crime in this neighborhood.

   PURPOSE: To describe the kinds of crime.

   LIKELY ORGANIZATION: *order of importance*

2. **TOPIC SENTENCE/THESIS:** Clothes selling at 60% off were all over the store.

   PURPOSE: To tell about where the clothes on sale are located

   LIKELY ORGANIZATION: *space order*

3. **TOPIC SENTENCE/THESIS:** In the last ten years, many different styles of jeans have been popular.

   PURPOSE: To describe jean styles over the last ten years

   LIKELY ORGANIZATION: *time order*

As you write your classification, use **transitions** to move your readers smoothly from one category to another.

Common Transitions in Classification

another	for example
another kind	for instance
first, second, third,	last
and so on	one example/another example

PRACTICE 4   **USING TRANSITIONS IN CLASSIFICATION** . . . .

Read the paragraph that follows and fill in the blanks with transitions. You are not limited to the ones listed in the preceding box.
Answers may vary. Possible answers shown.

    Every day, I get three kinds of e-mail: work, personal, and junk. The ____*first kind*____ of e-mail, work, I have to read carefully and promptly. Sometimes, the messages are important ones directed to me, but mostly they are group messages about meetings, policies, or procedures. ____*For example, For instance*____, it seems as if the procedure for leaving the building during a fire alarm is always changing. ____*The second kind,*____ ____*Another kind*____ of e-mail, personal, is from friends or my mother. These I read when I get a chance, but I read them quickly and delete any that are jokes or messages that have to be sent to ten friends for good luck. ____*The third kind, The last kind*____ of e-mail is the most common and most annoying: junk. I get at least thirty junk e-mails a day, advertising all kinds of things that I'm not interested in, like life insurance or baby products. Even when I reply asking that the company stop sending me these messages, they keep coming. Sometimes, I wish e-mail didn't exist.

Read and Understand Classification

■ **READING SELECTIONS:**
For further examples of and activities for classification, see Chapter 46.

Reading examples of classification to understand their structure and content will help you write your own. The first example, a paragraph, is followed by questions about the structure of classification. The second example, an essay, has questions in the margin to help you read closely. It is followed by questions about both structure and content, along with writing assignments. These activities will help you practice your critical reading and thinking skills.

Classification Paragraph: Textbook

■ **TIP:** For advice on building your vocabulary, see Appendix B.

Psychoactive drugs have been classified into three main categories: depressants, stimulants, and hallucinogens. **Depressants** are drugs that slow down the central nervous system, body functions, and behavior. Among the most widely used depressants are alcohol, barbiturates, and tranquilizers. **Stimulants** are drugs that increase the activity of the nervous system. The mostly widely used stimulants are caffeine, nicotine, amphetamines, and cocaine. **Hallucinogens** are drugs that modify a person's perceptual experiences and produce hallucinations. LSD, marijuana, and ecstasy are hallucinogens.

—From John W. Santrock, *Human Adjustment* (McGraw-Hill, 2006)

VOCABULARY DEVELOPMENT
Underline these words as you read the classification paragraph.

psychoactive: *affecting the brain or mind*

perceptual: *related to seeing or feeling*

hallucinations: *visions of things that aren't real*

1. Double-underline the **topic sentence**.

2. What categories does the paragraph sort psychoactive drugs into?
    depressants, stimulants, hallucinogens

3. Underline the **examples of items** in each category.

4. What words does the author consider important? *depressants, stimulants, hallucinogens*

    How can you tell? *They are in bold type.*

VOCABULARY DEVELOPMENT
Underline these words as you read the classification essay.

skeptical: *doubtful*

validity: *worth*

trendsetter: *one that starts a new style or movement*

ruthless: *without pity*

compassionate: *sympathetic*

adaptable: *able to adjust to a variety of situations*

tactful: *polite*

procrastinate: *to delay doing something*

Classification Essay: Student

Blood Type and Personality
Danny Fitzgerald

In Japan, the question "What's your blood type?" is as common as "What's your sign?" in the United States. Some Japanese researchers claim that people's personalities can be classified by their blood types. You may be skeptical about this method of classification, but don't judge its validity before you read the descriptions the researchers have put together. Do you see yourself?

If you have blood type O, you are a leader. When you see something you want, you strive to achieve your goal. You are passionate, loyal, and self-confident, and you are often a trendsetter. Your enthusiasm for projects and goals spreads to others who happily follow your lead. When you want something, you may be ruthless about getting it or blind to how your actions affect others.

Another blood type, A, is a social, "people" person. You like people and work well with them. You are sensitive, patient, compassionate, and affectionate. You are a good peacekeeper because you

1   **PREDICT:** What do you think this essay will discuss?

2   ■ **TEAMWORK:** If most students know their blood type, form groups according to blood type and have students determine if they have the traits discussed in the essay. They could then write a classification essay on their own blood type's characteristics.

3

want everyone to be happy. In a team situation, you resolve conflicts and keep things on a smooth course. Sometimes, type A's are stubborn and find it difficult to relax. They may also find it uncomfortable to do things alone.

People with type B blood are usually individualists who like to do things on their own. You may be creative and adaptable, and you usually say exactly what you mean. Although you can adapt to situations, you may not choose to do so because of your strong independent streak. You may prefer working on your own to being part of a team.

4

The final blood type is type AB. If you have AB blood, you are a natural entertainer. You draw people to you because of your charm and easygoing nature. AB's are usually calm and controlled, tactful and fair. On the downside, though, they may take too long to make decisions. And they may procrastinate, putting off tasks until the last minute.

5

Classifying people's personalities by blood type seems very unusual until you examine what researchers have found. Most people find the descriptions fairly accurate. When you think about it, classification by blood type isn't any more far-fetched than classification by horoscope sign. What will they think of next? Classification by hair color?

6

IDENTIFY: What are the four blood types?

_____

_____

■ **TIP:** For reading advice, see Chapter 1.

CRITICAL THINKING: READING

1. Double-underline the **thesis statement**.

2. What are the categories Danny uses? _blood types (O, A, B, AB)_

3. Underline the sentences where he introduces each category.

4. Circle the **transitions**.

5. Each paragraph describes not only the general characteristics of a blood type but also _each type's positive and negative traits._

6. In most of the final paragraph, Danny seems to believe in the blood type/personality connection. However, two sentences give a different impression. Underline them. Do you think these sentences help or hurt his conclusion? _Answers will vary. Possible answer: The last two sentences seem to contradict the rest of the paragraph._

7. Where does Danny get his information? _You can't tell—he doesn't cite a source._ How does this affect how seriously you take his essay? _Answers will vary._

CRITICAL THINKING: WRITING

Choose one of the following topics and respond in a paragraph or essay.

■ **TIP:** Look back at your idea-journal entry (p. 162) for ideas.

1. If you know your blood type, write about whether the Japanese system describes you and how it does or doesn't. If you don't know your type, write about what category you *think* you are and why.

2. Some people would not take this essay seriously. Others would be open to its ideas. Would you describe yourself as open or skeptical? Why? Give examples.

3. Describe a time when you were skeptical about something you heard or read. What made you skeptical and why?

Write Your Own Classification

In this section, you will write your own classification paragraph or essay based on your (or your instructor's) choice among three assignments.

To complete your classification, follow this sequence:

1. Review the Four Basics of Good Classification (p. 162).
2. Choose your assignment.
3. If you are asked to complete Assignment 3, read Solving Problems, Appendix D.
4. Write your classification using the Checklist: How to Write Classification (pp. 175–76).

CLASSIFICATION AT A GLANCE

Topic sentence (paragraph) or thesis statement (essay)
- the topic + organizing principle
- the topic + organizing principle + categories
OR
- the topic + categories

↓

First category
Examples/explanations of first category

↓

Second category
Examples/explanations of second category

↓

Third category
Examples/explanations of third category

↓

Conclusion
Refers back to the classification's purpose/categories and makes an observation

■ **ASSIGNMENT 1 WRITING ABOUT COLLEGE, WORK, AND EVERYDAY LIFE** . . . .

Write a classification on one of the following topics.

COLLEGE

PARAGRAPH	ESSAY
Types of	Types of
• Teachers	• Courses offered
• Students in your class	• Degree/certificate programs
• Assignments in this class	• Resources in a college library

WORK

PARAGRAPH	ESSAY
Types of	Types of
• Bosses	• Positions at your company
• Work you like (or dislike)	• Customers
• Skills needed to do your last job	• Clothing people wear at work

EVERYDAY LIFE

PARAGRAPH	ESSAY
Types of	Types of
• Challenges you face	• Drivers
• Fast-food restaurants	• Friends
• Stress	• Music you like

■ **ASSIGNMENT 2   WRITING ABOUT IMAGES** . . . .

Visualize yourself at the grocery store. What kinds of foods do you most like to buy? What kinds of foods do you think you should buy but don't?

■ **ASSIGNMENT 3   WRITING IN THE REAL WORLD/SOLVING A PROBLEM** . . . .

PROBLEM: You need a car loan. The loan officer gives you an application that asks for your monthly income and expenses. Since every month you find yourself short on money, you realize that you need to see how you spend your money. You decide to make a monthly budget that categorizes the kinds of expenses you have.

ASSIGNMENT: Working with a group or on your own, break your monthly expenses into categories, thinking of everything that you spend money on. Then, review the expenses carefully to see which ones might be reduced. Next, write a classification paragraph or essay for the loan officer that classifies your monthly expenses, with examples, and ends with one to two suggestions about how you might reduce your monthly spending. You might start with this sentence:

■ **TEAMWORK:** For more detailed guidance on group work, see *Practical Suggestions.*

My monthly expenses fall. into ____*(number)*____ basic categories: _____, _____, and _____.

You may want to refer to the problem-solving steps in Appendix D.

CHECKLIST: HOW TO WRITE CLASSIFICATION

STEPS IN CLASSIFICATION	HOW TO DO THE STEPS
☐ **Focus.**	• Think about what you want to classify and your purpose for classifying.
☐ **Narrow and explore your topic.** See Chapter 3.	• Prewrite to get ideas for categories and for things that fit into those categories. • Review your prewriting and choose the categories that best serve your purpose.
☐ **Write a topic sentence (paragraph) or thesis statement (essay).** See Chapter 4.	• State your topic, the categories you are using to sort it, and/or your organizing principle.
☐ **Support your point.** See Chapter 5.	• Prewrite to find examples or explanations of things that fit into your categories.
☐ **Make a plan.** See Chapter 6.	• Arrange your categories to best suit your purpose and help your readers to understand the topic.
☐ **Write a draft.** See Chapter 7.	**FOR A PARAGRAPH** • Write a paragraph with your topic sentence, categories, and examples or explanations of things that fit into those categories. Use complete sentences. **FOR AN ESSAY** • Consider using one of the introduction types in Chapter 7. Include your thesis statement in your introduction. • Using your plan, write topic sentences for each of the categories. • Write paragraphs that give examples or explanations of what is in each category.

continued

STEPS IN CLASSIFICATION	HOW TO DO THE STEPS
☐ **Write a draft.** See Chapter 7.	**FOR PARAGRAPHS AND ESSAYS** • Write a conclusion that reminds your readers of your topic and makes an observation based on what you have written. • Write a title that previews your main point but doesn't repeat it.
☐ **Revise your draft, making at least four improvements.** See Chapter 8.	• Get feedback from others using the peer-review guide for classification at **bedfordstmartins.com/realwriting**. • Read to make sure that the categories all follow the same organizing principle. • Add any other examples or explanations that you think of. • Add transitions to move readers from one category to the next.
☐ **Edit your revised draft.** See Parts Four through Seven.	• Correct errors in grammar, spelling, word use, and punctuation.
☐ **Ask yourself:**	• Does my paper have the Four Basics of Good Classification (see p. 162)? • Is this the best I can do?

Chapter Review

1. Classification is writing that _organizes/sorts people or items into categories._

2. The organizing principle is _how you sort the people or items._

3. What are the Four Basics of Good Classification?

   It makes sense of a group of people or items by organizing them into categories.

   It has a purpose for sorting the people or items.

   It categorizes using a single organizing principle.

   It gives detailed examples or explanations of what fits into each category.

4. Choose five of the vocabulary words on page 171 and use each in a sentence.

■ **LEARNING JOURNAL:**
Reread your idea-journal entry (p. 162) on the kinds of students in this class or the kinds of friends you have. Make another entry on the same topic, using what you have learned about classification.

14

Definition

Writing That Tells What Something Means

Understand What Definition Is

Definition is writing that explains what a term or concept means.

■ ■
■ ■ **FOUR BASICS OF GOOD DEFINITION**

1. It tells readers what is being defined.
2. It presents a clear basic definition.
3. It uses examples to show what the writer means.
4. It gives details about the examples that readers will understand.

In the following paragraph, each number corresponds to one of the Four Basics of Good Definition.

A **1** stereotype **2** is a conventional idea or image that is much over-simplified—and often wrong, particularly when it is applied to people or groups of people. Stereotypes can prevent us from seeing people as they really are because they blind us with preconceived notions about what a certain type of person is like. **3** For example, I had a stereotyped notion of Native Americans until I met my friend Daniel, a Chippewa Indian. **4** I thought all Indians wore feathers and beads, had long black hair, and avoided all contact with non-Native Americans because they resented their land being taken away. Daniel, however, wears jeans and T-shirts, and we talk about everything—even our different ancestries. After meeting him, I understood that my stereotype of Native Americans was completely wrong. **3** Not only was it wrong, but it set up an us-them concept in my mind that made me feel that I, as a non-Native American, would never have anything in common with Native Americans. My stereotype would not have allowed me to see any Native American as an individual: I would have seen him or her as part of a group that I thought was all alike, and all different from me. From now on, I won't assume that any individual fits my stereotype; I'll try to see that person as I'd like them to see me: as myself, not a stereotyped image.

You can use definition in many practical situations:

COLLEGE	On a math exam, you are asked to define *exponential notation*.
WORK	On an application that says, "Choose one word that describes you," you must define yourself in a word and give examples that support this definition. (This is also a very common interview question.)
EVERYDAY LIFE	In a relationship, you define for your partner what you mean by *commitment* or *communication*.

Profile of Success: Definition in the Real World

Walter Scanlon
Program and Workplace
Consultant

■ **RESOURCES:** For a discussion of how to use the profiles in Part Two, see *Practical Suggestions*.

■ **READING SELECTIONS:** Students might also be interested in Walter Scanlon's "It's Time I Shed My Ex-Convict Status," which appears on page 597 of the Readings section.

The following profile shows how a business consultant uses definition on the job.

BACKGROUND: I grew up in a working-class neighborhood in New York City, in a family with a long history of alcohol problems. From my earliest days in grammar school, I assumed the role of class clown, somehow managing to just get by academically. By the time I reached high school, I was using drugs and alcohol and I soon dropped out of school. For the next ten years, I was in and out of hospitals and prisons. When I wasn't in an institution, I lived on the streets—in abandoned buildings and deserted cars.

At one point after being released from yet another prison, I knew I had to do something different if I was to survive. Instead of looking for a drink or a drug this time out of jail, I joined Alcoholics Anonymous.[1] That was the beginning of a new life for me.

I earned a GED, and took a pre-college reading course to improve my reading skills. Then, I took one college-level course, never intending to earn a degree but just to say I went to college. I didn't do all that well in the first course, but I kept taking courses and got a bachelor's degree. I then went on for a master's and, finally, a Ph.D. Now, I run my own successful consulting business in which I work with companies' employee assistance programs, private individual clients, and families with a wide range of complex problems. I have also published two books and professional articles.

COLLEGE(S)/DEGREES: B.A., Pace University; M.B.A., New York Institute of Technology; Ph.D., Columbus University

EMPLOYER: Self

WRITING AT WORK: I do all kinds of writing in my job: letters, proposals, presentations, articles, books, training programs, e-mails, memos, and more. I take my writing very seriously because I know that's how people will judge me. Often I have only a few minutes to present myself, so I work hard to make my point early on, and very clearly. I believe that if you write clearly,

[1] **Alcoholics Anonymous:** an organization in which people support each other to stay sober.

you think clearly. In most situations, there are many factors that I can't control, but I can always control my writing and the message it gives people.

I sometimes get e-mails that have all kinds of grammar mistakes in them, and believe me, I notice them and form opinions about the sender. (For an example of an e-mail that Walter received and his reaction to it, see Chapter 23, p. 000.)

HOW WALTER USES DEFINITION: As I work with clients, I often have to define a term so that they can understand it before I explain its relevance to the situation within which we're working.

WALTER'S DEFINITION

In the following paragraph, Walter defines *employee assistance program* for a client.

Employee Assistance Program

The "employee assistance program" (EAP) is a confidential, early-intervention workplace counseling service designed to help employees who are experiencing personal problems. It is a social service within a work environment that can be found in most major corporations, associations, and government organizations. EAP services are always free to the employee and benefit the organization as much as the employee. Employees who are free of emotional problems are far more productive than those who are not. An employee whose productivity is negatively affected by a drinking problem, for example, might seek help through the EAP. He/she would be assessed by a counselor and then referred to an appropriate community resource for additional services. The *employee* is helped through the EAP while the *employer* is rewarded with improved productivity. An EAP is a win-win program for all involved.

1. Double-underline the **topic sentence**.

2. Fill in the blanks with the term defined in the paragraph and the definition.

   Term: *employee assistance program*

   Definition: *a confidential, early-intervention workplace counseling service designed to help employees who are experiencing personal problems*

3. Underline an **example** of what an EAP might do.

4. Double-underline the sentence that makes a final observation about the topic.

■ **TIP:** For other possible patterns for a topic sentence, see page 180.

Main Point in Definition

In definition, the **main point** usually defines a term or concept. The main point is related to your purpose: to help your readers understand the term or concept as you are using it.

When you write your definition, don't just copy the dictionary definition; write it in your own words as you want your readers to understand it. To help you, you might first complete the following sentence:

I want readers to understand that this term means . . .

Then, based on your response, write a topic sentence (paragraph) or thesis statement (essay). These sentences can follow several different patterns.

(1) | Term | + | *means / is* | + | Basic definition | = | Topic sentence Thesis statement |

| Assertiveness | is | standing up for your rights. |
| Insomnia | means | sleeplessness. |

"Class" is the larger group the term belongs to.

■ **TIP:** Once you have a basic statement of your definition, try revising it to make it stronger, clearer, or more interesting.

(2) | Term | + | Class | + | Detail | = | Topic sentence Thesis statement |

| Insomnia | is a sleep disorder | that prevents people from sleeping. |
| A jet ski | is a jet-propelled craft | that races across water. |

■ **PRACTICE 1   WRITING A STATEMENT OF YOUR DEFINITION** . . . . . .

For each of the following terms, write a definition statement using the pattern indicated in brackets. You may need to use a dictionary.

EXAMPLE:

Cirrhosis [term + class + detail]:

Cirrhosis is a liver disease often caused by alcohol abuse.
Answers will vary. Possible answers shown.

1. Stress [term + class + detail]: *Stress is an emotionally upsetting condition that can have physical effects.*

2. Vacation [term + *means/is* + basic definition]: *Vacation means taking time off to relax.*

3. Confidence [term + class + detail]: *Confidence is a feeling of trust or faith.*

4. Conservation [term + *means/is* + basic definition]: *Conservation means preserving something from damage, loss, or neglect.*

5. Marriage [term + *means/is* + basic definition]: *Marriage is a union that requires respect, communication, and the ability to compromise.*

Support in Definition

Support in definition explains what a term or concept means by providing specific examples and giving details about the examples so that your readers understand what you mean.

If a friend says, "Don't take that class; it's terrible," you won't really know what she means by *terrible* until she explains it. Let's say she adds, "The teacher sometimes falls asleep, his lectures put the students to sleep, and the bathroom next door floods the room." These examples support her definition so you have no doubt about what she means.

■ **PRACTICE 2   SELECTING EXAMPLES AND DETAILS TO EXPLAIN THE DEFINITION** . . . .

List three examples or pieces of information that you could use to explain each of the following definitions.

EXAMPLE:

Insomnia means sleeplessness.

a. *hard to fall asleep*

b. *wake up in the middle of the night*

c. *wake up without feeling rested in the morning*
Answers will vary. Possible answers shown.

1. Confidence is feeling that you can conquer any obstacle.

   a. *You focus on chances of success.*

   b. *You know you have the needed skills.*

   c. *You let others know you are optimistic.*

2. A true vacation is not just time off from work.

   a. *need to relax*

   b. *need to have something fun and unusual to do*

   c. *need enough time to unwind*

3. A family is a group you always belong to, no matter what.

   a. *You can always count on family.*

   b. *Distance, divorce, even death won't change it.*

   c. *Sometimes you might want to escape, but you can't.*

■ **COMPUTER:** In computer classrooms, have students type one example into their computers and then move to the next computer, add an example for the topic there, and continue until there are three examples for each definition.

■ **DISCUSSION:** Ask students, "How has the definition of *family* changed in the last decade?"

Organization in Definition

■ **TIP:** For more on order of importance, see page 66.

The examples in definition are often organized by **order of importance**, meaning that the example that will have the most impact on readers is saved for last.

Transitions in definition move readers from one example to the next. Use transitions within a paragraph and also to move from one paragraph to another to link the paragraphs. Here are some transitions you might use in definition, though many others are possible, too.

Common Definition Transitions

another; one/another	for example
another kind	for instance
first, second, third, and so on	

■ PRACTICE 3   **USING TRANSITIONS IN DEFINITION** . . . .

Read the paragraph that follows and fill in the blanks with transitions. You are not limited to the ones listed in the preceding box.
Answers may vary. Possible answers shown.

Each year, *Business Week* publishes a list of the most family-friendly companies to work for. The magazine uses several factors to define the organizations as family-friendly. _____*One*_____ factor is whether the company has flextime, allowing employees to schedule work hours that better fit family needs. _____*For example*_____, a parent might choose to work from 6:30 to 2:30 to be able to spend time with children. _*Another, A second*_ factor is whether family leave programs are encouraged. In addition to maternity leaves, _____*for example*_____, does the company encourage paternity leaves and leaves for care of elderly parents? A final factor is whether the company makes allowances for one-day or part-day absences for a child's illness, parent-teacher conferences, and other important family duties. Increasingly, companies are trying to become more family-friendly to attract and keep good employees.

Read and Understand Definition

Reading examples of definition to understand their structure and content will help you write your own. The first example, a paragraph, is followed by questions about the structure of definition. The second example, an essay, has questions in the margin to help you read closely. It is followed by questions about both structure and content, along with writing assignments. These activities will help you practice your critical reading and thinking skills.

Definition Paragraph: Textbook

Many of us are anxious or depressed occasionally, and that is normal. When anxiety and depression are not appropriate to the situations we face, they may be signs of a **psychological disorder**, a disturbance of psychological functioning resulting in emotional distress or abnormal behavior. For example, it is normal to be anxious before a job interview or a final exam. It is *not* normal to be anxious when one is looking out of a sixth-story window or about to receive a harmless vaccination. It is normal to feel down or depressed for a time because of a poor performance on a test. It is *not* normal to be depressed when things are going well.

> —Adapted from Jeffrey S. Nevid, Spencer A. Rathus, and Hannah R. Rubenstein, *Health in the New Millennium* (Worth, 1998)

1. Double-underline the **topic sentence**.

2. Underline the examples that explain the definition.

3. If you were studying for a test in a class using this textbook, what sentence would you underline or highlight? *the topic sentence*

Definition Essay: Textbook

Need for Achievement

Some students persist in their studies despite distractions. Some people strive relentlessly to get ahead, to "make it," to earn vast sums of money, to invent, to achieve the impossible. Such people are said to have a strong **need for achievement**, a psychological need to accomplish external goals.

People with a strong need for achievement earn higher grades than people of comparable ability but with a lower need for achievement. They are more likely to earn high salaries and be promoted than less motivated people with similar opportunities.

■ **READING SELECTIONS:** For further examples of and activities for definition, see Chapter 47.

VOCABULARY DEVELOPMENT Underline these words in the definition paragraph.

anxious: *uneasy or fearful* (anxiety *is the state of being anxious*)

depressed: *sad or discouraged* (depression *is the state of being depressed.*)

abnormal: *not normal or ordinary*

vaccination: *an injection that prevents a disease*

■ **TIP:** For advice on building your vocabulary, **see** Appendix B.

VOCABULARY DEVELOPMENT Underline these words as you read the definition essay.

persist: *to work toward a goal even when difficulties arise*

distractions: *things that take one's attention*

strive: *work hard*

relentlessly: *steadily*

characterized: *to have the qualities of*

1　PREDICT: What do you think this essay will discuss?

2

Most college graduates with strong needs for achievement take po-   3
sitions characterized by risk, decision making, and the chance of great
success. For example, they may enter business management or sales or
establish businesses of their own. People with a strong need for achievement prefer challenges and are willing to take on reasonable risks to
achieve their goals.

The need for achievement is a basic human need, according to   4
Maslow's hierarchy of needs.[2] However, the strength of this need varies
greatly from one individual to the next. Students should not, for example,
feel lazy if they are not as ambitious as another person. A normal need
for achievement is satisfied by a sense of always striving to do one's best,
even if the rewards are not measured in fame or money.

— Adapted from Jeffrey S. Nevid, Spencer A. Rathus, and Hannah R.
Rubenstein, *Health in the New Millennium* (Worth, 1998)

IDENTIFY: What is one of your goals?
_____

_____

■ **TIP:** For reading advice, see Chapter 1.

CRITICAL THINKING: READING

1. Double-underline the **thesis statement**. In your own words, what is
the need for achievement? *Answers will vary.* _____

2. Give three examples of how people with a strong need for achievement
behave. *Answers will vary. Possible answers: They earn high grades and*
salaries, get promoted, take risks, and like challenges.

3. If you were using this textbook in a class, what sentence would you
highlight or underline as you read? *the thesis statement*
What terms or concepts would you highlight or underline?
Answers will vary. Possible answers: need for achievement, Maslow's Hierarchy
of needs

4. How do you think a strong need for achievement could be damaging?
_____ *Answers will vary.* _____ Mention a movie or a time in real life when this
happened. *Answers will vary.* _____

5. How might a person with a moderate need for achievement behave?
Answers will vary. _____

■ **TEACHING TIP:** You might
tell students that Maslow's hierarchy includes the following
needs: physiological, safety,
love and belonging, esteem,
and self-actualization.

[2] **Maslow's hierarchy of needs:** a sequence of human needs, from basic survival needs
to having a satisfying life.

CRITICAL THINKING: WRITING

Choose one of the following topics and respond in a paragraph or essay.

1. How would you describe your own need for achievement: Strong? Moderate? Low? Give examples to support your characterization.
2. Aside from achievement, what do you think is another basic human need? Explain.
3. Define and give examples of *one* of the following terms: *lazy, ambitious, rewards.*

Write Your Own Definition

In this section, you will write your own definition paragraph or essay based on your (or your instructor's) choice among three assignments.

To complete your definition, follow this sequence:

1. Review the Four Basics of Good Definition (p. 177).
2. Choose your assignment.
3. If you are asked to complete Assignment 3, read Solving Problems, Appendix D.
4. Write your definition using the Checklist: How to Write Definition (pp. 187–88).

ASSIGNMENT 1   WRITING ABOUT COLLEGE, WORK, AND EVERYDAY LIFE . . . .

Write a definition on one of the following terms (in italics) or topics.

COLLEGE

PARAGRAPH	ESSAY
• *Course syllabus*	• *Cheating*
• *Good student* or *bad student*	• *Plagiarism*
• *Academic probation*	• *Learning*

WORK

PARAGRAPH	ESSAY
• A good job	• A positive work environment
• *Internship*	• *Growth opportunities*
• A term used in your work	• *Entrepreneur*

EVERYDAY LIFE

PARAGRAPH	ESSAY
• *Scam*	• *Success*
• *Addiction*	• A good relationship
• *Common sense*	• *Heroism*

DEFINITION AT A GLANCE

Topic sentence (paragraph) or thesis statement (essay)
Defines term or concept

↓

First example explaining the definition
Details about the first example

↓

Second example explaining the definition
Details about the second example

↓

Third example explaining the definition
Details about the third example

↓

Conclusion
Refers back to the defined term/concept and makes an observation about it based on what you have written

■ **ESL:** Suggest that students define a common term in their language that has no direct counterpart in English.

■ **ASSIGNMENT 2   WRITING ABOUT IMAGES** . . . .

Write a definition of what it means to be more than a test score. You might start with this sentence:

I am not just a test score; I am _____.

■ **ASSIGNMENT 3   WRITING IN THE REAL WORLD/SOLVING A PROBLEM** . . . .

■ **RESOURCES:** Reproducible peer-review guides for different kinds of papers are available in *Additional Resources.*

PROBLEM: You see a news report that cites a recent survey of business managers who were asked what skills or traits are most important to employers. The top five skills and traits cited were (1) motivation, (2) interpersonal skills, (3) initiative, (4) communication skills, and (5) maturity.

You have a job interview next week, and you want to be able to present yourself well. Before you can do that, though, you need to have a better understanding of the five skills and traits noted above and what examples you might be able to give to demonstrate that you have them.

ASSIGNMENT: Working in a group or on your own, come up with definitions of three of the five terms and think of some examples of how the skills or traits could be used at work. Then, do one of the following assignments:

For a paragraph: Choose one of the terms and give examples of how you have demonstrated the trait.

For an essay: Write about how you have demonstrated the three traits.

You might begin with the following sentence:

I am a person who is (or has) _____.

■ **RESOURCES:** All chapters in Part Two have writing checklists, which are reproduced in *Additional Resources.* You can photocopy and distribute them if you want students to hand in the checklists with their assignments.

■ **TEAMWORK:** For more detailed guidance on group work, see *Practical Suggestions.*

CHECKLIST: HOW TO WRITE DEFINITION

STEPS IN DEFINITION	HOW TO DO THE STEPS
☐ **Focus.**	• Think about the term you want to define and the meaning you want to give your readers.
☐ **Explore your topic.** See Chapter 3.	• Prewrite about the term or concept and its definition as you are using it. • Review your prewriting and choose a definition.
☐ **Write a topic sentence (paragraph) or thesis statement (essay).** See Chapter 4.	• Write a sentence using one of the patterns on page 180.
☐ **Support your definition.** See Chapter 5.	• Prewrite to get examples that will show what you mean by the term or concept.
☐ **Make a plan.** See Chapter 6.	• Organize your examples, saving for last the one that you think will have the most impact on readers.
☐ **Write a draft.** See Chapter 7.	**FOR A PARAGRAPH** • Write a paragraph that includes a topic sentence and defines your term or concept, showing what you mean through examples. Use complete sentences. **FOR AN ESSAY** • Consider using one of the introduction types in Chapter 7. Include your thesis statement in your introduction. • Using your plan, write topic sentences for each of the examples. • Write paragraphs that give details about the examples.

continued

STEPS IN DEFINITION	HOW TO DO THE STEPS
☐ **Write a draft.** See Chapter 7.	**FOR PARAGRAPHS AND ESSAYS** • Write a conclusion that restates the term or concept and makes an observation about it based on what you have written. • Write a title that previews your main point but doesn't repeat it.
☐ **Revise your draft, making at least four improvements.** See Chapter 8.	• Get feedback from others using the peer-review guide for definition at **bedfordstmartins.com/realwriting**. • Reread your definition of the term or concept to make sure that it clearly states your meaning. • Add any other examples that you can think of, and delete any that do not clearly show the meaning of the term or concept. • Add transitions to move readers from one example to the next.
☐ **Edit your revised draft.** See Parts Four through Seven.	• Correct errors in grammar, spelling, word use, and punctuation.
☐ **Ask yourself:**	• Does my paper include the Four Basics of Good Definition (p. 177)? • Is this the best I can do?

Chapter Review

1. Definition is writing that *explains what a term or concept means.*

2. What are the Four Basics of Good Definition?

   It tells readers what term is being defined.

   It presents a clear basic definition.

   It uses examples to show what the writer means.

   It gives details about the examples that readers will understand.

3. Choose five of the vocabulary words on page 183 and use each in a sentence.

■ **LEARNING JOURNAL:**
Reread your idea-journal entry from page 177. Write another entry on the same topic, using what you have learned about definition.

15

Comparison and Contrast

Writing That Shows Similarities and Differences

Understand What Comparison and Contrast Are

Comparison is writing that shows the similarities among subjects — people, ideas, situations, or items; **contrast** shows the differences. In conversation, people often use the word *compare* to mean either compare or contrast, but as you work through this chapter, the terms will be separated.

■ **IDEA JOURNAL:** Write about some of the differences between men and women.

Compare	=	Similarities

Contrast	=	Differences

■■
■■ **FOUR BASICS OF GOOD COMPARISON AND CONTRAST**

1. It uses subjects that have enough in common to be compared/contrasted in a useful way.
2. It serves a purpose — either to help readers make a decision or to help them understand the subjects.
3. It presents several important, parallel points of comparison/contrast.
4. It arranges points in a logical order.

In the following paragraph each number corresponds to one of the Four Basics of Good Comparison and Contrast.

1 Grocery stores in wealthy suburbs are **2** much better than the **1** ones in poor, inner-city neighborhoods. **3** Suburban stores are large, bright, and stocked with many varieties of each food. In contrast, inner-city stores are often cramped, dark, and limited in choice. For example,

4 Organized by order of importance

189

the cereal section in suburban stores often runs for an entire aisle, with hundreds of choices, ranging from the sugary types to the organic, healthy brands. The inner-city stores often stock only the very sugary cereals. Another way in which suburban stores are better is in the quality and freshness of the produce. The fruits and vegetables are plentiful and fresh in typical suburban markets. In inner-city neighborhoods, the choices are again limited, fruits are bruised, and vegetables are often limp and soft. A more important difference between the suburban and inner-city stores is in the prices. You might expect that the prices in wealthy suburban groceries would be high and that those in the poor neighborhoods would be lower. However, the reverse is true: Wealthy suburban shoppers actually pay less for a nicer environment, more choice, and higher-quality food than shoppers at inner-city stores. Grocery stores are just one example of how "the rich get richer, and the poor get poorer."

Many situations require you to understand similarities and differences:

COLLEGE	In a pharmacy course, you compare and contrast the side effects of two drugs prescribed for the same illness.
WORK	You are asked to contrast this year's sales with last year's.
EVERYDAY LIFE	At the supermarket, you contrast brands of the same food to decide which to buy.

Profile of Success: Comparison and Contrast in the Real World

Brad Leibov
President,
New Chicago Fund, Inc.

The following profile shows how a company president uses comparison and contrast in his job.

BACKGROUND: In high school, I put very little effort into completing my coursework. When I first enrolled at Oakton Community College, I wasn't motivated and soon dropped all my courses. An instructor from Project Succeed contacted me after my first year, and this program helped me recognize that I really wanted to put in the effort necessary to succeed.

A few years later, I earned a B.A. degree from a four-year university. After working for a few years in community development, I was accepted into a top-tier graduate program in urban planning and policy, from which I graduated with a perfect grade-point average. Later, I started my own urban planning and development company to help revitalize inner-city commercial areas.

COLLEGE(S)/DEGREES: B.A., DePaul University; M.A., University of Illinois, Chicago

WRITING AT WORK: I write contracts, proposals, marketing materials, etc.

HOW BRAD USES COMPARISON AND CONTRAST: I often give examples of how my company can improve a community—kind of before-and-after contrasts.

BRAD'S COMPARISON AND CONTRAST

The following paragraph describes how Brad's company restored a special service area (SSA), a declining community targeted for improvements.

■ **RESOURCES:** For a discussion of how to use the profiles in Part Two, see *Practical Suggestions.*

New Chicago Fund, Inc., is an expert at advising and leading organizations through all the steps necessary to establish an SSA with strong local support. <u>Our experience acting as a liaison among various neighborhood groups and individuals affected by an SSA helps us plan for and address the concerns of residents and property owners.</u> In 2005, New Chicago Fund assisted the Uptown Community Development Corporation with establishing an SSA in Uptown, Chicago. Uptown's commercial area was estimated to lose approximately $506 million annually in consumer expenditures to neighboring commercial districts and suburban shopping centers. Community leaders recognized that Uptown's sidewalks were uninviting with litter, hazardous with unshoveled snow, and unappealing in the lack of pedestrian-friendly amenities found in neighboring commercial districts. The Uptown SSA programs funded the transformation of the commercial area. The sidewalks are regularly cleaned and are litter-free. People no longer have to walk around uncleared snow mounds and risk slipping on the ice because maintenance programs provide full-service clearing. Additionally, SSA funds provided new pedestrian-friendly amenities such as benches, trash receptacles, flower planters, and street-pole banners. The Uptown area is now poised for commercial success.

1. Double-underline the **topic sentence.**

2. What subjects are being contrasted and what are the points of contrast? *an area before and after SSA improvements; sidewalk features*

3. What is the purpose of the statement? *to sell services of the New Chicago Fund*

4. What are the points of contrast? *buildings, street activities, feelings of residents*

Main Point in Comparison and Contrast

The **main point** in a comparison/contrast paragraph or essay is related to your **purpose**. Comparing or contrasting subjects can serve different purposes:

- to help readers make a decision about the subjects
- to help readers understand the subjects
- to show your understanding of the subjects

To help you discover your main point, complete the following sentence:

I want my readers to _____ **after reading my comparison or contrast.**

Then, write a topic sentence (paragraph) or thesis statement (essay) that identifies the subjects and states the main point you want to make about them.

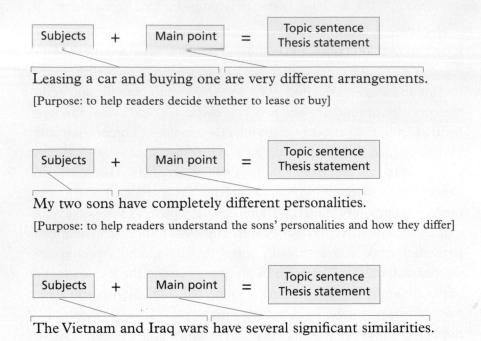

Leasing a car and buying one are very different arrangements.

[Purpose: to help readers decide whether to lease or buy]

My two sons have completely different personalities.

[Purpose: to help readers understand the sons' personalities and how they differ]

The Vietnam and Iraq wars have several significant similarities.

[Purpose: to demonstrate your understanding of the wars and their similarities]

Support in Comparison and Contrast

The **support** in comparison/contrast demonstrates your main point by showing how your subjects are the same or different. To find support, many people make a list with two columns, one for each subject, with parallel points of comparison or contrast.

TOPIC SENTENCE/THESIS STATEMENT: The two credit cards I'm considering offer very different financial terms.

BIG CARD	MEGA CARD
no annual fee	$35 annual fee
$1 fee per cash advance	$1.50 fee per cash advance
30 days before interest charges begin	25 days before interest charges begin
15.5% finance charge	17.9% finance charge

Choose points that will be convincing and understandable to your readers, and explain them with facts, details, or examples.

■   **PRACTICE 1   FINDING POINTS OF CONTRAST** . . . .

Each of the following items lists some points of contrast. Fill in the blanks
with more.

EXAMPLE:

CONTRAST: Hair lengths

Long hair	*Short hair*
takes a long time to dry	dries quickly
can be worn a lot of ways	*only one way to wear it*
doesn't need to be cut often	needs to be cut every five weeks
gets tangled, needs brushing	*low maintenance*

1. **CONTRAST:** Snack foods

Potato chips	*Pretzels*
high fat	low fat
Answers will vary but should	twists or sticks
focus on differences.	_____

2. **CONTRAST:** Ethnic foods

Mexican	*Chinese*
beans as a starch	_____
_____	common condiment: soy sauce
_____	_____

3. **CONTRAST:** Buildings

The most modern one in town	*An older building*
lots of glass	_____
_____	only a few stories tall
_____	_____

4. **CONTRAST:** Dancing and other forms of exercise

Dancing	*Other forms of exercise*
purpose: social, for fun	_____
_____	done at a gym
_____	_____

PRACTICE 2   FINDING POINTS OF COMPARISON . . . .

Each of the following items lists some points of comparison. Fill in the blanks with more.

1. **COMPARE:** Sports

Basketball	*Soccer*
team sport	team sport
Answers will vary but	_____
should focus on similarities.	_____

2. **COMPARE:** Ethnic foods

Mexican	*Chinese*
relatively inexpensive	_____
can be mild or spicy	_____
_____	_____

3. **COMPARE:** Dancing and other forms of exercise

Dancing	*Other forms of exercise*
done to music	done to music
_____	_____
_____	_____
_____	_____

Organization in Comparison and Contrast

Comparison/contrast can be organized in two ways: a **point-by-point** organization presents one point of comparison or contrast between the subjects and then moves to the next point. A **whole-to-whole** organization presents all the points of comparison or contrast for one subject and then all the points for the next subject. (For charts illustrating these two methods, see page 201.) Consider which organization will best explain the similarities or differences to your readers. Whichever organization you choose, stay with it throughout your writing.

 PRACTICE 3   ORGANIZING A COMPARISON/CONTRAST . . . .

The first outline that follows is for a comparison paper using a whole-to-whole organization. Reorganize the ideas and create a new outline (#2) using a point-by-point organization. The first blank has been filled in for you.

The third outline is for a contrast paper using a point-by-point organization. Reorganize the ideas and create a new outline (#4) using a whole-to-whole organization. The first blank has been filled in for you.

■ **TEACHING TIP:** Point out that in a whole-to-whole essay, there usually needs to be a strong transition when the essay moves from subject 1 to subject 2.

1. COMPARISON PAPER USING WHOLE-TO-WHOLE ORGANIZATION

MAIN POINT: My daughter is a lot like I was at her age.

a. Me
   - Not interested in school
   - Good at sports
   - Hard on myself

b. My daughter
   - Does well in school but doesn't study much or do more than the minimum
   - Plays in a different sport each season
   - When she thinks she has made a mistake, she gets upset with herself

2. COMPARISON PAPER USING POINT-BY-POINT ORGANIZATION

MAIN POINT: My daughter is a lot like I was at her age.

a. Interest in school
   - Me: *Not interested in school*
   - My daughter: _____

b. _____
   - Me: _____
   - My daughter: _____

c. _____
   - Me: _____
   - My daughter: _____

3. CONTRAST PAPER USING POINT-BY-POINT ORGANIZATION

MAIN POINT: My new computer is a great improvement over my old one.

a. Weight and portability
   - New computer: *small and light*
   - Old computer: *heavy, not portable*

b. *Speed*
   - New computer: *fast*
   - Old computer: *slow*

c. *Cost*
   - New computer: *inexpensive*
   - Old computer: *expensive*

4. CONTRAST PAPER USING WHOLE-TO-WHOLE ORGANIZATION

MAIN POINT: My new computer is a great improvement over my old one.

a. New computer
   - *small and light*
   - _____
   - _____

b. Old computer
   - _____
   - _____
   - _____

■ **TIP:** For more on order of importance, see page 66.

Comparison/contrast is often organized by **order of importance**, meaning that the most important point is saved for last.

Using **transitions** in comparison/contrast is very important, to move readers from one subject to another and from one point of comparison or contrast to the next.

Common Comparison/Contrast Transitions

COMPARISON	CONTRAST
both	in contrast
like	most important difference
most important similarity	now/then
one similarity/another similarity	one difference/another difference
similarly	unlike
	while

■ **PRACTICE 4   USING TRANSITIONS IN COMPARISON AND CONTRAST**

Read the paragraph that follows and fill in the blanks with transitions. You are not limited to the ones listed in the preceding box.

Answers may vary. Possible answers shown.

College is much more difficult than high school. _One difference_ is that students have to pay for college classes, while high school is free. As a result, many college students have to work, take out loans, or both, making staying in school much more of a challenge. _Another difference_ is that there is a lot more work in college than in high school. College students have to spend more time out of class doing schoolwork than they had to in high school. Also, _in contrast_ to the content of high school classes, college courses are much more difficult. Often, students have to get help from their professors during office hours. _The most important_ difference between college and high school is that college professors expect students to do the assignments without being reminded. In high school, teachers remind students to do their homework and ask why if students don't do it. In college, students have to take responsibility for their own success or failure.

· ·

Read and Understand Comparison and Contrast

Reading examples of comparison and contrast to understand their structure and content will help you write your own. The first example, a paragraph, is followed by questions about the structure of comparison and contrast. The second example, an essay, has questions in the margin to help you read closely. It is followed by questions about both structure and content, along with writing assignments. These activities will help you practice your critical reading and thinking skills.

Comparison and Contrast Paragraph: Student

When they get lost while driving, women and men have very different ways to find the right route.[1] As soon as a woman thinks she might be lost, she will pull into a store or gas station and ask for directions. As she continues on, if she's still not sure of the directions,[2] she will stop again and ask someone else for help. Until they know they are on the right track,[3] women will continue to ask for directions.[1] In contrast, men would rather turn around and go home than stop and ask for directions. First, a man doesn't readily admit he is lost.[2] When it is clear that he is, he will pull over and consult a map. If he still finds himself lost, he will again pull out that map. Either the map will finally put the man on the right route, or—[3]as a last resort—he will reluctantly stop at a store or gas station and let his wife go in and ask for directions. Many battles of the sexes have raged over what to do when lost while driving.

1. Double-underline the **topic sentence**.

2. Is the **purpose** of the paragraph to help readers make a decision or to help them understand the subjects better? *to help them understand*

3. Underline **each point of contrast** in the sample paragraph. Give each parallel, or matched, point the same number.

4. Which organization (point-by-point or whole-to-whole) does the writer of the sample paragraph use? *whole-to-whole*

5. Circle the **transitions** in the paragraph.

■ **READING SELECTIONS:** For further examples of and activities for comparison and contrast, see Chapter 48.

VOCABULARY DEVELOPMENT
Underline these words as you read the comparison and contrast paragraph.

consult: *look at*

last resort: *final step*

reluctantly: *with hesitation; unwillingly*

■ **TIP:** For advice on building your vocabulary, see Appendix B.

VOCABULARY DEVELOPMENT
Underline these words in the comparison and contrast essay.

boycotts: *organized efforts against buying from or dealing with*

perceptions: *understandings of*

inferior: *of poor quality*

durable: *lasting*

hip: *fashionable; trendy*

villain: *an evil person*

sweatshops: *factories with poor working conditions and pay*

PREDICT: What do you think this essay will discuss?

_____

_____

IDENTIFY: Outside sources are in parentheses. Put a check mark by these.

Comparison and Contrast Essay: Student

Target and Wal-Mart: Not as Different as You Think
Lou Enrico

Keep Wal-Mart Out! That's what you hear from a lot of people who think Wal-Mart is just plain bad, while Target is good. Communities organize to prevent Wal-Mart from building new stores, and groups promote boycotts of the whole chain. In contrast, Target, the fourth biggest retailer in the United States, is welcome anywhere. However, the two stores are more alike than different; the biggest difference is in people's perceptions about them. 1

One perceived difference is in the quality of the merchandise of the two chains. Many people think that low quality comes with Wal-Mart's low prices. They believe that the store's clothing will fall apart because of poor workmanship and inferior fabrics. They think its electronics will fail just after the warrantee expires. Target, on the other hand, is perceived as carrying stylish, high-quality merchandise at affordable prices. People think that the clothing and shoes are as durable as they are hip and that the furniture could be found in expensive department stores. However, there is no proof at all that the clothing, electronics, furniture, food—anything—at Target is higher quality than anything at Wal-Mart. 2

Another perceived difference is in the business practices of the two chains. The media are always running reports that make Wal-Mart look like a villain: Wal-Mart employees are poorly paid. Wal-Mart buys from sweatshops in third-world countries. Wal-Mart discourages unions (Borosage and Peters). Recently, the American Federation of Teachers urged a boycott of Wal-Mart because of its "dismal record" on worker pay, benefits, and rights ("Join"). In contrast, Target is rarely in the news, so we assume that its practices are better. However, there is no proof that Target employees make any more than Wal-Mart workers, and Target discourages unionization (Bhatnagar; Jones). Target also buys products from foreign sources that may not pay and treat their workers fairly. In reality, Wal-Mart has made many positive changes to its business practices, while Target has not, probably because it has not been criticized by the media. Wal-Mart has changed sources of foreign suppliers, for one thing. Also, it was recently named one of the thirty best companies for diversity by *Black Enterprise*. 3

One of the biggest perceived differences concerns Wal-Mart's <u>effect on local economies</u>. People accuse Wal-Mart of putting small retailers out of business and destroying downtowns that once had many family businesses (Borosage and Peters). It is said to be personally responsible for changing the U.S. economy for the worse. In contrast, people are happy to hear that Target is opening a new store. It is true that some Wal-Marts do put local retailers out of business. The stores are big, they are not located in downtown areas, and they carry a whole range of merchandise that used to be spread throughout many smaller businesses. However, Target also takes business away from smaller stores. Yet Wal-Mart, in contrast to Target, often helps rural towns by opening stores where people previously had to drive long distances to shop. You won't find many Targets in these kinds of areas. Target wants to locate in richer communities.   4

The fact that Wal-Mart is the largest retailer has certainly led to all of the negative publicity it is getting. This makes me wonder how else the media changes people's perceptions. Is perception reality?   5

Works Cited

Bhatnagar, Parija. "Just Call It 'Teflon' Target." *CNN/Money* 20
      Apr. 2005. 6 Dec. 2005 <http://money.cnn.com/2005/04/
      20/news/fortune500/target_walmart>.

Borosage, Robert L., and Troy Peters. "Target Wal-Mart."
      TomPaine.com. 14 Nov. 2005. 5 Dec. 2005 <http://www
      .tompaine.com/articles/20051114/target_walmart.php>.

"Join the 'Send Wal-Mart Back to School' Campaign." American
      Federation of Teachers. 6 Dec. 2005 <http://www.aft.org/
      news/2005/back-to-school.htm>.

Jones, Sandra. "Target's Image Trumps Wal-Mart's." *Chicago
      Business*. 11 Apr. 2005. 6 Dec. 2005 <http://chicagobusiness
      .com/cgi-bin/news.pl?id=16077>.

CRITICAL THINKING: READING

1. Double-underline the **thesis statement**. Put the author's main point in your own words. *Answers will vary. Possible answer: Wal-Mart and Target are very much alike, but people think of them differently.*

2. Underline the **points of contrast** in the essay.

■ **TIP:** For reading advice, see Chapter 1.

3. Why does the writer think people have certain perceptions?

Answers will vary but should include the media's negative reports on Wal-Mart.

4. What larger point does the writer make at the end of the essay?

Answers will vary but could refer to how much the media influences people.

5. The writer has cited four outside sources. What other sources or outside information might have been useful? *Answers will vary but could include sources with quotes from Wal-Mart officials, quotes from Target officials, or quotes from employees of either chain.*

CRITICAL THINKING: WRITING

Choose one of the following topics and respond in a paragraph or essay.

1. Go to a Wal-Mart and a Target and compare or contrast three things about them.

2. Listen to the news or read an online news story. Choose one story and write about how its observations may be perception rather than fact.

3. Look at an advertisement and write about how it creates a certain perception of a product or service.

4. Write about how the media shapes people's beliefs. Include at least three specific examples.

Write Your Own Comparison and Contrast

In this section you will write your own comparison/contrast paragraph or essay based on your (or your instructor's) choice among three assignments. To complete your comparison/contrast, follow this sequence:

■ **TIP:** Look back at your idea-journal entry (p. 189) for ideas.

1. Review the Four Basics of Good Comparison and Contrast (p. 189).

2. Choose your assignment.

3. If you are asked to complete Assignment 3, read Solving Problems, Appendix D.

4. Write your comparison/contrast using the Checklist: How to Write Comparison and Contrast (pp. 204–05).

ASSIGNMENT 1   WRITING ABOUT COLLEGE, WORK, AND EVERYDAY LIFE

Write a comparison/contrast on one of the following topics.

COLLEGE

PARAGRAPH	ESSAY
• Taking a test when you've studied versus when you haven't	• High school and college
• Two teachers	• Your best versus your worst course
• Two kinds of tests	• Successful versus unsuccessful student behaviors

WORK

PARAGRAPH	ESSAY
• Two bosses	• Two kinds of customers
• A job you liked versus one you didn't	• The job you have versus the job you'd like to have
• Good employee behavior versus bad employee behavior	• A job versus a career

EVERYDAY LIFE

PARAGRAPH	ESSAY
• How you dress now/how you dressed five years ago	• Two types of music
• Healthy foods/unhealthy foods	• Two television shows
• Two friends or family members	• Your life now/How you would like your life to be in five years

ASSIGNMENT 2   WRITING ABOUT IMAGES

Contrast the lives of the poor and the rich. If you like, use the two figures in the following photograph. Give detailed examples of both ways of life and include possible attitudes of one group toward another.

You might start with this sentence:

The lives of the poor and rich differ in several important ways.

COMPARISON/CONTRAST: POINT-BY-POINT

Topic sentence (paragraph) or thesis statement (essay)
Sets up the comparison/contrast

Point 1
Subject 1
Subject 2

Point 2
Subject 1
Subject 2

Point 3
Subject 1
Subject 2

Conclusion
Reminds readers of the main point and makes an observation based on it

COMPARISON/CONTRAST: WHOLE-TO-WHOLE

Topic sentence (paragraph) or thesis statement (essay)
Sets up the comparison/contrast

Subject 1
Point 1
Point 2
Point 3

Subject 2
Point 1
Point 2
Point 3

Conclusion
Reminds readers of the main point and makes an observation based on it

ASSIGNMENT 3   WRITING IN THE REAL WORLD/SOLVING A PROBLEM

PROBLEM: You need a new cell phone, and you want to make sure you get the best one for your money. Before ordering one, you want to do some research.

ASSIGNMENT: Working with a group or on your own, consult the rating chart that follows or an online one. Identify three points that are contrasted in the chart (or that you identify on your own), and make notes about why each point is important to you. Then, choose the model you would buy, based on these points. Finally, write a contrast paragraph or essay that explains your decision and contrasts your choice versus another model. Make sure to support your choice based on the three points you considered.

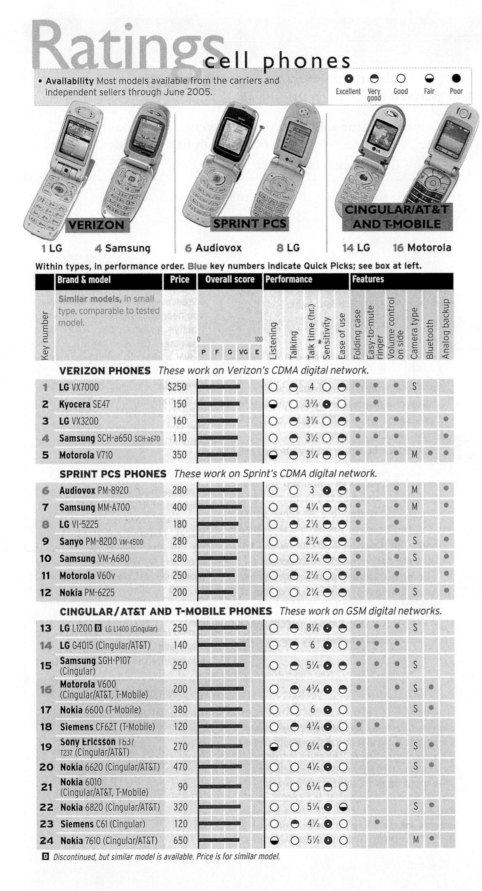

Ratings cell phones

• **Availability** Most models available from the carriers and independent sellers through June 2005.

Excellent   Very good   Good   Fair   Poor

VERIZON
1 LG   4 Samsung

SPRINT PCS
6 Audiovox   8 LG

CINGULAR/AT&T AND T-MOBILE
14 LG   16 Motorola

Within types, in performance order. **Blue** key numbers indicate Quick Picks; see box at left.

Key number	Brand & model (Similar models, in small type, comparable to tested model.)	Price	Overall score (0–100 P F G VG E)	Listening	Talking	Talk time (hr.)	Sensitivity	Ease of use	Folding case	Easy-to-mute ringer	Volume control on side	Camera type	Bluetooth	Analog backup
VERIZON PHONES *These work on Verizon's CDMA digital network.*														
1	**LG** VX7000	$250		○	◐	4	○	◐	•	•	•	S		
2	**Kyocera** SE47	150		◑	○	3¾	●	○		•				
3	**LG** VX3200	160		○	◐	3¼	○	◐	•	•	•			•
4	**Samsung** SCH-a650 SCH-a670	110		○	◐	3½	○	◐	•	•	•			•
5	**Motorola** V710	350		◑	●	3¼	◐	◐	•		•	M	•	•
SPRINT PCS PHONES *These work on Sprint's CDMA digital network.*														
6	**Audiovox** PM-8920	280		○	○	3	●	◐	•		•	M		•
7	**Samsung** MM-A700	400		○	◐	4¼	◐	◐	•		•	M		•
8	**LG** VI-5225	180		○	◐	2½	◐	◐	•		•			
9	**Sanyo** PM-8200 VM-4500	280		○	◐	2¾	◐	◐	•		•	S		•
10	**Samsung** VM-A680	280		○	○	2¾	◐	◐	•		•	S		•
11	**Motorola** V60v	250		○	◐	2½	◐	○	•		•			•
12	**Nokia** PM-6225	200		○	○	2¼	◐	◐			•	S		•
CINGULAR/AT&T AND T-MOBILE PHONES *These work on GSM digital networks.*														
13	**LG** L1200 🄳 LG L1400 (Cingular)	250		○	◐	8½	◐	◐	•	•	•	S		
14	**LG** G4015 (Cingular/AT&T)	140		○	◑	6	●	○	•	•	•			
15	**Samsung** SGH-P107 (Cingular)	250		○	◐	5¼	●	◐	•	•	•	S		
16	**Motorola** V600 (Cingular/AT&T, T-Mobile)	200		○	◐	4¾	●	◐		•	•	S	•	
17	**Nokia** 6600 (T-Mobile)	380		○	○	6	●	○				S	•	
18	**Siemens** CF62T (T-Mobile)	120		○	◐	4¾	●	○	•	•				
19	**Sony Ericsson** T637 T237 (Cingular/AT&T)	270		◑	○	6¼	●	○		•		S	•	
20	**Nokia** 6620 (Cingular/AT&T)	470		○	○	4½	●	○				S	•	
21	**Nokia** 6010 (Cingular/AT&T, T-Mobile)	90		○	○	6¾	●	○						
22	**Nokia** 6820 (Cingular/AT&T)	320		○	○	5¼	●	◑				S	•	
23	**Siemens** C61 (Cingular)	120		○	◐	4½	●	○	•					
24	**Nokia** 7610 (Cingular/AT&T)	650		◑	○	5½	●	○				M	•	

🄳 *Discontinued, but similar model is available. Price is for similar model.*

■ **RESOURCES:** Reproducible peer-review guides for different kinds of papers are available in the *Additional Resources.*

CHECKLIST: HOW TO WRITE COMPARISON AND CONTRAST	
STEPS	**HOW TO DO THE STEPS**
☐ **Focus.**	• Think about what you want to compare or contrast and your purpose for doing so.
☐ **Narrow and explore your topic.** See Chapter 3.	• Choose specific subjects to compare/contrast, making sure they have enough in common to result in a meaningful paper. • Write down some ideas about the subjects.
☐ **Write a topic sentence (paragraph) or thesis statement (essay).** See Chapter 4.	• Include the subjects and your main point about them. • Make sure the sentence serves your purpose.
☐ **Support your main point.** See Chapter 5.	• Prewrite to find similarities or differences. Try making a two-column list (see p. 192). • Add details that will help your readers see the similarity or difference in each point of comparison or contrast.
☐ **Make a plan.** See Chapter 6.	• Decide whether to use point-by-point or whole-to-whole organization. • Make an outline with the points of comparison or contrast in the order you want to present them.
☐ **Write a draft.** See Chapter 7.	**FOR A PARAGRAPH** • Write a paragraph that includes a topic sentence and detailed points of comparison or contrast. Use complete sentences. **FOR AN ESSAY** • Consider using one of the introduction types in Chapter 7. Include your thesis statement in your introduction. • Using your plan, write topic sentences for each of the points of comparison or contrast. • Write paragraphs with details about each of the points of comparison and contrast. **FOR PARAGRAPHS AND ESSAYS** • Write a conclusion that reminds readers of your main point and makes an observation based on what you have written. • Write a title that previews your main point but doesn't repeat it.
☐ **Revise your draft, making at least four improvements.** See Chapter 8.	• Get feedback from others using the peer-review guide for comparison and contrast at **bedfordstmartins.com/realwriting**. • Reread to make sure that all points of comparison or contrast are parallel and relate to your main point.

STEPS	HOW TO DO THE STEPS
☐ **Revise your draft, making at least four improvements.** See Chapter 8.	• Add any points and details that will help show readers the similarities or differences. • Add transitions to move readers from one point or subject to the next.
☐ **Edit your revised draft.** See Parts Four through Seven.	• Correct errors in grammar, spelling, word use, and punctuation.
☐ **Ask yourself:**	• Does my paper include the Four Basics of Good Comparison and Contrast (p. 189)? • Is this the best I can do?

Chapter Review

1. What are the four basics of good comparison and contrast?

   It uses subjects that have enough in common to be compared/contrasted in a

   useful way.

   It serves a purpose — either to help readers make a decision or to help them

   understand the subjects.

   It presents several important, parallel points of comparison/contrast.

   It arranges points in a logical order.

2. The topic sentence (paragraph) or thesis statement (essay) in comparison/contrast should include what two basic parts? *the subjects being compared or contrasted and the main point of the comparison*

3. What are the two ways to organize comparison/contrast? *point-by-point or whole-to-whole*

4. In your own words, explain what these organizations are. *Answers will vary.*

5. Choose five of the vocabulary words on pages 197 or 198 and use each in a sentence.

   ■ **LEARNING JOURNAL:**
   Reread your idea-journal entry (p. 189) on the differences between men and women. Make another entry on the same topic, using what you have learned about comparison and contrast.

You Know This

You consider causes and effects every day:

- You explain to a boss or a companion what caused you to be late.
- You consider the possible effects of calling in sick.
- After eating, you feel ill and try to figure out the cause.

16

Cause and Effect

Writing That Explains Reasons or Results

■ **IDEA JOURNAL:** Write about a time that you did something that caused someone to be happy or unhappy.

■ **TEACHING TIP:** Explain to students the differences between *effect* (noun) and *affect* (verb).

Understand What Cause and Effect Are

A **cause** is what made an event happen. An **effect** is what happens as a result of the event.

▪▪ FOUR BASICS OF GOOD CAUSE AND EFFECT

1. The main point reflects the writer's purpose: to explain causes, effects, or both.
2. If the purpose is to explain causes, it presents real causes.
3. If the purpose is to explain effects, it presents real effects.
4. It gives readers detailed examples or explanations of the causes or effects.

In the following paragraph, each number corresponds to one of the Four Basics of Good Cause and Effect.

1 The next time you get a cold, don't blame the weather; blame your hands. While many people think that cold weather causes colds, the weather is not the real cause. **2** Colds are caused by viruses that are transmitted primarily from the hands to the eyes or nose. When you come in contact with someone who has a cold, or just with something they have touched, **3** you often pick up germs from that person on your hands. **4** For example, when a cashier with a cold gives you change, the coins may well carry the cold germ. When you later **2** rub your eyes or nose, you **3** pass the germ on to yourself. Elementary schools and day-care centers are cold breeding grounds **2** because children are in close contact with each other, in confined spaces; they touch the same desks, computer keyboards, and lunch tables, and each other. **3** Those same children can then infect their family members at home. Colds are more common in the winter only **2** because during the cold weather, windows are closed and less fresh air circulates. There are only two known ways to cut down on getting colds: Never come into contact with anyone or anything, or wash your hands with warm water and soap, often. The choice seems pretty clear.

When you are writing about causes and effects, make sure that you don't confuse something that happened before an event with a real cause or something that happened after an event with a real effect. For example, if you have pizza on Monday and get the flu on Tuesday, the pizza is not the cause of the flu just because it happened before you got the flu, nor is the flu the effect of eating pizza—you just happened to get the flu the next day.

Jim Rice of Quinsigamond Community College helps his students visualize the cause/effect relationship by suggesting that they think of three linked rings:

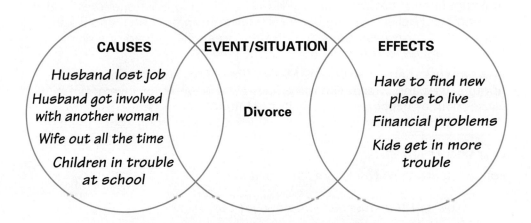

You use cause and effect in many situations:

COLLEGE	In a nutrition course, you are asked to identify the consequences (effects) of poor nutrition.
WORK	A car comes into your auto shop with a flat tire, and you are asked to determine the cause of the flat.
EVERYDAY LIFE	You explain to your child why a certain behavior is not acceptable by warning him or her about the negative effects of that behavior.

Profile of Success: Cause and Effect in the Real World

Mary LaCue Booker
Singer, Actor
(stage name: La Q)

■ **RESOURCES:** For a discussion of how to use the profiles in Part Two, see *Practical Suggestions.*

The following profile shows how a rap singer uses cause and effect in her work.

BACKGROUND: I grew up in a very small town in Georgia but always had big dreams that I followed. Those dreams included becoming a nurse, then a teacher, then a singer and actor. Before becoming a nurse and teacher, I went to college, studying both nursing and psychology. Later, I followed my dream of performing and left Georgia to attend the very competitive American Academy of Dramatic Arts in Los Angeles.

I returned to Georgia and combined teaching and performance as chair of the Fine Arts Department at Columbia Middle School. I wrote rap songs for my students, and my first one, "School Rules," was an immediate hit in Atlanta. I now have two CDs and have been cast in a Hollywood movie, *We Must Go Forward,* about African American history. In addition to performing, I also am busy giving motivational speeches.

COLLEGE(S)/DEGREES: A.A., DeKalb College; B.S., Brenau Women's College; M.Ed., Cambridge College

WRITING AT WORK: When I taught, I wrote lesson plans, reports for students, and communications with parents. Now, I write song lyrics, speeches, and screenplays. I believe writing is critical. I write from the heart, and it's a good outlet for my emotions. Sometimes, I freewrite around one word, like *mischievous,* which is the name of my new CD.

HOW LA Q USES CAUSE AND EFFECT: Many of my songs and speeches are about causes and effects, like the effects of how we act or love or what causes pain or happiness. I wrote "School Rules" for my students, who didn't listen to regular rules but would listen to a rap song about them.

LA Q'S CAUSE AND EFFECT

Following are some lyrics from "School Rules."

> *Now get this, now get this, now get this.*
> If ya wanna be cool, obey the rules
> Cause if ya don't, it's your future you lose.
>
> I'm a school teacher from a rough school.
> I see students every day breakin' the rules.
> Here comes a new boy with a platinum grill
> Makin' trouble, ringin' the fire drill.
>
> There goes anotha' fool wanna run the school,
> Breakin' all the damn school rules.
> Runnin' in the halls, writin' graffiti on the walls,
> Tellin' a lie without blinkin' an eye,
> Usin' profanity, pleadin' insanity,
> Callin' names, causin' pain,
> Joinin' gangs like it's fame,

Dissin' the teacha and each otha.

Regardless of color, they're all sistas and brothas.

Now get this, now get this, now get this, now get this.

Boys and girls are <u>skippin' class,</u>

Cause they <u>late with no hall pass.</u>

They wanna have their say, and that's okay,

But they're outta their minds if they wanna have their way.

Now get this, now get this, now get this.

If ya wanna be free, school's not the place ta be.

But if ya wanna degree, you gotta feel me.

So if you wanna be cool, obey the rules

Cause if ya don't, it's your future you lose.

1. What is La Q's **purpose?** *to tell students that breaking the rules will prevent them from getting a degree*

2. What are the **effects** of breaking the rules? *not getting a degree, losing your future*

3. Underline the **causes** that lead to these effects.

4. With a partner, or as a class, translate this rap into formal English.

> ■ **TIP:** For more on using formal English, see Chapter 2.

Main Point in Cause and Effect

The **main point** in cause and effect reflects your purpose. For example, your purpose might be to explain the effects of Hurricane Katrina on the nation's economy.

> Hurricane Katrina had devastating effects on the national economy.

To help you discover your main point, complete the following sentence:

(Your topic) causes (or caused) . . .
(Your topic) resulted in (or results in) . . .

The topic sentence (paragraph) or thesis statement (essay) usually includes the topic and an indication of whether the author will present causes, effects, or both.

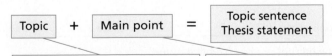

Weak car emissions standards are destroying our air quality.

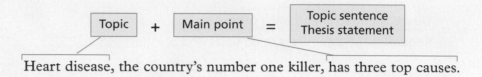

Heart disease, the country's number one killer, has three top causes.

■ PRACTICE 1   CHOOSING DIRECT CAUSES AND EFFECTS

For each of the situations that follow, create a ring diagram. Write three possible causes in the left ring and three possible effects in the right one. There is no one correct set of answers, but your choices should be logical, and you should be prepared to explain how your answers were direct causes and effects.   *Answers will vary.*

EXAMPLE:

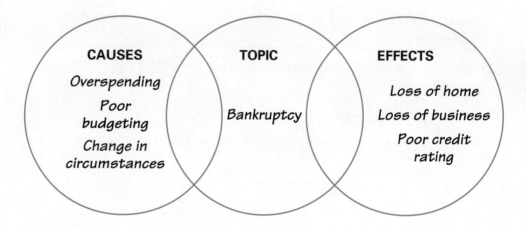

1. **TOPIC:** A fire in someone's home

2. **TOPIC:** An A in this course

3. **TOPIC:** A car accident

■ PRACTICE 2   STATING YOUR MAIN POINT

For each of the topics in Practice 1, review your causes and effects, and write a sentence that states a main point. First look at the following example and at the list of causes for the topic (bankruptcy) in the example in Practice 1.

EXAMPLE:

TOPIC: Bankruptcy

MAIN POINT: *Although many different kinds of people declare bankruptcy each year, the causes for bankruptcy are often the same.*

1. **TOPIC:** A fire in someone's home

   MAIN POINT: _Answers will vary._

2. **TOPIC:** An A in this course

   MAIN POINT: _____

3. **TOPIC:** A car accident

   MAIN POINT: _____

. . . .

Support in Cause and Effect

In cause/effect writing, **support** consists of detailed examples or explanations of the causes or effects.

Your reader may not immediately understand how one event or situation caused another or what particular effects resulted from a certain event or situation. You need to give specific examples and details to explain the relationship.

▮ PRACTICE 3   GIVING EXAMPLES AND DETAILS . . . .

Look at your answers to Practices 1 and 2. Choose two causes or two effects for each of the three items, and give an example or detail that explains each cause or effect.

EXAMPLE:

TOPIC: Bankruptcy

CAUSE 1: _Overspending_

    EXAMPLE/DETAIL: _bought a leather jacket I liked and charged it_

CAUSE 2: _Poor budgeting_

    EXAMPLE/DETAIL: _never keeping track of monthly expenses versus monthly_

income

1. **TOPIC:** A fire in someone's home

   CAUSE/EFFECT 1: _Answers will vary._

       EXAMPLE/DETAIL: _____

   CAUSE/EFFECT 2: _____

       EXAMPLE/DETAIL: _____

2. **TOPIC:** An A in this course

    CAUSE/EFFECT 1: _____

        EXAMPLE/DETAIL: _____

    CAUSE/EFFECT 2: _____

        EXAMPLE/DETAIL: _____

3. **TOPIC:** A car accident

    CAUSE/EFFECT 1: _____

        EXAMPLE/DETAIL: _____

    CAUSE/EFFECT 2: _____

        EXAMPLE/DETAIL: _____

Organization in Cause and Effect

■ **TIP:** For more on the different orders of organization, see pages 65–66.

Cause and effect can be organized in a variety of ways, depending on your purpose.

MAIN POINT	PURPOSE	ORGANIZATION
Hurricane Katrina had devastating effects on the national economy.	to explain Katrina's effects on the U.S. economy	order of importance, saving the most important effect for last
Hurricane Katrina caused devastation throughout New Orleans.	to describe the destruction	space order
Hurricane Katrina destroyed New Orleans in two distinct stages, first as the storm ripped through the city and then when the levees broke.	to describe the effects of the storm over time	time order

Note: If you are explaining both causes and effects, you would present the causes first and the effects later.

Use **transitions** to move readers smoothly from one cause to another, from one effect to another, or from causes to effects. Because cause and effect can use any method of organization depending on your purpose, the following list shows just a few of the transitions that you might use.

Common Cause and Effect Transitions

also	more important/serious cause/effect
as a result	most important/serious cause/effect
because	one cause/effect; another cause/effect
the final cause/effect	a primary cause; a secondary cause
the first, second, third cause/effect	a short-term effect; a long-term effect

---

▪ **PRACTICE 4   USING TRANSITIONS IN CAUSE AND EFFECT** . . . . . .

Read the paragraph that follows and fill in the blanks with transitions.
Answers may vary. Possible answers shown.

Recently, neuroscientists, who have long been skeptical about meditation,[1] confirm that it has numerous positive outcomes. *One, The first* is that people who meditate can maintain their focus and attention longer than people who do not. This ability to stay "on task" was demonstrated among students who had been practicing meditation for several weeks. They reported more effective studying and learning because they were able to pay attention. *Another, A second* positive outcome was the ability to relax on command. While meditating, people learned how to reduce their heart rates and blood pressure so that they could relax more easily in all kinds of situations. *A third, The most important* outcome was a thickening of the brain's cortex. Meditators' cortexes were uniformly thicker than nonmeditators'. Because the cortex enables memorization and the production of new ideas, this last outcome is especially exciting, particularly in fighting Alzheimer's disease and other dementias.

. . . .

Read and Understand Cause and Effect

Reading examples of cause and effect to understand their structure and content will help you write your own. The first example, a paragraph, is followed by questions about the structure of cause and effect. The second example, an essay, has questions in the margin to help you read closely. It is followed by questions about both structure and content, along with writing assignments. These activities will help you practice critical reading and thinking skills.

▪ **READING SELECTIONS:** For further examples of and activities for cause and effect, see Chapter 49.

[1] **meditation:** to focus the mind through exercises or other means.

Cause and Effect Paragraph: Student

VOCABULARY DEVELOPMENT
Underline these words as
you read the cause and
effect paragraph.
hounded: *bothered*
aggressive: *forceful*
shopping spree: *making
many purchases*

■ **TIP:** For advice on building your vocabulary, see
Appendix B.

VOCABULARY DEVELOPMENT
Underline these words as
you read the cause and
effect essay.
aerobic: *using a lot of oxygen (as when running)*
neurotransmitters: *chemicals that send nerve im-
pulses*
euphoria: *great happiness*
endorphins: *a group of
brain hormones that reduce
pain sensations*
narcotic: *an addictive drug
that reduces pain, alters
mood, and causes sleepiness*
compensate: *to offset or
counterbalance*

PREDICT: Will the text discuss causes or effects?
_____
_____

Much to her surprise, lottery winner Sylvia Lee found that sudden wealth was a mixed blessing—the results were both good and bad. After her win was announced, she was constantly hounded by people who wanted to sell her something. She got an unlisted telephone number, but the more aggressive salespeople just camped out on her doorstep. Another negative result was that people started treating her differently. "I was shocked," said Lee. "Everyone from the checkout clerk at the grocery store where I've shopped for years to my next-door neighbor acted as though I had changed. I'm still the same; I've just got money now." Lee admits, though, that most of the changes have been positive. "It really is a relief not worrying about money all the time. I actually went on my first shopping spree ever, and it was great." Lee expects that other new and unexpected results of her sudden wealth are yet to come, but she's not discouraged: So far, at least, the plusses far outweigh the minuses.

1. Double-underline the **topic sentence**.

2. Does the paragraph present causes, effects, or both? *effects* _____

3. Underline **each cause or effect** in the sample paragraph.

4. Circle the **transitions** in the sample paragraph.

5. Double underline the sentence at the end that reminds the reader of the main point.

Cause and Effect Essay: Textbook

Effects of Exercise

People who exercise regularly report positive changes in their moods. They may feel less tense, anxious, and depressed during and after workouts. They are generally more relaxed and self-confident than inactive people. They are also more likely to engage in health-ful behaviors and avoid harmful substances. The connection be-tween improved mood and exercise is so strong that health professionals often encourage depressed people to exercise.   1

Exercise also provides a break from the strains of everyday life, which can help combat stress. Aerobic exercise helps normalize levels of neurotransmitters that are believed to play a role in depres-   2 sion. Exercise can also be enjoyable, which is another reason that it may help combat depression. Exercise can give us a sense of mastery and accomplishment, which boosts our self-image and self-confidence and may help us overcome the feelings of helplessness that are often associated with depression.

Some runners report feelings of euphoria known as "runner's high." The phenomenon has been linked to the release of *endorphins*. Endorphins are the body's natural painkillers. They function in a similar way to the narcotic morphine.

3

Regular exercise has numerous positive effects, both physical and psychological. Although it is difficult to find time to exercise regularly, once people develop the habit, they find that their increased energy and productivity more than compensate for the time taken. In starting to exercise, as with most things, the first step is the hardest.

4 **REFLECT:** Can you name other effects of exercise?

———

———

—Adapted from Jeffrey S. Nevid, Spencer A. Rathus, and Hannah R. Rubenstein, *Health in the New Millennium* (Worth, 1998)

CRITICAL THINKING: READING

1. Double-underline the **thesis statement.**

2. What are four effects of regular exercise? *Answers will vary but could* _____ *include reduced tension, anxiety, depression, and stress; increased self-* _____ *confidence; better self-image; and improved mood.* _____

■ **TIP:** For reading advice, see Chapter 1.

3. Some people who exercise regularly describe themselves as "exercise addicts." Why do you think they may become addicted? *Answers will vary.* _____ As discussed in this essay, what effect of exercise might cause such addiction? *the release of endorphins* _____

4. What makes up for the time devoted to exercise? *Exercisers find that* _____ *they are more energetic and productive.* _____

5. Highlight the essay, which is from a health textbook, as if you were reading it for a health class.

CRITICAL THINKING: WRITING

Choose one of the following topics and respond in a paragraph or essay.

1. Why, in your experience, is the first step the hardest in all things? Explain, describing a difficult first step you took and what resulted from it.

2. Do you think exercise is worth the time people devote to it? Why or why not? Agree with or argue against points made in the previous essay.

3. Discuss why you exercise (and what you do) or why you don't exercise.

Write Your Own Cause and Effect

■ **TIP:** Look back at your idea-journal entry (p. 206) for ideas.

In this section you will write your own cause/effect paragraph or essay based on your (or your instructor's) choice among three assignments.

To complete your cause/effect writing, follow this sequence:

1. Review the Four Basics of Good Cause and Effect (p. 206).
2. Choose your assignment.
3. If you are asked to complete Assignment 3, read Solving Problems, Appendix D.
4. Write your cause/effect paper using the Checklist: How to Write Cause and Effect (pp. 218–19).

**CAUSE AND EFFECT
AT A GLANCE**

**Topic sentence
(paragraph) or thesis
statement (essay)**
Indicates causes,
effects, or both

Cause 1 or effect 1
Detailed explanation or
example of the first
cause or effect

Cause 2 or effect 2
Detailed explanation or
example of the second
cause or effect

Cause 3 or effect 3
Detailed explanation or
example of the third
cause or effect

Conclusion
Reminds readers of
your main point and
makes an observation
about it based on what
you have written

■ **ASSIGNMENT 1   WRITING ABOUT COLLEGE, WORK,
AND EVERYDAY LIFE** . . . .

Write a cause/effect paper on one of the following topics.

COLLEGE

PARAGRAPH	ESSAY
• Causes or effects of not studying for an exam	• Effects of getting a college degree
• Causes of getting a failing grade in a course	• Causes/effects of plagiarism
• Effects of being a good student	• Causes of your interest in a particular course or major

WORK

PARAGRAPH	ESSAY
• Causes of frequent absences	• Causes of job satisfaction/ dissatisfaction
• Effects of a task you perform	• Causes/effects of stress at work
• Causes of stress at work	• Effects of having a minimum-wage job

EVERYDAY LIFE

PARAGRAPH	ESSAY
• Causes/effects of not getting enough sleep	• Causes or effects of a major change in your life
• Causes/effects of stress	• Effects of a good decision you made
• Causes/effects of a difficult decision	• Effects of having children

■ **ESL:** Suggest that students write about the cause or effect of a cultural misunderstanding.

ASSIGNMENT 2   WRITING ABOUT IMAGES . . . .

Write a paragraph or an essay about the causes and effects that are the main point of the cartoon below.

GARBAGE IN...

ASSIGNMENT 3   WRITING IN THE REAL WORLD/SOLVING A PROBLEM . . . .

PROBLEM: You've learned of a cheating ring at school that uses cell phones to give test answers to students taking the test. A few students in your math class, who are also friends of yours, think this is a great idea and are planning to participate in the ring during a test you will be taking next week. You have decided not to participate, partly because you

■ **RESOURCES:** All chapters in Part Two have writing checklists, which are reproduced in *Additional Resources.* You can photocopy and distribute them if you want students to hand in the checklists with their assignments.

■ **RESOURCES:** Reproducible peer-review guides for different kinds of papers are available in the *Additional Resources.*

■ **TEAMWORK:** For more detailed guidance on group work, see *Practical Suggestions.*

fear getting caught, but also because you think cheating is wrong. Now you want to convince your friends not to take part in the ring, because you think your teacher will find out, and you don't want them to get caught and possibly kicked out of school. How do you make your case?

ASSIGNMENT: Working in a group or on your own, list the various effects of cheating—both immediate and long-term—that you could use to convince your friends. Then, write a cause/effect paragraph or essay that identifies and explains some possible effects of cheating. You might start with this sentence:

Cheating on tests or papers is not worth the risks.

. . . .

CHECKLIST: HOW TO WRITE CAUSE AND EFFECT	
STEPS	**HOW TO DO THE STEPS**
☐ **Focus.**	• Think about your topic and whether you want to describe what caused it or what resulted from it.
☐ **Narrow and explore your topic.** See Chapter 3.	• Choose a topic that is narrow enough that you can present all important causes and/or effects. • Prewrite to get ideas about the narrowed topic.
☐ **Write a topic sentence (paragraph) or thesis statement (essay).** See Chapter 4.	• Include your topic and an indication of whether you will discuss causes, effects, or both.
☐ **Support your main point.** See Chapter 5.	• Prewrite to find causes and/or effects. • Choose the most significant causes and/or effects. • Explain the causes/effects with detailed examples.
☐ **Make a plan.** See Chapter 6.	• Arrange the causes/effects in a logical order (space, time, or importance).
☐ **Write a draft.** See Chapter 7.	**FOR A PARAGRAPH** • Write a paragraph that includes a topic sentence, your cause(s), effect(s), and detailed examples. Use complete sentences. **FOR AN ESSAY** • Consider using one of the introduction types in Chapter 7. Include your thesis statement in your introduction. • Using your plan, write topic sentences for each of the causes or effects. • Write paragraphs with detailed examples of the causes and effects.

STEPS	HOW TO DO THE STEPS
☐ **Write a draft.** See Chapter 7.	**FOR PARAGRAPHS AND ESSAYS** • Write a conclusion that reminds readers of your main point and makes an observation based on what you have written. • Write a title that previews your main point but doesn't repeat it.
☐ **Revise your draft, making at least four improvements.** See Chapter 8.	• Get feedback from others using the peer-review guide for cause and effect at **bedfordstmartins.com/realwriting**. • Cut anything that doesn't directly explain what caused or resulted from the situation or event. • Add examples and details that help readers understand the causes and/or effects. • Add transitions to move readers from one cause or effect to the next or from causes to effects.
☐ **Edit your revised draft.** See Parts Four through Seven.	• Correct errors in grammar, spelling, word use, and punctuation.
☐ **Ask yourself:**	• Does my paper include the Four Basics of Good Cause and Effect (p. 206)? • Is this the best I can do?

Chapter Review

1. A cause is *what made an event happen* _____.

2. An effect is *what happens as a result of the event* _____.

3. What are the Four Basics of Good Cause and Effect?

   The main point reflects the writer's purpose: to explain causes, effects, or both.

   If the purpose is to explain causes, it presents real causes.

   If the purpose is to explain effects, it presents real effects.

   It gives readers detailed examples or explanations of the causes or effects.

4. Choose five of the vocabulary words on page 214 and use each in a sentence.

■ **LEARNING JOURNAL:** Reread your idea-journal entry (p. 206) on a time you caused someone to be happy or unhappy. Make another entry on this topic, using what you have learned about cause and effect.

You Know This

You often try to persuade others or make your opinion known:

- You convince your partner that it's better to save some money than to buy a new television.
- The college announces a tuition increase, and you want to protest.
- You persuade someone to lend you money or let you borrow a car.

17

Argument

Writing That Persuades

Understand What Argument Is

Argument is writing that takes a position on an issue and gives supporting evidence to persuade someone else to accept, or at least consider, the position. Argument is also used to convince someone to take (or not take) an action.

Argument helps you persuade people to see things your way, or at least to understand your position. Most of us have experienced the feeling of being a helpless victim—just standing by while something that we don't want to happen happens. Although knowing how to argue won't eliminate all such situations, it will help you to stand up for what you want. You may not always win, but you will sometimes, and you'll at least be able to put up a good fight.

■ **IDEA JOURNAL:** Persuade a friend who has a dead-end job to take a course at your college.

■ **TEACHING TIP:** Explain to students that argument is not like bickering or fighting. It is a reasonable defense of a position.

■■
■■ **FOUR BASICS OF GOOD ARGUMENT**

1. It takes a strong and definite position.
2. It gives good reasons and supporting evidence to defend the position.
3. It considers opposing views.
4. It has enthusiasm and energy from start to finish.

In the following paragraph, each number corresponds to one of the Basics of Good Argument.

4 Argument is enthusiastic and energetic

1 The state government should not require all citizens, particularly young people, to have health insurance. I am a recent college graduate and have a decent job, but my company does not provide health insurance. To require me to buy an individual policy is not fair or reasonable. **2** One reason is that such a policy would be very expensive and would take most of my income. As someone just starting out, my income barely covers my rent and food. If I had to buy health insurance, I would have to take another job, find another roommate, or try to find a cheaper apartment. Another reason is that any policy I could buy would have such a high deductible that I would have to pay most of my own expenses anyway. Most inexpensive policies have deductibles of $250 to $1,000, so I would be paying that on top of a high monthly premium. The most important reason that young people should not be required to buy individual health insurance is that, statistically, we are not likely to need expensive medical treatment. So why should we be expected to pay for it? **3** Although the people who want everyone to have insurance hope that the state will provide lower rates for low-income families and children, they haven't considered how such a requirement will penalize the many young people who are just getting started. A new system may be needed, but not one that is unfair to a whole generation of citizens.

Knowing how to make a good argument is one of the most useful skills you can develop. Consider the following examples:

COLLEGE   You might argue for or against makeup exams for students who don't do well the first time.

WORK   You need to leave work an hour early one day a week for twelve weeks to take a course. You must persuade your boss to allow you to do so.

EVERYDAY LIFE   You try to negotiate a better price on an item you want to buy.

Profile of Success: Argument in the Real World

Sandro Polo
Graduate Student in
Architecture

The following profile shows how an architect uses argument on the job.

BACKGROUND: I was born in Peru and moved to California with my family when I was sixteen. It took me about five years to learn English. I enrolled at Solano Community College but was kicked out twice for a low grade point average. To continue there, I had to go before the president of the college and make a case for my reinstatement. I told the president, "I know I can do it," and two years later, I graduated with honors. I went on to the University of California, Davis, where I received a B.S. in design. After working in several interior design/architectural firms, I decided that I wanted my architecture degree, so I'm pursuing an M.S. at the University of Southern California.

COLLEGE(S)/DEGREES: A.A., Solano Community College; B.S., University of California, Davis. Pursuing M.S. at the University of Southern California.

WRITING AT WORK: I write to clients, engineers, contractors, and city officials. Everything about a project has to be accurately documented so that the project is successfully designed and built.

■ **RESOURCES:** For a discussion of how to use the profiles in Part Two, see *Practical Suggestions*.

HOW SANDRO USES ARGUMENT: Often, some aspect of a building project turns out to be more expensive than was originally budgeted. I then have to present a case for spending more money than was originally allocated.

SANDRO'S ARGUMENT

To: Johnson Clark

Fr: Sandro Polo

Re: Justification for additional costs, HVAC (heat, ventilation, air conditioning)

The HVAC system we recommend will more than pay for itself within one year and is a sound investment. Although the system is more expensive than originally estimated, it is well worth the additional cost for several reasons.

The new system is more energy efficient, resulting in two economic plusses for you. First, with the cost of energy skyrocketing, a system that uses less fuel will save significant money immediately. In addition, because of the efficiency, your company will receive a tax credit, reducing your taxes this year and in the future.

Additionally, the new system is more adaptable to your future needs. Older, less expensive systems are not designed for adaptability or expansion. As your needs change, the older system would need to be updated with parts that would be both costly and inefficient. Because of design and technology, the new system allows changes with minimal additional costs and no redesign.

Finally, and most important, we believe the quality of the newer system will save money by increasing employee productivity. Its superior filtration has documented results indicating a much healthier environment for occupants. "Sick building" complaints have been eliminated in buildings with this HVAC system, reducing employee absences and medical claims.

For all of the above reasons, we firmly believe that your costs will be reduced with the new system, more than justifying the additional expense. If you have further questions, please do not hesitate to contact me.

1. Double-underline the **thesis statement**.

2. What are three **reasons** Sandro gives to support his thesis?
   Answers will vary but should mention energy efficiency, adaptability,
   and savings through increased productivity.

3. Underline the sentence that considers the opposing view.

Main Point in Argument

Your **main point** in argument is the position you take on the issue (or topic) you are writing about. When you are free to choose an issue, choose something you care about. When you are assigned an issue, try to find some part of it that matters to you. You might try starting with a "should" or "should not" sentence:

> Young people should/should not be required to buy health insurance.

If you have trouble seeing how an issue matters, talk about it with a partner, or write down ideas about it using the following tips.

TIPS FOR BUILDING ENTHUSIASM AND ENERGY

- Imagine yourself arguing your position with someone you always disagree with (who, naturally, holds the opposite position).
- Imagine that your whole grade rests on persuading your professor of your position.
- Imagine how this issue could affect you or your family personally.
- Imagine that you are representing a large group of people who care about the issue very much and whose lives will be forever changed by it. It's up to you to win their case.

In argument, the topic sentence (paragraph) or thesis statement (essay) usually includes the issue/topic and the writer's position about it.

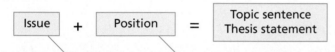

```
┌─────────┐        ┌──────────┐        ┌─────────────────────┐
│  Issue  │   +    │ Position │   =    │   Topic sentence    │
└─────────┘        └──────────┘        │  Thesis statement   │
                                       └─────────────────────┘
```

Day-care facilities should be provided by companies at a low cost to employees.

Many good topic sentences or thesis statements in argument use words like these:

could (not)	ought (not)
must (not)	requires
must have	should (not)
needs	would

When you have a statement of your position, try revising it to make it sound stronger, clearer, or more interesting. Here are progressively stronger revisions:

■ **TIP:** For more on revising, see Chapter 8.

1. Day-care facilities should be provided by companies.
2. Companies should provide day-care facilities at a low cost to employees.
3. Employees are entitled to low-cost, company-sponsored day care.

■ **TIP:** If your students are comfortable using the Web, have them type some key words about their topic into a search engine (e.g., <www.google.com>)—for instance *animal testing* and *pros and cons*. Seeing the points others have raised about an issue can help them consider the various sides. However, they should take care to consult only reliable sources. For more information, see Chapter 19.

■ **PRACTICE 1**   **WRITING A STATEMENT OF YOUR POSITION** . . . . . .

Write a statement of your position for each item. *Answers will vary. Possible answers shown.*

EXAMPLE:

ISSUE: Prisoners' rights

POSITION STATEMENT: *Prisoners should not have more rights and privileges than law-abiding citizens.*

1. **ISSUE:** Lab testing on animals

    POSITION STATEMENT: *Animals should continue to be used for lab testing.*

2. **ISSUE:** Use of cell phones

    POSITION STATEMENT: *Cell phone signals should be blocked in theaters.*

3. **ISSUE:** Athletes' salaries

    POSITION STATEMENT: *Limits should be placed on major league baseball players' salaries.*

Support in Argument

A strong position must be **supported** with convincing reasons and evidence. Remember that you want to persuade readers that your position is the right one. Use strong reasons and supporting evidence that will be convincing to your audience, consider opposing views, and end on a strong note.

Reasons and Evidence

■ **TEACHING TIP:** Go over the concept of evidence carefully. Students' arguments are often weak because of poor evidence or lack of evidence.

The primary support for your position is the **reasons** you give. Your reasons need to be supported by **evidence**, such as *facts, examples,* and *expert opinions.*

*   **FACTS:** Statements or observations that can be proved. Statistics—real numbers from actual studies—can be persuasive factual evidence.
*   **EXAMPLES:** Specific information or experiences that support your position.
*   **EXPERT OPINIONS:** The opinion of someone who is considered an expert in the area you are writing about. The person must be known for his or her expertise in your topic. For example, the opinion of the head of the FBI about the benefits of a low-fat diet isn't strong evidence. The FBI director isn't an expert in the field of nutrition.

In the following examples, a reason and appropriate evidence support each position.

POSITION: It pays to stay in college.

REASON: College graduates earn more than people without degrees.

EVIDENCE/FACT: Community-college graduates earn 58 percent more than high-school graduates and 320 percent more than high-school dropouts.

POSITION: Genetically modified foods should be banned until they have been thoroughly tested for safety.

REASON: Currently, nobody is certain about the effects of such foods on humans and animals.

EVIDENCE/EXAMPLE: The government and the biotech industry have not produced convincing evidence that such foods are as safe or nutritious as foods that have not been genetically modified.

POSITION: The drug Ritalin is overprescribed for attention-deficit/hyperactivity disorder (ADHD) in children.

REASON: It is too often considered a "wonder drug."

EVIDENCE/EXPERT OPINION: Dr. Peter Jensen, a pediatric specialist, warns, "I fear that ADHD is suffering from the 'disease of the month' syndrome, and Ritalin is its 'cure.'"

As you choose reasons and evidence to support your position, consider what your audience is likely to think about your view of the issue. Are they likely to agree with you, to be uncommitted, or to be hostile? Think about what kinds of reasons and evidence would be most convincing to a typical member of your audience.

When writing an argument, it's tempting to cite as evidence something that "everyone" knows or believes or does. But be careful of "everyone" evidence; everyone usually doesn't know or believe it. It is better to use facts (including statistics), specific examples, and expert opinions.

■ **TIP:** To find good reasons and strong evidence, you may want to consult outside sources, either at the library or on the Internet. For more on using outside sources, see Chapter 19

■ PRACTICE 2   **FINDING EVIDENCE** . . . .

For each of the following positions, give the type of evidence indicated (you may have to make up the evidence).

EXAMPLE:

POSITION: Pesticides should not be sprayed from planes.

REASON: They can cause more damage than they prevent.

EVIDENCE/FACT: *Scientific studies prove that both plant life and people are harmed.*

■ **COMPUTER:** If you are working in a lab setting, have each student list the evidence for his or her topic on the computer. Then, have each student move to another student's computer and write down opposition to the evidence that is listed. Students should then return to their own computers and try to answer the objections.

1. **POSITION:** The parking situation on this campus is impossible.

   REASON: There are too few spaces for the number of students.

   EVIDENCE/EXAMPLE: *Answers will vary.*

2. **POSITION:** People should be careful when dieting.

   REASON: Losing weight quickly is unhealthy.

   EVIDENCE/FACT: _____

3. **POSITION:** Smoking is harmful to smokers and nonsmokers alike.

   REASON: Even secondhand smoke can cause lung damage.

   EVIDENCE/EXPERT OPINION: _____

· ·

Your reasons and evidence may be convincing to you, but will they persuade your readers? Review the support for your argument by using these strategies.

TESTING YOUR REASONS AND EVIDENCE

DISCUSSION: Model the opponent's perspective in class. Put a topic and some evidence on the board. Ask for ideas about how the opposition would try to knock down the evidence.

- Reread your reasons and evidence from your opponent's perspective, looking for ways to knock them down. Anticipate your opponent's objections, and include evidence to answer them.

- Ask someone else to cross-examine your reasons, trying to knock them down.

- Stay away from generalities. Statements about what everyone else does or what always happens are easy to disprove.

- Make sure that you have considered every important angle of the issue. Take the time to present good support for your position; your argument depends on the quality of your reasons and evidence.

- Reread your reasons and evidence to make sure that they support your position. They must be relevant to your argument.

PRACTICE 3 REVIEWING THE EVIDENCE · · · · · · · · · · · · · ·

For each of the following positions, one piece of evidence is weak: It does not support the position. Circle the letter of the weak evidence, and in the space provided state why it is weak.

EXAMPLE:

POSITION: Advertisements should not use skinny models.

REASON: Skinny should not be promoted as ideal.

   a. Three friends of mine became anorexic trying to get skinny.

   (b.) Everyone knows that most people are not that thin.

c. A survey of young girls shows that they think they should be as thin as models.

d. People can endanger their health trying to fit the skinny "ideal."

Not strong evidence because *"everyone knows" is not strong evidence; everyone*

obviously doesn't know that.

1. **POSITION:** People who own guns should not be allowed to keep them at home.

    REASON: It is dangerous to keep a gun in the house.

    a. Guns can go off by accident.

    b. Keeping guns at home has been found to increase the risk of home suicides and adolescent suicides.

    c. Just last week a story in the newspaper told about a man who, in a fit of rage, took his gun out of the drawer and shot his wife.

    (d.) Guns can be purchased easily.

    Not strong evidence because *it is irrelevant; it doesn't support the position* .

2. **POSITION:** Schoolchildren in the United States should go to school all year.

    REASON: Year-round schooling promotes better learning.

    (a.) All of my friends would like to end the long summer break.

    b. A survey of teachers across the country showed that children's learning improved when they had multiple shorter vacations rather than entire summers off.

    c. Many children are bored and restless after three weeks of vacation and would be better off returning to school.

    d. Test scores improved when a school system in Colorado went to year-round school sessions.

    Not strong evidence because *wanting it doesn't mean it should happen; also this*

    is a personal preference, not evidence.

3. **POSITION:** The "three strikes and you're out" law that forces judges to send people to jail after three convictions should be revised.

    REASON: Basing decisions about sentencing on numbers alone is neither reasonable nor fair.

    a. A week ago, a man who stole a slice of pizza was sentenced to eight to ten years in prison because it was his third conviction.

    b. The law makes prison overcrowding even worse.

    (c.) Judges always give the longest sentence possible anyway.

    d. The law too often results in people getting major prison sentences for minor crimes.

    Not strong evidence because *it is a generality; not all judges do this.*

The Conclusion

Your conclusion is your last opportunity to convince readers of your position. Make it memorable and dramatic. Remind your readers of the issue, your position, and the rightness of your position.

Before writing your conclusion, build up your enthusiasm again. Then reread what you have written. As soon as you finish reading, write the most forceful ending you can think of. Aim for power; you can tone it down later.

Organization in Argument

■ **TIP:** For more on order of importance, see pages 65–66.

Most arguments are organized by **order of importance**, saving the most convincing reason and evidence for last.

Use **transitions** to move your readers smoothly from one reason to another. Here are some of the transitions you might use in your argument.

Common Argument Transitions

above all	more important
also	most important
best of all	one fact/another fact
especially	one reason/another reason
for example	one thing/another thing
in addition	remember
in fact	the first (second, third) point
in particular	worst of all
in the first (second, third) place	

■ **PRACTICE 4   USING TRANSITIONS IN ARGUMENT** . . . .

Read the paragraph that follows and fill in the blanks with transitions. You are not limited to the ones in the preceding box. *Answers may vary. Possible answers shown.*

Daylight savings time should not be extended for an additional two months. Supporters of this change believe that it will save energy, but the savings are doubtful, and there are definite disadvantages. _For one thing,_ _In the first place_, while it would be light later into the evening, the morning hours would be darker. Many experts do not believe that there will be much difference in the amount of energy used. _Also, In the second_ _place, One important disadvantage is that_ the cost of the change could be extremely high. For example, computers are now set to change with the usual schedule of daylight savings. These computers run hospitals, transportation systems, and a whole range of operations, and updating them would be very expensive. _The biggest disadvantage is that, Worst of all,_ children would be placed at risk. They would be going to school in darkness, increasing the chance of crime or accidents. I support changes that make sense, but changing the schedule of daylight savings is not one of them.

Read and Understand Argument

Reading examples of argument to understand their structure and content will help you write your own. The first example, a paragraph, is followed by questions about the structure of argument. The second example, an essay, has questions in the margin to help you read closely. It is followed by questions about both structure and content, along with writing assignments. These activities will help you practice critical reading and thinking skills.

■ **READING SELECTIONS:**
For further examples of and activities for argument, see Chapter 50.

Argument Paragraph: Student

The student loan program should not be one of the cuts in the federal budget because such cuts would hurt the economy, students, and the nation as a whole. One reason for keeping the current level of funding for loans is that it helps the banks that loan the money. Banks need the business that loans provide. If they lose business, the economy is hurt. Another reason is that, more than ever, students rely on loans to help them go to college. Today, most students work while they go to school, but the work they have is usually low-paid. To get better jobs, they need college training and college degrees. The most important reason for not cutting the loan program is that the country needs a trained, professional workforce. People without training will be drains on the economy rather than contributors. Students are the future of our global economy, and keeping them from going to college hurts everyone. The student loan program is important for all of us.

VOCABULARY DEVELOPMENT
Underline this word in the argument paragraph.
rely: _depend on_

■ **TIP:** For advice on building your vocabulary, see Appendix B.

1. Double-underline the **topic sentence**.

2. Underline the three **reasons** that support the main point.

3. Circle the **transitions**.

4. What one of the Four Basics of Good Argument does the paragraph lack?
   the third basic

Argument Essay: Professional

We Must Stop the War on Medical Marijuana
Dr. Andrew Weil

Today, in dozens of cities and towns across the United States,   1
something remarkable happened: Thousands of people battling
cancer, AIDS, and other terrible illnesses, their families, friends, and
supporters delivered cease-and-desist orders to the federal Drug Enforcement Administration to stop it from blocking their access to a
needed medication.

Their request was so simple, so obviously correct, that it is heart-   2
breaking that people—many very seriously ill—were forced to deliver their message in this way, with many risking arrest. But as
individuals who have found that medical marijuana relieves their
symptoms when conventional medicines fail, they felt they had no
choice: The federal government continues to fight an irrational war
against medical marijuana, and the sick and struggling are its principal victims.

Make no mistake: The government's demonization of marijuana   3
is irrational. When I first published a study in the journal *Science*
on marijuana's physical and psychological effects back in 1968, I
was certain that medical use of the plant would be legal within five
years. This is, after all, a medicinal plant for which no fatal dose has
ever been established and that has been used in folk medicine for
millennia.

Like all medicines, marijuana has its drawbacks, particularly in   4
smoked form. It is not a panacea. I support research into safer delivery systems such as low-temperature vaporizers or inhalers, which
offer the fast action of inhaled medicine without the irritants found
in smoke. Still, I have seen in my own studies that marijuana is less
toxic than most pharmaceutical drugs in current use and is certainly
helpful for some patients, including those with wasting syndromes,
chronic muscle spasticity, and intractable nausea.

Unfortunately, the only legal substitute available now—a prescription pill containing a synthetic THC, marijuana's main psychoactive component—is not effective enough for many patients. I hear regularly from patients that the pill does not work as well as the natural herb and causes much greater intoxication.

5

I am far from alone in this view. The Institute of Medicine, in a report commissioned by the White House "drug czar," concluded in 1999 that there is convincing evidence of marijuana's value in relieving nausea, weight loss, and other symptoms caused by diseases such as AIDS, cancer, and multiple sclerosis, as well as by the harsh drugs often used to treat these conditions. The institute concluded that for some patients, the potential benefits clearly outweigh the risks, and that ways should be found to make marijuana available to them.

6   **IDENTIFY:** Underline the evidence presented in this paragraph.

As a physician, I am frustrated that I cannot prescribe marijuana for patients who might benefit from it. At the very least, I would like to be able to refer them to a safe, reliable, quality-controlled source.

7

But both the Clinton and Bush administrations have pursued a policy that the *New England Journal of Medicine* has called "misguided, heavy-handed, and inhumane." They have declined to act on the Institute of Medicine's recommendation and have conducted a series of raids on medical marijuana cooperatives operating legally under California law. Sick people are forced to turn to street sources or simply suffer without relief.

8

So it comes to this: Desperately ill people, their friends, families, and loved ones, standing outside DEA offices, pleading with their government not to deprive them of medicine that relieves their suffering. It should never have been necessary, and one can only hope that the administration and Congress will listen.

9

> —From the *Arizona Daily Star*, June 5, 2002. Andrew Weil is director
> of the Program in Integrative Medicine of the College of Medicine
> at the University of Arizona. He has written several books,
> including *Eight Weeks to Optimum Health* (Knopf, 1997).

CRITICAL THINKING: READING

■ **TIP:** For reading advice, see Chapter 1.

1. Double-underline the **thesis statement**.

2. Is the author a reliable authority on the use of medical marijuana?
   Yes, as indicated by the note at the end of the essay.

3. Weil does not consider the opposing view in this essay. What do you think that is? *People will abuse marijuana.*

4. Do you think that Weil's failure to consider the opposing view hurts his essay? Why or why not? *Answers will vary.*

5. The conclusion could use a strong final sentence. Write one.
Answers will vary.

CRITICAL THINKING: WRITING

Choose one of the following topics and respond in a paragraph or essay.

1. Argue for or against the use of medical marijuana. Your argument might be in the form of a letter to Dr. Weil.

2. Should doctors who believe that laws governing medical practice are wrong ignore those laws? (Consider, for example, laws against physician-assisted suicide or use of medicinal marijuana.) Why or why not?

3. Write a letter to your congressional representative supporting Weil.

4. Choose another medical issue (for example, physician-assisted suicide, human cloning, maintaining life support for brain-dead patients) and argue for or against it.

Write Your Own Argument

■ **TIP:** Look back at your idea-journal entry (p. 220) for ideas.

In this section, you will write your own argument paragraph or essay based on your (or your instructor's) choice among four assignments.

To complete your argument, follow this sequence:

1. Review the Four Basics of Good Argument (p. 220).

2. Choose your assignment.

3. If you are asked to complete Assignment 3, read Solving Problems, Appendix D.

4. Write your argument using the Checklist: How to Write Argument (pp. 234–36).

■ **ESL:** Some cultures (many Asian ones, for example) are not as direct as U.S. culture is. Emphasize to students that their positions must be clear, direct, and supported by evidence.

■ **ASSIGNMENT 1 WRITING ABOUT COLLEGE, WORK, AND EVERYDAY LIFE** . . . .

Write an argument paragraph or essay on one of the following topics.

COLLEGE

PARAGRAPH	ESSAY
• Take a position on a controversial issue on your campus.	• Take a position on the law that requires students to stay in school until they are sixteen.
• Argue that textbooks cost too much.	• Argue that student evaluations should/should not determine teachers' pay raises.
• Persuade your teacher to raise your grade.	• Argue for or against affirmative action in college admissions.

WORK

PARAGRAPH	ESSAY
• Take a position on a controversial issue in your workplace. • Persuade your boss to give you a raise. • Argue for a change at work.	• Persuade someone to buy your company's product or service. • Argue that "my e-mail is private." • Argue that a company policy isn't fair.

EVERYDAY LIFE

PARAGRAPH	ESSAY
• Take a position on a controversial issue in your community. • Argue for or against smoking restrictions. • Argue that something should be banned.	• Argue for or against a government spying on its citizens. • Argue for or against mandatory health insurance. • Take a position on any issue you feel strongly about.

ARGUMENT AT A GLANCE

Topic sentence (paragraph) or thesis statement (essay)
Includes the issue (topic) and your position on it

↓

Reason 1
Supporting examples, facts, examples, and expert opinions (with response to opposing views)

↓

Reason 2
Supporting examples, facts, examples, and expert opinions (with response to opposing views)

↓

Reason 3
Supporting examples, facts, examples, and expert opinions (with response to opposing views)

↓

Conclusion
Reminds readers of your position and makes a strong last attempt to convince them of that position, based on the reasons you have presented

■ **ASSIGNMENT 2   WRITING ABOUT IMAGES** . . . .

See the spoof (or joke) advertisement below. What does it mean? Agree or disagree with the message. As you think about your position, consider how you get news (for example, from *The Daily Show,* network television, or on-line) and whether it is reliable or distorted.

■ **ASSIGNMENT 3   WRITING IN THE REAL WORLD/SOLVING A PROBLEM**

PROBLEM: Your friend/child/relative has just turned sixteen and is planning to drop out of high school. He's always done poorly, and if he drops out he can increase his hours at the restaurant where he works. You think this is a terrible idea for many reasons.

   ASSIGNMENT: In a group or on your own, come up with various reasons in support of your decision. Consider, too, your friend's/child's/relative's possible objections to your argument, and account for those. Then, write an argument paragraph or essay to persuade him to complete high school. Give at least three solid reasons and support your reasons with good evidence or examples.

■ **TEACHING TIP:** Suggest to students that they make journal entries on some of the topics that they don't write about for this assignment.

■ **TEAMWORK:** For more detailed guidance on group work, see *Practical Suggestions.*

■ **TIP:** For more on timed writing, see Appendix A.

■ **ASSIGNMENT 4 WRITING ARGUMENT FOR A WRITING TEST** . . . . .

Many states and colleges require students to take a writing test. Often, the test calls for an argument paragraph or essay on an assigned topic, and students must argue for or against something, as directed. Many people believe that a good writer should be able to argue either side of an issue regardless of his or her personal feelings. Choose one of the following topics, come up with reasons and evidence to support both sides of the issue, and write a paragraph or an essay defending each side. If your instructor gives you a time limit, make sure to budget your time carefully: Allow enough time to decide on your position for each side, write a topic sentence (paragraph) or thesis statement (essay), and develop strong reasons and evidence to support your position.

■ **DISCUSSION:** Organize debates on some of these topics. Poll the class on the issues, divide students into groups to develop arguments, and suggest using the library to gather evidence. Devote a class period to the debates and a discussion of the effectiveness of the arguments.

1. People convicted of drunk driving should lose their license forever.

2. Recently a popular and well-respected high school teacher in Illinois was dismissed from his position because people found out that when he was a high-school student he had been charged with possession of marijuana (two joints). The law in the state says that no one convicted of any drug crime may serve as a teacher in a public school, so the principal had no choice but to dismiss the teacher despite his superb record of fifteen years of teaching. Argue for and against the law.

3. A conviction for first-degree murder should carry a mandatory death penalty.

4. The government should make it more difficult for couples to divorce.

5. College students should be penalized for poor attendance.

. . . .

CHECKLIST: HOW TO WRITE ARGUMENT	
STEPS	**HOW TO DO THE STEPS**
☐ **Focus.**	• Think about topics/issues that interest you.
☐ **Narrow and explore your topic.** See Chapter 3.	• Choose a particular issue that you care about. (If your topic has been assigned, think of an angle that interests you.) • Write down some ideas about the issue.
☐ **Write a topic sentence (paragraph) or a thesis statement (essay).** See Chapter 4.	• Build energy by thinking about how you are personally affected by the issue. • Write your topic sentence or thesis statement, including your position. • Rewrite the topic sentence or thesis statement to make it more definite and confident.

STEPS	HOW TO DO THE STEPS
☐ **Support your position.** See Chapter 5.	• Prewrite to come up with reasons and evidence. • Use facts, examples, and expert opinions. • Consider what your readers' position on the issue might be and what types of reasons and evidence will most likely convince them. • Consider opposing views and anticipate objections.
☐ **Make a plan.** See Chapter 6.	• Arrange the reasons in order of importance, saving the most important for last.
☐ **Write a draft.** See Chapter 7.	**FOR A PARAGRAPH** • Write a paragraph that includes a topic sentence, the reasons for your position, and supporting evidence. Use complete sentences. **FOR AN ESSAY** • Consider using one of the introduction types in Chapter 7. Include your thesis statement in your introduction. • Using your plan, write topic sentences for each of the reasons that support your position. • Write paragraphs with supporting evidence for each of the reasons.
☐ **Write a draft.** See Chapter 7.	**FOR PARAGRAPHS AND ESSAYS** • Write a conclusion that reminds readers of your position and makes a strong last attempt to convince them of that position, based on the reasons you have presented. • Write a title that previews your main point but doesn't repeat it.
☐ **Revise your draft, making at least four improvements.** See Chapter 8.	• Get feedback from others using the peer-review guide for argument at **bedfordstmartins.com/realwriting**. • Cut any reasons that don't directly support your position or that are weak. • Add reasons and evidence that help readers understand your position. Read your argument as if you hold the opposing view, and try to anticipate any criticisms. • Check to make sure the essay is organized by order of importance, with the most convincing reason presented last. • Add transitions to move readers from one point or subject to the next.
☐ **Edit your revised draft.** See Parts Four through Seven.	• Correct errors in grammar, spelling, word use, and punctuation.

continued

STEPS	HOW TO DO THE STEPS
☐ **Ask yourself:**	• Does my paper include the Four Basics of Good Argument (page 220)? • Is this the best I can do?

Chapter Review

1. Argument is writing _that takes a position on an issue and gives evidence to support it_ .

2. What are the Four Basics of Good Argument?

   It takes a strong and definite position.

   It gives good reasons and supporting evidence to defend the position.

   It considers opposing views.

   It has enthusiasm and energy from start to finish.

3. The topic sentence (paragraph) or thesis statement (essay) in an argument should include what two elements? _an issue and the writer's position on that issue_

4. What three types of information make good evidence? _facts, examples, expert opinions_

5. Why do you need to be aware of opposing views? _to anticipate attacks that may damage the strength of your argument_

6. Choose five of the vocabulary words on pages 229 or 230 and use each in a sentence.

■ **LEARNING JOURNAL:** Reread your idea-journal entry (p. 220) on why your friend should take a college course. Make another entry on this topic, using what you have learned about argument.

■ **RESOURCES:** All chapters in Part Two have writing check-lists, which are reproduced in *Additional Resources.* You can photocopy and distribute them if you want students to hand in the checklists with their assignments.

■ **RESOURCES:** Reproducible peer-review guides for differ-ent kinds of papers are avail-able in *Additional Resources.*

Part Three
Special College Writing Projects

18

Writing Summaries and Reports

Condensing Important Information

Write a Summary

A **summary** is a condensed, or shortened, version of a longer piece of writing, a conversation, or a situation. It presents the main ideas and major support, stripping down the information to its essential elements.

■■ FOUR BASICS OF A GOOD SUMMARY

1. It has a topic sentence (paragraph) or a thesis statement (essay) that states what is being summarized and its main idea.
2. It identifies the major support points.
3. It includes any final observations or recommendations made in the original piece.
4. It is written in your own words and presents information without your opinions.

1 The essay "Target and Wal-Mart: Not as Different as You Think" states that while Wal-Mart is often villainized and Target is welcomed, the two large chains are more similar than different. 2 The first similarity the author presents is the quality of the merchandise, which, she says, is perceived as poor at Wal-Mart and high at Target. However, there is no proof for this perception, she notes. The second similarity concerns the business practices of the two chains. While Wal-Mart is often criticized for its low pay, anti-union activities, and so on, Target is not blamed for its negative business practices. The author cites improvements Wal-Mart has made in its practices. The third similarity is the effect on local economies. Both chain stores can have a negative effect on small businesses, but Wal-Mart, not Target, is fought by local communities. The author gives examples of how Wal-Mart has helped local

■ **TIP:** The essay "Target and Wal-Mart: Not as Different as You Think" is on pages 198–199.

4 Summary is in the writer's own words

economies, while Target has not. **3** The author concludes by saying that Wal-Mart is singled out for bad publicity because of its large size. He wonders about other ways in which the media shapes people's views.

There are many uses for summarizing.

COLLEGE	A test question asks you to summarize a particular procedure or finding.
WORK	You write a summary of a telephone conversation to send to a client and your boss.
EVERYDAY LIFE	You summarize a car accident for your insurance company.

The Reading Process for Summaries

To write a summary, you must first understand it. The easiest way to prepare to write a summary is to note what's important as you read. You might follow this process:

READING TO SUMMARIZE

1. Double-underline the main point and write "main point" in the margin next to it.
2. Underline each major support point. This support may be a sentence or a group of sentences. For each major support point, write "major support" in the margin.
3. Underline the final observations, recommendations, or conclusions, and write "conclusion" in the margin.
4. After you finish reading, write a sentence or two, in your own words, about what's important about the piece.

NOTE: Instead of underlining, you could use two different-colored highlighters for steps 1 and 2.

Here is the paragraph from the Four Basics of a Good Summary, underlined and annotated using the steps of the reading process.

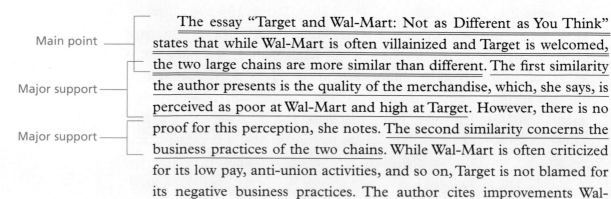

Main point

Major support

Major support

The essay "Target and Wal-Mart: Not as Different as You Think" states that while Wal-Mart is often villainized and Target is welcomed, the two large chains are more similar than different. The first similarity the author presents is the quality of the merchandise, which, she says, is perceived as poor at Wal-Mart and high at Target. However, there is no proof for this perception, she notes. The second similarity concerns the business practices of the two chains. While Wal-Mart is often criticized for its low pay, anti-union activities, and so on, Target is not blamed for its negative business practices. The author cites improvements Wal-

Mart has made in its practices. The third similarity is the effect on local economies. Both chain stores can have a negative effect on small businesses, but Wal-Mart, not Target, is fought by local communities. The author gives examples of how Wal-Mart has helped local economies, while Target has not. The author concludes by saying that Wal-Mart is singled out for bad publicity because of its large size. He wonders about other ways in which the media shapes people's views.

— Major support

— Conclusion

WHAT'S IMPORTANT: The writer argues that Wal-Mart is really no worse than Target, yet Wal-Mart has been criticized even as it has tried to improve its business practices.

 PRACTICE 1   READING TO SUMMARIZE . . . .

Read the following essay and mark it according to the four steps of reading to summarize.

In 2005, Judge Samuel Alito was nominated to the Supreme Court by President George W. Bush. Although Judge Alito was confirmed by Congress in January 2006, his confirmation hearings were marked by conflict as questioners tried to find out how he would rule on several controversial issues.

— Main point

One issue was how much power Alito thought a president should have. During the hearings, news broke that the government was listening in on the telephone conversations of U.S. citizens without seeking court approval. Many people believe that Bush had overstepped his authority in allowing this. Bush, on the other hand, defended both the practice and his authority to act without permission, citing the powers to fight terrorism extended to his office after September 11, 2001. Questioners reviewed Alito's past rulings, trying to predict how he would rule on domestic spying and future questions about executive powers.

— Major support

The most controversial issue was a woman's right to an abortion, which was upheld in 1973, in the landmark case *Roe v. Wade*. The country—and the Senate—was sharply divided between so-called pro-life and right-to-choose groups. After each day of rigorous questioning on Alito's opinion of *Roe v. Wade,* each group claimed that something he had said indicated his opinion and his likely ruling on future cases regarding abortion rights. Both supporters and opponents of Judge Alito

— Major support

spent millions of dollars on research, outreach, and advertisements to make their case.

Enduring times of brutal questioning and attacks that made his wife cry and leave the room, Alito remained calm. His responses to questions, while direct, never gave a true sense of how he might rule on controversial cases. The overall impression he created was that of an extremely intelligent, experienced, and guarded jurist. In the end, Judge Alito was confirmed to a lifetime Supreme Court seat on January 31, 2006, and no one can be sure how his rulings will influence the future of this country.

Conclusion

WHAT'S IMPORTANT: *Answers will vary but should indicate that Alito was confirmed despite tough questioning that didn't give any clues about how he might rule in Supreme Court cases.*

■ **PRACTICE 2   READING TO SUMMARIZE** . . . .

Read the textbook excerpt on page 214 and mark it according to the four steps of reading to summarize.

The Writing Process for Summaries

Use the following checklist to help you write summaries.

CHECKLIST: HOW TO WRITE A SUMMARY	
STEPS	**HOW TO DO THE STEPS**
☐ Focus.	• Think about why you are writing the summary and for whom. How much information will your audience need?
☐ Read the selection carefully.	• Underline the main idea, the major support, and the conclusion(s), noting each in the margin.
☐ Write a short statement about what you've read.	• In your own words, write what is important about the piece.
☐ Reread the sections you underlined and annotated, along with your written statement.	• Make additional notes or annotations.

STEPS	HOW TO DO THE STEPS
☐ **For an essay-length summary, make an outline.**	• Include a thesis statement with the name of what you are summarizing. • Arrange the support points in the order you will mention them.
☐ **Draft the summary.**	• Refer to the original piece, but use your own words. • Work in the points you have annotated, using your outline if you wrote one.
☐ **Revise the summary.**	• Read your draft, making sure it includes the main point and major support. • Add transitions to move readers smoothly from one point to another. • Make sure the summary is all in your own words.
☐ **Edit your work.**	• Check for errors in grammar, spelling, and punctuation. (See Parts Four through Seven of this book.)
☐ **Ask yourself:**	• Does my paper have the Four Basics of a Good Summary?

Summary Assignments

Choose one of the following assignments and complete it using the previous checklist.

- Using your notes from Practice 1, write a summary of the piece in Practice 1.
- Summarize a section of a textbook from one of your other courses.
- Summarize an editorial from a print or online magazine or newspaper.
- Summarize an entry from a blog that you have read.
- Summarize the plot of a movie or television program.
- Summarize one of the essays in Chapters 9–17 under "Read and Analyze."

Write a Report

A **report** usually begins with a short summary of a piece of writing, a conversation, or a situation. Then, it analyzes the information, providing reactions, opinions, or recommendations. Unlike a summary, a report often includes the writer's opinions.

■ **TIP:** Note that the present tense is used to describe the action in essays and literary works.

■■ FOUR BASICS OF A GOOD REPORT

1. It states the title and author of the piece in the first sentence or paragraph.

2. It summarizes the original piece, conversation, or event, including the main idea and major support points.

3. It then moves to the writer's reactions to the piece and reasons for those reactions.

4. It has a conclusion that usually includes a general comment from the writer. The writer may give an opinion (such as whether the piece is good or bad) or make a general observation.

NOTE: Reports often use specific passages or quotations from a piece. For more information on citing and documenting source material, see Chapter 19.

"A Brother's Murder": A Painful Story That's as True as Ever

1 In the essay "A Brother's Murder," Brent Staples writes about his younger brother, Blake, who took a very different path in life than Staples did. 2 The essay starts with a phone call in which Staples learns that Blake has been murdered, shot six times by a former friend (517). The essay goes on to tell about the conditions in which Blake grew up. The neighborhood in which the brothers lived was violent, and young men grew into dangerous adults. Staples recalls a conversation he overheard there between two Vietnam veterans, in which one of them said how much he preferred to fight with young men from the inner city, who wear "their manhood on their sleeves." They weren't afraid to fight, believing that violence proved they were *real* men (518).

The author leaves the neighborhood to go to college, and he never returns. Blake, however, stays, and the author recalls a visit home when he sees that his brother has been transformed and now hangs out with drug dealers and gangs (518). When Staples notices a wound on his brother's hand, Blake shrugs it off as "kickback from a shotgun" (519). The author wants to help his brother and makes a date to see him the next night (519). Blake does not show up, and the author returns to Chicago, where he lives. Sometime later, he gets the phone call that announces Blake's death and regrets that he had not done something to help his brother.

3 "A Brother's Murder" is a moving and sad story about how men growing up in the inner city are destroyed. Although the essay was written in 1986, its message is at least as true today as it was more than twenty years ago. Staples shows how his brother is sucked into the routine violence of the streets, shooting and being shot because that is what he knows, and that is how a man shows he is a man.

Main point

Direct reference

Summary with major support/events

Direct reference

4 Today, thousands of young men live this life and die before they are thirty. This essay makes me wonder why this continues, but it also makes me wonder how two brothers could go such different ways. What happened to save Brent Staples? Could he have saved Blake? What can we do to stop the violence? "A Brother's Murder" is an excellent and thought-provoking essay about a very dangerous and growing societal problem.

Writer's reaction in conclusion

Works Cited

Staples, Brent. "A Brother's Murder." *Outlooks and Insights: A Reader for College Writers*. Ed. Paul Eschholz and Alfred Rosa. 4th ed. Bedford/ St. Martin's, Boston: 1995.

You may need to write a report in a number of situations:

COLLEGE	You are assigned to write a book report.
WORK	You have to write a report on a patient's condition. You are asked to report on a product or service your company is considering.
EVERYDAY LIFE	You write an e-mail to a friend describing the key events in a movie.

The Reading Process for Reports

Reading to write a report is like reading to write a summary except that in the last step you write your response to the piece instead of just noting what's important about it.

READING TO REPORT

1. Double-underline the main point and write "main point" in the margin next to it.
2. Underline each major support point. This support may be a sentence or a group of sentences. For each major support, write "major support" in the margin.
3. Underline the final observations, recommendations, or conclusions, and write "conclusion" in the margin.
4. After you finish reading, write a sentence or two, in your own words, about how you responded to the piece and why.

NOTE: Instead of underlining, you could use two different-colored highlighters for steps 1 and 2.

■   **PRACTICE 3   READING TO REPORT** . . . .

Read the essay "Blood Type and Personality" on page 171. Or, if you are using the version of this book with readings, read the essay "Supersize It" in Chapter 43. Then, mark whichever essay you select according to the four steps of reading to report.

The Writing Process for Reports

Use the following checklist to help you write reports.

CHECKLIST: HOW TO WRITE A REPORT	
STEPS	**HOW TO DO THE STEPS**
☐ **Focus.**	• Think about why you are writing the report and for whom. What do you think of the piece, and how can you get that view across to readers?
☐ **Read the selection carefully.**	• Underline the main idea, the major support, and the conclusion(s), noting each in the margin.
☐ **Write a short statement about what you've read.**	• In your own words, write your reactions to the piece and reasons for those reactions.
☐ **Reread your underlinings, marginal notes, and reactions.**	• Make additional notes, and look for specific statements from the piece you might use in your report.
☐ **For an essay-length report, make an outline.**	• Include a thesis statement with the name of what you are reporting on. • Arrange the support points in the order you will mention them. • Put your reactions last.
☐ **Draft the report.**	• Refer to the original piece, but use your own words. • Start with a summary, and make sure you include the major support points. • Work from your outline if you wrote one, and make sure to include your reactions.
☐ **Revise the report.**	• Read your draft, making sure it includes the main point and major support. • Make sure that your response is clear and that you give reasons for your response. • Add transitions to move readers smoothly from one point to another.

STEPS	HOW TO DO THE STEPS
☐ **Revise the report.**	• Make sure the report (aside from quotations) is all in your own words.
☐ **Edit your work.**	• Check for errors in grammar, spelling, and punctuation. (See Parts Four through Seven of this book.)
☐ **Ask yourself:**	• Does my paper have the Four Basics of a Good Report?

Report Assignments

Choose one of the following assignments and complete it using the previous checklist.

- Using your notes from Practice 3, write a report on the piece in Practice 3.
- Report on a movie or a concert you have seen recently.
- Report on an event in your community.
- Report on an article in a print or online magazine or news source.
- Report on another essay in this book, either from Chapters 9–17 or Chapters 41–51 (if you are using the version of this book with readings).
- Report on a class or an exam.

Chapter Review

1. How is a summary different from a report? _A summary is objective, while a report includes the writer's responses._

2. What are the Four Basics of a Good Summary?
   1. _It has a topic sentence (paragraph) or a thesis statement (essay) that states what is being summarized and its main idea._
   2. _It identifies the major support points._
   3. _It includes any final observations or recommendations made in the original piece._
   4. _It is written in your own words and presents information without your opinions._

3. What is different about the Four Basics of a Good Report? _The fourth basic calls for the writer's opinion/ response._

You Know This

You have done research
and reported on it:

- You go online to find information about some-
  thing you want to do
  or buy.
- You ask a coworker
  about how to do a
  certain job, and you
  take notes.

19

Writing the Research Essay

Using Outside Sources in Your Writing

In all areas of your life, doing research makes you better informed and strengthens any point you want to make. In college, you will need to use outside sources to write papers in many different courses. Here are some situations in which you might use research skills:

COLLEGE	In a criminal justice course, you are asked to write about whether the death penalty deters crime.
WORK	You are asked to do some research about a major office product (such as a phone or computer system) that your company wants to purchase.
EVERYDAY LIFE	Your child's doctor has prescribed a certain medication, and you want information about it.

This chapter will explain the major steps of writing a college research essay: how to make a schedule; choose a topic and guiding research question; and find, evaluate, and document sources. A checklist guides you through the process of writing a research essay.

Make a Schedule

Writing a college research essay takes time: It cannot be started and finished in a day or two. To make sure you allow enough time, make a schedule, and stick to it.

You can use the following schedule as a model for making your own.

SAMPLE RESEARCH ESSAY SCHEDULE

Assignment: (Write out what your instructor has assigned.) _____

_____

Number of outside sources required: _____

Length (if specified): _____

Draft due date: _____

Final due date: _____

My general topic: _____

My narrowed topic: _____

STEP	DO BY
Choose a topic.	_____
Find and evaluate sources; decide which ones to use.	_____
Take notes, keeping publication information for each source.	_____
Write a working thesis statement by answering a research question.	_____
Review all notes; choose the best support for your working thesis.	_____
Make an outline that includes your thesis and support.	_____
Write a draft, including a title.	_____
Review the draft; get feedback; add more support if needed.	_____
Revise the draft.	_____
Prepare a list of works cited using correct documentation form.	_____
Edit the revised draft.	_____
Submit the final copy.	_____

Choose a Topic

Your instructor may assign a topic or want you to think of your own topic for a research paper assignment. If you are free to choose your own topic, find a subject that you are personally interested in or curious about. Ask yourself some questions like the following.

1. What is going on in my own life that I want to know more about?

2. What do I daydream about? What frightens me? What do I see as a threat to me or my family? What inspires or encourages me?

3. What am I interested in doing in the future, either personally or professionally, that I could investigate?

4. What famous person or people interest me?

5. What current issue do I care about?

■ **TEACHING TIP:** Have students write an "I-search" paper—a proposal in which they report on what they are interested in learning and explain why they are interested in it. In the I-search papers, have students tell you what they know about their topics already and the specific questions they want answers to.

■ **TEACHING TIP:** Have students choose three of these topics to write about in their journals.

Here are some current topics that you might want to research.

Abortion laws	Obesity in the United States
Affirmative action	Online dating services
Antiterrorism measures	Privacy and the Internet
Assisted suicide	Road rage
Behavior disorders	School issues: home schooling, charter schools, school choice, school funding
Environmental issues: pollution, global warming, auto emissions	
Gay/lesbian marriage	Stem-cell research
Government wiretapping of U.S. citizens	Stolen identities
	Travel: good deals, cruises, places
Health issues	
Medical issues	Violence in the media
Music/musical groups	Volunteer opportunities

When you have an idea for a general topic, write answers to these questions.

1. Why is this topic important to me or of interest to me? How does it affect me? What do I hope to gain by exploring it?
2. What do I know about the topic? What do I want to find out?

Although a research essay may be a bit longer than some of the other essays you have written, the topic still needs to be narrow enough to write about in the assigned length. For more on narrowing your topic, see Chapter 3.

Before writing a working thesis statement, you need to learn more about your topic. It helps to come up with a **guiding research question** about your narrowed topic. This question—often a variation of "What do I want to find out?"—will help to guide and focus your research. Following is one student's research question.

> **MARCUS SHANKS'S GUIDING RESEARCH QUESTION:** Marcus chose the topic of the mandatory registration of sex offenders. He asked this guiding research question: **Should registration of sex offenders be mandatory?**

Find Sources

With both libraries and the Internet available to you, finding information is not a problem. Knowing how to find good, reliable sources of information, however, can be a challenge. The following strategies will help you.

Consult a Reference Librarian

The Internet does not reduce the need for reference librarians, who are essential resources in helping to find appropriate information in both print and electronic forms. In fact, with all of the information available to you, librarians are a more important resource than ever, saving you time and possible frustration in your search for relevant material.

If your library allows, schedule an appointment with a librarian. Before your appointment, write down some questions to ask, such as the following. Begin your conversation by telling the librarian your research topic.

QUESTIONS FOR THE LIBRARIAN

- How do I use an online catalog or a card catalog? What information will the library's catalog give me?
- Can I access the library catalog and article databases from home or other locations?
- What other reference tools would you recommend as a good starting place for research on my topic?
- Once I identify a source that might be useful, how do I find it?
- Can you recommend an Internet search engine that will help me find information on my topic? Can you also recommend some useful key words?
- How can I tell whether a Web site is reliable?
- I've already found some articles related to my topic. Can you suggest some other places to look for sources?

Use the Online Catalog or Card Catalog

Most libraries now list their holdings online rather than in a card catalog, but both systems give the same information: titles, authors, subjects, publication data, and call numbers. If you are working with a librarian, he or she may offer step-by-step instructions for using the online catalog. If you are working on your own, the online catalog help is usually easy to find (generally on the screen or in a Help menu) and easy to follow. Catalogs allow you to search by author, title, subject, or key word. If you are just beginning your research, you will probably use the keyword search because you may not know specific authors or titles.

Marcus Shanks, who wrote a research essay on mandatory registration of sex offenders (see the excerpt on pages 268–69), searched his library's online catalog using the key words *sex offender registration*. Here is one source he found:

Author:	Illinois State Police
Title:	A Guide to Sex Offender Registration and Community Notification in Illinois.
Published:	Springfield: Illinois State Police, ©1997
Location:	State Library Stacks

■ **TEACHING TIP:** If the library offers group training on library resources, schedule such a session for the class since many students will have the same questions.

■ **RESOURCES:** For reproducible research handouts, see *Additional Resources.*

■ **TIP:** For more on conducting keyword searches, see page 254.

Call #:   HQ72.U53 G843 1997

Status: Available

Description: 1 v.; 28 cm.

Contents: History of sex offender registration in Illinois, 730 ILCS
              150 — Qualifying sex offenses — Court/probation —
              Illinois Department of Corrections facility or other
              penal institution — Penalty for failure to register —
              Access to sex offender registration records.

OCLC #:   ocm40706307

A call number is a book's identification number. Knowing the call number will help you to locate a source in the library. Once you do locate the source, browse the nearby shelves. Since a library's holdings are organized by subject, you may find other sources related to your topic.

If the book is available only at another library, you can ask a librarian to have the book sent to your library.

Look at Your Library's Web Site

Many libraries have Web sites that can help researchers find useful information. The home page may have links to electronic research sources that the library subscribes to and that are free to library users. It will also list the library's hours and resources, and it may offer research tips and other valuable information. It is a good idea to save the Web site's address for future use.

Use Other Reference Materials

The reference section of the library has many resources that will help you find information on your topic. Here is a sampling of common reference sources. Most are available online or on CD-ROM.

Periodical Indexes and Databases

Magazines, journals, and newspapers are called *periodicals*. Periodical indexes help you locate information published in these sources. Online periodical indexes are called *periodical databases* and often include the full text of magazine, journal, or newspaper articles. Here are some of the most popular periodical indexes and databases:

- *InfoTrac*
- *LexisNexis*
- *NewsBank*
- *New York Times Index*
- *ProQuest*
- *Readers' Guide to Periodical Literature*

Encyclopedias

Encyclopedias can give you an overview of a subject, although most instructors will want you to use more specialized sources such as those listed previously. You might also consult the bibliographies of other useful sources that conclude most encyclopedia entries. Some encyclopedias, like the *Encyclopedia Britannica,* are available in print, online, and on CD-ROM.

In addition to general encyclopedias, your library may have specialized encyclopedias that give more detailed information on your topic. For instance, you might consult the *Encyclopedia of Psychology* for a research paper in a psychology course.

■ **TEAMWORK:** Send groups of students on a collaborative research trip to the library, asking each group to find and report to the rest of the class on one of the reference sources listed here. (First make sure that the library has these sources.) Students should be able to explain how the source they reported on could be relevant to their classmates' research projects.

Statistical Sources

Statistical data, or facts and figures, that are directly related to your research question can provide sound support. As one example, the *Statistical Abstract of the United States* (published annually by the U.S. Census Bureau) can help you locate useful statistics related to social issues, population trends, economics, and other topics. Visit **<www.census.gov>**, the official Web site of the U.S. Census Bureau, for current state and national statistical data related to population, economics, and geography.

Use the Internet

The Internet provides access to all kinds of information. The biggest part of the Internet is called the World Wide Web, which allows users to jump from site to site using links. If the Web seems overwhelming to you, this section will offer some basics on finding what you need. You might also want to work with a librarian, a writing-center tutor, or a knowledgeable friend to help you navigate the Web. To get started, you can go to some sites that categorize information on the Web, such as the Internet Public Library **<www.ipl.org>** or the Librarians' Internet Index **<lii.org>**.

NOTE: Some Internet sites charge fees for information (such as archived newspaper or magazine articles). Before using any of these, check to see if the sources are available free through your library's database.

Uniform Resource Locator (URL)

Every Web site has an address, called a uniform resource locator (URL). You may already be familiar with some frequently advertised URLs, such as **<www.amazon.com>** (the Internet address for bookseller Amazon.com) or the URL for your college's Web site. If you know the URL of a Web site that you think would be helpful, enter it into the address field of your Web browser. (Web browsers, like Microsoft Internet Explorer, Firefox, and Netscape Navigator, are software programs that allow a computer to read Web pages.) If you do not know the URL of a particular site you want to visit, or if you want to look at multiple Web sites related to your topic, you will need to use a search engine.

Search Engines and Searching with Key Words

■ **TEACHING TIP:** Ask students to test three different search engines by typing in key words related to their research paper. Which search engine seemed most effective for their research needs? Why?

Of the following commonly used search engines, Google is the most popular:

- AltaVista **<www.altavista.com>**
- Ask Jeeves **<www.askjeeves.com>**
- Excite **<www.excite.com>**
- Google **<www.google.com>**
- HotBot **<www.hotbot.com>**
- Lycos **<www.lycos.com>**
- Yahoo! **<www.yahoo.com>**

To use a search engine, type in key words from your subject. Because the Web is so large (Google searches more than 4 billion pages), adding more specific key words or phrases and using an Advanced Search option may narrow the number of entries (called *hits*) you have to sift through to find relevant information. Also, search engines typically have a Help feature that offers guidance in using the engine, selecting key words, and refining your search. Adding additional search terms can narrow a search even more.

When you discover a Web site that you might want to return to, save the URL so that you don't have to remember it each time you want to go to the site. Different browsers have different ways of saving URLs; use the Bookmarks menu in Netscape or Firefox, or the Favorites menu in Microsoft Internet Explorer.

Online Research Sites

Online research sites are another valuable source of information on how to do research. For example, the publisher of this book hosts The Bedford Research Room (at **bedfordstmartins.com/researchroom**), which includes guided tutorials on research processes; advice on finding, evaluating, and documenting sources; tips on avoiding plagiarism; and more.

Other useful sites include:

- **Citing Electronic Sources** (from the Internet Public Library) at **<www.ipl.org/div/farq/netciteFARQ.html>**. This site contains links to various sources that explain how to document information found online.
- **Evaluating Web sites** (from the Ohio State University) at **<gateway .lib.ohio-state.edu/tutor/les1/>**. This site gives tips on finding and evaluating Internet sources.
- **OWL** (from Purdue University) at **<owl.english.purdue.edu>**. This site offers a variety of materials and resources for writers, including research information.

Interview People

Personal interviews can be excellent sources of information. Before interviewing anyone, however, plan carefully. First, consider what kind of person to interview. Do you want information from an expert on the subject, or from someone directly affected by the issue? The person should be knowledgeable about the subject and have firsthand experience. When you have decided whom to interview, schedule an appointment.

Next, to get ready for the interview, prepare a list of five to ten questions. Ask more open-ended questions (What do you think of the proposal to build a new library?) than closed ones that require only a simple "yes" or "no" response (Are you in favor of building a new library?). Leave space for notes about the person's responses and for additional questions that may occur to you during the interview. Include the person's full name and qualifications and the date of the interview in your research notes.

As you conduct the interview, listen carefully and write down any important ideas. If you plan to use any of the person's exact words, put them in quotation marks in your notes. Doing so will help you remember if your notes are the exact words of the person you interviewed, your interpretation of something he or she said, or a thought you had during the interview. For more on using direct quotations, see page 263 of this chapter and Chapter 38.

NOTE: Recording what a person says without asking is unethical and, in some states, against the law. If you plan to record an interview, get your subject's permission first.

■ **TEAMWORK:** Have students interview each other on their research topics. They can write a short summary of the interview using both direct quotations and paraphrases.

Evaluate Sources

Evaluating sources means judging them to determine how reliable and appropriate for your topic they are. Reliable sources present accurate, up-to-date information written by authors with appropriate credentials for the subject matter. Reliable sources support claims with evidence and use objective, reasonable language. Research materials found in a college library (books, journals, and newspapers, for example) are generally considered reliable sources.

Don't assume that an Internet source is reliable just because it exists online; anyone can create a Web site and put whatever he or she wants on it. If you are searching the Web for information about drugs for migraine headaches, for example, you will find a range of sources. These include reliable ones, such as an article published by the *Journal of the American Medical Association* or a report by faculty at Johns Hopkins University, and questionable ones sponsored by manufacturers of migraine drugs. Whether you are doing research for a college course, a work assignment, or personal reasons, make sure that the sources you use are reliable and appropriate for your purpose.

When you're viewing a Web site, try to determine its purpose. A Web site set up solely to provide information might be more reliable than an online product advertisement. A keyword search on "how to lose weight," for example, would point a researcher to thousands of sites; the two shown

Site sponsored by the makers of Hoodia Maxx to promote the product

No names are supplied. Quotes on the right seem to imply celebrity use, but there are no actual endorsements.

Unrealistic claims

above and on page 257 are just samples. Which do you think contains more reliable information?

Here are some questions you can ask to evaluate a source. If you answer "no" to any of these questions, think twice about using the source.

■ **TIP:** For more information on evaluating sources, visit **bedfordstmartins.com/researchroom**.

■ **TEACHING TIP:** Evaluating Internet sources is difficult for students. Have them apply these questions to an article or Web site printout that you (or they) bring to class. Decide as a class whether the source is reliable.

QUESTIONS FOR EVALUATING A PRINT OR ELECTRONIC SOURCE

- Is the source reliable? Is it from a well-known magazine or publisher or from a reputable Web site? (For Web sites, also consider the URL extension; see the box on page 257 for guidance.)
- Is the information appropriate for your research topic?
- Is the author qualified to write reliably about the subject? If there is no biographical information, try an online search using the author's name.
- Who sponsored the publication or Web site? Be aware of the sponsor's motives (for example, to market a product) and how they might affect the type of information presented.
- Does the information seem fair and objective? If there is a bias, does the author state his or her position up front?
- Does the author provide adequate support for key points, and does he or she cite the sources of this support?

Guide to URL Extensions

EXTENSION	TYPE OF SITE	HOW RELIABLE?
.com	A commercial, or business, organization	Varies. Consider whether you have heard of the organization, and be sure to read its home page or "About us" link carefully.
.edu	An educational institution	Reliable, but may include materials of varying quality.
.gov	A government agency	Reliable.
.net	A commercial or business organization, or a personal site	Varies. This extension indicates just the provider, not anything about the source. Go to the source's home page to find out what you can about the author or the sponsor.
.org	A nonprofit organization	Generally reliable, although each volunteer or professional group promotes its own view or interests.

Avoid Plagiarism

■ **ESL:** In some cultures, copying someone else's work is a gesture of respect. Be very clear with students about what constitutes plagiarism.

Plagiarism is passing off someone else's ideas and information as your own. Turning in a paper written by someone else, whether it is from the Internet or written by a friend or family member who gives you permission, is deliberate plagiarism. Sometimes, however, students plagiarize by mistake because the notes they have taken do not indicate which ideas are theirs and which were taken from outside sources. As you find information for your research essay, do not rely on your memory to recall details about your sources; take good notes from the start.

NOTE: This section's advice on recording source information, and on citing and documenting sources, reflects Modern Language Association (MLA) style, the preferred style for English classes and other humanities courses.

Keep a Running Bibliography

■ **TEACHING TIP:** Have students practice citing and documenting sources throughout the semester. For example, if they write summaries of readings from this textbook, articles, or Web sites, ask them to use in-text citations and to include a list of Works Cited at the end of each summary.

■ **TEACHING TIP:** Ask students to bring in a draft bibliography after they have gathered their sources but before they have finished writing the research paper. This will allow you to make sure they have enough good sources with the right publication information.

A **bibliography** is a complete list, alphabetized by author, of the outside sources you consult. A **Works Cited** list is a complete list, alphabetized by author, of the outside sources that you actually use in your essay. Most instructors require a list of Works Cited at the end of a research essay. Some may require a bibliography as well.

You can keep information for your bibliography and Works Cited list on notecards or on your computer. Whatever method you use, be sure to record complete publication information for each source at the time you consult it, even if you are not sure you will use it; this will save you from having to look up this information again when you are preparing your list of Works Cited.

Following is a list of information to record for each source. For Marcus Shanks's Works Cited list, see page 269.

BOOKS	ARTICLES	WEB SITES
Author name(s)	Author name(s)	Author name(s) (if any)
Title and subtitle	Title of article and page number(s)	Title of page or site
Year of publication	Title of magazine, journal, or newspaper	Date of publication or latest update (if available)
Publisher and location of publisher	Year, month, day of publication (2006 Jan. 4)	Name of sponsoring organization
		Date on which you accessed the source
		URL (online address) in angle brackets (</>)

You will probably integrate source material by summary, paraphrase, and direct quotation. As you take notes, record which method you are using so you don't accidentally plagiarize.

The chart on page 260 explains each method, describes its typical use, and shows how a single source was summarized, paraphrased, and quoted to support a thesis. Note how the writer cites the source in each case; full publication information for the source is provided in a Works Cited entry. Note also how the writer clearly connects the source information to the thesis. Following are tips for summarizing, paraphrasing, and using direct quotations.

Indirect Quotation: Summary

Be careful if you choose to summarize (or paraphrase). It is easy to think you are using your own words when you are actually using only some of your own and some of the author's or speaker's. When you summarize, follow these guidelines:

- Don't look at the source while you are writing the summary.
- Check your summary against the original source to make sure you have not used the author's words or copied the author's sentence structure.
- Make sure to introduce the outside source when it's first mentioned — for example, "In an article in *Psychological Bulletin,* Lita Furby stated that sex offenders are more likely . . ."
- Include in parentheses the page number(s), if available, of the entire section you have summarized. (You will need to provide full publication information later, in the Works Cited list.)

SUMMARY OF AN ARTICLE

In their article in *Psychological Bulletin* titled "Sex Offender Recidivism[1]: A Review," Lita Furby, Mark Weinrott, and Lyn Blackshaw present data on the repeat offenses of sex offenders (3–4). They collected data from all fifty states, documenting the type of offense, type of punishment, whether upon release the sex offender returned to the same area or a new one, how many offenders repeated a sexual crime, the time lapsed between the first crime and the next one, and whether the nature of the repeat crime episode was similar or different from the first. They also compared the repeat rate of sex-offender crime with the rate of other types of crime. While the authors report that fewer than half of all convicted sex offenders repeat their crimes, they note that the rate is higher than most kinds of crime and that methods of tracking the whereabouts of sex offenders are essential to curb recidivism.

— Identifying information

— Page reference

■ **TIP:** For more on writing summaries, see Chapter 18.

---

[1] **recidivism:** repeating of crimes.

Student Thesis: While many people experience unfair treatment, few know how to complain in such a way that they get satisfaction.

Indirect Quotation: Summary: A condensed (shortened) form of a piece of writing that presents only the main points in your own words.

- **TYPICAL USE:** Use indirect quotations to briefly note major evidence from a source that supports your thesis.

- **WHAT TO FOCUS ON IN YOUR SOURCE:** Focus on the major points that support your thesis—in this case, how complicated complaining can be. See the blue highlighting in the facing article.

- **EXAMPLE:** The student's own thoughts—the "glue" connecting the source information to the thesis—is in blue.

  Recognizing the difficulty of complaining effectively, *Consumer Reports* presented experts with some common situations and asked them how consumers might get satisfaction (6).

Indirect Quotation: Paraphrase: A restatement of someone else's ideas in your own words. A paraphrase has more of the original ideas from a passage than a summary does.

- **TYPICAL USE:** In contrast to a summary, a paraphrase focuses more on particular details that show some aspect of the issue—for example, why retail stores have tightened up on return policies.

- **WHAT TO FOCUS ON IN YOUR SOURCE:** Focus on details that give specific reasons, examples, and other evidence. The example below focuses on the yellow paragraph in the facing article.

- **EXAMPLE:** Again, the student's own words glue the paraphrase to the thesis. These words are in blue.

Retail stores are much less likely than in the past to accept returns, especially of expensive technology products. According to Joseph Beaulieu, a retail analyst, stores have stricter return policies because some people buy items, such as videocams, use them, and then return them (*Consumer Reports* 6).

Direct Quotation: Exact words from a source. Put these in quotation marks (" ").

- **TYPICAL USE:** Quotations are used when the original author's or speaker's words offer particularly strong support for the thesis.

- **WHAT TO FOCUS ON IN YOUR SOURCE:** Look for a sentence or two that offer strong direct support for your thesis. See the green section of the facing article.

- **EXAMPLE:** Again, note the student's own connecting words, which are in blue.

  Effective complaining may require persistence as well as technique, according to Lynn Dralle, an author and expert complainer. Dralle says if at first you don't get satisfaction, try another branch of the same store. "You may find a manager who's more sympathetic" (*Consumer Reports* 6).

Works Cited Entry: When you summarize, paraphrase, or quote, you need to give publication information at the end of your paper for all sources you have cited. Here's the MLA-style Works Cited entry for the facing article.

Title   Publication/author   Date

"The New Art of Complaining." <u>Consumer Reports</u> Mar. 2006: 6-7.——— Page numbers

The new art of complaining

How to take your complaints to the next level and get fast results.

Your steak was cold. Your flight sat on the tarmac for two hours. Your credit-card payment was one day late, and you got dinged with a $39 fee.

You'll want to vent your spleen. But it's not always so easy to get results these days. With more companies outsourcing their customer-service department overseas and installing endless phone trees, the distance between you and the people with the power to solve your problems continues to grow. And even if you find a sympathetic ear, it can be harder to get satisfaction.

It's no wonder that many consumers are too intimidated or irritated to try. Complicating matters further is the fact that the most effective strategy will vary with the situation: What works with a department store won't necessarily work with a telemarketer. To arm you for the new consumer battlefield, we described five common scenarios to industry experts and consumer advocates and asked how they'd handle each situation. (See "What Works, What Doesn't," on the facing page.)

▶ **Your flight was late, and you missed your connection.** On time performance by U.S. airlines worsened slightly last year, with nearly one in five flights pulling into the gate late, according to the U.S. Department of Transportation. If you're aboard one of those unfortunate laggards, be aware that legally, the airline doesn't owe you a thing, even if mechanical problems caused the delay.

You might be tempted to hotfoot it to a hotel and make your flight arrangements by phone. Don't. "Talk to a person at the airport, not to a nameless, faceless reservations agent who can fabricate a confirmation number to get you off the call," says Terry Trippler, an airline-industry expert for CheapSeats.com.

Go directly to a customer-service agent at any open counter serving your airline. Ask to be rebooked on the next available flight, and make sure you're not on standby. Get a confirmation number. Not happy with what you're offered? Request a flight on another carrier with which the airline has a ticketing agreement.

If you end up getting stuck overnight, the airline has no legal obligation to pay for your lodging, taxi fare, or incidental expenses. Ask for them anyway. Trippler suggests saying, "You got me here late, and now I have to stay overnight. I followed your rules, got to the airport on time, and now I'm stranded."

If you can't get a voucher for a hotel stay, ask to get the airline's discounted hotel rate. (And when you finally get home, fire off a letter to the airline's consumer-affairs department. Include the date, flight number and time, name of the agent who "helped" you, and the reason for your continued dissatisfaction. You might get a check, frequent-flyer miles, or free tickets. Of course, if the airline is financially in the hole, you might get a letter thanking you for your comments.

▶ **The product isn't working as promised, and the store won't take it back.** Stores are getting more restrictive about returns in certain product categories, according to Joseph Beaulieu, a retail analyst with Morningstar, the Chicago publisher of financial information. For example, video and digital cameras may have smaller return windows than other

products because unscrupulous consumers buy them, use them to record special events, and then return them, he says.

But if you have a legitimate return that falls outside a store's parameters, you should know your rights. In one incident we recently witnessed at an office-supply store, a customer tried to return a personal-digital assistant (PDA) that a salesclerk had assured her would work with her Internet provider. When the customer discovered that it didn't, the store refused to refund her money, pointing to a statement on the back of the receipt specifying that open PDAs could not be returned.

If the customer had known about the "implied warranty of fitness for a particular purpose," she would have had a leg to stand on. Its point: If you rely on a salesperson's judgment that a product suits your needs for a certain task, you can return the item if it falls short. The "implied warranty of merchantability" says that the goods sold will do what they're supposed to do and that there's nothing significantly wrong with them. Web sites often disclaim those and similar laws, but retailers rarely do, and in some states such as Connecticut the disclaimers are illegal.

How does this help when you're butting heads with a store manager? Simply uttering "implied warranty of fitness" may send the message that you're not to be messed with, and you get what you want.

If that doesn't work, try returning the item to a different branch. "You may find a manager who's more sympathetic," says Lynn Dralle, a self-proclaimed champion complainer and author of "The 100 Best Things I've Sold on eBay" (All Aboard Inc., 2003). Call first and say that you're a steady customer who wants to make a return. "It's better than catching the manager off guard in the middle of the sales floor," she says.

ILLUSTRATION BY BOB ECKSTEIN

COMPLAINTS

Indirect Quotation: Paraphrase

To paraphrase responsibly, use these guidelines:

- Don't look at the source as you write the paraphrase.
- Check your paraphrase against the original source to make sure you have not used too many of the author's words or copied the author's sentence structure.
- Make sure to introduce the outside source—for example, "District Attorney Joseph P. Conti stated that . . ."
- Include in parentheses the page number, if available, of the section you have paraphrased.

Following are examples of unacceptable and acceptable paraphrases.

ORIGINAL SOURCE

Reliance on measures of repeat crimes as reflected through official criminal justice system data obviously omits offenses that are not cleared through an arrest or those that are never reported to the police. This distinction is critical in the measurement of the frequency of repeated crimes among sex offenders. For a variety of reasons, sexual assault is a vastly underreported crime. The National Crime Victimization Survey (Bureau of Justice Statistics) conducted in 2000 indicates that only 32 percent (one out of three) of sexual assaults against persons 12 or older are reported to law enforcement. No current studies indicate the rate of reporting for child sexual assault, although it is generally assumed that these assaults are equally underreported. Many victims are afraid to report sexual assault to the police. They may fear that reporting will lead to further trauma.

—Center for Sex Offender Management (CSOM), "Recidivism of Sex Offenders," May 2001

UNACCEPTABLE PARAPHRASE, TOO CLOSE TO ORIGINAL

Relying on reports of repeated crimes based on the official police data clearly don't show unreported offenses. In the case of sex offenders, this is an important distinction because sexual assault is often not reported. A survey by the Bureau of Justice Statistics in 2000 showed that only 32 percent of victims of sexual assault aged 12 or over report the crime. It is likely that assaults on children also are underreported for fear of more stress on the child.

This paraphrase is unacceptable for several reasons:

- The first sentence uses the same structure and some of the same words as the first sentence of the original.
- The paraphrase too closely follows the sentences and ideas of the original source.

- The writer hasn't included the page numbers of the source.
- The writer has obviously written the paraphrase while looking at the original source rather than expressing the ideas in his or her own words.

ACCEPTABLE PARAPHRASE

The Center for Sex Offender Management cautions that using po- — Identifying phrase
lice data to assess the rate of repeated sex offenses may not be accurate
because many sexual assaults go unreported (CSOM 3-4). The report — Publication and page reference
cites the National Crime Victimization Survey (2000), which found that
32 percent of sexual assaults on adolescents and adults are not reported,
and assaults on children probably have a similar percentage of unreported crimes.

The acceptable paraphrase presents the basic ideas, but in the writer's own words and structures. It also includes a parenthetical reference. The writer carefully read the original paragraph but then wrote the paraphrase without looking at the original. Then, the writer checked the original again to make sure he hadn't missed any ideas or repeated words or sentence structures.

Direct Quotation

Use these guidelines when you write direct quotations:

- Record the exact words of the source.
- Include the name of the writer or speaker. If there is more than one author or speaker, record all names.
- Enclose the writer's or speaker's words in quotation marks.
- For print sources, include the page number, if available, on which the quote appeared in the original source. The page number should go in parentheses after the end quotation mark but before the period. If the person quoted is not the author of the book or the article, give the author's name in parentheses along with the page number. If there are two or three authors, give all names.
- If a direct quotation is more than five typed lines, indent the whole quotation and do not use quotation marks.

DIRECT QUOTATION

According to Erie County, Pennsylvania, District Attorney Joseph P. — Identifying phrase
Conti, "I believe strongly in mandatory registration of sex offenders. Be- — Quotation in quotation marks
cause sex offenders may repeat their heinous crimes, our citizens need a
means of protecting themselves" (Schmitz 5). — Page reference

Cite and Document Your Sources

■ **TIP:** For more information on documenting sources, visit **bedfordstmartins.com/researchroom**.

As discussed on page 258, you need to document, or give credit to, your sources at the end of your research essay in a **Works Cited** list; your instructor may also require a bibliography. In addition, you need to include in-text citations of sources as you use them in the essay.

No one can remember the specifics of correct citation and documentation, so be sure to refer to this section or a reference that your instructor directs you to. Include all of the correct information, and pay attention to where punctuation marks such as commas, periods, and quotations should go.

There are several different systems of documentation. Most English professors prefer the Modern Language Association (MLA) system, which is used in this chapter. However, when you are writing a research paper in another course, you may be required to use another system. When in doubt, always ask your instructor.

Use In-Text Citations Within Your Essay

In-text citations like the ones shown below are used for books and periodicals. For Web sites and other electronic sources, you typically will not be able to include page numbers, although you can note any screen or paragraph numbers used in place of page numbers.

When you refer to the author (or authors) in an introductory phrase, write just the relevant page number(s), if available, in parentheses at the end of the quotation.

> **DIRECT QUOTATION:** In an article by Jon Schmitz, Erie County, Pennsylvania, District Attorney Joseph P. Conti was quoted as saying, "I believe strongly in mandatory registration of sex offenders. Because sex offenders may repeat their heinous crimes, our citizens need a means of protecting themselves" (5).

> **INDIRECT QUOTATION:** In an article by Jon Schmitz, Erie Country, Pennsylvania, District Attorney Joseph P. Conti stated that citizens needed special protection from sex offenders, who may again commit crimes (5).

When you do not refer to the author(s) in an introductory phrase, write the author's name followed by the page number(s), if available, at the end of the quotation. If an author is not named, use the title of the source.

> **DIRECT QUOTATION:** "Many victims are afraid to report sexual assault to the police. They may fear that reporting will lead to further trauma" (CSOM 3-4).

> **INDIRECT QUOTATION:** Fear of being harmed further may prevent sexual-assault victims from telling police what happened to them (CSOM 3-4).

For personal interviews, include the name of the person interviewed unless the speaker does not want his or her name used, in which case write "anonymous."

PERSONAL INTERVIEW CITATION

> Tarisha Moldovado and her three children lived next door to a child molester for two years without knowing of his offense. She said the neighbor kept to himself and was not a problem, but she wishes she had known so that she could have kept closer watch over her children (personal interview).

Use a Works Cited List at the End of Your Essay

Following are model Works Cited entries for major types of sources. At the end of your paper, you will need to include such entries for each source you cite in the body of the paper.

■ **TIP:** If you have additional questions about MLA style—especially on how to cite electronic sources—visit the MLA Web site at <**www.mla.org**>.

Books

1. BOOK WITH ONE AUTHOR

Full title

Anker, Susan. Real Writing: Paragraphs and Essays for College, Work, and
    Everyday Life. 4th ed. Boston: Bedford/St. Martin's, 2007.

Author, last name first | Edition number | Place of publication | Publisher | Publication date

All lines after first line of entry are indented.

2. BOOK WITH TWO OR THREE AUTHORS

Levitt, Steven D., and Stephen J. Dubner. Freakonomics: A Rogue Economist Explores
    the Hidden Side of Everything. New York: Morrow, 2005.

Quigley, Sharon, Gloria Florez, and Thomas McCann. You Can Clean Almost Anything.
    New York: Sutton, 1999.

3. BOOK WITH FOUR OR MORE AUTHORS (*ET AL.* MEANS "AND OTHERS")

Henretta, James A., et al. America: A Concise History. 3rd ed. Boston: Bedford/
    St. Martin's, 2006.

4. BOOK WITH AN EDITOR

Tate, Parson, ed. Most Romantic Vacation Spots. Cheyenne: Chandler, 2000.

5. WORK IN AN ANTHOLOGY

Wilson, Kathy. "Dude Looks Like a Lady." ReMix: Reading and Composing Culture.
    Catherine G. Latterell. Bedford/St. Martin's, 2006. 21–23.

6. ENCYCLOPEDIA ARTICLE

"Boston Common." The Encyclopedia of New England. 2005.

Periodicals

■ **TIP:** For a model entry for a journal article, see page 269.

7. MAGAZINE ARTICLE

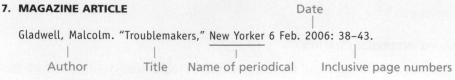

Gladwell, Malcolm. "Troublemakers," New Yorker 6 Feb. 2006: 38–43.

Author   Title   Name of periodical   Inclusive page numbers

8. NEWSPAPER ARTICLE

Lipton, Eric. "White House Knew of Levee's Failure on Night of Storm." New York Times
     10 Feb. 2006: A1.

9. EDITORIAL IN A MAGAZINE OR NEWSPAPER

Jackson, Derrick Z. "America's One-Sided Prayers." Editorial. Boston Globe 9 Apr.
     2003: A19.

Electronic Sources

Electronic sources include Web sites; databases or subscription services such as ERIC, InfoTrac, LexisNexis, and ProQuest; and electronic communications such as e-mail. Because electronic sources change often, always note the date you accessed or read the source as well as the date on which the source was posted or updated online, if this information is available.

10. AN ENTIRE WEB SITE   Title of Web site   Date of publication or most recent update

The Owl at Purdue. 6 Feb. 2006. Purdue University. 11 Feb. 2006
     <http://owl.english.purdue.edu/owl/>.

URL   Sponsor of site, if listed   Date of access

11. PART OF A LARGER WEB SITE

Purdue Owl. "Evaluating Sources of Information." The Owl at Purdue. 2 Feb. 2006.
     Purdue University. 11 Feb. 2006 **<http://owl.english.purdue.edu/owl/>.**

12. ARTICLE FROM A DATABASE   Author   Article title   Publication title

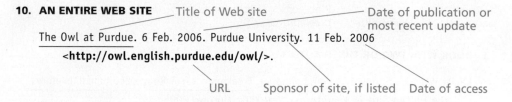

Rivero, Lisa. "Secrets of Successful Homeschooling." Understanding Our Gifted.

Volume and issue numbers   Date   Inclusive pages

     15.4 (2003): 8–11. ERIC. CSA Internet Database Service. Boston Public Lib.,
     Boston, MA. 4 Apr. 2006. **<http://ca1.csa.com>.**   Database title   Name of provider

Name and location of library   Access date   Main URL

13. ARTICLE IN AN ONLINE PERIODICAL   Author   Article title

Weine, Stevan M. "Survivor Families and Their Strengths: Learning from Bosnians after
     Genocide." Other Voices: The (e)Journal of Cultural Criticism. 2.1 (2000).

Name of online periodical   1 May 2006 **<http://www.othervoices.org/2.1/weine/bosnia.html>.**

Access date   URL   Volume number and publication date

14. E-MAIL OR ONLINE POSTING

Eisenhauer, Karen. "Learning Styles." E-mail to Susan Anker. 24 Apr. 2006.

White, Verna. "Working with Course Management Systems." Online posting. 14 Dec. 2005. CBW Listserv. 3 May 2006 <cbw-l@tc.umn.edu>.

Other Sources

15. PERSONAL INTERVIEW

Okayo, Margaret. Personal interview. 16 Apr. 2006.

16. SPEECH

Pennington, Karen. "Reading between the Lines." College Reading and Learning Association Conf. Hilton Long Beach, Long Beach, CA. 3 Nov. 2005.

17. FILM, VIDEO, OR DVD

Brokeback Mountain. Dir. Ang Lee. Perf. Heath Ledger, Jake Gyllenhaal. Universal, 2005.

18. TELEVISION OR RADIO PROGRAM

"The Sister Act." The OC. Fox. KTTV, Los Angeles. 19 Jan. 2006.

19. RECORDING

West, Kanye. "Wake Up Mr. West." Late Registration. Roc-a-Fella, 2005.

EXCERPT FROM A STUDENT RESEARCH ESSAY

Here is the first page and Works Cited page from Marcus Shanks's research essay, with annotations showing various standard characteristics of content, documentation, and formatting.

1/2" margin between top of page and header

Shanks 1

Marcus Shanks

Dr. Yesu

English 99

November 23, 2005

Sex Offender Registration: Our Right to Know

In 1994, seven-year-old Megan Nicole Kanka was raped and murdered by a paroled sex offender living in her neighborhood ("Megan's Law"). On May 17th, 1996, President Bill Clinton signed Megan's Law, which requires every state to develop a system for notifying people when a convicted sex offender has moved into their neighborhoods. Since that time, different states have enacted different procedures, but the law is controversial. But Megan's Law is essential, and the citizens of the United States have a right to know any and all information about sex offenders in their communities. Sex offender registries should be mandatory in every state, for every offender.

People have a right to know where sex offenders live, for the safety of themselves and their children. Sex offenders, especially pedophiles, are more likely than many other criminals to repeat their crimes. The reported percentage of pedophiles who repeat their crimes ranges from as low as 10 percent to as high as 40 percent (Furby, Weinrott, and Blackshaw 17–19). For this reason, states require registries. For example, according to Chapter 566 of Missouri law, any convicted sex offender who has been a resident of the United States since July 1, 1979, is required to be registered under both federal and military law for the safety of the citizenry ("Sex Offender Registry"). The parole officer in charge is responsible for making sure that the convicted felon completes the Missouri offender registration forms so that the public has information such as the felon's name, offense, and state of residence.

It is essential that states enforce the registration of sex offenders, and this takes interstate cooperation. Sex offenders, like everyone else, have the right to change their residences, but they are more likely than the average citizen to move in order to escape their past (Furby, Weinrott, and Blackshaw 3). The State of Missouri requires that convicted felons have ten days to report their new addresses and telephone numbers to their parole officers. Convicted felons must also verify their addresses every ninety days in order to conform with the conditions of their release or parole. However, states are not equally vigilant about tracking felons and sharing information with other state registries. Without this cooperation, innocent people are put at risk.

Annotations (left margin):

Student's last name and page number on top of each page

Identification of student, professor, course, and date

Title centered

Introduction

Thesis statement

Topic sentence

In-text citation

Topic sentence

In-text citation

Shanks 2

Works Cited

Furby, Lucas, Mark Weinrott, and Lyn Blackshaw. "Sex Offender Recidivism: A ———————— Journal article
    Review." <u>Psychological Bulletin</u> 105.1 (1989): 3–30.

"Megan's Law State by State." Klaas Kids Foundation. 15 Nov. 2005 ———————— Organization Web site
    <http://www.klaaskids.org/pg-legmeg.htm>.

Schmitz, Jon. "Megan's Law Debated before High Court." <u>Post-Gazette.com</u>.
    17 Sept. 1998. 14 Nov. 2005 **<http://www.postgazette.com/** ———————— Online newspaper
    regionstate/19980917megan4.asp>.

"Sex Offender Registry." <u>Missouri State Highway Patrol</u>. State of Missouri. ———————— Government Web site
    13 Nov. 2005 **<http//www.mshp.dps.missouri.gov>**.

To write a research essay, use the checklist below.

CHECKLIST: HOW TO WRITE A RESEARCH ESSAY	
STEPS	**HOW TO DO THE STEPS**
☐ **Make a schedule.** (See the model on pp. 248–49.)	• Include the due date and dates for doing the research, finishing a draft, and revising.
☐ **Choose a topic.** (See pp. 249–50.)	• Ask yourself the five questions on page 249. • Choose a topic that you are interested in. • Make sure the topic is narrow enough to cover in a paper of the assigned length.
☐ **Ask a guiding research question.** (See p. 250.)	• Ask a question about your topic that you will begin to answer as you do your initial research.
☐ **Find sources.** (See pp. 250–55.)	• Go to the library and find out what resources are available to you, both in print and online.
☐ **Evaluate your sources.** (See pp. 255–57.)	• Particularly for Web sites, look for the sponsor and judge whether the site is reliable and accurate.
☐ **Avoid plagiarism.** (See p. 258.)	• As you make notes from your sources, write down the publication information you will need.

☐ **Write a thesis statement.** (For more on writing a thesis, see Chapter 4.)	• Based on what you have read so far, write a thesis statement that includes the main idea of your research essay.
	• Try turning your guiding research question into a statement:
	    Research question: Should registration of sex offenders be mandatory?
	    Thesis: Sex offender registries should be mandatory.
	    Revised: Sex offender registries should be mandatory in every state, for every offender.

☐ **Support your thesis.** (For more on supporting your point, see Chapter 5.)	• Review all of your notes and choose the points that best support your thesis. • If you do not have enough support to make your point, do a little more reading.
☐ **Make an outline.** (For more on making an outline, see Chapter 6.)	• Include your thesis and the major support, arranged by order of importance.
☐ **Write a draft essay.** (For more on writing a draft, see Chapter 7.)	• Write an introduction that includes your thesis statement. • Write topic sentences for each major support and include supporting evidence.

STEPS	HOW TO DO THE STEPS
☐ **Write a draft essay.** (For more on writing a draft, see Chapter 7.)	• Write a conclusion that reminds readers of your thesis, reviews the evidence you have provided, and makes a final observation in support of your main point.
☐ **Cite and document your sources.** (See pp. 264–67.)	• Cite sources in the body of your essay and provide full publication information at the end, in the list of Works Cited.
☐ **Revise your draft.** (For more on revising, see Chapter 8.) Consider getting comments from a peer first. For more information, see page 90.	Ask yourself: • Does each topic sentence support my thesis? • Does the support in each of my body paragraphs directly support the thesis? • Do I have enough support that my readers are likely to understand my position on my topic? • Have I included transitions that will help readers move smoothly from one point to the next? • Does my conclusion make my point again, strongly? • Have I integrated source material smoothly into the essay? Do I need to smooth out anything that seems to be just dumped in? • Are all sources documented correctly? • What else can I do to make the essay stronger?
☐ **Edit your essay.**	• Reread your essay, looking for errors in grammar, spelling, and punctuation.
☐ **Ask yourself:**	• Is this the best I can do?

Part Four
The Four Most Serious Errors

20

The Basic Sentence

An Overview

The Four Most Serious Errors

This book focuses first on four grammar errors that people most often notice.

THE FOUR MOST SERIOUS ERRORS

1. Fragments
2. Run-ons
3. Problems with subject-verb agreement
4. Problems with verb form and tense

If you can edit your writing to correct these four errors, your grades will improve.

This chapter reviews the basic sentence elements that you will need to understand to do the later chapters covering the four most serious errors.

The Parts of Speech

There are seven basic parts of speech:

1. **Noun:** names a person, place, or thing.
2. **Pronoun:** replaces a noun in a sentence. *He, she, it, we,* and *they* are pronouns.
3. **Verb:** tells what action the subject does or links a subject to another word that describes it.
4. **Adjective:** describes a noun or pronoun.
5. **Adverb:** describes an adjective, a verb, or another adverb.

275

6. **Preposition:** connects a noun, pronoun, or verb with some other information about it. *Across, at, in, of,* and *around* are prepositions.

7. **Conjunction:** connects words. *And, but, for, nor, or, so,* and *yet* are conjunctions.

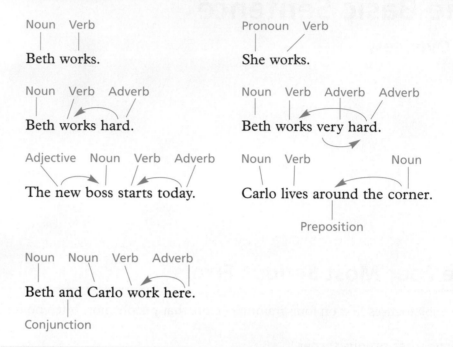

Noun   Verb

Beth works.

Pronoun   Verb

She works.

Noun   Verb   Adverb

Beth works hard.

Noun   Verb   Adverb   Adverb

Beth works very hard.

Adjective   Noun   Verb   Adverb

The new boss starts today.

Noun   Verb   Noun

Carlo lives around the corner.

Preposition

Noun   Noun   Verb   Adverb

Beth and Carlo work here.

Conjunction

> **Language Note:** One of the previous sentences ("The new boss starts today") uses the word *the* before the noun. *The, a,* and *an* are called *articles*. To be clear on which article to use with which nouns, or if you often forget to use an article, see page 485.
>
> Some languages, such as Chinese, Vietnamese, and Russian, do not use articles before nouns. If your native language doesn't, check all nouns in your writing to see if they need an article.

■ PRACTICE 1   USING THE PARTS OF SPEECH . . . .

Fill in the blanks with the part of speech indicated.

EXAMPLE: More and more wild animals are coming into towns and cities, making life ___*challenging*___ (adjective) for them and humans.

Answers will vary. Possible answers shown.

1. Two ___*rare*___ (adjective) hawks built a ___*nest*___ (noun) on the roof ___*of*___ (preposition) a city apartment building.

2. The female laid ___*eggs*___ (noun) there, and ___*they*___ (pronoun) hatched a few days later, releasing four ___*extremely*___ (adverb) noisy chicks.

3. Some of the building's residents ___*complained*___ (verb) about the hawks, ___*but*___ (conjunction) others loved to stand ___*across*___ (preposition) the street from the birds and watch ___*them*___ (pronoun).

4. Because of the complaints, the ___*nest*___ (noun) was removed, ___*but*___ (conjunction) the people who liked the hawks got ___*very*___ (adverb) upset.

5. The supporters ___*of*___ (preposition) the birds eventually won, and the hawks were allowed to ___*return*___ (verb) to rebuild their ___*nest*___ (noun).

The Basic Sentence

A **sentence** is the basic unit of written communication. A complete sentence in written standard English must have these three elements:

- A **subject**
- A **verb**
- A **complete thought**

Subjects

The **subject** of a sentence is the person, place, or thing that a sentence is about. The subject of a sentence can be a noun or a pronoun. For a complete list of pronouns, see page 334.

To find the subject, ask yourself, **Who or what is the sentence about?**

PERSON AS SUBJECT   <u>Isaac</u> <u>arrived</u> last night.

[**Whom** is the sentence about? *Isaac*]

THING AS SUBJECT   The <u>roller coaster</u> <u>has closed</u>.

[**What** is the sentence about? The *roller coaster*]

> ■ **TIP:** In the examples in this chapter, subjects are underlined once, and verbs are underlined twice.

> **Language Note:** Formal English has many sentence patterns, but they all build on just three basic structures.
>
>   Subject   Verb
> 1. <u>Deshawn</u> <u>paints</u>.
>
>   Subject   Verb   Direct object
> 2. <u>Deshawn</u> <u>painted</u> three houses last summer.
>
> A **direct object** receives the action of a verb.

> ■ **TEACHING TIP:** Have students look back at a recent paper and underline the subjects of sentences in a few paragraphs. If they are working on a computer, they can use the underline function.

continued

Subject   Verb   Direct object   Indirect object

3. Deshawn gave the extra paint to Rudy.

An **indirect object** is the person to whom or for whom the action is performed.

A **compound subject** consists of two (or more) subjects joined by *and, or,* or *nor.*

TWO SUBJECTS   Kelli and Kate love animals of all kinds.

SEVERAL SUBJECTS   The baby, the cats, and the dog play well together.

Again, a **preposition** connects a noun, pronoun, or verb with some other information about it. A **prepositional phrase** is a word group that begins with a preposition and ends with a noun or pronoun, called the **object of a preposition**. The subject of a sentence is *never* in a prepositional phrase.

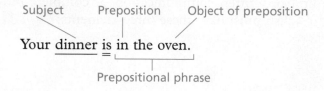

Subject   Preposition   Object of preposition

Your dinner is in the oven.

Prepositional phrase

Language Note: English sentences always have a subject, *separate* from the verb.

INCORRECT   Hates cleaning.

CORRECT   **He** hates cleaning.

Exception: Commands do not include a subject because it is understood that the subject is *you:*

[**You**] Come early.

PREPOSITION	OBJECT	PREPOSITIONAL PHRASE
from	the bakery	from the bakery
to	the next stoplight	to the next stoplight
under	the table	under the table

Language Note: *In* and *on* can be tricky prepositions for people whose native language is not English. Keep these definitions and examples in mind:

in = inside of (in the box, in the office) or at a certain time (in January, in the fall, in three weeks)

> **on** = on top of (on the table, on my foot), located in a certain place (on the page, on Main Street), or at a certain time (on January first)
>
> If you have trouble deciding what prepositions to use, see Chapter 32.

Common Prepositions

about	before	for	on	until
above	behind	from	out	up
across	below	in	outside	upon
after	beneath	inside	over	with
against	beside	into	past	within
along	between	like	since	without
among	by	near	through	
around	down	next to	to	
at	during	of	toward	
because of	except	off	under	

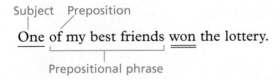

Subject   Preposition

One of my best friends won the lottery.

Prepositional phrase

Although you might think the word *friends* is the subject of the sentence, it isn't. *One* is the subject. The word *friends* can't be the subject because it is in the prepositional phrase *of my best friends.* When you are looking for the subject of a sentence, cross out the prepositional phrase.

PREPOSITIONAL PHRASE CROSSED OUT

One ~~of the students~~ won the science prize.

The rules ~~about the dress code~~ are very specific.

The sound ~~of water dripping~~ drives me crazy.

■ **PRACTICE 2**   **IDENTIFYING SUBJECTS AND PREPOSITIONAL PHRASES**

In each of the following sentences, cross out any prepositional phrases and underline the subject of the sentence.

EXAMPLE: The head ~~of the company~~ earned a very high salary.

1. A company ~~without a chief executive officer~~ conducted a search to find a new leader.

■ **ESL:** Give students a list of common prepositional phrases that they may not be familiar with (*over the hill, up a creek, beat around the bush,* and so on).

■ **TIP:** For more practices on sentence basics, visit Exercise Central at **bedfordstmartins .com/realwriting**.

■ **RESOURCES:** *Additional Resources* contains supplemental exercises for this chapter.

2. The policy ~~of the corporate board~~ was to find an experienced CEO.

3. The people ~~on the short list of candidates~~ had all run other companies.

4. Their work ~~at other businesses~~ had not always made the companies more successful.

5. One man ~~from a bankrupt firm~~ had earned a ten-million-dollar salary.

6. His payments ~~in stock options~~ had been even higher.

7. His appearance ~~before the members of the board~~ did not convince them.

8. One member ~~of the board~~ suggested looking further.

9. The workforce ~~within the company~~ included many talented executives.

10. A vice president ~~from the marketing division~~ became the company's new CEO.

Verbs

Every sentence has a **main verb**, the word or words that tell what the subject does or that link the subject to another word that describes it. Verbs do not always immediately follow the subject: Other words may come between the subject and the verb. There are three kinds of verbs: action verbs, linking verbs, and helping verbs.

Action Verbs

An **action verb** tells what action the subject performs.

To find the main action verb in a sentence, ask yourself, **What action does the subject perform?**

■ **TEACHING TIP:** Have a verb contest. Call out a subject and ask students to write as many action verbs as possible to go with it. Suggest that they work through the alphabet.

ACTION VERBS   The band played all night.

The alarm rings very loudly.

Linking Verbs

A **linking verb** connects (links) the subject to another word or group of words that describes the subject. Linking verbs show no action. The most common linking verb is *be*, along with all its forms (*am, is, are,* and so on). Other linking verbs, such as *seem* and *become,* can usually be replaced by a form of the verb *be,* and the sentence will still make sense.

To find linking verbs, ask yourself, **What word joins the subject and the words that describe the subject?**

LINKED VERBS The bus is late.

I feel great today. (I am great today.)

My new shoes look shiny. (My new shoes are shiny.)

The milk tastes sour. (The milk is sour.)

Some words can be used as either action verbs or linking verbs, depending on how the verb is used in a particular sentence.

ACTION VERB Justine smelled the flowers.

LINKING VERB The flowers smelled wonderful.

Common Linking Verbs

FORMS OF BE	FORMS OF SEEM AND BECOME	FORMS OF SENSE VERBS
am	seem, seems, seemed	look, looks, looked
are		
is	become, becomes, became	appear, appears, appeared
was		
were		smell, smells, smelled
		taste, tastes, tasted
		feel, feels, felt

Language Note: Forms of *be* are required in English to complete sentences like the following:

INCORRECT Tonya well now.

CORRECT Tonya **is** well now.

The word *be* must come with other verbs, as in:

She **could be** late.   He **will be waiting**.   They **must be notified**.

Helping Verbs

A **helping verb** joins the main verb in the sentence to form the **complete verb**. The helping verb is often a form of the verbs *be, have,* or *do*. A sentence may have more than one helping verb along with the main verb.

Helping Verb   +   Main verb   =   Complete verb

Sharon was listening to the radio as she was studying for the test.

[The helping verb is *was;* the complete verbs are *was listening* and *was studying.*]

I am saving my money for a car.

Colleen might have borrowed my sweater.

You must pass this course before taking the next one.

You should stop smoking.

Common Helping Verbs

FORMS OF *BE*	FORMS OF *HAVE*	FORMS OF *DO*	OTHER
am	have	do	can
are	has	does	could
been	had	did	may
being			might
is			must
was			should
were			will
			would

Before you begin Practice 3, look at these examples to see how action, linking, and helping verbs are different.

ACTION VERB   Kara graduated last year.

[The verb *graduated* is an action that Kara performed.]

LINKING VERB   Kara is a graduate.

[The verb *is* links Kara to the word that describes her: *graduate.* No action is performed.]

HELPING VERB   Kara is graduating next spring.

[The helping verb *is* joins the main verb *graduating* to make the complete verb *is graduating,* which tells what action the subject is taking.]

Language Note: Notice the position of helping verbs in negative statements and questions.

NEGATIVE STATEMENT   They **do not want** a break. They **don't want** a break.

The baby **has not slept** in his own bed for a week.

QUESTIONS	**Do** they **want** a break? **Don't** they [do they not] **want** a break?
	Has the baby **slept** in his own bed? **Hasn't** the baby [has the baby not] **slept** in his own bed?

Remember: If a sentence already has a negative, such as *never* or *none*, do not use another negative.

INCORRECT	They don't never want a break.
CORRECT	They **don't ever want** a break.

■ **PRACTICE 3   IDENTIFYING THE VERB (ACTION, LINKING, OR HELPING VERB + MAIN VERB)** . . . .

In the following sentences, underline each subject and double-underline each verb. Then, identify each verb as an action verb, a linking verb, or a helping verb + a main verb.

Helping verb + main verb
EXAMPLE: Bowling was created a long time ago.

Action verb
1. The ancient Egyptians invented bowling.

Linking verb
2. Dutch settlers were responsible for bowling's introduction to North America.

Action verb
3. They bowled outdoors on fields of grass.

Helping verb + main verb
4. One area in New York City is called Bowling Green because the Dutch *Action verb* bowled there in the 1600s.

Action verb
5. The first indoor bowling alley in the United States opened in 1840 in New York.

Linking verb
6. Indoor bowling soon became popular across the country.

Action verb
7. The largest bowling alley in the United States offers over a hundred lanes.

Helping verb + main verb
8. Visitors to Las Vegas can bowl there.

Helping verb + main verb
9. Most people would not think of bowling as more popular than basketball.

Action verb
10. However, more Americans participate in bowling than in any other sport.

Complete Thoughts

A **complete thought** is an idea, expressed in a sentence, that makes sense by itself, without other sentences. An incomplete thought leaves readers wondering what's going on.

INCOMPLETE THOUGHT	because my alarm didn't go off
COMPLETE THOUGHT	I was late because my alarm didn't go off.
INCOMPLETE THOUGHT	the people who won the lottery
COMPLETE THOUGHT	The people who won the lottery were very old.

To determine whether a thought is complete, ask yourself, **Do I have to ask a question to understand?**

INCOMPLETE THOUGHT	in my wallet

[You would have to ask a question to understand, so this is not a complete thought.]

COMPLETE THOUGHT	My ticket is in my wallet.

PRACTICE 4   IDENTIFYING COMPLETE THOUGHTS

Some of the following items contain complete thoughts, and others do not. In the space to the left of each item, write either "C" for complete thought or "I" for incomplete thought. If you write "I," add words to make a sentence. *Answers will vary. Possible answers shown.*

EXAMPLE: __I__ A person I know. *is a private detective*

__I__ 1. *I will wait until* ~~Until~~ the store closes at midnight.

__I__ 2. At the next meeting. *you should say what you think*

__C__ 3. My keys are missing.

__I__ 4. The apartment on the third floor. *was for rent*

__C__ 5. I rented it.

__I__ 6. *The Starmode Lounge is where* ~~Where~~ everyone goes on Saturday night.

__C__ 7. I bought a blue dress.

__C__ 8. You ought to exercise.

__I__ 9. *Mary joined a book club because* ~~Because~~ she likes novels.

__C__ 10. The baby is awake.

Chapter Review

1. List the seven parts of speech. *nouns, pronouns, verbs, adjectives, adverbs, prepositions, and conjunctions*

2. Write three sentences using all the parts of speech. Label the parts. *Answers will vary.*

3. A **sentence** must have three things: *a subject, a verb, and a complete thought* .

4. A ___*subject*___ is the person, place, or thing that the sentence is about.

5. A *noun* is *a word that names a person, place, or thing* .

6. A *prepositional phrase* is *a word group that begins with a preposition and ends with a noun or pronoun* .

7. What are five common prepositions? *Answers will vary.*

8. Write an example of a prepositional phrase (not from one of the examples presented earlier):
   Answers will vary.

9. An action verb tells *what action the subject performs* .

10. A linking verb *links the subject to a word or a group of words that describe the subject* .

11. A helping verb *joins the main verb in the sentence to form the complete verb* .

Chapter Test

Circle the correct choice for each of the following items.

■ **TIP:** For advice on taking tests, see Appendix A.

1. Identify the underlined part of speech in this sentence.

   Devon <u>walks</u> so fast that I can never keep up with him.
   a. Noun   (b.) Verb   c. Preposition   d. Adjective

■ **RESOURCES:** *Testing Tool Kit,* a CD-ROM available with this book, has even more tests.

2. Identify the underlined part of speech in this sentence.

   When you sent Gita a birthday present, did <u>she</u> send you a thank-you note?
   a. Noun   b. Verb   (c.) Pronoun   d. Conjunction

3. Identify the underlined part of speech in this sentence.

   In spring, the trees around our house are a <u>beautiful</u> shade of green.
   (a.) Adjective   b. Adverb   c. Preposition   d. Verb

4. Identify the underlined part of speech in this sentence.

   I ran for the bus, <u>but</u> it drove away before I reached it.
   a. Noun   b. Verb   c. Pronoun   (d.) Conjunction

5. Identify the underlined part of speech in this sentence.

   <u>Shopping</u> is Jerimiah's favorite hobby.

   (a.) Noun   b. Verb   c. Adjective   d. Adverb

6. Identify the type of verb in this sentence.

   The baby always <u>seems</u> tired after lunch.

   a. Action verb   (b.) Linking verb   c. Helping verb

7. Identify the type of verb in this sentence.

   Katarina <u>swims</u> five miles every day.

   (a.) Action verb   b. Linking verb   c. Helping verb

8. Identify the type of verb in this sentence.

   He <u>has</u> flown small planes in several countries.

   a. Action verb   b. Linking verb   (c.) Helping verb

9. Choose the item that is a complete sentence.

   a. Driving to the store.

   (b.) Driving to the store, I hit a squirrel.

   c. Driving to the grocery store last Wednesday.

10. Choose the item that is a complete sentence.

    (a.) Whenever I feel sick, I take aspirin.

    b. Whenever I feel sick.

    c. Takes me to the doctor whenever I feel sick.

21

Fragments

Incomplete Sentences

Ever Thought This?

"When my sentence gets too long, I think it probably needs a period, so I put one in, even though I'm not sure it goes there."
—Naomi Roman, Student

This chapter

- explains what fragments are
- gives you practice finding and correcting five common kinds of fragments

Understand What Fragments Are

A **fragment** is a group of words that is missing parts of a complete sentence.

SENTENCE   I was late, so I ate some cold pizza and drank a whole liter of Pepsi.

FRAGMENT   I was late, so I ate some cold pizza. *And drank a whole liter of Pepsi.*

[*And drank a whole liter of Pepsi* contains a verb (*drank*) but no subject.]

■ **TIP:** In the examples in this chapter, subjects are underlined once, and verbs are underlined twice.

> **Language Note:** Remember that any idea that ends with a period needs a subject and verb to be complete. For a review of subjects and verbs, see pages 277–83.

In the Real World, Why Is It Important to Correct Fragments?

SITUATION: Jeff is applying for a job at a building development corporation. He sends his résumé along with a cover letter to the human resources office. Although he really wants a job with this company, his cover letter hurts his chances. Here is a portion of the letter:

> I have a B.S. from Denver Community College, where I took classes in drafting. ^*and*^ Also in computer-assisted design. I studied engineering and engineering graphics., ^*both*^ Both of which I enjoyed and did well in. I would like the opportunity to speak with you in person regarding a position ^*in*^ at Richmond Homes. ^*of Richmond Homes*^ In the architecture department. I have good skills, ^

■ **TEACHING TIP:** Students should underline the fragments for Practice 1, page 288, and correct them for Practice 10, page 302.

and I am a very dedicated, hard worker. I think I could be an asset to the company.

> **RESPONSE:** Alan Whitehead, vice president of architecture, responded in the following way to this letter:
>
> I don't need perfect grammar; our business is building, not writing. But I noticed the errors in the letter right away. The résumé looks decent, but those kinds of mistakes tell me that Jeff is either sloppy or lacking in basic writing skills. I'm not a perfect writer myself, so I always have to spend time proofreading my writing before sending it. I don't need staff who can't write or who don't take the time to do things right; we have lots of applicants for every position.

Alan Whitehead

Home Development
Company Vice President

(See Alan's Profile of Success on p. 122.)

■ **RESOURCES:** *Additional Resources* contains tests and supplemental exercises for this chapter as well as a transparency master for the summary chart at the end of the chapter.

■ **TEACHING TIP:** Consider having students use different-colored highlighters to indicate subjects and verbs.

People outside the English classroom notice major grammar errors, and though they may not assign you a course grade, they do judge you by your communication skills.

Practice Finding and Correcting Fragments

Fragments are missing a subject, a verb, or a complete thought. To find fragments in your own writing, look for the five trouble spots in this chapter. They often signal fragments.

When you find a fragment in your own writing, you can usually correct it in one of two ways.

BASIC WAYS TO CORRECT A FRAGMENT

- Add what is missing (a subject, a verb, or both).
- Attach the fragment to the sentence before or after it.

■ **PRACTICE 1**   **FINDING FRAGMENTS** . . . .

Find and underline the three fragments in Jeff's letter on page 287.

. . . .

■ **TIP:** Remember, the subject of a sentence is *never* in a prepositional phrase (see p. 278).

1. Fragments That Start with Prepositions

Whenever a preposition starts what you think is a sentence, check for a subject, a verb, and a complete thought. If the group of words is missing any of these three elements, it is a fragment.

> **FRAGMENT**   <u>I pounded</u> as hard as I could. *Against the door.*
>
> [*Against the door* lacks both a subject and a verb.]

Correct a fragment that starts with a preposition by connecting it to the sentence either before or after it. If you connect such a fragment to the sentence after it, put a comma after the fragment to join it to the next sentence.

FINDING AND FIXING FRAGMENTS:
Fragments That Start with a Preposition

■ **TIP:** An audiovisual tutorial on finding and fixing fragments is available on a CD-ROM with this book.

Find

I pounded as hard as I could. (Against) the door.

1. **Circle** any preposition that starts a word group.

2. **Ask:** Is there a subject in the word group? *No.*   A verb? *No.*
   Underline any subject, and **double-underline** any verb.

3. **Ask:** Does the word group express a complete thought? *No.*

4. If the word group is missing a subject or verb or doesn't express a complete thought, it is a fragment. *This is a fragment.*

Fix

a

I pounded as hard as I could, Against the door.

5. **Correct the fragment** by joining it to the sentence before or after it.

Common Prepositions

about	before	for	on	until
above	behind	from	out	up
across	below	in	outside	upon
after	beneath	inside	over	with
against	beside	into	past	within
along	between	like	since	without
among	by	near	through	
around	down	next to	to	
at	during	of	toward	
because of	except	off	under	

■ **TIP:** For more practice correcting fragments, visit Exercise Central at **bedfordstmartins .com/realwriting**. Also, the Writing Guide Software with this book has tutorials on fragments.

■ **RESOURCES:** To gauge students' skills in correcting fragments, use the *Testing Tool Kit* CD-ROM available with this book.

■ **PRACTICE 2   CORRECTING FRAGMENTS THAT START WITH PREPOSITIONS** . . . .

In the following items, circle any preposition that appears at the beginning of a word group. Then, correct fragments by connecting them to the previous or the next sentence.

> **EXAMPLE:** (For) several years when they are young. Children often
> have imaginary friends.   *Answers may vary. Possible edits shown.*

1. Some parents worry/ (About) their children's imaginary companions.

2. Other parents think the imaginary friend is a sign/ (Of) the child's creativity.

3. Some parents think imaginary companions are a waste/ (Of) time and energy.

4. When children behave badly, they may blame the imaginary friend/ (For) their actions.

5. Children should be taught the difference/ (Between) lies and imagination.

6. (During) the time when a child has an imaginary friend/, Parents can learn a lot about the child.

7. A child may not want to admit to being afraid/ (Of) the dark.

8. Children may use imaginary friends to tell their parents/ (About) their fears.

9. Children usually give up their imaginary companions/ (After) grade school.

10. (After) its disappearance/ , Parents who have gotten interested in the imaginary friend may be sorry to see it go.

. . . .

2. Fragments That Start with Dependent Words

A **dependent word** (also called a **subordinating conjunction**) is the first word in a dependent clause.

> **SENTENCE WITH A**
> **DEPENDENT WORD**   We arrived early *because* we left early.
>
> [*Because* is a dependent word introducing the dependent clause *because we left early.*]

A dependent clause cannot be a sentence because it doesn't express a complete thought, even though it has a subject and a verb. Whenever a dependent word starts what you think is a sentence, stop to check for a subject, a verb, and a complete thought.

FRAGMENT   *Since I moved.* I have eaten out every day.

[*Since I moved* has a subject (*I*) and a verb (*moved*), but it doesn't express a complete thought.]

> ## Common Dependent Words
>
> | | | |
> |---|---|---|
> | after | now that | what(ever) |
> | although | once | when(ever) |
> | as/as if | since | where |
> | because | so that | whether |
> | before | that | which |
> | even if/though | though | while |
> | how | unless | who/whose |
> | if/if only | until | |

When a word group starts with *who, whose,* or *which,* it is not a complete sentence unless it is a question.

FRAGMENT   That is the police officer. *Who gave me a ticket last week.*

QUESTION   *Who* gave you a ticket last week?

FRAGMENT   He is the goalie. *Whose team is so bad.*

QUESTION   *Whose* team are you on?

FRAGMENT   Sherlene went to the HiHo Club. *Which does not serve alcohol.*

QUESTION   *Which* club serves alcohol?

> **Language Note:** For more help with forming questions, see Chapter 32.

Correct a fragment that starts with a dependent word by connecting it to the sentence before or after it. If the dependent clause is joined to the sentence before it, you do not usually need to put a comma in front of it. If the dependent clause is joined to the sentence after it, put a comma after the dependent clause.

■ **DISCUSSION:** Ask students to jot down what they think the word *dependent* means in the real world and to give an example. After getting some responses, ask how *dependent* in *dependent clause* is similar to *dependent* in the real world.

■ **COMPUTER:** Suggest that students become aware of the dependent words they use most by doing a computer search for them as they edit their own writing. They can then make sure that dependent clauses are attached to sentences.

FINDING AND FIXING FRAGMENTS:
Fragments That Start with a Dependent Word

Find

(Because) a job search is important. People should take the
time to do it right.

1. **Circle** any dependent word that starts either word group.

2. **Ask:** Is there a subject in the word group? *Yes.* A verb? *Yes.* **Underline** any
   subject, and **double-underline** any verb.

3. **Ask:** Does the word group express a complete thought? *No.*

4. If the word group is missing a subject or verb or doesn't express a complete
   thought, it is a fragment. *This is a fragment.*

Fix

Because a job search is important, People should take the
time to do it right.

5. **Correct the fragment** by joining it to the sentence before or after it. Add a
   comma if the dependent word group comes first.

■ **TIP:** For more on commas
with dependent clauses, see
Chapters 29 and 36.

■ **PRACTICE 3**   **CORRECTING FRAGMENTS THAT BEGIN WITH
DEPENDENT WORDS** . . . .

In the following items, circle any dependent word that appears at the beginning of a word group. Then, correct fragments by connecting them to the
previous or the next sentence.

> **EXAMPLE:** Online personal trainers are great for people. (Who)
> *who*
> don't have the time or money for an in-person trainer.

1. Going to a gym does not work for some people. (Because) their sched-
   because
   ules do not allow it.

2. Others may be embarrassed to work out in public. (If) they are out of
   if
   shape.

3. (Since) online trainers usually charge less than in-person trainers. Some
   , some
   people train online for the savings.

4. A person's online trainer can also be in contact/~~Whenever~~ *whenever* the person
   is on the Internet.

5. People who use online training say they will not exercise/ ~~Unless~~ *unless*
   someone holds them accountable for it.

6. Some regular personal trainers don't see/ ~~How~~ *how* online training can be
   effective.

7. ~~While~~ online trainers push clients to exercise/ ~~Many~~ *, many* people believe
   this is not as intimidating as having an in-person trainer.

8. ~~Whether~~ or not people want to stay fit/ ~~They~~ *, they* can always find excuses
   to avoid exercising.

9. ~~Before~~ anyone selects an online trainer/ ~~He~~ *, he* or she must be serious
   about exercising.

10. Nobody will benefit from training/~~Until~~ *until* it is taken seriously.

. . . .

3. Fragments That Start with *-ing* Verb Forms

An **-ing verb form** (also called a **gerund**) is the form of a verb that ends
in *-ing: walking, writing, running*. Unless it has a helping verb (*was walking, was writing, was running*), it can't be a complete verb in a sentence.
Sometimes an *-ing* verb form is used at the beginning of a complete
sentence.

> **SENTENCE**   <u>Walking</u> is good exercise.
>
> [The *-ing* verb form *walking* is the subject; *is* is the verb. The sentence expresses a com-
> plete thought.]

Sometimes, an *-ing* verb form introduces a fragment. When an *-ing* verb
form starts what you think is a sentence, stop and check for a subject, a verb,
and a complete thought.

> **FRAGMENT**   I was <u>running</u> as fast as I could. *Hoping to get there on time.*
>
> [*Hoping to get there on time* lacks a subject and a verb.]

Correct a fragment that starts with an *-ing* verb form either by adding
whatever sentence elements are missing (usually a subject and a helping
verb) or by connecting it to the previous or the next sentence. Usually, you
will need to put a comma before or after the fragment to join it to the complete sentence.

FINDING AND FIXING FRAGMENTS:
Fragments That Start with *-ing* Verb Forms

↓

Find

I was running as fast as I could. (Hoping) to get there on time.

1. **Circle** any *-ing* verb that starts a word group.

2. **Ask:** Is there a subject in the word group? *No.*   A verb? *Yes.* **Underline** any subject and **double-underline** any verb.

3. **Ask:** Does the word group express a complete thought? *No.*

4. If the word group is missing a subject or verb or doesn't express a complete thought, it is a fragment. *This is a fragment.*

↓

Fix

h
I was running as fast as I could/,Hoping to get there on time.
                                ^

I was still hoping
I was running as fast as I could. ~~Hoping~~ to get there on time.
                                      ^

5. **Correct the fragment** by joining it to the sentence before or after it. **Alternative:** Add the missing sentence elements.

■ PRACTICE 4   **CORRECTING FRAGMENTS THAT START WITH *-ING* VERB FORMS** . . . .

In the following items, circle any *-ing* verb that appears at the beginning of a word group. Then, correct fragments by adding the missing sentence elements or by connecting them to the previous or the next sentence.

EXAMPLE: People sometimes travel long distances in unusual ways.
They are trying
(Trying) to set new world records.
^

Answers may vary. Possible edits shown.

1. In 1931, Plennie Wingo set out on an ambitious journey/, (Walking)
                                                       w
backward around the world.

2. (Wearing) sunglasses with rearview mirrors/, ~~H~~e set out on his trip early
                                    h
                                    ^
one morning.

3. After eight thousand miles, Wingo's journey was interrupted by a war/,
h
(Halting) his progress in Pakistan.
^

4. Hans Mullikin spent two and a half years during the late 1970s travel-
He was crawling
ing to the White House. (Crawling) from Texas to Washington, D.C.
^

5. Mullikin's trip took so long because he lingered/, (Taking) *t* time out to
^
earn money as a logger and a Baptist minister.

6. (Taking) unusual transportation to the White House/, *P* rotesters have
^
often been able to get publicity.

7. Farmers hoping for government help traveled from the Great Plains to
They were driving
Washington. (Driving) large, slow-moving harvesting machines.
^
Reporters covered
8. The farmers' cause was helped by the media. (Covering) their trip from
^
beginning to end.

9. Americans may also have heard the story of Alvin Straight/, *l* (Looking)
^
for his long-lost brother as he traveled across the Midwest.

10. (Suffering) from increasingly poor eyesight/, Straight made his trip on a
riding lawn mower.

. . . .

4. Fragments That Start with *to* and a Verb

When what you think is a sentence begins with *to* and a verb (called the *in-finitive* form of the verb), you need to make sure that it is not a fragment.

FRAGMENT	Each week the <u>newspaper</u> <u>runs</u> a consumer watch. *To tell readers about potential scams.*[1]
CORRECTED	Each week the <u>newspaper</u> <u>runs</u> a consumer watch to tell readers about potential <u>scams</u>.

If a word group begins with *to* and a verb, it must have another verb, or it is not a complete sentence. When you see a word group that begins with *to* and a verb, first check to see if there is another verb. If there is not an-other verb, it is a fragment.

SENTENCE	*To run* a complete marathon <u>was</u> my goal.

[*To run* is the subject; *was* is the verb.]

FRAGMENT	<u>Cheri</u> <u>got</u> underneath the car. *To change the oil.*

[There is not another verb in the word group that begins with *to change*.]

[1] **scams:** plans to trick people, usually to get their money.

Language Note: Do not confuse the infinitive (*to* before the verb) with *that*.

INCORRECT	My brother wants *that* his girlfriend cook.
CORRECT	My brother wants his girlfriend *to cook*.

To correct a fragment that starts with *to* and a verb, join it to the sentence before or after it, or add the missing sentence elements.

FINDING AND FIXING FRAGMENTS:
Fragments That Start with *to* and a Verb

Find

Cheri got underneath the car. ⟨To change⟩ the oil.

1. **Circle** any *to*-plus-verb combination that starts a word group.

2. **Ask:** Is there a subject in the word group? *No.*   A verb? *Yes.* **Underline** any subject and **double-underline** any verb.

3. **Ask:** Does the word group express a complete thought? *No.*

4. If the word group is missing a subject or verb or doesn't express a complete thought, it is a fragment. *This is a fragment.*

Fix

Cheri got underneath the car, to change the oil.

To change the oil,
Cheri got underneath the car. ~~To change the oil.~~

She needed to
Cheri got underneath the car. ~~To change the oil.~~

5. **Correct the fragment** by joining it to the sentence before or after it. If you put the *to*-plus-verb word group first, put a comma after it. **Alternative:** Add the missing sentence elements.

■ **PRACTICE 5 CORRECTING FRAGMENTS THAT START WITH *TO***
AND A VERB

In the following items, circle any examples of *to* and a verb that begin a word group. Then, correct fragments by adding the missing sentence elements or by connecting them to the previous or next sentence.

EXAMPLE: There was a time when someone had to be famous./ (To be) on a postage stamp.
to
^

1. Now it is easy./ (To put) just about any face or object on a stamp.
to
^

2. Special Web sites show you how./ (To make) personalized stamps.
to
^

3. It is not necessary./ (To use) a photo of a face.
to
^

4. Try using a picture of a flower or a cute pet./ (To make) a stamp.
to
^

5. It is not acceptable./ (To choose) a photo of a famous person or to show anything offensive.
to
^

6. (To be placed) on a stamp,/ ~~The~~ photo must be in digital format.
the
^

7. Some people use the stamps./ (To personalize) invitations to weddings and other events.
to
^

8. Most grandparents would be happy./ (To receive) personalized stamps showing their grandchildren.
to
^

9. (To get) the personalized stamps,/ ~~One~~ has to pay a price.
one
^

10. It costs more than twice as much as regular stamps./ (To order) stamps with personal photos.
to
^

5. Fragments That Start with Examples or Explanations

As you reread what you have written, pay special attention to groups of words that are examples or explanations of information you presented in the previous sentence. They may be fragments.

FRAGMENT I thought of other ways to get out of my locked apartment. *For example, through the window.*

FRAGMENT I hate climbing out of windows. *Especially from the third floor.*

[*For example, through the window,* and *Especially from the third floor* lack subjects, verbs, and complete thoughts.]

This last type of fragment is harder to recognize because there is no single word or kind of word to look for. Here are a few starting words that may signal a fragment, but fragments that are examples or explanations do not always start with these words.

especially   for example   like   such as

When a group of words that you think is a sentence gives an example of information in the previous sentence, stop to check it for a subject, a verb, and a complete thought.

■ **TIP:** *Such as* and *like* do not often begin complete sentences.

FRAGMENT	<u>I</u> <u>decided</u> to call someone who could help me get out of my apartment. *Like a locksmith.*
FRAGMENT	An answering <u>machine</u> <u>answered</u> my call. *Not the locksmith.*
FRAGMENT	<u>I</u> <u>considered</u> getting out of my apartment by using the fire escape. *The one outside my window.*

[*Like a locksmith, Not the locksmith,* and *The one outside my window* lack verbs and complete thoughts.]

Correct a fragment that starts with an example or explanation by connecting it to the previous or the next sentence. Sometimes, you can add whatever sentence elements are missing (a subject or verb or both) instead. When you connect the fragment to a sentence, you may need to change some punctuation. For example, fragments that are examples and fragments that are negatives are often set off by a comma.

FINDING AND FIXING FRAGMENTS:
Fragments That Are Examples or Explanations

Find

I decided to call someone who could help me get out of my apartment. (Like a locksmith.)

1. **Circle** the word group that is an example or explanation.
2. **Ask:** Does the word group have a subject, a verb, and a complete thought? *No.*
3. If the word group is missing a subject or verb or doesn't express a complete thought, it is a fragment. *This is a fragment.*

↓

Fix

I decided to call someone who could help me get out of my apartment/, ~~Like~~ *like* a locksmith.

You may need to add some words to correct fragments:

I considered getting out of my apartment by using the fire escape. The one outside my window. *was strong enough to hold me*
∧

4. **Correct the fragment** by joining it to the sentence before or after it or by adding the missing sentence elements.

■ PRACTICE 6   **CORRECTING FRAGMENTS THAT ARE EXAMPLES OR EXPLANATIONS** . . . .

In the following items, circle any word groups that are examples or explanations. Then, correct fragments by connecting them to the previous or the next sentence or by adding the missing sentence elements.

EXAMPLE: It can be difficult to be a smart consumer/, (~~Especially~~ *especially* when making major purchases.)

Answers will vary. Possible edits shown.

1. At car dealerships, important information, *like financing charges,* is often in small type.
∧
(~~Like financing charges.~~)

2. Advertisements also put negative information, *such as drug side effects,* in fine print. (~~Such as drug side effects.~~)
∧

3. Sometimes, the costs that are really important are not widely known. (For instance, the cost of printing each page for an inkjet printer) *is not often considered by consumers.*
∧

4. Yet, over a printer's lifetime, the per-page cost can be higher than any other expenses/, (~~Such~~ *such* as the cost of the printer itself.)
∧

5. A consumer must be careful with everyday purchases/, (~~Like~~ *like* groceries or car maintenance.)
∧

6. Oil-change businesses may try to sell you things you don't need. (For example, an air filter when yours is still clean.) *they might try to sell you*
∧

7. Car maintenance might be cheaper elsewhere/. ~~Especially~~ *especially* if you have a trusted mechanic.

8. Purchases can also be costly because of high credit-card expenses/, ~~Such~~ *such* as interest charges and late fees.

9. Those who pay their entire credit card balance every month get a great deal. ~~Essentially,~~ *they get* a free loan.

10. Finally, it's a good idea to check that phone and cable bills don't charge for services not used/. ~~Like~~ *like* caller I.D. and premium cable.

▦ PRACTICE 7 CORRECTING VARIOUS TYPES OF FRAGMENTS . . . . .

In the following items, circle each word group that is a fragment. Then, correct fragments by connecting them to the previous or the next sentence or by adding the missing sentence elements.

EXAMPLE: With the high cost of producing video games/, ~~Game~~ *game* publishers are turning to a new source of revenue.

Answers will vary. Possible edits shown.

1. To add to their income/, ~~Publishers~~ *publishers* are placing advertisements in their games.

2. Sometimes, the ads show a character using a product. For example, *a character might be shown* drinking a specific brand of soda to earn health points.

3. One character, a racecar driver, drove his ad-covered car/ ~~Across~~ *across* the finish line.

4. When a warrior character picked up a sword decorated with an athletic-shoe logo/, ~~Some~~ *some* players complained.

5. Worrying that ads are distracting/, ~~Some~~ *some* publishers are trying to limit the number of ads per game.

6. But most players do not seem to mind seeing ads in video games/. ~~If~~ *if* there are not too many of them.

7. These players are used to seeing ads in all kinds of places/. ~~Like~~ *like* grocery carts and restroom walls.

8. For video game publishers/, ~~The~~ *the* goal is making a profit, but most publishers also care about the product.

9. (To strike a balance between profitable advertising and high game quality) ~~That~~ is what publishers want.

10. (Doing market research) ~~Will~~ help publishers find that balance.

Edit Paragraphs and Your Own Writing

Use the chart, Finding and Fixing Fragments, on page 305 to help you complete the practices in this section and edit your own writing.

■ **PRACTICE 8   EDITING PARAGRAPHS FOR FRAGMENTS**

Find and correct fragments in the following paragraphs.
Answers may vary. Possible edits shown.

1. (1) Wilma Rudolph was born in 1940 in Tennessee. (2) When she was four, she became ill with scarlet fever and pneumonia. (3) ~~So~~ *She was so* sick that everyone thought she would die. (4) She survived, but one of her legs was damaged. (5) She was told that she would never walk again. (6) Rudolph did manage to walk again despite the doctors' predictions. (7) After years of treatment, braces, and hard work/, (8) *s*She started running for exercise. (9) In 1960, Rudolph became the second American woman in history to win three gold medals in a single Olympics.

2. (1) Louis Braille was born in France in 1809. (2) In a tragic accident, he hurt one of his eyes when he was three. (3) Infection set in, and he lost sight in both eyes. (4) He attended a special school for the blind where students were taught a system of communication. (5) *It was a* ~~A~~ very complicated and difficult system. (6) Becoming interested in the idea of inventing a writing system the blind could read/, (7) Braille worked for two years on his own idea. (8) *He* ~~To~~ develop*ed* the raised dot system, called Braille, that is used universally.

3. (1) Most people think of Thomas Edison as a famous inventor/ (2) ~~The man~~ who invented the light bulb. (3) Most people don't know that Edison was considered learning disabled as a child. (4) An illness had prevented him from entering school until he was eight, and his teachers told his parents that he couldn't learn. (5) His parents took him

■ **TEAMWORK:** Divide the class into small groups and have each group present a corrected paragraph. Compare the different ways that the groups correct the fragments.

out of school/ (6) ᵇBecause they did not believe the teachers. (7) He was then homeschooled/ (8) ᵇBy his very determined mother. (9) By the age of ten, Edison was already experimenting with what would become his great inventions.

■ **TIP:** For more advice on using formal English, see Chapter 2. For advice on choosing appropriate words, see Chapter 33.

■ PRACTICE 9   EDITING FRAGMENTS AND USING FORMAL ENGLISH

Your friend wants to send this thank-you note to an employer she interviewed with for a job. She knows the note has problems and has asked for your help. Correct the fragments in the note. Then, edit the informal English in it.   *Answers will vary. Possible edits shown.*

Dear Ms. Hernandez,

(1) Thank you so much for taking the time/ (2) ᵗTo meet with me this past Wednesday. (3) I am more ~~psyched~~ excited than ever about the administrative assistant position at Fields Corporation. (4) Learning more about the ~~stuff I would need to do. Was very cool.~~ challenges and requirements of the job was very valuable to me. (5) Also, I enjoyed meeting you and the other managers. (6) With my strong organizational skills, professional experience, and friendly personality, (7) I'm sure that I would be ~~awesome for the job.~~ an asset to the company. (8) Because ~~I'm totally jazzed about the position.~~ of my strong interest in the position, I hope you will keep me in mind. (9) Please let me know if you need any other ~~info.~~ information, like (10) ~~Like~~ references or a writing sample. (11) ~~Thank U much,~~ Thanks again for your time.

Sincerely,

Terri Hammons

■ PRACTICE 10   EDITING JEFF'S LETTER

Look back at Jeff's letter on page 287. You may have already underlined the fragments in his letter; if not, do so now. Next, using what you've learned in this chapter, correct each fragment in the letter.

■ PRACTICE 11   EDITING YOUR OWN WRITING FOR FRAGMENTS

■ **LEARNING JOURNAL:** What kind of fragments do you find most often in your writing? What are some ways to avoid or correct this mistake?

As a final practice, edit fragments in a piece of your own writing—a paper you are working on for this class, a paper you've already finished, a paper for another course, or a recent piece of writing from your work or everyday life. Use the chart on page 305 to help you.

Chapter Review

1. A *sentence* is a group of words that has a ____subject____, a ____verb____, and *expresses a* _____
complete thought _____.

2. A ____fragment____ seems to be a complete sentence but is only a piece of one. It lacks a ____subject____,
a ____verb____, or a ____complete thought____.

3. What are the five trouble spots that signal possible fragments?

   A word group that starts with a preposition

   A word group that starts with a dependent word

   A word group that starts with an -ing verb form

   A word group that starts with to and a verb

   A word group that starts with an example or explanation

4. What are the two basic ways to correct fragments?

   Add what is missing (a subject, a verb, or both).

   Attach the fragment to the sentence before or after it.

Chapter Test

Circle the correct choice for each of the following items.

■ **TIP:** For advice on taking tests, see Appendix A.

1. If an underlined portion of this sentence is incorrect, select the revision that fixes it. If the sentence is correct as written, choose d.

   Natalie did not go on our bike trip. Because she could not ride a bike.
   .......................A..................B...............................C

   a. go. On
   b. trip because
   c. ride; a
   d. No change is necessary.

■ **RESOURCES:** *Testing Tool Kit,* a CD-ROM available with this book, has even more tests.

2. Choose the item that has no errors.

   a. Since Gary is the most experienced hiker here, he should lead the way.

   b. Since Gary is the most experienced hiker here. He should lead the way.

   c. Since Gary is the most experienced hiker here; he should lead the way.

3. If an underlined portion of this sentence is incorrect, select the revision that fixes it. If the sentence is correct as written, choose d.

   Planting fragrant flowers will attract wildlife. Such as butterflies.
   _____ A _____ B _____ C

   a. When planting   c. wildlife, such
   b. flowers; will   d. No change is necessary.

4. Choose the item that has no errors.

   a. To get to the concert hall; take exit 5 and drive for three miles.
   b. To get to the concert hall. Take exit 5 and drive for three miles.
   c. To get to the concert hall, take exit 5 and drive for three miles.

5. If an underlined portion of this sentence is incorrect, select the revision that fixes it. If the sentence is correct as written, choose d.

   Buying many unnecessary groceries. Shows that you felt deprived as a child.
   _____ A _____ B _____ C

   a. groceries shows   c. deprived. As
   b. that: you   d. No change is necessary.

6. If an underlined portion of this sentence is incorrect, select the revision that fixes it. If the sentence is correct as written, choose d.

   Some scientists predict that people will soon take vacation cruises. Into space.
   _____ A _____ B _____ C

   a. predict, that   c. cruises into
   b. soon; take   d. No change is necessary.

7. Choose the item that has no errors.

   a. Walking for ten miles after her car broke down. Pearl became tired and frustrated.
   b. Walking for ten miles after her car broke down; Pearl became tired and frustrated.
   c. Walking for ten miles after her car broke down, Pearl became tired and frustrated.

8. Choose the item that has no errors.

   a. Many people find it hard. To concentrate during stressful times.
   b. Many people find it hard to concentrate during stressful times.
   c. Many people find it hard, to concentrate during stressful times.

9. If an underlined portion of this sentence is incorrect, select the revision that fixes it. If the sentence is correct as written, choose d.

   Growing suspicious, the secret agent discovered a tiny recording device
   _____ A _____ B
   inside a flower vase.
   _____ C

   a. Growing, suspicious   c. inside, a vase
   b. agent. Discovered   d. No change is necessary.

10. If an underlined portion of this sentence is incorrect, select the revision that fixes it. If the sentence is correct as written, choose d.

    <u>Early in</u> their training, <u>doctors learn</u> there is a fine <u>line. Between</u> life and
        A   B   C

    death.

    a. Early, in

    b. doctors. Learn

    c. line between

    d. No change is necessary.

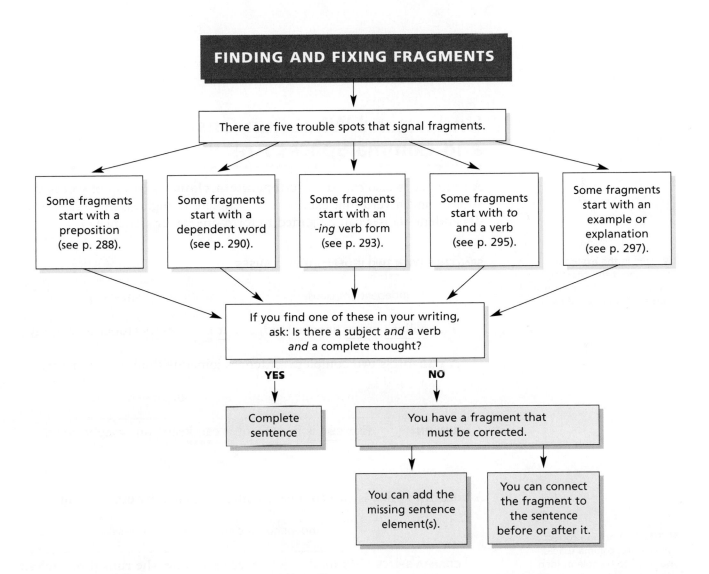

Ever Thought This?

"I tried putting in commas instead of periods, so I wouldn't have fragments. But now my papers get marked for 'comma splices.'"

—Jimmy Lester, Student

This chapter

- explains what run-ons and comma splices are
- gives you practice finding them and shows four ways to correct them

22
Run-Ons and Comma Splices
Two Sentences Joined Incorrectly

Understand What Run-Ons and Comma Splices Are

A sentence is also called an **independent clause**, a group of words with a subject and a verb that expresses a complete thought. Sometimes, two independent clauses can be joined to form one larger sentence.

■ **TIP:** In the examples throughout this chapter, subjects are underlined once, and verbs are underlined twice.

SENTENCE WITH TWO INDEPENDENT CLAUSES

Independent clause · · · · · Independent clause

The college offers financial aid, and it encourages students to apply.

A **run-on** is two complete sentences joined without any punctuation.

Independent clause · · · · · Independent clause

RUN-ON   Exercise is important it can keep your weight down.

↑ no punctuation

A **comma splice** is two complete sentences joined by only a comma.

Independent clause · · · · · Independent clause

COMMA SPLICE   My mother jogs every morning, she runs three miles.

Comma ↑

■ **TIP:** To find and correct run-ons and comma splices, you need to be able to identify a complete sentence. For a review, see Chapter 20.

When you join two sentences, you must use the proper punctuation. If you join them with no punctuation or with only a comma, you create a run-on or comma splice error.

CORRECTIONS   Exercise is important; it can keep your weight down.

My mother jogs every morning; she runs three miles.

In the Real World, Why Is It Important to Correct Run-Ons and Comma Splices?

SITUATION: Naomi is applying to a special program for returning students at Cambridge College. Here is one of the essay questions on the application, followed by a paragraph from Naomi's response.

STATEMENT OF PURPOSE: In two hundred words or less, describe your intellectual and professional goals and how a Cambridge College education will assist you in achieving them.

For many years, I did not take control of my life; I just drifted along without any purpose or goals. I realized one day as I was meeting with my daughter's guidance counselor that I hoped my daughter would not turn out like me. From that moment, I decided I would focus my energy on doing something to help myself and others. I set a goal of becoming a teacher. To begin on that path, I took a course in math at night school, and then I took another in science. I passed both courses. With hard work, I know I can do well in the Cambridge College program. I am committed to the professional goal I finally found. It has given new purpose to my whole life.

RESPONSE: When Mary La Cue Booker, a master's degree recipient from Cambridge College, read Naomi's answer, she noticed the errors and made the following comment:

Cambridge College takes these essays very seriously. It wants students who are thoughtful, hardworking, and mature. Although Naomi's essay indicates that she has some of these qualities, her writing gives another impression. She makes several noticeable errors; I wonder if she took the time to really think about this essay. If she is careless on a document that represents her for college admission, will she be careless in other areas as well? It's too bad, because her qualifications are quite good otherwise.

Mary La Cue Booker
Recording artist, actress
(See Mary's Profile of Success on p. 208).

Run-ons and comma splices, like sentence fragments, are errors that people notice and consider major mistakes.

Practice Finding and Correcting Run-Ons and Comma Splices

To find run-ons and comma splices, focus on each sentence in your writing, one at a time. Until you get used to finding them (or until you don't make the errors anymore), this step will take extra time. But if you spend the extra time, your writing will improve.

■ **PRACTICE 1   IDENTIFYING RUN-ONS AND COMMA SPLICES** . . . . .

Find and underline the four run-ons or comma splices in Naomi's writing on page 307.

. . . .

Once you have found a run-on, there are four ways to correct it.

FOUR WAYS TO CORRECT RUN-ONS AND COMMA SPLICES

- Add a period.
- Add a semicolon.
- Add a comma and a coordinating conjunction.
- Add a dependent word.

Add a Period

You can correct run-ons and comma splices by adding a period to make two separate sentences. After adding the period, capitalize the letter that begins the new sentence. Reread your two sentences to make sure they each contain a subject, a verb, and a complete thought.

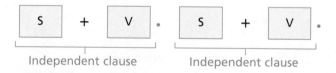

| S | + | V | . | S | + | V | . |

    Independent clause   Independent clause

RUN-ON (CORRECTED)   I interviewed a candidate for a job. $\overset{S}{\underset{\wedge}{she}}$ gave me the "dead fish" handshake.

COMMA SPLICE (CORRECTED)   The "dead fish" is a limp handshake$\underset{\wedge}{,}\overset{T}{the}$ person plops her hand into yours.

Add a Semicolon

■ **TEACHING TIP:** Remind students that a semicolon balances two independent clauses. What is on either side of it must be able to stand alone as a complete sentence.

A second way to correct run-ons and comma splices is to use a semicolon (;) to join the two sentences. Use a semicolon only when the two sentences express closely related ideas. A semicolon can be used only where a period could also be used; the words on each side of the semicolon must be able to stand alone as a complete sentence. Do not capitalize the word that follows a semicolon unless it is the name of a specific person, place, or thing that is usually capitalized — for example, Mary, New York, or Eiffel Tower.

RUN-ON (CORRECTED)   Slouching creates a terrible impression; it makes a person seem uninterested, bored, or lacking in self-confidence.

COMMA SPLICE (CORRECTED)   It is important in an interview to hold your head up; it is just as important to sit up straight.

A semicolon is sometimes used before a transition from one sentence to another, and the transition word is then followed by a comma.

Semicolon   Transition   Comma

I stopped by the market; however, it was closed.

Semicolon   Transition   Comma

Sharon is a neighbor; actually, she is my friend.

FINDING AND FIXING RUN-ONS AND COMMA SPLICES:
Adding a Period or Semicolon

Find

Few people know the history of many popular holidays Valentine's Day is one of these holidays.

1. To see if there are two independent clauses in a sentence, **underline** the subjects and **double-underline** the verbs.

2. **Ask:** If there two independent clauses in the sentence, are they separated by either a period or a semicolon?   *No. It is a run-on.*

Fix

Few people know the history of many popular holidays. Valentine's Day is one of these holidays.

Few people know the history of many popular holidays; Valentine's Day is one of these holidays.

3. **Correct** the error by adding a period or a semicolon.

■ **TIP:** An audiovisual tutorial on finding and fixing run-ons and comma splices is available on the CD-ROM available with this book.

■ **TEACHING TIP:** You may want to warn students that if they have written a sentence that is longer than two lines, they should look at it closely to see if it has errors.

■ **TIP:** For more practices on run-ons and comma splices, visit Exercise Central at **bedfordstmartins.com/ realwriting**.

■ **RESOURCES:** To gauge students' skills in correcting run-ons and comma splices, use the *Testing Tool Kit* CD-ROM available with this book.

■ **PRACTICE 2 CORRECTING A RUN-ON OR COMMA SPLICE BY ADDING A PERIOD OR A SEMICOLON** . . . .

For each of the following items, indicate in the space to the left whether it is a run-on ("RO") or a comma splice ("CS"). Then, correct the error by adding a period or a semicolon. Capitalize the letters as necessary to make two sentences.

EXAMPLE: <u>CS</u> Valentine's Day is a time to celebrate love. legends
^L^

say that the holiday dates back to ancient Rome.

Edits will vary. Possible answers shown.

<u>RO</u>   1. The holiday we now call Valentine's Day was celebrated in the Roman Empire on February 15 it was called Lupercalia.

<u>RO</u>   2. At that time the woods around Rome were full of wolves. Romans asked their god Lupercus to remove the animals.

<u>CS</u>   3. The Romans held a festival to honor Lupercus this was the feast of Lupercalia.

<u>RO</u>   4. The Romans had traditional ways of celebrating Lupercalia. one custom involved choosing sweethearts.

<u>RO</u>   5. The night before the feast, all of the young women wrote their names on pieces of paper. they put the names in a jar.

<u>CS</u>   6. Then, each young man chose a name this woman would be his sweetheart for the year.

<u>RO</u>   7. The emperor ordered his soldiers not to get married. he was afraid they would want to stay home instead of going to war.

<u>CS</u>   8. A Christian priest named Valentine married several couples secretly. he was arrested.

<u>CS</u>   9. The emperor had Valentine killed on February 14. later the priest was declared a saint.

_CS_   10. The Romans became Christians and stopped celebrating

the feast honoring Lupercus/ they began to celebrate

St. Valentine's Day on February 14.

Add a Comma and a Coordinating Conjunction

A third way to correct run-ons is to add a comma and a coordinating conjunction: *and, but, or, nor, so, for,* or *yet.* Think of a coordinating conjunction as a link that joins independent clauses to form one sentence.

A comma splice already has a comma, so you need to add only a conjunction. Before adding a conjunction, read the independent clauses aloud to see which word best expresses the relationship between them.

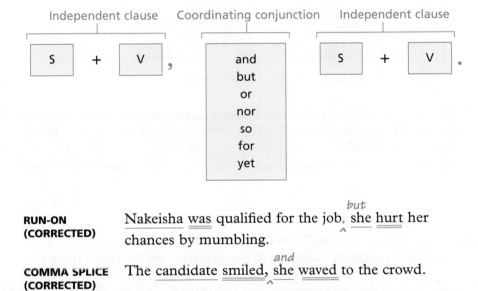

■ **TIP:** Notice that the comma does not follow the conjunction. The comma follows the word before the conjunction.

RUN-ON (CORRECTED)   Nakeisha was qualified for the job, *but* she hurt her chances by mumbling.

COMMA SPLICE (CORRECTED)   The candidate smiled, *and* she waved to the crowd.

Coordinating conjunctions need to connect two independent clauses. They are not used to join a dependent and an independent clause.

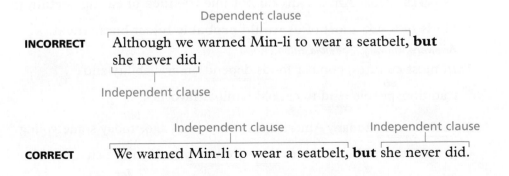

INCORRECT   Although we warned Min-li to wear a seatbelt, **but** she never did.

CORRECT   We warned Min-li to wear a seatbelt, **but** she never did.

FINDING AND FIXING RUN-ONS AND COMMA SPLICES:
Using a Comma and a Coordinating Conjunction

Find

Foods <u>differ</u> from place to place your favorite <u>treat</u> <u>might disgust</u> someone from another culture.

1. To see if there are two independent clauses in a sentence, **underline** the subjects and **double-underline** the verbs.
2. **Ask:** If there are two independent clauses in the sentence, are they separated by either a period or a semicolon? *No. It is a run-on.*

Fix

Foods <u>differ</u> from place to place, *and* your favorite <u>treat</u> <u>might disgust</u> someone from another culture.

3. **Correct a run-on** by adding a comma and a coordinating conjunction between the two independent clauses. Correct a comma splice by adding just a coordinating conjunction.

PRACTICE 3 CORRECTING RUN-ONS AND COMMA SPLICES BY ADDING A COMMA AND/OR A COORDINATING CONJUNCTION

Correct each of the following run-ons by adding a comma, if necessary, and an appropriate coordinating conjunction. First, underline the subjects and double-underline the verbs.

EXAMPLE: Most <u>Americans</u> <u>do</u> not <u>like</u> the idea of eating certain kinds of food, *and* most of <u>us</u> <u>would</u> probably <u>reject</u> horse meat.
Answers will vary. Possible edits shown.

1. In most cultures, popular <u>foods</u> <u>depend</u> on availability and tradition, *so* <u>people</u> <u>tend</u> to eat old familiar favorites.

2. <u>Sushi</u> <u>shocked</u> many Americans twenty years ago, *but* today some young <u>people</u> in the United States <u>have</u> <u>grown</u> up eating raw fish.

3. In many societies, certain <u>foods</u> <u>are</u> <u>allowed</u> to age, *for* this <u>process</u> <u>adds</u> flavor.

4. Icelanders <u>bury</u> eggs in the ground to rot for months, *and* these aged <u>eggs</u> <u>are considered</u> a special treat.

5. As an American, <u>you</u> <u>might</u> not like such eggs, *or* the <u>thought</u> of eating them <u>might</u> even <u>revolt</u> you.

6. In general, aged <u>foods</u> <u>have</u> a strong taste, *so* the <u>flavor</u> <u>is</u> unpleasant to someone unaccustomed to those foods.

7. Many <u>Koreans</u> <u>love</u> to eat kimchee, a spicy aged cabbage, *but* <u>Americans</u> often <u>find</u> the taste odd and the smell overpowering.

8. <u>Herders</u> in Kyrgyzstan <u>drink</u> kumiss, *and* this <u>beverage</u> <u>is made</u> of aged horse's milk.

9. <u>Americans</u> on a visit to Kyrgyzstan <u>consider</u> themselves brave for tasting kumiss, *but* local <u>children</u> <u>drink</u> it regularly.

10. <u>We</u> <u>think</u> of familiar foods as normal, *yet* favorite American <u>foods</u> <u>might</u> <u>horrify</u> people in other parts of the world.

. . . .

Add a Dependent Word

A fourth way to correct run-ons and comma splices is to make one of the complete sentences a dependent clause by adding a dependent word, such as *after, because, before, even though, if, though, unless,* and *when*. (For a more complete list of these words, see the graphic on p. 314.) Choose the dependent word (also called a **subordinating conjunction**) that best expresses the relationship between the two clauses.

Use a dependent word when the clause it begins is less important than the other clause or explains the other clause, as in the following sentence.

When <u>I</u> <u>get</u> to the train station, <u>I'll</u> <u>call</u> Josh.

The italicized clause is dependent (subordinate) because it just explains when the most important part of the sentence — calling Josh — will happen. It begins with the dependent word *when*.

Because a dependent clause is not a complete sentence (it has a subject and verb but does not express a complete thought), it can be joined to a sentence without creating a run-on. When the dependent clause is the second clause in a sentence, you usually do not need to put a comma before it unless it is showing contrast.

TWO SENTENCES

Halloween <u>was</u> originally a religious holiday. <u>People</u> <u>worshiped</u> the saints.

DEPENDENT CLAUSE: NO COMMA NEEDED

Halloween <u>was</u> originally a religious holiday *when <u>people</u> <u>worshiped</u> the saints.*

■ **TIP:** For more on using commas with dependent clauses, see Chapters 29 and 36.

DEPENDENT CLAUSE SHOWING CONTRAST: COMMA NEEDED

Many <u>holidays</u> <u>have</u> religious origins, *though the <u>celebrations</u> <u>have moved</u> away from their religious roots.*

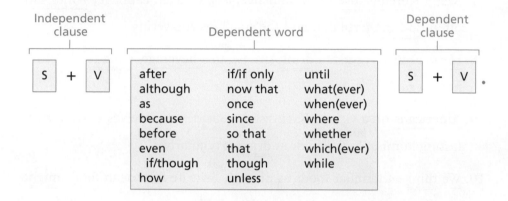

RUN-ON (CORRECTED)   Your final <u>statement</u> <u>should express</u> your interest in the position ^*,although* you <u>don't want</u> to sound desperate.

[The dependent clause *although you don't want to sound desperate* shows contrast, so a comma comes before it.]

COMMA SPLICE (CORRECTED)   <u>It</u> <u>is</u> important to end an interview on a positive note*,* ^*because* that final <u>impression</u> <u>is</u> what the interviewer will re-member.

You can also put the dependent clause first. When the dependent clause comes first, be sure to put a comma after it.

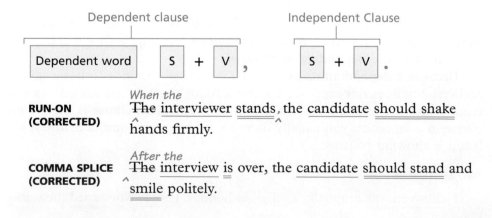

RUN-ON (CORRECTED)   *When the* ^T̶h̶e̶ <u>interviewer</u> <u>stands</u> ^, the <u>candidate</u> <u>should shake</u> hands firmly.

COMMA SPLICE (CORRECTED)   *After the* ^T̶h̶e̶ <u>interview</u> <u>is</u> over, the <u>candidate</u> <u>should stand</u> and smile politely.

FINDING AND FIXING RUN-ONS AND COMMA SPLICES:
Making a Dependent Clause

Find

Alzheimer's disease <u>is</u> a heartbreaking illness, <u>it</u> <u><u>causes</u></u> a steady decrease in brain capacity.

1. To see if there are two independent clauses in a sentence, **underline** the subjects and **double-underline** the verbs.

2. **Ask:** If there are two independent clauses in the sentence, are they separated by a period, a semicolon, or a comma and a coordinating conjunction? *No. It is a comma splice.*

Fix

                                      because
Alzheimer's disease is a heartbreaking illness, ^ it causes a steady decrease in brain capacity.

3. If one part of the sentence is less important than the other, or if you want to make it so, add a dependent word to the less important part.

PRACTICE 4   CORRECTING A RUN-ON OR COMMA SPLICE BY MAKING A DEPENDENT CLAUSE

Correct run-ons or comma splices by adding a dependent word to make a dependent clause. First, underline the subjects and double-underline the verbs.

              As wildflowers
EXAMPLE: ~~<u>Wildflowers</u>~~ <u><u>become</u></u> endangered in northeastern
           ^ America's woodlands, part of our natural <u>heritage</u>

           <u><u>is threatened</u></u>.   *Answers will vary. Possible edits shown.*

Although many
1. ~~<u>Many</u>~~ spring <u>wildflowers</u> once <u><u>grew</u></u> in these woods, many <u>fewer</u>
  ^

    <u><u>are appearing</u></u> now.

2. <u>Wildflowers</u> like Virginia bluebells, spring beauties, and pink lady's

                 because
    slippers <u><u>are</u></u> harder to find, ^ <u>they</u> <u><u>are being crowded</u></u> out and eaten.

  When
3. <u>Japanese honeysuckle</u> and other invasive <u>plants</u> quickly <u><u>cover</u></u> large
  ^

    areas of forest, many native <u>wildflowers</u> <u><u>cannot survive</u></u>.

Even though many
4. ~~Many~~ people like deer, they are another deadly enemy of wildflowers.

after
5. The number of native wildflowers in an area usually decreases the number of deer goes up.

whenever
6. More wildflowers are lost woodlands are cleared to build new homes.

where
7. Pollution and nonnative worms can also harm woods/ wildflowers are already struggling to survive.

When some
8. ~~Some~~ woodland wildflowers cannot bloom even for one spring, they never reappear.

until
9. Other wildflowers will not bloom invasive plants or other threats are removed.

unless
10. Much of our forests' beauty and diversity will soon be gone we do more to protect these native wildflowers.

. . . .

A Word That Can Cause Run-Ons and Comma Splices: *Then*

Many run-ons and comma splices are caused by the word *then*. You can use *then* to join two sentences, but if you add it without the correct punctuation or added words, your sentence will be a run-on or comma splice. Often, writers use just a comma before *then,* but that makes a comma splice.

COMMA SPLICE   I picked up my laundry, then I went home.

Use any of the four methods you have just practiced to correct errors caused by *then.* These methods are shown in the following examples.

T
I picked up my laundry/. then I went home.

;
I picked up my laundry/ then I went home.

and
I picked up my laundry, then I went home.

before
I picked up my laundry/ ~~then~~ I went home.

■ PRACTICE 5 CORRECTING VARIOUS TYPES OF RUN-ONS AND COMMA SPLICES · · · · · · · · · · · · · · · · · · ·

In the following items, correct any run-ons or comma splices. Use each method of correcting such errors—adding a period, adding a semicolon, adding a comma and a coordinating conjunction, or adding a dependent word—at least twice.

EXAMPLE: Most people expect to be cramped in an airplane
seat ‸*, but* more spacious seating is on the way.

Answers will vary. Possible edits shown.

1. *Even though jumbo*
   ~~Jumbo~~-sized airplanes can hold up to 900 people, they are now being
   ‸
   designed with only 500 seats.

2. This allows space for on-board lounges ‸*, and* it provides room for passengers
   to walk around.

3. Another way to add room is to eliminate the phones on the seatbacks
   since
   ‸ hardly anyone uses those phones anyway.

4. This moves the upper seatback two inches farther from the person behind it ‸*;* that will make a surprising difference in comfort.

5. New design features will also make passengers feel more comfortable ‸ .
   T
   ‸ ‸hese include softer lighting and larger overhead luggage bins.

6. Also, the bathrooms will be bigger ‸*;* this change will be welcomed by
   many passengers.

7. The most noticeable difference in the new planes will be the large win-
   T
   dows ‸‸*.* ‸hey will be 19 inches high and 11 inches wide.

8. This is twice the size of normal airplane portholes ‸*, so* passengers will get
   better views of the sky and land.

9. There is something about being able to see more of our surroundings
   that puts us at ease ‸*;* at least that is what the airlines hope.

10. Nevertheless, added spaciousness will not matter to some travelers
    because
    ‸ plenty of people will never fly for any reason.

· ·

Edit Paragraphs and Your Own Writing

Use the chart, Finding and Fixing Run-ons and Comma Splices, on page 322 to help you complete the practices in this section and edit your own writing.

■ **PRACTICE 6   EDITING PARAGRAPHS FOR RUN-ONS AND COMMA SPLICES** . . . .

Find and correct the run-ons and comma splices in the following paragraphs.   *Answers will vary. Possible answers shown.*

1. (1) Few people like talking about saliva/ in fact, many think it's disgusting. (2) Yet the use of saliva may someday save people from the need to have blood tests, an often painful procedure. (3) Nine laboratories across the United States are now attempting to create tools to detect the molecular components of saliva. *T*hey are part of a program funded by the National Institute of Dental and Craniofacial Research. (4) The goal is to develop new tests to diagnose diseases *, and* saliva tests may be possible because saliva has much in common with blood. (5) Basically, what is in blood is also in saliva, including DNA, proteins, germs, viruses, and many other molecules helpful in detecting diseases. (6) This similarity has been understood for some time *, but* in saliva the quantities of these components are much smaller, making them hard to detect. (7) *Although this* This problem has been challenging to overcome, engineers recently developed extremely precise detectors for tiny amounts of molecules.

2. (1) Having a blood test is an experience nobody enjoys *. The* the use of needles can also transmit infections. (2) In contrast, a diagnostic test using saliva would be noninvasive; all patients would have to do is spit. (3) Furthermore, saliva could be checked often to quickly detect changes. *A* a person could easily take a saliva test a dozen times during a day. (4) *Because not* Not many people want to submit to blood tests this often, many developing problems go undetected and untreated. (5) Some saliva tests are already in use; they check for HIV and substance abuse. (6) Scientists are now attempting to create "saliva profiles" for several potentially deadly diseases/ *. These* these conditions include breast cancer,

Type 2 diabetes, and ovarian cancer. (7) In the future, a visit to the dentist might include a saliva test to check for signs of certain diseases.

Before their

(8) ^ Their teeth are cleaned, patients will give the dentist a drop of saliva.

so that

(9) This will be inserted into a machine ^ the saliva's components can be detected. (10) When the visit is over, patients will get a printout indicating whether they are at risk for certain diseases *, and* ^ they will take this printout to their regular doctor.

■ **PRACTICE 7   EDITING RUN-ONS AND COMMA SPLICES AND USING FORMAL ENGLISH** . . . .

Your brother has been overcharged for an MP3 reader he ordered online, and he is about to send this e-mail to the seller's customer-service department. Help him by correcting the run-ons and comma splices in the e-mail. Then, edit the informal English in it.   *Answers will vary. Possible edits shown.*

to you because   *overcharged*

(1) I'm writing ~~2U cuz~~ I was seriously ~~ripped off~~ for the Star 3 MP3 player I ordered from your Web site last week. (2) *You* ~~U~~ listed the price as

, but   *If you check*

$150 ^ $250 was charged to my credit card. (3) ~~Check~~ out any competi-

you   *to pay that much money for the Star model. The*

tors' sites, ~~U~~ will see that no one expects people ~~2 cough up that much~~

Because

~~cash for the Star model, the~~ prices are never higher than $165. (4) I

a large amount for this product,

overpaid ~~big bucks on this,~~ I want my money back as soon as possible.

Sincerely, ^

(5) ~~Seriously bummin',~~

^

Chris Langley

■ **TIP:** For more advice on using formal English, see Chapter 2. For advice on choosing appropriate words, see Chapter 33.

■ **PRACTICE 8   EDITING NAOMI'S APPLICATION ANSWER** . . . .

Look back at Naomi's writing on page 307. You may have already underlined the run-ons and comma splices; if not, underline them now. Then, correct each error.

■ **LEARNING JOURNAL:** What kind of run-ons and comma splices do you find most often in your writing? What are some ways to avoid or correct these mistakes?

■ **PRACTICE 9   EDITING YOUR OWN WRITING FOR RUN-ONS AND COMMA SPLICES** . . . .

As a final practice, edit a piece of your own writing—a paper you are working on for this course, a paper you've already finished, a paper for another course, or a recent piece of writing from your work or everyday life. Use the chart on page 322 to help you.

Chapter Review

1. A sentence can also be called an <u>*independent clause*</u>.

2. A <u>*run-on*</u> is two complete sentences joined without any punctuation.

3. A <u>*comma splice*</u> is two complete sentences joined by only a comma.

4. What are the four ways to correct run-ons and comma splices?

   <u>*Add a period.*</u>

   <u>*Add a semicolon.*</u>

   <u>*Add a comma and a coordinating conjunction.*</u>

   <u>*Add a dependent word.*</u>

5. What word in the middle of a sentence may signal a run-on or comma splice? <u>*then*</u>

Chapter Test

Circle the correct choice for each of the following items.

■ **TIP:** For advice on taking tests, see Appendix A.

1. Choose the item that has no errors.
   a. Please fill this prescription for me, it is for my allergies.
   b. Please fill this prescription for me. It is for my allergies. *(circled)*
   c. Please fill this prescription for me it is for my allergies.

■ **RESOURCES:** *Testing Tool Kit,* a CD-ROM available with this book, has even more tests.

2. If an underlined portion of this sentence is incorrect, select the revision that fixes it. If the sentence is correct as written, choose d.

   Harlan is busy <u>now ask</u> <u>him</u> if he can do his <u>report next</u> week.
               A   B   C

   a. now, so *(circled)*   c. report; next
   b. him, if   d. No change is necessary.

3. Choose the item that has no errors.
   a. You cut all the onion slices to the same thickness, they will finish cooking at the same time.
   b. You cut all the onion slices to the same thickness they will finish cooking at the same time.
   c. If you cut all the onion slices to the same thickness, they will finish cooking at the same time. *(circled)*

4. Choose the correct answer to fill in the blank.

I've told Jervis several times not to tease the baby ——————— he

never listens.

   a. ,   c. No word or punctuation is necessary.

   (b.) , but

5. Choose the item that has no errors.

   a. I am in no hurry to get a book I order it online.

   b. I am in no hurry to get a book, I order it online.

   (c.) When I am in no hurry to get a book, I order it online.

6. If an underlined portion of this sentence is incorrect, select the revision
that fixes it. If the sentence is correct as written, choose d.

<u>Many people</u> think a tomato is a <u>vegetable it is</u> <u>really a</u> fruit.
       A   B   C

   a. Many, people   c. really; a

   (b.) vegetable; it   d. No change is necessary.

7. Choose the item that has no errors.

   (a.) Although air conditioning makes hot days more comfortable, it will
increase your energy bills.

   b. Air conditioning makes hot days more comfortable it will increase
your energy bills.

   c. Air conditioning makes hot days more comfortable, it will increase
your energy bills.

8. If an underlined portion of this sentence is incorrect, select the revision
that fixes it. If the sentence is correct as written, choose d.

In northern Europe, bodies that are thousands of years <u>old have</u> been
                                                         A

found in <u>swamps, some</u> bodies are so well preserved that they <u>look like</u>
            B   C

sleeping people.

   a. old, have   c. look, like

   (b.) swamps. Some   d. No change is necessary.

9. Choose the item that has no errors.

   a. Don't be shy about opening doors for strangers, courtesy is always
appreciated.

   (b.) Don't be shy about opening doors for strangers; courtesy is always
appreciated.

   c. Don't be shy about opening doors for strangers courtesy is always
appreciated.

10. Choose the correct answer to fill in the blank.

You can ride with me to work _____ you can take the train.

(a.) , or   c.   No word or punctuation is necessary.

b.   if

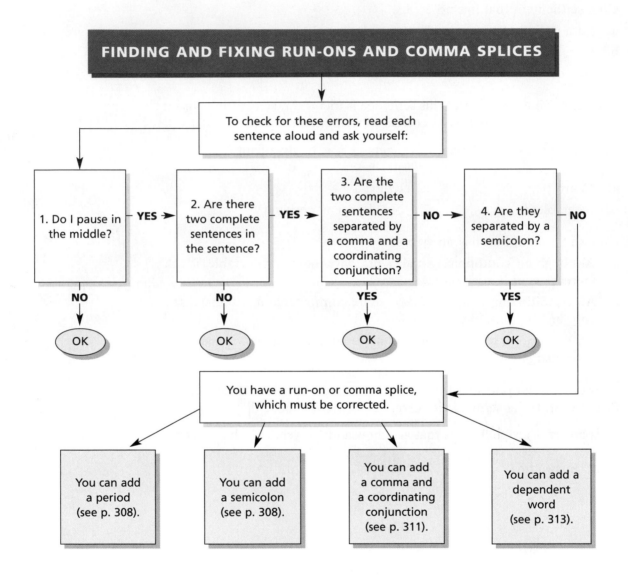

FINDING AND FIXING RUN-ONS AND COMMA SPLICES

To check for these errors, read each sentence aloud and ask yourself:

1. Do I pause in the middle? — **YES** → 2. Are there two complete sentences in the sentence? — **YES** → 3. Are the two complete sentences separated by a comma and a coordinating conjunction? — **NO** → 4. Are they separated by a semicolon? — **NO**

1. **NO** → OK

2. **NO** → OK

3. **YES** → OK

4. **YES** → OK

You have a run-on or comma splice, which must be corrected.

You can add a period (see p. 308).

You can add a semicolon (see p. 308).

You can add a comma and a coordinating conjunction (see p. 311).

You can add a dependent word (see p. 313).

23

Problems with Subject-Verb Agreement

When Subjects and Verbs Don't Match

Ever Thought This?

"I know sometimes the verb is supposed to end with -s and sometimes it isn't, but I always get confused."
— Mayerlin Fana, Student

This chapter

- explains what *agreement* between subjects and verbs is
- explains the simple rules for *regular verbs*
- identifies five trouble spots that can cause confusion
- gives you practice finding and fixing errors in subject-verb agreement

Understand What Subject-Verb Agreement Is

In any sentence, the **subject and the verb must match—or agree—**in number. If the subject is singular (one person, place, or thing), then the verb must also be singular. If the subject is plural (more than one), the verb must also be plural.

SINGULAR The skydiver jumps out of the airplane.

PLURAL The skydivers jump out of the airplane.

Regular verbs (with forms that follow standard English patterns) have two forms in the present tense: one that ends in -*s* and one that has no ending. The third-person subjects *he, she, it,* and singular nouns always use the form that ends in -*s*. First-person subjects (*I*), second-person subjects (*you*), and plural subjects use the form with no ending.

■ **TIP:** To find and correct errors in subject-verb agreement, you must be able to identify subjects and verbs. For a review, see Chapter 20.

	SINGULAR	PLURAL
First person	I walk.	We walk.
Second person	You walk.	You walk.
Third person	He (she, it) walks.	They walk.
	Joe walks.	Joe and Alice walk.
	The student walks.	The students walk.

First person / Second person: } no -*s*

Third person (He, Joe, The student): } all end in -*s*

■ **TIP:** In the examples throughout this chapter, subjects are underlined, and verbs are double-underlined.

Language Note: Some nouns that don't end in -*s* are plural and thus need plural verbs. For example, *children* and *people* don't end in -*s*, but they indicate more than one child or person, so they are plural.

INCORRECT These children is making me crazy.

CORRECT These children are making me crazy.

In the Real World, Why Is It Important to Correct Errors in Subject-Verb Agreement?

SITUATION: Regina Toms (name changed) wrote the following brief report about a company employee whom she was sending to the employee assistance program. (These programs help workers with various problems, such as alcoholism or mental illness, that may affect their job performance.)

> Mr. XXX, who has been a model employee of the company for five years, ~~have~~ *has* recently behaved in ways that ~~is~~ *are* inappropriate. For example, last week he was very rude when a colleague asked him a question. He has been late to work several times and has missed work more often than usual. When I spoke to him about his behavior and asked if he ~~have~~ *has* problems, he admitted that he had been drinking more than usual. I would like him to speak to someone who understand*s* more about this than I do.

Walter Scanlon
Program and workplace consultant

(See Walter's Profile of Success on p. 178.)

RESPONSE: When Walter Scanlon received Regina's report, he responded in this way:

I immediately formed an opinion of her based on this short piece of correspondence: that she was either not very well educated or not very considerate of the addressee. Ms. Toms may indeed be intelligent and considerate, but those qualities are not reflected in this report. In this fast-paced world we live in, rapid-fire faxes, e-mails, and brief telephone conversations are likely to be our first mode of contact. Since one never gets a second chance to make a first impression, make the first one count!

Practice Finding and Correcting Errors in Subject-Verb Agreement

To find problems with subject-verb agreement in your own writing, look for five trouble spots that often signal these problems.

1. The Verb Is a Form of *Be, Have,* or *Do*

The verbs *be, have,* and *do* do not follow the rules for forming singular and plural forms; they are **irregular verbs**.

FORMS OF THE VERB *BE*

PRESENT TENSE	SINGULAR	PLURAL
First person	I am	we are
Second person	you are	you are
Third person	she, he, it is	they are
	the student is	the students are

PAST TENSE		
First person	I was	we were
Second person	you were	you were
Third person	she, he, it was	they were
	the student was	the students were

FORMS OF THE VERB *HAVE*, **PRESENT TENSE**

	SINGULAR	PLURAL
First person	I have	we have
Second person	you have	you have
Third person	she, he, it has	they have
	the student has	the students have

FORMS OF THE VERB *DO*, **PRESENT TENSE**

	SINGULAR	PLURAL
First person	I do	we do
Second person	you do	you do
Third person	she, he, it does	they do
	the student does	the students do

■ TEACHING TIP: Misuse of the verb *be* is a very common error among some groups of students. If your students often use *be* for all forms and tenses of the verb *be*, you may want to have them flag or paperclip this chart for ease of reference.

These verbs cause problems for writers who in conversation use the same form in all cases (*He do the cleaning; they do the cleaning*). People also sometimes use the word *be* instead of the correct form of *be* (*She be on vacation*).

In college and at work, use the correct forms of these verbs, making sure that they agree with the subject in number. If you confuse the forms, refer to the charts until you feel confident that your use is correct.

They is sick today. *[are]*

She be at the library every morning. *[is]*

Carlos do the laundry every Wednesday. *[does]*

Joan have the best jewelry. *[has]*

■ **TIP:** An audiovisual tutorial on finding and fixing subject-verb agreement errors is available on a CD-ROM with this book.

> ## FINDING AND FIXING PROBLEMS WITH SUBJECT-VERB AGREEMENT: Making Subjects and Verbs Agree When the Verb Is *Be, Have,* or *Do*

> ### Find
>
> <u>I</u> (am / is / are) a believer in naps.
>
> 1. **Underline** the subject.
> 2. **Ask:** Is the subject in the first (*I*), second (*you*), or third person (*he/she*)? *First person.*
> 3. **Ask:** Is the subject singular or plural? *Singular.*

> ### Fix
>
> I ((am) / is / are) a believer in naps.
>
> 4. **Choose** the verb by matching it to the form of the subject (first person, singular).

PRACTICE 1   IDENTIFYING PROBLEMS WITH SUBJECT-VERB AGREEMENT . . . .

Find and underline the four problems with subject-verb agreement in Regina Toms's paragraph on page 324.

PRACTICE 2   CHOOSING THE CORRECT FORM OF *BE, HAVE,* OR *DO* . .

■ **TIP:** For more practices on subject-verb agreement, visit Exercise Central at **bedfordstmartins.com/ realwriting**.

In each sentence, underline the subject of the verb *be, have,* or *do,* and circle the correct form of the verb.

EXAMPLE: Most <u>people</u> (does /(do)) not get enough sleep.

1. <u>Sleep</u> ((is)/ are) necessary for people to function well.

2. Most <u>people</u> (has /(have)) to get eight hours or more of sleep to be completely alert.

3. Electric <u>lights</u> (was /(were)) once uncommon, so people usually went to bed when the sun went down.

4. Today, <u>darkness</u> ((does)/ do) not make us go to sleep.

5. Almost every <u>home</u> ((has)/ have) electricity, so people stay up long after sundown.

6. Modern <u>Americans</u> (has /(have)) such busy lives that they often sleep less than they should.

7. A working college <u>student</u> ((doesn't)/ don't) often have time to get eight hours of sleep.

8. Job <u>duties</u> (has /(have)) to be done, but schoolwork is equally important.

9. If you study when <u>you</u> (be /(are)) tired, you remember less information.

10. Busy people today try to get by on very little sleep, but <u>it</u> ((is)/ are) unhealthy to be sleep-deprived.

■ **PRACTICE 3   USING THE CORRECT FORM OF _BE, HAVE,_ OR _DO_** . . . .

In each sentence, underline the subject of the verb _be, have,_ or _do,_ and fill in the correct form of the verb indicated in parentheses.

■ **RESOURCES:** To gauge students' understanding of subject-verb agreement, use the _Testing Tool Kit_ CD-ROM available with this book.

> **EXAMPLE:** She _____has_____ (_have_) often looked at the stars on clear, dark nights.

1. <u>Stars</u> _____are_____ (_be_) clustered together in constellations.

2. Every <u>constellation</u> _____has_____ (_have_) a name.

3. <u>I</u> _____do_____ (_do_) not know how they got their names.

4. Most <u>constellations</u> _____do_____ (_do_) not look much like the people or creatures they represent.

5. <u>You</u> _____have_____ (_have_) to use your imagination to see the pictures in the stars.

6. Twelve <u>constellations</u> _____are_____ (_be_) signs of the zodiac.

7. <u>One</u> _____is_____ (_be_) supposed to look like a crab.

8. Other star <u>clusters</u> _____have_____ (_have_) the names of characters from ancient myths.

9. <u>Orion</u>, the hunter, _____is_____ (_be_) the only one I can recognize.

10. <u>He</u> _____does_____ (_do_) not look like a hunter to me.

2. Words Come between the Subject and the Verb

When the subject and verb aren't right next to each other, it is more difficult to find them and to make sure they agree. Most often, either a prepositional phrase or a dependent clause comes between the subject and the verb.

Prepositional Phrase between the Subject and the Verb

A **prepositional phrase** starts with a preposition and ends with a noun or pronoun: I took my bag *of books* and threw it *across the room*.

The subject of a sentence is never in a prepositional phrase. When you are looking for the subject of a sentence, you can cross out any prepositional phrases. This strategy should help you to find the real subject and decide whether it agrees with the verb.

> A volunteer ~~in the Peace Corps~~ (serve/<u>serves</u>) two years.

> The <u>speaker</u> ~~of the U.S. House of Representatives~~ (give/<u>gives</u>) many interviews.

> **FINDING AND FIXING PROBLEMS WITH SUBJECT-VERB AGREEMENT:** Making Subjects and Verbs Agree When They Are Separated by a Prepositional Phrase

> **Find**
>
> <u>Learners</u> ~~with dyslexia~~ (face / faces) many challenges.
>
> 1. **Underline** the subject.
> 2. **Cross out** any prepositional phrase that follows the subject.
> 3. **Ask:** Is the subject singular or plural? *Plural.*

> **Fix**
>
> Learners with dyslexia ((face)/ faces) many challenges.
>
> 4. **Choose** the form of the verb that matches the subject.

■ **PRACTICE 4   MAKING SUBJECTS AND VERBS AGREE WHEN THEY ARE SEPARATED BY A PREPOSITIONAL PHRASE** . . . . . .

In each of the following sentences, cross out the prepositional phrase between the subject and the verb, and circle the correct form of the verb. Remember, the subject of a sentence is never in a prepositional phrase.

■ **COMPUTER:** Have students highlight prepositional phrases in their writing and read only the nonhighlighted parts of their sentences.

■ **TIP:** For a list of common prepositions, see page 279.

EXAMPLE: Life in these fast-paced times ((does)/ do) not leave much time for rest.

1. Stress from a job or family commitments ((makes) / make) sleeping difficult for some.

2. Crying fits after midnight (wakes /(wake)) parents of small children, giving the parents little rest.

3. Also, people with cable television often (wants /(want)) to stay up to see their favorite shows.

4. A recent report on sleeping habits ((is)/ are) revealing.

5. People from all parts of our society (is /(are)) going to bed late.

6. One out of every three adult Americans ((gets)/ get) to bed after midnight during the week.

7. Adults across America also (sleeps /(sleep)) less than people from many other countries.

8. The report on sleeping habits ((shows)/ show) that 19 percent of Americans sleep six or fewer hours a night.

9. But most of us (needs /(need)) about eight hours of sleep a night to function well.

10. Even a nap during afternoons ((helps)/ help) a person to feel refreshed.

. . . .

Dependent Clause between the Subject and the Verb

A **dependent clause** has a subject and a verb, but it does not express a complete thought. When a dependent clause comes between the subject and the verb, it usually starts with the word *who, whose, whom, that,* or *which.*

The subject of a sentence is never in a dependent clause. When you are looking for the subject of a sentence, you can cross out any dependent clauses. This strategy should make it easier for you to find the real subject and decide whether it agrees with the verb.

The <u>coins</u> that I found last week (<u>seem</u>/seems) very valuable.

The <u>person</u> who delivers our street's newspapers (throw/<u>throws</u>) them everywhere but on people's porches.

> ## FINDING AND FIXING PROBLEMS WITH
> ## SUBJECT-VERB AGREEMENT: Making Subjects and Verbs
> Agree When They Are Separated by a Dependent Clause

Find

The security <u>systems</u> ~~that shopping sites on the Internet provide~~ (is / are) surprisingly effective.

1. **Underline** the subject.
2. **Cross out** any dependent clause that follows the subject. (Look for the words *who, whose, whom, that,* or *which* because they can signal such a clause.)
3. **Ask:** Is the subject singular or plural? *Plural.*

Fix

The security systems that shopping sites on the Internet provide (is / (are)) surprisingly effective.

4. **Choose** the form of the verb that matches the subject.

■ **PRACTICE 5   MAKING SUBJECTS AND VERBS AGREE
WHEN THEY ARE SEPARATED BY A DEPENDENT CLAUSE** . . . .

In each of the following sentences, cross out any dependent clauses. Then, correct any problems with subject-verb agreement. If there is no problem, write "OK" next to the sentence.

> EXAMPLE: My cousins ~~who immigrated to this country from~~
>   *have*
>   ~~Ecuador~~ has jobs in a fast-food restaurant.
>   ^

1. The restaurant ~~that hired my cousins~~ *is* ~~are~~ not treating them fairly.

2. People ~~who work in the kitchen~~ *have* ~~has~~ to report to work at 7:00 A.M.

3. The boss ~~who supervises the morning shift~~ tells the workers not to punch in until 9:00 A.M. *OK*

4. The benefits ~~that full-time workers earn~~ have not been offered to my cousins. *OK*

5. Ramón, ~~whose hand was injured slicing potatoes~~, need to have physical

   therapy.

6. No one ~~who works with him~~ has helped him file for worker's compen-

   sation. *OK*

7. The doctors ~~who cleaned his wound and put in his stitches at the hos-

   pital~~ expects him to pay for the medical treatment.

8. The managers ~~who run the restaurant~~ insists that he is not eligible for

   medical coverage.

9. My cousins, ~~whose English is not yet perfect~~, feels unable to leave

   their jobs.

10. The restaurant ~~that treats them so badly~~ offers the only opportunity

    for them to earn a living. *OK*

. . . .

3. The Sentence Has a Compound Subject

A **compound subject** is two (or more) subjects joined by *and, or,* or *nor.* If two subjects are joined by *and,* they combine to become a plural subject, and the verb must be plural too.

Plural subject = Plural verb

The teacher *and* her aide grade all of the exams.

If two subjects are separated by the word *or* or *nor,* they are not combined. The verb should agree with whichever subject is closer to it.

Subject *or* Singular subject – Singular verb

Either the teacher *or* her aide grades all of the exams.

Subject *or* Plural subject = Plural verb

The teacher *or* her aides grade all of the exams.

Subject *nor* Plural subject = Plural verb

Neither the teacher *nor* her aides grade all of the exams.

■ **TIP:** Whenever you see a compound subject joined by *and,* try replacing it in your mind with *they.*

FINDING AND FIXING PROBLEMS WITH SUBJECT-VERB AGREEMENT: Making Subjects and Verbs Agree in a Sentence with a Compound Subject

---

Find

Watermelon (or) cantaloupe (makes / make) a delicious and healthy snack.

1. **Underline** the subjects.
2. **Circle** the word between the subjects.
3. **Ask:** Does that word join the subjects to make them plural or keep them separate? *Keeps them separate.*
4. **Ask:** Is the subject that is closer to the verb singular or plural? *Singular.*

Fix

Watermelon or cantaloupe ((makes) / make) a delicious and healthy snack.

5. **Choose** the verb form that agrees with the subject that is closer to the verb.

■ **PRACTICE 6   CHOOSING THE CORRECT VERB IN A SENTENCE WITH A COMPOUND SUBJECT** . . . .

In each of the following sentences, underline the word (*and* or *or*) that joins the parts of the compound subject. Then, circle the correct form of the verb.

> **EXAMPLE:** My mother <u>and</u> my sister (has /(have)) asked a nutritionist for advice on a healthy diet.

1. A tomato <u>and</u> a watermelon (shares /(share)) more than just red-colored flesh.

2. A cooked tomato <u>or</u> a slice of watermelon ((contains)/ contain) a nutrient called lycopene that seems to protect the human body from some diseases.

3. Fruits <u>and</u> vegetables (is /(are)) an important part of a healthy diet, most experts agree.

4. Nutrition experts and dieticians (believes /(believe)) that eating a variety of colors of fruits and vegetables is best for human health.

5. Collard greens or spinach ((provides)/ provide) vitamins, iron, and protection from blindness to those who eat them.

6. Carrots and yellow squash (protects /(protect)) against cancer and some kinds of skin damage.

7. Too often, a busy college student or worker ((finds)/ find) it hard to eat the recommended five to nine servings of fruits and vegetables a day.

8. A fast-food restaurant or vending machine ((is)/ are) unlikely to have many fresh vegetable and fruit selections.

9. A salad or fresh fruit ((costs)/ cost) more than a hamburger in many places where hurried people eat.

10. Nevertheless, a brightly colored vegetable and fruit (adds /(add)) vitamins and healthy fiber to any meal.

. . . .

4. The Subject Is an Indefinite Pronoun

An **indefinite pronoun** replaces a general person, place, or thing or a general group of people, places, or things. Indefinite pronouns are often singular, though there are some exceptions, as shown in the chart on page 334.

SINGULAR   Everyone wants the semester to end.

PLURAL   Many want the semester to end.

SINGULAR   Either of the meals is good.

Often, an indefinite pronoun is followed by a prepositional phrase or dependent clause. Remember that the verb of a sentence must agree with the subject of the sentence, and the subject of a sentence is *never in a prepositional phrase or dependent clause*. To choose the correct verb, focus on the indefinite pronoun—you can cross out the prepositional phrase or dependent clause.

Everyone in all of the classes (want/wants) the term to end.

Few of the students (is/are) looking forward to exams.

Several who have to take the math exam (is/are) studying together.

Indefinite Pronouns

ALWAYS SINGULAR			MAY BE SINGULAR OR PLURAL
another	everybody	no one	all
anybody	everyone	nothing	any
anyone	everything	one (of)	none
anything	much	somebody	some
each (of)★	neither (of)★	someone	
either (of)★	nobody	something	

★When one of these words is the subject, mentally replace it with *one*. *One* is singular and takes a singular verb.

FINDING AND FIXING PROBLEMS WITH SUBJECT-VERB AGREEMENT: Making Subjects and Verbs Agree When the Subject Is an Indefinite Pronoun

Find

One ~~of my best friends~~ (lives / live) in California.

1. **Underline** the subject.
2. **Cross out** any prepositional phrase or dependent clause that follows the subject.
3. **Ask:** Is the subject singular or plural? *Singular.*

Fix

One of my best friends (lives)/ live) in California.

4. **Choose** the verb form that agrees with the subject.

PRACTICE 7   CHOOSING THE CORRECT VERB WHEN THE SUBJECT IS AN INDEFINITE PRONOUN . . . .

In each of the following sentences, cross out any prepositional phrase or dependent clause that comes between the subject and the verb. Then, underline the subject, and circle the correct verb.

EXAMPLE: One ~~of the strangest human experiences~~ (results/result) from the "small-world" phenomenon.

1. Everyone (remembers / remember) an example of a "small-world" phenomenon.

2. Someone ~~whom you have just met~~ (tells / tell) you a story.

3. During the story, one ~~of you~~ (realizes / realize) that you are connected somehow.

4. One ~~of your friends~~ (lives / live) next door to the person.

5. Someone ~~in your family~~ (knows / know) someone in the person's family.

6. Each ~~of your families~~ (owns / own) a home in the same place.

7. One ~~of your relatives~~ (plans / plan) to marry his cousin.

8. Some (believes / believe) that if you know one hundred people and talk to someone who knows one hundred people, together you are linked to one million people through friends and acquaintances.

9. Someone ~~in this class~~ probably (connects / connect) to you in one way or another.

10. Each ~~of you~~ probably (knows / know) a good "small-world" story of your own.

. . . .

5. The Verb Comes before the Subject

In most sentences, the subject comes before the verb. Two kinds of sentences often reverse the usual subject-verb order: questions and sentences that begin with *here* or *there*. In these two types of sentences, you need to check for errors in subject-verb agreement.

Questions

In questions, the verb or part of the verb comes before the subject. To find the subject and verb, you can turn the question around as if you were going to answer it.

Where is the bookstore? / The bookstore is . . .

Are you excited? / You are excited.

When is the bus going to leave? / The bus is going to leave . . .

■ **TEAMWORK:** Divide the class down the middle. One side asks questions (students go in turns according to where they are sitting). The other side turns the questions around (anyone can answer by raising his or her hand or calling out the answer). Keep a fairly fast pace.

> **Language Note:** For reference charts on forming questions, see Chapter 32.

Sentences That Begin with Here or There

When a sentence begins with *here* or *there*, the subject often follows the verb. Turn the sentence around to find the subject and verb.

> *Here* is your key to the apartment. / Your key to the apartment is here.

> *There* are four keys on the table. / Four keys are on the table.

> **Language Note:** *There is* and *there are* are common in English. These expressions have the general meaning of *have/has*.
>
> There is time to finish = We have time to finish.

FINDING AND FIXING PROBLEMS WITH SUBJECT-VERB AGREEMENT: Making Subjects and Verbs Agree When the Verb Comes before the Subject

---

Find

What classes (is / are) the professor teaching?

1. If the sentence is a question, **turn the question into a statement:** *The professor (is / are) teaching the classes.*

There (is / are) two good classes in the music department.

2. If the sentence begins with *here* or *there*, **turn it around:** *Two good classes (is / are) in the music department.*

3. **Identify** the subject in each of the two new sentences. *It's "professor" in the first sentence and "classes" in the second.*

4. **Ask:** Is the subject singular or plural? *"Professor" is singular; "classes" is plural.*

Fix

The professor (is / are) teaching the classes.

Two good classes (is / are) in the music department.

5. **Choose** the form of the verb in each sentence that matches the subject.

■ **PRACTICE 8   CORRECTING A SENTENCE WHEN THE VERB COMES BEFORE THE SUBJECT** . . . .

Correct any problem with subject-verb agreement in the following sentences. If a sentence is already correct, write "OK" next to it.

> **EXAMPLE:** What electives ~~do~~ *does* the school offer?

1. What ~~are~~ *is* the best reason to study music?

2. There ~~is~~ *are* several good reasons.

3. There is evidence that music helps students with math. *OK*

4. What is your favorite musical instrument? *OK*

5. Here ~~is~~ *are* a guitar, a saxophone, and a piano.

6. There ~~is~~ *are* very few people with natural musical ability.

7. What time of day ~~does~~ *do* you usually practice?

8. There is no particular time. *OK*

9. What musician ~~does~~ *do* you admire most?

10. Here ~~are~~ *is* some information about the importance of regular practice.

■ **PRACTICE 9   CORRECTING VARIOUS PROBLEMS WITH SUBJECT-VERB AGREEMENT** . . . .

In the following sentences, identify any verb that does not agree with its subject. Then, correct the sentence using the correct form of the verb.

> **EXAMPLE:** Thousands of people ~~is~~ *are* actually being paid to go shopping.

1. The shoppers who take on this work ~~earns~~ *earn* money for checking on a store's quality of service.

2. There ~~is~~ *are* two names for these people: mystery shoppers and secret shoppers.

3. Chain stores across the nation ~~hires~~ *hire* mystery shoppers.

4. Fast-food restaurants and retail stores ~~uses~~ *use* these shoppers the most.

5. What reasons ~~motivates~~ *motivate* a person to become a mystery shopper?

6. Mystery shoppers with a good heart ~~says~~ *say* they do their work to make sure consumers are treated well.

7. Others say they ~~has~~ *have* only one reason: the money they are paid.

8. The pay and benefits ~~appeals~~ *appeal* to many mystery shoppers; they typically get $7 to $30 per store visit, plus money to cover purchases.

9. One ~~do~~ *does* not have to pay a fee to become a mystery shopper.

10. Anybody who likes the idea of getting paid to visit stores ~~are~~ *is* advised to visit www.mysteryshop.org.

Edit Paragraphs and Your Own Writing

Use the chart, Finding and Fixing Problems with Subject-Verb Agreement, on page 342 to help you complete the practices in this section and edit your own writing.

PRACTICE 10 EDITING PARAGRAPHS FOR SUBJECT-VERB AGREEMENT

Find and correct any problems with subject-verb agreement in the following paragraphs.

1. (1) A study I came across while doing research for my sociology class rate*s* U.S. cities by "most things to do." (2) The categories ~~be~~ *are* sun, sea, snow, nature, sports, and culture. (3) Each of the cities ~~were~~ *was* assigned a total from 0 to 100 points in each category. (4) The points were determined by the number of recreational activities available. (5) Los Angeles and San Diego, which share a warm, coastal climate, have perfect scores. (6) Either of these places ~~are~~ *is* a good place to visit. (7) Miami, New York, and Washington, D.C., are the other cities ranked in the top five.

2. (1) Another study measures the fastest and slowest talkers. (2) Postal workers in different cities talk*s* at different speeds when explaining the class of mail. (3) Workers in Columbus, Ohio, speak the fastest. (4) Atlanta and Detroit ~~has~~ *have* the next fastest talkers. (5) There ~~is~~ *are* also fast talkers in Boston and Bakersfield, California. (6) The slowest talkers in the country are in Sacramento, California. (7) Other postal workers who

speak very slowly lives in Los Angeles; Shreveport, Louisiana; and Chat-

tanooga, Tennessee. (8) How do you think your city ranks?

PRACTICE 11   EDITING SUBJECT-VERB AGREEMENT ERRORS AND COMMA SPLICES AND USING FORMAL ENGLISH . . . .

A friend of yours has been turned down for a course because of high enrollment, even though she registered early. She knows her e-mail to the instructor teaching the course has problems. Help her by correcting the subject-verb agreement errors in it. Then, edit the informal English in the e-mail.
Answers will vary. Possible edits shown.

TIP: For more advice on using formal English, see Chapter 2. For advice on choosing appropriate words, see Chapter 33.

Professor
(1) Dear ~~Prof~~ Harper,

am writing ^   *allow me to enter*
(2) I ~~is write~~ to see if there is any chance that you would ~~be cool with~~
  ^   ^
~~me entering~~ your Human Development Course this semester. (3) I
                                                    have
signed up on the first day of registration. (4) Also, my grades ~~has~~ been
         Students   *are*   ^
good so far. (5) ~~Guys~~ I know who ~~is~~ taking your class now says it's really
             ^   ^
great, and the idea of learning about how humans grow and develop
interests me greatly.   *want*
~~interest me a bunch.~~ (6) Because I ~~wants~~ to become a sociology major,
  ^   ^   *is*
taking the class next semester or waiting until next year ~~are~~ not ideal.
  Are   ^
(7) ~~Is~~ you able to accommodate me? (8) Please let me know.
  ^

Thanks,

Kari Estrada

PRACTICE 12   EDITING REGINA'S LETTER . . . .

Look back at Regina Toms's report on page 324. You may have already underlined the subject-verb agreement errors; if not, do so now. Next, using what you've learned in this chapter, correct each error.

PRACTICE 13   EDITING YOUR OWN WRITING FOR SUBJECT-VERB AGREEMENT . . . .

Use your new skill at editing for subject-verb agreement on a piece of your own writing—a paper you are working on for this class, a paper you've already finished, a paper for another course, or a recent piece of writing from your work or everyday life. Use the chart on page 342 to help you.

LEARNING JOURNAL: What kinds of problems with subject-verb agreement do you find most often in your writing? What are some ways to avoid or correct these mistakes?

Chapter Review

1. The ___subject___ and the ___verb___ in a sentence must agree (match) in terms of number. They must both be ___singular___, or they must both be plural.

2. ___Five___ trouble spots can cause errors in subject-verb agreement:

   • When the verb is a form of ___be___, ___have___, or ___do___.

   • When a ___prepositional phrase___ or a ___dependent clause___ comes between the subject and the verb.

   • When there is a ___compound___ subject joined by *and, or,* or *nor.*

   • When the subject is an ___indefinite___ pronoun.

   • When the ___verb___ comes ___before___ the subject.

Chapter Test

Circle the correct choice for each of the following items.

■ **TIP:** For advice on taking tests, see Appendix A.

1. If an underlined portion of this sentence is incorrect, select the revision that fixes it. If the sentence is correct as written, choose d.

   <u>There is</u> only certain times when <u>you can</u> call <u>to get</u> technical support
     A   B   C
   for this computer.

   ■ **RESOURCES:** *Testing Tool Kit,* a CD-ROM available with this book, has even more tests.

   (a.) There are   c. getting
   b. you could   d. No change is necessary.

2. Choose the correct word to fill in the blank.

   Dana's dog Bernard _____ just a puppy, but he moves so slowly that he seems old.

   a. be   c. being
   b. am   (d.) is

3. If an underlined portion of this sentence is incorrect, select the revision that fixes it. If the sentence is correct as written, choose d.

   The <u>umpire was</u> not happy to see that <u>everyone were</u> watching him
        A   B
   <u>argue with</u> the baseball player.
        C

   a. umpire were   c. argues with
   (b.) everyone was   d. No change is necessary.

4. Choose the correct word to fill in the blank.

   The woman who rented us our kayaks _____ now paddling her
   own kayak down the river.

   a. are   b. be   (c.) is

5. Choose the item that has no errors.

   a. Alex and Dane likes to travel now that they have retired from
      their jobs.

   b. Alex and Dane liking to travel now that they have retired from
      their jobs.

   (c.) Alex and Dane like to travel now that they have retired from
      their jobs.

6. Choose the correct word to fill in the blank.

   The builders of this house _____ used the best materials they
   could find.

   (a.) have   b. having   c. has

7. Choose the correct word to fill in the blank.

   The calm before hurricanes _____ most people with anxiety.

   a. fill   b. filling   (c.) fills

8. Choose the item that has no errors.

   (a.) Sheryl and her sons go to the beach whenever they can find the
      time.

   b. Sheryl and her sons goes to the beach whenever they can find the
      time.

   c. Sheryl and her sons is going to the beach whenever they can find
      the time.

9. Choose the correct word to fill in the blank.

   Where _____ the children's wet swimsuits?

   (a.) are   b. is   c. be

10. If an underlined portion of this sentence is incorrect, select the revision
    that fixes it. If the sentence is correct as written, choose d.

    Anybody who <u>can</u> speak several languages <u>are</u> in great demand for
                  A   **B**

    government <u>work</u>, especially positions in foreign embassies.
               C

    a. could   c. working
    (b.) is   d. No change is necessary.

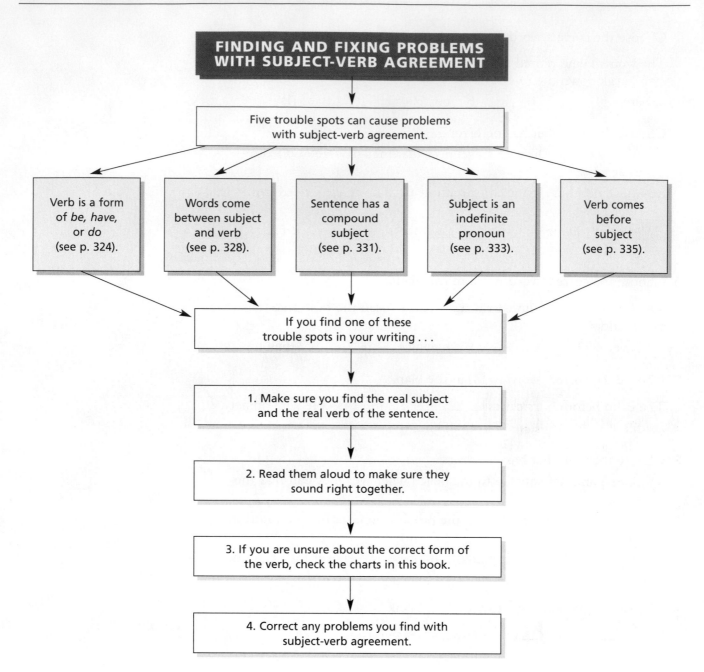

FINDING AND FIXING PROBLEMS WITH SUBJECT-VERB AGREEMENT

Five trouble spots can cause problems with subject-verb agreement.

Verb is a form of *be, have,* or *do* (see p. 324).

Words come between subject and verb (see p. 328).

Sentence has a compound subject (see p. 331).

Subject is an indefinite pronoun (see p. 333).

Verb comes before subject (see p. 335).

If you find one of these trouble spots in your writing . . .

1. Make sure you find the real subject and the real verb of the sentence.

2. Read them aloud to make sure they sound right together.

3. If you are unsure about the correct form of the verb, check the charts in this book.

4. Correct any problems you find with subject-verb agreement.

Verb Tense

Using Verbs to Express Different Times

Understand What Verb Tense Is

Verb tense tells *when* an action happened: in the past, in the present, or in the future. Verbs change their form and use the helping verbs *have* or *be* to indicate different tenses.

PRESENT TENSE	Rick hikes every weekend.
PAST TENSE	He hiked ten miles last weekend.
FUTURE TENSE	He will hike again on Saturday.

■ **TIP:** In the examples throughout this chapter, subjects are underlined, and verbs are double-underlined.

> **Language Note:** Remember to include needed endings on present-tense and past-tense verbs, even if they are not noticed in speech.
>
> | | |
> |---|---|
> | **PRESENT TENSE** | Nate listens to his new iPod wherever he goes. |
> | **PAST TENSE** | Nate listened to his iPod while he walked the dog. |
>
> For reference charts and more practices on the various verb tenses, see Chapter 32.

In the Real World, Why Is It Important to Use the Correct Verb Tense?

SITUATION: Gabriel is an intern in an architectural firm. He'd like to get a part-time job there during the school year because he is studying computer-assisted design and knows the experience would help him get a job after graduation. He sends this e-mail to his supervisor.

I have work hard since coming to T.L.M. Associates and learn many new things. I enjoy learning about architecture and know that it help me in

■ **TIP:** To find and correct problems with verbs, you need to be able to identify subjects and verbs. For a review, see Chapter 20.

■ **TEACHING TIP:** Students should underline the verb errors for Practice 1, on page 344, and correct them for Practice 17 on page 363.

Sandro Polo

Graduate Student in
Architecture

*(See Sandro's Profile of
Success on p. 221.)*

the future. Mr. Partnoy says that he <u>like</u> my work, and I think you do, too. Therefore, I would like to continue after my summer internship. If there is a part-time position available in the fall, I hope that you <u>consider</u> me.

Thank you for your consideration.

> **RESPONSE:** If Sandro Polo had received Gabriel's e-mail, he would have been torn. While Gabriel showed motivation in writing, his e-mail has several obvious grammar errors. Architecture is a very precise business, and not understanding how to use verbs to correctly indicate present, past, or future work could cause major problems. For that reason, Sandro probably would not hire Gabriel, even part-time.

Using verbs incorrectly is an error that people notice.

Practice Using Correct Verbs

This section will teach you about verb tenses and give you practice with using them. The best way to learn how to use the various verb tenses correctly, however, is to read, write, and speak them as often as possible.

 PRACTICE 1   IDENTIFYING VERB ERRORS . . . .

Find and underline the five verb errors in Gabriel's e-mail on page 343.

. . . .

Regular Verbs

Most verbs in English are **regular verbs** that follow standard rules about what endings to use to express time.

Two Regular Present-Tense Endings: -s and No Ending

The **present tense** is used for actions that are happening at the same time that they are being written about (the present) and for things that happen all the time. Present-tense, regular verbs end either in *-s,* or they have no ending added.

-S ENDING	NO ENDING
jumps	jump
walks	walk
lives	live

Use the -*s* ending when the subject is *he, she, it,* or the name of one person or thing. Use no ending for all other subjects.

Regular Verbs in the Present Tense

	SINGULAR	PLURAL
First person	I jump.	We jump.
Second person	You jump.	You jump.
Third person	She (he, it) jumps.	They jump.
	The child jumps.	The children jump.

■ **TIP:** For more about making verbs match subjects, see Chapter 23.

■ **PRACTICE 2   USING PRESENT-TENSE REGULAR VERBS CORRECTLY**

In each of the following sentences, first underline the subject, and then circle the correct verb form.

EXAMPLE: I (tries /(try)) to keep to my budget.

■ **TIP:** For more practices on verb problems, visit Exercise Central at **bedfordstmartins .com/realwriting**.

1. My classes (requires /(require)) much of my time these days.

2. In addition to attending school, I (works /(work)) twenty hours a week in the college library.

3. The other employees (agrees /(agree)) that the work atmosphere is pleasant.

4. Sometimes, we even (manages /(manage)) to do homework at the library.

5. The job ((pays) / pay) a fairly low wage, however.

6. My roommate ((helps)/ help) with the rent on the apartment.

7. Because he isn't in school, he often ((wonders)/ wonder) how I get by.

8. I (uses /(use)) my bicycle to get everywhere I need to go.

9. The bicycle ((allows)/ allow) me to stay in shape both physically and financially.

10. I know that I won't be in school forever, so for now, life on a budget ((satisfies)/ satisfy) me.

■ **RESOURCES:** To gauge students' skills in using verbs, use the *Testing Tool Kit* CD-ROM available with this book.

■ **DISCUSSION:** A common error is using only the present tense in writing. If your students do this, ask why. A common answer is that they know the present form and are less certain about others. Point out that using the present-tense form of a verb where the past tense is correct is as serious an error as using an incorrect past form.

One Regular Past-Tense Ending: -ed

The **past tense** is used for actions that have already happened. An -ed ending is needed on all regular verbs in the past tense.

	PRESENT TENSE	PAST TENSE
First person	I avoid her.	I avoided her.
Second person	You help me.	You helped me.
Third person	He walks fast.	He walked fast.

■ **TIP:** If a verb already ends in -e, just add -d: dance/danced. If a verb ends in -y, usually the -y changes to -i when -ed is added: spy/spied; try/tried.

■ **PRACTICE 3   USING THE PAST TENSE OF REGULAR VERBS CORRECTLY** . . . .

In each of the following sentences, fill in the correct past-tense forms of the verbs in parentheses.

(1) Last winter, I ____displayed____ (*display*) the clear signs of a cold. (2) I ____sneezed____ (*sneeze*) often, and I ____developed____ (*develop*) a sore throat. (3) The congestion in my nose and throat ____annoyed____ (*annoy*) me, and it ____seemed____ (*seem*) that blowing my nose was useless. (4) However, I ____visited____ (*visit*) with my friends and ____attended____ (*attend*) classes at college. (5) I ____assumed____ (*assume*) that I could not give anyone else my cold once I showed the symptoms. (6) Unfortunately, many people ____joined____ (*join*) me in my misery because of my ignorance. (7) Later, I ____learned____ (*learn*) that I ____remained____ (*remain*) contagious for several days after I first showed symptoms. (8) My doctor ____explained____ (*explain*) to me that I ____started____ (*start*) spreading my cold about one day after I became infected with it. (9) However, after my symptoms ____disappeared____ (*disappear*), I ____passed____ (*pass*) on my cold to others for up to three days more. (10) I ____wanted____ (*want*) to apologize to everyone I had infected, but I also ____realized____ (*realize*) that others had given me their colds as well.

. . . .

One Regular Past Participle Ending: -ed

The **past participle** is a verb that is used with a helping verb, such as *have*. For all regular verbs, the past-participle form is the same as the past-tense form: It uses an -ed ending. (To learn about when past participles are used, see pages 355–60.)

PAST TENSE	PAST PARTICIPLE
My kids watched cartoons.	They have watched cartoons before.
George visited his cousins.	He has visited them every year.

■ PRACTICE 4   USING THE PAST PARTICIPLE OF REGULAR VERBS CORRECTLY ·

In each of the following sentences, underline the helping verb (a form of *have*), and fill in the correct form of the verb in parentheses.

> **EXAMPLE:** Because of pressure to keep up with others, families <u>have</u> ___*started*___ (*start*) to give fancier and fancier birthday parties.

1. We <u>have</u> all ___*received*___ (*receive*) invitations to simple birthday parties where children played games and had cake, but those days are gone.

2. Kids' birthday parties <u>have</u> ___*turned*___ (*turn*) into complicated and expensive events.

3. Price tags for some of these parties <u>have</u> ___*climbed*___ (*climb*) to $1,000 or more.

4. By the time she'd finished planning her daughter's birthday, one mother <u>had</u> ___*devoted*___ (*devote*) hundreds of dollars to the event.

5. She discovered that she <u>had</u> ___*handed*___ (*hand*) out $50 for a clubhouse rental, $200 for a cotton-candy maker, and $300 for an actor dressed as the Little Mermaid.

6. The money spent on gifts <u>has</u> ___*increased*___ (*increase*) as well.

7. At the end of each year, many parents find that they <u>have</u> ___*purchased*___ (*purchase*) an average of twenty gifts costing $20 dollars each—$400 total!

8. However, some families <u>have</u> ___*decided*___ (*decide*) to go against the trend.

9. My best friend <u>has</u> ___*saved*___ (*save*) money and effort by having small birthday parties for her son.

10. The savings <u>have</u> ___*reached*___ (*reach*) $500, and she is putting the money toward his college education.

Irregular Verbs

Irregular verbs do not follow the regular pattern for endings. Practice using these verbs so that you learn to use the correct forms in your writing.

Irregular Verbs

PRESENT TENSE	PAST TENSE	PAST PARTICIPLE (USED WITH HELPING VERB)
be (am/are/is)	was/were	been
become	became	become
begin	began	begun
bite	bit	bitten
blow	blew	blown
break	broke	broken
bring	brought	brought
build	built	built
buy	bought	bought
catch	caught	caught
choose	chose	chosen
come	came	come
cost	cost	cost
dive	dived, dove	dived
do	did	done
draw	drew	drawn
drink	drank	drunk
drive	drove	driven
eat	ate	eaten
fall	fell	fallen
feed	fed	fed
feel	felt	felt
fight	fought	fought
find	found	found
fly	flew	flown
forget	forgot	forgotten
get	got	gotten
give	gave	given
go	went	gone
grow	grew	grown

PRESENT TENSE	PAST TENSE	PAST PARTICIPLE (USED WITH HELPING VERB)
have/has	had	had
hear	heard	heard
hide	hid	hidden
hit	hit	hit
hold	held	held
hurt	hurt	hurt
keep	kept	kept
know	knew	known
lay	laid	laid
lead	led	led
leave	left	left
let	let	let
lie	lay	lain
light	lit	lit
lose	lost	lost
make	made	made
mean	meant	meant
meet	met	met
pay	paid	paid
put	put	put
quit	quit	quit
read	read	read
ride	rode	ridden
ring	rang	rung
rise	rose	risen
run	ran	run
say	said	said
see	saw	seen
seek	sought	sought
sell	sold	sold
send	sent	sent
shake	shook	shaken
show	showed	shown
shrink	shrank	shrunk

■ **TEACHING TIP:** Give students a few minutes in class, or ask them as a homework assignment, to review the list of irregular verbs and underline the fifteen verbs they use most frequently.

continued

PRESENT TENSE	PAST TENSE	PAST PARTICIPLE (USED WITH HELPING VERB)
shut	shut	shut
sing	sang	sung
sink	sank	sunk
sit	sat	sat
sleep	slept	slept
speak	spoke	spoken
spend	spent	spent
stand	stood	stood
steal	stole	stolen
stick	stuck	stuck
sting	stung	stung
strike	struck	struck, stricken
swim	swam	swum
take	took	taken
teach	taught	taught
tear	tore	torn
tell	told	told
think	thought	thought
throw	threw	thrown
understand	understood	understood
wake	woke	woken
wear	wore	worn
win	won	won
write	wrote	written

Present Tense of Two Irregular Verbs

BE		HAVE	
I am	we are	I have	we have
you are	you are	you have	you have
he, she, it is	they are	he, she, it has	they have
the editor is	the editors are		
Beth is	Beth and Christina are		

■ **PRACTICE 5   USING *BE* AND *HAVE* IN THE PRESENT TENSE** . . . . . .

In each of the following sentences, fill in the correct form of the verb indicated in parentheses.

> **EXAMPLE:** Because of my university's internship program, I ___*am*___ (*be*) able to receive academic credit for my summer job.

1. I ___*have*___ (*have*) a job lined up with a company that provides private security to businesses and residential developments.

2. The company ___*has*___ (*have*) a good record of keeping its clients safe from crime.

3. The company ___*is*___ (*be*) part of a fast-growing industry.

4. Many people no longer ___*have*___ (*have*) faith in the ability of the police to protect them.

5. People with lots of money ___*are*___ (*be*) willing to pay for their own protection.

6. Concern about crime ___*is*___ (*be*) especially noticeable in so-called gated communities.

7. In these private residential areas, no one ___*has*___ (*have*) the right to enter without permission.

8. If you ___*are*___ (*be*) a visitor, you must obtain a special pass.

9. Once you ___*have*___ (*have*) the pass, you show it to the security guard when you reach the gate.

10. In a gated community, the residents ___*are*___ (*be*) likely to appreciate the security.

. . . .

Irregular verbs do not use the *-ed* ending for the past-tense form. They show the past tense with a change in spelling or in some other way.

PRESENT TENSE	PAST TENSE
I begin today.	I began yesterday.
You sleep very soundly.	You slept late this morning.
I let the dog in today.	I let the dog in yesterday.

The verb *be* is tricky because it has two different forms for the past tense: *was* and *were*.

The Verb Be, *Past Tense*

	SINGULAR	PLURAL
First person	I was	we were
Second person	you were	you were
Third person	he, she, it was	they were
	the student was	the students were

There is no simple rule for how to form irregular verbs in the past tense. Until you memorize them, consult the chart on pages 348–50.

PRACTICE 6   USING *BE* IN THE PAST TENSE

In the paragraph that follows, fill in each blank with the correct past tense of the verb *be*.

> **EXAMPLE:** During college, my sister _____*was*_____ excited about a big decision she'd made.

(1) My sister _____*was*_____ always afraid of visits to the doctor. (2) Therefore, my parents and I _____*were*_____ very surprised when she announced that she wanted to become a doctor herself. (3) We thought that medicine _____*was*_____ a strange choice for her. (4) "Since you _____*were*_____ a little girl, you have disliked doctors," I reminded her. (5) I _____*was*_____ sure she would change her mind very quickly. (6) She admitted that she _____*was*_____ still afraid, but she hoped that understanding medicine would help her overcome her fears. (7) Her pre-medical courses in college _____*were*_____ very difficult, but finally she was accepted into medical school. (8) We _____*were*_____ very proud of her that day, and we knew that she would be a great doctor.

PRACTICE 7   USING IRREGULAR VERBS IN THE PAST TENSE

In each of the following sentences, fill in the past tense of the irregular verb in parentheses. If you do not know the answer, find the word in the chart of irregular verb forms on pages 348–50.

EXAMPLE: It _____*took*_____ (*take*) many years for baseball players
in the Negro Leagues to get recognized for their abilities.

1. The Negro Leagues _____*began*_____ (*begin*) in 1920, founded by
pitcher Andrew "Rube" Foster.

2. Segregation _____*made*_____ (*make*) it impossible for black players to
play on the all-white major league teams at that time.

3. The Negro Leagues _____*gave*_____ (*give*) black athletes the opportunity to play professional baseball.

4. Some Negro League players _____*became*_____ (*become*) legendary.

5. People across the country _____*knew*_____ (*know*) the name of Satchel
Paige, the pitcher for the Kansas City Monarchs.

6. The Kansas City Monarchs's infielder, Jackie Robinson, _____*laid*_____
(*lay*) the groundwork for all future black baseball players.

7. Robinson _____*left*_____ (*leave*) the Negro Leagues in 1947 to
become the first black player to join a major league team, the Brooklyn
Dodgers.

8. Other Negro League players _____*hit*_____ (*hit*) home runs and
_____*stole*_____ (*steal*) bases but did not become famous.

9. The Negro Leagues _____*shut*_____ (*shut*) down in 1960.

10. Supporters _____*built*_____ (*build*) the Negro Leagues Baseball
Museum in Kansas City, Missouri.

■ **PRACTICE 8   USING IRREGULAR VERBS IN THE PAST TENSE** · · · · ·

In the following paragraph, replace any incorrect present-tense verbs with
the correct past tense of the verb.

(1) In 1900, my great-grandfather ~~grows~~ *grew* wheat and raised a few
cattle on his farm in Wyoming. (2) When my grandmother and her
brothers were young, they ~~go~~ *went* to the fields every day to help their father.
(3) The family ~~does~~ *did* not have much money, and they hoped for good
weather every year. (4) Droughts and damaging storms often cost them

a lot. (5) One year, high winds ~~blew~~ ^{*blew*} down the barn, and hailstones
~~break~~ ^{*broke*} their windows. (6) Another year, very little rain ~~falls~~ ^{*fell*}, and they almost ~~lose~~ ^{*lost*} the farm. (7) Somehow, they ~~keep~~ ^{*kept*} going in spite of their difficulties. (8) Their life was hard, but the whole family ~~understands~~ ^{*understood*} that
the rewards of owning their own land were worthwhile.

. . . .

For irregular verbs, the past participle is often different from the past tense.

	PAST TENSE	PAST PARTICIPLE
REGULAR VERB	I <u>walked</u> home.	I <u>have walked</u> home before.
IRREGULAR VERB	I <u>drove</u> home.	I <u>have driven</u> home before.

It is difficult to predict how irregular verbs form the past participle. Until
you are familiar with them, find them in the chart on pages 348–50.

■ PRACTICE 9 USING IRREGULAR VERBS IN THE PAST PARTICIPLE · · ·

In each of the following sentences, fill in the correct helping verb (a form of
have) and the correct past-participle form of the verb in parentheses. If you
do not know the correct form, find the word in the chart on pages 348–50.

> **EXAMPLE:** For some time, Rob Wrubel and George Lichter
> ___*had known*___ (*know*) that their stressful jobs were damaging
> their health.

1. They were top executives of an Internet search engine company, and
   their lives ___*had become*___ (*become*) full of work and travel.

2. For a long time, their bodies ___*had been*___ (*am/are/is*) telling them
   that they were paying a high price for their busy schedules.

3. Lichter ___*had begun*___ (*begin*) to feel pain in his back and legs, and
   Wrubel had gained a lot of weight and had high blood pressure.

4. By the time the two executives met, each of them ___*had found*___ (*find*)
   relief in practicing yoga.

5. Late in 2001, the two men discussed new business opportunities, saying how they ___*had grown*___ (*grow*) tired of stressful work.

6. By this time, they ___*had left*___ (*leave*) their companies.

7. Now, they ___*have put*___ (*put*) their business skills and passion for yoga to work in creating a new corporation.

8. They ___*have built*___ (*build*) a small chain of yoga studios and hope to open locations nationwide.

9. For several years now, their company, Yoga Works, ___*has run*___ (*run*) fourteen studios in California and New York.

10. Wrubel and Lichter ___*have shown*___ (*show*) that hard work and a little imagination can turn a negative situation into a positive one.

■ **TEACHING TIP:** As you introduce this section, remind students that the purpose of this chapter is not to memorize the terms but to use verbs correctly in writing.

Using Past Participles

A **past participle**, by itself, cannot be the main verb of a sentence. But when a past participle is combined with another verb, called a **helping verb**, it can be used to make the present perfect tense and the past perfect tense.

Have/Has + *Past Participle* = *Present Perfect Tense*

The **present perfect** tense is used for an action that began in the past and either continues into the present or was completed at some unknown time in the past.

Present tense of
have (helping verb)   Past participle

PRESENT PERFECT TENSE   My car has stalled several times recently.

[This sentence says the stalling began in the past but may continue into the present.]

PAST TENSE   My car stalled.

[This sentence says that the car stalled once and that it's over.]

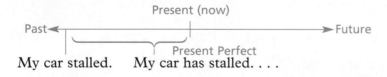

Past ←   Present (now)   → Future

Present Perfect

My car stalled.   My car has stalled. . . .

> **Language Note:** Be careful not to leave out *have* when it is needed for the present perfect. Time-signal words like *since* and *for* may mean that the present perfect is required.
>
> **INCORRECT**   I been driving since 1985.   We been waiting for two hours.
>
> **CORRECT**   I **have** been driving since 1985.   We **have** been waiting for two hours.

■   **PRACTICE 10   USING THE PRESENT PERFECT TENSE** . . . .

In each of the following sentences, circle the correct verb tense.

> **EXAMPLE:** For many years now, the laws of most states (allowed /(have allowed)) only doctors to write prescriptions for patients.

1. In the past few years, a number of states (began /(have begun)) to allow physician assistants and nurse practitioners to write prescriptions.

2. Before the changes in the laws, physician assistants and nurse practitioners ((saw)/ have seen) patients with common illnesses.

3. However, if the patients ((needed)/ have needed) a prescription, a doctor had to write it.

4. Many doctors (said /(have said)) that the changes are a good idea.

5. Physician assistants and nurse practitioners (spent /(have spent)) years in training by the time they get their licenses.

6. Since the new laws took effect, physician assistants and nurse practitioners (wrote /(have written)) many common prescriptions.

7. Recently, some people (expressed /(have expressed)) concern that physician assistants and nurse practitioners might make mistakes in writing prescriptions.

8. However, the possibility of a mistake in a prescription (always existed / (has always existed)).

9. For the past several years, pharmacists (kept /(have kept)) track of prescription errors.

10. Doctors made all but one of the mistakes they (found /(have found)) so far.

. . . .

Had + *Past Participle* = *Past Perfect Tense*

Use *had* plus the past participle to make the **past perfect tense**. The past perfect tense is used for an action that began in the past and ended before some other past action.

Had (helping verb)   Past participle

PAST PERFECT TENSE   My car had stalled several times before I called the mechanic.

[This sentence says that both the *stalling* and *calling the mechanic* happened in the past, but the stalling happened before the calling.]

Present (now)

Past ◄─────┼───────────┼───────────┼───────────────────► Future
          car   mechanic
         stalled   called

■ **PRACTICE 11   USING THE PAST PERFECT TENSE** . . . .

In each of the following sentences, circle the correct verb tense.

EXAMPLE: When musician Ray Charles was born in September 1930, the Depression already (caused /(had caused)) many Americans to lose hope.

1. His family (was /(had been)) poor even before the Depression started.

2. Until he was four years old, Ray ((enjoyed)/ had enjoyed) normal vision.

3. However, by the time he was seven, he (became /(had become)) totally blind.

4. When he ((tripped)/ had tripped) over furniture and asked for his mother's help, often she just watched him and remained silent.

5. In this way, she ((encouraged)/ had encouraged) him to learn how to help himself to get back up.

6. She (come/(had come)) to recognize how important it was for Ray to find his way on his own.

7. Ray later ((spent)/ had spent) several years in Florida's state school for the deaf and blind.

8. By the time he left the school, he (developed /(had developed)) his unusual gift for playing, composing, and arranging music.

9. After many more years as a struggling musician, Ray Charles ((refined)/ had refined) his unique musical style and become a star.

10. By the time of his death in 2004, Charles understood that he (inspired /(had inspired)) many people.

- -

Be + *Past Participle* = *Passive Voice*

A sentence that is written in the **passive voice** has a subject that does not perform an action. Instead, the subject is acted upon. To create the passive voice, combine a form of the verb *be* with a past participle.

Form of *be*   Past participle
(helping verb)

PASSIVE   The <u>newspaper</u> <u>was thrown</u> onto the porch.

[The subject, *newspaper*, did not throw itself onto the porch. Some unidentified person threw the newspaper.]

Most sentences are written in the **active voice**, which means that the subject performs the action.

ACTIVE   The <u>delivery person</u> <u>threw</u> the newspaper onto the porch.

[The subject, *delivery person*, performed the action: He or she threw the newspaper.]

Use the passive voice when no one person performed the action, when you don't know who performed the action, or when you want to emphasize the receiver of the action. Do not overuse the passive voice. When you know who performed the action, it is usually preferable to identify the actor.

ACTIVE   The <u>bandleader</u> <u>chose</u> Kelly to do a solo.

PASSIVE   <u>Kelly</u> <u>was chosen</u> to do a solo.

[If you wanted to emphasize Kelly's being chosen rather than the bandleader's choice, you might decide to use the passive voice.]

FINDING AND FIXING VERB-TENSE ERRORS:
Changing from Active to Passive Voice

↓

Find

<u>He</u> <u>sent</u> the payment over two weeks ago.

1. **Underline** the subject, and **double-underline** the verb.
2. **Ask:** What word in the sentence is receiving the action? *Payment.*
3. **Cross out** the subject.

↓

↓

Fix

The payment
He sent ~~the payment~~ over two weeks ago.
  ^

4. Make the word that is receiving the action the subject by moving it to the beginning of the sentence.

The payment was
He sent ~~the payment~~ over two weeks ago.
  ^

5. Add the correct form of the verb *be* in front of the main verb.

The payment was   *by him*
He sent ~~the payment~~ over two weeks ago.
  ^   ^

6. You can either delete the performer of the action or put this information after the verb and the word *by*.

NOTE: If the original sentence uses a form of *have* followed by a past participle, form the passive voice by using a form of *have* + *been* + the past participle:

The payment   been
He has sent . ~~the payment.~~
  ^   ^   ^

Language Note: Avoid confusing passive voice and the present perfect tense, which does not use *been* except in sentences with *be* as main verb.

INCORRECT   My <u>aunt</u> and <u>uncle</u> <u>have been trained</u> the dogs.

CORRECT   My <u>aunt</u> and <u>uncle</u> **have trained** the dogs.
          (present perfect)

CORRECT   The <u>dogs</u> **have been trained** by my aunt and uncle.
          (passive)

■   PRACTICE 12   **USING THE PASSIVE VOICE** . . . .

Rewrite the following sentences in the passive voice.

My bill was
EXAMPLE: ~~You~~ added ~~my bill~~ incorrectly.
          ^

The Civil war was
1. ~~Soldiers~~ fought ~~the Civil War~~ from 1861 to 1865.
   ^
The movie   been
2. ~~Critics~~ had praised ~~the movie~~ highly even before its opening day.
   ^
Paint was   ^
3. ~~Vandals~~ smeared ~~paint~~ on the statues in the park.
   ^

We were
4. An anonymous caller told us the good news at 7:00 this morning.
    ^

The winner   been
5. A voice has announced the winner.
    ^   ^

Consistency of Verb Tense

Consistency of verb tense means that all actions in a sentence that happen (or happened) at the same time are in the same tense. If all of the actions happen in the present or happen all the time, use the present for all verbs in the sentence. If all of the actions happened in the past, use the past tense for all verbs.

When you edit your writing, make sure that any time a verb tense changes it is because the action the verb describes happened at a different time. Otherwise, the shift in tenses causes an inconsistency.

INCONSISTENT The movie started just as we take our seats.

[The actions both happened at the same time, but *started* is in the past tense, and *take* is in the present tense.]

CONSISTENT, The movie starts just as we take our seats.
PRESENT TENSE

[The actions and verb tenses are both in the present.]

CONSISTENT, The movie started just as we took our seats.
PAST TENSE

[The actions *started* and *took* both happened in the past, and both are in the past tense.]

■ **PRACTICE 13   USING CONSISTENT VERB TENSE** . . . .

In each of the following sentences, double-underline the verbs and correct any unnecessary shifts in verb tense. Write the correct form of the verb in the blank space provided.

EXAMPLE: _____*have*_____ Although some people dream of having their picture taken by a famous photographer, not many had the chance.

1. _____*wants*_____ Now, special stores in malls take magazine-quality photographs of anyone who wanted one.

2. _____*heard*_____ The founder of one business got the idea when she hear friends complaining about how bad they looked in family photographs.

3. _____*felt*_____ They feel they were always blinking or making a funny face.

4. _____*decided*_____ She ~~decide~~ to open a business to take studio-style photographs that <u>didn't</u> cost a lot of money.

5. _____*offered*_____ Her first store <u>included</u> special lighting and ~~offers~~ different sets, such as colored backgrounds, outdoor scenes, or room backgrounds.

6. _____*want*_____ Now, her stores even <u>have</u> makeup studios for people who ~~wanted~~ a special look for their pictures.

7. _____*advise*_____ Some stores even <u>provide</u> consultants who ~~advised~~ customers on the best colors to <u>wear</u> and poses to <u>take</u>.

8. _____*keep*_____ These locations ~~kept~~ extra clothing on hand in case a customer <u>chooses</u> to wear a more flattering color.

9. _____*like*_____ All the stores <u>use</u> professional photographers who ~~liked~~ the high volume of business they get at mall studios.

10. _____*charges*_____ A set of ten headshots from a mall studio <u>costs</u> about $50, while a typical professional photographer ~~charged~~ hundreds of dollars for this type of package.

■ **PRACTICE 14   CORRECTING VARIOUS VERB PROBLEMS** . . . .

In the following sentences, find and correct any verb problems.

EXAMPLE: Sheena ~~be~~ *is* tired of the tattoo on her left shoulder.

1. Many of Sheena's friends ~~was~~ *were* getting tattoos ten years ago.

2. Sheena had never consider*ed* a tattoo until several of her friends got them.

3. Sheena was twenty-two when she ~~goes~~ *went* to the tattoo parlor.

4. After looking at many designs, she ~~choose~~ *chose* a purple rose, which she gave to the tattoo artist.

5. Her sister liked the tattoo, but her mother faint*ed*.

6. Tattoos ~~are~~ *were* very popular among young Americans in the 1990s.

7. Today, however, a typical person with a ten-year-old tattoo express*es* some regret about following that 1990s trend.

8. Many people who *have* now reached their thirties want to get rid of their tattoos.

9. Dermatologists have ~~saw~~ *seen* the development of a new trend toward tattoo removal.

10. A few years ago, when a person *had* decided to have a tattoo removed, doctors had to cut out the design.

11. That technique ~~leaved~~ *left* scars.

12. Today, doctors ~~using~~ *use* laser light to break up the ink molecules in the skin.

13. Six months ago, Sheena start*ed* to have treatments to remove her tattoo.

14. The procedure hurt~~ed~~ every time she saw the doctor, but she hoped it would be worth the pain.

15. Purple ink ~~have~~ *has* longer staying power than black, blue, and red, so Sheena's treatments will continue for more than two years.

Edit Paragraphs and Your Own Writing

Use the chart, Finding and Fixing Verb-Tense Errors, on page 366 to help you complete the practices in this section and edit your own writing.

PRACTICE 15   **EDITING PARAGRAPHS FOR CORRECT VERBS** . . . . .

Find and correct any problems with verb tense in the following paragraphs.

1. (1) When Teresa saw her friend Jan drop makeup into her bag, she frown*ed*. (2) She ~~know~~ *knew* that Jan was stealing. (3) She also ~~knowed~~ *knew* that Jan would be mad if Teresa said anything. (4) What if someone from security had seen Jan! (5) As they ~~leave~~ *left* the store, Teresa's heart beat~~ed~~ hard. (6) When nothing happened, she was relieve*d*. (7) Still, she ~~feel~~ *felt* bad, so she spoke to Jan. (8) Jan ~~say~~ *said* she was sorry and ~~has~~ returned the makeup. (9) Teresa ~~be feeling~~ *felt* much better.

2. (1) George Crum, a Native American chef, invent*ed* potato chips in 1853. (2) A customer ~~has~~ *had* returned an order of french fries with a note that they were too thick. (3) Crum decide*d* to make superthin fries to get even. (4) The customer loved the thin fries, and since then they *have* become

a favorite snack. (5) In the 1920s, Herman Lay ~~brang~~ *brought* the potato chip to grocery stores. (6) The chips sold first in the South, and their popularity quickly spread. (7) Since then, people ~~ate~~ *have eaten* millions of chips.

3. (1) Many people in the world ~~be~~ *are* consumers of the same energy-boosting drug. (2) For centuries, people have ~~use~~ *used* caffeine as a stimulant. (3) Caffeine ~~have~~ *has* the power to increase both physical and mental alertness. (4) The sodas and chocolate bars that children have ~~be~~ *been* eating for years contain this habit-forming drug. (5) It ~~is~~ *was* only about 150 years ago that chemists discovered that coffee and tea contain the same effective ingredient. (6) Back then, boiling water for coffee or tea ~~reduces~~ *reduced* disease among workers in crowded cities. (7) The caffeine also ~~keep~~ *kept* workers awake at their machinery. (8) In a sense, caffeine has ~~make~~ *made* today's fast-paced world possible. (9) Scientists have found~~ed~~ that consuming caffeine at moderate levels is not dangerous. (10) A moderate level ~~meant~~ *means* one to two 12-ounce cups of coffee or a few cans of soda a day.

■ **PRACTICE 16   EDITING VERB PROBLEMS AND USING FORMAL ENGLISH** . . . .

Your sister has a bad case of laryngitis and wants to bring a note about her condition to her doctor. Help her by correcting the verb problems in the note. Then, edit the informal English.   *Answers will vary. Possible edits shown.*

■ **TIP:** For more advice on using formal English, see Chapter 2. For advice on choosing appropriate words, see Chapter 33.

> Dear Dr. Kerrigan,
>
> (1) ~~What's up,~~ Doc ~~Kerrigan?~~
>
> (2) Your assistant ~~ask~~ *asked* me to tell you about my symptoms, so I ~~describe~~ *will* them as well as I can. (3) I ~~becomed~~ *became* sick about a day ago. (4) Now, my throat ~~hurt~~ *hurts* every time I swallow~~ed~~, and I can't speak. (5) Also, I ~~has~~ *have* a very high fever, and I ~~be wicked~~ *am very* tired. (6) I don't think I ~~has~~ *have* ever ~~feeled~~ *felt* so ~~crappy~~ *bad* before. (7) I ~~looked~~ *look* forward to seeing you during my appointment.
>
> (8) Thanks ~~mucho,~~ *very much,*
>
> Corrine Evans

■ **PRACTICE 17   EDITING MARTINA'S NOTE** . . . .

Look back at Gabriel's note on page 343. You may have already underlined the five verb errors; if not, do so now. Next, using what you've learned in this chapter, correct each error.

■ **PRACTICE 18** **EDITING YOUR OWN WRITING FOR VERB TENSE** . . . .

■ **LEARNING JOURNAL:**
What kind of verb problems
do you find most often in
your writing? What are some
ways to avoid or correct these
mistakes?

Edit verbs in a piece of your own writing—a paper you are working on for this class, a paper you've already finished, a paper for another course, or a recent piece of writing from your work or everyday life. Use the chart on page 366 to help you.

Chapter Review

1. Verb ____*tense*____ indicates when the action in a sentence happens (present or past).

2. What are the two present-tense endings for regular verbs? *-s and no ending*

3. How do regular verbs in the past tense end? *-ed ending*

4. The past participle is used with a ____*helping*____ verb.

5. Verbs that do not follow the regular pattern for verbs are called ____*irregular*____.

6. An action that started in the past but might continue into the present uses the ___*present perfect tense*___.

7. An action that happened in the past before something else that happened in the past uses the *past perfect tense* .

8. You should usually avoid using the ____*passive*____ voice, which has a subject that performs no action but is acted upon.

9. Verb tenses are consistent when actions that happen at the same ____*time*____ are in the same ____*tense*____ .

Chapter Test

Circle the correct choice for each of the following items.

■ **TIP:** For advice on taking tests, see Appendix A.

1. If an underlined portion of this sentence is incorrect, select the revision that fixes it. If the sentence is correct as written, choose d.

   It has <u>became</u> difficult to tell whether Trisha is <u>tired</u> of her work or <u>tired</u>
       A   B   C
   of her boss.

   ■ **RESOURCES:** *Testing Tool Kit*, a CD-ROM available with this book, has even more tests.

   (a.) become   c. tiring

   b. be   d. No change is necessary.

2. Choose the item that has no errors.

   a. By the time we arrived, Michelle already gave her recital.

   (b.) By the time we arrived, Michelle had already given her recital.

   c. By the time we arrived, Michelle has already given her recital.

3. If an underlined portion of this sentence is incorrect, select the revision that fixes it. If the sentence is correct as written, choose d.

   I <u>likes</u> Manuel's new car, but I <u>wish</u> he wouldn't park it in my space
       A   **B**

   when he <u>comes</u> home from work.
            C

   (a.) like   c. came

   b. wishing   d. No change is necessary.

4. Choose the item that has no errors.

   (a.) Patrick has such a bad memory that he has to write down everything he is supposed to do.

   b. Patrick had such a bad memory that he has to write down everything he is supposed to do.

   c. Patrick had such a bad memory that he having to write down everything he is supposed to do.

5. Choose the correct word(s) to fill in the blank.

   For many years, Steven _____ the manual typewriter that his grandfather gave to him.

   a. keeped   (b.) kept   c. was keeping

6. Choose the item that has no errors.

   a. I have be cutting back on the amount of coffee I drink.

   b. I has been cutting back on the amount of coffee I drink

   (c.) I have been cutting back on the amount of coffee I drink.

7. Choose the correct word(s) to fill in the blank.

   We had intended to visit Marina's parents while we _____ in town, but we didn't have time.

   a. was   b. had were   (c.) were

8. Choose the correct word(s) to fill in the blank.

   Each family _____ a dish and brought it to our knitting club's annual dinner.

   a. prepares   (b.) prepared   c. have prepared

9. If an underlined portion of this sentence is incorrect, select the revision that fixes it. If the sentence is correct as written, choose d.

The boy <u>jumped</u> out of the way just before the car <u>is</u> about to <u>hit</u> him.
           A   B   C

a. jumping   c. hitted

(b.) was   d. No change is necessary.

10. Choose the correct word to fill in the blank.

Who has _____ the train to New York before?

(a.) taken   b. take   c. taked

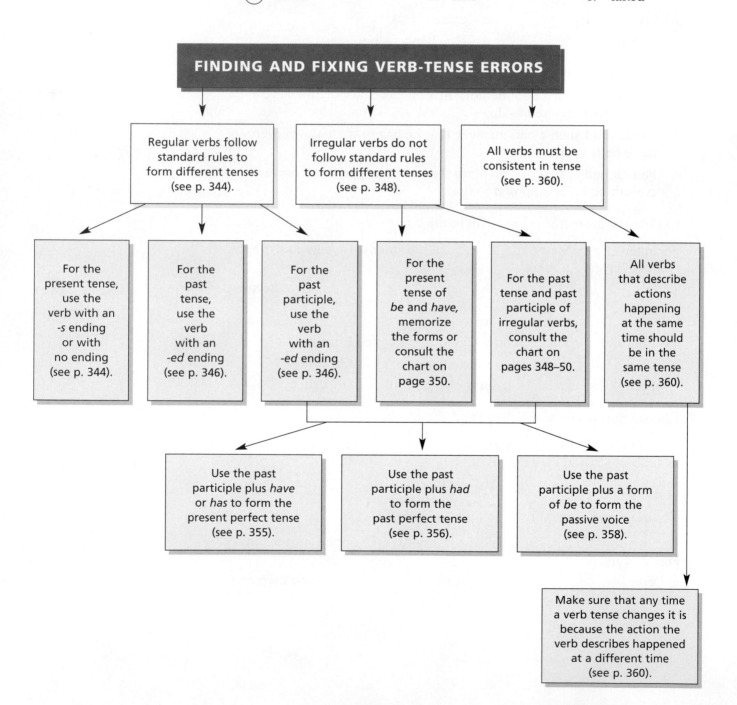

FINDING AND FIXING VERB-TENSE ERRORS

Regular verbs follow standard rules to form different tenses (see p. 344).

Irregular verbs do not follow standard rules to form different tenses (see p. 348).

All verbs must be consistent in tense (see p. 360).

For the present tense, use the verb with an -s ending or with no ending (see p. 344).

For the past tense, use the verb with an -ed ending (see p. 346).

For the past participle, use the verb with an -ed ending (see p. 346).

For the present tense of be and have, memorize the forms or consult the chart on page 350.

For the past tense and past participle of irregular verbs, consult the chart on pages 348–50.

All verbs that describe actions happening at the same time should be in the same tense (see p. 360).

Use the past participle plus have or has to form the present perfect tense (see p. 355).

Use the past participle plus had to form the past perfect tense (see p. 356).

Use the past participle plus a form of be to form the passive voice (see p. 358).

Make sure that any time a verb tense changes it is because the action the verb describes happened at a different time (see p. 360).

Part Four Test
The Four Most Serious Errors

PART I

Following are two paragraphs. Read them carefully, and circle the correct answers to the questions that follow them. Use some of the reading strategies from Chapter 1.

1 Versailles, the famous palace first occupied in the 1600s by King Louis XIV, is now one of France's biggest tourist attractions. 2 Ten million people visit the palace every year, but never on Mondays, when it <u>was</u> closed. 3 That is when the clockmaker walks around to check out the palace's many clocks. 4 Most of these clocks are very elaborate. 5 Which is in keeping with the elegance of the palace. 6 One clock, built by an engineer and astronomer, has golden rings inside a glass sphere. 7 The rings track the movement of the planets, the clock is a calendar that can show the date until the year 9999. 8 The palace's oldest clock can put on a mechanical show in which two eagles flap their wings and a king on a throne pops out. 9 This part of the clock is usually turned off because nearby drivers who see the clock pauses, causing traffic jams. 10 Clocks were important for the royal court even in the seventeenth century. 11 Louis XIV had fixed times when he get up in the morning, said prayers, held meetings, and ate his meals. 12 The king had four clockmakers working for him, and when he traveled, the clockmakers and many clocks went with him. 13 Today, only one timekeeper maintains the palace's clocks. 14 He himself wears a common wristwatch that runs on a battery.

1. Which of the following should be used in place of the underlined word in sentence 2?

    a. were

    (b.) is

    c. be

    d. been

2. Which of the following changes is needed in sentence 5?

    a. Add a period after "elegance."

    b. Join it to sentence 6 to avoid a fragment.

    c. Change "with" to "to."

    (d.) Join it to sentence 4 to avoid a fragment.

3. Which of the following sentences should be revised because it is a comma splice?

    a. Sentence 3

    b. Sentence 4

    (c.) Sentence 7

    d. Sentence 10

4. Which of the following changes is needed in sentence 9?
   a. Change "is" to "be."
   b. Change "turned" to "turn."
   c. Change "see" to "sees."
   d. Change "pauses" to "pause." *(circled)*

5. Which of the following changes is needed in sentence 11?
   a. Change "get" to "got." *(circled)*
   b. Change "held" to "hold."
   c. Change "ate" to "eat."
   d. Change "ate" to "eating."

■ **RESOURCES:** *Additional Resources* includes reproducible answer keys for the tests that conclude Parts Four through Seven. For each question, the keys list the section of *Real Writing* that students should study if they missed the question.

1 Team-building is important in many companies, and some businesses are willing to take unusual steps to encourage it. 2 For many years, trainers hired to help with team building has involved employees in group games outdoors. 3 Now, a new set of team-building exercises has become popular. 4 Executives and other employees are now competing in cooking contests, performing in musical groups, and solving fake crimes together. 5 Teamwork is essential in the crime games because everyone needed to share clues and information to solve a case. 6 While searching the location of the fake crime, team members get evidence such as hair and blood samples or possible murder weapons. 7 They then hold a dinner where they try to find the suspect who matches all the clues. 8 Another popular team-building activity is grape stomping teams of managers compete to see which group produces the most juice. 9 Some teammates stomp the grapes in a barrel. 10 Others try to guide the juice through a spout, and anyone in close range gets splashed. 11 Exercises like this can bring employees closer together. 12 For instance, an owner of a national hotel chain once squeezed into a barrel with some of his managers to stomp grapes. 13 When they were done. 14 The owner drank some of the juice they'd made. 15 No one is certain. 16 Whether these exercises actually change employees' behavior back on the job.

6. What revision should be made to the underlined section of sentence 2?
   a. has been involved
   b. have involved *(circled)*
   c. has involve
   d. No change is necessary.

7. What revision should be made to the underlined section of sentence 5?
   a. needs to *(circled)*
   b. need to
   c. needing to
   d. No change is necessary.

8. What revision should be made to the underlined section of sentence 8?
   a. stomping, teams
   b. stomping Teams
   c. stomping. Teams *(circled)*
   d. No change is necessary.

9. What revision should be made to the underlined sections of sentences 13 and 14?

   a. done; the owner

   b. done the owner

   c. done, the owner

   d. No change is necessary.

10. What revision should be made to the underlined sections of sentences 15 and 16?

   a. certain; whether

   b. certain whether

   c. certain, whether

   d. No change is necessary.

PART II

Circle the correct choice for each of the following items.

1. Choose the correct word(s) to fill in the blank.

   If you want to use your cell phone, you _____ to leave the theater.

   a. has

   b. had

   c. have

   d. have had

2. Choose the item that has no errors.

   a. When he stepped on the brake to stop. The brake pedal went all the way to the floor.

   b. When he stepped on the brake to stop, the brake pedal went all the way to the floor.

   c. When he stepped on the brake to stop; the brake pedal went all the way to the floor.

3. If an underlined portion of this item is incorrect, select the revision that fixes it. If the item is correct as written, choose d.

   Amy's leg injury prevented her from jogging for months she decided to

                                                          A   **B**

   watch her diet so she wouldn't gain too much weight.

            C

   a. jogging; for

   b. months. She

   c. diet, so

   d. No change is necessary.

4. Choose the correct word(s) to fill in the blank.

   By the time I got around to responding to the invitation, the party _____ occurred.

   a. had already

   b. has

   c. have already

5. Choose the item that has no errors.

   a. Our local bookstore went out of business the owner said she couldn't compete with the huge chain bookstore down the street.

   b. Our local bookstore went out of business, the owner said she couldn't compete with the huge chain bookstore down the street.

   c. Our local bookstore went out of business. The owner said she couldn't compete with the huge chain bookstore down the street.

6. Choose the correct words to fill in the blank.

   To learn a foreign _____ is helpful to live in a country in which that language is spoken.

   a. language; it
   b. language. It
   c. language, it (circled)

7. If an underlined portion of this item is incorrect, select the revision that fixes it. If the item is correct as written, choose d.

   The large, fluffy <u>dog with</u> the dirty paws <u>have</u> just <u>run through</u> a mud
               A   B   C
   puddle.

   a. dog. With
   b. has (circled)
   c. run, through
   d. No change is necessary.

8. If an underlined portion of this item is incorrect, select the revision that fixes it. If the item is correct as written, choose d.

   Marija has <u>choosed</u> to <u>practice</u> a form of martial arts called aikido so she
                 A   B
   can <u>protect</u> herself.
        C

   a. chosen (circled)
   b. practiced
   c. protected
   d. No change is necessary.

9. Choose the item that has no errors.

   a. Walking two miles a day. Ben got in shape for his hike.
   b. Walking two miles a day, Ben got in shape for his hike. (circled)
   c. Walking two miles a day; Ben got in shape for his hike.

10. If an underlined portion of this item is incorrect, select the revision that fixes it. If the item is correct as written, choose d.

    It's too bad you <u>missed</u> the club <u>meeting because</u> Marcos <u>had showed</u>
                    A   B   C
    us pictures from his trip to China.

    a. miss
    b. meeting. Because
    c. showed (circled)
    d. No change is necessary.

11. Choose the correct words to fill in the blank.

    Ms. Fleming's resume is _____ she is not qualified for this job.

    a. impressive however
    b. impressive However
    c. impressive; however, (circled)

12. Choose the item that has no errors.

    a. Randall is happy that he gets weekends off. (circled)
    b. Randall happy that he gets weekends off.
    c. Randall be happy that he gets weekends off.

13. Choose the item that has no errors.
    a. There is at least five people in that car.
    (b.) There are at least five people in that car.
    c. There be at least five people in that car.

14. If an underlined portion of this item is incorrect, select the revision that fixes it. If the item is correct as written, choose d.

    Martha <u>knew she</u> should call in <u>an expert</u> at computer <u>repairs. Like</u>
           A   **B**   **C**
    Betsy.
    a. knew, she   (c.) repairs, like
    b. an. Expert   d. No change is necessary.

15. Choose the correct word to fill in the blank.

    Your dogs or my cat _____ wrecking the neighbors' flowers.
    a. are   b. be   (c.) is

16. Choose the item that has no errors.
    (a.) Many people see ads for certain drugs, and they ask their doctors for those drugs.
    b. Many people see ads for certain drugs they ask their doctors for those drugs.
    c. Many people see ads for certain drugs, they ask their doctors for those drugs.

17. Choose the item that has no errors.
    a. James wrecked the van. During his long road trip.
    (b.) James wrecked the van during his long road trip.
    c. James wrecked the van; during his long road trip.

18. Choose the correct word to fill in the blank.

    A doughnut and an apple do not _____ the same calorie content.
    a. has   (b.) have   c. had

19. If an underlined portion of this item is incorrect, select the revision that fixes it. If the item is correct as written, choose d.

    Becca <u>found it</u> wasn't as easy as she'd <u>expected. To</u> get a good grade
           A   **B**
    <u>in biology.</u>
     C

    a. found, it   c. in, biology
    (b.) expected to   d. No change is necessary.

20. Choose the correct word(s) to fill in the blank.

    Some people say that playing video games improves a person's hand-eye coordination, but I _____ always disagreed with that.
    (a.) have   b. has   c. have had

Part Five
Other Grammar Concerns

25

Pronouns

Using Substitutes for Nouns

Understand What Pronouns Are

Pronouns replace nouns or other pronouns in a sentence so that you do not have to repeat them.

>   *her*
> Sheryl got into ~~Sheryl's~~ car.
>   *He* ^
> I like Mario. ~~Mario~~ is a good dancer.
>   ^

In most cases, a pronoun refers to a specific noun or pronoun mentioned nearby.

> Noun
> |
> I picked up my new glasses. They are cool.
> |
> Pronoun replacing noun

■ **RESOURCES:** *Additional Resources* contains tests and supplemental exercises for this chapter as well as a transparency master for the chart at the end.

Practice Using Pronouns Correctly

Identify Pronouns

Before you practice finding and correcting common pronoun errors, it will help you to practice identifying pronouns.

Common Pronouns

PERSONAL PRONOUNS	POSSESSIVE PRONOUNS	INDEFINITE PRONOUNS	
I	my	all	much
me	mine	any	neither (of)
you	your/yours	anybody	nobody
she/he	hers/his	anyone	none (of)
her/him	hers/his	anything	no one
it	its	both	nothing
we	our/ours	each (of)	one (of)
us	our/ours	either (of)	some
they	their/theirs	everybody	somebody
them	their/theirs	everyone	someone
		everything	something
		few (of)	

■ **PRACTICE 1   IDENTIFYING PRONOUNS** . . . .

■ **TIP:** For more practice with pronoun usage, visit Exercise Central at **bedfordstmartins .com/realwriting**.

In each of the following sentences, circle the pronoun, underline the noun it refers to, and draw an arrow from the pronoun to the noun.

> **EXAMPLE:** In 2002, a gold coin made news when it sold for the highest price of any coin in history.

■ **RESOURCES:** To gauge students' skills in pronoun usage, use the *Testing Tool Kit* CD-ROM available with this book.

1. When the U.S. mint began to make gold coins in 1850, they had a face value of twenty dollars.

2. The sculptor Augustus Saint-Gaudens redesigned the gold pieces in 1907, so Americans began to call the coins "saints" after him.

3. After President Franklin Roosevelt took the country off the gold standard in 1933, he ordered all 1933 "saints" to be melted down.

4. Two coins were given to the Smithsonian Institution, and they were supposed to be the only surviving 1933 gold twenty-dollar pieces.

5. A coin stolen from the mint somehow ended up with the delegates of the royal family of Egypt; they asked for permission to take the coin to Egypt.

6. Probably by mistake, the Treasury Department granted its permission to the request.

7. When Egypt's King Farouk, a coin collector, obtained the world's rarest coin, (he) must have felt quite lucky.

8. When Farouk was deposed, (his) coin collection was sold, and the coin disappeared.

9. Stephen Fenton, a later owner of the coin, had to go to court in the United States to prove that (he) had the right to sell the gold piece.

10. When the "saint" was auctioned in 2002, (it) brought a price of over 6.6 million dollars.

■ **ESL:** ESL students may have particular trouble with pronouns and benefit from extra practice exercises.

- -

Check for Pronoun Agreement

A pronoun must agree with (match) the noun or pronoun it refers to in number. **Number** is the amount of something, which is either one (singular) or more than one (plural).

If a pronoun is singular, it must also match the noun or pronoun it refers to in gender (*he, she,* or *it*).

CONSISTENT   Magda sold *her* old television set.

[*Her* agrees with *Magda* because both are singular and feminine.]

CONSISTENT   The Wilsons sold *their* old television set.

[*Their* agrees with the *Wilsons* because both are plural.]

Watch out for singular, general nouns. If a noun is singular, the pronoun that refers to it must be singular as well.

INCONSISTENT   Any student can tell you what *their* least favorite course is.

[*Student* is singular, but the pronoun *their* is plural.]

CONSISTENT   Any student can tell you what *his* or *her* least favorite course is.

[*Student* is singular, and so are the pronouns *his* or *her.*]

To avoid using the awkward phrase *his* or *her,* make the subject plural.

CONSISTENT   Most students can tell you what *their* least favorite course is.

Two types of words often cause errors in pronoun agreement: indefinite pronouns and collective nouns.

Indefinite Pronouns

An **indefinite pronoun** does not refer to a specific person, place, or thing: It is general. Indefinite pronouns often take singular verbs. Whenever a pronoun refers to an indefinite pronoun, check for agreement.

Someone left ~~their~~ *her* purse in the cafeteria.

The monks got up at dawn. Everybody had ~~their~~ *his* chores for the day.

Indefinite Pronouns

ALWAYS SINGULAR			MAY BE PLURAL OR SINGULAR
another	everyone	nothing	all
anybody / anyone	everything	one (of)	any
anything	much	somebody	none
each (of)	neither (of)	someone	some
either (of)	nobody	something	
everybody	no one		

NOTE: Many people object to use of only the masculine pronoun *he* when referring to a singular indefinite pronoun, such as *everyone.* Although grammatically correct, using the masculine form alone to refer to an indefinite pronoun is considered sexist. Here are two ways to avoid this problem:

1. Use *his or her.*

   Someone posted *his or her* e-mail address to the Web site.

2. Change the sentence so that the pronoun refers to a plural noun or pronoun.

   Some students posted *their* e-mail addresses to the Web site.

■ PRACTICE 2   USING INDEFINITE PRONOUNS

Circle the correct pronoun or group of words in parentheses.

(1) Anyone who wants to start (their /(his or her)) own business had better be prepared to work hard. (2) One may find, for example, that ((his or her)/ their) work is never done. (3) There is always something waiting, with ((its)/ their) own peculiar demands. (4) Nothing gets done on (their /

(its) own. (5) Anybody who expects to have more freedom now that (he or she no longer works)/ they no longer work) for a boss may be disappointed. (6) After all, when you work as an employee for a company, there is always someone above you who must make decisions as (they see /(he or she sees)) fit. (7) When you are your own boss, there is no one else to place (themselves /(himself or herself)) in the position of final responsibility.

(8) Somebody starting a business may also be surprised by how much tax (they /(he or she)) must pay. (9) Each employee at a company pays only about half as much toward social security as what (they /(he or she)) would pay if self-employed. (10) And neither medical nor dental coverage can be obtained as inexpensively as ((it)/ they) can when a person is an employee at a corporation.

. . . .

Collective Nouns

A **collective noun** names a group that acts as a single unit.

Common Collective Nouns		
audience	company	group
class	crowd	jury
college	family	society
committee	government	team

Collective nouns are usually singular, so when you use a pronoun to refer to a collective noun, it too must usually be singular.

The team had ~~their~~ *its* sixth consecutive win of the season.

The jury returned ~~their~~ *its* verdict.

If the people in a group are acting as individuals, however, the noun is plural and should be used with a plural pronoun.

The class brought *their* papers to read.

FINDING AND FIXING PRONOUN PROBLEMS:
Using Collective Nouns and Pronouns

Find

The <u>committee</u> changed (its / their) meeting time.

1. **Underline** any collective nouns.
2. **Ask:** Is the collective noun singular (a group acting as a single unit) or plural (people in a group acting as individuals)? *Singular.*

Fix

The committee changed (its)/ their) meeting time.

3. **Choose** the pronoun that agrees with the subject.

■ PRACTICE 3   **USING COLLECTIVE NOUNS AND PRONOUNS** . . . .

Fill in the correct pronoun in each of the following sentences.

> **EXAMPLE:** In 1884, a Swiss company called Victorinox began selling a new kind of knife that _____*it*_____ had invented.

1. A large group of customers sent _____*their*_____ thanks to Victorinox, in letters praising the knife's quality and the tools included with it.

2. The company had found a way to add a screwdriver, a punch, and a can opener to _____*its*_____ knife.

3. The Swiss military at that time issued plain knives with wooden handles, but many army officers went to Victorinox to buy _____*its*_____ knives.

4. The Swiss army officially began equipping _____*its*_____ soldiers with Victorinox's knives in 1896.

5. In 1908, a committee from a rival company submitted _____*its*_____ bid to sell the company's own knives to the Swiss army.

6. The Swiss government awarded half of _____*its*_____ knife order to this company, called Wenger.

7. Wenger's corporate board raised _____*their*_____ voices in a cheer.

8. Victorinox got the other half of the order, and _____*it*_____ was pleased that it kept at least some of the business.

9. Recently, a team of executives from both companies announced _____*its*_____ decision to merge the two businesses.

10. My brother's family, all of whom like to hike and hunt, buy _____*their*_____ own custom knives from a small manufacturer.

Make Pronoun Reference Clear

If the reader isn't sure what noun or pronoun a pronoun refers to, the sentence may be confusing. Look for and edit any sentence that has an ambiguous, vague, or repetitious pronoun reference.

An **ambiguous pronoun reference** is one in which the pronoun could refer to more than one noun.

AMBIGUOUS   Enrico told Jim *he* needed a better résumé.

[Did Enrico tell Jim that Enrico himself needed a better résumé? Or did Enrico tell Jim that Jim needed a better résumé?]

EDITED   Enrico advised Jim to revise his résumé.

AMBIGUOUS   I put the glass on the shelf, even though *it* was dirty.

[Was the glass or the shelf dirty?]

EDITED   I put the dirty glass on the shelf.

A **vague pronoun reference** is one in which the pronoun does not refer clearly to any particular person, place, or thing. To correct a vague pronoun reference, use a more specific noun instead of the pronoun.

VAGUE   When Tom got to the clinic, *they* told him it was closed.

[Who told Tom the clinic was closed?]

EDITED   When Tom got to the clinic, the nurse told him it was closed.

VAGUE   Before I finished printing my report, *it* ran out of paper.

[What was out of paper?]

EDITED   Before I finished printing my report, the printer ran out of paper.

FINDING AND FIXING PRONOUN PROBLEMS:
Avoiding Ambiguous or Vague Pronoun References

Find

The <u>cashier</u> said (they) were out of milk.

1. **Underline** the subject.
2. **Circle** the pronoun.
3. **Ask:** Who or what does the pronoun refer to? *No one. "They" does not refer to "cashier."*

Fix

The <u>cashier</u> said ~~they were~~ out of milk.
the store was

4. **Correct the pronoun reference** by revising the sentence to make the pronoun more specific.

PRACTICE 4   AVOIDING AMBIGUOUS OR VAGUE PRONOUN REFERENCES

Edit each sentence to eliminate ambiguous or vague pronoun references. Some sentences may be revised in more than one way.

Answers may vary. Possible edits shown.

> **EXAMPLE:** I'm always looking for good advice on controlling my
> *experts*
> weight, but ~~they~~ have provided little help.

1. My doctor referred me to a physical therapist, ~~and she~~ said I needed to
   who
   exercise more.

2. I joined a workout group and did exercises with the members, but ~~it~~
   exercising
   did not solve my problem.

3. I tried a lower fat diet along with the exercising, but ~~it~~ did not really
   this combination
   work either.

   Some nutritionists
4. ~~They~~ used to say that eliminating carbohydrates is the easiest way to
   lose weight.

5. Therefore I started eating fats again and stopped consuming carbs,
   these methods were
   but, ~~this was~~ not a permanent solution.

   this low-carb diet
6. Although I lost weight and loved eating fatty foods, ~~it~~ did not keep me
   from eventually gaining the weight back.

7. Last week, I overheard my Uncle Kevin talking to my brother, and ~~he~~ *my uncle*
explained how he stayed slender even while traveling a lot.

8. Uncle Kevin eats fruit and vegetables instead of junk food while traveling, and ~~it~~ *this diet* has kept off the pounds.

9. He says it's not hard to pack carrots or apples for a trip, so anyone can
~~do this.~~ *plan in advance,*

10. I now try to plan better, eat less at each meal, and ignore all diet
books, and I hope ~~it works.~~ *these three ideas work.*

. . . .

A **repetitious pronoun reference** is one in which the pronoun repeats a reference to a noun rather than replacing the noun.

> The nurse at the clinic ~~he~~ told Tom that it was closed.

> The newspaper, ~~it~~ says that the new diet therapy is promising.

■ **ESL:** Repetitious pronoun reference is a very common error among ESL students. Read aloud some sentences with this problem (from their own writing, if possible), and ask students to raise their hands when they hear a repetitious pronoun reference.

> **Language Note:** In some languages, like Spanish, it is correct to re-peat a noun with a pronoun. In formal English, however, a pronoun is used to replace a noun, not to repeat it.
>
> **INCORRECT**   My instructor he gives us lots of homework.
>
> **CORRECT**   My instructor gives us lots of homework.

FINDING AND FIXING PRONOUN PROBLEMS:
Avoiding Repetitious Pronoun References

↓

Find

Television advertising (it) sometimes has a negative influence on young viewers.

1. **Underline** the subject and **double-underline** the verb.

2. **Circle** any pronouns in the sentence.

3. **Ask:** What noun does the pronoun refer to? *Advertising.*

4. **Ask:** Do the noun and the pronoun that refers to it share the same verb? *Yes.* Does the pronoun just repeat the noun rather than replace it? *Yes.* If the answer to one or both questions is yes, the pronoun is repetitious.

↓

↓

┌───┐
│   **Fix**   │
│   │
│ Television advertising ~~it~~ sometimes has a negative influence │
│ on young viewers.   │
│   │
│ 5. **Correct the sentence** by crossing out the repetitious pronoun. │
└───┘

■ **PRACTICE 5   AVOIDING REPETITIOUS PRONOUN REFERENCES** . . . . .

Correct any repetitious pronoun references in the following sentences.

> **EXAMPLE:** Car commercials ~~they~~ want viewers to believe that buying a certain brand of car will bring happiness.

1. Young people ~~they~~ sometimes take advertisements too literally.

2. ~~In a~~ beer advertisement, ~~it~~ might imply that drinking alcohol makes people more attractive and popular.

3. People who see or hear an advertisement ~~they~~ have to think about the message.

4. Parents should help their children understand why advertisements ~~they~~ don't show the real world.

5. A recent study, ~~it~~ said that parents can help kids overcome the influence of advertising.

. . . .

Use the Right Type of Pronoun

Three important types of pronouns are **subject pronouns**, **object pronouns**, and **possessive pronouns**. Notice their uses in the following sentences.

Object Subject
pronoun pronoun

The dog barked at *him,* and *he* laughed.

Possessive
pronoun

As Josh walked out, *his* phone started ringing.

■ **TIP:** Never put an apostrophe in a possessive pronoun.

Pronoun Types

	SUBJECT	OBJECT	POSSESSIVE
First-person singular/plural	I/we	me/us	my, mine/ our, ours
Second-person singular/plural	you/you	you/you	your, yours/ your, yours
Third-person singular	he, she, it	him, her, it	his, her, hers, its
Third-person plural	they who/who	them whom/whom	their, theirs its, whose

Language Note: Notice that pronouns have gender (*he/she, him/her, his/her/hers*). The pronoun must agree with the gender of the noun it refers to.

INCORRECT   Carolyn went to see *his* boyfriend.

CORRECT   Carolyn went to see *her* boyfriend.

Also, notice that English has different forms for subject and object pronouns, as shown in the previous chart.

Read the following sentence and replace the underlined noun, Andreas, with pronouns. Note that the pronouns are all different.

When Andreas made an A on ~~Andreas's~~ *his* final exam, ~~Andreas~~ *he* was proud of himself, and the teacher congratulated ~~Andreas~~ *him*.

Subject Pronouns

A **subject pronoun** serves as the subject of a verb.

You live next door to a graveyard.

I opened the door too quickly.

Language Note: Do not use *you* to mean *people*.

INCORRECT   The instructor says that you have to turn in your homework.

CORRECT   The instructor says that **students** have to turn in **their** homework.

Object Pronouns

Object pronouns either receive the action of a verb or are part of a prepositional phrase.

| OBJECT OF THE VERB | Jay gave *me* his watch. |
| OBJECT OF THE PREPOSITION | Jay gave his watch to *me*. |

■ **TIP:** For a list of prepositions, see page 279.

Possessive Pronouns

Possessive pronouns show ownership.

Dave is *my* uncle.

That book is *yours*.

Three trouble spots make it difficult to know what type of pronoun to use.

THREE PRONOUN TROUBLE SPOTS

- Compound subjects and objects
- Comparisons
- Sentences that need *who* or *whom*

Pronouns Used with Compound Subjects and Objects

A **compound subject** has more than one subject joined by a conjunction such as *and* or *or*. A **compound object** has more than one object joined by a conjunction. (For a list of conjunctions, see p. 276.)

| COMPOUND SUBJECT | Chandler and *I* worked on the project. |
| COMPOUND OBJECT | My boss gave the assignment to Chandler and *me*. |

■ **TIP:** When you are writing about yourself and someone else, always put yourself after everyone else. *My friends and I went to a club,* not *I and my friends went to a club.*

To decide what type of pronoun to use in a compound construction, try leaving out the other part of the compound and the conjunction. Then, say the sentence aloud to yourself.

Compound subject

J̶o̶a̶n̶ ̶a̶n̶d̶ (me / Ⓘ) went to the movies last night.

[Think: *I* went to the movies last night.]

■ **TIP:** Many people make the mistake of using *I* in the phrase *between you and I.* The correct pronoun with *between* is the object *me.*

Compound object

The car was headed right for T̶o̶m̶ ̶a̶n̶d̶ (she / (her)).

[Think: The car was headed right for *her*.]

If a pronoun is part of a compound object in a prepositional phrase, use an object pronoun.

Compound object

I will keep that information just between you and (I / me).

[*Between you and me* is a prepositional phrase, so an object pronoun, *me*, is required.]

FINDING AND FIXING PRONOUN PROBLEMS:
Using Pronouns in Compound Constructions

Find

My friend and me talk at least once a week.

1. **Underline** the subject and **double-underline** the verb, and **circle** any object or objects.

2. **Ask:** Is there a compound subject or object? *Yes — "friend and me" is a compound subject.*

3. **Ask:** Do the nouns in the compound construction share a verb? *Yes, "talk".*

4. **Cross out** one of the subjects so that only the pronoun remains.

5. **Ask:** Does the sentence sound right with just the pronoun as the subject? *No.*

Fix

                        I
My friend and me talk at least once a week.

6. **Correct the sentence** by replacing the incorrect pronoun with the correct one.

■ PRACTICE 6   EDITING PRONOUNS IN COMPOUND CONSTRUCTIONS

Edit each sentence using the proper type of pronoun. If a sentence is already correct, write a "C" next to it.

> **EXAMPLE:** Don King approached Zaire's President Mobutu, and
>   *he*
>   Mobutu and him reached an agreement.

1. In 1974, George Foreman was the heavyweight boxing champion, and
   he
   him and Muhammad Ali agreed to a fight for the title.

2. President Mobutu of Zaire wanted to make his country famous, so the
                                         him
   financial backing for the fight came from he and the people of Zaire.

3. Because American officials considered Mobutu a strong anticommu-

   they and he
   nist, ~~them and him~~ were allies, but Mobutu was a dictator who stole
          ^

   money intended for his impoverished country.

4. According to the agreement with Mobutu, he and Don King guaran-

   teed Foreman and Ali five million dollars each for the championship

   fight. *C*

5. Foreman angered the people of Zaire immediately when ~~him~~ and his
                                                        ^
                                                       he

   German shepherd dog were seen getting off the airplane.

6. German shepherds were part of Zaire's unhappy past, when the streets

   were patrolled by them and the Belgian colonial police; people were

   afraid of the dogs. *C*

                                                        him
7. The people loved Muhammad Ali, and pictures of ~~he~~ and his group in
                                                  ^

   Zaire showed adoring crowds everywhere.

8. Foreman was younger and stronger, so most boxing fans believed that

   in a fight between him and Ali, Foreman would win an easy victory. *C*

                                                      he
9. Ali may have feared losing the fight, but when ~~him~~ and Foreman
                                                  ^

   finally got in the ring, Ali took punch after punch.

                                                             him
10. Foreman became so tired that the end of the fight came for ~~he~~ and Ali
                                                               ^

    in the eighth round; Ali knocked out the champion and regained the

    world heavyweight title.

. . . .

Pronouns Used in Comparisons

■ **TEACHING TIP:** Have each
student write a sentence that
uses implied words in a comparison. Then, have the students read the sentences aloud
and ask other class members to
supply the missing words.

Using the right type of pronoun in comparisons is particularly important
because using the wrong type changes the meaning of the sentence. Editing
comparisons can be tricky because they often imply words that aren't actually included in the sentence.

■ **TIP:** To find comparisons,
look for the words *than* or *as*.

Bob trusts Donna more than *I.*

[This sentence means Bob trusts Donna more than I trust her. The implied words are
trust her.]

Bob trusts Donna more than *me.*

[This sentence means Bob trusts Donna more than he trusts me. The implied words are
he trusts.]

To decide whether to use a subject or object pronoun in a comparison, try adding the implied words and saying the sentence aloud.

The registrar is much more efficient than (us / we).

[Think: The registrar is much more efficient than *we are*.]

Susan rides her bicycle more than (he / him).

[Think: Susan rides her bicycle more than *he does*.]

■ **TIP:** Add the additional words to the comparison when you speak and write. Then others will not think you are incorrect.

FINDING AND FIXING PRONOUN PROBLEMS:
Using Pronouns in Comparisons

Find

The other band attracts a bigger audience than us on Friday nights.

1. **Circle** the word that indicates a comparison.
2. **Ask:** What word or words that would come after the comparison word are implied but missing from the sentence? *Do.*
3. **Ask:** If you add the missing word or words, does the pronoun make sense? *No.*

Fix

we (do)
The other band attracts a bigger audience than ~~us~~ on Friday nights.
                                                    ^

4. **Correct the sentence** by replacing the incorrect pronoun with the correct one.

■ **PRACTICE 7   EDITING PRONOUNS IN COMPARISONS** . . . .

Edit each sentence using the correct pronoun type. If a sentence is correct, put a "C" next to it.

■ **TEACHING TIP:** Have students read the sentences aloud, adding the implied words.

EXAMPLE: The camping trip we were planning did not seem dangerous to Hannah, so she was not as nervous about it as ~~me~~.
                                                                                                                    I
                                                                                                                    ^

1. In addition, I was nowhere near as well equipped for camping as ~~her~~.
                                                                    she
                                                                    ^

2. In the sporting goods store, it was Hannah rather than ~~me~~ who did all
                                                           I
                                                           ^
   the talking for us.

3. At the campground, I could see that some of the other camping

groups were not as prepared as we. *c*

4. As the park ranger came around to collect everyone's camping fees, he

chatted with the other campers more than ~~we~~. *us*
^

5. He seemed to believe that we were more experienced than ~~them~~. *they*
^

6. On the hiking trail, the other campers sure walked faster than we. *c*

7. They all hurried past us, but Hannah kept hiking just as slowly

as ~~me~~. *I*
^

8. Our boots had been crunching on the trail for hours when we

suddenly heard that a group ahead was being much louder than ~~us~~. *we*
^

9. When Hannah and I saw the group running back toward us, I was

more alarmed than ~~her~~. *she*
^

10. But when we spotted the bear that was chasing the other hikers,

Hannah ran to hide a lot faster than I. *c*

. . . .

Choosing between Who *and* Whom

Who is always a subject; *whom* is always an object. If a pronoun performs an action, use the subject form *who*. If a pronoun does not perform an action, use the object form *whom*.

■ **TIP:** In the examples here, subjects are underlined, and verbs are double-underlined.

> **WHO = SUBJECT**   I would like to know *who* delivered this package.
>
> **WHOM = OBJECT**   He told me to *whom* I should report.

■ **TIP:** *Whoever* is a subject pronoun; *whomever* is an object pronoun.

In sentences other than questions, when the pronoun (*who* or *whom*) is followed by a verb, use *who*. When the pronoun (*who* or *whom*) is followed by a noun or pronoun, use *whom*.

The pianist (who / whom) played was excellent.

[The pronoun is followed by the verb *played*. Use *who*.]

The pianist (who / whom) I saw was excellent.

[The pronoun is followed by another pronoun: *I*. Use *whom*.]

■ **PRACTICE 8   CHOOSING BETWEEN *WHO* AND *WHOM*** . . . .

In each sentence, circle the correct word, *who* or *whom*.

> **EXAMPLE:** Police officers (who)/ whom) want to solve a crime—or prevent one—are now relying more than ever on technology.

1. Face-recognition software, now being introduced, is supposed to identify possible criminals (who / (whom)) cameras have photographed in public places.

2. Use of such software, which can compare security camera images with photos from a criminal database, can help law enforcement officials determine (who / (whom)) they want to question about a crime.

3. Police will try to detain any person ((who)/ whom) is identified by the software as a criminal.

4. There are bound to be innocent people ((who)/ whom) resemble criminals closely enough that the software will single them out.

5. However, police and nervous Americans are hopeful that this method can help to identify terrorists ((who)/ whom) appear in airports or other locations.

. . . .

Make Pronouns Consistent in Person

Person is the point of view a writer uses—the perspective from which he or she writes. Pronouns may be in first person (*I, we*), second person (*you*), or third person (*he, she,* or *it*). (See the chart on p. 385.)

> **INCONSISTENT PERSON**   *I* wanted to sign up for a computer class, but the person said *you* had to know word processing.

[The sentence starts in the first person (*I*) but shifts to the second person (*you*).]

> **CONSISTENT PERSON**   *I* wanted to sign up for a computer class, but the person said *I* had to know word processing.

[The sentence stays with the first person, *I*.]

> **INCONSISTENT PERSON**   As soon as *a shopper* walks into the store, *you* can tell it is a weird place.

[The sentence starts with the third person (*a shopper*) but shifts to the second person (*you*).]

CONSISTENT PERSON   As soon as *a shopper* walks into the store, *he* or *she* can tell it is a weird place.

CONSISTENT PERSON, PLURAL   As soon as *shoppers* walk into the store, *they* can tell it is a weird place.

FINDING AND FIXING PRONOUN PROBLEMS:
Making Pronouns Consistent in Person

Find

I had the right answer, but to win the tickets (you) had to be the ninth caller.

1. **Underline** all of the subject nouns and pronouns in the sentence.
2. **Circle** any pronouns that refer to another subject noun or pronoun in the sentence.
3. **Ask:** Is the subject noun or pronoun that the circled pronoun refers to in the first (*I, we*), second (*you*), or third person (*he, she,* or *it*)? *First person.*
4. **Ask:** What person is the pronoun in? *Second.*

Fix

I had the right answer, but to win the tickets ~~you~~ *I* had to be the ninth caller.

5. **Correct the sentence** by changing the pronoun to be consistent with the noun or pronoun it refers to.

■ **PRACTICE 9**   **MAKING PRONOUNS CONSISTENT IN PERSON** . . . . .

In the following items, correct the shifts in person. There may be more than one way to correct some sentences.   *Answers may vary. Possible edits shown.*

> EXAMPLE: Many college students have access to a writing center where ~~you~~ *they* can get tutoring.

1. A writing tutor must know ~~your~~ *his or her* way around college writing assignments.

2. I have gone to the writing center at my school because sometimes ~~you~~ *I* need a second pair of eyes to look over a paper.

3. Students signing up for tutoring at the writing center may not be in
their
~~your~~ first semester of college.
   ^

4. Even a graduate student may need help with *his or her* ~~your~~ writing at times.
   ^

5. The writing-center tutor is very careful not to correct *his or her* ~~their~~ students'
   ^

papers.

6. My tutor told me that *I* ~~you~~ had to learn to edit a paper.
   ^

7. Every student has to learn to catch *his or her* ~~your~~ own mistakes.
   ^

8. A student's tutor is not like *his or her* ~~your~~ English professor.
   ^

9. No student gets *his or her* ~~their~~ grade on a paper from a writing tutor.
   ^

10. Tutors don't judge but simply help students with *their* ~~your~~ papers.
    ^

■ **PRACTICE 10   CORRECTING VARIOUS PRONOUN PROBLEMS** · · · · ·

In the following sentences, find and correct problems with pronoun use. You
may be able to revise some sentences in more than one way, and you may
need to rewrite some sentences to correct errors.
Answers may vary. Possible edits shown.

EXAMPLE: *Students with busy schedules have* ~~Everyone with a busy schedule has~~ probably been
          ^
tempted to take shortcuts on their coursework.

1. My class received *their* ~~its~~ term paper grades yesterday.
   ^

2. My friend Gene and *I* ~~me~~ were shocked to see that he had gotten an F
   ^
for his paper.

3. I usually get better grades than *he* ~~him~~, but he doesn't usually fail.
   ^

4. Mr. Padilla, the instructor, *whom* ~~who~~ most students consider strict but fair,
   ^
scheduled an appointment with Gene.

5. When Gene went to the department office, *the office assistant* ~~they~~ told him where to find
   ^
Mr. Padilla.

6. Mr. Padilla *didn't think that Gene* ~~told Gene that he didn't think he~~ had written the paper.
   ^

7. The paper ~~it~~ contained language that was unusual for Gene.

8. The instructor said that *he* ~~you~~ could compare Gene's in-class writing
   ^
with this paper and see differences.

9. Mr. Padilla, whom had typed some passages from Gene's paper into a search engine, found two online papers containing sentences that were also in Gene's paper.

10. Gene ~~told Mr. Padilla~~ *admitted* that he had made a terrible mistake.

11. Gene told my girlfriend and ~~I~~ *me* later that he did not realize that borrowing sentences from online sources was plagiarism.

12. We looked at the paper, and ~~you~~ *we* could tell that parts of it did not sound like Gene's writing.

13. Anyone doing Internet research must be especially careful to document ~~their~~ *the* sources, as Gene now knows.

14. The department decided ~~that they would~~ *to* not suspend Gene from school.

15. Mr. Padilla will let Gene take his class again and will help him avoid accidental plagiarism, and Gene said that no one had ever been more relieved than ~~him~~ *he* to hear that news.

Edit Paragraphs and Your Own Writing

■ **PRACTICE 11** **EDITING PARAGRAPHS FOR PRONOUN USE** . . . .

Find and correct any problems with pronoun use in the following paragraphs. You may want to use the chart, Finding and Fixing Pronoun Problems, on page 398. *Answers may vary. Possible edits shown.*

■ **TEACHING TIP:** Have students underline every pronoun in their paragraphs and draw an arrow to the word or words each pronoun refers to.

1. (1) Can a person make ~~their~~ *his or her* own luck? (2) People ~~whom~~ *who* consider themselves lucky may actually be luckier than those who think they are unlucky. (3) If you and ~~me~~ *I* feel optimistic and in control of the future, we are more likely to have good luck. (4) Some people try to increase their chances of having good luck by carrying good-luck charms. (5) Rabbit feet are common charms, but ~~they~~ *people* say ~~they~~ *the feet* didn't bring the rabbit any luck! (6) Seventy percent of students ~~they~~ believe that good-luck charms bring academic success. (7) "Lucky" rituals are also common among students; for example, ~~you~~ *they* might wear the same shirt for

every test. (8) Experts say that people who want good luck should try to meet new people who might bring them a lucky break.

2. (1) In the early 1980s, a group of young Canadians who walked on stilts ~~they~~ started a street theater group. (2) People loved the group's performances so much that ~~it~~ <u>the shows</u> inspired other street artists. (3) The theater group's big opportunity came in 1984, when Canada was celebrating the 450th anniversary of ~~their~~ <u>its</u> discovery. (4) The group decided that ~~they~~ <u>it</u> would present a show, *Cirque du Soleil,* in Quebec City to celebrate the anniversary. (5) The show was a big success, and today almost everyone ~~have~~ <u>has</u> heard of the group, now called *Cirque du Soleil.* (6) *Cirque du Soleil* has become a favorite of people ~~whom~~ <u>who</u> like circuses or acrobatics. (7) Fans enjoy the show so much that ~~you~~ <u>they</u> have to tell everyone about it. (8) *Cirque du Soleil* recently set a Guinness World Record when it featured the largest number of people ever to walk on stilts (544) at the same time and place. (9) No one likes this performing group more than ~~me~~ <u>I</u>. (10) Next week, my brother and ~~me~~ <u>I</u> are going to see our fifth *Cirque du Soleil* show.

■ **PRACTICE 12 EDITING YOUR OWN WRITING FOR PRONOUN USE** . . .

As a final practice, edit a piece of your own writing for pronoun use. It can be a paper you are working on for this course, a paper you've already finished, a paper for another course, or a recent piece of writing from your work or everyday life. Use the chart on page 398 to help you. Record in your learning journal any problem sentences you find, along with a corrected version of these sentences.

■ **LEARNING JOURNAL:** Do you understand the terms *pronoun agreement* and *pronoun reference*? How would you explain them to someone else?

Chapter Review

1. Pronouns replace ____*nouns*____ or other ___*pronouns*___ in a sentence.

2. A pronoun must agree with (match) the noun or pronoun it replaces in ___*number*___ and ___*gender*___.

3. In an ___*ambiguous*___ pronoun reference, the pronoun could refer to more than one noun.

4. Subject pronouns serve as the subject of a verb. Write a sentence using a subject pronoun. _Answers will_
   vary. Possible answer: We went to the movies last night.

5. What are two other types of pronouns? _object pronouns and possessive pronouns_

6. What are three trouble spots in pronoun use?

   compound subjects and objects

   comparisons

   sentences that need who or whom

Chapter Test

Circle the correct choice for each of the following items.

■ **TIP:** For advice on taking tests, see Appendix A.

1. Choose the item that has no errors.
   a. When he skis, Jim never falls down as much as me.
   b. When he skis, Jim never falls down as much as I.
   c. When he skis, Jim never falls down as much as mine.

■ **RESOURCES:** *Testing Tool Kit*, a CD-ROM available with this book, has even more tests.

2. Choose the correct word(s) to fill in the blank.

   Everyone hopes the jury will deliver _____ verdict by the end
   of this week.
   a. his or her   b. their   c. its

3. If an underlined portion of this sentence is incorrect, select the revision
   that fixes it. If the sentence is correct as written, choose d.

   She is the one who Jake always calls whenever he wants a favor.
     A   B   C

   a. Her   c. him
   b. whom   d. No change is necessary.

4. If an underlined portion of this sentence is incorrect, select the revision
   that fixes it. If the sentence is correct as written, choose d.

   Somebody has left their camera here, and we do not know to whom it
                     A   B   C
   belongs.
   a. his or her   c. who
   b. us   d. No change is necessary.

5. Choose the item that has no errors.
   a. Becky told Lydia that she needed to help clean up after the party.
   b. Becky told Lydia to help clean up after the party.
   c. Becky told Lydia that she needed to help clean up after it.

6. Choose the item that has no errors.

   a. When I applied for the tour operator job, I was told that you needed a special certificate.

   b. When I applied for the tour operator job, you were told that you needed a special certificate.

   (c.) When I applied for the tour operator job, I was told that I needed a special certificate.

7. Choose the correct word(s) to fill in the blank.

   Nicole's _____ must be lonely because he barks all the time.

   a. dog he   b. dog him   (c.) dog

8. Choose the correct words to fill in the blank.

   The other players in my soccer club like me because _____ agree on the importance of teamwork.

   (a.) they and I   b. them and me   c. them and I

9. If an underlined portion of this sentence is incorrect, select the revision that fixes it. If the sentence is correct as written, choose d.

   I think my next-door neighbor has mice in him house because he keeps
   _____   _____
        A   B

   asking me to lend him my cat.
                 _____
                     C

   a. me next-door   c. lend he

   (b.) his house   d. No change is necessary.

10. Choose the item that has no errors.

    a. Any lifeguard can tell you about a scary experience they have had on the job.

    b. Any lifeguard can tell you about a scary experience her have had on the job.

    (c.) Most lifeguards can tell you about a scary experience they have had on the job.

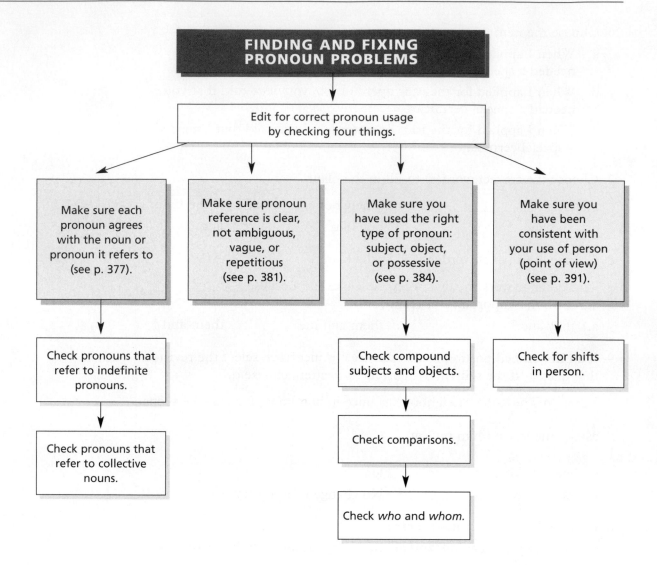

26

Adjectives and Adverbs

Using Descriptive Words

Understand What Adjectives and Adverbs Are

Adjectives describe or modify nouns (words that name people, places, or things) and pronouns (words that replace nouns). They add information about *what kind, which one,* or *how many.*

The *final* exam was today.

It was *long* and *difficult.*

The *three shiny new* coins were on the dresser.

■ **TIP:** To understand this chapter on adjectives and adverbs, you need to know what nouns and verbs are. For a review, see Chapter 20.

> **Language Note:** In English, adjectives do not indicate whether the words they describe are singular or plural.
>
> **INCORRECT**   The three babies are *adorables.*
>
> [The adjective *adorables* should not end in *-s.*]
>
> **CORRECT**   The three babies are *adorable.*

Adverbs describe or modify verbs (words that tell what happens in a sentence), adjectives, or other adverbs. They add information about *how, how much, when, where, why,* or *to what extent.*

MODIFYING VERB	Sharon *enthusiastically* accepted the job.
MODIFYING ADJECTIVE	The *very* young lawyer handled the case.
MODIFYING ANOTHER ADVERB	The team played *surprisingly* well.

Adjectives usually come before the words they modify; adverbs come before or after. You can use more than one adjective or adverb to modify a word.

> **Language Note:** The *-ed* and *-ing* forms of adjectives are sometimes confused. Common examples include *bored/boring, confused/confusing, excited/exciting,* and *interested/interesting.*
>
> **INCORRECT** Janelle is interesting in ghosts and ghost stories.
>
> **CORRECT**   Janelle is interested in ghosts and ghost stories.
>
> **CORRECT**   Janelle finds ghosts and ghost stories interesting.
>
> Often, the *-ed* form describes a person's reaction, while the *-ing* form describes the thing being reacted to.

Practice Using Adjectives and Adverbs Correctly

Choosing between Adjectives and Adverbs

Many adverbs are formed by adding *-ly* to the end of an adjective.

ADJECTIVE	ADVERB
She received a *quick* answer.	Her sister answered *quickly.*
The *new* student introduced himself.	The couple is *newly* married.
That is an *honest* answer.	Please answer *honestly.*

To decide whether to use an adjective or an adverb, find the word being described. If that word is a noun or pronoun, use an adjective. If it is a verb, adjective, or another adverb, use an adverb.

■ **DISCUSSION:** To get students focused on adjectives and adverbs, throw out a few sentences containing adjectives, with students in the class as the subjects (*Dan is wearing a black leather jacket*). Ask the student in the sentence what the adjectives are.

■ **TIP:** For more practice with adjective and adverb usage, visit Exercise Central at **bedfordstmartins.com/ realwriting**.

■ **PRACTICE 1**   **CHOOSING BETWEEN ADJECTIVES AND ADVERBS** . . .

In each sentence, underline the word in the sentence that is being described or modified, and then circle the correct word in parentheses.

> **EXAMPLE:** People are (common / commonly) <u>aware</u> that smoking causes health risks.

1. Many <u>smokers</u> are (stubborn / stubbornly) about refusing to quit.

2. Others who are thinking about quitting may <u>decide</u> (sudden / suddenly) that the damage from smoking has already been done.

3. In such cases, the (typical)/ typically) smoker sees no reason to stop.

4. The news about secondhand smoke may have made some smokers stop (quick /(quickly)) to save the health of their families.

5. Now, research shows that pet lovers who smoke can have a (terrible)/ terribly) effect on their cats.

6. Cats who live with smokers (frequent /(frequently)) develop cancer.

7. Veterinarians point out that the cats of smokers may smell (strong / (strongly)) of smoke.

8. Cats like to have their fur ((clean)/ cleanly), and they lick the fur to groom themselves.

■ **RESOURCES:** *Additional Resources* contains tests and supplemental practice exercises for this chapter as well as a transparency master for the chart at the end.

9. When they are grooming, cats may inhale a ((large)/ largely) dose of tobacco smoke.

10. Perhaps some smokers who feel that it's too late for their own health will (serious /(seriously)) consider quitting for the sake of their pets.

Using Comparative and Superlative Forms

To compare two persons, places, or things, use the **comparative** form of adjectives or adverbs. Comparisons often use the word *than*.

> Carol ran *faster* than I did.
> Johan is *more intelligent* than his sister.

To compare three or more persons, places, or things, use the **superlative** form of adjectives or adverbs.

> Carol ran *fastest* of all the women runners.
> Johan is the *most intelligent* of the five children.

If an adjective or adverb is short (one syllable), add the endings *-er* to form the comparative and *-est* to form the superlative. Also use this pattern for adjectives that end in *-y* (but change the *-y* to *-i* before adding *-er* or *-est*).

If an adjective or adverb has more than one syllable, add the word *more* to make the comparative and the word *most* to make the superlative.

■ **TIP:** For more on changing a final *-y* to *-i* when adding endings, and on other spelling changes involving endings, see Chapter 35.

Forming Comparatives and Superlatives

ADJECTIVE OR ADVERB	COMPARATIVE	SUPERLATIVE
ADJECTIVES AND ADVERBS OF ONE SYLLABLE		
tall	taller	tallest
fast	faster	fastest
ADJECTIVES ENDING IN -Y		
happy	happier	happiest
silly	sillier	silliest
ADJECTIVES AND ADVERBS OF MORE THAN ONE SYLLABLE		
graceful	more graceful	most graceful
gracefully	more gracefully	most gracefully
intelligent	more intelligent	most intelligent
intelligently	more intelligently	most intelligently

Use either an ending (*-er* or *-est*) or an extra word (*more* or *most*) to form a comparative or superlative—not both at once.

Lance Armstrong is the ~~most~~ greatest cyclist in the world.

■ PRACTICE 2   USING COMPARATIVES AND SUPERLATIVES · · · · · · ·

In the space provided in each sentence, write the correct form of the adjective or adverb in parentheses. You may need to add *more* or *most* to some adjectives and adverbs.

■ **TEACHING TIP:** This is a good practice to do aloud so students can hear the correct choice.

EXAMPLE: It was one of the ____*scariest*____ (scary) experiences of my life.

1. I was driving along Route 17 and was ____*more relaxed*____ (relaxed) than I ought to have been.

2. Knowing it was a busy highway, I was ____*more careful*____ (careful) than usual to be sure my cell phone was ready in case of an accident.

■ **RESOURCES:** To gauge students' skills in adjective and adverb usage, use the *Testing Tool Kit* CD-ROM available with this book.

3. I had run the cord for the phone's ear bud over my armrest, where it would be in the ____*easiest*____ (easy) place to reach if the phone rang.

4. I was in the ____*heaviest*____ (heavy) traffic of my drive when the cell phone rang.

5. I saw that the ear bud was ____*harder*____ (hard) to reach than before because the cord had fallen between the front seats of the car.

6. When I reached down to get the ear bud, a pickup truck to my right
   suddenly started going _____*faster*_____ (fast).

7. The truck swerved toward my lane, coming _____*closer*_____ (close)
   than I wanted it to be.

8. _____*Quicker*_____ (Quick) than I thought possible, I shifted to the left
   lane and just barely avoided the pickup.

9. _____*Calmer*_____ (Calm) now, I decided to give up on trying to find the
   ear bud.

10. I wanted the cell phone ready for safety's sake, but I now think that
    concentrating on my driving is the _*most intelligent*_ (intelligent) thing
    to do.

. . . .

Using *Good, Well, Bad,* and *Badly*

Four common adjectives and adverbs have irregular forms: *good, well, bad,*
and *badly.*

Forming Irregular Comparatives and Superlatives

	COMPARATIVE	SUPERLATIVE
ADJECTIVE		
good	better	best
bad	worse	worst
ADVERB		
well	better	best
badly	worse	worst

■ **TIP:** *Irregular* means not following a standard rule.

People often get confused about whether to use *good* or *well. Good* is an
adjective, so use it to describe a noun or pronoun. *Well* is an adverb, so use
it to describe a verb or an adjective.

ADJECTIVE   She has a *good* job.

ADVERB   He works *well* with his colleagues.

Well can also be an adjective to describe someone's health: I am not *well* today.

■ PRACTICE 3   USING *GOOD* AND *WELL* . . . .

Complete each sentence by circling the correct word in parentheses. Underline the word that *good* or *well* modifies.

> **EXAMPLE:** A (good/ well) pediatrician spends as much time talking with parents as he or she does examining patients.

1. The ability to communicate (good / well) is something that many parents look for in a pediatrician.

2. With a firstborn child, there is a (good)/ well) chance that every visit to the doctor will cause the parent at least some anxiety.

3. Parents can become particularly worried when their infant doesn't feel (good /(well) because the child can't say what the problem is.

4. Doctors today have (good)/ well) diagnostic tools, however.

5. An otoscope helps a doctor see (good /(well) when he or she looks into a patient's ear, for example.

6. A fever and an inflamed eardrum are (good)/ well) signs of a middle-ear infection.

7. Children who have many ear infections may not hear as (good /(well) as children who have fewer infections.

8. If the pediatrician presents clear options for treatment, parents can make a (good /(well)-informed decision about treating their child's illness.

9. Some parents decide that ear-tube surgery is a (good)/ well) solution to the problem of frequent ear infections.

10. Within an hour after ear-tube surgery, most children are (good /(well) enough to go home.

■ PRACTICE 4   **USING COMPARATIVE AND SUPERLATIVE FORMS OF** *GOOD* **AND** *BAD* . . . .

Complete each sentence by circling the correct comparative or superlative form of *good* or *bad* in parentheses.

> **EXAMPLE:** Men tend to sleep (better)/ best) than women do.

1. One of the (worse / worst) gaps in human knowledge about sleep disorders used to be that little research had been done using female subjects.

2. Until the 1990s, most scientists considered male subjects a (better / best) choice than female ones for sleep research.

3. Now that (better / best) research on sleep disorders in women is available, scientists know that women suffer more than men from certain kinds of sleep problems.

4. One of the (worse / worst) problems for new mothers is loss of sleep.

5. Whether because of habit or some biological cause, women are (better / best) than men at hearing the sound of a child crying in the middle of the night.

6. New sleep research shows that women suffer (worse / worst) than men do from insomnia, whether they are parents or not.

7. In the past, many women who complained of being tired were diagnosed with depression instead of with sleep disorders; the treatment often failed to help and sometimes made the problems (worse / worst).

8. So far, the (better / best) explanation that researchers can offer for women's sleep problems is that sleeplessness may be related to levels of hormones.

9. However, hormone therapies, according to some scientists, can create health problems that are (worse / worst) than the ones they are supposed to solve.

10. No one is certain yet of the (better / best) solution for insomnia and sleep problems in women, but the increasing availability of information will probably improve the situation.

Edit Paragraphs and Your Own Writing

 PRACTICE 5   EDITING PARAGRAPHS FOR CORRECT ADJECTIVES AND ADVERBS . . . .

■ TEAMWORK: Copy an article from the newspaper or some other source, and have students find all the adjectives and adverbs, drawing arrows from the modifiers to the words they modify. This can be done in small groups in class or assigned as homework and gone over the next day in class.

Find and correct any problems with adjectives and adverbs in the following paragraphs. You may want to use the chart, Editing for Correct Usage of Adjectives and Adverbs, on page 409 to help you.

1. (1) One of the jobs *most commonly* ~~commonliest~~ held by teenagers is a position in a fast-food restaurant. (2) Managers of fast-food franchises consider hiring teenagers a *good* ~~well~~ idea. (3) Teens will work for ~~more~~ lower pay than many other workers, so the restaurant can keep its prices down. (4) The jobs do not require a lot of skills, so the restaurants do not need to spend money offering training to *new* ~~newly~~ workers. (5) Jobs in fast food are not glamorous, but they are plentiful; a teenager who wants to work in a fast-food restaurant can usually find a job *quickly* ~~quick~~. (6) However, few teenagers, and probably even fewer of their parents, realize that fast-food work has a drawback: It can be *more* dangerous than many other summer jobs. (7) Fast-food restaurants keep large amounts of cash on hand, and this fact is known *well* ~~good~~ by people who want to commit a robbery. (8) Today, fast-food franchises are robbed more often than convenience stores because criminals have a *worse* ~~worser~~ chance of success in a convenience-store holdup. (9) Many teenagers think that a fast-food job is a boring but *harmless* ~~harmlessly~~ way to spend a summer. (10) Unfortunately, a robbery can make a fast-food job *more exciting* ~~excitinger~~ than any worker wants it to be.

2. (1) One of the *most important* ~~importantest~~ things I've learned since starting college is to avoid waiting until the last minute to begin my work. (2) I used to think that I could successfully write a paper the night before it was due. (3) This technique worked *well* ~~good~~ for me in high school. (4) However, when I tried it in my history class during my first year in college, I received a bad grade, much *worse* ~~badder~~ than I had expected. (5) I promised myself that I would do *better* ~~gooder~~ than that in the future. (6) I've also learned to work *persistently* ~~persistent~~ at a task, even when I feel frustrated. (7) If a task is ~~more~~ harder than I expected, I will arrange to ask the professor

or a tutor for help. (8) This often turns out to be the ~~faster~~ *fastest* way of all to
solve the problem. (9) If no outside help is available, I will usually put
the work away for a few hours, or overnight, and start again when I feel
~~more~~ better about my ability to concentrate.

■ **PRACTICE 6   EDITING YOUR OWN WRITING FOR CORRECT
ADJECTIVES AND ADVERBS** . . . .

As a final practice, edit a piece of your own writing for correct use of adjectives and adverbs. It can be a paper you are working on for this course, a
paper you've already finished, a paper for another course, or a recent piece
of writing from your work or everyday life. Record in your learning journal
any problem sentences you find, along with their corrections. You may want
to use the chart on page 409 to help you.

■ **LEARNING JOURNAL:**
What mistake in using adjectives or adverbs do you make
most often in your writing?
What are some ways to avoid
or correct this mistake?

Chapter Review

1. Adjectives modify ____*nouns*____ and ____*pronouns*____ .

2. Adverbs modify _____*verbs*_____ , _____*adjectives*_____ , or ___*other adverbs*___ .

3. Many adverbs are formed by adding an _____*-ly*_____ ending to an adjective.

4. The comparative form of an adjective or adverb is used to compare how many people, places, or
    things? _____*two*_____

5. The superlative form of an adjective or adverb is used to compare how many people, places, or things?
    _*three or more*_____

6. What four words have irregular comparative and superlative forms? *good, well, bad, badly*_____

Chapter Test

Circle the correct choice for each of the following items.

■ **TIP:** For advice on taking
tests, see Appendix A.

1. Choose the correct word to fill in the blank.

    We performed _____ in the debate, so we will have to be better
    prepared next time.
    a. bad   b. worse   (c.) badly

■ **RESOURCES:** *Testing Tool
Kit*, a CD-ROM available with
this book, has even more tests.

2. If an underlined portion of this sentence is incorrect, select the revision that fixes it. If the sentence is correct as written, choose d.

   After the beautiful wedding, the groom danced happy down the church's
   ⎯⎯⎯⎯⎯ A   ⎯⎯⎯⎯⎯ B

   stone steps.
   ⎯⎯⎯⎯⎯ C

   a. beautifully   c. stonily
   (b.) happily   d. No change is necessary.

3. Choose the item that has no errors.
   (a.) Sarah's foot is healing well, and she is making a good recovery.
   b. Sarah's foot is healing good, and she is making a good recovery.
   c. Sarah's foot is healing good, and she is making a well recovery.

4. Choose the correct word(s) to fill in the blank.

   With Kenneth's wild imagination, he is a _____ choice than Conor for writing the play's script.

   a. gooder   (b.) better   c. more good

5. If an underlined portion of this sentence is incorrect, select the revision that fixes it. If the sentence is correct as written, choose d.

   When asked about the thoughtfulest person I know, I immediately gave
   ⎯⎯⎯⎯⎯⎯⎯⎯⎯ A

   the name of my best friend, who is kind to everyone.
   ⎯⎯⎯⎯⎯ B   ⎯⎯⎯⎯⎯ C

   (a.) most thoughtful   c. kindest
   b. bestest   d. No change is necessary.

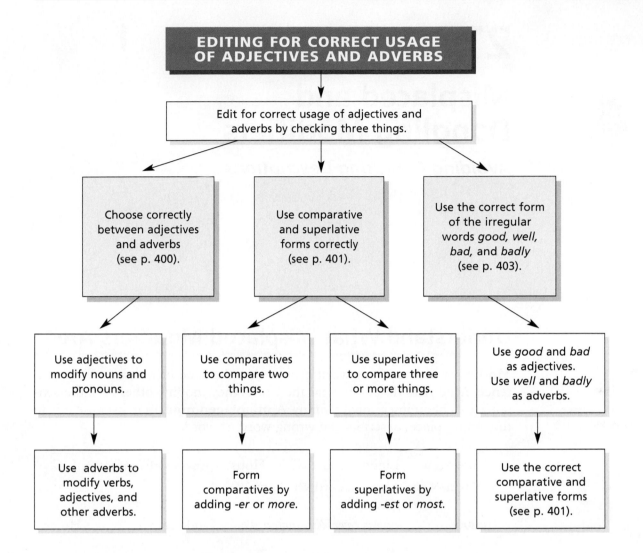

EDITING FOR CORRECT USAGE OF ADJECTIVES AND ADVERBS

Edit for correct usage of adjectives and adverbs by checking three things.

Choose correctly between adjectives and adverbs (see p. 400).

Use comparative and superlative forms correctly (see p. 401).

Use the correct form of the irregular words *good, well, bad,* and *badly* (see p. 403).

Use adjectives to modify nouns and pronouns.

Use comparatives to compare two things.

Use superlatives to compare three or more things.

Use *good* and *bad* as adjectives. Use *well* and *badly* as adverbs.

Use adverbs to modify verbs, adjectives, and other adverbs.

Form comparatives by adding *-er* or *more.*

Form superlatives by adding *-est* or *most.*

Use the correct comparative and superlative forms (see p. 401).

27

Misplaced and Dangling Modifiers

Avoiding Confusing Descriptions

Understand What Misplaced Modifiers Are

Modifiers are words or word groups that describe other words in a sentence. Modifiers should be near the words they modify; otherwise, the sentence can be unintentionally funny. A **misplaced modifier**, because it is in the wrong place, describes the wrong word or words.

TIP: For a review of basic sentence elements, see Chapter 20.

> **MISPLACED**   Linda saw the White House *flying over Washington, D.C.*
>
> [Was the White House flying over Washington?]
>
> **CLEAR**   *Flying over Washington, D.C.,* Linda saw the White House.

To correct a misplaced modifier, place the modifier as close as possible to the word or words it modifies, often directly before it.

Wearing my bathrobe,
I went outside to get the paper. ~~wearing my bathrobe~~.

Four constructions in particular often lead to misplaced modifiers.

1. **Modifiers such as *only, almost, hardly, nearly,* and *just*.**   These words need to be right before — not just close to — the words or phrases they modify.

   only
   I ~~only~~ found two old photos in the drawer.

   [The intended meaning is that just two photos were in the drawer.]

   almost
   Joanne ~~almost~~ ate the whole cake.

   [Joanne actually ate; she didn't "almost" eat.]

   nearly
   Thomas ~~nearly~~ spent two hours waiting for the bus.

   [Thomas spent close to two hours waiting; he didn't "nearly spend" them.]

RESOURCES: *Additional Resources* contains tests and supplemental practice exercises for this chapter as well as a transparency master for the chart at the end.

410

2. **Modifiers that are prepositional phrases.**

from the cash register
The cashier found money on the floor ~~from the cash register~~.
                                    ^

for the front door
Kayla hid the key under the rock. ~~for the front door.~~
                                ^   ^

3. **Modifiers that start with *-ing* verbs.**

Using jumper cables,
Darlene started the car. ~~using jumper cables.~~
                       ^   ^
[The car wasn't using jumper cables; Darlene was.]

Wearing flip flops,
Javier climbed the mountain. ~~wearing flip flops.~~
                           ^
[The mountain wasn't wearing flip flops; Javier was.]

4. **Modifier clauses that start with *who, whose, that,* or *which.***

that was infecting my hard drive
Joel found the computer virus attached to an e-mail message. ~~that was~~
                                                           ^   ^
~~infecting my hard drive.~~

[What was infecting the hard drive, the virus or the message?]

who was crying
The baby on the bus ~~who was crying~~ had curly hair.
                  ^
[The bus wasn't crying; the baby was.]

Practice Correcting Misplaced Modifiers

■ **PRACTICE 1   CORRECTING MISPLACED MODIFIERS** . . . .

Find and correct misplaced modifiers in the following sentences.

> *only*
> **EXAMPLE:** I write things in my blog that I used to ~~only~~ tell my best
>   ^
> friends.

in a diary
1. I still write about all kinds of personal things and private observations.
                      ^   ^
~~in a diary.~~

nearly
2. Now, I ~~nearly~~ write the same things in my blog.
        ^

that is entertaining
3. Any story might show up in my blog. ~~that is entertaining.~~
                                ^
of my cousin Tim's birthday
4. The video I was making was definitely something I wanted to write
                         ^
about in my blog. ~~of my cousin Tim's birthday.~~

Wanting the video to be funny,
5. I had invited to the birthday party my loudest, wildest friends. ~~wanting~~
 ^   ^
~~the video to be funny.~~

■ **TEAMWORK:** As homework, have each student write a sentence that is funny because of a misplaced or dangling modifier. Collect the sentences and read some aloud, asking the class for corrections.

■ **TIP:** For more practice correcting misplaced and dangling modifiers, visit Exercise Central at **bedfordstmartins.com/realwriting**.

■ **RESOURCES:** To gauge students' skills in correcting misplaced and dangling modifiers, use the *Testing Tool Kit* CD-ROM available with this book.

6. We jumped off of tables, had mock swordfights, and ~~almost~~ used ten *almost* cans of whipped cream in a food fight.

7. Unfortunately, the battery in the video recorder died. *that Tim loaned me* ~~that Tim loaned me.~~

8. *Apologizing to Tim,* I told ~~Tim~~ *him* that I would write a blog about the party anyway. ~~apologizing to him.~~

9. I explained how I would include *in the blog* the funny story about the failed videotaping. ~~in the blog.~~

10. Tim ~~hardly~~ said he *hardly* could wait until we tried again to make the video.

- -

Understand What Dangling Modifiers Are

A **dangling modifier** "dangles" because the word or words it modifies are not in the sentence. Dangling modifiers usually appear at the beginning of a sentence and seem to modify the noun or pronoun that immediately follows them; however, they are really modifying another word or group of words.

DANGLING	*Rushing to class,* the books fell out of my bag.

[The books weren't rushing to class.]

CLEAR	*Rushing to class,* I dropped my books.

There are two basic ways to correct dangling modifiers. Use the one that makes the most sense. You can add the word being modified right after the opening modifier so that the connection between the two is clear.

Trying to eat a hot dog, *I* ~~my bike~~ swerved *on my bike.*

Or you can add the word being modified in the opening modifier itself.

While I was trying ~~Trying~~ to eat a hot dog, my bike swerved off the path.

Practice Correcting Dangling Modifiers

PRACTICE 2   CORRECTING DANGLING MODIFIERS . . . .

Find and correct any dangling modifiers in the following sentences. If a sentence is correct, write a "C" next to it. It may be necessary to add new words or ideas to some sentences.   *Answers may vary. Possible edits shown.*

Because I had invited

EXAMPLE: ~~Inviting~~ my whole family to dinner, the kitchen was filled
^
with all kinds of food.

While I was preparing
1. ~~Preparing~~ a big family dinner, the oven suddenly stopped working.
^

2. In a panic, we searched for Carmen, who can solve any problem. *C*

With everyone trying
3. ~~Trying~~ to help, the kitchen was crowded.
^

we could see that
4. Looking into the oven, the turkey was not done.

we almost ^cancelled dinner.
5. Discouraged, ~~the dinner was about to be cancelled.~~

As I was staring^
6. ~~Staring~~ out the window, a pizza truck went by.
^

7. Using a credit card, Carmen ordered six pizzas. *C*

One   *and*
8. ~~With one~~ quick phone call,/ six large pizzas solved our problem.

^When I returned   ^
9. ~~Returning~~ to the crowd in the kitchen, family members still
^

surrounded the oven.

they cheered.
10. Delighted with Carmen's decision, ~~cheers filled the room.~~
^

. . . .

Edit Paragraphs and Your Own Writing

**PRACTICE 3   EDITING PARAGRAPHS FOR MISPLACED AND
DANGLING MODIFIERS** . . . .

Find and correct any misplaced or dangling modifiers in the following
paragraphs. You may want to refer to the chart, Editing for Misplaced and
Dangling Modifiers, on page 416.   *Answers may vary. Possible edits shown.*

1. (1) Believing they can do nothing to make a difference in the en-
people often waste   *who make environmentally good choices*
vironment, energy. ~~is often wasted.~~ (2) Individuals can have an effect.
^   ^   *, such as buying a gas-^guzzling car or SUV,* ^
~~who make environmentally good choices.~~ (3) Bad choices can have an

effect too/.~~such as buying a gas-guzzling car or SUV.~~ (4) By saving
^   *that cost more up front*
energy, consumers can also save money. (5) Some products will save
^
people money for many years. ~~that cost more up front.~~ (6) With solar
^
shingles installed on their roofs, homeowners who paid more for the

shingles will have dramatically lower energy bills for the life of the house.

(7) Rated for energy efficiency, household appliances can help the

who do the right thing for the environment

environment and the owner's budget. (8) Individuals can make a difference. ~~who do the right thing for the environment.~~
^

2. Dear Mr. Bolton:

(1) I am responding to your advertisement in the *Courier-Ledger*
seeking a summer intern for your law practice. (2) A hard worker, ~~my~~

I have strong

qualifications. ~~are strong.~~ (3) I am currently working on a bachelor's de-

nearly

gree in political science and ~~nearly~~ have taken fifty credit hours of
^

courses, including classes in jurisprudence, law and public policy, and

business law.

, while sitting in class,

(4) Business law is especially of interest to me. (5) Sometimes I
^

dream of becoming a corporate attorney. ~~while sitting in class.~~ (6) Some-

I am already

day, I'd like to work for one of the major firms in New York. (7) ~~Already~~
^

and

planning to go on to law school, my grade point average is in the top 10
^

percent of my class.

(8) I realize that I will not earn much money as an intern. (9) How-

someday

ever, ~~someday~~ I am confident that I will be able to find a good-paying
^

I find

job. (10) Thinking of the experience I could gain, a summer job at your
^

firm ~~is~~ highly appealing.

■ **PRACTICE 4   EDITING YOUR OWN WRITING FOR MISPLACED AND
DANGLING MODIFIERS** . . . .

As a final practice, edit a piece of your own writing for misplaced and dangling modifiers. It can be a paper you are working on for this course, a paper
you've already finished, a paper for another course, or a recent piece of
writing from your work or everyday life. Record in your learning journal any
problem sentences you find, along with their corrections. You may want to
use the chart on page 416.

■ **LEARNING JOURNAL:**
Which is more difficult for
you, finding misplaced and
dangling modifiers or correcting them? What can you do to
help yourself find or correct
them more easily?

Chapter Review

1. ___Modifiers___ are words or word groups that describe other words in a sentence.

2. A ___misplaced modifier___ describes the wrong word or words.

3. When an opening modifier does not modify any word in the sentence, it is a ___dangling modifier___ .

Chapter Test

Circle the correct choice for each of the following items.

■ **TIP:** For advice on taking tests, see Appendix A.

1. If an underlined portion of this sentence is incorrect, select the revision that fixes it. If the sentence is correct as written, choose d.

   <u>Annoyed</u> by the flashing cameras, <u>the limousine drove the celebrity</u> away
       A   B

   from the crowd <u>in front of the restaurant.</u>
                              C

■ **RESOURCES:** *Testing Tool Kit*, a CD-ROM available with this book, has even more tests.

   a. Annoying

   (b.) the celebrity got into the limousine, which drove

   c. the restaurant in front of

   d. No change is necessary.

2. Choose the item that has no errors.

   a. The thief found the code in the bank clerk's desk for the alarm system.

   (b.) The thief found the code for the alarm system in the bank clerk's desk.

   c. For the alarm system, the thief found the code in the bank clerk's desk.

3. If an underlined portion of this sentence is incorrect, select the revision that fixes it. If the sentence is correct as written, choose d.

   <u>Talking</u> on <u>his cell phone,</u> <u>his shopping cart rolled</u> over my foot.
       A   B   C

   a. Talking and concentrating too much

   b. his cell phones

   (c.) he rolled his shopping cart

   d. No change is necessary.

4. If an underlined portion of this sentence is incorrect, select the revision that fixes it. If the sentence is correct as written, choose d.

   <u>I only bought</u> two tickets <u>to the game,</u> so one <u>of the three of</u> us cannot go.
           A   B   C

   (a.) bought only   c. of the us three of

   b. to go to the game   d. No change is necessary.

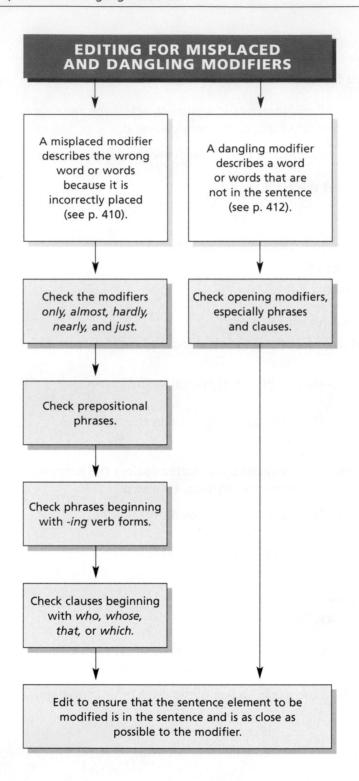

EDITING FOR MISPLACED AND DANGLING MODIFIERS

A misplaced modifier describes the wrong word or words because it is incorrectly placed (see p. 410).

A dangling modifier describes a word or words that are not in the sentence (see p. 412).

Check the modifiers *only, almost, hardly, nearly,* and *just.*

Check opening modifiers, especially phrases and clauses.

Check prepositional phrases.

Check phrases beginning with *-ing* verb forms.

Check clauses beginning with *who, whose, that,* or *which.*

Edit to ensure that the sentence element to be modified is in the sentence and is as close as possible to the modifier.

28

Coordination

Joining Sentences with Related Ideas

Understand What Coordination Is

Coordination is used to join two sentences with related ideas, and it can make your writing less choppy. The sentences remain complete and independent, but they are joined with a comma and a coordinating conjunction.

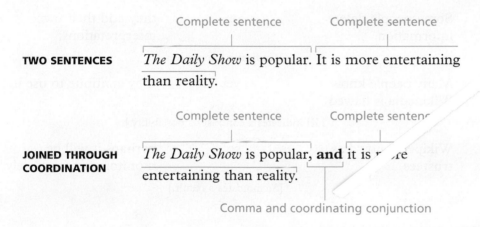

	Complete sentence	Complete sentence

TWO SENTENCES   *The Daily Show* is popular. It is more entertaining than reality.

	Complete sentence	Complete sentence

JOINED THROUGH COORDINATION   *The Daily Show* is popular, **and** it is more entertaining than reality.

Comma and coordinating conjunction

◢ **TIP:** To understand this chapter, you need to be familiar with basic sentence elements. For a review, see Chapter 20.

Practice Using Coordination

Coordination Using Coordinating Conjunctions

Conjunctions join words, phrases, or clauses. **Coordinating conjunctions** (*and, but, for, nor, or, so,* and *yet*) join ideas of equal importance. (You can remember them by thinking of FANBOYS—*for, and, nor, but, or, yet, so.*) To join two sentences through coordination, put a comma and one of these conjunctions between the sentences. Choose the conjunction that makes the most sense for the meaning of the two sentences.

■ **RESOURCES:** *Additional Resources* contains tests and supplemental practice exercises for this chapter as well as a transparency master for the chart at the end.

■ **TIP:** For more on the use of commas, see Chapter 36.

■ **TEACHING TIP:** Emphasize that conjunctions are not interchangeable (*but* can't fill in for *so*, for example). Write two independent clauses on the board (*Tom was hungry/he had a sandwich*). Ask students which conjunctions would work. Ask how the sentence would have to change to use others.

Complete sentence	, for , and , nor , but , or , yet , so	Complete sentence

Wikipedia is a popular encyclopedia	, for	it is easily available online.

[*For* indicates a reason or cause.]

The encyclopedia is open to all	, and	anyone can add information to it.

[*And* simply joins two ideas.]

Often, inaccurate entries cannot be stopped	, nor	is there any penalty for them.

[*Nor* indicates a negative.]

People have complained about errors	, but	the mistakes may or may not be fixed.

[*But* indicates a contrast.]

Some people delete information	, or	they add their own interpretations.

[*Or* indicates alternatives.]

Many people know Wikipedia is flawed	, yet	they continue to use it.

[*Yet* indicates a contrast or possibility.]

Wikipedia now has trustees	, so	perhaps it will be monitored more closely.

[*So* indicates a result.]

PRACTICE 1   JOINING IDEAS WITH COORDINATING CONJUNCTIONS

In each of the following sentences, fill in the blank with an appropriate coordinating conjunction. There may be more than one correct answer for some sentences.   *Answers will vary. Possible answers shown.*

■ **TIP:** For more practice with coordination and subordination, visit Exercise Central at **bedfordstmartins.com/ realwriting**.

EXAMPLE: Companies want workers with diverse skills, ____*but*____ parents may find that child-rearing experience does not always impress potential employers.

1. Parents who quit work to care for children may worry about making enough money, ____*or*____ they may fear that small children will be hard to deal with all day long.

2. Those problems can cause people to think twice about leaving their jobs, _____*yet*_____ the real problem for many people may come when they want to go back to work.

■ **RESOURCES:** To gauge students' skills with coordination, use the *Testing Tool Kit* CD-ROM available with this book.

3. Finding a job can be difficult in any circumstances, _____*so*_____ a job-seeker's résumé needs to be impressive.

4. Résumé experts say that every gap in employment should be explained, _____*for*_____ employers want to know what a person did during that time.

5. Many parents fear that employers will see that the job-seekers have spent a few years raising children, _____*and*_____ their résumés won't receive consideration.

6. Employers may not realize that parenting requires all kinds of skills, _____*so*_____ a person returning to work after raising young children must make employers see that the experience was valuable.

7. The wrong description can make child care sound like dull, unimaginative work, _____*but*_____ a good résumé can demonstrate how challenging and diverse the job of raising children can be.

8. Some parents who want to return to careers find ways to fill gaps on their résumés, _____*and*_____ others come up with ways to get around the problem of résumés altogether.

9. Skills that a worker had before leaving a career can be used in a new business, _____*so*_____ a person who starts a business does not have to worry about creating a perfect résumé.

10. Parents who leave careers have new challenges to consider, _____*but*_____ they can get jobs when they decide to return to work.

■ PRACTICE 2   **COMBINING SENTENCES WITH COORDINATING CONJUNCTIONS** . . . .

Combine each pair of sentences into a single sentence by using a comma and a coordinating conjunction. In some cases, there may be more than one correct answer.   *Answers may vary. Possible edits shown.*

EXAMPLE: E-mail has become common in business communication. People should mind their e-mail manners.
, so people

1. Many professionals use e-mail to keep in touch with clients and
   so businesspeople
   contacts/, ~~They~~ must be especially careful not to offend anyone with
   their e-mail messages.

2. However, anyone who uses e-mail should be cautious/, *for it* ~~It~~ is danger-
   ously easy to send messages to the wrong person.

3. Employees may have time to send personal messages from work/, *but they* ~~They~~
   should remember that employers often have the ability to read their
   workers' messages.

4. R-rated language and jokes may be deleted automatically by a
   or they
   company's server/, ~~They~~ may be read by managers and cause problems
   for the employee sending or receiving them.

5. No message should be forwarded to everyone in a sender's address
   and senders
   book/, ~~Senders~~ should ask permission before adding someone to a
   mass-mailing list.

6. People should check the authenticity of mailings about lost children,
   for most
   dreadful diseases, and terrorist threats before passing them on/, ~~Most~~
   such messages are hoaxes.

7. Typographical errors and misspellings in e-mail make the message
   yet using
   appear less professional/, ~~Using~~ all capital letters—a practice known as
   shouting—is usually considered even worse.

   and these files
8. Many people do not like attachments/, ~~They~~ are likely to be deleted
   unread.

   but no
9. Viruses are a major problem with attachments/, ~~No~~ one wants to
   receive even a harmless attachment if it takes a long time to download.

   so they
10. People who use e-mail for business want to be taken seriously/, ~~They~~
    should make their e-mails as professional as possible.

■ **TEACHING TIP:** Remind
students that a semicolon balances two independent clauses;
what's on either side must be
able to stand alone as a complete sentence.

Coordination Using Semicolons

A **semicolon** is a punctuation mark that can join two sentences through coordination. Use semicolons *only* when the ideas in the two sentences are
very closely related. Do not overuse semicolons.

Complete sentence	;	Complete sentence

Antarctica is a mystery	;	no one knows too much about it.
Its climate is extreme	;	few people want to endure it.
My cousin went there	;	he loves to explore the unknown.

A semicolon alone does not tell readers much about the relationship between the two ideas. To give more information about the relationship, use a **conjunctive adverb** after the semicolon. Put a comma after the conjunctive adverb.

Complete sentence	; also, ; as a result, ; besides, ; however, ; in addition, ; in fact, ; instead, ; still, ; then, ; therefore, ; yet,	Complete sentence

■ **TIP:** When you connect two sentences with a conjunctive adverb, the statement following the semicolon remains a complete thought. If you use a subordinating word such as *because,* however, the second statement becomes a dependent clause and a semicolon is not needed: *It receives little rain because it is incredibly cold.*

Antarctica is largely unexplored	; as a result,	it is unpopulated.
It receives little rain	; also,	it is incredibly cold.
It is a huge area	; therefore,	scientists are becoming more interested in it.

■ **PRACTICE 3 JOINING IDEAS WITH SEMICOLONS** . . . .

Join each pair of sentences by using a semicolon alone.

> **EXAMPLE:** Tanning booths can cause skin to age/. ~~They~~ *they* may also promote cancer.

1. Too much exposure to the sun can cause skin cancer/. ~~Using~~ *using* tanning booths has similar risks.

2. Using a tanning booth does not mean that you will definitely harm yourself/. ~~What~~ *what* it does mean is that you are taking a chance.

3. It's easy to ignore long-term health dangers/. ~~The~~ *the* desire to look good is tempting.

4. Some people wear no clothes in a tanning booth/;~~This~~ *this* behavior can damage skin that is normally covered by a bathing suit.

5. Ultraviolet light can injure the eyes/;~~Tanning~~-*tanning-*salon patrons should always wear protective goggles.

■ **PRACTICE 4   COMBINING SENTENCES WITH SEMICOLONS AND CONNECTING WORDS (CONJUNCTIVE ADVERBS)** . . . .

Combine each pair of sentences by using a semicolon and a conjunctive adverb. In some cases, there may be more than one correct answer.
Answers may vary. Possible edits shown.

EXAMPLE: Seventy percent of mothers now work outside the home/ *; as a result, family* ~~Family~~ life in the United States has changed.

1. Only 40 percent of mothers worked outside the home in 1970/; *then, the* ~~The~~ American workforce changed.

2. Many families today need two incomes to survive/; *however, mothers* ~~Mothers~~ often feel guilty about spending too little time with their children.

3. A new study shows that children of working parents don't necessarily feel neglected/; *in fact, they* ~~They~~ think they get to spend enough time with their mothers and fathers.

4. Children whose parents work and children with a parent at home rate their parents about equally/; *still, children* ~~Children~~ with working parents want their parents to be less tired.

5. Compared with earlier generations, parents today generally have fewer children/; *in addition, fathers* ~~Fathers~~ today may spend more time parenting.

6. Many Americans work longer hours than their parents did/; *as a result, they* ~~They~~ think their children want them to work less.

7. For most children, their parents' jobs are not the problem/; *however, they* ~~They~~ want their time with their parents to be more relaxed.

8. Children think that their fathers should be more available/; *yet, most* ~~Most~~ children think their fathers are teaching them important values.

9. Most working parents try not to give up time with their families/; *instead, they* ~~They~~ cut out personal time and hobbies.

10. A parent's relationship with a child is more important than the
number of hours they spend together/;~~Parents~~ should try to find out
therefore, parents
^
what is going on in the lives of their children.

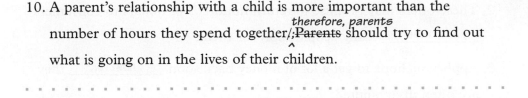

EDITING FOR COORDINATION
Joining Sentences with Related Ideas

Find

I go to bed very late at night. I get up early in the morning.

1. **Ask:** Should the sentences be joined by a coordinating conjunction (FANBOYS) or a semicolon and a conjunctive adverb? *These sentences should be joined by a coordinating conjunction.*

2. **Ask:** What coordinating conjunction or conjunctive adverb best expresses the relationship between the two sentences? *"And" could join the two ideas; "but" could show a contrast.*

Edit

I go to bed very late at night/ I get up early in the morning.
, and
^

I go to bed very late at night/ I get up early in the morning.
; but
^

3. **Join the two sentences** with a coordinating conjunction or a semicolon and a conjunctive adverb.

■ **PRACTICE 5   CHOOSING THE RIGHT COORDINATING CONJUNCTIONS AND CONJUNCTIVE ADVERBS** . . . .

Fill in the blanks with a coordinating conjunction or conjunctive adverb that makes sense in the sentence. Make sure to add the correct punctuation. *Answers may vary. Possible answers shown.*

EXAMPLE: Rebates sound like a good deal _____ *, but* _____ they rarely are.

1. Rebate offers are common _____ *, and* _____ you have probably seen many of them on packages for appliances and electronics.

2. These offers may promise to return hundreds of dollars to consumers ___*; as a result,*___ many people apply for them.

3. Applicants hope to get a lot of money back soon ___*; however,*___ they are often disappointed.

4. They might have to wait several months ___*, or*___ they might not get their rebate at all.

5. Rebate applications are not short ___*, nor*___ are they easy to fill out.

6. One applicant compared completing a rebate form to filling out tax forms ___*, for*___ he spent more than an hour on the process.

7. Manufacturers sometimes use rebates to move unpopular products off the shelves ___*; then,*___ they can replace these products with newer goods.

8. Only about 10 to 30 percent of people who apply for a rebate eventually get it ___*; therefore,*___ consumer groups are warning people to be careful.

9. Problems with rebates are getting more attention ___*, so*___ companies that offer them might have to improve their processes for giving refunds.

10. Manufacturers have received a lot of complaints about rebates ___*; yet,*___ they will probably never stop making these offers.

. . . .

Edit Paragraphs and Your Own Writing

PRACTICE 6   EDITING PARAGRAPHS FOR COORDINATION . . . . . .

In the following paragraphs, join the underlined sentences using coordinating conjunctions, semicolons, or conjunctive adverbs. You may want to use the chart, Editing for Coordination, on page 427.
Answers may vary. Possible edits shown.

     1. (1) Candies, hamburgers, and soft drinks all used to come in familiar, standard sizes/ *, but now* (2) Now, snack and fast-food companies offer

many extra-large products. (3) Some nutritionists say that this trend is worrisome. (4) They point out that when people are offered more, they eat more/ ~~(5) Bigger~~ ^; bigger^ portions make bigger consumers. (6) One candy maker's response to this argument is that the idea for larger portions came from consumers. (7) The company recently offered consumers a trial of super-sized pieces of a popular chocolate candy/ ~~(8) One~~ ^; as a result, one^ out of every three callers to the company asked if the candy could be made into a regular product.

2. (1) In recent years, encounters between hikers and black bears have ~~increased. (2) Several~~ ^increased, and several^ people have been seriously injured. (3) A few hikers have even been killed by out-of-control bears. (4) Bears usually try to avoid any contact with people/ ~~(5) Bears~~ ^; however, bears^ that associate people with food can become aggressive. (6) To help hikers and campers to fully enjoy their outdoor experience, wildlife experts offer a few tips. (7) The most important tip seems ~~obvious. (8) It~~ ^obvious; it^ is to never feed bears or any other wild animals. (9) In addition, don't keep food in tents or leave it lying around in easy reach. (10) Do not burn or bury garbage/ ^, for bears^ ~~(11) Bears~~ will smell it and dig it up. (12) Place all food and garbage in airtight containers, dumpsters, or a locked car. (13) Coolers are not ~~air-tight. (14) Bears~~ ^airtight, and bears^ often associate them with food. (15) Keep your campsite and tools clean, especially cooking and eating utensils. (16) Finally, report any bear damage to wildlife officials/ ~~(17) They~~ ^, so they^ can keep an eye on any bears that might be dangerous.

■ **PRACTICE 7   EDITING YOUR OWN WRITING FOR COORDINATION** · · · ·

As a final practice, edit a piece of your own writing for coordination. It can be a paper you are working on for this course, a paper you've already finished, a paper for another course, or a recent piece of writing from your work or everyday life. Record in your learning journal any choppy sentences you find, along with the edited versions. You may want to use the chart on page 427.

■ **LEARNING JOURNAL:**
How would you explain coordination to someone who had never heard of it?

Chapter Review

1. What word will help you remember what the coordinating conjunctions are? _FANBOYS_

2. What are two ways to join sentences through coordination?

   Use a comma and a coordinating conjunction.

   Use a semicolon alone or a semicolon and a conjunctive adverb.

3. Use a semicolon *only* when the sentences are _very closely related_ .

4. List six conjunctive adverbs that you are most likely to use. _Answers could include any adverbs from_

   the list on page 421.

5. If you use a semicolon and a conjunctive adverb to join two sentences, what punctuation must you use,

   and where? _a comma after the conjunctive adverb_

Chapter Test

Circle the correct choice to fill in each blank.

■ **TIP:** For advice on taking tests, see Appendix A.

1. We were delighted when Eva was transferred to our department, _____ she does not seem pleased with the change.

   a. or   b. and   (c.) but

■ **RESOURCES:** *Testing Tool Kit*, a CD-ROM available with this book, has even more tests.

2. Daniel is very clever _____ he can convince anyone that he is right.

   a. , but   (b.) ;   c. ,

3. I do not have to pay extra for long-distance cell phone calls; _____ I use my cell phone for all my out-of-state calls.

   a. besides,   b. then,   (c.) as a result,

4. I did not like the teacher's criticism of my paper; _____ I must admit that everything she said was right.

   a. as a result,   b. in addition,   (c.) still,

5. Jenna is the best speaker in the class, _____ she will give the graduation speech.

   a. or   (b.) so   c. yet

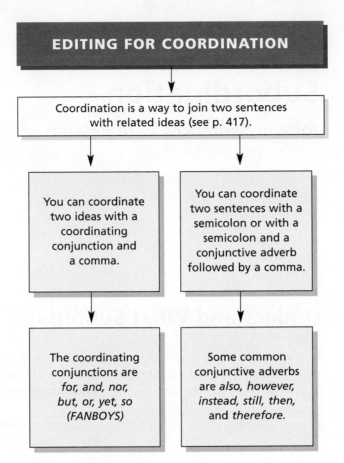

EDITING FOR COORDINATION

Coordination is a way to join two sentences with related ideas (see p. 417).

You can coordinate two ideas with a coordinating conjunction and a comma.

You can coordinate two sentences with a semicolon or with a semicolon and a conjunctive adverb followed by a comma.

The coordinating conjunctions are *for, and, nor, but, or, yet, so (FANBOYS)*

Some common conjunctive adverbs are *also, however, instead, still, then,* and *therefore.*

29

Subordination

Joining Sentences with Related Ideas

Understand What Subordination Is

Like coordination, **subordination** is a way to join short, choppy sentences with related ideas into a longer sentence. With subordination, you put a dependent word (such as *after, although, because,* or *when*) in front of one of the sentences. The resulting sentence will have one complete sentence and one dependent clause, which is no longer a complete sentence.

■ **TIP:** To understand this chapter, you need to be familiar with basic sentence elements. For a review, see Chapter 20.

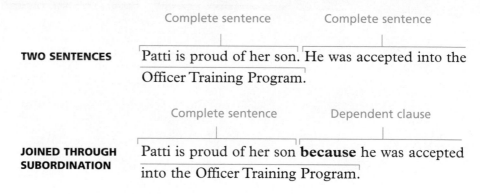

	Complete sentence	Complete sentence
TWO SENTENCES	Patti is proud of her son.	He was accepted into the Officer Training Program.

	Complete sentence	Dependent clause
JOINED THROUGH SUBORDINATION	Patti is proud of her son	**because** he was accepted into the Officer Training Program.

Practice Using Subordination

■ **TEACHING TIP:** Write two sentences on the board and have students suggest how the sentences would have to change to accommodate different subordinating conjunctions.

To join two sentences through subordination, use a **subordinating conjunction**. Choose the conjunction that makes the most sense with the two sentences. Here are some of the most common subordinating conjunctions.

Complete sentence	after	now that	Dependent clause
	although	once	
	as	since	
	as if	so that	
	because	unless	
	before	until	
	even if/ though	when	
		whenever	
	if	where	
	if only	while	

■ **TEACHING TIP:** Point out that unlike the conjunctive adverbs on page 421, these subordinating conjunctions are never used with a semicolon in front of them or a comma after.

I love music	because	it makes me relax.
It is hard to study at home	when	my children are screaming.

When a dependent clause ends a sentence, it usually does not need to be preceded by a comma unless it is showing a contrast.

You can also put a subordinating conjunction and dependent clause at the beginning of a new sentence. When the dependent clause comes first, use a comma to separate it from the rest of the sentence.

Subordinating conjunction	Dependent clause	,	Complete sentence
When	I eat out	,	I usually have steak.
Although	it is harmful	,	young people still smoke.

EDITING FOR SUBORDINATION:
Joining Ideas with Related Ideas

↓

Find

It is hard to sleep in the city. It is always very noisy.

1. **Ask:** What is the relationship between the two complete sentences? *The second sentence explains the first.*

2. **Ask:** What subordinating conjunctions express that relationship? *"Because," "as," or "since."*

↓

Edit

because it
It is hard to sleep in the city. It is always very noisy.
^

3. **Join the two sentences** with a subordinating conjunction that makes sense.

PRACTICE 1   JOINING IDEAS THROUGH SUBORDINATION . . . . . .

In the following sentences, fill in the blank with an appropriate subordinating conjunction. There may be more than one correct choice.
Answers may vary. Possible answers shown.

EXAMPLE: ___*When*___ the Treasury Department redesigned the twenty-dollar bill, many people thought that it looked like play money.

1. The Treasury Department decided to change the design of American paper money ___*because*___ it was too easy for criminals to copy.

2. ___*Since*___ security was the only reason for the change, the basic elements of each bill remain the same.

3. The portrait on each denomination shows the same person as the old bills did ___*so that*___ the new money is familiar.

4. ___*Although*___ the person in the portrait is the same, the portraits themselves are different.

5. ___*While*___ discussing the security measures, Treasury Department officials considered changing the color of the bills.

6. The bills are printed on the same paper as they were before ___*because*___ people can tell by the feel if the bills are real.

7. ___*When*___ you look closely at one of the new bills, you can see security fibers printed with the bill's amount.

8. The paper also has a watermark that is invisible ___*unless*___ you hold the bill up to the light.

9. The new bills do have simpler graphics ___*because*___ the new security measures take more space than the original design did.

10. ___*After*___ so many years of the old design, the new bills seem strange to many people.

PRACTICE 2   COMBINING SENTENCES THROUGH SUBORDINATION . .

Combine each pair of sentences into a single sentence by using an appropriate subordinating conjunction either at the beginning of or between the two sentences. Use a conjunction that makes sense with the two sentences and add commas where necessary.   *Answers may vary. Possible edits shown.*

EXAMPLE: Most business executives now type their own letters,/ *because composing*

~~Composing~~ on a computer is faster than writing

by hand.

1. Almost all college students used typewriters until the 1980s,/ *when computers* ~~Computers~~

became more affordable.

2. Typewriters were used less often,/ *after computers* ~~Computers~~ became more wide-

spread.

3. Computers offer many advantages,/, *although there* ~~There~~ are also some drawbacks.

4. *If you* ~~You~~ have not saved what you have written,/, *a* ~~A~~ power outage could

cause you to lose your work.

5. *When computers* ~~Computers~~ became widely used in the 1980s,/, *professors* ~~Professors~~ were sur-

prised to hear students say, "The computer ate my paper."

6. *When you* ~~You~~ have written a rough draft of a paper,/, *you* ~~You~~ should print it out.

7. Some people like to print out a document to proofread it,/ *because they* ~~They~~ fail to

catch all their mistakes on the screen.

8. *While the* ~~The~~ quality of computer screens is getting better,/, *people* ~~People~~ still complain

about eyestrain.

9. *Even though spell-checking* ~~Spell-checking~~ programs prevent many errors,/, *only* ~~Only~~ a person is able to

recognize sound-alikes such as *their* and *there*.

10. Using a grammar-check program can also cause problems,/ *if writers* ~~Writers~~

assume that the computer understands grammar rules and do not

check their work themselves.

PRACTICE 3   USING SUBORDINATION . . . .

Complete each of the following sentences.
Answers will vary. Possible answers shown.

EXAMPLE: **Although most people may live to one hundred in the**

future, *those days are a long way off* _____.

1. *We have all heard stories of people who lived long lives* _____ even though

they smoked, ate meat every day, and drank alcohol regularly.

2. When someone lives to one hundred or older, *the story usually makes it into the news*
.

3. Because very elderly people are unusual, *scientists are studying them to learn from their secrets*
.

4. *We will not understand why certain people live so long* until researchers learn more about the genetics of these individuals.

5. While some say it may be possible to develop drugs that greatly extend our lives, *many others are skeptical*
.

6. *For now, most people will not live past one hundred* unless they are very lucky.

7. *You will hear a lot of different stories* if you ask very old people what they do every day to stay happy and healthy.

8. After my ninety-nine-year-old great-aunt wakes up every morning, *she reads the paper and takes a walk*
.

9. Before she goes to bed, *she watches her favorite TV shows and has a beer*.

10. *I plan to do exactly what she does* so that I can live to at least one hundred.

Edit Paragraphs and Your Own Writing

PRACTICE 4   **EDITING PARAGRAPHS FOR SUBORDINATION**

In the following paragraphs, join the underlined sentences through subordination. Do not forget to punctuate correctly. You may want to use the chart, Editing for Subordination, on page 435.
Answers may vary. Possible edits shown.

1. (1) Why are there expiration dates on some products and not on others? (2) For example, not all manufacturers of sunscreen give expiration dates./ (3) ~~There~~ *because there* are no federal regulations requiring these dates on sunscreen. (4) Bike helmets never come with expiration dates. (5) ~~Most~~ *Although most* professionals believe it's not necessary to replace a bike helmet regularly,/ (6) ~~It's~~ *it's* best to get a new helmet if the wearer has fallen on his

or her head. (7) According to industry experts, bottled water is safe to use indefinitely when it is stored properly, but bottled water always has an expiration date because of state laws. (8) Car tires, which eventually start disintegrating, should be replaced within five years, *even though tires* (9) ~~Tires~~ never have expiration dates.

2. (1) Most people don't expect to get a stunning view of Jupiter while they are out for a walk. (2) Nevertheless, some do, thanks to the sidewalk astronomers movement. (3) *When a* A volunteer sidewalk astronomer sets up a telescope on a city ~~sidewalk.~~ *sidewalk, anybody* (4) ~~Anybody~~ who comes by is invited to take a look. (5) Recently, a woman walking with her two grandsons in New York City's Greenwich Village got an excellent look at the equatorial bands of Jupiter. (6) *As her* ~~Her~~ grandsons gazed through the ~~tele-scope. (7) Other~~ *telescope, other* people lined up to see for themselves. (8) Sidewalk astronomy was first made popular in the late 1960s by John Dobson. (9) *After he* ~~He~~ sanded down a 12-inch piece of porthole glass into a reflecting telescope ~~mirror. (10) He~~ *mirror, he* made a mount for the scope out of a plywood box, some pieces of cardboard, and roof shingles. (11) He had little money at the time, so he had to use materials that cost nothing. (12) *When he* ~~He~~ pointed the telescope at the ~~moon. (13) He~~ *moon, he* found that the scope made the moon's craters, mountains, and ridges appear to be right in front of him. (14) Eventually, his design for this affordable telescope would be named the Dobsonian. (15) He wheeled the telescope around the streets of San ~~Francisco. (16) He~~ *Francisco, where he* loaned it to kids and taught them how to make their own telescopes.

■ PRACTICE 5   EDITING YOUR OWN WRITING FOR SUBORDINATION   . .

Edit a piece of your own writing for subordination. It can be a paper you are working on for this course, a paper you've already finished, a paper for another course, or a recent piece of writing from your work or everyday life. You may want to use the chart on page 435.

■ **LEARNING JOURNAL:**
How would you explain subordination to someone who had never heard of it?

Chapter Review

1. With subordination, you put a __*dependent word*__ in front of one of two related sentences.

2. List five common subordinating conjunctions. *Possible answers:* although, because, since, if, unless

Chapter Test

Circle the correct choice to fill in each blank.

■ **TIP:** For advice on taking tests, see Appendix A.

1. _____ the candidate stepped up to the podium, a group of protesters began to shout criticisms of her.

   a. So that   b. As if   c.) As

■ **RESOURCES:** *Testing Tool Kit*, a CD-ROM available with this book, has even more tests.

2. There were now neat rows of suburban homes _____ there had once been orange groves.

   a.) where   b. as if   c. before

3. _____ you are sure that the lightning has stopped, don't let the kids get back into the pool.

   a.) Until   b. Before   c. As if

4. Matt speaks out against glorifying college sports _____ he himself is the star of our football team.

   a. until   b.) even though   c. unless

5. _____ we bought a snowblower, my son hasn't complained about having to shovel after storms.

   a.) Since   b. Where   c. Unless

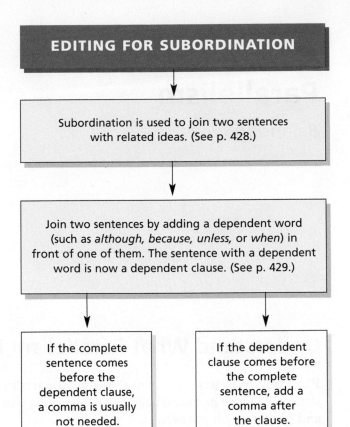

EDITING FOR SUBORDINATION

Subordination is used to join two sentences with related ideas. (See p. 428.)

Join two sentences by adding a dependent word (such as *although, because, unless,* or *when*) in front of one of them. The sentence with a dependent word is now a dependent clause. (See p. 429.)

If the complete sentence comes before the dependent clause, a comma is usually not needed.

If the dependent clause comes before the complete sentence, add a comma after the clause.

30

Parallelism

Balancing Ideas

Understand What Parallelism Is

■ **TIP:** To understand this chapter, you need to be familiar with basic sentence elements, such as nouns and verbs. For a review, see Chapter 20.

Parallelism in writing means that similar parts in a sentence have the same structure: Their parts are balanced. Use nouns with nouns, verbs with verbs, and phrases with phrases.

> **NOT PARALLEL**   I enjoy <u>basketball</u> more than <u>playing video games</u>.
>
> [*Basketball* is a noun, but *playing video games* is a phrase.]
>
> **PARALLEL**   I enjoy <u>basketball</u> more than <u>video games</u>.
>
> **NOT PARALLEL**   Last night, I <u>worked</u>, <u>studied</u>, and was <u>watching television</u>.
>
> [Verbs must be in the same tense to be parallel. *Was watching television* has a different structure from *worked* and *studied*.]
>
> **PARALLEL**   Last night, I <u>worked</u>, <u>studied</u>, and <u>watched television</u>.
>
> **NOT PARALLEL**   This weekend we can go <u>to the beach</u> or <u>walking in the mountains</u>.
>
> [*To the beach* should be paired with another prepositional phrase: *to the mountains*.]
>
> **PARALLEL**   This weekend we can go <u>to the beach</u> or <u>to the mountains</u>.

Practice Writing Parallel Sentences

Parallelism in Pairs and Lists

When two or more items in a series are joined by the words *and* or *or*, use a similar form for each item.

NOT PARALLEL The professor assigned a <u>chapter to read</u>, <u>practices to do</u>, and <u>writing a paper</u>.

PARALLEL The professor assigned a <u>chapter to read</u>, <u>practices to do</u>, and <u>a paper to write</u>.

NOT PARALLEL The story was <u>in the newspaper</u>, <u>on the radio</u>, and <u>the television</u>.

[*In the newspaper* and *on the radio* are prepositional phrases. *The television* is not.]

PARALLEL The story was <u>in the newspaper</u>, <u>on the radio</u>, and <u>on the television</u>.

PRACTICE 1 USING PARALLELISM IN PAIRS AND LISTS . . . .

In each sentence, underline the parts of the sentence that should be parallel. Then, edit the sentence to make it parallel.
Answers may vary. Possible edits shown.

EXAMPLE: Coyotes roam the <u>western mountains</u>, the <u>central plains</u>, and <s>they are in the suburbs of</s> the East Coast of the United States. *suburbs*

1. Wild predators, such as wolves, are vanishing because people <u>hunt</u>
them and <s>are taking</s> over their land. *take*

2. Coyotes are <u>surviving</u> and <s>they do</s> well in the modern United States. *doing*

3. The success of the coyote is due to its <u>varied diet</u> and <s>adapting easily</s>. *adaptability*

4. Coyotes are sometimes <u>vegetarians</u>, sometimes <u>scavengers</u>, and sometimes <s>they hunt</s>. *hunters*

5. Today, they are <u>spreading</u> and <s>populate</s> the East Coast for the first time. *populating*

6. The coyotes' appearance <u>surprises</u> and <s>is worrying</s> many people. *worries*

7. The animals have chosen an area <s>that is more populated and it's not as wild as</s> their traditional home. *more populated and less wild than*

8. Coyotes can adapt to <u>rural</u>, <u>suburban</u>, or <s>even living in a city</s>. *urban life.*

9. One coyote was <u>identified</u>, <u>tracked</u>, and <s>they</s> <u>captured</u> <s>him</s> in Central Park in New York City.

10. Suburbanites are getting used to the <u>sight</u> of coyotes. <s>and hearing them.</s> *and sound*

■ **TIP:** For more practice with making sentences parallel, visit Exercise Central at **bedfordstmartins.com/ realwriting**.

■ **RESOURCES:** *Additional Resources* contains tests and supplemental practice exercises for this chapter as well as a transparency master for the chart at the end.

■ **TEACHING TIP:** Doing this practice orally allows students to hear problems with parallelism. The same is true of Practices 2, 3, and 5.

Parallelism in Comparisons

In comparisons, the items being compared should have parallel structures. Comparisons often use the words *than* or *as*. When you edit for parallelism, make sure that the items on either side of those words are parallel.

NOT PARALLEL	<u>Driving downtown</u> is as fast as <u>the bus</u>.
PARALLEL	<u>Driving downtown</u> is as fast as <u>taking the bus</u>.
NOT PARALLEL	<u>To admit a mistake</u> is better than <u>denying it</u>.
PARALLEL	<u>To admit a mistake</u> is better than <u>to deny it</u>.
	<u>Admitting a mistake</u> is better than <u>denying it</u>.

Sometimes you need to add or delete a word or two to make the parts of a sentence parallel.

NOT PARALLEL	<u>A tour package</u> is less expensive than <u>arranging every travel detail yourself</u>.
PARALLEL, WORD ADDED	*Buying* <u>a tour package</u> is less expensive than <u>arranging every travel detail yourself</u>.
NOT PARALLEL	The <u>sale price of the shoes</u> is as low as <u>paying the regular price for two pairs</u>.
PARALLEL, WORDS DROPPED	The <u>sale price of the shoes</u> is as low as <u>the regular price for two pairs</u>.

■ **RESOURCES:** To gauge students' skills with parallelism, use the *Testing Tool Kit* CD-ROM available with this book.

■ **PRACTICE 2 USING PARALLELISM IN COMPARISONS** . . . .

In each sentence, underline the parts of the sentence that should be parallel. Then, edit the sentence to make it parallel.
Answers may vary. Possible edits shown.

    EXAMPLE: <u>Leasing a new car</u> may be less expensive than t̶o̶ b̶u̶y̶ *buying* one.

1. Car dealers often require less money down for leasing a car than <u>for</u>
    t̶h̶e̶ p̶u̶r̶c̶h̶a̶s̶e̶ o̶f̶ *purchasing* one.

2. The <u>monthly payments</u> for a leased car may be as low as p̶a̶y̶i̶n̶g̶ f̶o̶r̶ *loan payments*
    a̶ l̶o̶a̶n̶.

3. You should check the <u>terms of leasing</u> to make sure they are as favor-
    able as t̶o̶ b̶u̶y̶ *the terms of buying*.

4. You may find that t̶o̶ l̶e̶a̶s̶e̶ *leasing* is a safer bet than <u>buying</u>.

5. You will be making less of a financial commitment by leasing a car
    by owning
   than ~~to own~~ it.
        ^

    leasing
6. Buying a car may be better than ~~a lease on~~ one if you plan to keep it

   for several years.

7. A used car can be more economical than ~~getting~~ a new one.

    maintaining
8. However, ~~maintenance of~~ a new car may be easier than taking care of
        ^

   a used car.

9. A used car may not be as impressive as ~~buying~~ a brand-new vehicle.

10. To get a used car from a reputable source can be a better decision than
    to buy
    a new vehicle that loses value the moment you drive it home.
        ^

Parallelism with Certain Paired Words

When a sentence uses certain paired words, called **correlative conjunctions**, the items joined by them must be parallel. These words link two equal elements and show the relationship between them. Here are the paired words:

both . . . and	neither . . . nor	rather . . . than
either . . . or	not only . . . but also	

When you use the first part of a pair, be sure you always use the second part, too.

NOT PARALLEL   Bruce wants *both* freedom *and* wealthy.

[*Both* is used with *and*, but the items joined by them are not parallel.]

PARALLEL   Bruce wants *both* freedom *and* wealth.

NOT PARALLEL   He can *neither* fail the course and quitting his job is also impossible.

PARALLEL   He can *neither* fail the course *nor* quit his job.

PRACTICE 3   USING PARALLELISM WITH CERTAIN PAIRED WORDS

In each sentence, circle the paired words and underline the parts of the sentence that should be parallel. Then, edit the sentence to make it parallel. You may need to change one of the paired elements to make the sentence parallel.   *Answers may vary. Possible edits shown.*

■ **COMPUTER:** Students can use the find or search function to locate the first word in correlative conjunctions. They should read the sentences with those constructions carefully to make sure the second word is present and that parallel structure is used.

EXAMPLE: A cell phone can be (either) a lifesaver (or) ~~it can be~~
an annoyance
~~annoying~~.
                    ^

1. Fifteen years ago, most people (neither) had cell phones (nor) ~~did they~~
wanted
~~want~~ them.
    ^

2. Today, cell phones are (not only) used by people of all ages (but also) ~~are~~
carried everywhere.

3. Cell phones are not universally popular: Some commuters would
                                                                    be
(rather) ban cell phones on buses and trains (than) ~~being~~ forced to listen
                                                         ^
to other people's conversations.

4. No one denies that a cell phone can be (both) useful (and) ~~convenience is~~
                                                     convenient
                                                          ^
~~a factor~~.

5. A motorist stranded on a deserted road would (rather) have a cell phone
    be forced
(than) to walk to the nearest gas station.
    ^

6. When cell phones were first introduced, some people feared that they
(either) caused brain tumors (or) ~~they~~ were a dangerous source of
radiation.

7. Most Americans today (neither) worry about radiation from cell phones
    fear
(nor) other injuries.
    ^

8. The biggest risk of cell phones is (either) that drivers are distracted by
                that people get
them (or) ~~people getting~~ angry at someone talking too loudly in public
              ^
on a cell phone.

9. Cell phones probably do not cause brain tumors, but some experiments on human cells have shown that energy from the phones may
(both) affect people's reflexes (and) ~~it might~~ alter the brain's blood vessels.

10. Some scientists think that these experiments show that cell phone use
                                                    also mental ones
might have (not only) physical effects on human beings (but) ~~it also~~ ~~could~~
                                                                  ^
~~influence mental processes~~.

PRACTICE 4   **COMPLETING SENTENCES WITH PAIRED WORDS** . . . .

For each sentence, complete the correlative conjunction and add more information. Make sure that the structures on both sides of the correlative
conjunction are parallel.   *Answers will vary. Possible answers shown.*

EXAMPLE: I am both impressed by your company *and enthusiastic to*
work for you   .

1. I could bring to this job not only youthful enthusiasm *but also relevant*

   experience   .

2. I am willing to work either in your main office *or in your San Francisco*

   office   .

3. My current job neither encourages initiative *nor allows flexibility*   .

4. I would rather work in a challenging job *than work in a boring one*   .

5. In college, I learned a lot both from my classes *and from other students*

                                                 .

Edit Paragraphs and Your Own Writing

PRACTICE 5   EDITING PARAGRAPHS FOR PARALLELISM

Find and correct any problems with parallelism in the following paragraphs.
You may want to refer to the chart, Editing for Parallelism, on page 444.
Answers will vary. Possible edits shown.

1. (1) Karaoke started about thirty years ago in Japan, found many
fans in that country, and ~~it~~ became a popular form of entertainment
around the world. (2) The word *karaoke* combines part of the word
kara, meaning "empty," with part of the word *okesutura,* ~~which means~~ *meaning*
"orchestra." (3) A karaoke recording of a song contains the music without vocals, and karaoke performers sing the lyrics. (4) In Japan, where
houses are small, close together, and ~~they are~~ not soundproofed, people
travel to special karaoke rooms to sing. (5) Karaoke rooms allow customers to sing, relax, and ~~they can~~ enjoy being the center of attention
for a little while. (6) Many Westerners are surprised to learn that most
Japanese are neither reluctant nor ~~do they find it embarrassing~~ *embarrassed* to sing in
public. (7) Japanese karaoke singers know that they can entertain either
by singing well or ~~they can sing~~ *by singing* badly. (8) To them, ~~to entertain~~ *entertaining* is more
important than showing off a beautiful voice.

2. (1) As a young man, Sigmund Freud, the founder of psychoanalysis,

> ■ **TEAMWORK:** Have students
> form small groups. Then, have
> each group write five sentences
> that are not parallel. Each
> group should then exchange
> sentences with another group
> and correct the other group's
> sentences.

wanted to use scientific methods to unlock the secrets of human behavior. (2) However, as biographer Peter Gay explains, the effort was slow, time-consuming, and ~~that it was~~ often discouraging. (3) In the 1890s, Freud, a medical doctor by training, began studying and ~~to document~~ *documenting* causes of hysteria, and he discovered that many of his female patients had been sexually abused by their fathers. (4) Through this discovery, Freud came to understand how traumatic events from childhood that are ignored or ~~one forgets them~~ *forgotten* can cause emotional problems later.

(5) To test his theories, Freud analyzed himself. (6) Studying his own behavior was frightening and ~~disturbed him~~ *disturbing*. (7) However, it was deeply rewarding as well, not only to Freud as a scientist but also *to* Freud as an individual. (8) His neurotic symptoms gradually disappeared. (9) Soon, he published his most famous book, *The Interpretation of Dreams*. (10) Here, he describes how even in sleep the subconscious mind often distorts and ~~is disguising~~ *disguises* forbidden wishes so that they become unrecognizable. (11) A dream takes on meaning only when understood symbolically—"interpreted" through the methods of psychoanalysis.

■ PRACTICE 6   **EDITING YOUR OWN WRITING FOR PARALLELISM** . . . .

■ **LEARNING JOURNAL:**
How would you explain parallelism to someone who had never heard of it? How would you explain how to edit for it?

As a final practice, edit a piece of your own writing for parallelism. It can be a paper you are working on for this course, a paper you've already finished, a paper for another course, or a recent piece of writing from your work or everyday life. Record in your learning journal any problem sentences you find, along with their corrections. You may want to use the chart on page 444.

Chapter Review

1. Parallelism in writing means that <u>similar parts in a sentence are balanced</u>.

2. In what three situations do problems with parallelism most often occur? <u>with pairs and lists, with comparisons, and with certain paired words</u>

3. What are two pairs of correlative conjunctions? <u>Possible answers: both/and, neither/nor</u>

Chapter Test

Circle the correct choice for each of the following items.

■ **TIP:** For advice on taking tests, see Appendix A.

1. If an underlined portion of this sentence is incorrect, select the revision that fixes it. If the sentence is correct as written, choose d.

   For our home renovation, we're planning to <u>expand the kitchen</u>,
   A

   <u>retile the bathroom</u>, and we also want to <u>add a bedroom</u>.
   B   C

   a. add space to the kitchen   (c.) add a bedroom

   b. replace the tile in the bathroom   d. No change is necessary.

■ **RESOURCES:** *Testing Tool Kit*, a CD-ROM available with this book, has even more tests.

2. Choose the correct word(s) to fill in the blank.

   In my personal ad, I said that I like taking long walks on the beach, dining over candlelight, and _____ sculptures with a chainsaw.

   a. to carve   (b.) carving   c. carved

3. If an underlined portion of this sentence is incorrect, select the revision that fixes it. If the sentence is correct as written, choose d.

   To get <u>her elbow</u> back into shape, she wants <u>exercising</u> and not <u>to take pills</u>.
   A   B   C

   a. To getting   c. taking pills

   (b.) to do exercises   d. No change is necessary.

4. Choose the correct word(s) to fill in the blank.

   The first-time homebuyer course teaches that _____ a home is often less expensive than renting one over the long term.

   (a.) owning   b. have owned   c. to own

5. Choose the correct words to fill in the blank.

   You can travel by car, by plane, or _____.

   a. boating is fine   (b.) by boat   c. on boat

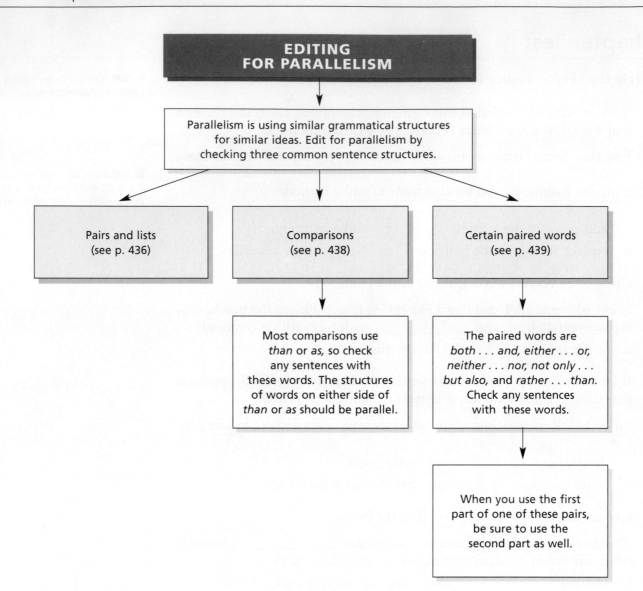

EDITING FOR PARALLELISM

Parallelism is using similar grammatical structures for similar ideas. Edit for parallelism by checking three common sentence structures.

Pairs and lists
(see p. 436)

Comparisons
(see p. 438)

Certain paired words
(see p. 439)

Most comparisons use *than* or *as,* so check any sentences with these words. The structures of words on either side of *than* or *as* should be parallel.

The paired words are *both . . . and, either . . . or, neither . . . nor, not only . . . but also,* and *rather . . . than.* Check any sentences with these words.

When you use the first part of one of these pairs, be sure to use the second part as well.

31

Sentence Variety

Putting Rhythm in Your Writing

Understand What Sentence Variety Is

Having **sentence variety** in your writing means using different sentence patterns, lengths, and rhythms. Sometimes, writers use too many short, simple sentences, thinking that short is always easier to understand than long. In fact, that is not true, as you can see in these examples, where the writing doesn't have any rhythm.

WITH SHORT, SIMPLE SENTENCES

Many people do not realize how important their speaking voice is. This is particularly true in a job interview. What you say is important. How you say it is nearly as important. The way you say it is what creates the impression of you. Mumbling while slouching is a particularly bad way of speaking. It makes the speaker appear sloppy and lacking in confidence. It also makes it difficult for the interviewer to hear. Talking too fast is another bad speech behavior. The speaker runs his or her ideas together. The interviewer can't follow them or distinguish what's important. A third common bad speech behavior concerns what are called verbal "tics." Verbal tics are things like saying "um" or "like" or "you know" all the time. Practice for an interview. Sit up straight. Look the person to whom you're speaking directly in the eye. Speak up. Slow down. One good way to find out how you sound is to leave yourself a voice-mail message. If you sound bad to yourself, you need practice speaking aloud. Don't let poor speech behavior interfere with creating a good impression.

WITH SENTENCE VARIETY

Many people do not realize how important their speaking voice is, particularly in a job interview. What you say is important, but how you say it is nearly as important because that is what creates the impression of you. Mumbling while slouching is a particularly bad way of speaking. Not only does this make the speaker appear sloppy and lacking in confidence, but it also makes it difficult for the interviewer to hear. Talking

■ **COMPUTER:** Students can get a visual measure of the length of their sentences by inserting two returns after every period in a paragraph. (They can search for periods to do this.)

too fast is another bad speech behavior. The speaker runs his or her ideas together, and the interviewer can't follow them or distinguish what's important. A third common bad speech behavior concerns what are called verbal "tics," like saying "um" or "like" or "you know" all the time. When you practice for an interview, sit up straight, look the person to whom you're speaking directly in the eye, speak up, and slow down. One good way to find out how you sound is to leave yourself a voice-mail message. If you sound bad to yourself, you need practice speaking aloud. Don't let poor speech behavior interfere with creating a good impression.

Sentence variety is what gives your writing good rhythm and flow.

Practice Creating Sentence Variety

■ **RESOURCES:** *Additional Resources* contains tests and supplemental practice exercises for this chapter as well as a transparency master for the chart at the end.

To create sentence variety, write sentences of different types and lengths. Most writers tend to write short sentences that start with the subject, so this chapter will focus on techniques for starting with something other than the subject and for writing a variety of longer sentences. Two additional techniques for achieving sentence variety—coordination and subordination—are covered in Chapters 28 and 29.

Remember that the goal is to use variety to achieve a good rhythm. Do not just change all your sentences from one pattern to another pattern, or you still won't have variety.

Start Some Sentences with Adverbs

■ **TIP:** For more about adverbs, see Chapter 26.

Adverbs are words that describe verbs, adjectives, or other adverbs; they often end with *-ly.* As long as the meaning is clear, adverbs can be placed at the beginning of a sentence instead of in the middle. Adverbs at the beginning of a sentence are usually followed by a comma.

ADVERB IN MIDDLE	Stories about haunted houses *frequently* surface at Halloween.
ADVERB AT BEGINNING	*Frequently,* stories about haunted houses surface at Halloween.
ADVERB IN MIDDLE	These stories *often* focus on ship captains lost at sea.
ADVERB AT BEGINNING	*Often,* these stories focus on ship captains lost at sea.

■ **PRACTICE 1**   **STARTING SENTENCES WITH AN ADVERB** . . . .

■ **TIP:** For more practice with sentence variety, visit Exercise Central at **bedfordstmartins .com/realwriting**.

Edit each sentence so it begins with an adverb.

EXAMPLE: *Unfortunately, rabies*
Rabies ~~unfortunately~~ remains a problem in the United States.

1. *Once, rabies*

   ~~Rabies once~~ was a major threat to domestic pets in this country.

2. *Now, the*

   ~~The~~ disease is ~~now~~ most deadly to wildlife such as raccoons, skunks,

   and bats.

3. *Frequently, people*

   ~~People frequently~~ fail to have their pets vaccinated against rabies.

4. *Mistakenly, they believe*

   ~~They believe mistakenly~~ that their dogs and cats are no longer in

   danger.

5. *Worriedly, veterinarians note*

   ~~Veterinarians note worriedly~~ that wildlife with rabies can infect pets

   and people.

■ **PRACTICE 2   STARTING SENTENCES WITH AN ADVERB** . . . .

In each sentence, fill in the blank with an adverb that makes sense. Add a
comma when necessary. There may be several good choices for each item.
Answers will vary. Possible answers shown.

    EXAMPLE: _____*Luckily,*_____ a new method of vaccination may help

              reduce the amount of rabies in some wild animals.

1. _____*Recently,*_____ an oral vaccine that prevents rabies in raccoons and

   skunks has been developed.

2. _____*Often,*_____ the vaccine can be placed in bait that the animals like

   to eat.

3. _____*Thankfully,*_____ this method of vaccination has stopped the spread of

   rabies in coyotes in southern Texas.

4. _____*Additionally,*_____ it has saved humans' and pets' lives, public health

   officials agree.

5. _*Unfortunately,*_ the problem of rabies in bats has not yet been solved.

■ **PRACTICE 3   WRITING SENTENCES THAT START WITH AN ADVERB** . .

Write three sentences that start with an adverb. Use commas as necessary.
Choose among the following adverbs: *often, sadly, amazingly, luckily, lovingly,
aggressively, gently, frequently, stupidly.*

1. *Answers will vary.* _____

2. _____

3. _____

Join Ideas Using an *-ing* Verb

One way to combine sentences is to use a verb that ends in *-ing* to make one of the sentences into a phrase.

The *-ing* verb form indicates that the two parts of the sentence are happening at the same time. Add an *-ing* verb to the less important of the two sentences.

■ **TEACHING TIP:** Explain to students that in their own writing they will need to consider the context when deciding which sentence contains the more important idea.

TWO SENTENCES	A pecan roll from our bakery is not dietetic. It contains eight hundred calories.
JOINED WITH *-ING* VERB FORM	*Containing* eight hundred calories, a pecan roll from our bakery is not dietetic.

To combine sentences this way, add *-ing* to the verb in one of the sentences and delete the subject. You now have a phrase that can be added to the beginning or the end of the other sentence, depending on what makes the most sense.

The fat content is also high/. ~~It equals~~ *equaling* the fat in a huge country breakfast.

If you add a phrase starting with an *-ing* verb to the beginning of a sentence, put a comma after it. If you add the phrase to the end of a sentence, you will usually need to put a comma before it, as in the preceding example, unless the phrase is essential to the meaning of the sentence.

If you put a phrase starting with an *-ing* verb at the beginning of a sentence, be sure the word that the phrase modifies follows immediately. Otherwise, you will create a dangling modifier.

■ **TIP:** For more on finding and correcting dangling modifiers, see Chapter 27, and for more on joining ideas, see Chapters 28 and 29.

TWO SENTENCES	I ran through the rain. My raincoat got all wet.
DANGLING MODIFIER	Running through the rain, my raincoat got all wet.
EDITED	Running through the rain, I got my raincoat all wet.

■ PRACTICE 4   JOINING IDEAS USING AN *-ING* VERB . . . .

■ **TEACHING TIP:** Doing this practice orally will help students hear the correct formation. The same is true of Practices 7, 8, 10, 12, and 14.

Combine each pair of sentences into a single sentence by using an *-ing* verb. Add or delete words as necessary.   *Answers may vary. Possible edits shown.*

EXAMPLE: Some people read faces very well/. ~~They interpret~~ *interpreting* nonverbal cues that other people miss.

1. ~~A recent study tested~~ *Testing* children's abilities to interpret facial expressions/, ^*a recent* ~~The~~ study made headlines.

2. ~~Physically~~ abused children ~~participated in the study. They~~ *Participating in the study, physically* saw photographs of faces changing from one expression to another.

3. The children told researchers what emotion was most obvious in each
   choosing
   face/, ~~The children chose~~ among fear, anger, sadness, happiness, and
          ^
   other emotions.

                                                serving
4. Nonabused children also looked at the faces/, ~~They served~~ as a control
                                                 ^
   group for comparison with the other children.

5. All of the children in the study were equally good at identifying most
        responding
   emotions/, ~~They all responded~~ similarly to happiness or fear.
            ^

6. Battered children were especially sensitive to one emotion on the
      identifying
   faces/, ~~These children identified~~ anger much more quickly than the
         ^
   other children could.
   Having   *the abused children*
7. ~~The abused children have~~ learned to look for anger/, ~~They~~ protect
 ^   ^
   themselves with this early-warning system.

8. Their sensitivity to anger may not help the abused children later in
      perhaps hurting
   life/, ~~It perhaps hurts~~ them socially.
        ^
   Tending   *abused children*
9. ~~The abused children tend~~ to run from anger they observe/, ~~They~~ have
 ^   ^
   difficulty connecting with people who exhibit anger.

                                                   often hanging
10. The human brain works hard to acquire useful information/, ~~It often~~
                                                             ^
    ~~hangs~~ on to the information after its usefulness has passed.

▇ **PRACTICE 5   JOINING IDEAS USING AN *-ING* VERB** . . . .

Fill in the blank in each sentence with an appropriate *-ing* verb.
Answers will vary. Possible answers shown.

EXAMPLE: __*Approaching*__ the plate, Hernandez eyed the pitcher
calmly.

1. The pitcher stepped off the mound, ____*delaying*____ his first pitch.

2. ____*Clutching*____ his bat, Hernandez waited.

3. ____*Striding*____ back onto the mound, the pitcher released his
   devastating fastball.

4. Hernandez swung too late, ____*missing*____ the ball.

5. "Strike," called the umpire, ____*pointing*____ his finger sharply.

■ **PRACTICE 6   JOINING IDEAS USING AN *-ING* VERB** . . . .

Write two sets of sentences and join them using an *-ing* verb form.

EXAMPLE: a. *Carol looked up.*

b. *She saw three falling stars in the sky.*

COMBINED: *Looking up, Carol saw three falling stars in the sky.*

1. a. _____ Answers will vary. _____

b. _____

COMBINED: _____

2. a. _____

b. _____

COMBINED: _____

· ·

Join Ideas with a Past Participle

■ **TIP:** For more on helping verbs, see Chapters 20 and 24. Chapter 24 also covers past participles.

Another way to combine sentences is to use a past participle (often, a verb ending in *-ed*) to make one of the sentences into a phrase.

TWO SENTENCES	Henry VIII was a powerful English king. He is *remembered* for his many wives.
JOINED WITH A PAST PARTICIPLE	*Remembered* for his many wives, Henry VIII was a powerful English king.

Past participles of irregular verbs do not end in *-ed;* they take different forms.

TWO SENTENCES	Tim Treadwell was *eaten* by a grizzly bear. He showed that wild animals are unpredictable.
JOINED WITH A PAST PARTICIPLE	*Eaten* by a grizzly bear, Tim Treadwell showed that wild animals are unpredictable.

Note that sentences can be joined this way when one of them has a form of *be* along with a past participle (*is remembered* in the first Henry VIII example and *was eaten* in the first Tim Treadwell example).

To combine sentences this way, delete the subject and the *be* form from the sentence that has the *be* form and the past participle. You now have a phrase that can be added to the beginning or the end of the other sentence, depending on what makes the most sense.

Henry VIII was ~~determined~~ to divorce one of his wives~~.~~ ~~He~~ created the Church of England because Catholicism does not allow divorce.

If you add a phrase that begins with a past participle to the beginning of a sentence, put a comma after it. If you add the phrase to the end of the sentence, put a comma before it.

If you put a phrase starting with a past participle at the beginning of a sentence, be sure the word that the phrase modifies follows immediately. Otherwise, you will create a dangling modifier. Sometimes, as in the example, you will need to change the word that the phrase modifies from a pronoun to a noun.

▉ PRACTICE 7   JOINING IDEAS WITH A PAST PARTICIPLE · · · · · · · · ·

Combine each pair of sentences into a single sentence by using a past participle.   *Answers may vary. Possible edits shown.*

EXAMPLE: *Forced*
The oil company was forced to take the local women's
objections seriously/. *the oil* The company had to close for ten days during their protest.

1. *Angered by British colonial rule in 1929, the*
The women of southern Nigeria were angered by British colonial rule in 1929. They organized a protest.

2. *Covered with pipelines and oil wells,*
Nigeria is now one of the top ten oil-producing countries. The nation is covered with pipelines and oil wells.

3. *Pumped*
The oil is pumped by American and other foreign oil companies/. *the* The oil often ends up in wealthy Western economies.

4. *Stolen by corrupt rulers in many cases, the*
The money from the oil seldom reaches Nigeria's local people. The cash is stolen by corrupt rulers in many cases.

5. *Polluted*
The Nigerian countryside is polluted by the oil industry/. *the Nigerian countryside* The land then becomes a wasteland.

6. *Insulted*
Many Nigerians are insulted by the way the oil industry treats them/.
^many Nigerians
They want the oil companies to pay attention to their problems.

7. *Inspired*
Local Nigerian women were inspired by the 1929 women's protests/.
^local Nigerian women
They launched a series of protests against the oil industry in the summer of 2002.

8. The women prevented workers from entering or leaving two oil company offices/. The offices were located in the port of Warri.

9. *Concerned*
Workers at the oil company were concerned about the women's threat
many workers at the oil company
to take their clothes off/. Many workers told company officials that

such a protest would bring a curse on the company and shame to its employees.

10. The company eventually agreed to hire more local people and to invest in local projects/, ~~The projects are~~ intended to supply electricity and provide the villagers with a market for fish and poultry.

PRACTICE 8   JOINING IDEAS WITH A PAST PARTICIPLE . . . .

Fill in the blank in each sentence with an appropriate past participle.
Answers will vary. Possible answers shown.

EXAMPLE: _____*Trusted*_____ by people around the world for centuries, herbs can be powerful medical tools.

1. Common American plants are made into medicine, such as St. John's wort, _____*taken*_____ as an antidepressant.

2. _____*Made*_____ in laboratories, popular herbs are widely available in capsule form.

3. _____*Regarded*_____ as "natural" medicines, herbs are often believed to be harmless.

4. _____*Uninformed*_____ about the effects of herbal medicines, some people take them without understanding possible consequences.

5. Some herbs may interact badly with other drugs _____*prescribed*_____ by a doctor.

PRACTICE 9   JOINING IDEAS WITH A PAST PARTICIPLE . . . .

Write two sets of sentences and join them with a past participle.

EXAMPLE: a. *Chris is taking intermediate accounting.*
            b. *It is believed to be the most difficult course in the major.*

COMBINED: *Chris is taking intermediate accounting, believed to be the*
            most difficult course in the major.

1. a. *Answers will vary.* _____

   b. _____

   COMBINED: _____

2. a. _____

    b. _____

    COMBINED: _____

. . . .

Join Ideas Using an Appositive

An **appositive** is a noun or noun phrase that renames a noun. Appositives can be used to combine two sentences into one.

■ **TEACHING TIP:** Say aloud a sentence that has as its subject something familiar to students in the class (for example, the president, a celebrity). Ask them to suggest a good appositive.

TWO SENTENCES	Fen-Phen was found to be toxic. It was a very popular diet drug.
JOINED WITH AN APPOSITIVE	Fen-Phen, a very popular diet drug, was found to be toxic.

[The phrase *a very popular diet drug* renames the noun *Fen-Phen*.]

To combine two sentences this way, turn the sentence that renames the noun into a noun phrase by dropping the subject and verb. The appositive phrase can appear anywhere in the sentence, but it should be placed before or after the noun it renames. Use a comma or commas to set off the appositive.

        , a dangerous compound,
The drug caused a few deaths. ~~It was a dangerous compound.~~
      ^

■ **PRACTICE 10   JOINING IDEAS USING AN APPOSITIVE** . . . .

Combine each pair of sentences into a single sentence by using an appositive. Be sure to use a comma or commas to set off the appositive.
Answers may vary. Possible edits shown.

              , perhaps the most famous work clothes in the world,
    EXAMPLE: Levi's jeans have looked the same for well over a century. ~~They are perhaps the most famous work clothes in the world.~~
        ^

1. Jacob Davis, ~~was~~ a Russian immigrant working in Reno, Nevada/. ~~He~~ was the inventor of Levi's jeans.
    ^

2. Davis came up with an invention that made work clothes last longer.
                              , the riveted seam,
    ~~The invention was the riveted seam.~~
      ^

3. Davis bought denim from a wholesaler/. ~~The wholesaler was~~ Levi Strauss.
     ^

4. In 1870, he offered to sell the rights to his invention to Levi Strauss for the price of the patent/. ~~Patents then cost~~ about seventy dollars.
     ^

5. Davis joined the firm in 1873 and supervised the final development of its product/~~The product was~~ the famous Levi's jeans.

6. Davis oversaw a crucial design element/~~The jeans all had~~ orange
   ^
   stitching.

   Another
7. ~~The curved stitching on the back pockets was another~~ choice Davis
   ^   *, the curved stitching on the back pockets,*
   made/ ~~It~~ also survives in today's Levi's.
         ^
   A   *the stitching on the pockets*
8. ~~The stitching on the pockets has been a~~ trademark since 1942/,~~It~~ is
   ^   ^
   very recognizable.

9. During World War II, Levi Strauss temporarily stopped adding the pocket stitches because they wasted thread/,~~It was~~ a valuable resource.

10. Until the war ended, the pocket design was added with a less valuable material/,~~The company used~~ paint.

PRACTICE 11   JOINING IDEAS USING AN APPOSITIVE · · · · · · · ·

Fill in the blank in each sentence with an appropriate appositive.
Answers will vary. Possible answers shown.

> **EXAMPLE:** The off-campus housing office, *a small room crowded with* *desperate students*, offered little help.

1. My sister, *a college freshman*, needed to find an apartment before she started school.

2. As she looked for a place to live, she faced a serious problem, *sky-high rents*.

3. Searching for apartments in the area near the campus, *a quiet, tree-lined neighborhood*, she found nothing suitable.

4. She applied for housing in a dormitory, *a high-rise on the campus*, but the waiting list already contained sixty-two names.

5. She finally found a place she could afford, *a dark, cramped apartment*, in a neighborhood with a high crime rate.

Join Ideas Using an Adjective Clause

An **adjective clause** is a group of words with a subject and a verb that describes a noun. An adjective clause often begins with the words *who, which,* or *that,* and it can be used to combine two sentences into one.

TWO SENTENCES	Lauren has won many basketball awards. She is captain of her college team.
JOINED WITH AN ADJECTIVE CLAUSE	Lauren, *who is captain of her college team,* has won many basketball awards.

To join sentences this way, use *who, which,* or *that* to replace the subject in a sentence that describes a noun in the other sentence. You now have an adjective clause that you can move so that it follows the noun it describes. The sentence with the more important idea (the one you want to emphasize) should become the main clause. The less important idea should be in the adjective clause.

Main clause   Adjective clause

which

Rocío attributes her success to the Puente Project./ It helped her meet the challenges of college.

[The more important idea here is that Rocío gives the Puente Project credit for her success. The less important idea is that the Puente Project helped her cope with college.]

NOTE: If an adjective clause can be taken out of a sentence without completely changing the meaning of the sentence, put commas around it.

Lauren, *who is captain of her college team,* has won many basketball awards.

[The phrase *who is captain of her college team* adds information about Lauren, but it is not essential; the sentence *Lauren has won many basketball awards* means almost the same thing as the sentence in the example.]

If an adjective clause is an essential part of a sentence, do not put commas around it.

Lauren is an award-winning basketball player who overcame childhood cancer.

[*Who overcame childhood cancer* is an essential part of this sentence. The sentence *Lauren is an award-winning basketball player* is very different in meaning from the whole sentence in the example.]

PRACTICE 12   JOINING IDEAS USING AN ADJECTIVE CLAUSE · · · ·

Combine each pair of sentences into a single sentence by using an adjective clause beginning with *who, which,* or *that.*   *Answers will vary. Possible edits shown.*

, who has been going to college for the past three years,

EXAMPLE: My friend Erin had her first child last June. ~~She has been going to college for the past three years.~~

TIP: For more about adjectives, see Chapter 26.

TEACHING TIP: Explain to students that in their own writing they will need to consider the context when deciding which sentence contains the more important idea.

TIP: Use *who* to refer to a person, *which* to refer to places or things (but not to people), and *that* for places or things.

1. While Erin goes to classes, her baby boy stays at a day-care center/
   which,
   ~~The day-care center~~ costs Erin about $100 a week.
   ^

2. Twice when her son was ill, Erin had to miss her geology lab/ ~~The lab~~
   , which
   ^
   is an important part of her grade for that course.

3. Occasionally, Erin's parents come up and watch the baby while Erin is
   , who live about seventy miles away,
   ^
   studying. ~~They live about seventy miles away.~~

4. Sometimes Erin feels discouraged by the extra costs/ ~~The costs~~ have
   that
   ^
   come from having a child.

5. She feels that some of her professors aren't very sympathetic. ~~These~~
   who have never been parents themselves
   ^
   ~~are the ones who have never been parents themselves.~~

6. Erin understands that she must take responsibility for both her child
   , who wants to be a good mother and a good student,
   ^
   and her education. ~~She wants to be a good mother and a good~~
   ~~student.~~

7. Her grades have suffered somewhat since she had her son. ~~They were~~
   , which were once straight A's,
   ^
   ~~once straight A's.~~

8. Erin wants to graduate with honors. ~~She hopes to go to graduate~~
   , who hopes to go to graduate school someday,
   ^
   ~~school someday.~~

9. Her son is more important than an A in geology. ~~He is the most~~
   , who is the most important thing to her,
   ^
   ~~important thing to her.~~

10. Erin still expects to have a high grade point average/ ~~She~~ has simply
    , who
    ^   ^
    given up expecting to be perfect.

■ **PRACTICE 13   JOINING IDEAS WITH AN ADJECTIVE CLAUSE** . . . . .

Fill in the blank in each of the following sentences with an appropriate adjective clause. Add commas, if necessary.
Answers will vary. Possible edits shown.

EXAMPLE: The firefighters _____*who responded to the alarm*_____
entered the burning building.

1. A fire ___*that was probably caused by faulty wiring*___ began in our house in
   the middle of the night.

2. The members of my family ___*who were home at the time of the fire*___
   were all asleep.

3. My father _____ *, who has always been a light sleeper,* _____ was the first to

   smell smoke.

4. He ran to our bedrooms _____ *, which were on the second floor,* _____ and

   woke us up with his shouting.

5. The house *, which was the only home I had ever lived in,* was damaged, but

   everyone in my family reached safety.

Edit Paragraphs and Your Own Writing

PRACTICE 14   EDITING PARAGRAPHS

Create sentence variety in the following paragraphs by joining at least two sentences in each of the paragraphs. Try to use several of the techniques covered in this chapter. You may want to refer to the chart, Editing for Sentence Variety, on page 460.   *Answers will vary. Possible edits shown.*

1. (1) Immunizations have saved countless lives in this century. *, which* ,

   (2) ~~Immunizations~~ have recently become controversial. (3) A few children *a very small minority,* have reactions to the vaccines. (4) ~~They are a very small minority.~~ *Worrying* (5) ~~Some parents worry~~ that vaccinations are harmful. *, some parents* (6) ~~They~~ are

   speaking out against routine immunization. (7) Without immunization,

   however, more children would have terrible childhood diseases. (8) Im-

   munization is slightly risky but necessary.

2. (1) Movies were made possible by Thomas Edison. (2) ~~He was~~

   the inventor of the motion picture camera. (3) One of the first films

   showed scenes of an oncoming train. *, which* (4) ~~The scenes~~ frightened audi-

   ences early in the twentieth century. (5) Audiences today are not as eas-

   ily frightened. (6) They are accustomed to the magic of movies.

   (7) One type of magic gets more amazing as technology improves. *Called* *this magic* (8) ~~This magic is called~~ "special effects." (9) ~~Magic~~ is not cheap. (10)

   Blockbuster movies get more expensive every year because they have

   bigger and flashier special effects. (11) Hollywood studios are corpora- *, which* tions trying to earn a profit. (12) ~~They~~ spend millions to make block-

   busters. (13) They do everything they can to make sure that people see the movies. (14) The studios do not necessarily want new and unusual products.

(15) There is another kind of magic in moviemaking/ (16) ~~This magic~~ *that* makes us remember why we loved movies in the first place. (17) A great movie does not necessarily need special effects. (18) It may be small and personal/, (19) ~~It may capture~~ *capturing* our imagination or our hearts. (20) The movies we love may show us the invention of a completely new world/, (21) ~~It can be a world~~ unimagined even by Thomas Edison.

■ **PRACTICE 15**   **EDITING YOUR OWN WRITING FOR SENTENCE VARIETY**

■ **LEARNING JOURNAL:** Do you tend to write short, similar-sounding sentences? Which strategies from this chapter do you think you will use most often when you are editing for sentence variety?

As a final practice, edit a piece of your own writing for sentence variety. It can be a paper you are working on for this course, a paper you've already finished, a paper for another course, or a recent piece of writing from your work or everyday life. Record in your learning journal any examples of short, choppy sentences you find, along with the edited versions of these sentences. You may want to use the chart on page 460.

Chapter Review

1. Having sentence variety means <u>*using different sentence patterns, lengths, and rhythms*</u>.

2. If you tend to write short, similar-sounding sentences, what five techniques should you try?
    <u>*starting some sentences with adverbs, combining sentences using an -ing verb, combining sentences with a past*</u>
    <u>*participle, combining sentences using an appositive, and combining sentences using an adjective clause*</u>

3. An <u>*appositive*</u> is a noun or noun phrase that renames a noun.

4. An <u>*adjective*</u> clause often starts with *who*, <u>*which*</u>, or <u>*that*</u>. It describes a noun or pronoun.

5. Use commas around an adjective clause when the information in it is (essential / (not essential)) to the meaning of the sentence.

Chapter Test

For each of the following sentence pairs, choose the answer that joins the sentences logically using one of the strategies in this chapter.

■ **TIP:** For advice on taking tests, see Appendix A.

■ **RESOURCES:** *Testing Tool Kit*, a CD-ROM available with this book, has even more tests.

1. Luis straightened his tie. He waited to be called in for his job interview.
    a. Straightened his tie, Luis waited to be called in for his job interview.
    (b.) Straightening his tie, Luis waited to be called in for his job interview.

2. The auditorium was noisy and chaotic. It was filled with people in Superman outfits.
    (a.) Filled with people in Superman outfits, the auditorium was noisy and chaotic.
    b. Filled with people in Superman outfits; the auditorium was noisy and chaotic.

3. My niece is a star softball player. She loves to watch baseball on TV.
    (a.) My niece, a star softball player, loves to watch baseball on TV.
    b. Starring as a softball player, my niece loves to watch baseball on TV.

4. Chocolate is a favorite sweet worldwide. It has compounds that might lower the risk of certain diseases.
    a. Chocolate is a favorite sweet worldwide, for it has compounds that might lower the risk of certain diseases.
    (b.) Chocolate, a favorite sweet worldwide, has compounds that might lower the risk of certain diseases.

5. The lawyer believed passionately in his client's innocence. He convinced the jury to come to a verdict of not guilty.
    (a.) The lawyer, who believed passionately in his client's innocence, convinced the jury to come to a verdict of not guilty.
    b. The lawyer believed passionately in his client's innocence, yet he convinced the jury to come to a verdict of not guilty.

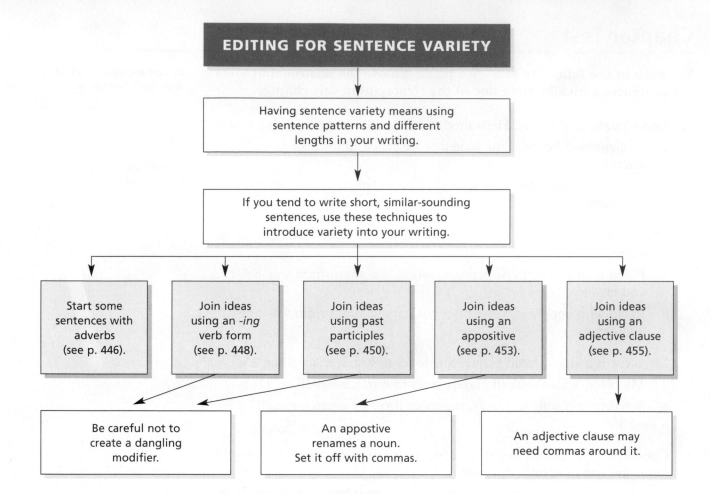

32

Formal English and ESL Concerns

Grammar Trouble Spots for Multilingual Students

Academic, or formal, English is the English you will be expected to use in college and in most work situations, especially in writing. If you are not used to using formal English, or if English is not your native language, this chapter will help you avoid the most common problems with key sentence parts.

NOTE: In this chapter, we use the word *English* to refer to formal English.

■ **TIP:** For more on using formal English, see Chapter 2. In this chapter, subjects are underlined, and verbs are double-underlined.

Subjects

- **Every sentence in English must have a subject and a verb.** The most basic sentence pattern is **SUBJECT-VERB (S-V).**

             S V

  EXAMPLE: The <u>dog</u> <u>ate</u>.

To find the subject in a sentence, ask, "Who or what is doing the main action of the sentence?" In the previous example, the answer is the *dog*. To find the verb in a sentence, ask, "The subject did what?" In the previous example, the answer is *ate*.

Other English sentence patterns build on the **S-V** structure. One of the most common patterns is **SUBJECT-VERB-OBJECT (S-V-O).** The object in the **S-V-O** pattern is called a **direct object** because it directly receives the action of the verb.

               S   V   DO

      EXAMPLE: The <u>dog</u> <u>ate</u> the food.

To find the direct object in a sentence, ask "What?" of the verb. For the previous example, the question would be "ate what?" The answer is the *food*.

- **A complete subject can be more than one word.** The complete subject includes all the words that make up the subject.

■ **TEACHING TIP:** You may wish to assign this chapter to your class as a whole, especially if you have native students who speak nonstandard English. Even if they know the parts of speech, many students need extra practice with how those parts function in writing.

■ **TIP:** For more on English sentence patterns, see Chapter 20.

EXAMPLES: Smoky Mountain National Park is in Tennessee.
The old apple tree produced a lot of fruit.

- **Some sentences can have more than one subject.** Consider these three cases:

1. Subjects joined by *and* or *or*

   EXAMPLES: Taxes **and** tests are not on anyone's list of fun things to do.
   Tatiana **or** Bill will wash the car.

2. Sentences that are really two sentences joined with the words *and, but, for, or, so, nor,* or *yet*

■ **TIP:** For more on how to join sentences with these words, see Chapters 22 and 28.

   EXAMPLES: Kim went to English class, **and** Dan went to math.
   Kim went to English class, **but** she was late.

3. Sentences joined by dependent words, such as *after, before, if, since, unless, until,* and *while*

■ **TIP:** For a more complete list of dependent words, see page 291.

   EXAMPLES: Dan went to math class *before* he ate lunch.
   Dan did his homework *after* he ate.

IMPORTANT: The subject of a sentence can never be in a prepositional phrase. For more information, see pages 278–79.

▮ PRACTICE 1   USING THE RIGHT WORD ORDER IN SENTENCES . . . .

Underline the complete subject in each sentence. If there is no subject, add one and underline it. If the sentence pattern is incorrect, rewrite the sentence using either the S-V or S-V-O patterns.

Answers may vary. Possible edits shown.

                              Edward Albee is
EXAMPLE: Is a famous American playwright.
                  ^

                                                    entered
1. At the age of twelve, the young man private ~~entered~~ school.
   The school   ^
2. ₯ismissed him for poor attandance.
   ^
                                   dismissed
3. In fact, three different schools him .~~dismissed.~~
                    ^   ^   ^
              was
4. Even so, writing his ~~was~~ passion.
                        ^
                                        completed
5. At the age of thirty, Albee his first major play ~~completed.~~
   The title was   ^
6. ~~Was~~ *The Zoo Story.*
   ^
                              refused
7. New York theaters to stage the play ~~refused.~~
              the play ^
8. However, was a hit in Europe.
           ^

9. *Who's Afraid of Virginia Woolf?* ^is^ the playwright's most famous play. ~~is.~~

10. In 1994, this famous writer ^received^ his third Pulitzer Prize ~~received~~.

■ **TIP:** For more practice, visit Exercise Central at **bedfordstmartins.com/ realwriting**.

■ **RESOURCES:** For additional support and exercises for ESL students, see *The Bedford/St. Martin's ESL Workbook* available with this text. For tests on particular ESL trouble spots, see the *Testing Tool Kit* CD-ROM.

Pronouns

Pronouns replace nouns (or other pronouns) in a sentence so that you do not have to repeat them. There are three kinds of pronouns: subject pronouns, object pronouns, and possessive pronouns, and it is important not to confuse them.

Subject pronouns serve as the subject of the verb in a sentence; remember, *every English sentence must have a subject.* **Object pronouns** either receive the action of the verb or are part of a prepositional phrase. **Possessive pronouns** show ownership. The chart below lists the type of pronouns.

Pronoun Types

SUBJECT		OBJECT		POSSESSIVE	
SINGULAR	**PLURAL**	**SINGULAR**	**PLURAL**	**SINGULAR**	**PLURAL**
I	we	me	us	my/mine	our/ours
you	you	you	you	your/yours	your/yours
he/she/it	they	him/her/it	them	his/her/hers/ its	theirs

NOTE: Most singular third-person pronouns (*he/she, him/her, his/hers*) show gender. *He, him,* and *his* are masculine. *She, her,* and *hers* are feminine. Here are some examples of common pronoun errors, with corrections.

■ **TIP:** For more on pronouns, see Chapter 25.

- **Confusing subject and object pronouns.** Use a subject pronoun for the subject of the sentence, the word that performs the action.

INCORRECT   Joseph is in my class. **Him** failed the test.

[*Him* is the subject of the verb *failed* in the second sentence. The sentence needs a subject pronoun: *he.*]

CORRECT   Joseph is in my class. **He** failed the test.

INCORRECT   My teacher is Professor Smith. I gave the homework to **she**.

[In the second sentence, *I* is correct: It is a subject pronoun. *She* is not the subject of the verb *gave*. An object pronoun should be used: *her.*]

CORRECT   My teacher is Professor Smith. I gave the homework to **her**.

- **Confusing gender in pronouns.** If the pronoun replaces a masculine noun, the pronoun must be masculine. A pronoun that replaces a feminine noun must be feminine.

INCORRECT   Gloriana is my cousin. **He** lives in Buenos Aires.

[Gloriana is female, so the pronoun must be feminine: *she*.]

CORRECT   Gloriana is my cousin. **She** lives in Buenos Aires.

INCORRECT   The jacket belongs to David. Janice gave it to **her**.

[David is male, so the pronoun must be masculine: *him*.]

CORRECT   The jacket belongs to David. Janice gave it to **him**.

- **Leaving a pronoun out.** In some sentences, the subject is *it*. Remember, all English sentences have subjects, so do not leave the word *it* out.

INCORRECT   Is cold today.

[The sentence has no subject.]

CORRECT   **It** is cold today.

INCORRECT   The soccer game was cancelled. Will be played next week.

[The second sentence has no subject.]

CORRECT   The soccer game was cancelled. **It** will be played next week.

Earlier, you learned that a common English sentence pattern is subject-verb-object. To find the direct object in a sentence, ask, "What?" of the subject. Sometimes, the object is an object pronoun that cannot be left out.

INCORRECT   I skied for the first time, and I liked very much.

[I liked what? An object pronoun is needed.]

CORRECT   I skied for the first time, and I liked **it** very much.

- **Using a pronoun to repeat the subject.** Pronouns are used to replace nouns or pronouns, not to repeat them.

INCORRECT   The driver **he** hit another car.

[*Driver* is the subject noun, and *he* just repeats it.]

CORRECT   The driver hit another car.

■ **PRACTICE 2**   **USING CORRECT PRONOUNS** . . . .

Using the chart of pronouns on page 463, fill in the blanks with the correct pronoun.   *Answers may vary. Possible answers shown.*

> **EXAMPLE:** Tennis is popular, for _____*it*_____ is an exciting sport.

1. Since the first time I played tennis, I liked _____*it*_____ very much.

2. _____*My*_____ favorite player is John McEnroe.

3. _____*He*_____ is famous for his bad temper.

4. Even though he is now middle-aged, _____*his*_____ serve is perfect.

5. No matter how much I practice, _____*my*_____ serve will never be
   as good.

6. McEnroe got a lot of publicity when _____*he*_____ challenged Venus
   and Serena Williams to a match.

7. _____*They*_____ declined.

8. Venus said she didn't know if she could fit him into _____*her*_____
   schedule.

9. Both of the sisters were busy with _____*their*_____ tournament matches.

10. Who is _____*your*_____ favorite tennis player?

Verbs

English verbs, like verbs in most other languages, have different tenses to
show when something happened: in the past, present, or future.

Present (now)

Past ◄———————————|———————————► Future

This section covers the most common tenses. The discussions of each
tense start with a chart that tells you what time the tense is used for. The
chart then shows how to use the tense in statements, negative sentences, and
questions. You can use the verb charts both to learn tenses and to edit your
own writing. Following the charts are lists of common errors to avoid.

■ **TIP:** For more on the kinds
of English verbs (action, linking, and helping) see Chapter
20. For more on irregular verb
forms, see pages 348–50.

The Simple Tenses

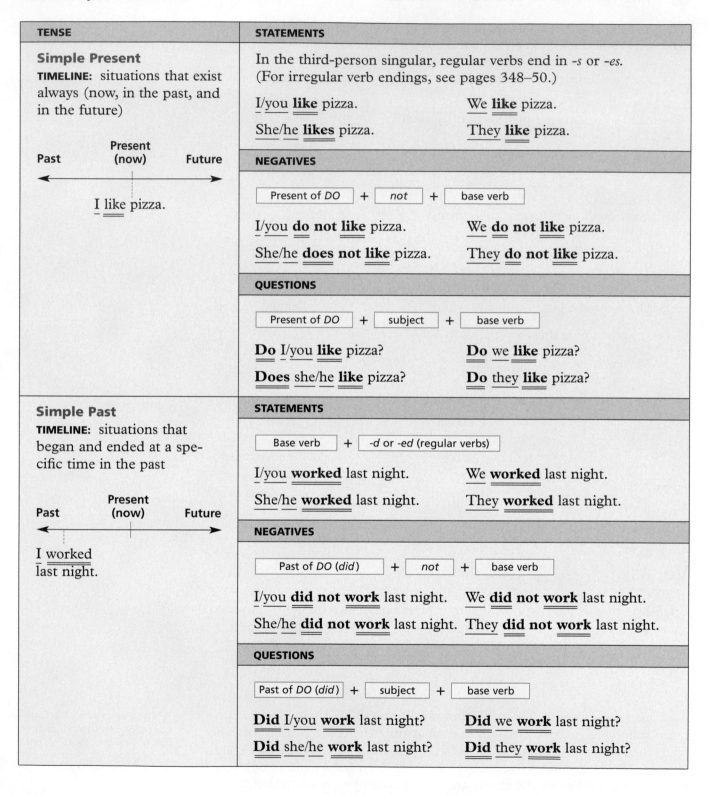

TENSE	STATEMENTS
Simple Present **TIMELINE:** situations that exist always (now, in the past, and in the future) Past — Present (now) — Future I like pizza.	In the third-person singular, regular verbs end in *-s* or *-es*. (For irregular verb endings, see pages 348–50.) I/you **like** pizza. We **like** pizza. She/he **likes** pizza. They **like** pizza.

NEGATIVES

Present of *DO* + *not* + base verb

I/you **do not like** pizza. We **do not like** pizza.
She/he **does not like** pizza. They **do not like** pizza.

QUESTIONS

Present of *DO* + subject + base verb

Do I/you **like** pizza? **Do** we **like** pizza?
Does she/he **like** pizza? **Do** they **like** pizza?

TENSE	STATEMENTS
Simple Past **TIMELINE:** situations that began and ended at a specific time in the past Past — Present (now) — Future I worked last night.	Base verb + *-d* or *-ed* (regular verbs) I/you **worked** last night. We **worked** last night. She/he **worked** last night. They **worked** last night.

NEGATIVES

Past of *DO* (*did*) + *not* + base verb

I/you **did not work** last night. We **did not work** last night.
She/he **did not work** last night. They **did not work** last night.

QUESTIONS

Past of *DO* (*did*) + subject + base verb

Did I/you **work** last night? **Did** we **work** last night?
Did she/he **work** last night? **Did** they **work** last night?

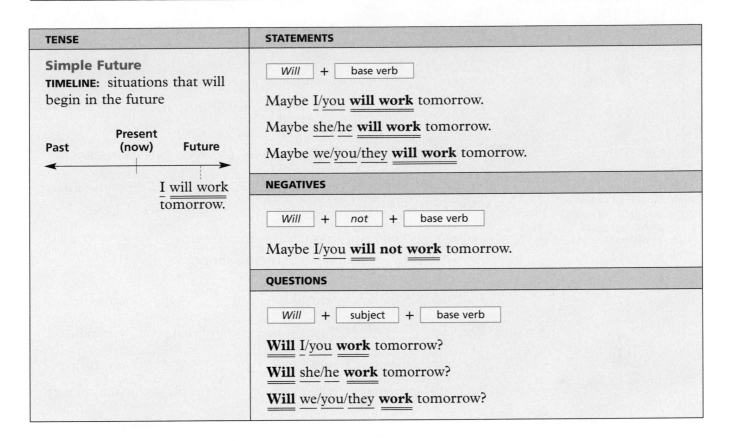

TENSE	STATEMENTS
Simple Future TIMELINE: situations that will begin in the future Past — Present (now) — Future I will work tomorrow.	*Will* + base verb Maybe I/you **will work** tomorrow. Maybe she/he **will work** tomorrow. Maybe we/you/they **will work** tomorrow.
	NEGATIVES
	Will + *not* + base verb Maybe I/you **will not work** tomorrow.
	QUESTIONS
	Will + subject + base verb **Will** I/you **work** tomorrow? **Will** she/he **work** tomorrow? **Will** we/you/they **work** tomorrow?

Following are some common errors in using simple tenses.

Simple Present

- **Forgetting to add -s or -es to verbs that go with third-person singular subjects (*she/he/it*)**

    INCORRECT   She know the manager.

    CORRECT   She knows the manager.

> ■ **TIP:** Subject and verbs must agree in number. For more on subject-verb agreement, see Chapter 23.

Simple Past

- **Forgetting to add -d or -ed to regular verbs**

    INCORRECT   Gina work late last night.

    CORRECT   Gina worked late last night.

- **Forgetting to use the correct past form of irregular verbs (see the chart of irregular verb forms on pages 348–50)**

    INCORRECT   Gerard speaked to her about the problem.

    CORRECT   Gerard **spoke** to her about the problem.

- **Forgetting to use the base verb without an ending for negative sentences**

INCORRECT   She <u>does</u> not [doesn't] <u>wants</u> money for helping.

CORRECT   She <u>does</u> not **want** money for helping.

■ PRACTICE 3   USING THE SIMPLE PRESENT AND THE SIMPLE PAST . . .

■ **TIP:** Double negatives (*Johnetta will **not** call **no one***) are not standard in English. One negative is enough (*Johnetta will **not** call **any-body***).

Fill in the correct simple present or simple past form of the verb in parentheses after the blank.

EXAMPLE: When radio was first invented, ships ____*used*____ (use) it to communicate with the shore.

1. By 1925, 5.5 million households ____*had*____ (have) radios.

2. People ____*listened*____ (listen) to a variety of things on their radios.

3. For example, when Charles Lindbergh ____*returned*____ (return) from his first solo transatlantic flight, millions of people across the country tuned in.

4. In the 1930s and 1940s, many programs ____*were*____ (is) popular, such as *The Shadow* and *The Lone Ranger*.

5. The quiz show *Truth or Consequences* ____*ran*____ (run) for seventeen years on the radio.

6. Many popular radio shows later ____*became*____ (become) television shows.

7. The invention of static-free FM ____*made*____ (make) radio ideal for playing music.

8. Today, many people ____*complain*____ (complain) about the lack of variety on the radio.

9. It ____*seems*____ (seem) no matter where you go in the country, you find the same types of stations.

10. Internet radio now ____*offers*____ (offer) a greater range of choice.

■   **PRACTICE 4   FORMING NEGATIVE STATEMENTS AND QUESTIONS** . . .

Rewrite the following sentences as indicated.

1. Tanya plays with the baby. Make the sentence a question: *Does Tanya*
    play with the baby?

2. They like to vacation in Florida. Make the sentence a negative
    statement: *They do not like to vacation in Florida.*

3. Shelly played her flute in the orchestra. Make the sentence a question:
    Did Shelly play her flute in the orchestra?

4. They will ride with us to the store. Make the sentence a negative
    statement: *They will not ride with us to the store.*

5. David walked five miles this morning. Make the sentence into a
    question: *Did David walk five miles this morning?*

The Progressive Tenses

TENSE	STATEMENTS
Present Progressive **TIMELINE:** a situation that is in progress now but that started in the past Past Present (now) Future ← → I am typing.	Present of *BE (am/is/are)* + base verb ending in *-ing* I **am typing**. We **are typing**. You **are typing**. They **are typing**. She/he **is typing**.
	NEGATIVES
	Present of *BE (am/is/are)* + *not* + base verb ending in *-ing* I **am not typing**. We **are not typing**. You **are not typing**. They **are not typing**. She/he **is not typing**.
	QUESTIONS
	Present of *BE (am/is/are)* + subject + base verb ending in *-ing* **Am** I **typing**? **Are** we **typing**? **Are** you **typing**? **Are** they **typing**? **Is** she/he **typing**?

continued

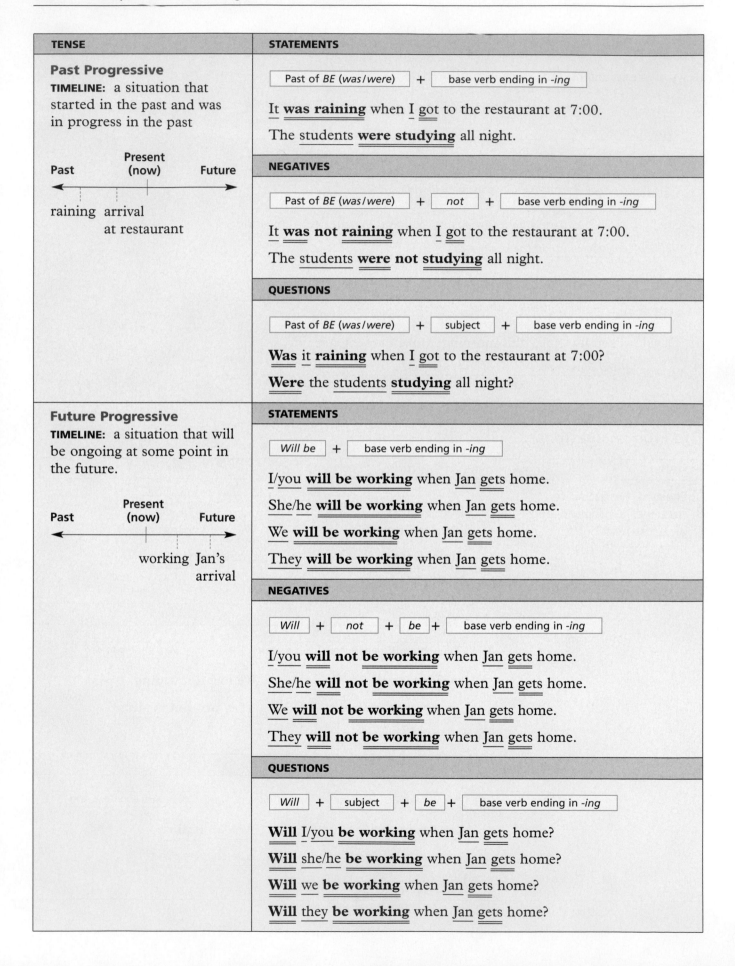

TENSE	STATEMENTS
Past Progressive **TIMELINE:** a situation that started in the past and was in progress in the past **Past** — **Present (now)** — **Future** raining arrival at restaurant	Past of *BE* (*was*/*were*) + base verb ending in *-ing* It **was raining** when I got to the restaurant at 7:00. The students **were studying** all night.
	NEGATIVES
	Past of *BE* (*was*/*were*) + *not* + base verb ending in *-ing* It **was not raining** when I got to the restaurant at 7:00. The students **were not studying** all night.
	QUESTIONS
	Past of *BE* (*was*/*were*) + subject + base verb ending in *-ing* **Was** it **raining** when I got to the restaurant at 7:00? **Were** the students **studying** all night?
Future Progressive **TIMELINE:** a situation that will be ongoing at some point in the future. **Past** — **Present (now)** — **Future** working Jan's arrival	**STATEMENTS** *Will be* + base verb ending in *-ing* I/you **will be working** when Jan gets home. She/he **will be working** when Jan gets home. We **will be working** when Jan gets home. They **will be working** when Jan gets home.
	NEGATIVES
	Will + *not* + *be* + base verb ending in *-ing* I/you **will not be working** when Jan gets home. She/he **will not be working** when Jan gets home. We **will not be working** when Jan gets home. They **will not be working** when Jan gets home.
	QUESTIONS
	Will + subject + *be* + base verb ending in *-ing* **Will** I/you **be working** when Jan gets home? **Will** she/he **be working** when Jan gets home? **Will** we **be working** when Jan gets home? **Will** they **be working** when Jan gets home?

Following are some common errors in forming the present progressive.

- **Forgetting to add *-ing* to the verb**

INCORRECT	CORRECT
I am type now.	I am typ**ing** now.
She/he is not work now.	She/he is not work**ing** now.

- **Forgetting to include a form of *be* (*am / is / are*)**

INCORRECT	CORRECT
He typing now.	He **is** typing now.
They typing now.	They **are** typing now.

- **Forgetting to use a form of *be* (*am / is / are*) to start questions**

INCORRECT   They typing now?

CORRECT   **Are** they typing now?

■ **PRACTICE 5   USING THE PROGRESSIVE TENSE** . . . .

Fill in the correct progressive form of the verb in parentheses after each blank.

EXAMPLE: My friend Maria and I are _____*trying*_____ (try) to be healthier.

1. First, we are _____*starting*_____ (start) to walk every day.

2. Why are we _____*making*_____ (make) this change?

3. Last week, when Maria _____*was visiting*_____ (visit) me, she said I didn't seem like myself.

4. I answered, "Yes, I am _____*feeling*_____ (feel) kind of sad."

5. "Are you _____*sleeping*_____ (sleep) well?" she asked.

6. "Oh, yes," I said. "I _____*am getting*_____ (get) plenty of sleep."

7. "What about your diet? Are you _____*eating*_____ (eat) right?" she asked.

8. "I eat in the cafeteria," I explained. "They're always _____*cooking*_____ (cook) healthy options."

9. "What about activities? Are you ___*exercising*___ (exercise) at all?"

10. "Not really, unless you count my brain while I'm ___*studying*___ (study)!" I admitted.

■ **PRACTICE 6   FORMING NEGATIVE STATEMENTS AND QUESTIONS** . . .

Rewrite the following sentences as indicated.

1. Betsy is golfing today. Make the sentence a question: _*Is Betsy golfing*_ *today?*

2. It was snowing when we got up. Make the sentence a negative statement: _*It was not snowing when we got up.*_

3. You are going to the mall. Make the sentence a question: *Are you going to the mall?*

4. They are losing the game. Make the sentence a negative statement: *They are not losing the game.*

5. Meriam was eating when you arrived. Make the sentence into a question: *Was Meriam eating when you arrived?*

. . . .

Modal Auxiliaries/Helping Verbs

■ **TIP:** For more on helping verbs, see Chapter 20.

If you have taken an English-as-a-second-language course, you might recognize the term **modal auxiliary,** a type of helping verb that expresses a writer's view about an action. As shown in the following chart, these helping verbs join with a main (base) verb to make a complete verb.

HELPING VERB (MODAL AUXILIARY)	STATEMENTS
General formulas For all modal auxilaries. (More helping verbs shown below.)	**Present:** Subject + helping verb + base verb Dumbo can fly. **Past:** Forms vary—see below.
	NEGATIVES
	Present: Subject + helping verb + *not* + base verb Dumbo cannot fly. **Past:** Forms vary—see below.
	QUESTIONS
	Present: Helping verb + subject + base verb Can Dumbo fly? **Past:** Forms vary—see below.
Can Means *ability*	**STATEMENTS**
	Present: Beth **can** work fast. **Past:** Beth **could** work fast.
	NEGATIVES
	Present: Beth **can**not work fast. **Past:** Beth **could** not work fast.
	QUESTIONS
	Present: Can Beth work fast? **Past: Could** Beth work fast?
Could Means *possibility*. It can also be the past tense of *can*.	**STATEMENTS**
	Present: Beth **could** work fast if she had more time. **Past:** Beth **could** have worked fast if she had more time.
	NEGATIVES
	Can is used for present negatives. (See above.) **Past:** Beth **could not** have worked fast.
	QUESTIONS
	Present: Could Beth work fast? **Past: Could** Beth have worked fast?

continued

HELPING VERB (MODAL AUXILIARY)	STATEMENTS
May Means *permission* For past-tense forms, see *might*.	**Present:** You **may** borrow my car.
	NEGATIVES
	Present: You **may not** borrow my car.
	QUESTIONS
	Present: **May** I borrow your car?
Might Means *possibility.* It can also be the past tense of *may*.	**STATEMENTS**
	Present (with *be*): Lou **might** be asleep. **Past** (with *have* + past participle of *be*): Lou **might** have been asleep. **Future:** Lou **might** sleep.
	NEGATIVES
	Present (with *be*): Lou **might** not be asleep. **Past** (with *have* + past participle of *be*): Lou **might** not have been asleep. **Future:** Lou **might** not sleep.
	QUESTIONS
	Might in questions is very formal and not often used.
Must Means *necessary*	**STATEMENTS**
	Present: We **must** try. **Past** (with *have* + past participle of base verb): We **must** have tried.
	NEGATIVES
	Present: We **must** not try. **Past** (with *have* + past participle of base verb): We **must** not have tried.
	QUESTIONS
	Present: **Must** we try? Past-tense questions with *must* are unusual.

HELPING VERB (MODAL AUXILIARY)	STATEMENTS
Should Means *duty* or *expectation*	**Present:** They **should** call. **Past** (with *have* + past participle of base verb): They **should** have called.
	NEGATIVES
	Present: They **should** not call. **Past** (with *have* + past participle of base verb): They **should** not have called.
	QUESTIONS
	Present: Should they call? **Past** (with *have* + past participle of base verb): **Should** they have called?
Will Means *intend to* (future) For past-tense forms, see *might*.	**STATEMENTS**
	Future: I **will** succeed.
	NEGATIVES
	Future: I **will** not succeed.
	QUESTIONS
	Future: Will I succeed?
Would Means *prefer* or used to start a future request. It can also be the past tense of *will*.	**STATEMENTS**
	Present: I **would** like to travel. **Past** (with *have* + past participle of base verb): I **would** have traveled if I had the money.
	NEGATIVES
	Present: I **would** not like to travel. **Past** (with *have* + past participle of base verb): I **would** not have traveled if it hadn't been for you.
	QUESTIONS
	Present: Would you like to travel? *Or* to start a request: **Would** you help me? **Past** (with *have* + past participle of base verb): **Would** you have traveled with me if I had asked you?

Following are some common errors in using modal auxiliaries.

- **Using more than one helping verb**

  INCORRECT They **will can** help.

  CORRECT They **will** help. (future intention)
  They **can** help. (are able to)

- **Using *to* between the helping verb and the main (base) verb**

  INCORRECT Emilio **might to** come with us.

  CORRECT Emilio **might** come with us.

- **Using *must* instead of *had to* in the past**

  INCORRECT She **must** work yesterday.

  CORRECT She **had to** work yesterday.

- **Forgetting to change *can* to *could* in the past negative**

  INCORRECT Last night, I **can**not sleep.

  CORRECT Last night, I **could** not sleep.

- **Forgetting to use *have* with *could/should/would* in the past tense**

  INCORRECT Tara **should** called last night.

  CORRECT Tara **should have** called last night.

- **Using *will* instead of *would* to express a preference in the present tense**

  INCORRECT I **will** like to travel.

  CORRECT I **would** like to travel.

▪ **PRACTICE 7 USING MODAL AUXILIARIES** · · · · · · · · · · · · · · ·

Fill in modal auxiliaries (helping verbs) in the sentences below.
Answers may vary. Possible answers shown.
EXAMPLE: Lilly _____*would*_____ like to help the homeless.

1. What _____*should*_____ she do?

2. First, she _____*can*_____ find out what programs exist in her community.

3. For example, there _____*might*_____ be a chapter of Habitat for
Humanity.

4. Religious organizations _____*might*_____ have started soup kitchens.

5. If she _____*cannot*_____ find anything in her community, she should
contact a national organization, such as the National Coalition for the
Homeless.

6. The organization _____*could*_____ definitely give her some ideas.

7. Also, she _____*should not*_____ feel as though she must do this alone.

8. Surely, there are other people who _____*will*_____ want to help.

9. How _____*can*_____ she get them involved?

10. She _____*must*_____ spread the word, perhaps through e-mail.

▮ PRACTICE 8 FORMING NEGATIVE STATEMENTS AND QUESTIONS · · ·

Rewrite the following sentences as indicated.

1. You can help me. Make the sentence a question: *Can you help me?*

2. We might take the train to New York. Make the sentence a negative
statement: *We might not take the train to New York.*

3. They should learn how to cook. Make the sentence a question:
Should they learn how to cook?

4. They could take care of the dog. Make the sentence a negative
statement: *They could not take care of the dog.*

5. Terrell would like to join us. Make the sentence into a question:
Would Terrell like to join us?

The Perfect Tenses

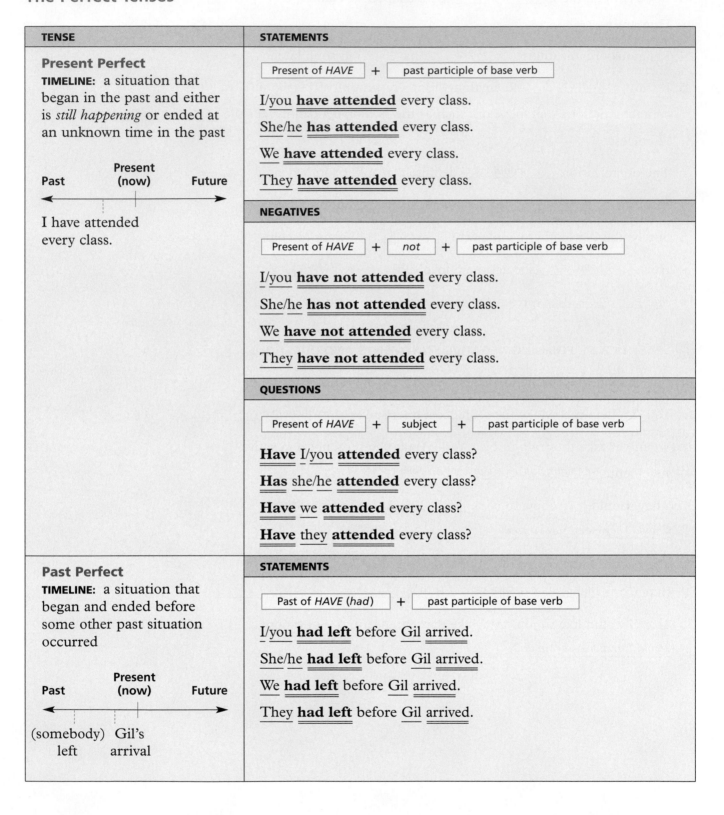

TENSE	STATEMENTS
Present Perfect **TIMELINE:** a situation that began in the past and either is *still happening* or ended at an unknown time in the past Past — Present (now) — Future I have attended every class.	Present of *HAVE* + past participle of base verb I/you **have attended** every class. She/he **has attended** every class. We **have attended** every class. They **have attended** every class.
	NEGATIVES
	Present of *HAVE* + *not* + past participle of base verb I/you **have not attended** every class. She/he **has not attended** every class. We **have not attended** every class. They **have not attended** every class.
	QUESTIONS
	Present of *HAVE* + subject + past participle of base verb **Have** I/you **attended** every class? **Has** she/he **attended** every class? **Have** we **attended** every class? **Have** they **attended** every class?
Past Perfect **TIMELINE:** a situation that began and ended before some other past situation occurred Past — Present (now) — Future (somebody) Gil's left arrival	**STATEMENTS** Past of *HAVE (had)* + past participle of base verb I/you **had left** before Gil arrived. She/he **had left** before Gil arrived. We **had left** before Gil arrived. They **had left** before Gil arrived.

TENSE	NEGATIVES
Past Perfect	Past of *HAVE (had)* + *not* + past participle of base verb

Usually used for "if" situations

If you **had not left**, you would have seen him.

If she/he **had not left**, she/he would have seen him.

If we **had not left**, we would have seen him.

If they **had not left**, they would have seen him.

QUESTIONS

Past of *HAVE (had)* + subject + past participle of base verb

Had I/you **left** before Gil arrived?

Had she/he **left** before Gil arrived?

Had we **left** before Gil arrived?

Had they **left** before Gil arrived?

Future Perfect	**STATEMENTS**

TIMELINE: a situation that will be completed in the future before another future situation

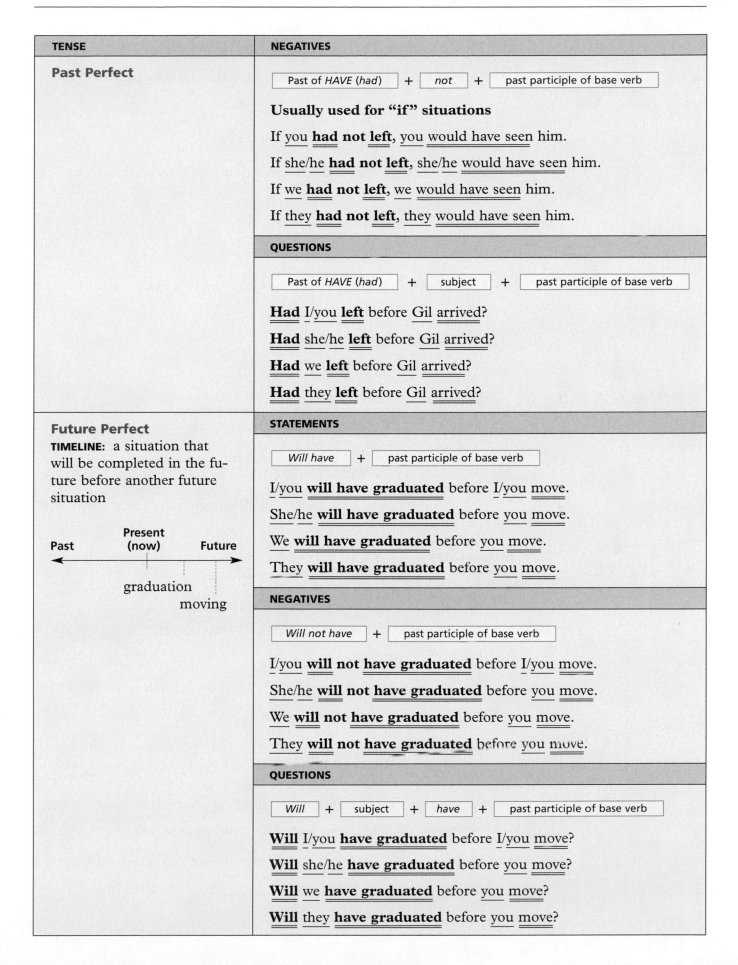

```
Present
Past        (now)        Future
◄──────────┼──────────►
         graduation
              moving
```

Will have + past participle of base verb

I/you **will have graduated** before I/you move.

She/he **will have graduated** before you move.

We **will have graduated** before you move.

They **will have graduated** before you move.

NEGATIVES

Will not have + past participle of base verb

I/you **will not have graduated** before I/you move.

She/he **will not have graduated** before you move.

We **will not have graduated** before you move.

They **will not have graduated** before you move.

QUESTIONS

Will + subject + *have* + past participle of base verb

Will I/you **have graduated** before I/you move?

Will she/he **have graduated** before you move?

Will we **have graduated** before you move?

Will they **have graduated** before you move?

Following are some common errors in forming the perfect tense.

■ **TIP:** For more on the perfect tense, see Chapter 24. For a list of irregular verbs and their forms, see pages 348–50.

• **Using *had* instead of *has* or *have* for the present perfect**

INCORRECT   We **had** lived here since 2003.

CORRECT   We **have** lived here since 2003.

• **Forgetting to use past participles (with *-d* or *-ed* endings for regular verbs)**

INCORRECT   She has attend every class.

CORRECT   She has attend**ed** every class.

• **Using *been* between *have* or *has* and the past participle of a base verb**

INCORRECT   I have **been** attended every class.

CORRECT   I have attended every class.

INCORRECT   I will have **been** graduated before I move.

CORRECT   I will have graduated before I move.

■ **PRACTICE 9   USING PERFECT TENSES** . . . .

Fill in the correct perfect tense of the verb in parentheses after each blank. Add helping verbs as needed.

EXAMPLE: _____*Have*_____ you ever _____*seen*_____ (see) a UFO?

1. All around the globe, there _____*have been*_____ (be) sightings.

2. However, witnesses often _____*have*_____ not _____*wanted*_____ (want) their names to be publicized.

3. In 1976, four men who _____*had met*_____ (meet) in college saw a UFO in the Allagash wilderness in northern Maine.

4. Likewise, many people _____*have claimed*_____ (claim) to have been abducted by aliens.

5. In 1995, a doctor in California removed an object from a woman who _____*had experienced*_____ (experience) what she believed to be an alien abduction.

6. After examining the object, the doctor claimed that it was made from materials that _____*had*_____ not _____*come*_____ (come) from earth.

7. If they were not from earth, where ____*had*____ the materials
____*come*____ (come) from?

8. Skeptics say a person who remembers being abducted might
__*have imagined*__ (imagine) the whole thing.

9. In addition, no one ___*has provided*___ (provide) proof that intelligent life
exists in outer space.

10. Nevertheless, it is possible that skeptics __*will have changed*__ (change)
their minds by the time they have finished reading a convincing
abduction story.

■ **PRACTICE 10   USING THE CORRECT TENSE** . . . .

Fill in the blanks with the correct verbs, adding helping verbs as needed.
Refer to the verb charts if you need help.
Answers may vary. Possible answers shown.

EXAMPLE: Many critics ___*have argued*___ (argue) that *Citizen Kane*,
directed by Orson Welles, is the greatest movie ever
made.

1. ____*Have*____ you ____*seen*____ (see) it?

2. If not, you ___*should rent*___ (rent) it right away!

3. You might not want to watch a movie from 1941, but *Citizen Kane*
___*will convince*___ (convince) you to give older films a chance.

4. The story ____*begins*____ (begin) with the death of Charles Foster
Kane, who was once very powerful.

5. By the time of his death, Kane ____*had lost*____ (lose) much of his
power.

6. When he ____*died*____ (die), he was alone in his mansion.

7. Charles's parents were very poor, but he ___*inherited*___ (inherit) a lot
of money as a child.

8. His mother ____*sent*____ (send) him east to live with a guardian,
who was put in charge of the boy's fortune.

9. Kane ____*would*____ not ____*have*____ (have) access to the money
until his twenty-fifth birthday.

10. Kane's fortune _____did_____ (do) not _____consist_____ (consist) only of money.

11. He also inherited a failing newspaper, *The Inquirer,* and _____turned_____ (turn) it into a success.

12. In the beginning, his marriage was also a success, but his wife divorced him when she discovered he _____was having_____ (have) an affair.

13. At the time of the discovery, Kane _____was running_____ (run) for governor.

14. Because of the scandal, he _____lost_____ (lose) the election.

15. Kane married his mistress, but he _____was_____ (be) very controlling with her.

16. She was so unhappy, she _____tried_____ (try) to commit suicide.

17. Her suicide attempt showed that he _should have been_ (be) kinder to her.

18. Eventually, his second wife _____left_____ (leave) him, too.

19. Kane's last word was "Rosebud." What _____could_____ (can) he _____have meant_____ (mean) by that?

20. You _____must watch_____ (watch) the movie to find out!

▨ **PRACTICE 11   USING THE CORRECT TENSE** . . . .

Fill in the blanks with the correct verbs, adding helping verbs as needed. Refer to the verb charts if you need help.
Answers may vary. Possible answers shown.

EXAMPLE: _____*Have*_____ you _____*heard*_____ (hear) of snow boarding?

(1) Snowboarding is like skiing, except snowboarders _____strap_____ (strap) a single fiberglass board, instead of skis, onto their feet. (2) It is a winter sport because snowboarders, like skiers, _____must wait_____ (wait) for snow. (3) In a November 5, 2002, article in *National Geographic Today,* Zoltan Istvan _____reported_____ (report) on a new sport: volcano boarding. (4) Volcano boarders _____do_____ not _____need_____ (need) to wait for snow. (5) If you _____are looking_____ (look) for adventure, an active volcano will never disappoint you.

(6) Istvan first _____got_____ (get) the idea in 1995, when he _____was sailing_____ (sail) past Mt. Yasur, an active volcano on an island off

the coast of Australia. (7) For centuries, Mt. Yasur ____*has had*____ (have) the reputation of being a dangerous volcano. (8) For example, it regularly ____*spits*____ (spit) out lava bombs. (9) These large molten rocks ____*have*____ often ____*struck*____ (strike) visitors on the head. (10) ____*Can*____ you ____*imagine*____ (imagine) how much that ____*would hurt*____ (hurt)?

(11) There is a village at the base of Mt. Yasur. (12) When Istvan arrived with his snowboard, the villagers ____*did*____ not ____*know*____ (know) what to think. (13) He ____*made*____ (make) his way to the volcano, ____*hiked*____ (hike) up the highest peak, and rode his board all the way down. (14) After he ____*reached*____ (reach) the bottom, Istvan admitted that volcano boarding is more difficult than snow boarding. (15) Luckily, no lava bombs ____*fell*____ (fall) from the sky, though the volcano ____*had erupted*____ (erupt) seconds before his descent. (16) Istvan hopes this new sport ____*will become*____ (become) popular with snowboarders around the world.

Gerunds and Infinitives

A **gerund** is a verb form that ends in *-ing* and acts as a noun. An **infinitive** is a verb form that is preceded by the word *to.* Gerunds and infinitives cannot be the main verbs in sentences; each sentence must have another word that is the main verb.

GERUND   Mike loves **swimming**.

[*Loves* is the main verb, and *swimming* is a gerund.]

INFINITIVE   Mike loves **to run**.

[*Loves* is the main verb, and *to run* is an infinitive.]

How do you decide whether to use a gerund or an infinitive? The decision often depends on the main verb in a sentence. Some verbs can be followed by either a gerund or an infinitive.

Verbs That Can be Followed by Either an Infinitive or a Gerund

begin	hate	remember	try
continue	like	start	
forget	love	stop	

■ **TIP:** To improve your ability to write and speak standard English, read magazines and your local newspaper, and listen to television and radio news programs. Also, read magazines and newspaper articles aloud; this will help your pronunciation.

Sometimes, using an infinitive or gerund after one of these verbs results in the same meaning.

GERUND   Joan likes **playing** the piano.

INFINITIVE   Joan likes **to play** the piano.

Other times, however, the meaning changes depending on whether you use an infinitive or a gerund.

GERUND   Carla stopped **to help** me.

[This means that Carla stopped what she was doing and helped me.]

■ **TIP:** For other problems with verbs, see Chapter 24.

INFINITIVE   Carla stopped **helping** me.

[This means that Carla no longer helps me.]

Verbs That Are Followed by an Infinitive Only

agree	decide	need	refuse
ask	expect	offer	want
beg	fail	plan	
choose	hope	pretend	
claim	manage	promise	

Aunt Sally wants **to help**.

Cal hopes **to become** a millionaire.

Verbs That Are Followed by a Gerund Only

admit	discuss	keep	risk
avoid	enjoy	miss	suggest
consider	finish	practice	
deny	imagine	quit	

The politician risked **losing** her supporters.

Sophia considered **quitting** her job.

A FINAL NOTE: Make sure to use a gerund or infinitive, not the base form of a verb, when a noun is intended.

In the following sentence, the writer's intended meaning is that the act of gambling (a noun) can be addictive.

INCORRECT   Gamble can be addictive.

[*Gamble* is a verb, but the subject must be a noun.]

CORRECT	**Gambling** <u>can</u> be addictive. Or **to gamble** can be addictive.

[*Gambling* is a gerund and *to gamble* is an infinitive. Both serve as nouns here.]

■ PRACTICE 12   USING GERUNDS AND INFINITIVES · · · · · · · · · · ·

Read the paragraph and fill in the blanks with either a gerund or an infinitive as appropriate.   *Answers may vary. Possible answers shown.*

EXAMPLE: If you want _____*to be*_____ (be) an actor, be aware that the profession is not all fun and glamor.

(1) When you were a child, did you pretend _____*to be*_____ (be) famous people? (2) Did you imagine _____*playing*_____ (play) roles in movies or on television? (3) Do you like _____*to take*_____ (take) part in plays? (4) If so, you might want _____*to make*_____ (make) a career out of acting.

(5) Be aware of some drawbacks, however. (6) If you hate _____*working*_____ (work) with others, acting may not be the career for you. (7) Also, if you don't enjoy _____*repeating*_____ (repeat) the same lines over and over, you will find acting dull. (8) You must practice _____*speaking*_____ (speak) lines to memorize them. (9) Despite these drawbacks, you will gain nothing if you refuse _____*to try*_____ (try). (10) Anyone who hopes _____*to become*_____ (become) an actor has a chance at succeeding through hard work and determination.

■ **TEACHING TIP:** Have students submit (anonymously, if they prefer) paragraphs from one of their rough drafts. Then, copy and distribute the paragraphs, and, as a whole class, edit the paragraphs with attention to verb forms.

Articles

Articles announce a noun. English uses only three articles—*a*, *an*, and *the*—and the same articles are used for both masculine and feminine nouns.

To use the correct article, you need to know whether the noun being announced is count or noncount. **Count nouns** name things that can be counted, and count nouns can be made plural, usually by adding *-s* or *-es*. **Noncount nouns** name things that cannot be counted, and they are usually singular. They can't be made plural.

COUNT NOUN/SINGLE	I <u>got</u> a **ticket** for the concert.
COUNT NOUN/PLURAL	I <u>got</u> two **tickets** for the concert.

NONCOUNT NOUN   The <u>Internet</u> <u>has</u> all kinds of **information**.

[You would not say, *The Internet has all kinds of informations*.]

Here are some count and noncount nouns. This is just a brief list; all nouns in English are either count or noncount.

COUNT	NONCOUNT	
apple/apples	beauty	money
chair/chairs	flour	postage
dollar/dollars	furniture	poverty
letter/letters	grass	rain
smile/smiles	grief	rice
tree/trees	happiness	salt
	health	sand
	homework	spaghetti
	honey	sunlight
	information	thunder
	jewelry	wealth
	mail	
	milk	

Use the chart that follows to determine when to use *a*, *an*, *the*, or no article.

Articles with Count and Noncount Nouns

COUNT NOUNS	ARTICLE USED
SINGULAR	
Identity known ⟶	**the**
	I want to read **the book** on taxes that you recommended.
	[The sentence refers to one particular book: the one that was recommended.]
	I can't stay in **the sun** very long.
	[There is only one sun.]
Identity not known ⟶	**a** *or* **an**
	I want to read **a** book on taxes.
	[It could be any book on taxes.]
PLURAL	
Identity known ⟶	**the**
	I enjoyed **the books** we read.
	[The sentence refers to a particular group of books: the ones we read.]

Identity not known or a general category	→	no article or some

I usually enjoy **books**.

[The sentence refers to books in general.]

She found **some books**.

[I don't know which books she found.]

NONCOUNT NOUNS		**ARTICLE USED**
SINGULAR		

Identity known	→	the

I put away **the food** we bought.

[The sentence refers to particular food: the food we bought.]

Identity not known or a general category	→	no article or some

There is **food** all over the kitchen.

[The reader doesn't know what food the sentence refers to.]

Give **some food** to the neighbors.

[The sentence refers to an indefinite quantity of food.]

PRACTICE 13   USING ARTICLES CORRECTLY . . . .

Fill in the correct article (*a, an,* or *the*) in each of the following sentences. If no article is needed, write "no article."

EXAMPLE: I can't go out tonight because I have _____*a*_____ ton of homework.

1. _____*The*_____ school I attend is the best in the region.

2. The professors expect you to do a lot of _____*no article*_____ homework every night.

3. I don't mind because I've always enjoyed reading _____*no article*_____ books.

4. The school also has _____*an*_____ excellent reputation for sports.

5. For example, our football team has ranked in _____*the*_____ top ten of our conference for forty years straight.

■ **TEACHING TIP:** Have students, in small groups, create two separate lists: one of count nouns and the other of non-count nouns. Then, ask students to write two brief stories, each using all the words from one of the lists.

6. Three years ago, we won _____*the*_____ conference championship, but we have not been able to win it again.

7. It is very exciting to go to _____*a*_____ football game during a winning season.

8. _____*The*_____ view from the stadium is nice, too. You can see all the way to the mountains.

9. When I first arrived, I made _____*no article*_____ friends quickly.

10. I will always remember _____*the*_____ good times I had here.

■ **PRACTICE 14 USING ARTICLES CORRECTLY** . . . .

Edit the following paragraphs, adding, revising, or deleting articles as necessary.

EXAMPLE: Jhumpa Lahiri is ~~the~~ fine writer.
(a inserted above "the")

(1) Have you ever heard of ~~an~~ author Jhumpa Lahiri? *(the inserted above "an")* (2) Before she won *the* 2000 Pulitzer Prize for her short story collection, *Interpreter of Maladies*, she was unknown. (3) However, *Interpreter of Maladies* has been translated into twenty-nine different languages and became ~~the~~ best-seller around the world. *(a inserted above "the")*

(4) Lahiri was born in ~~the~~ England and raised in ~~the~~ Rhode Island, but her parents were from ~~the~~ Calcutta, India, and held onto many traditions from the old country. (5) Although Lahiri visited India many times, she felt removed from *the* country's culture as a child. (6) On the other hand, Lahiri admitted that, while growing up in America, she felt that ~~an~~ "Indian part" of her was "unacknowledged." *(the inserted above "an")* (7) She identified neither as ~~the~~ American nor as ~~the~~ Indian. *(an inserted above each "the")* (8) She had to create *a* cultural identity for herself.

. . . .

Prepositions

A **preposition** is a word (such as *of, above, between, about*) that connects a noun, pronoun, or verb with other information about it. The correct preposition to use is often determined by idiom or common practice rather than by the preposition's actual meaning.

An **idiom** is any combination of words that is always used the same way, even though there is no logical or grammatical explanation for it. The best way to learn English idioms is to listen and read as much as possible and then to practice writing and speaking the correct forms.

Adjectives with Prepositions

Adjectives are often followed by prepositions. Here are some common examples.

■ **TIP:** For more on prepositions, see Chapter 20.

afraid of	full of	scared of
ashamed of	happy about	sorry about/sorry for
aware of	interested in	tired of
confused by	proud of	
excited about	responsible for	

Peri is afraid ^of^ ~~to~~ walking alone.

We are happy ^about^ ~~of~~ Dino's promotion.

Verbs with Prepositions

Many verbs consist of a verb plus a preposition (or adverb). The meaning of these combinations is not usually the meaning the verb and the preposition would each have on its own. Often, the meaning of the verb changes completely depending on which preposition is used with it.

You must **take out** the trash. [*take out* = bring to a different location]

You must **take in** the exciting sights of New York City. [*take in* = observe]

Sometimes, words can come between the verb and preposition; other times, this isn't logical in English. Here are some examples of combinations that can and can't be separated.

SEPARABLE VERB/PREPOSITION COMBINATIONS

call off (cancel)	They *called off* the pool party. [They *called **it** off*.]
fill in (refill)	Please *fill in* the holes in the ground. [Please *fill **them** in*.]
fill out (complete)	Please *fill out* this application form. [Please *fill **it** out*.]
fill up (make something full)	Don't *fill up* the tank all the way. [Don't *fill **it** up* all the way.]
find out (discover)	Did you *find out* her name? [Did you *find **it** out*?]
give up (forfeit; stop)	Don't *give up* your place in line. [Don't *give **it** up*.]

hand in (submit)	You may *hand in* your homework now. [You may *hand **it** in* now.]
lock up (secure)	Don't forget to *lock up* the house. [Don't forget to *lock **it** up*.]
look up (check)	I *looked up* the word in the dictionary. [I *looked **it** up*.]
pick out (choose)	Sandy *picked out* a dress. [She *picked **it** out*.]
pick up (take or collect)	When do you *pick up* the keys? [When do you *pick **them** up*?]
put off (postpone)	I often *put off* chores. [I often *put **them** off*.]
sign up (register for)	I want to sign up for the contest. [Please *sign **me** up* for the contest.]

INSEPARABLE VERB/PREPOSITION COMBINATIONS

call on (choose)	The teacher always *calls on* me.
drop in (visit)	*Drop in* when you are in the area.
fight against (combat)	He tried to *fight against* the proposal.
fight for (defend)	We need to *fight for* our rights.
go over (review; travel to)	He wants to *go over* our speeches. I want to *go over* to Lisa's place on Saturday.
grow up (mature)	All children *grow up*.

PRACTICE 15   EDITING PREPOSITIONS . . . .

Edit the following sentences to make sure that the correct prepositions are used. Some sentences are correct; put "C" next to them.

EXAMPLE: My instructor, Mr. Johnson, always calls ~~out~~ me.

(on)

1. Of course, my classmates are aware ~~at~~ this trend. *(of)*

2. I'm so tired ~~with~~ them teasing me. *(of)*

3. I wish they would grow up, and I've told them that. *C*

4. One day, I dropped ~~over~~ at Mr. Johnson's office when he was about to leave. *(in)*

5. "Hello, Seth!" he said. "Did you forget to hand ~~up~~ your paper in class?" *(in)*

6. "No," I said, "I just want to say that your calling on me so much makes me a bit uncomfortable." *C*

7. "Oh," said Mr. Johnson thoughtfully. "I'm sorry *~~of~~* that."
   ^*about*^

8. "Maybe you could start asking more of the other students to participate," I suggested. "I would certainly be happy *~~of~~* that."
   ^*about*^

9. "Sure," said Mr. Johnson. "It will make them more responsible *~~on~~*
   ^*for*^
   their homework, anyway."

10. "Thanks for your time," I said. "I'll go and let you lock *~~out~~* now."
    ^*up*^

■ **PRACTICE 16   EDITING PREPOSITIONS** . . . .

Edit the following paragraph to make sure that the correct prepositions are used.

EXAMPLE: Lucy is excited *~~for~~* the coming weekend.
^*about*^

(1) She is almost finished with her English paper and will hand it *~~to~~* on Friday. (2) She has been working hard on the paper and has begun to grow tired *~~with~~* it. (3) At one point last week, she was so frustrated she almost gave up. (4) Now, however, she's glad she fought *~~through~~* that urge.

(5) As for this weekend, Lucy has a million things she wants to do. (6) Her friend Sylvie asked her to drop *~~over~~* Friday night for a visit. (7) Saturday morning, she plans to sign *~~on~~* for a gym membership. (8) Also, she might go *~~in~~* to the theater to see a movie. (9) Lucy was going to check out an event in the park on Sunday, but it has been called *~~out~~*.

(10) Lucy is proud *~~with~~* herself for finishing her paper. (11) She deserves a little rest and relaxation.

[Editing marks: (1) in ^; (2) of; (4) against ^; (6) in ^; (7) up ^; (8) over ^; (9) off ^; (10) of ^]

. . . .

Chapter Review

1. What is a pronoun? *a word that replaces a noun or another pronoun*

   What are the three types of English pronouns? *subject, object, possessive*

   Use each of the types in a sentence. *Answers will vary.*

What are five common pronouns? *Answers will vary.*

2. Rewrite this sentence in the simple past and the simple future. Melinda picks flowers every morning.

   Past: *Melinda picked flowers yesterday (or some other past time).*

   Future: *Melinda will pick flowers in the spring (or some other future time).*

3. Using the progressive tenses, rewrite this sentence first as a question, then in the past tense and in the future tense.

   Chris is learning Spanish.

   Question: *Is Chris learning Spanish?*

   Past: *Was Chris learning Spanish?*

   Future: *Will Chris be learning Spanish?*

4. Rewrite these sentences so that they use the modal auxiliary correctly.

   Jennifer should to help her mother. *Jennifer should help her mother.*

   Yesterday, I cannot work. *Yesterday, I could not work.*

5. Rewrite this sentence so that it uses the perfect tense correctly.

   They have call an ambulance. *They have called an ambulance.*

6. What is a gerund? *a verb form that ends in -ing and acts as a noun*

   Write a sentence with a gerund in it. *Answers will vary.*

7. What is an infinitive? *a verb form that is preceded by the word to*

   Write a sentence with an infinitive in it. *Answers will vary.*

8. Give an example of a count noun. *Answers will vary.*   Give an example of a noncount noun.
   Answers will vary.   Use each of the nouns in a sentence, using the correct article.

9. What is a preposition? *a word that connects a noun, pronoun, or verb with other information about it*

   Write a sentence using a preposition. *Answers will vary.*

Chapter Test

Circle the correct choice for each of the
following items.

■ **TIP:** For advice on taking
tests, see Appendix A.

■ **RESOURCES:** *Testing Tool
Kit*, a CD-ROM available with
this book, has even more tests.

1. Choose the correct word(s) to fill in the blank.

   You need _____ me if you have a problem.

   a. telling   (b.) to tell   c. told

2. Choose the sentence that has no errors.

   a. I have been written to my congressman three times, but I never
      heard back from him.
   b. I have been writing to my congressman three times, but I never
      heard back from him.
   (c.) I have written to my congressman three times, but I never heard
      back from him.

3. Choose the sentence that has no errors.

   (a.) I walked five miles yesterday.
   b. I walk five miles yesterday.
   c. I walking five miles yesterday.

4. Choose the correct word to fill in the blank.

   In January, they _____ to vacation in Florida.

   a. going   b. is going   (c.) are going

5. If an underlined portion of this sentence is incorrect, select the revision
   that fixes it. If the sentence is correct as written, choose d.

   Pasquale <u>might</u> to get a job <u>at</u> his father's <u>construction</u> business.
          A   B   C

   (a.) might   c. constructing
   b. on   d. No change is necessary.

6. Choose the correct word to fill in the blank.

   Elena tells the funniest jokes. _____ always makes me laugh.

   a. Her   b. Him   (c.) She

7. Choose the sentence that is in the correct order.

   a. One pound of chocolate I ate last week.
   (b.) I ate one pound of chocolate last week.
   c. Chocolate one pound I ate last week.

8. If an underlined portion of this sentence is incorrect, select the revision that fixes it. If the sentence is correct as written, choose d.

The <u>healths</u> of our employees <u>is</u> very important.
  A   B   C

  a. A   c. were

  (b.) health   d. No change is necessary.

9. Choose the sentence that has no errors.

  (a.) Was it snowing when you got to the mountain?

  b. Snowing it was when you got to the mountain?

  c. When you got to the mountain snowing it was?

10. Choose the correct word to fill in the blank.

Because it rained, we called _____ the picnic.

  a. on   b. in   (c.) off

Part Five Test
Other Grammar Concerns

PART I

Following are two paragraphs. Read them carefully and circle the correct answers to the questions that follow them. Use some of the reading strategies from Chapter 1.

1 For years, computer professionals have pondered a hardest question that most of us never think about: How many buttons should be on a computer mouse? 2 Steven P. Jobs, cofounder and chief executive of Apple Computer, used to say that the answer is <u>one</u>. 3 The user will automatically push the right button. 4 Now, however, both Apple and Windows PC computers use mice with multiple buttons. 5 <u>Original</u> computer mouse was invented by Douglas Engelbart and <u>William English</u> at a company then called Stanford Research Institute. 6 The first mouse had three buttons, but Mr. Engelbart has said that ten buttons would have been preferable to he. 7 The user would need training, but the mouse would be more useful with the additional buttons. 8 In the early 1970s, researchers at Xerox's Palo Alto Research Center developed a three-button mouse with a roller ball, which replaced the original mouse's two wheels. 9 Jobs and others at Apple Computer introduced the one-button mouse in the early 1980s, Apple recently introduced mice with multiple touch sensors. 10 Microsoft added a scroll wheel to its mouse in the mid 1990s. 11 This change allowed Internet users to scroll through long pages. 12 Some computer experts now think that the mice of the future will have no buttons; they will somehow sense what we want them do.

1. Which of the following revisions is needed in sentence 1?
   a. Change "have" to "has."
   b. Change "that" to "than."
   (c.) Change "hardest" to "hard."
   d. Change "hardest" to "harder."

2. Which of the following revisions would correctly join sentences 2 and 3?
   a. Change "one. The" to "one; because the."
   (b.) Change "one. The" to "one because the."
   c. Change "one. The" to "one. Because the."
   d. Change "one. The" to "one, the."

3. Which of the following should be used in place of the underlined word in sentence 5?
   a. Originally,   (c.) The original
   b. Is original   d. His original

4. Which of the following sentences contains an incorrect pronoun?
    a. Sentence 2
    (c.) Sentence 6
    b. Sentence 4
    d. Sentence 7

5. Which of the following changes is needed in sentence 9?
    (a.) Change "1980s, Apple" to "1980s; however, Apple."
    b. Change "Computer introduced" to "Computer, introduced."
    c. Change "1980s, Apple" to "1980s; therefore, Apple."
    d. Change "mouse in" to "mouse. In."

■ RESOURCES: *Additional Resources* includes reproducible answer keys for the tests that conclude Parts Four through Seven. For each question, the keys list the section of *Real Writing* that students should study if they missed the question.

1 The banana is in trouble. 2 The version of the banana, the Cavendish, that many Americans add to their breakfast cereal could be headed for extinction. 3 In 1992, a fungus that is dangerous to the Cavendish began spreading through plantations in Indonesia, Malaysia, Australia, and Taiwan. 4 Since that time, the fungus has spread throughout much of Southeast Asia. 5 Some scientists are especially concerned; them say that the fungus will eventually kill all the Cavendish bananas in the world. 6 Banana growers, shippers, and retailers stand to lose billions of dollars a year. 7 The most popular fruit, each American consumes 26.2 pounds of bananas a year. 8 By comparison, the average yearly consumption of the second-most-popular fruit, apples, is 16.7 pounds per person. 9 Scientists and growers are attempting to save the banana on two fronts. 10 In one of the efforts, scientists are trying to genetically alter the Cavendish to help it resist the fungus. 11 However, many consumers may reject a genetically altered banana. 12 Growers are making a separate effort, attempting to develop a different type of banana that looks, tastes, and it smells like the Cavendish. 13 Most growers are aware to the fact that this was tried before. 14 Until the 1960s, Americans ate a banana called the Gros Michel. 15 Many experts say it was larger and tastier than the Cavendish. 16 However, a different fungus killed off the Gros Michel bananas, and growers replaced them with the Cavendish. 17 It was a successful switch. 18 Most Americans never noticed the difference.

6. Which of the following should be used in place of the underlined word in sentence 5?
    a. them all
    c. it
    (b.) they
    d. No change is necessary.

7. Which of the following should be used in place of sentence 7?
    (a.) Each American consumes 26.2 pounds of bananas a year, making it the most popular fruit.
    b. The most popular fruit, Americans every year consume 26.2 pounds of bananas.
    c. Consuming 26.2 pounds a year, bananas are Americans' most popular fruit.
    d. No change is necessary.

8. Which of the following should be used in place of the underlined section of sentence 12?
   a. looks, tastes, and smells
   b. looks, it tastes and smells
   c. looks, tastes, and be smelling
   d. No change is necessary.

9. Which of the following should be used in place of the underlined word in sentence 13?
   a. of
   b. for
   c. at
   d. No change is necessary.

10. Which of the following revisions would correctly join sentences 14 and 15?
    a. Gros Michel, many experts
    b. Gros Michel, and many experts
    c. Gros Michel many experts
    d. Gros Michel; however, many experts

PART II

Circle the correct choice for each of the following items.

1. Choose the item that has no errors.
   a. I have been play the lottery several times, but I've never won.
   b. I have been playing the lottery several times, but I've never won.
   c. I have played the lottery several times, but I've never won.

2. If an underlined portion of this sentence is incorrect, select the revision that fixes it. If the sentence is correct as written, choose d.

   The school superintendent said she wanted she wanted to plan the new
                                                 ‾‾‾‾‾‾‾‾‾‾‾‾‾‾‾‾   ‾‾‾‾
                                                       A   B

   school year most carefully than had been done previously.
                    ‾‾‾‾‾‾‾‾‾‾‾‾‾
                          C

   a. wanted plan
   b. newer
   c. more carefully
   d. No change is necessary.

3. Choose the correct word(s) to fill in the blank.

   Everyone loves to have _____ picture in the newspaper.
   a. their
   b. he or she
   c. his or her

4. Choose the item that has no errors.
   a. I have four umbrellas at home, but I have none at work.
   b. I have four umbrellas at home, I have none at work.
   c. I have four umbrellas at home, nor I have none at work.

5. If an underlined portion of this sentence is incorrect, select the revision that fixes it. If the sentence is correct as written, choose d.

He is not <u>qualified</u> <u>to be</u> our company's vice <u>president he</u> is the son of
         A   B   C
our company's owner.

a. qualify

(c.) president, even though he

b. be

d. No change is necessary.

6. Choose the item that has no errors.

a. I found my old elementary school pictures searching through the attic.

(b.) Searching through the attic, I found my old elementary school pictures.

c. I found my old elementary school pictures, searching through the attic.

7. Choose the correct words to fill in the blank.

Tim told Bob that _____ needed a vacation.

a. he

b. him

(c.) he, Tim,

8. Choose the item that has no errors.

a. When spring finally arrives. All the flowers and trees burst out with color and new life.

(b.) When spring finally arrives, all the flowers and trees burst out with color and new life.

c. Spring finally arrives, all the flowers and trees burst out with color and new life.

9. Choose the correct word(s) to fill in the blank.

Jennie was walking in her sleep, so I _____ led her back to her bed.

(a.) gently

b. gentle

c. most gentle

10. Choose the correct word(s) to fill in the blank.

I want _____ him if he needs help.

a. asking

(b.) to ask

c. ask

11. If an underlined portion of this sentence is incorrect, select the revision that fixes it. If the sentence is correct as written, choose d.

We will get to the <u>stadium</u> <u>faster</u> than our <u>neighbors</u> as if my aunt drives.
                  A   B   C

a. stadium

(c.) neighbors if

b. more fast

d. No change is necessary.

12. Choose the item that has no errors.
    a. Looking out a window, a pack of stray dogs ran down the block.
    b. Looking out a window, I saw a pack of stray dogs run down the block.
    c. Looking out a window, a block was run down by a pack of stray dogs.

13. Choose the item that is most logical.
    a. Borrowing money is putting yourself in a risky position, but stealing it is illegal.
    b. Borrowing money is risky, but stealing it is illegal.
    c. Borrowing money is risky, but stealing it is definitely against the law.

14. If an underlined portion of this sentence is incorrect, select the revision that fixes it. If the sentence is correct as written, choose d.

    Shelly wanted to play varsity basketball, she had to plan her study time
                   A   **B**

    carefully.
      C

    a. play
    b. basketball, so she
    c. careful
    d. No change is necessary.

15. Choose the correct word to fill in the blank.

    Our school had the _____ debating team in the competition.
    a. worse
    b. worsetest
    c. worst

16. Choose the item that has no errors.
    a. I like my new camera for work projects, nor it's also great for family snapshots.
    b. I like my new camera for work projects, it's also great for family snapshots.
    c. I like my new camera for work projects, but it's also great for family snapshots.

17. If an underlined portion of this sentence is incorrect, select the revision that fixes it. If the sentence is correct as written, choose d.

    For our daughter's wedding, we're going to call an events planner, hire
                                             A   **B**

    a band, and we'll also order lots of food.
                  C

    a. calling
    b. to hire
    c. order
    d. No change is necessary.

18. Choose the correct word(s) to fill in the blank.

Whenever a club member wants to use the auditorium, _____ must reserve it ahead of time.

   (a.) he or she   b. they   c. them

19. Choose the item that has no errors.

   a. Working carelessly, the paint got all over my clothes and my face.

   (b.) Working carelessly, I got paint all over my clothes and my face.

   c. Working carelessly, my clothes and face got paint all over them.

20. Choose the item that means that one piece of cake is desired.

   a. I only want one piece of Shirley's lemon cake.

   (b.) I want only one piece of Shirley's lemon cake.

   c. I want one piece of Shirley's only lemon cake.

Part Six
Word Use

33

Word Choice

Using the Right Words

Understand the Importance of Choosing Words Carefully

In conversation, you show much of your meaning through facial expression, tone of voice, and gestures. In writing, you have only the words on the page to make your point, so you must choose them carefully. If you use vague or inappropriate words, your readers may not understand you. Carefully chosen words tell your readers exactly what you mean.

Two resources will help you find the best words for your meaning: a dictionary and a thesaurus.

Dictionary

You need a dictionary. A good paperback dictionary does not cost much, and a number of good dictionaries are now available free online. Dictionaries give you all kinds of useful information about words: spelling, division of words into syllables, pronunciation, parts of speech, other forms of words, definitions, and examples of use. Following is a sample dictionary entry.

spelling and end-of-line division	pronunciation	parts of speech	other forms

con • crete (kon´krēt, kong´-, kon-krēt´), *adj., n., v.* **-cret • ed,**
-cret • ing, *adj.* **1.** constituting an actual thing or instance; real; — definition
perceptible; substantial: *concrete proof.* **2.** pertaining to or concerned with — example
realities or actual instances rather than abstractions; particular as
opposed to general: *concrete proposals.* **3.** referring to an actual substance
or thing, as opposed to an abstract quality: The words *cat, water,* and
teacher are concrete, whereas the words *truth, excellence,* and *adulthood*
are abstract. . . .

—*Random House Webster's College Dictionary*

■ **RESOURCES:** *Additional Resources* contains tests and supplemental practice exercises for this chapter.

■ **TIP:** Several online dictionaries are available. Just a few of them are <**dictionary.reference.com**>, <**yourdictionary.com**>, and <**m-w.com**> (Merriam-Webster OnLine). Online thesauruses include <**www.thesaurus.reference.com**> and <**www.bartleby.com/thesauri**>. The Merriam-Webster site also offers an online thesaurus.

■ **ESL:** ESL students may want to use a dictionary written especially for nonnative speakers (such as the *Longman Dictionary of American English*) in addition to a standard English dictionary.

Thesaurus

A thesaurus gives **synonyms** (words that have the same meaning) for the word you look up. It comes in inexpensive and even electronic editions. Use a thesaurus when you can't find the right word for what you mean. Be careful, however, to choose a word that has the precise meaning you intend. If you are not sure how a word should be used, look it up in the dictionary.

Concrete, *adj.* 1. Particular, specific, single, certain, special, unique, sole, peculiar, individual, separate, isolated, distinct, exact, precise, direct, strict, minute; definite, plain, evident, obvious; pointed, emphasized; restrictive, limiting, limited, well-defined, clear-cut, fixed, finite; determining, conclusive, decided.

—J. I. Rodale, *The Synonym Finder*

Language Note: Make sure to use the right kinds of words in sentences: nouns when a person, place, or thing is meant, and adjectives when a description is meant.

INCORRECT	Everyone in the world wants happy. [*Happy* is an adjective, but a noun is needed in this case.] Smoking is not health. [*Health* is a noun, but an adjective is needed in this case.]
CORRECT	Everyone in the world wants **happiness**. Smoking is not **healthy**.

Practice Avoiding Four Common Word-Choice Problems

Four common problems with word choice may make it hard for you to get your point across.

Vague and Abstract Words

Your words need to create a clear picture for your readers. Vague and abstract words are too general. They don't give your readers a clear idea of what you mean. Here are some common vague and abstract words.

VAGUE AND ABSTRACT WORDS

a lot	dumb	old	very
amazing	good	pretty	whatever
awesome	great	sad	young
bad	happy	small	
beautiful	nice	terrible	
big	OK (okay)	thing	

■ **COMPUTER:** Tell students they can use a computer's search or find function to locate these words in their own writing.

When you see one of these words or another general word in your writing, try to replace it with a concrete or more specific word. A **concrete** word names something that can be seen, heard, felt, tasted, or smelled. A **specific** word names a particular individual or quality. Compare these two sentences:

VAGUE AND ABSTRACT	An old man crossed the street.
CONCRETE AND SPECIFIC	An eighty-seven-year-old priest stumbled along Main Street.

The first version is too general to be interesting. The second version creates a clear, strong image. Some words are so vague that it is best to avoid them altogether.

VAGUE AND ABSTRACT	It's awesome.

[This sentence is neither concrete nor specific.]

> ■ **TEACHING TIP:** Take students to a spot on campus and have them write descriptions of the same scene. Then, have them compare what they wrote, noting the use of concrete and specific language as well as of vague and abstract words.

■ PRACTICE 1   AVOIDING VAGUE AND ABSTRACT WORDS . . . .

In the following sentences, underline any words that are vague or abstract. Then, edit each sentence by replacing the vague or abstract words with concrete, specific ones. You may invent any details you like.
Answers will vary. Possible edits shown.

> ■ **TIP:** For more practice on choosing words effectively, visit Exercise Central at **bedfordstmartins.com/ realwriting**.

         Bronx Zoo   *neighborhood sprawls over hundreds of acres.*
EXAMPLE: The ~~zoo~~ in my ~~city is big~~.

1. I visit the *Bronx Zoo at least twice a year.*
   ~~local zoo a lot.~~

2. The animals ~~seem happy there.~~ *behave as they would in the wild instead of pacing restlessly.*

3. Living in a cage would be ~~awful~~, *painfully boring and uncomfortable* but the ~~zoo in my city~~ *Bronx Zoo* doesn't have cages.

4. The new gorilla habitat is ~~nice.~~ *like the gorillas' native habitat.*

5. The zoo has ~~some~~ *two different species of* ~~very pretty~~ birds/ *with purple and turquoise feathers.*

6. ~~Sometimes,~~ *Every spring,* the zoo has ~~young~~ *newborn* animals.

7. Watching the bats is ~~great.~~ *like watching a creepy old movie or a thrilling air show.*

8. The zoo raises money to ~~do good things~~ *preserve natural habitats* for wildlife around the world.

9. The ~~zoo has a lot of information available for~~ visitors/ *zoo's exhibits teach* *about wildlife conservation.*

10. Working at a zoo would be ~~awesome.~~ *challenging and rewarding.*

> ■ **RESOURCES:** To gauge students' word-choice skills, use the *Testing Tool Kit* CD-ROM available with this book.

Slang

■ **TEAMWORK:** Students can collaborate to list slang words and then translate them into edited English.

Slang, informal and casual language, should be used only in informal situations. Avoid it when you write, especially for college classes or at work. Use language that is appropriate for your audience and purpose.

SLANG	EDITED
If I don't get this job, I'll be *bummed.*	If I don't get this job, I will be disappointed.
Dawg, I don't deserve this grade.	Professor, I don't deserve this grade.

■ PRACTICE 2   AVOIDING SLANG · · · · · · · · · · · · · · · · · · ·

In the following sentences, underline any slang words. Then, edit the sentences by replacing the slang with language appropriate for a formal audience and purpose. Imagine that you are writing to a supervisor at work.
Answers will vary. Possible edits shown.

> **EXAMPLE:** I want to know why you have been ~~on my case so much~~
> *so critical of me*
> recently.

1. I don't see why it is necessary for you to ~~chew me out~~ so often.
   reprimand me

2. During my last evaluation you asked me to ~~get my act together~~, and I
   improve my performance
   believe that I have done so.

3. I was really ~~fired up~~ about the last project I worked on.
   enthusiastic

4. I wish that our relationship could be more ~~laid back~~.
   relaxed

5. This is a ~~sweet gig,~~ and I'd like to ~~hang around~~ here for at least
   good job, *remain*
   another year.

6. ~~I'm buddies~~ with all of my coworkers in this department.
   I get along well

7. Jim Hoffman and I did once ~~get into it over~~ scheduling.
   have a disagreement about

8. Working with him was tense for a while, but ~~we're cool~~ now.
   we get along fine

9. If anyone has been ~~talking me down~~, I would like to know about it.
   complaining about me

10. If you see a problem with my work, please ~~give me the 411.~~
    tell me about it.

· ·

Wordy Language

People sometimes use too many words to express their ideas. They may think that using more words will make them sound smart, but too many words can weaken a writer's point.

WORDY	I'm not interested *at this point in time*.
EDITED	I'm not interested now.

[The phrase *at this point in time* uses five words to express what could be said in one word: *now*.]

WORDY	*In the opinion of this writer,* I think the directions are clear.

[The phrase *in the opinion of this writer* is not necessary and weakens the statement.]

WORDY	The suspect was *evasive* and *avoided answering the questions*.
EDITED	The suspect was evasive.

[The words *evasive* and *avoided answering the questions* repeat the same idea without adding anything new.]

COMMON WORDY EXPRESSIONS

WORDY	EDITED
As a result of	Because
Due to the fact that	Because
In spite of the fact that	Although
It is my opinion that	I think (*or just make the point*)
In the event that	If
The fact of the matter is that	(*Just state the point.*)
A great number of	Many
At that time	Then
In this day and age	Now
At this point in time	Now
In this paper I will show that . . .	(*Just make the point; don't announce it.*)
Utilize	Use

■ **COMPUTER:** Students can use a computer's search or find function to locate these phrases (or others like them) in their writing.

■ **PRACTICE 3 AVOIDING WORDY LANGUAGE** . . . .

In the following sentences, underline the wordy or repetitive language. Then, edit each sentence to make it more concise. Some sentences may contain more than one wordy phrase. *Answers may vary. Possible edits shown.*

EXAMPLE: Television has had a huge effect on politics ~~as a result of~~ *because*
~~the fact that~~ it ~~brings~~ *has brought* politicians into people's homes.

1. ~~It is a well-known fact that~~ ~~television~~ *Television* helped Richard Nixon lose the 1960 presidential election.

2. *Many*
   ~~A great number of~~ voters disliked Nixon's appearance during televised
   debates with John F. Kennedy.

3. *Although*
   ~~In spite of the fact that~~ technicians encouraged Nixon to wear makeup
   for the debate, he refused.

4. He *looked*
   ~~gave the appearance of being~~ sweaty and pale next to tanned, calm
   Kennedy.

5. ~~The fact of the matter is that~~ Nixon did not look much better on
   television during his presidency from 1968 to 1974.

6. Like Kennedy, President Ronald Reagan ~~was a chief executive who~~
   looked good on television.

7. He had experience standing in front of cameras *because* ~~due to the fact that~~ he
   had been an actor.

8. Reagan's ~~cheerful, happy~~ smile made people forget questions they had
   about his political experience.

9. *Some*
   ~~In this day and age, some~~ people have pointed out that looking good
   on television is one of the *most important* requirements ~~of the most paramount impor-
   tance~~ for future presidents.

10. Anyone who does not resemble a news anchorperson ~~in appearance~~ is
    not likely to go far in national politics *now.* ~~at this point in time.~~

. . . .

Clichés

Clichés are phrases used so often that people no longer pay attention to
them. To get your point across and to get your readers' attention, replace
clichés with fresh language.

CLICHÉS	EDITED
I can't *make ends meet.*	I don't have enough money to live on.
My uncle *worked his way up the corporate ladder.*	My uncle started as a shipping clerk but ended up as a regional vice president.
This roll is *as hard as a rock.*	This roll is so hard I could bounce it.

COMMON CLICHÉS

as big as a house	light as a feather
the best/worst of times	no way on earth
better late than never	110 percent
break the ice	playing with fire
crystal clear	spoiled brat/rotten
a drop in the bucket	starting from scratch
easier said than done	sweating blood/bullets
few and far between	too little, too late
hell on earth	work like a dog
last but not least	

■ **COMPUTER:** Students can use a computer's search or find function to locate these phrases (or others like them) in their writing.

■ PRACTICE 4   AVOIDING CLICHÉS . . . .

In the following sentences, underline the clichés. Then, edit each sentence by replacing the clichés with fresh language.   *Answers will vary. Possible edits shown.*

EXAMPLE: Riding a bicycle one hundred miles a day can be ~~hell on~~ *excruciating*

~~earth~~ unless you're willing to ~~give 110 percent.~~ *work extremely hard.*

1. You have to persuade yourself to ~~sweat blood and work like a dog~~ for *devote every bit of your strength to the challenge*

   up to ten hours.

2. *It is impossible to* ~~There's no way on earth you can~~ do it without extensive training.

3. Staying on your bike until ~~the bitter end,~~ *the very last mile,* of course, is ~~easier said than~~ *an enormously difficult* ~~done.~~ *task.*

4. It is important to ~~keep the fire in your belly~~ *maintain your determination* and keep your goal of fin-

   ishing the race ~~crystal clear~~ *always present* in your mind.

5. No matter how long it takes you to cross the finish line, remind your-

   self that ~~it's better late than never.~~ *finishing at all is a tremendous achievement.*

6. Even if you aren't a champion racer, training for a bike race will keep

   you ~~fit as a fiddle.~~ *in top physical condition.*

7. It may take discipline to make yourself train, but you should ~~keep your~~ *continue to*

   ~~nose to the grindstone.~~ *work hard.*

8. Bike racers should always ~~play it safe~~ *protect themselves* by wearing helmets.

9. When you train for road racing, ~~keep an eye peeled~~ *watch carefully* for cars.

10. You don't want to end up ~~flat on your back~~ *injured* in the hospital or ~~six feet~~ *killed!* ~~under!~~

. . . .

■ **TIP:** See Chapter 25 for more advice on using pronouns.

A FINAL NOTE: Language that favors one gender over another or that assumes that only one gender performs a certain role is called *sexist*. Such language should be avoided.

SEXIST   A doctor should politely answer *his* patients' questions.

[Not all doctors are male, as suggested by the *his* pronoun.]

REVISED   A doctor should politely answer *his or her* patients' questions.

Doctors should politely answer *their* patients' questions.

[The first revision changes *his* to *his or her* to avoid sexism. The second revision changes the subject to a plural noun (*Doctors*) so that a genderless pronoun (*their*) can be used. Usually, it's preferable to avoid *his or her*.]

Edit Paragraphs and Your Own Writing

■ **PRACTICE 5   EDITING PARAGRAPHS FOR WORD CHOICE** . . . .

Find and edit any examples of vague and abstract language, slang, wordy language, or clichés in the following paragraphs. You may want to refer to the chart, Editing for Word Choice, on page 513.

Answers will vary. Possible edits shown.

1. (1) Space travel is not available to ~~the average Joe at this point in~~ *ordinary citizens now,* ~~time,~~ but that situation may change. (2) In ~~the year~~ 1997, Congress *legalized* ~~declared the legality of~~ private manned space flights. (3) ~~A lot of~~ *Many* entrepreneurs are ~~betting the farm~~ *speculating* that space tourism will happen ~~pretty~~ soon. (4) But a vacation on the moon won't ~~come cheap, however.~~ *be inexpensive.* (5) Only people ~~with deep pockets~~ *wealthy* will be able to afford half a million *dollars* ~~smackers~~ for a cruise around the moon. (6) ~~This one~~ *One* company plans a moon community, and a night at the hotel there will cost $1,500. (7) If anyone is interested in a more permanent visit to space, an option already exists. (8) For ~~a cost of~~ $4,800, people who want to ~~spend eter-~~ *be buried* ~~nity in space~~ can have their ashes launched from a rocket.

2. (1) Throughout recorded history, humans have done ~~bad~~ *devastating* things to the environment. (2) For example, the need for firewood ~~really—~~

destroyed
~~screwed up~~ the forests of Europe. (3) ~~Due to the fact that~~ *Because* wood has
^   ^
a high carbon-to-hydrogen ratio, the burning of wood is a dirty and in-
used
efficient source of fuel. (4) Coal was ~~utilized~~ as an alternative, but ~~as we~~
                           also harmful to the environment.   ^   *When*
~~know,~~ coal is ~~not so nice either.~~ (5) ~~At this point in time when~~ oil fur-
         ^   ^
naces began to replace coal furnaces, the air in many cities slowly be-

came somewhat cleaner.
                Amazingly,
        (6) ~~Another thing that blows my mind is that~~ whales were the main
            ^
source of fuel for lamps for much of the nineteenth century. (7) Each

year, thousands of whales were killed, until ~~the time came when~~ they

were almost extinct. (8) When petroleum oil was discovered in 1859,

people thought that their energy problems were over ~~forever after.~~
                                                          ^   *significant*
(9) However, ~~in my opinion I feel that~~ our dependence on oil is a ~~big-~~
                                                                     ^
~~time~~ problem. (10) During the energy crisis of the 1970s, for example,
        restrict our fuel consumption.   *foolish*
we really had to ~~bite the bullet.~~ (11) It is ~~dumb~~ to continue to use fos-
                 ^   ^
sil fuels when scientists have shown that these fuels contribute to global

warming.

■ PRACTICE 6   EDITING YOUR OWN WRITING FOR WORD CHOICE . . . .

As a final practice, edit a piece of your own writing for word choice. It can
be a paper you are working on for this course, a paper you've already finished, a paper for another course, or a recent piece of writing from your work
or everyday life. Record in your learning journal any problem sentences you
find, along with their corrections. You may want to use the chart on page 513.

■ **LEARNING JOURNAL:**
Which of the four common
problems with word choice do
you have trouble with? Why
do you think you have this
problem? How can you avoid
it in your writing?

Chapter Review

1. What two resources will help you choose the best words for your meaning? *a dictionary and a thesaurus*

2. What are four common word-choice problems? *vague and abstract words, slang, wordy language, and clichés*

3. Replace vague and abstract words with _____*concrete*_____ and _____*specific*_____ words.

4. When is it appropriate to use slang in college writing or in writing at work? _____*never*_____

5. Give an example of two wordy expressions. *Answers will vary.*

Chapter Test

For each of the following items, choose words or sentences that are specific and appropriate for a formal (academic or work) audience.

■ **TIP:** For advice on taking tests, see Appendix A.

■ **RESOURCES:** *Testing Tool Kit*, a CD-ROM available with this book, has even more tests.

1. Choose the item that uses words most effectively.
   a. My dorm is just an OK place to study.
   (b.) My dorm is so noisy and full of activity that it's difficult to study there.
   c. My dorm is not where I go when I want to study.

2. Choose the best words to fill in the blank.

   I'm afraid all of your hard work did not _____.
   (a.) solve our problem   b. do the trick   c. do it for us

3. Choose the best word(s) to fill in the blank.

   Kevin was extremely _____ about his new job.
   a. juiced   b. turned on   (c.) enthusiastic

4. Choose the item that uses words most effectively.
   a. I really like that thing Nikki does whenever she scores a goal.
   b. I really like the way Nikki goes nuts whenever she scores a goal.
   (c.) I really like the way Nikki does a triple back flip whenever she scores a goal.

5. Choose the item that uses words most effectively.
   a. In the event that you are ever in River City, stop by to see me.
   (b.) If you are ever in River City, stop by to see me.
   c. If by chance you are ever in River City, stop by to see me.

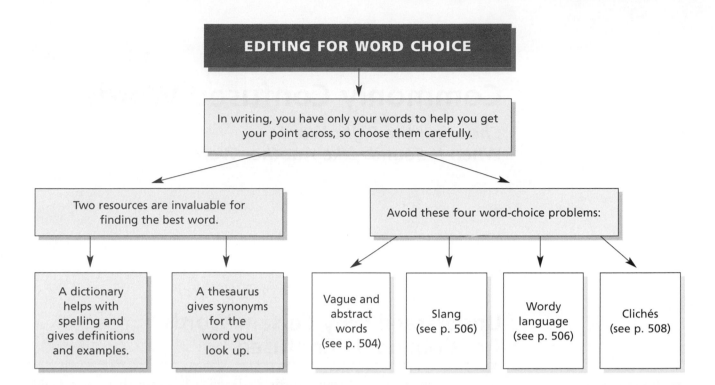

EDITING FOR WORD CHOICE

In writing, you have only your words to help you get your point across, so choose them carefully.

Two resources are invaluable for finding the best word.

Avoid these four word-choice problems:

A dictionary helps with spelling and gives definitions and examples.

A thesaurus gives synonyms for the word you look up.

Vague and abstract words (see p. 504)

Slang (see p. 506)

Wordy language (see p. 506)

Clichés (see p. 508)

34

Commonly Confused Words

Choosing the Right Word
When It Sounds Like Another Word

Understand Why Certain Words Are Commonly Confused

People often confuse certain words in English because they sound alike and may have similar meanings. In speech, words that sound alike are not a problem. In writing, however, words that sound alike may be spelled differently, and readers rely on the spelling to understand what you mean. Edit your writing carefully to make sure that you have used the correct words.

- **Proofread carefully**, using the techniques discussed on page 527.
- **Use a dictionary** to look up any words you are unsure about.
- **Focus on finding and correcting mistakes** you make with the twenty-seven sets of commonly confused words covered in this chapter.
- **Develop a personal list of words** you confuse often. In your learning journal, record words that you confuse in your writing and their meanings. Before you turn in any piece of writing, consult your personal word list to make sure you have used words correctly.

Practice Using Commonly Confused Words Correctly

Study the different meanings and spellings of these twenty-seven sets of commonly confused words. Complete the sentence after each set of words, filling in each blank with the correct word.

A/An/And

a: used before a word that begins with a consonant sound

A friend of mine just won the lottery.

an: used before a word that begins with a vowel sound

An old friend of mine just won the lottery.

and: used to join two words

My friend *and* I went out to celebrate.

A friend *and* I ate at *an* Italian restaurant.

Other lottery winners were _____*an*_____ algebra teacher _____*and a*_____ bowling team.

Accept/Except

accept: to agree to receive or admit (verb)

I will *accept* the job offer.

except: but, other than

All the stores are closed *except* the Quik-Stop.

I *accept* all the job conditions *except* the low pay.

Do not _____*accept*_____ gifts from clients _____*except*_____ those who are also personal friends.

Advice/Advise

advice: opinion (noun)

I would like your *advice* before I make a decision.

advise: to give an opinion (verb)

Please *advise* me what to do.

Please *advise* me what to do; you always give me good *advice*.

If you don't like my _____*advice*_____, please _____*advise*_____ me how to proceed.

■ **TIP:** For more practice using commonly confused words correctly, visit Exercise Central at **bedfordstmartins.com/ realwriting**.

Affect/Effect

affect: to make an impact on, to change something (verb)

The whole city was *affected* by the hurricane.

effect: a result (noun)

What *effect* will the hurricane have on the local economy?

Although the storm will have many negative *effects*, it will not *affect* the price of food.

The _____*effect*_____ of the disaster will _____*affect*_____ many people.

Are/Our

■ **TEACHING TIP:** It is helpful to complete these sentences as a class or to assign them as homework and then go over them in class. Have students read the sentences aloud so they can focus on differences in pronunciation.

are: a form of the verb *be*

  The workers *are* about to go on strike.

our: a pronoun showing ownership

  The children played on *our* porch.

My relatives *are* staying at *our* house.

___*Our*___ new neighbors ___*are*___ moving in today.

By/Buy

by: next to or before

  Meet me *by* the entrance.

  Make sure the bill is paid *by* the fifteenth of the month.

buy: to purchase (verb)

  I would like to *buy* a new CD player.

When I walk *by* the cottage, I know I'd like to *buy* it.

___*By*___ next year, I will be able to ___*buy*___ a washing machine.

Conscience/Conscious

■ **TIP:** Remember that one of the words is *con-science;* the other is not.

conscience: a personal sense of right and wrong (noun)

  Jake's *conscience* wouldn't allow him to cheat.

conscious: awake, aware (adjective)

  The coma patient is now *conscious.*

  I am *conscious* that it's getting late.

The judge was *conscious* that the accused had acted according to his *conscience* even though he had broken the law.

The man said he was not ___*conscious*___ that what he had done was illegal, or his ___*conscience*___ would not have let him do it.

Fine/Find

fine: of high quality (adjective); feeling well (adverb); a penalty for breaking a law (noun)

  This jacket is made of *fine* leather.

  After a day in bed, Jacob felt *fine.*

  The *fine* for exceeding the speed limit is fifty dollars.

find: to locate, to discover (verb)

  Did Clara *find* her glasses?

I *find* gardening to be a *fine* pastime.

Were you able to ___*find*___ a place to store your ___*fine*___ jewelry?

Its/It's

its: a pronoun showing ownership

The dog chased *its* tail.

it's: a contraction of the words *it is*

It's about time you got here.

■ **TIP:** If you are not sure whether to use *its* or *it's* in a sentence, try substituting *it is*. If the sentence doesn't make sense with *it is*, use *its*.

It's very hard for a dog to keep *its* teeth clean.

_____It's_____ no surprise that the college raised _____its_____ tuition.

Knew/New/Know/No

knew: understood; recognized (past tense of the verb *know*)

I *knew* the answer, but I couldn't think of it.

new: unused, recent, or just introduced (adjective)

The building has a *new* security code.

know: to understand; to have knowledge of (verb)

I *know* how to bake bread.

no: used to form a negative

I have *no* idea what the answer is.

I never *knew* how much a *new* car costs.

The _____new_____ teacher _____knew_____ many of her students already.

There is _____no_____ way Tom could _____know_____ where Celia is hiding.

I _____know_____ that there is _____no_____ cake left.

Loose/Lose

loose: baggy; relaxed; not fixed in place (adjective)

In hot weather, people tend to wear *loose* clothing.

lose: to misplace; to forfeit possession of (verb)

Every summer I *lose* about three pairs of sunglasses.

If the ring is too *loose* on your finger, you might *lose* it.

I _____lose_____ my patience with _____loose_____ rules in schools.

Mind/Mine

mind: to object to (verb); the thinking or feeling part of one's brain (noun)

Toby doesn't *mind* if I borrow his CDs.

Estela has a good *mind,* but often she doesn't use it.

mine: belonging to me (pronoun); a source of ore and minerals (noun)

That coat is *mine.*

My uncle worked in a coal *mine* in West Virginia.

That writing problem of *mine* was on my *mind*.

If you don't ___mind___, the gloves you just took are ___mine___.

Of/Have

of: coming from; caused by; part of a group; made from (preposition)

> The leader *of* the band played bass guitar.

have: to possess (verb; also used as a helping verb)

> I *have* one more course to take before I graduate.
>
> I should *have* started studying earlier.

The president *of* the company should *have* resigned.

Sidney could ___have___ been one ___of___ the winners.

NOTE: Do not use *of* after *would, should, could,* and *might.* Use *have* after those words.

Passed/Past

passed: went by or went ahead (past tense of the verb *pass*)

> We *passed* the hospital on the way to the airport.

past: time that has gone by (noun); gone by, over, just beyond (preposition)

> In the *past,* I was able to stay up all night and not be tired.
>
> The snow fell *past* my window.

This *past* school year, I *passed* all of my exams.

Trish ___passed___ me as we ran ___past___ the one-mile marker.

Peace/Piece

peace: no disagreement; calm

> Could you quiet down and give me a little *peace*?

piece: a part of something larger

> May I have a *piece* of that pie?

The feuding families found *peace* after they sold the *piece* of land.

To keep the ___peace___, give your sister a ___piece___ of candy.

Principal/Principle

principal: main (adjective); head of a school or leader of an organization (noun)

> Brush fires are the *principal* risk in the hills of California.

Ms. Edwards is the *principal* of Memorial Elementary School.

Corinne is a *principal* in the management consulting firm.

principle: a standard of beliefs or behaviors (noun)

Although tempted, she held on to her moral *principles*.

The *principal* questioned the delinquent student's *principles*.

The __*principal*__ problem is that you want me to act against my __*principles*__ .

Quiet/Quite/Quit

quiet: soft in sound; not noisy (adjective)

The library was very *quiet*.

quite: completely; very (adverb)

After cleaning all the windows, Alex was *quite* tired.

quit: to stop (verb)

She *quit* her job.

After the band *quit* playing, the hall was *quite quiet*.

If you would __*quit*__ shouting and be __*quiet*__ , you would find that the scenery is __*quite*__ pleasant.

■ **COMPUTER:** Tell students that although a spell checker won't help them with the spelling of most of these words, they can use the search or find function to find every instance of the words they have trouble with.

Right/Write

right: correct; in a direction opposite from left (adjective)

You definitely made the *right* choice.

When you get to the stoplight, make a *right* turn.

write: to put words on paper (verb)

Will you *write* your phone number for me?

Please *write* the *right* answer in the space provided.

You were __*right*__ to __*write*__ to the senator.

Set/Sit

set: a collection of something (noun); to place an object somewhere (verb)

Paul has a complete *set* of Johnny Cash records.

Please *set* the package on the table.

sit: to rest with one's rear end supported by a chair or other surface

I need to *sit* and rest for a few minutes.

If I *sit* down now, I won't have time to *set* the plants outside.

Before you __*sit*__ on that chair, __*set*__ the magazines on the floor.

Suppose/Supposed

suppose: to imagine or assume to be true
I *suppose* you would like something to eat.
Suppose you won a million dollars.

supposed: past tense of *suppose;* intended
Karen *supposed* Thomas was late because of traffic.

I *suppose* you know that Rita was *supposed* to be home by 6:30.

I ___*suppose*___ you want to leave soon because we are ___*supposed*___ to arrive before the guests.

Than/Then

than: a word used to compare two or more things or persons
It's colder inside *than* outside.

then: at a certain time; next in time
I got out of the car and *then* realized the keys were still in it.

Clara ran more miles *than* she ever had before, and *then* she collapsed.

Back ___*then*___, I smoked more ___*than*___ three packs a day.

Their/There/They're

■ **TIP:** If you aren't sure whether to use *their* or *they're,* substitute *they are.* If the sentence doesn't make sense, use *their.*

their: a pronoun showing ownership
I borrowed *their* clippers to trim the hedges.

there: a word indicating location or existence
Just put the keys *there* on the desk.
There are too many lawyers.

they're: a contraction of the words *they are*
They're about to leave.

There is a car in *their* driveway, which indicates that *they're* home.

___*Their*___ beach house is empty except for the one week that ___*they're*___ vacationing ___*there*___.

Though/Through/Threw

though: however; nevertheless; in spite of (conjunction)
Though he's short, he plays great basketball.

through: finished with (adjective); from one side to the other (preposition)

I'm *through* arguing with you.

The baseball went right *through* the window.

threw: hurled; tossed (past tense of the verb *throw*)

She *threw* the basketball.

Even *though* it was illegal, she *threw* the empty cup *through* the window onto the road.

_____Though_____ she didn't really believe it would bring good luck, Jan _____threw_____ a penny _____through_____ the air into the fountain.

To/Too/Two

to: a word indicating a direction or movement (preposition); part of the infinitive form of a verb

Please give the message *to* Sharon.

It is easier *to* ask for forgiveness than *to* get permission.

too: also; more than enough; very (adverb)

I'm tired *too*.

Dan ate *too* much and felt sick.

That dream was *too* real.

two: the number between one and three (noun)

The lab had only *two* computers.

They went *to* a restaurant and ordered *too* much food for *two* people.

When Marty went _____to_____ pay for his meal, the cashier charged him _____two_____ dollars _____too_____ much.

Use/Used

use: to employ or put into service (verb)

How do you plan to *use* that blueprint?

used: past tense of the verb *use*. *Used to* can indicate a past fact or state, or it can mean "familiar with."

He *used* his lunch hour to do errands.

He *used* to go for a walk during his lunch hour.

She *used* to be a chef, so she knows how to *use* all kinds of kitchen gadgets.

She is also *used* to improvising in the kitchen.

Tom _____used_____ the prize money to buy a boat; his family hoped he would _____use_____ it for his education, but Tom was _____used_____ to getting his way.

Who's/Whose

■ **TIP:** If you aren't sure whether to use *whose* or *who's,* substitute *who is.* If the sentence doesn't make sense, use *whose.*

who's: a contraction of the words *who is*
> *Who's* at the door?

whose: a pronoun showing ownership
> *Whose* shoes are these?

Who's the person *whose* car sank in the river?

The student _____*whose*_____ name is first on the list is the one _____*who's*_____ in charge.

Your/You're

■ **TIP:** If you aren't sure whether to use *your* or *you're,* substitute *you are.* If the sentence doesn't make sense, use *your.*

your: a pronoun showing ownership
> Did you bring *your* wallet?

you're: a contraction of the words *you are*
> *You're* not telling me the whole story.

You're going to have *your* third exam tomorrow.

_____*Your*_____ teacher says _____*you're*_____ very good with numbers.

■ **PRACTICE 1   USING THE RIGHT WORD** . . . .

In each of the following items, circle the correct word in parentheses.

1. I just can't (accept)/ except) your decision.

2. She (use /used) to live next door.

3. (Their / There /They're) on (their)/ there / they're) way to the mountains.

4. The baby has more toys (than)/ then) he knows what to do with.

5. You should always act in accordance with your (principals /principles).

6. After cheating on the test, she had a very guilty (conscience)/ conscious).

7. His enthusiasm (knows)/ nos) (know /no) bounds.

8. Are you going to (your)/ you're) class today?

9. I should (of /have) left (are /our) car at the garage.

10. I need to (buy)/ by) some food for dinner.

Edit Paragraphs and Your Own Writing

■ **PRACTICE 2 EDITING PARAGRAPHS FOR COMMONLY CONFUSED WORDS** . . . .

Edit the following paragraphs to correct errors in word use.

1. (1) More and more women are purchasing handguns, against the ~~advise~~ *advice* of law enforcement officers. (2) Few of these women are criminals or plan to commit crimes. (3) They ~~no~~ *know* the risks of guns, and they ~~except~~ *accept* those risks. (4) They buy weapons primarily because ~~their~~ *they're* tired of feeling like victims. (5) They don't want to contribute ~~too~~ *to* the violence in ~~are~~ *our* society, but they also realize that women are the victims of violent attacks far ~~to~~ *too* often. (6) Many women ~~loose they're~~ *lose their* lives because they can't fight off ~~there~~ *their* attackers. (7) Some women have made a ~~conscience~~ *conscious* decision to arm themselves for protection.

(8) But does buying a gun make things worse rather ~~then~~ *than* better? (9) Having a gun in ~~you're~~ *your* house makes it three times more likely that someone will be killed there—and that someone is just as likely to be you or one of your children as a ~~assailant~~ *criminal*. (10) Most young children can't tell the difference between a real gun and a toy gun when they ~~fine~~ *find* one. (11) Every year, ~~their~~ *there* are tragic examples of children who accidentally shoot and even kill other youngsters while they are playing with guns. (12) A mother ~~who's~~ *whose* children are injured while playing with her gun will never again think that a gun provides ~~piece~~ *peace* of mind. (13) Reducing the violence in ~~are~~ *our* society may be a better solution.

■ **PRACTICE 3 EDITING YOUR OWN WRITING FOR COMMONLY CONFUSED WORDS** . . . .

As a final practice, edit a piece of your own writing for commonly confused words. It can be a paper you are working on for this course, a paper you've already finished, a paper for another course, or a recent piece of writing from your work or everyday life. Add any misused words you find to your personal list of the words you confuse most often.

■ **LEARNING JOURNAL:** Record the words from this chapter that often confuse you when writing. As you edit your writing, look for these words and make sure you have used them correctly.

■ **TEACHING TIP:** Ask students for a few more commonly confused words. Start them off by putting one set on the board and then list others that they suggest.

Chapter Review

1. What are four strategies you can use to avoid confusing words that sound alike or have similar meanings?

   Proofread carefully, use a dictionary to look up any words you are unsure about, find and correct mistakes you make

   with the twenty-seven sets of commonly confused words, develop a personal list of words you confuse often.

2. What are the top five commonly confused words on your personal list?

   Answers will vary.

Chapter Test

Use the words in parentheses to correctly fill in the blanks in each of the following sentences.

■ **TIP:** For advice on taking tests, see Appendix A.

1. The coin machine will ___*accept*___ any coins ___*except*___ foreign ones. (*accept, except*)

■ **RESOURCES:** *Testing Tool Kit*, a CD-ROM available with this book, has even more tests.

2. ___*They're*___ going to arrive ___*there*___ late, but they will be sure to bring all of ___*their*___ tools. (*their, there, they're*)

3. There is ___*too*___ much confusion in our department now that ___*two*___ supervisors have been asked ___*to*___ perform the same job. (*to, too, two*)

4. Everyone thinks ___*you're*___ going to get a perfect score on ___*your*___ exam. (*your, you're*)

5. The veterinarian told me ___*it's*___ not necessary to wash a cat because a cat keeps ___*its*___ own fur clean. (*its, it's*)

35

Spelling

Using the Right Letters

Understand the Importance of Spelling Correctly

Some very smart people are very poor spellers. Unfortunately, spelling errors are easy for readers to spot, and they make a bad impression. If you want to improve your spelling, you need to have two important tools—a dictionary and a spelling list—and use them.

Dictionary

A dictionary contains the correct spellings of words, along with information on how the words are pronounced, what they mean, and where they came from. Buy a dictionary; everyone needs one. You might also use one of the many dictionaries that are now available online.

When proofreading your papers, consult a dictionary whenever you are unsure about the spelling of a word. *Checking a dictionary is the single most important thing you can do to improve your spelling.* For a sample dictionary entry, see page 503.

Buy a current dictionary rather than an old one because current editions have up-to-date definitions and words that are new to the language. If you have trouble finding words in a regular dictionary, get a spelling dictionary, which is designed to help you find a word even if you have no idea how to spell it.

Spelling List

Most people misspell the same words over and over. Keeping a list of these words will show you what your problem words are and will help you learn to spell them correctly.

■ **TEACHING TIP:** Keep at least two dictionaries in the classroom. Let students know where they are, but also emphasize that they should buy their own.

■ **TIP:** Online dictionaries can also help you with spelling. Merriam-Webster OnLine, at <**m-w.com**>, has a feature called the "wild card search" in which you can substitute a "?" for any single character you don't know and an "*" for any string of characters. The search engine then returns a list of possible words for you to choose from.

■ **RESOURCES:** *Additional Resources* contains tests and supplemental exercises for this chapter.

Set aside a section of your course notebook or learning journal for your spelling list. Every time you edit a paper, write down the words that you misspelled. Put the correct spelling first, and then in parentheses put the way you actually wrote it. After you have recorded the spelling errors for three pieces of writing, ask yourself:

- What words have I misspelled more than once?
- What do I get wrong about them? Do I always misspell them the same way?
- What are my personal spelling "demons"? ("Demons" are the five to ten words that you tend to spell wrong over and over.)
- What other mistakes do I tend to make repeatedly (leaving the final -*s* off words, for example)?

■ **TEACHING TIP:** Telling students they will have to turn in their spelling lists reinforces the importance of their making them. If you have time, you can make up individualized spelling quizzes. Premade quizzes are included in the *Testing Tool Kit* CD-ROM available with this book.

Write your demon words (five to ten words), spelled correctly, on an index card, and keep the card somewhere handy so that you can consult it whenever you write.

Every couple of weeks, go back to your spelling list to see if your problem words have changed. Are you misspelling fewer words in each paper? What are your current spelling demons?

Practice Spelling Correctly

You can improve your spelling in several ways. First, learn to find and correct spelling mistakes in your writing by using three strategies.

Three Strategies for Finding and Correcting Mistakes

Every time you write a paper, proofread it for spelling errors by focusing only on spelling. Don't try to correct your grammar, improve your message, and check your spelling at the same time. Remember to check the dictionary whenever you are unsure about the spelling of a word and to add all the spelling mistakes you find to your personal spelling list.

Use a Spell Checker

All word-processing programs have spell checkers. A spell checker finds and highlights a word that may be misspelled, suggests other spellings, and gives you the opportunity to change the spelling of the word. (Most word-processing programs automatically highlight potentially misspelled words.) Use a spell checker after you have completed a piece of writing but before you print it out.

Never rely on a spell checker to do your editing for you. A spell checker ignores anything it recognizes as a word, so it will not help you find words that are misused or misspellings that are also words. For example, a spell checker would not highlight any of the problems in these phrases:

Just *to* it.   (Correct: Just *do* it.)

pain in the *nick*   (Correct: pain in the *neck*)

my writing *coarse*   (Correct: my writing *course*)

Use Proofreading Techniques

Use some of the following proofreading techniques to focus on the spelling of one word at a time. Different techniques work for different people, so try them all and then decide which ones work best for you.

- Print out your paper before proofreading. (Many writers find it easier to detect errors on paper than on a computer screen.)
- Put a piece of paper under the line that you are reading.
- Cut a "window" in an index card that is about the size of a long word (such as *misunderstanding*), and place it over your writing to focus on one word at a time.
- Proofread your paper backward, one word at a time.
- Print out a version of your paper that looks noticeably different: Make the words larger, make the margins larger, triple-space the lines, or do all of these.
- Read your paper aloud. This strategy will help you if you tend to leave words out.
- Exchange papers with a partner and proofread each other's papers, identifying only possible misspellings. The writer of the paper should be responsible for checking the spelling and correcting any errors.

Check Your Personal Spelling List

After you have proofread each word in your paper, look at your personal spelling list and your list of demon words one more time. Have you used any of these words in your paper? If so, go back and check their spelling again. You may be surprised to find that you missed seeing the same old spelling mistakes.

▇ **PRACTICE 1   FINDING AND CORRECTING SPELLING ERRORS** . . . . .

Take the last paper you wrote—or one that you are working on now—and use the three techniques for finding and correcting spelling mistakes. How many spelling mistakes did you find? Were you surprised? How was the experience different from what you normally do to edit for spelling? How confident are you that your paper now contains no spelling mistakes?

■ **TIP:** For more spelling practice, visit Exercise Central at **bedfordstmartins.com/ realwriting**.

Four Strategies for Becoming a Better Speller

Learning to find and correct spelling mistakes that you have already made is only half the battle. You also need to become a better speller so that you do not make so many mistakes in the first place. Here are four strategies.

Master Ten Troublemakers

The ten words in the following list were identified by writing teachers around the United States, as the words most commonly misspelled by students of all ages and backgrounds. Master these and you will be ahead of the crowd. Because there are only ten, you should be able to memorize them.

A phrase related to the spelling of a word often helps people remember the correct spelling. Silly as these memory aids may seem, they can work, so try them or think of your own.

THE TEN TROUBLEMAKERS

TROUBLEMAKERS	COMMON MISSPELLINGS	MEMORY AIDS
1. **a lot**	alot	*a lot* is a lot of words
2. **develop**	develope	*lop* off the *e*
3. **receive**	recieve	*i* before *e* except after *c*, or when sounded like *a*, as in *neighbor* or *weigh*
4. **separate**	*seperate*	there's *a rat* in there
5. **until**	*untill*	sounds like *one l*
6. **light**	*lite*	light *is* right
7. **necessary**	necesary, nesesary	a *c* and two *s*'s are *necessary*
8. **argument**	arguement	no *gue* (pronounced *gooey*) arguments!
9. **definite**	definate, defenite	people *definitely* have two eyes (*i*'s)
10. **surprise**	surprize	*surprise* is no *prize*

Master Your Personal Spelling Demons

Once you know what your spelling demons are, you can start to conquer them. If your list of spelling demons is long, you may want to start by focusing on the top five or the top three. When you have mastered these, you can go on to the next few. Different techniques work for different people. Try them all, and then stick with the ones that work for you.

TECHNIQUES FOR MASTERING YOUR SPELLING DEMONS

- Create memory aids, like those shown for the ten troublemakers.
- Break the word into parts and try to master each part. You can break it into syllables (*Feb ru ar y*) or separate the prefixes and endings (*dis ap point ment*).
- Write the word (correctly) ten times.
- Say the letters of the word out loud. See if there's a rhythm or a rhyme you can memorize.

- Write a paragraph in which you use the word at least three times.

- Say the word out loud, emphasizing each letter and syllable even if that's not the way you normally say it. For example, say *pro bab ly* instead of *prob ly*. Try to pronounce the word this way in your head each time you spell it.

- Ask a partner to give you a spelling test.

Master Commonly Confused Words

Chapter 34 covers twenty-seven sets of words that are commonly confused because they sound similar, such as *write* and *right* or *its* and *it's*. If you can master these commonly confused words, you will avoid many spelling mistakes.

Learn Six Spelling Rules

This section covers spelling situations in which people often think, *What do I do here?* If you can remember the rules, you can correct many of the spelling errors in your writing.

Before the six rules, here is a quick review of vowels and consonants.

VOWELS: *a, e, i, o,* and *u*

CONSONANTS: *b, c, d, f, g, h, j, k, l, m, n, p, q, r, s, t, v, w, x,* and *z*.

The letter *y* can be either a vowel or a consonant. It is a vowel when it sounds like the *y* in *fly* or *hungry*. It is a consonant when it sounds like the *y* in *yellow*.

RULE 1:	*I* before *e*
	Except after *c*.
	Or when sounded like *a*
	As in *neighbor* or *weigh*.

Many people repeat this rhyme to themselves as they decide whether a word is spelled with an *ie* or an *ei*.

p**ie**ce (*i* before *e*)
rec**ei**ve (except after *c*)
eight (sounds like *a*)

EXCEPTIONS: *either, neither, foreign, height, seize, society, their, weird*

■ **TEAMWORK:** For each rule, have students give three additional examples of words that follow the rule. This can be done in small groups or pairs.

■ **PRACTICE 2   USING RULE 1** . . . .

In the spaces provided on the next page, write more examples of words that follow the rule. Do not use words that have already been covered.
Answers will vary. Possible answers shown.

1.	*niece*	4.	*deceive*
2.	*siege*	5.	*freight*
3.	*believe*	6.	*sieve*

. . . .

RULE 2:   **Drop the final *e*** when adding an ending that begins with a vowel.

   hop**e** + ing = hoping

   imagin**e** + ation = imagination

Keep the final *e* when adding an ending that begins with a consonant.

   achiev**e** + ment = achiev**e**ment

   definit**e** + ly = definit**e**ly

EXCEPTIONS: *argument, awful, simply, truly,* and others

▪ PRACTICE 3   USING RULE 2 . . . .

For each item, circle the first letter in the ending, and decide whether it is a consonant or a vowel. Then, add the ending to the word and write the new word in the space.

1. peace + (f)ul = *peaceful*	6. write + (i)ng = *writing*
2. separate + (l)y = *separately*	7. pure + (e)r = *purer*
3. believe + (i)ng = *believing*	8. create + (i)ve = *creative*
4. schedule + (e)d = *scheduled*	9. shame + (f)ul = *shameful*
5. value + (a)ble = *valuable*	10. converse + (a)tion = *conversation*

. . . .

RULE 3:   When adding an ending to a word that ends in *y*, **change the *y* to *i*** when a consonant comes before the *y*.

   lone**ly** + est = loneli**e**st

   hap**py** + er = happi**e**r

   apolo**gy** + ize = apolo**g**ize

   like**ly** + hood = likeli**hood**

Do not change the *y* when a vowel comes before the *y*.

   bo**y** + ish = boyish

   pa**y** + ment = payment

   surve**y** + or = surveyor

   bu**y** + er = buyer

EXCEPTIONS: 1. When adding *-ing* to a word ending in *y*, always keep the *y*, even if a consonant comes before it: stu**dy** + ing = studying.

2. Other exceptions include *daily, dryer, said,* and *paid.*

PRACTICE 4   USING RULE 3 . . . .

For each item, circle the letter before the *y*, and decide whether it is a vowel or a consonant. Then, add the ending to the word, and write the new word in the space provided.

1. pl**a**y + ful = *playful*   6. pl**a**y + ed = *played*

2. pl**i**y + ers = *pliers*   7. bu**r**y + al = *burial*

3. come**d**y + an = *comedian*   8. me**rr**y + ment = *merriment*

4. ca**rr**y + er = *carrier*   9. pu**ff**y + ness = *puffiness*

5. de**f**y + ant = *defiant*   10. pr**a**y + ers = *prayers*

. . . .

RULE 4:   When adding an ending that starts with a vowel to a one-syllable word, follow these rules.

Double the final consonant only if the word ends with a consonant-vowel-consonant.

> **trap** + ed = tra**pp**ed
> **drip** + ed = dri**pp**ed
> **knit** + ed = kni**tt**ed
> **fat** + er = fa**tt**er

Do not double the final consonant if the word ends with some other combination.

VOWEL-VOWEL-CONSONANT	VOWEL-CONSONANT-CONSONANT
clean + est = cleanest	sli**ck** + er = slicker
poor + er = poorer	tea**ch** + er = teacher
clear + ed = cleared	last + ed = lasted

RULE 5:   When adding an ending that starts with a vowel to a word with two or more syllables, follow these rules.

Double the final consonant only if the word ends with a consonant-vowel-consonant and the stress is on the last syllable.

> sub**mit** + ing = submi**tt**ing
> oc**cur** + ence = occu**rr**ence
> pre**fer** + ed = prefe**rr**ed

Do not double the final consonant in other cases.

problem + atic = problematic

understand + ing = understanding

offer + ed = offered

■ PRACTICE 5   USING RULES 4 AND 5

For each item, circle the last three letters in the main word, and decide whether they fit the consonant-vowel-consonant pattern. In words with more than one syllable, underline the stressed syllable. Then, add the ending to each word, and write the new word in the space provided.

1. lift + ed = *lifted*

2. happen + ed = *happened*

3. command + er = *commander*

4. omit + ed = *omitted*

5. cheap + er = *cheaper*

6. disgust + ed = *disgusted*

7. spot + ed = *spotted*

8. slip + ery = *slippery*

9. scrap + ed = *scrapped*

10. return + ed = *returned*

RULE 6:   **Add -s** to most words, including words that end in *o* preceded by a vowel.

MOST WORDS	WORDS THAT END IN VOWEL PLUS *O*
book + **s** = book**s**	vide**o** + **s** = video**s**
college + **s** = college**s**	stere**o** + **s** = stereo**s**
jump + **s** = jump**s**	radi**o** + **s** = radio**s**

Add -es to words that end in *o* preceded by a consonant and words that end in *s, sh, ch,* or *x.*

WORDS THAT END IN CONSONANT PLUS *O*	WORDS THAT END IN *S, SH, CH,* OR *X*
pota**to** + **es** = potato**es**	class + **es** = class**es**
he**ro** + **es** = hero**es**	pu**sh** + **es** = push**es**
go + **es** = go**es**	ben**ch** + **es** = bench**es**
	fa**x** + **es** = fax**es**

EXCEPTIONS: *pianos, solos,* and others

■ PRACTICE 6   USING RULE 6

For each word, circle the last two letters, and decide which of the Rule 6 patterns this word fits. Add *-s* or *-es* and write the new word in the space provided.

1. addre(ss) *addresses*
2. bicyc(le) *bicycles*
3. toma(to) *tomatoes*
4. chur(ch) *churches*
5. stret(ch) *stretches*

6. stud(io) *studios*
7. da(sh) *dashes*
8. constru(ct) *constructs*
9. discov(er) *discovers*
10. b(ox) *boxes*

One Hundred Commonly Misspelled Words

Use this list as an easy reference to check your spelling.

absence	convenient	height	receive
achieve	cruelty	humorous	recognize
across	daughter	illegal	recommend
aisle	definite	immediately	restaurant
a lot	describe	independent	rhythm
already	dictionary	interest	roommate
analyze	different	jewelry	schedule
answer	disappoint	judgment	scissors
appetite	dollar	knowledge	secretary
argument	eighth	license	separate
athlete	embarrass	lightning	sincerely
awful	environment	loneliness	sophomore
basically	especially	marriage	succeed
beautiful	exaggerate	meant	successful
beginning	excellent	muscle	surprise
believe	exercise	necessary	truly
business	fascinate	ninety	until
calendar	February	noticeable	usually
career	finally	occasion	vacuum
category	foreign	occurrence	valuable
chief	friend	perform	vegetable
column	government	physically	weight
coming	grief	prejudice	weird
commit-	guidance	probably	writing
ment	harass	psychology	written
conscious			

Edit Paragraphs and Your Own Writing

■ PRACTICE 7   EDITING PARAGRAPHS FOR SPELLING . . . .

Find and correct any spelling mistakes in the following paragraphs.

(1) In today's schools, there is a ~~rageing~~ *raging* argument about whether to ~~seperate~~ *separate* children of different ~~abilitys~~ *abilities* ^ into classes with others of similar *^achievement* ~~achievment~~ levels. (2) Some experts claim that children develop¢ and ^ learn best when they are in mixed-ability classes. (3) These same experts state that ~~divideing~~ *dividing* ^ students will ~~prejudise~~ *prejudice* ^ teachers against the slower students. (4) When students of lesser ability are grouped together, they don't learn as fast, their self-esteem drops, their ~~absenses~~ *absences* ^ increase, and they may drop out. (5) ~~Basicaly~~, *Basically,* the experts claim, students ~~loose~~ *lose* ^ all motivation to ~~acheive~~. *achieve* ^

(6) Other experts present another side of the ~~arguement~~. *argument* ^ (7) They say that grouping ~~buy~~ *by* ^ ability allows students ~~too~~ *to* ^ learn at a more natural rate. (8) Teachers ~~usally~~ *usually* ^ have ~~alot~~ *a lot* ^ more time to spend with students because they aren't trying to teach students of all abilities. (9) For example, if students with similar writing skills ~~our~~ *are* ^ together in class, the teacher either can spend a lot of time with grammar if the class needs it or can skip over it if the students have ~~masterred~~ *mastered* ^ the basic rules. (10) These experts claim that grouping by ability provides a more efficient learning ~~enviroment,~~ *environment,* gets a good class ~~rythym~~ *rhythm* ^ going, and results in the ~~happyest,~~ *happiest,^* most enthusiastic learners. ^

(11) Both sides have ~~intresting,~~ *interesting,* ^ persuasive arguments that they present to local, state, and federal ~~goverment~~ *government* ^ officials.

■ PRACTICE 8   EDITING YOUR OWN WRITING FOR SPELLING . . . . . .

■ **LEARNING JOURNAL:**
Record your spelling demons (spelled correctly) in your learning journal.

Edit a piece of your own writing for spelling. It can be a paper you are working on for this course, a paper you've already finished, a paper for another course, or a recent piece of writing from work or everyday life. Record in your learning journal any mistakes you find, along with their corrections.

Chapter Review

1. What are two important tools for good spelling? *a dictionary and a spelling list*

2. What three strategies can you use to find and correct spelling mistakes?
   Use a spell checker, use proofreading techniques, check your personal spelling list.

3. What four strategies can you use to become a better speller?
   Master the ten troublemakers, your personal spelling demons; commonly confused words, learn

   the six spelling rules.

Chapter Test

In each sentence, fill in the blank with the correctly spelled word.

■ **TIP:** For advice on taking tests, see Appendix A.

1. Your joining us for dinner is a pleasant _____.
   a. suprise
   b. surprize
   c.) surprise

■ **RESOURCES:** *Testing Tool Kit*, a CD-ROM available with this book, has even more tests.

2. When can I expect to _____ the package?
   a. recieve
   b.) receive
   c. reeceive

3. Is the fax _____ right now?
   a. transmiting
   b.) transmitting
   c. transsmiting

4. Is Colin's roommate _____ weird?
   a. definately
   b.) definitely
   c. definitly

5. After my doctor diagnosed my injury, she _____ me to a physical therapist.
   a. refered
   b. reffered
   c.) referred

Part Six Test
Word Use

Circle the correct choice for each of the following items.

1. Choose the correct word to fill in the blank.

   I asked the doctor if the drug would _____ my sleep.
   a. effect
   b. afect
   c. affect *(circled)*

2. Choose the correct word to fill in the blank.

   Are you _____ the book you're reading?
   a. liking *(circled)*
   b. likeing
   c. likking

3. If an underlined portion of this sentence is incorrect, select the revision that fixes it. If the sentence is correct as written, choose d.

   Carolyn's brother likes to <u>embarass</u> her, and I'm sure he will not
   A

   <u>disappoint</u> her on the <u>occasion</u> of her thirtieth birthday.
   B   **C**

   a. embarrass *(circled)*
   b. dissappoint
   c. ocasion
   d. No change is necessary.

4. Choose the most appropriate word(s) to fill in the blank.

   Did you get _____ just for parking in the wrong spot?
   a. nabbed
   b. busted
   c. in trouble *(circled)*

5. If an underlined portion of this sentence is incorrect, select the revision that fixes it. If the sentence is correct as written, choose d.

   I didn't <u>know</u> that you <u>new</u> we had just gotten <u>two</u> new puppies.
   A   **B**   **C**

   a. no
   b. knew *(circled)*
   c. too
   d. No change is necessary.

6. If an underlined portion of this sentence is incorrect, select the revision that fixes it. If the sentence is correct as written, choose d.

   Mandy did not <u>exaggerate</u> when she said that her new <u>jewelry</u> is <u>wierd</u>.
   A   **B**   **C**

   a. exagerate
   b. jewlry
   c. weird *(circled)*
   d. No change is necessary.

7. Choose the most appropriate word(s) to fill in the blank.

   Our trip to Montreal was _____.
   a. awful
   b. a bummer
   c. ruined because a truck hit our car. *(circled)*

■ **RESOURCES:** *Additional Resources* includes reproducible answer keys for the tests that conclude Parts Four through Seven. For each question, the keys list the section of *Real Writing* that students should study if they missed the question.

8. Choose the correct word to fill in the blank.

   I finally told Deborah the truth because my _____ was bothering me.

   a.) conscience   b. conscious   c. consience

9. Let's _____ the children if they start to fight in the back seat.

   a.) separate   b. seperete   c. seperate

10. If an underlined portion of this sentence is incorrect, select the revision that fixes it. If the sentence is correct as written, choose d.

    Donny's <u>new</u> haircut is <u>similar</u> to the one he <u>use</u> to have.
                 A   **B**   **C**

    a. knew   c.) used

    b. similiar   d. No change is necessary.

11. Choose the most appropriate words to fill in the blank.

    Summer jobs this year are _____.

    a. few and far between   c.) scarce and highly competitive

    b. as scarce as hen's teeth

12. If an underlined portion of this sentence is incorrect, select the revision that fixes it. If the sentence is correct as written, choose d.

    Because Derrell is the <u>friendlyest</u> person in <u>our</u> building, he has joined
                                    A   **B**

    the welcome <u>committee</u>.
                C

    a.) friendliest   c. comittee

    b. are   d. No change is necessary.

13. Choose the most appropriate word(s) to fill in the blank.

    That test was _____, so I am sure that I did well on it.

    a. a piece of cake   b. a breeze   c.) easy

14. Choose the correct word to fill in the blank.

    He says he is suing the company not to make money but because an important _____ is at stake.

    a. principal   b. princapal   c.) principle

15. Choose the correct word to fill in the blank.

Can you tell the officer how the accident _____?

a. ocured   b. occured   (c.) occurred

16. Fill in the blank with the most effective words.

_____ Christy's family is wealthy, she dresses as though she has no money at all.

a. In spite of the fact that

(b.) Although

c. Leaving aside the well-known fact that

17. If an underlined portion of this sentence is incorrect, select the revision that fixes it. If the sentence is correct as written, choose d.

I proudly <u>except</u> your award; however, I <u>prefer</u> to donate the two
             A   **B**

hundred <u>dollars</u> to our high school band.
       C

(a.) accept   c. dollers

b. proffer   d. No change is necessary.

18. Fill in the blank with the most effective words.

Derek's painting is _____.

a. really neat   (c.) full of jagged shapes and bright colors

b. truly amazing

19. If an underlined portion of this sentence is incorrect, select the revision that fixes it. If the sentence is correct as written, choose d.

Carly will not <u>receive</u> notification <u>until</u> next week about whether her
                  A   **B**

<u>arguement</u> won at the hearing.
    C

a. recieve   (c.) argument

b. untill   d. No change is necessary.

20. Fill in the blank with the most effective words.

The new registration process _____.

a. is dumb   c. is a real pain

(b.) is inefficient and confusing

Part Seven
Punctuation and Capitalization

36

Commas

> ,

Understand What Commas Do

Commas (,) are punctuation marks that help readers understand a sentence. Read aloud the following three sentences. How does the use of commas change the meaning?

NO COMMA	When you call Sarah I'll start cooking.
ONE COMMA	When you call Sarah, I'll start cooking.
TWO COMMAS	When you call, Sarah, I'll start cooking.

When you use a comma in a sentence, it signals a particular meaning to your readers, so it is important that you understand when and how to use it.

■ **RESOURCES:** *Additional Resources* contains supplemental exercises for this chapter.

Practice Using Commas Correctly

Commas between Items in a Series

Use commas to separate the items in a series (three or more items). This includes the last item in the series, which usually has *and* before it.

item	,	item	,	item	,	and	item

To get from South Dakota to Texas, we will drive through *Nebraska, Kansas,* and *Oklahoma.*

We can *sleep in the car, stay in a motel,* or *camp outside.*

As I drive I see many beautiful sights, such as *mountains, plains,* and *prairies.*

■ **TIP:** How does a comma change the way you read a sentence aloud? Most readers pause when they come to a comma.

■ **TEACHING TIP:** Write this incorrectly punctuated sentence on the board: *My daughter is a fast aggressive, and competitive soccer player.* Read it aloud (as if it were correctly punctuated), and ask students if they can hear where the missing comma should go.

■ **TIP:** For more practice using commas correctly, visit Exercise Central at **bedfordstmartins.com/ realwriting**.

■ **RESOURCES:** To gauge students' punctuation skills, use the *Testing Tool Kit* CD-ROM available with this book.

NOTE: In magazines and newspapers as well as in some business writing, the comma before the final item is sometimes left out. It is always best to include it, however, so that your meaning will be clear.

■ **PRACTICE 1   USING COMMAS IN SERIES** . . . .

Edit the following sentences by underlining the items in the series and adding commas where they are needed. If a sentence is already correct, put a "C" next to it.

EXAMPLE: Sales of our fruit juices have expanded in the Northeast, the South, and the Midwest.

1. Continued expansion depends on our ability to promote novelty beverages such as papaya, mango, and boysenberry juices in grocery stores and restaurants.

2. We also present juice as an alternative to beverages such as soda, beer, and water.

3. In Washington and California, we are doing well against our major competitors. *C*

4. In these areas, our increase in market share over the past three years has been 7 percent, 10 percent, and 7 percent.

5. In areas where our juice is new, we'd like increases of 10 percent, 20 percent, or 25 percent.

6. In each section of the country, the regional sales director will develop a plan, his or her assistant will communicate the plan, and local salespeople will implement the plan for that area.

7. We want to target New England states such as Connecticut, Massachusetts, and Maine, where attitudes about fruit juice are similar to those in Seattle, Portland, and other Northwest cities.

8. Our advertising should emphasize our small-scale production methods, our commitment to quality, and our juices' delicious flavor. *C*

9. We should set up displays, provide free samples of our juices, and sponsor contests.

10. <u>Careful planning</u>, <u>hard work</u>, and <u>individual initiative</u> will ensure the growth of our company. *C*

. . . .

Commas in Compound Sentences

A **compound sentence** contains two complete sentences joined by a coordinating conjunction: *and, but, for, nor, or, so, yet.* Use a comma before the joining word to separate the two complete sentences.

■ **TIP:** Remember what coordinating conjunctions are with FANBOYS: *for, and, nor, but, or, yet,* and *so.* For more information, see Chapter 28.

| Sentence | , | and, but, for, nor, or, so, yet | sentence. |

I called my best friend, and she agreed to drive me to work.

I asked my best friend to drive me to work, but she was busy.

I can take the bus to work, or I can call another friend.

> **Language Note:** Remember that a comma alone cannot separate two sentences in English. This creates an error known as a *comma splice* (see Chapter 22). A comma is *not* needed if a coordinating conjunction joins two sentence elements that are *not* complete sentences.

EDITING FOR CORRECT COMMA USAGE:
Using Commas in Compound Sentences

↓

Find

Many college <u>students</u> <u>are</u> the first in their families to go to college (and) their <u>relatives</u> <u>are</u> proud of them.

1. To determine if the sentence is compound, **underline** subjects and **double-underline** the verbs.
2. **Ask:** Is the sentence compound? *Yes.*
3. **Circle** the word that joins them.

↓

Edit

Many college students are the first in their families to go to college, and their relatives are proud of them.

4. **Put a comma** before the word that joins the two sentences.

■ **PRACTICE 2   USING COMMAS IN COMPOUND SENTENCES** . . . . . .

Edit the following compound sentences by adding commas where they are needed. If a sentence is already correct, put a "C" next to it.

> **EXAMPLE:** Marika wanted to get a college education,but her
> husband didn't like the idea.

1. Marika's hospital volunteer work had convinced her to become a physical therapist, but she needed a college degree to qualify. *C*

2. Deciding to apply to college was difficult for her,so she was excited when she was admitted.

3. She had chosen the college carefully,for it had an excellent program in physical therapy.

4. Marika knew the courses would be difficult,but she had not expected her husband to oppose her plan.

5. They had been married for twelve years, and he was surprised that she wanted a career. *C*

6. She tried to tell him about the exciting things she was learning,but he didn't seem interested.

7. It was hard for her to manage the house and keep up with her classes, but he would not help. *C*

8. Maybe he was upset that she wanted more education than he had,or perhaps he was afraid they would grow apart.

9. She didn't want to have to choose between her husband and an education,and she didn't have to.

10. They talked about their problems,and now he thinks her career might even help their marriage.

. . . .

■ **ESL:** Because different languages have different intonation patterns, students should not rely on intonation alone to decide where to put commas.

Commas after Introductory Word Groups

Use a comma after an introductory word or word group. An introductory word group can be a phrase or a clause. The comma lets your readers know when the main part of the sentence is starting.

| Introductory word or word group | **,** | main part of sentence. |

INTRODUCTORY WORD: *However,* the president is coming to visit our city.

INTRODUCTORY PHRASE: *By the way,* I don't have a babysitter for tomorrow.

INTRODUCTORY CLAUSE: *While I waited outside,* Susan went backstage.

PRACTICE 3   USING COMMAS AFTER INTRODUCTORY WORD GROUPS

In each item, underline introductory words or word groups. Then, add commas after introductory word groups where they are needed. If a sentence is already correct, put a "C" next to it.

> **EXAMPLE:** According to most medical researchers, the chance of the AIDS virus being spread through athletic contact is very low.

1. As we all know, AIDS is spread mainly through sexual contact and through drug use that involves the sharing of needles.

2. Nonetheless, some people feel that all college athletes should be tested for HIV.

3. Since basketball star Magic Johnson revealed in 1991 that he is HIV-positive, an NBA player must be removed from a game if he is bleeding.

4. Once the wound is properly bandaged, the player is allowed to return to the game.

5. Not surprisingly, many college sports follow similar rules.

6. However, requiring athletes to leave a contest when they are bleeding is quite different from forcing them to be tested for HIV. *C*

7. According to some student athletes, mandatory HIV testing would violate their civil liberties.

8. Using the same argument, many student athletes object to being tested for the use of drugs. *C*

9. <u>In their view</u>, student athletes should be treated no differently than other students. *C*

10. <u>In this case,</u> some would say that public health is more important than civil liberties.

. . . .

Commas around Appositives and Interrupters

An **appositive** comes directly before or after a noun or pronoun and re-names it.

■ **TIP:** For more on apposi-tives, see Chapter 31.

> Lily, *a senior*, will take her nursing exam this summer.
>
> The prices are outrageous at Beans, *the local coffee shop*.

An **interrupter** is an aside or transition that interrupts the flow of a sentence and does not affect its meaning.

> My sister, *incidentally*, has very good reasons for being late.
>
> Her child had a fever, *for example*.

Putting commas around appositives and interrupters tells readers that these elements give extra information but are not essential to the meaning of a sentence. If an appositive or interrupter is in the middle of a sentence, set it off with a pair of commas, one before and one after. If an appositive or interrupter comes at the beginning or end of a sentence, separate it from the rest of the sentence with one comma.

> *By the way*, your proposal has been accepted.
>
> Your proposal, *by the way*, has been accepted.
>
> Your proposal has been accepted, *by the way*.

NOTE: Sometimes an appositive is essential to the meaning of a sentence. When a sentence would not have the same meaning without the appositive, the appositive should not be set off with commas.

> The actor *John Travolta* has never won an Academy Award.
>
> [The sentence *The actor has never won an Academy Award* does not have the same meaning.]

EDITING FOR CORRECT COMMA USAGE: Using Commas to Set Off Appositives and Interrupters

Find

Tamara my sister-in-law moved in with us last week.

1. **Underline** the subject.

2. **Underline** any appositive (which renames the subject) or interrupter (which interrupts the flow of the sentence).

3. **Ask:** Is the appositive or interrupter essential to the meaning of the sentence?
   No.

Edit

Tamara, my sister-in-law, moved in with us last week.

4. If it is not essential, **set it off with commas.**

PRACTICE 4   USING COMMAS TO SET OFF APPOSITIVES AND INTERRUPTERS . . . .

Underline appositives and interrupters in the following sentences. Then, use commas to set them off. Some sentences may have more than one appositive or interrupter.

> **EXAMPLE:** Many homeowners, people of all ages and backgrounds, are nervous these days.

1. Gated communities, those fancy neighborhoods with a gate at the entrance, have been part of the American landscape for years.

2. Today, however, they are more popular than ever before.

3. The terrorist attacks of 2001, the hijackings and anthrax scares, have left many people feeling insecure.

4. Gates and guardhouses, visible symbols of protective authority, make anxious Americans feel safer at home.

5. The fear of crime may, in fact, be worse than crime itself in most parts of the United States.

6. Crime in gated communities, mainly vandalism and petty theft, occurs in spite of gates and guards.

7. The criminals behind such acts, often neighborhood teenagers, may live inside the gates.

8. Most gated communities, as it happens, do not even have walls around them.

9. The gate, a sign of a safe community, is nothing more than that, a sign.

10. Nervous residents use one mirage, the appearance of security, to help them overcome another, the fear of random violence.

Commas around Adjective Clauses

■ **TIP:** Use *who* to refer to a person, *which* to refer to places or things (but not to people), and *that* for places or things. For more on adjective clauses, see Chapter 31.

An **adjective clause** is a group of words that begins with *who, which,* or *that,* has a subject and verb, and describes a noun right before it in a sentence. Whether or not an adjective clause should be set off from the rest of the sentence by commas depends on its meaning in the sentence.

If an adjective clause can be taken out of a sentence without completely changing the meaning of the sentence, put commas around the clause.

Lily, *who is my cousin,* will take her nursing exam this summer.

Beans, *which is the local coffee shop,* charges outrageous prices.

I complained to Mr. Kranz, *who is the shop's manager.*

■ **TEACHING TIP:** Ask students to explain what is meant by "essential" in this context. Help them see that essential (restrictive) phrases and clauses generally answer the question "Which one?" If they are taken out, the meaning of the sentence can change completely.

If an adjective clause is essential to the meaning of a sentence, do not put commas around it. You can tell whether a clause is essential by taking it out and seeing if the meaning of the sentence changes significantly, as it would if you took the clauses out of the following examples.

The only grocery store *that sold good bread* went out of business.
Students *who do internships* often improve their hiring potential.
Salesclerks *who sell liquor to minors* are breaking the law.

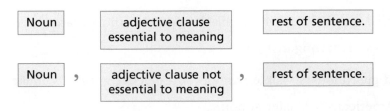

EDITING FOR CORRECT COMMA USAGE:
Using Commas to Set Off Adjective Clauses

Find

The woman <u>who is the CEO of eBay</u> is well respected.

1. **Underline** any adjective clause (a word group that begins with *who, which,* or *that*).
2. **Read** the sentence without this clause.
3. **Ask:** Does the meaning change significantly without the clause? *Yes.*

Edit

The woman who is the CEO of eBay is well respected.

4. If the meaning *does* change, as in this case, **do not put in commas.** (Add commas only if the meaning *does not* change.)

PRACTICE 5   USING COMMAS TO SET OFF ADJECTIVE CLAUSES . . .

Edit the following sentences by putting commas around adjective clauses where they are needed. Remember that if an adjective clause is essential to the meaning of a sentence, you should not use commas. If a sentence is already correct, put a "C" next to it.

> **EXAMPLE:** Elvis Presley, who died in 1977, still has fans around the
> world.

1. My mother, who has always loved music, was not a big fan of Elvis Presley when she was younger.

2. She considered the teenagers who were Elvis fans out of touch with popular music. *C*

3. The records that she bought as a teenager embarrass her now. *C*

4. I have looked through her collection, which includes hits by Barry Manilow and John Denver.

5. She started to listen to Elvis after a party that friends of hers held on the tenth anniversary of the King's death. *c*

6. The party, which featured local bands playing Elvis songs, changed her mind about the music.

7. My mother's best friend from high school, who also attended the party, introduced her to a handsome Elvis impersonator.

8. That man, who is still an Elvis impersonator today, is also my father.

9. My father's stage show, which now emphasizes the King's Las Vegas years, is only a little embarrassing to me.

10. The part that I like best about his performances is how impressed my friends are with my dad. *c*

- -

Other Uses for Commas

Commas with Quotation Marks

> **TIP:** For more on quotation marks, see Chapter 38.

Quotation marks are used to show that you are repeating exactly what someone said. Use commas to set off the words inside quotation marks from the rest of the sentence.

"Let me see your license," demanded the police officer.

"Did you realize," she asked, "that you were going eighty miles per hour?"

I exclaimed, "I didn't!"

Notice that a comma never comes directly after a quotation mark.

When quotations are not attributed to a particular person, commas may not be necessary.

"Pretty is as pretty does" never made sense to me.

Commas in Addresses

Use commas to separate the elements of an address included in a sentence. However, do not use a comma before a zip code.

My address is 2512 Windermere Street, Jackson, Mississippi 40720.

If a sentence continues after the address, put a comma after the address.

I moved here from Detroit, Michigan, when I was eighteen.

Commas in Dates

Separate the day from the year with a comma. If you give just the month and year, do not separate them with a comma.

> My daughter was born on November 8, 1992.

> The next conference is in August 2007.

If a sentence continues after the date, put a comma after the date.

> On April 21, 2008, the contract will expire.

Commas with Names

Put commas around the name of someone you are addressing by name.

> Don, I want you to come look at this.

> Unfortunately, Marie, you need to finish the report by next week.

Commas with Yes or No

Put commas around the word *yes* or *no* in response to a question.

> Yes, I believe you are right.

███ PRACTICE 6   **USING COMMAS IN OTHER WAYS** . . . .

Edit the following sentences by adding commas where they are needed. If a sentence is already correct, put a "C" next to it.

> EXAMPLE: On August 12, 2006, beachfront property was badly damaged by a fast-moving storm.

1. Some homeowners were still waiting to settle their claims with their insurance companies in January 2007. *C*

2. Rob McGregor of 31 Hudson Street, Wesleyville, is one of those homeowners.

3. Asked if he was losing patience, McGregor replied, "Yes, I sure am."

4. "I've really had it up to here," McGregor said. *C*

5. His wife said, "Rob, don't go mouthing off to any reporters."

6. "Betty, I'll say what I want to say," Rob replied.

7. An official of Value-Safe Insurance of Wrightsville, Ohio, said the company will process claims within the next few months.

8. "No, there is no way we can do it any sooner," the official said.
   ^

9. Customers unhappy with their service may write to Value-Safe Insurance, P.O. Box 225, Wrightsville, Ohio 62812. *c*

10. The company's home office in Rye, New York, can be reached by a
                                  ^   ^
    toll-free number.

Edit Paragraphs and Your Own Writing

■ PRACTICE 7   EDITING PARAGRAPHS FOR COMMAS . . . .

Edit the following paragraphs by adding commas where they are needed.

1. (1) According to etiquette experts, e-mail users need to practice
   good manners. (2) Yes, you can answer your e-mail in your bathrobe, but
   you should still be courteous. (3) Not everyone appreciates receiving
   jokes, electronic greeting cards, and bogus virus warnings regularly. (4)
   You should be careful, in particular, to avoid sending dozens of such
   e-mail messages to someone's office address. (5) E-mail is similar to a
   telephone call, a quick and informal way to keep in touch. (6) As a
   rule, you should not e-mail anyone more often than you would call. (7)
   In addition, you should use the subject header to let the recipient know
   whether or not the message is important. (8) Proper etiquette is not just
   for dinner parties, so do your part to improve the manners of the online
   community.

2. (1) In April 1990, the book *You Just Don't Understand* was published by William Morrow in New York, New York. (2) The subject of the
   book is the differences in the way men and women use language, including how they listen, how they speak, how they interact, and generally
   how they communicate. (3) It gives examples of how men and women
   misunderstand each other, and it describes the causes of and possible solutions to the differences in their language expectations. (4) Deborah
   Tannen, the author, starts with childhood experiences that shape the way
   girls and boys use language.

(5) Tannen writes, "Even if they grow up in the same house, girls and boys grow up in different worlds of words. (6) Although they often play together, boys and girls spend most of their time playing in same-sex groups. (7) And although some of their play activities are similar, their favorite games are different, and their ways of using language in their games are also different." (8) Tannen continues, "Boys tend to play outside, for example, in large groups that have a hierarchy. (9) Girls, on the other hand, play in small groups or pairs. (10) Many of their activities (such as playing house) don't have winners or losers."

(11) Later in life, these differences can cause disagreements between men and women.

■ **LEARNING JOURNAL:**
What mistake with commas do you make most often? Why do you think you make this mistake?

■ **PRACTICE 8 EDITING YOUR OWN WRITING FOR COMMAS** . . . .

As a final practice, edit a piece of your own writing for comma usage. It can be a paper you are working on for this course, a paper you've already finished, a paper for another course, or a recent piece of writing from your work or everyday life. In your learning journal, record any examples of sentences with comma problems that you find, along with edited versions of those sentences.

Chapter Review

1. A comma (,) is a _punctuation mark_ that helps readers understand your sentence.

2. How do you use commas in these three situations?

    In a series of items, _use a comma to separate three or more items_ .

    In a compound sentence, _use a coordinating conjunction and a comma to make two sentences into one_ .

    When there is an introductory word or word group, _use a comma after the word, clause, or phrase_ .

3. An appositive comes before or after a noun or pronoun and _renames the noun or pronoun_ .

4. An interrupter is an _aside or transition_ that interrupts the flow of a sentence.

5. Put commas around an adjective clause when it is _not essential_ to the meaning of a sentence.

6. How are commas used with quotation marks? _Use commas to set off the words inside quotation marks from the rest of the sentence_ .

7. In a date with the month, the day, and the year, a comma goes _between the day and the year_ .

Chapter Test

Circle the correct choice for each of the following items.

1. If an underlined portion of this sentence is incorrect, select the revision that fixes it. If the sentence is correct as written, choose d.

   The company <u>owners, for</u> your <u>information are</u> planning to inspect our
   A   B

   <u>department this</u> afternoon.
   C

   a. owners for   c. department, this

   (b.) information, are   d. No change is necessary.

■ **TIP:** For advice on taking tests, see Appendix A.

■ **RESOURCES:** *Testing Tool Kit*, a CD-ROM available with this book, has even more tests.

2. Choose the item that has no errors.

   a. Digital cameras are easy, to use but they don't necessarily improve people's pictures.

   (b.) Digital cameras are easy to use, but they don't necessarily improve people's pictures.

   c. Digital cameras are easy to use, but, they don't necessarily improve people's pictures.

3. Choose the item that has no errors.

   a. If you don't file your income tax forms by April 15, 2007 you could face penalties.

   (b.) If you don't file your income tax forms by April 15, 2007, you could face penalties.

   c. If you don't file your income tax forms by April 15 2007 you could face penalties.

4. If an underlined portion of this sentence is incorrect, select the revision that fixes it. If the sentence is correct as written, choose d.

   Henry's <u>favorite hobbies</u> <u>are watching birds,</u> collecting <u>stamps, and</u>
   A   B   C

   fixing up old cars.

   a. favorite, hobbies   c. stamps and

   b. are watching, birds   (d.) No change is necessary.

5. Choose the item that has no errors.

   (a.) Roger, who teaches dance at a local studio, will be my partner for the ballroom competition.

   b. Roger who teaches dance at a local studio will be my partner for the ballroom competition.

   c. Roger who teaches dance at a local studio, will be my partner for the ballroom competition.

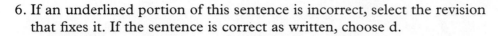
6. If an underlined portion of this sentence is incorrect, select the revision that fixes it. If the sentence is correct as written, choose d.

Feeling <u>adventurous, Alexia</u> tasted the guava, <u>mango and</u> passion fruit.
        A   B   C

  a. adventurous Alexia   (c.) mango, and

  b. tasted, the   d. No change is necessary.

7. Choose the item that has no errors.

  a. I discovered that Lansing, Michigan was the hometown of four people at the party.

  b. I discovered that Lansing Michigan, was the hometown of four people at the party.

  (c.) I discovered that Lansing, Michigan, was the hometown of four people at the party.

8. If an underlined portion of this sentence is incorrect, select the revision that fixes it. If the sentence is correct as written, choose d.

Just to be <u>different I decided to</u> wear a top <u>hat to</u> all of my classes today.
           A   B   C

  (a.) different, I   c. hat, to

  b. decided, to   d. No change is necessary.

9. Choose the item that has no errors.

  a. "If you follow my instructions precisely" said the manager, "I will consider you for a promotion."

  b. "If you follow my instructions precisely," said the manager "I will consider you for a promotion."

  (c.) "If you follow my instructions precisely," said the manager, "I will consider you for a promotion."

10. If an underlined portion of this sentence is incorrect, select the revision that fixes it. If the sentence is correct as written, choose d.

<u>No Bob,</u> I can't <u>swim, paddle</u> a <u>kayak, or</u> steer a sailboat.
   A   B   C

  (a.) No, Bob   c. kayak or

  b. swim paddle   d. No change is necessary.

37
Apostrophes

,

Understand What Apostrophes Do

An **apostrophe (')** is a punctuation mark that either shows ownership (*Susan's*) or indicates that a letter has been intentionally left out to form a contraction (*I'm, that's, they're*). Although an apostrophe looks like a comma **(,)**, it is not used for the same purpose, and it is written higher on the line than commas are.

apostrophe'   comma,

Practice Using Apostrophes Correctly

Apostrophes to Show Ownership

■ **TIP:** *Singular* means one; *plural* means more than one.

- **Add *-'s* to a singular noun to show ownership even if the noun already ends in *-s.***

  Karen's apartment is on the South Side.

  They all followed the *college's* rules.

  James's roommate is looking for him.

■ **RESOURCES:** *Additional Resources* contains tests and supplemental exercises for this chapter.

- **If a noun is plural and ends in *-s*, just add an apostrophe. If it is plural but does not end in *-s*, add *-'s.***

  My *books'* covers are falling off.

  [more than one book]

  The *twins'* father was building them a playhouse.

  [more than one twin]

The *children's* toys were broken.

The *men's* locker room is being painted.

- **The placement of an apostrophe makes a difference in meaning.**

  My *sister's* six children are at my house for the weekend.
  [one sister who has six children]

  My *sisters'* six children are at my house for the weekend.
  [two or more sisters who together have six children]

- **Do not use an apostrophe to form the plural of a noun.**

  Gina went camping with her *sister's* and their children.

  All of the *highway's* to the airport are under construction.

- **Do not use an apostrophe with a possessive pronoun.** These pronouns already show ownership (possession).

  Is that bag *your's*?   No, it is *our's*.

■ **TEACHING TIP:** Using an apostrophe with a possessive pronoun is a very common error; tell students to be especially careful of this problem when they edit. You may also want to have students discuss why this error is so common.

Possessive Pronouns

my	his	its	their
mine	her	our	theirs
your	hers	ours	whose
yours			

The single most common error with apostrophes and pronouns is confusing *its* (a possessive pronoun) with *it's* (a contraction meaning "it is"). Whenever you write *it's*, test correctness by replacing it with *it is* and reading the sentence aloud to hear if it makes sense.

■ **COMPUTER:** If some students often misuse apostrophes in possessive pronouns, advise them to use the search function to find and check all uses of *-'s* in papers before turning them in. Tell them to write "checked for *-'s*" on top of each paper.

■ PRACTICE 1   **USING APOSTROPHES TO SHOW OWNERSHIP** . . . . . .

Edit the following sentences by adding -'s or an apostrophe alone to show ownership and by crossing out any incorrect use of an apostrophe or -'s.

> EXAMPLE. People must respect other people's need's for personal
>
> space.

1. A person's feelings about personal space depend on his or her's culture.

2. Personal space is especially important in cultures' that are formal and
   reserved.

■ **TIP:** For more practice using apostrophes correctly, visit Exercise Central at **bedfordstmartins.com/ realwriting**.

3. Putting your face too close to another's is considered rude.

4. Fistfights often are preceded by someone's aggressive violation of someone else's space.

5. The expression "Get out of my face!" is a warning meant to prevent the confrontation's violent conclusion.

6. A dog's interaction with a member of it's own species can follow a similar pattern; dogs are determined to defend what is their's.

7. The hair on dogs' neck's may stand on end.

8. A researcher's recent work examines various species' personal space.

9. For example, seagulls' positions on a log follow a pattern similar to that of people lined up waiting for a bus.

10. Studies show that an animal's overcrowded environment can lead to violent behavior.

. . . .

Apostrophes in Contractions

■ **TIP:** Ask your instructor if contractions are acceptable in papers.

A **contraction** is formed by joining two words and leaving out one or more of the letters. When writing a contraction, put an apostrophe where the letter or letters have been left out, not between the two words.

She's on her way. = *She is* on her way.

I'll see you there. = *I will* see you there.

Be sure to put the apostrophe in the right place.

It *does/n't* really matter.

Language Note: Contractions including a *be* verb cannot be followed by the base form of a verb or another helping verb (like *can, does,* or *has*).

INCORRECT	I'm try to study.	He's can come.
CORRECT	**I'm trying** to study.	**He can** come.

Common Contractions

aren't = are not	she'll = she will
can't = cannot	she's = she is, she has
couldn't = could not	there's = there is
didn't = did not	they'd = they would, they had
don't = do not	they'll = they will
he'd = he would, he had	they're = they are
he'll = he will	they've = they have
he's = he is, he has	who'd = who would, who had
I'd = I would, I had	who'll = who will
I'll = I will	who's = who is, who has
I'm = I am	won't = will not
I've = I have	wouldn't = would not
isn't = is not	you'd = you would, you had
it's = it is, it has	you'll = you will
let's = let us	you're = you are
she'd = she would, she had	you've = you have

■ **ESL:** Because contractions are often new to ESL students, you may want to advise them to avoid all contractions in college work that they are submitting for a grade. They should use apostrophes only to show ownership.

■ PRACTICE 2   **USING APOSTROPHES IN CONTRACTIONS** . . . .

Read each sentence carefully, looking for any words that have missing letters. Edit these words by adding apostrophes where needed and crossing out incorrectly used apostrophes.

> **EXAMPLE:** Although we observe personal space boundaries in our daily lives, they're not something we spend much time thinking about.

1. You'll notice right away if a stranger leans over and talks to you so his face is practically touching yours.

2. Perhaps you'd accept this kind of behavior from a family member.

3. There isn't one single acceptable boundary we'd use in all situations.

4. An elevator has its own rules: Don't stand right next to a person if there is open space.

5. With coworkers, we're likely to keep a personal space of four to twelve feet.

■ **RESOURCES:** To gauge students' punctuation skills, use the *Testing Tool Kit* CD-ROM available with this book.

6. We'll accept a personal space of four feet down to eighteen inches with friends.

7. The last sixteen inches are reserved for people we're most intimate with.

8. When people hug or kiss, they're willing to surrender their personal space to each other.

9. A supervisor who's not aware of the personal space boundaries of his or her employees might make workers uncomfortable.

10. Even if the supervisor does'nt intend anything by the gestures, it's his or her responsibility to act appropriately.

Apostrophes with Letters, Numbers, and Time

- **Use -'s to make letters and numbers plural.** The apostrophe prevents confusion or misreading.

   In Scrabble games, there are more *e*'s than any other letter.

   In women's shoes, size *8*'s are more common than size *10*'s.

- **Use an apostrophe or -'s in certain expressions in which time nouns are treated as if they possess something.**

   She took four *weeks*' maternity leave after the baby was born.

   This year's graduating class is huge.

▮ **PRACTICE 3   USING APOSTROPHES WITH LETTERS, NUMBERS, AND TIME** . . . .

Edit the following sentences by adding apostrophes where needed and crossing out incorrectly used apostrophes.

   EXAMPLE: When I returned to work after two weeks' vacation, I had what looked like a decade's worth of work in my box.

1. I sorted letters alphabetically, starting with *A*'s.

2. There were more letters by names starting with *M*'s than any other.

3. When I checked my e-mail, the screen flashed 48's to show that I had forty-eight messages.

4. My voice mail wasn't much better, telling me that in two weeks' time I had received twenty-five messages.

5. I needed another week's time just to return all the phone calls.

Edit Paragraphs and Your Own Writing

■ **PRACTICE 4   EDITING PARAGRAPHS FOR APOSTROPHES** . . . .

Edit the following paragraphs by adding apostrophes where needed and crossing out incorrectly used apostrophes.

1. (1) An astronaut goes through extreme adjustment's in zero gravity. (2) The human body has a hard time keeping it's systems operating normally. (3) The brain can't tell up from down. (4) Immune cell's don't respond the way they should. (5) Heartbeats' can speed up and then slow down for no apparent reason. (6) Sleep is a problem for many astronauts, who may complain that they can't get their "z's." (7) The physical effects of a few week's' space travel can imitate what a body experiences after thirty years' aging. (8) These effects might help scientist's learn about treating illnesses associated with getting old.

2. (1) People's names often have strange stories attached to them. (2) Oprah Winfrey's first name, for example, is very unusual. (3) It's actually misspelled. (4) It was supposed to be Orpah, a biblical name, but a clerk's' error on the birth certificate resulted in Oprah. (5) Somehow, *The Orpah Winfrey Show* doesn't sound like a popular television program. (6) *Oprah,* on the other hand, with it's resemblance to *opera,* makes us think of a performer on stage. (7) Winfrey herself is certainly not upset that she didn't end up with her parents' choice of name; her production company's name is Harpo, which is Oprah spelled backward. (8) As Winfrey's example suggests, names on birth certificates are often mixed up. (9) If a clerk's a's look like o's, for example, Dana becomes Dona and

Jarvis becomes Jorvis. (10) But unusual names do'nt all result from mistakes. (11) You've probably heard of names such as Candy Cane or Stormy Winters. (12) Some people's names sound like job titles. (13) Think, for example, of a surgeon who's named Carver, or a dentist called Dr. Drill. (14) Early in his career, the baseball pitcher Eric Plunk was known for hitting batters' with his wild pitches. (15) There's no way to explain any of these names except by attributing them to pure chance. (16) Each name has its own meaning and origin; we're all affected by our names, whether we like them or not.

■ **PRACTICE 5**   **EDITING YOUR OWN WRITING FOR APOSTROPHES** . . .

■ **LEARNING JOURNAL:**
What type of mistake with apostrophes do you make most often? How can you avoid this mistake or be sure to edit for it?

As a final practice, edit a piece of your own writing for apostrophes. It can be a paper you are working on for this course, a paper you've already finished, a paper for another course, or a recent piece of writing from your work or everyday life. In your learning journal, record any examples of sentences with apostrophe problems that you find, along with edited versions of these sentences.

Chapter Review

1. An apostrophe (') is a punctuation mark that usually either shows _____ownership_____ or indicates where a letter or letters have been left out in a _____contraction_____.

2. To show ownership, add _____'s_____ to a singular noun, even if the noun already ends in -s. For a plural noun, add an _____apostrophe_____ alone if the noun ends in -s; add _____'s_____ if the noun does not end in -s.

3. Do not use an apostrophe with a _____possessive_____ pronoun.

4. Do not confuse *its* and *it's*. *Its* shows _____ownership_____; *it's* is a _____contraction_____ meaning "it is."

5. A _____contraction_____ is formed by joining two words and leaving out one or more of the letters.

6. Use -'s to make letters and numbers _____plural_____.

7. Use an apostrophe or -'s in certain expressions in which _____time nouns_____ are treated as if they possess something.

Chapter Test

Circle the correct choice for each of the following items.

■ **TIP:** For advice on taking tests, see Appendix A.

1. If an underlined portion of this sentence is incorrect, select the revision that fixes it. If the sentence is correct as written, choose d.

   I've always believed that <u>its</u> a crime to use software that you <u>haven't</u>
      A   B   C

   ■ **RESOURCES:** *Testing Tool Kit*, a CD-ROM available with this book, has even more tests.

   paid for.
   - a. Ive
   - (b.) it's
   - c. havent
   - d. No change is necessary.

2. Choose the item that has no errors.
   - a. The thicves boldness made them a lot of money, but it eventually landed them in jail.
   - b. The thieves's boldness made them a lot of money, but it eventually landed them in jail.
   - (c.) The thieves' boldness made them a lot of money, but it eventually landed them in jail.

3. Choose the item that has no errors.
   - a. By playing that slot machine, your throwing away money.
   - (b.) By playing that slot machine, you're throwing away money.
   - c. By playing that slot machine, youre' throwing away money.

4. If an underlined portion of this sentence is incorrect, select the revision that fixes it. If the sentence is correct as written, choose d.

   The house is now <u>Renee's</u>, but <u>she'll</u> regret having an address with five
                 A   B

   <u>3s</u> in it.
    C
   - a. Renees
   - b. sh'ell
   - (c.) 3's
   - d. No change is necessary.

5. Choose the item that has no errors.
   - (a.) Her eighteen months' service overseas has somehow made her seem older.
   - b. Her eighteen month's service overseas has somehow made her seem older.
   - c. Her eighteen months service overseas has somehow made her seem older.

38

Quotation Marks

" "

Understand What Quotation Marks Do

Quotation marks (" ") always appear in pairs. Quotation marks have two common uses in college writing: They are used with direct quotations, and they are used to set off titles.

Direct quotations exactly repeat, word for word, what someone said or wrote, and **indirect quotations** restate what someone said or wrote, not word for word. Quotation marks are used only for direct quotations.

> **DIRECT QUOTATION**   He said, "You should get the downtown bus."
>
> **INDIRECT QUOTATION**   He said that I should get the downtown bus.

Practice Using Quotation Marks Correctly

Quotation Marks for Direct Quotations

■ **RESOURCES:** *Additional Resources* contains tests and supplemental exercises for this chapter.

When you write a direct quotation, use quotation marks around the quoted words. These tell readers that the words used are exactly what was said or written.

1. "I don't know what she means," I said to my friend Lina.

2. Lina asked, "Do you think we should ask a question?"

3. "Excuse me, Professor Soames," I called out, "but could you explain that again?"

4. "Yes," said Professor Soames. "Let me make sure you all understand."

5. After further explanation, Professor Soames asked, "Are there any other questions?"

When you are writing a paper that uses outside sources, use quotation marks to indicate where you quote the exact words of a source.

■ **TIP:** For more on incorporating outside source material through quoting and other methods, see Chapter 19.

> We all need to become more conscientious recyclers. A recent editorial in the *Bolton Common* reported, "When recycling volunteers spot-checked bags that were supposed to contain only newspaper, they found a collection of nonrecyclable items such as plastic candy wrappers, aluminum foil, and birthday cards."

When quoting, writers usually use words that identify who is speaking, such as *I said to my friend Lina* in the first example on the previous page. The identifying words can come after the quoted words (example 1), before them (example 2), or in the middle of them (example 3). Here are some guidelines for capitalization and punctuation.

GUIDELINES FOR CAPITALIZATION AND PUNCTUATION

- Capitalize the first letter in a complete sentence that's being quoted, even if it comes after some identifying words (example 2 on the previous page).
- Do not capitalize the first letter in a quotation if it's not the first word in a complete sentence (*but* in example 3).
- If it is a complete sentence, and it's clear who the speaker is, a quotation can stand on its own (second sentence in example 4).
- Identifying words must be attached to a quotation; they cannot be a sentence on their own.
- Use commas to separate any identifying words from quoted words in the same sentence.
- Always put quotation marks after commas and periods. Put quotation marks after question marks and exclamation points if they are part of the quoted sentence.

■ **TEACHING TIP:** As you go over the first two rules on capitalization, put a sentence on the board without any quotation marks. Ask students where the quotation marks should go and which letters should be capitalized.

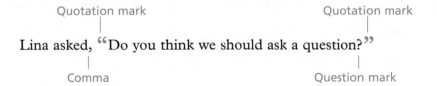

■ **TIP:** For more on commas with quotation marks, see Chapter 36.

- If a question mark or exclamation point is part of your own sentence, put it after the quotation mark.

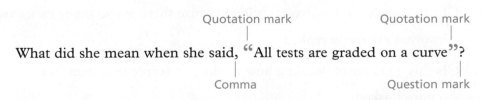

Setting Off a Quotation within Another Quotation

Sometimes, when you directly quote someone, part of what that person said quotes words that someone else said or wrote. Put single quotation marks (' ') around the quotation within a quotation so that readers understand who said what.

> The student handbook says, "Students must be given the opportunity to make up work missed for legitimate reasons."

> Terry told his instructor, "I'm sorry I missed the exam, but that isn't a reason to fail me for the term. Our student handbook says, 'Students must be given the opportunity to make up work missed for legitimate reasons,' and I have a good reason."

■ PRACTICE 1   PUNCTUATING DIRECT QUOTATIONS . . . .

Edit the following sentences by adding quotation marks and commas where needed.

■ **TIP:** For more practice using quotation marks correctly, visit Exercise Central at **bedfordstmartins.com/ realwriting**.

■ **RESOURCES:** To gauge students' punctuation skills, use the *Testing Tool Kit* CD-ROM available with this book.

EXAMPLE: A radio journalist asked a nurse at a critical-care facility, "Do you feel that the medical community needlessly prolongs the life of the terminally ill?"

1. "If I could quickly answer that question," the nurse replied, "I'd deserve an honorary degree in ethics."

2. She added, "But I see it as the greatest dilemma we face today."

3. "How would you describe that dilemma?" the reporter asked the nurse.

4. The nurse said, "It's a choice of when to use our amazing medical technology and when not to."

5. The reporter asked, "So there are times when you'd favor letting patients die on their own?"

6. "Yes," the nurse replied, "I would."

7. The reporter asked, "Under what circumstances should a patient be allowed to die?"

8. "I can't really answer that question because there are so many variables involved," the nurse replied.

9. "Is this a matter of deciding how to allocate scarce resources?" the reporter asked.

10. "In a sense, it is," the nurse replied. "As a colleague of mine says, 'We shouldn't try to keep everyone alive for as long as possible just because we can.'"

. . . .

No Quotation Marks for Indirect Quotations

When you report what someone said or wrote but do not use the person's exact words, you are writing an indirect quotation. Do not use quotation marks for indirect quotations. Indirect quotations often begin with the word *that*.

■ **TEAMWORK:** Have students interview one another on a controversial issue that you have chosen. The interviewer should write up the interview using direct and indirect quotations.

INDIRECT QUOTATION	DIRECT QUOTATION
Sam said that there was a fire downtown.	Sam said, "There was a fire downtown."
The police told us to move along.	"Move along," directed the police.
Tara told me that she is graduating.	Tara said, "I am graduating."

■ **PRACTICE 2   PUNCTUATING DIRECT AND INDIRECT QUOTATIONS** . . .

Edit the following sentences by adding quotation marks where needed and crossing out quotation marks that are incorrectly used. If a sentence is already correct, put a "C" next to it.

> **EXAMPLE:** Three days before her apartment was robbed, Jocelyn told a friend, "I have concerns about the safety of this building."

1. "Have you complained to the landlord yet?" her friend asked.

2. "Not yet," Jocelyn replied, "although I know I should."

3. Jocelyn phoned the landlord and asked him to install a more secure lock on the front door. *C*

4. The landlord said that "he felt the lock was fine the way it was."

5. When Jocelyn phoned the landlord after the burglary, she said, "I know this wouldn't have happened if that lock had been installed."

6. "I'm sorry," the landlord replied, "but there's nothing I can do about it now."

7. Jocelyn asked a tenants' rights group whether she had grounds for a lawsuit. *C*

8. The person she spoke to said that *"*she probably did.*"*

9. *"*If I were you,*"* the person said, *"*I'd let your landlord know about your plans.*"*

10. When Jocelyn told her landlord of the possible lawsuit, he said that he would reimburse her for the lost items. *C*

Quotation Marks for Certain Titles

When you refer to a short work such as a magazine or newspaper article, a chapter in a book, a short story, an essay, a song, or a poem, put quotation marks around the title of the work.

NEWSPAPER ARTICLE	"College Tuition to Rise 25 Percent"
SHORT STORY	"The Awakening"
ESSAY	"Why Are We So Angry?"

Usually titles of longer works, such as novels, books, magazines, newspapers, movies, television programs, and CDs, are underlined or italicized. The titles of sacred books such as the Bible or the Koran are neither underlined nor surrounded by quotation marks.

BOOK	The Good Earth or *The Good Earth*
NEWSPAPER	Washington Post or *Washington Post*

[Do not underline, italicize, or capitalize the word *the* before the name of a newspaper or magazine, even if it is part of the title: I saw that in the *New York Times*. But do capitalize *The* when it is the first word in titles of books, movies, and other sources.]

■ **TIP:** For more information on citing sources, see Chapter 19.

If you are writing a paper with many outside sources, your instructor will probably refer you to a particular system of citing sources. Follow that system's guidelines when you use titles in your paper.

NOTE: Do not enclose the title of a paragraph or an essay that you have written in quotation marks when it appears at the beginning of your paper. Do not underline it either.

■ **PRACTICE 3   USING QUOTATION MARKS FOR TITLES** . . . .

Edit the following sentences by adding quotation marks around titles as needed. Underline any book, magazine, or newspaper titles.

EXAMPLE: After the terrorist attacks of September 11, 2001, the 1,200 radio stations belonging to Clear Channel Communications were asked not to play songs with a political message, such as "Imagine" by John Lennon.

1. In 2002, Bruce Springsteen released his first new album in years, containing songs like "Worlds Apart" that dealt with the terrorist attacks on the United States.

2. "The Missing," a review of the Springsteen album in the New Yorker magazine, found Springsteen's new songs unusual because they did not include many specific details about people, as older Springsteen songs like "Born in the U.S.A." had done.

3. No one made that complaint about "John Walker's Blues," a song by Steve Earle based on the story of the young American captured while fighting for the Taliban in Afghanistan.

4. Earle was condemned by some for writing from Walker's point of view; a New York Post headline claimed, "Twisted Ballad Honors Tali-Rat."

5. As a Time magazine article, "Don't Even Tell These Guys About Eminem," pointed out, the controversy was peculiar because it occurred before Earle's song had even been released, and those objecting had apparently neither heard the song nor read its lyrics.

Edit Paragraphs and Your Own Writing

PRACTICE 4   EDITING PARAGRAPHS FOR QUOTATION MARKS . . . .

Edit the following paragraphs by adding quotation marks where needed and crossing out any incorrectly used quotation marks. Correct any errors in punctuation.

1. (1) When I first read Edgar Allan Poe's "The Tell-Tale Heart," I thought it was the scariest story ever written. (2) I told all my friends that "they should read it." (3) The narrator is a murderer who knows that readers will "think he is mad." (4) He admits, "True!—nervous—very, very dreadfully nervous I had been and am." (5) However, he insists that he is perfectly sane. (6) As proof, he points out that his sense of

hearing is good and says, "I heard all things in the heaven and in the earth,." (7) At the end of the story, the narrator confesses to the murder of an old man. (8) His guilt makes him imagine that he is hearing the dead man's heartbeart, so he tells the police that the sound is "the beating of his hideous heart!"

2. (1) When Ruiz first came into my office, he told me that he was a poor student. (2) I asked,"What makes you think that?"

(3) Ruiz answered,"I've always gotten bad grades, and I don't know how to get any better." (4) He shook his head. (5)"I've just about given up."

(6) I told him that "there were some resources on campus he could use and that we could work together to help him."

(7) "What kind of things are you talking about?" asked Ruiz. (8) "What exactly will I learn?"

(9) I said,"There are plenty of programs to help you. (10) You really have no excuse to fail."

(11)"Can you be a little more specific?"he asked.

(12)"Certainly,"I said. (13) I told him about the survival skills program. (14) I also pulled out folders on study skills, such as managing time, improving memory, taking notes, and having a positive attitude. (15)"Take a look at these,"I said.

(16) Ruiz said,"No, I'm not interested in that. (17) And I don't have time."

(18) I replied, "That's your decision, Ruiz, but remember that education is one of the few things that people are willing to pay for and not get." (19) I paused and then added,"Sounds to me like you're wasting the money you spent on tuition. (20) Why not try to get what you paid for?"

(21) Ruiz thought for a moment, while he looked out the window, and finally told me that "he'd try."

(22)"Good,"I said. (23)"I'm glad to hear it."

PRACTICE 5   EDITING YOUR OWN WRITING FOR QUOTATION MARKS

As a final practice, edit a piece of your own writing for quotation marks. It can be a paper you are working on for this course, a paper you've already finished, a paper for another course, or a recent piece of writing from your work or everyday life. In your learning journal, record any examples you find of mistakes in the use of quotation marks. Also, write down the edited versions of these sentences.

■ **LEARNING JOURNAL:** In your own words, explain the difference between direct quotations and indirect quotations. Write one example of each.

. . . .

Chapter Review

1. Quotation marks look like this: _____ " " . They always appear in (pairs)/ threes).

2. A direct quotation is the exact _____repetition_____ of what someone (or some outside source) said or wrote. (Use)/ Do not use) quotation marks around direct quotations.

3. An indirect quotation is a _____restatement of what someone said or wrote, but not word for word_____.
   (Use /Do not use) quotation marks with indirect quotations.

4. To set off a quotation within a quotation, use *single quotation marks* _____.

5. Put quotation marks around the titles of short works such as (give four examples) *Answers will vary.* _____
   Possible answers: short stories, poems, songs, articles _____.

6. For longer works such as magazines, novels, books, newspapers, and so on, either _____*italicize*_____ or
   _____*underline*_____ the titles.

Chapter Test

Circle the correct choice for each of the following items.

■ **TIP:** For advice on taking tests, see Appendix A.

1. If an underlined portion of this sentence is incorrect, select the revision that fixes it. If the sentence is correct as written, choose d.

   Do you think she was serious when she said, "Leave the building
   _____   A   _____   B
   immediately?"
   _____C_____

■ **RESOURCES:** *Testing Tool Kit*, a CD-ROM available with this book, has even more tests.

   a. "she"
   b. said "Leave
   c. immediately"?
   d. No change is necessary.

2. Choose the item that has no errors.

   a. "You need to strengthen that knee," Dr. Wheeler warned, "so be sure to do all of your exercises".

   b. "You need to strengthen that knee," Dr. Wheeler warned, so be sure to do all of your exercises.

   c. "You need to strengthen that knee," Dr. Wheeler warned, "so be sure to do all of your exercises."

3. Choose the item that has no errors.

   a. Eric pointed at an article titled 'New Alternative Fuel in Your Backyard.'

   b. Eric pointed at an article titled New Alternative Fuel in Your Backyard.

   c. Eric pointed at an article titled "New Alternative Fuel in Your Backyard."

4. If an underlined portion of this sentence is incorrect, select the revision that fixes it. If the sentence is correct as written, choose d.

   The man said, "I'm sorry, <u>officer,</u> but did I hear you correctly when you

                                         A

   said, <u>"Drive</u> into that <u>ditch'?"</u>

     B   C

   a. officer, "but   c. ditch?' "

   b. said, 'Drive   d. No change is necessary.

5. Choose the item that has no errors.

   a. Rachel told the security guard that she needed to enter the building for official business.

   b. Rachel told the security guard that "she needed to enter the building for official business."

   c. Rachel told the security guard that she "needed to enter the building for official business."

39

Other Punctuation

; : ( ) -- -

Understand What Punctuation Does

Punctuation helps readers understand your writing. If you use punctuation incorrectly, you send readers a confusing—or, even worse, a wrong—message. This chapter covers five punctuation marks that people sometimes use incorrectly because they aren't quite sure what they are supposed to do.

Practice Using Punctuation Correctly

Semicolon ;

Semicolons to Join Closely Related Sentences

Use a semicolon to join two very closely related sentences and make them into one sentence.

> In an interview, hold your head up and don't slouch; it is important to look alert.

> Make good eye contact; looking down is not appropriate in an interview.

■ **RESOURCES:** *Additional Resources* contains tests and supplemental exercises for this chapter.

Semicolons When Items in a List Contain Commas

Use semicolons to separate items in a list that itself contains commas. Otherwise, it is difficult for readers to tell where one item ends and another begins.

> For dinner, Bob ate an order of onion rings; a sixteen-ounce steak; a baked potato with sour cream, bacon bits, and cheese; a green salad; and a huge bowl of ice cream with fudge sauce.

> Because one item, *a baked potato with sour cream, bacon bits, and cheese,* contains its own commas, all items need to be separated by semicolons.

■ **TEACHING TIP.** Caution students not to use semicolons unless they feel certain about how they are used. Since many students use semicolons as a default solution when trying to increase sentence complexity, they end up overusing or misusing them.

Colon :

Colons before Lists

Use a colon after an independent clause to introduce a list. An independent clause contains a subject, a verb, and a complete thought. It can stand on its own as a sentence.

Many companies had booths at the computer fair: Apple, Microsoft, IBM, and Hewlett-Packard, to name just a few.

The fair featured a vast array of software: financial management applications, games, educational CDs, college-application programs, and so on.

Colons before Explanations or Examples

Use a colon after an independent clause to let readers know that you are about to provide an explanation or example of what you just wrote.

The fair was overwhelming: too much hype about too many things.

I picked up something I've been looking for: a new laptop.

A colon follows an independent clause. One of the most common misuses of colons is to use them after a phrase instead of an independent clause. Watch out especially for colons following the phrases *such as* or *for example*.

> **TIP:** See Commas (Chapter 36), Apostrophes (Chapter 37), and Quotation Marks (Chapter 38) for coverage of these punctuation marks. For more information on using semi-colons to join sentences, see Chapter 28.

INCORRECT	Tonya enjoys sports that are sometimes dangerous. For example: white-water rafting, wilderness skiing, rock climbing, and motorcycle racing.
CORRECT	Tonya enjoys sports that are sometimes dangerous: white-water rafting, wilderness skiing, rock climbing, and motorcycle racing.
INCORRECT	Jeff has many interests. Three are: bicycle racing, sculpting, and building musical instruments.
CORRECT	Jeff has many interests: bicycle racing, sculpting, and building musical instruments.

Colons in Business Correspondence and before Subtitles

Use a colon after a greeting (called a *salutation*) in a business letter and after the standard heading lines at the beginning of a memorandum.

Dear Mr. Hernandez:

To: Pat Toney
From: Susan Anker

Colons should also be used before subtitles—for example, "Running a Marathon: The Five Most Important Tips."

Parentheses ( )

Use parentheses to set off information that is not essential to the meaning of a sentence. Parentheses are always used in pairs and should be used sparingly.

> My grandfather's most successful invention (and also his first) was the electric blanket.

> When he died (at the age of ninety-six) he had more than 150 patents registered.

■ **TEACHING TIP:** Advise students that although an occasional set of parentheses is fine, too many are distracting.

Dash --

Dashes can be used like parentheses to set off additional information, particularly information that you want to emphasize. Make a dash by writing or typing two hyphens together. Do not put extra spaces around a dash.

> The final exam--worth 25 percent of your total grade--will be next Thursday.

> There will be no makeup exam--no exceptions--for this course.

A dash can also indicate a pause, much like a comma does.

> My uncle went on long fishing trips--without my aunt and cousins.

Hyphen -

Hyphens to Join Words That Form a Single Description

Writers often join two or more words that together form a single description of a person, place, or thing. To join the words, use a hyphen.

> Being a stockbroker is a high-risk career.

> Michelle is the ultimate decision-maker in our department.

> Jill was a lovely three-year-old girl.

When writing out numbers from twenty-one to ninety-nine, you should put a hyphen between the numbers.

> Seventy-five people participated in the demonstration.

Hyphens to Divide a Word at the End of a Line

Use a hyphen to divide a word when part of the word must continue on the next line.

> Critics accused the tobacco industry of increasing the amounts of nico-tine in cigarettes to encourage addiction and boost sales.

■ **TIP:** Most word processing programs automatically put a whole word on the next line rather than hyphenating it. When you write by hand, however, you need to hyphenate correctly.

■ **TIP:** For more practice using the types of punctuation covered in this chapter, visit Exercise Central at **bedfordstmartins.com/ realwriting**.

If you are not sure where to break a word, look it up in a dictionary. The word's main entry will show you where you can break the word: *dic • tio • nary*. If you still aren't confident that you are putting the hyphen in the right place, don't break the word; write it all on the next line.

Edit Paragraphs and Your Own Writing

■ **PRACTICE 1   EDITING PARAGRAPHS FOR OTHER PUNCTUATION MARKS**

Edit the following paragraphs by adding semicolons, colons, parentheses, dashes, and hyphens where needed. Circle the punctuation marks that you add. Keep in mind that in some places more than one type of punctuation may be acceptable.   *Answers may vary. Possible edits shown.*

1. (1) We already know that natural light can improve our mood; now it seems that light from the sun has other positive effects. (2) It may be possible for schools to improve student performance with one simple trick: letting the sun shine in. (3) One study indicates that natural light — even on a cloudy day — can help students learn. (4) The students in the study took standardized tests; those whose schools got more natural light had higher scores. (5) The scores improved by up to twenty-six percent, even when other factors affecting scores were taken into account. (6) In a related study, stores in a retail chain were compared; some had skylights and others did not. (7) The sun-filled stores had much higher sales — an average of forty percent higher. (8) Natural light in a building apparently makes people want to have more of any commodity (whether it is education or merchandise) the establishment offers.

2. (1) More than fifty thousand domestic adoptions take place in this country each year; despite minor difficulties, most of them go smoothly. (2) But a few years ago, the case of four-year-old Baby Richard highlighted an important issue: the rights of adoptive parents versus the rights of birth parents. (3) Richard was in a good situation: healthy, happy, loved by the couple who had adopted him at birth. (4) Then, Richard's other parents — the biological ones — appeared on the scene. (5) They were prepared to spend years battling the case in court; they desperately wanted their son back.

(6) Toward the end of her pregnancy, the birth mother felt alone, frightened, and confused; angry that her boyfriend had left her two weeks

before Richard was born⌢and unprepared for motherhood. (7) There-fore, a few days after the baby's birth, the baby was put up for adop-tion⌢his mother didn't want him. (8) When the boyfriend⌢the father of the baby⌢returned later, he was told that the baby had died. (9) Even-tually, however, the father discovered that his former girlfriend had lied⌢his son was still alive. (10) The biological parents found their long⌢lost child, who was living happily with his adoptive parents. (11) After years of legal arguments, the Illinois Supreme Court reached its ver-dict⌢Baby Richard belonged to the parents whose genes he shared. (12) The adoptive parents⌢the people who had loved and cared for Richard for his first four years⌢were bitterly disappointed.

PRACTICE 2   EDITING YOUR OWN WRITING FOR OTHER PUNCTUATION MARKS

As a final practice, edit a piece of your own writing for semicolons, colons, parentheses, dashes, and hyphens. It can be a paper you are working on for this course, a paper you've already finished, a paper for another course, or a piece of writing from your work or everyday life. You may want to try more than one way to use these punctuation marks in your writing. In your learn-ing journal, record any examples of sentences you edited, showing the sen-tences both before and after you edited them.

■ LEARNING JOURNAL:
What is one useful piece of in-formation you learned in this chapter?

Chapter Review

1. Semicolons (;) can be used to *join closely related sentences into one sentence* and to *separate items in a list that itself contains commas* .

2. Colons (:) can be used in what three ways?
   after an independent clause to introduce a list, after an independent clause to provide an explanation or example of what you just wrote, after a greeting in a business letter or memo heading and in subtitles

3. A colon in a sentence must always be used after an *independent clause* .

4. Parentheses ( ) set off information that is _____ *not essential* _____ to a sentence.

5. ___ *Dashes (--)* ___ also set off information in a sentence, usually information that you want to emphasize.

6. Hyphens (-) can be used to join two or more words that together *form a single description* and to _____ *break* _____ a word at the end of a line.

Chapter Test

Circle the correct choice for each of the following items.

■ **TIP:** For advice on taking tests, see Appendix A.

1. Choose the item that has no errors.

    a. Our car trip took us through Pittsburgh, Pennsylvania, Wheeling, West Virginia, and Bristol, Tennessee.

    b. Our car trip took us through Pittsburgh, Pennsylvania; Wheeling, West Virginia; and Bristol, Tennessee.

    c. Our car trip took us through Pittsburgh; Pennsylvania, Wheeling; West Virginia, and Bristol; Tennessee.

■ **RESOURCES:** *Testing Tool Kit*, a CD-ROM available with this book, has even more tests.

2. If an underlined portion of this sentence is incorrect, select the revision that fixes it. If the sentence is correct as written, choose d.

    Gary's dog (a seventeen-year-old easily won first prize in the Elderly
                        A

    Dog Show; she had the shiniest coat and the most youthful step.
        B   C

    a. (a seventeen-year-old)   c. coat: and

    b. Show-she   d. No change is necessary.

3. Choose the item that has no errors.

    a. As our computer specialist, you have three tasks: fixing malfunctioning computers, teaching people to use their computers, and not making any problem worse.

    b. As our computer specialist: you have three tasks, fixing malfunctioning computers, teaching people to use their computers, and not making any problem worse.

    c. As our computer specialist, you have three tasks: fixing malfunctioning computers, teaching people to use their computers (and not making any problem worse).

4. Choose the item that has no errors.

    a. Is there such a thing as a low-stress-job?

    b. Is there such a thing as a low-stress job?

    c. Is there such a thing as a low stress-job?

5. If an underlined portion of this sentence is incorrect, select the revision that fixes it. If the sentence is correct as written, choose d.

    You will have five and only five minutes to leave the office before the
                    A   B   C

    alarm sounds.

    a. five—and only five—   c. before; the

    b. to: leave   d. No change is necessary.

40

Capitalization
Using Capital Letters

Understand Three Rules of Capitalization

If you can remember the following rules, you will avoid the most common errors of capitalization.

THE THREE RULES OF CAPITALIZATION

Capitalize the first letter

- Of every new sentence
- In names of specific people, places, dates, and things
- Of important words in titles

■ **RESOURCES:** *Additional Resources* contains tests and supplemental exercises for this chapter.

Practice Capitalization

Capitalization of Sentences

Capitalize the first letter of each new sentence, including the first word of a direct quotation.

The superintendent was surprised.

He asked, "What's going on here?"

■ **PRACTICE 1   CAPITALIZING THE FIRST WORD IN A SENTENCE** . . . .

Edit the following paragraph, changing lowercase letters to capital letters as needed.

(1) Occasionally, a phrase or sentence uttered by a president is so memorable that it becomes part of American history. (2) one example occurred before the start of the Civil War, when Abraham Lincoln

■ **TEACHING TIP:** Remind students that they should not write or type in all capital letters because it will be more difficult for them to recognize and edit their capitalization errors.

581

■ **TIP:** For more practice
with capitalization, visit
Exercise Central at
**bedfordstmartins.com/
realwriting**.

stated, "~~a~~ A house divided against itself cannot stand." (3) ~~a~~ Almost seventy
years later, in the midst of the Great Depression, Franklin Roosevelt declared, "~~w~~ We have nothing to fear but fear itself."

Capitalization of Names of Specific People, Places, Dates, and Things

The general rule is to capitalize the first letter in names of specific people,
places, dates, and things. Do not capitalize a generic name such as *college* as
opposed to the specific name: *Carroll State College.* Look at the examples for
each group.

People

■ **TEACHING TIP:** Have students come up with their own
"specific" and "not specific"
examples.

Capitalize the first letter in names of specific people and in titles used with
names of specific people.

SPECIFIC	NOT SPECIFIC
Jean Heaton	my neighbor
Professor Fitzgerald	your math professor

SPECIFIC	NOT SPECIFIC
Dr. Cornog	the doctor
Aunt Pat, Mother	my aunt, your mother

The name of a family member is capitalized when the family member is
being addressed directly: Happy Birthday, *Mother.* In other instances, do not
capitalize: It is my *mother's* birthday.

The word *president* is not capitalized unless it comes directly before a
name as part of that person's title: *President* George W. Bush.

Places

Capitalize the first letter in names of specific buildings, streets, cities, states,
regions, and countries.

SPECIFIC	NOT SPECIFIC
Bolton Town Hall	the town hall
Arlington Street	our street
Dearborn Heights	my hometown
Arizona	this state
the South	the southern region
Spain	that country

Do not capitalize directions in a sentence.

Drive *south* for five blocks.

Dates

Capitalize the first letter in the names of days, months, and holidays. Do not capitalize the names of the seasons (winter, spring, summer, fall).

SPECIFIC	NOT SPECIFIC
Wednesday	tomorrow
June 25	summer
Thanksgiving	my birthday

> **Language Note:** Some languages, such as Spanish, French, and Italian, do not capitalize days, months, and languages. In English, such words must be capitalized.
>
> **INCORRECT**   I study russian every monday, wednesday, and friday from january through may.
>
> **CORRECT**   I study **Russian** every **Monday, Wednesday**, and **Friday** from **January** through **May**.

■ **ESL:** Ask ESL students to identify any English capitalization rules that differ from the rules in their first language.

Organizations, Companies, and Groups

SPECIFIC	NOT SPECIFIC
Taft Community College	my college
Microsoft	that software company
Alcoholics Anonymous	the self-help group

Languages, Nationalities, and Religions

SPECIFIC	NOT SPECIFIC
English, Greek, Spanish	my first language
Christianity, Buddhism	your religion

The names of languages should be capitalized even if you aren't referring to a specific course.

I am taking psychology and *Spanish.*

Courses

SPECIFIC	NOT SPECIFIC
Composition 101	a writing course
Introduction to Psychology	my psychology course

Commercial Products

SPECIFIC	NOT SPECIFIC
Diet Pepsi	a diet cola
Skippy peanut butter	peanut butter

■ PRACTICE 2   CAPITALIZING NOUNS

Edit the following sentences by adding capitalization as needed or removing capitalization where it is inappropriate.

EXAMPLE: New york is one of the best Cities for a vacation.
(Y over y; c over C)

1. Unlike most american cities, New York has a great Mass Transportation system, so visitors don't need a car.
(A; m; t)

2. That's fortunate, for most visitors would not want to drive on the Streets of Manhattan.
(s)

3. You can arrive by Train at pennsylvania station or grand central station.
(t; P; S; G; C; S)

4. New york is famous as the home of the Statue of liberty.
(Y; L)

5. There are many internationally known buildings, such as the empire state building.
(E; S; B)

6. If you like Museums, New York has more than its share: the metropolitan museum of art, the american museum of natural history, and the guggenheim museum, to name just a few.
(m; M; M; A; A; M; N; H; G; M)

7. One of the best things about the city is the Restaurants, which serve food from all over the world.
(r)

8. You can dine on indian, ethiopian, cuban, or italian food within the space of a few blocks.
(I; E; C; I)

9. Famous new yorkers include gwyneth Paltrow, Woody allen, and al sharpton.
(N; Y; G; A; A; S)

10. The new york stock exchange on wall street is watched around the world.
(N; Y; S; E; W; S)

Capitalization of Titles

When you write the title of a book, movie, television program, magazine, newspaper, article, story, song, paper, poem, and so on, capitalize the first word and all important words. The only words that do not need to be capitalized (unless they are the first word) are *the, a, an,* coordinating conjunctions (*and, but, for, nor, or, so, yet*), and prepositions.

■ **TIP:** For more on punctuating titles, see Chapter 38. For a list of common prepositions, see Chapter 20.

I Love Lucy was a long-running television program.

Both *USA Today* and the *New York Times* are popular newspapers.

"Once More to the Lake" is one of Chuck's favorite essays.

■ **PRACTICE 3 CAPITALIZING TITLES** . . . .

Edit the following sentences by capitalizing titles as needed.

EXAMPLE: Some people believe that the myth of the American West
began with movie westerns like *shane* and *stagecoach.* (*S*, *S*)

1. The American West has been a common topic in popular culture since early films like *the big trail.* (*T B T*)

2. Western songs, including Gene Autry's version of "back in the saddle again" and "the yellow rose of texas," were radio favorites. (*B S A T Y R T*)

3. Television, too, relied on westerns in its early years, making *gunsmoke* (*G*) one of the longest-running shows of all time.

4. Clint Eastwood first became famous in the TV western *rawhide.* (*R*)

5. John Ford movies, including *the searchers* and *she wore a yellow ribbon,* (*T S S W Y R*) popularized an image of the West.

. . . .

Edit Paragraphs and Your Own Writing

■ **PRACTICE 4 EDITING PARAGRAPHS FOR CAPITALIZATION** . . . . . .

Edit the following paragraphs by capitalizing as needed and removing unnecessary capitalization.

(1) The names and accomplishments of some presidents of the united states are familiar to almost every american. (*U S A*) (2) Most people are

familiar with george washington or abraham lincoln, for example. (3) being president is no guarantee that a person will have lasting fame, however. (4) How many of us could recall anything about millard fillmore, the thirteenth president of the united states? (5) The millard fillmore society celebrates his birthday every year on january 7. (6) It also publishes a magazine called *milestones with millard* and sponsors an essay contest. (7) Nevertheless, the facts about fillmore are known mainly to students of history.

(8) Fillmore was the whig party's candidate for vice president in 1848. (9) The candidate for president was zachary taylor, a hero of the mexican war. (10) american voters were divided on the subject of slavery, and the democrats and the free soil party took opposite sides on the issue. (11) Taylor, who remained neutral, was elected, but he died in office, so fillmore became president in 1850. (12) The whig party decided to nominate another mexican war hero, winfield scott, instead of fillmore in 1852, so fillmore was never elected president of the united states. (13) The newspaperman h.l. mencken wrote a column in the *new york evening mail* in 1917 claiming that fillmore had installed the white house's first bathtub. (14) Mencken had intended the column as a joke, but many people believed it. (15) poor millard fillmore—when he is remembered at all, it is usually to be given credit for something he didn't really do.

■   PRACTICE 5   **EDITING YOUR OWN WRITING FOR CAPITALIZATION** . . .

■ **LEARNING JOURNAL:**
What problem with capitalization do you have most often? How can you edit more effectively for this problem in the future?

As a final practice, edit a piece of your own writing for capitalization. It can be a paper you are working on for this course, a paper you've already finished, a paper for another course, or a recent piece of writing from your work or everyday life. In your learning journal, record any examples of sentences with capitalization problems that you find, along with edited versions of these sentences.

Chapter Review

1. Capitalize the ___*first letter*___ of every new sentence.

2. Capitalize the first letter in names of specific ___*people*___, ___*places*___, ___*dates*___, and ___*things*___.

3. Capitalize the first letter of ___*important words*___ in titles.

Chapter Test

Circle the correct choice for each of the following items.

■ **TIP:** For advice on taking tests, see Appendix A.

1. Choose the item that has no errors.
    a. My daughter's school, Spitzer High School, no longer sells pepsi and other sodas in its vending machines.
    b. My daughter's school, Spitzer high school, no longer sells pepsi and other sodas in its vending machines.
    c. My daughter's school, Spitzer High School, no longer sells Pepsi and other sodas in its vending machines.

■ **RESOURCES:** *Testing Tool Kit*, a CD-ROM available with this book, has even more tests.

2. If an underlined portion of this sentence is incorrect, select the revision that fixes it. If the sentence is correct as written, choose d.

    Will our company <u>President</u> speak at the <u>annual meeting</u>, or will
                    A   B

    <u>Dr. Anders</u>?
      C

    a. president
    b. Annual Meeting
    c. doctor Anders
    d. No change is necessary.

3. Choose the item that has no errors.
    a. Which Library do you go to, Hill Library or Barry Township Library?
    b. Which library do you go to, Hill Library or Barry Township Library?
    c. Which library do you go to, Hill library or Barry Township library?

4. If an underlined portion of this sentence is incorrect, select the revision that fixes it. If the sentence is correct as written, choose d.

    In my <u>english 99</u> class <u>last summer</u>, we read some interesting essays by
            A   B

    <u>famous authors</u>.
       C

    a. English 99
    b. Summer
    c. Famous Authors
    d. No change is necessary.

5. If an underlined portion of this sentence is incorrect, select the revision that fixes it. If the sentence is correct as written, choose d.

Of the states in the $\underset{\text{A}}{\underline{\text{East}}}$, one can travel the farthest $\underset{\text{B}}{\underline{\text{North}}}$ in $\underset{\text{C}}{\underline{\text{Maine}}}$.

a. east   c. maine

b. north   d. No change is necessary.

Part Seven Test
Punctuation and Capitalization

Circle the correct choice for each of the following items.

1. If an underlined portion of this sentence is incorrect, select the revision that fixes it. If the sentence is correct as written, choose d.

   When <u>geese landed</u> in our <u>backyard our</u> three-year-old chased <u>them away</u>.
          A   B   C

   a. geese, landed   c. them, away
   (b.) backyard, our   d. No change is necessary.

2. Choose the correct words to fill in the blank.

   I grew up just a few miles from our college, but my roommate is from

   _____.

   (a.) Columbus, Ohio   c. columbus, Ohio
   b. columbus, ohio

3. Choose the correct words to fill in the blank.

   "I make all my phone calls from my _____ Rita, "and it costs nothing."
   a. computer, said   (c.) computer," said
   b. computer", said

4. If an underlined portion of this sentence is incorrect, select the revision that fixes it. If the sentence is correct as written, choose d.

   The <u>politicians: those who are honest: will tell</u> <u>you that</u> our town must
                               A   B
   stop <u>businesses</u> from moving out.
        C

   (a.) —those who are honest—   c. Businesses
   b. you, "that   d. No change is necessary.

5. If an underlined portion of this sentence is incorrect, select the revision that fixes it. If the sentence is correct as written, choose d.

   We are renting this house, so it is not <u>Ryan's</u>, the <u>Douglas's</u>, or <u>our's</u>.
                                         A   B   C

   a. Ryans   (c.) ours
   b. Douglas'   d. No change is necessary.

6. If an underlined portion of this sentence is incorrect, select the revision that fixes it. If the sentence is correct as written, choose d.

Lincoln's famous Gettysburg <u>Address which</u> he delivered in about two
                                       A

<u>minutes, followed</u> a two-hour <u>speech that</u> hardly anyone remembers.
    B   **C**

(a.) Address, which   c. speech, that

b. minutes followed   d. No change is necessary.

7. Choose the correct words to fill in the blank.

I include in my salads some of my favorite _____, red peppers, mushrooms, and scallions.

a. foods lettuce   (c.) foods: lettuce

b. foods. Lettuce

8. Choose the correct words to fill in the blank.

That ash tree may be only four feet tall _____ it will eventually be eighty feet tall.

(a.) now, but   b. now but,   c. now, but,

9. If an underlined portion of this sentence is incorrect, select the revision that fixes it. If the sentence is correct as written, choose d.

Whenever I hear your car pass by, <u>its</u> just too loud, so <u>it's</u> time to have
                                 A   **B**

<u>its</u> muffler replaced.
C

(a.) it's   c. it's

b. its   d. No change is necessary.

10. If an underlined portion of this sentence is incorrect, select the revision that fixes it. If the sentence is correct as written, choose d.

Susannah reminded us <u>that her</u> teacher said <u>that</u> "tonight is <u>Amateur</u>
                      A   **B**   **C**

Ballroom Dancers' Night.

a. that "her   c. "Amateur

(b.) that tonight   d. No change is necessary.

11. Choose the correct words to fill in the blank.

On _____ people around the world realized that the feared Y2K problem was no problem at all.

a. January, 1, 2000   (c.) January 1, 2000,

b. January 1, 2000

■ **RESOURCES:** *Additional Resources* includes reproducible answer keys for the tests that conclude Parts Four through Seven. For each question, the keys list the section of *Real Writing* that students should study if they missed the question.

12. If an underlined portion of this sentence is incorrect, select the revision that fixes it. If the sentence is correct as written, choose d.

For <u>history 101</u>, I wrote a paper <u>about why</u> and how the
          A   B
<u>Washington Monument</u> was built.
          C

    (a.) History 101   c. Washington monument
    b. about, why   d. No change is necessary.

13. If an underlined portion of this sentence is incorrect, select the revision that fixes it. If the sentence is correct as written, choose d.

<u>Johann wants</u> <u>to paint</u> the walls, the <u>ceiling and the</u> floor of his living
          A   B   C
room black.

    a. Johann, wants   (c.) ceiling, and the
    b. to, paint   d. No change is necessary.

14. If an underlined portion of this sentence is incorrect, select the revision that fixes it. If the sentence is correct as written, choose d.

My <u>sister, who</u> makes beautiful quilts, gets <u>vintage textiles</u> and other
          A   B
<u>hard to find</u> fabrics on eBay.
          C

    a. sister who   (c.) hard-to-find
    b. vintage-textiles   d. No change is necessary.

15. Choose the correct word to fill in the blank.

Marisa promised that in three _____ time, we would see plenty
of A's on her report card.

    a. month's   b. months   (c.) months'

16. Choose the correct word to fill in the blank.

"Please don't try to pet the cat," said Thomas. _____ might
scratch you."

    a. "he   (b.) "He   c. He

17. Choose the correct words to fill in the blank.

That athlete ____ _____ can't seem to win an Olympic medal.

    (a.) , a national champion in her own country,
    b. ; a national champion in her own country
    c. a national champion in her own country

18. If an underlined portion of this sentence is incorrect, select the revision that fixes it. If the sentence is correct as written, choose d.

the TV technician said, "A new TV would cost about as much as the
<u>the</u> ... <u>technician</u> ... <u>"A</u>
  A   B   C

repair of this old one."

a. The   c. a

b. Technician   d. No change is necessary.

19. Choose the correct item to fill in the blank.

A record number of runners _____ ran in this year's Green Hills Marathon.

a. : 1,254   b. ; 1,254   c. (1,254)

20. Choose the correct punctuation to fill in the blank.

Mr. Ferrantino is a famous painter _____ his son is even more talented.

a. ,   b. ;   c. :

Part Eight
Readings for Writers

41

Introduction to the Readings

In this part of the book, you will find twenty essays (in Chapters 42–50) that demonstrate the types of writing you studied in Part Two of this book. Chapter 51 presents a mini-casebook of readings on the theme of stereotypes.

These readings are more than just good models of writing. They also tell great stories, argue passionately about controversial issues, and present a wide range of perspectives and information. These essays can also provide you with ideas for your own writing, both in and out of school. Most important, they offer you a chance to become a better reader and writer by seeing how others write.

How Can These Readings Help You?

Reading the essays in this part of the book will help you develop several different abilities.

Your Ability to Write

The essays in this section are good examples of the types of writing you are doing in your writing course. By looking at how someone else states main ideas, provides supporting details, organizes ideas, and introduces and concludes an essay, you gain a better sense of how you might write a similar type of essay. The essays can also help you choose writing topics. As you react to an author's ideas, you may discover ideas of your own to explore. It's a good idea to keep a reading journal to record these ideas.

Your Ability to Read Critically

To get the most out of what you read, you need to read critically. Critical reading means that you ask yourself why writers have made the points they did and whether you agree. To help you read critically, the essays in this section contain many notes and questions. For more on critical reading, see Chapter 1.

Your Ability to Understand Other Experiences and Points of View

The authors of these readings vary in age, gender, race, culture, and experience, and their writing reflects their many differences. In a rapidly changing world, your ability to understand, appreciate, and interact with people whose outlooks differ from your own is essential.

Increasingly, employers value social skills, communication skills, and the ability to work as part of a team. Being able to understand new and different viewpoints can help you work well in a group. Another benefit may be more personal: As you read more and learn to see things through other people's eyes, you may discover new perspectives on your own life.

Your Ability to Help Yourself

Much practical information is in written form, either print or electronic. As a good reader, you will be able to find out whatever you need to know to get what you want from life. The list of topics is endless: making money, investing, starting your own business, finding a job, raising a family, buying a car at the best price, protecting yourself from unfairness, and so on.

42

Narration

Each essay in this chapter uses narration to get its main point across to the reader. As you read these essays, consider how they achieve the four basics of good narration that are listed below and discussed in Chapter 9 of this book.

■■ FOUR BASICS OF GOOD NARRATION

1. It reveals something of importance to the writer (the main point).

2. It includes all of the major events of the story (primary support).

3. It brings the story to life with details about the major events (secondary support).

4. It presents the events in a clear order, usually according to when they happened.

Walter Scanlon

It's Time I Shed My Ex-Convict Status

Walter F. Scanlon (b. 1937) began working with alcohol and drug abusers after he had himself sought out and entered a twelve-step program upon his release from prison. Scanlon had dropped out of high school and then spent more than a decade in hospitals, in jail, and on the streets. Today, he holds a bachelor's degree from Pace University, an M.B.A. from the New York Institute of Technology, and a Ph.D. in psychology from Columbus University. In addition to being a specialist in workplace and family interventions for individuals with drug, alcohol, and other problems, he lectures widely. Recently, with Nick Lessa, he coauthored *Wiley Concise Guides to Mental Health: Substance Use Disorders* (2005).

Scanlon observes that "there were long periods in my life when most decisions were made for me, not by me. Writing gave me a way to circumvent all that was happening around me and better understand what was happening within me." In the following essay, Scanlon tells the story of the changes in his life over the past thirty years. (For more on Walter Scanlon and an example of his writing at work, see pp. 178–179.)

GUIDING QUESTION
Why does Scanlon feel that he should be able to shed his ex-convict status? Is his personal story convincing?

■ **IDEA JOURNAL:** Tell about a time when you overcame a difficulty in your life.

REFLECT: What is the purpose of the background information in paragraphs 1 and 2? Is it effective?

_____

_____

_____

IDENTIFY: Put an X by Scanlon's educational and job accomplishments in this paragraph.

REFLECT: Why does Scanlon give the reader these details?

_____

_____

_____

IDENTIFY: Underline the sentence that explains why Scanlon was not eligible for higher-level positions.

Thirty years ago I decided to drastically turn my life around. With a state-issued olive suit on my back, a high-school equivalency diploma and $40 travel money in my pocket, I became an ex-convict. I had done my time—almost five years in all—and now had the opportunity to redeem myself. I felt almost optimistic. As the huge outer gate of New York state's Clinton Prison slammed behind me, the discharge officer bid me farewell: "Get your act together," he bellowed with a mix of sincerity and humor. "I don't want to see you back here any time soon." A Department of Corrections van sat rumbling at the prison's checkpoint—my ride to the Greyhound bus depot.

As we pulled away, the towering walls, razor wire, and iron gates of the prison grew even more awesome, and the looming gun towers more ominous.[1] It was a bright early autumn morning, my thirty-second birthday was days away, and the last ten years of my life had been spent in and out of men's shelters, hospitals, and prisons. I wanted to make it this time.

Alcohol and other drugs had been my failing. Realizing I would need help, I sought an organization of other recovering addicts. Within a few days I landed a job in a metal-plating factory and rented a tiny furnished room. *X* On the urging of a new friend who had a similar past, I soon took my first *X* college course. My first grade was a disappointing C, but before long I was *X* scoring A's and B's. I also got better jobs, eventually landing a counseling *X* job in a substance-abuse treatment program. On job applications, I left questions about past arrests and convictions blank. I'd read that this would probably go unnoticed and, if it didn't, it would be better to discuss such matters in person. Time passed and, in a few short years, I completed college. I went on to get my master's degree and, using my graduate thesis as *X* its foundation, I wrote a book on drugs in the workplace. *X*

Today I live a full life, enjoying what most people enjoy: movies, books, theater, good food, and good friends. My significant other is a South Asian woman and her diverse circle of friends has enriched my life. My annual income as a substance-abuse specialist is adequate, my standing in the community solid, and my commitment to continued recovery is permanent.

All of these qualities notwithstanding, I remain, irrevocably,[2] an ex-convict. Although the years have removed all but hazy memories of addiction, hospitalizations, street living, and prison, I secretly carry the baggage of a former offender. As my qualifications for higher-level positions grew, so, too, did the potential for a more detailed scrutiny[3] of my past. Opportunities for better jobs that colleagues took for granted were not so available to

---

[1] **ominous:** threatening

[2] **irrevocably:** permanently

[3] **scrutiny:** inspection

me. On virtually every job application, the question continued to haunt me: "Have you ever been convicted of a felony or misdemeanor or denied bond in any state?" Staring blankly at the application, I would often wonder, will this nightmare ever end? For minorities, who have a higher rate of incarceration, the nightmare is even more likely to occur.

To the average person, the ex-convict is an individual of questionable character. And without the experience of meeting a rehabilitated offender, there is little chance that this image will change. It is reinforced by the fact that the only thing usually newsworthy about an ex-convict is bad news— another arrest.

6

■ **TEACHING TIP:** Point out to students how Scanlon gives plenty of examples in the course of telling his story—for instance, examples of how he turned his life around after prison and of the challenges he faced while doing so.

Yet the real news is that many former offenders are, like me, rehabilitated members of society. No one would guess at our pasts. We don't deserve kudos[4] for not committing crimes, but our failings should not supersede[5] decades of personal growth and responsible citizenship. Unfortunately, that's often what happens.

7

Under employment discrimination laws, hiring decisions cannot be made on the basis of age, sex, or the color of a person's skin. A job applicant does not have to reveal a disability or medical condition, including former drug dependence. Employability is based on the ability to perform the essential function of the job. Yet the former offender, whose past may be directly related to substance abuse, is expected to reveal his transgression.

8

No one is born an ex-convict; the title is earned and the individual must accept responsibility. Yet wouldn't it be nice if there were an ex-ex-con status? It would feel good not to panic at the sight of a job application and that dreaded question: "Have you ever been convicted of a felony or misdemeanor or denied bond in any state?" This question, without exclusionary criteria ([for example,] within the last ten years), serves no one's interest. To those of us who have paid our debt to society, it's a form of discrimination that undermines our efforts to continue to rebuild our lives.

9

REFLECT: How might discrimination against ex-convicts hurt their efforts "to continue to rebuild" their lives?

■ **SUMMARIZE AND RESPOND** . . . .

In your reading journal or elsewhere, summarize the main point of "It's Time I Shed My Ex-Convict Status." Then, go back and check off the support for this main idea. Next, write a brief summary of the essay. Finally, write a brief response to the reading. Should ex-convicts, like Scanlon, be able to shed their status?

■ **CHECK YOUR COMPREHENSION** . . . .

1. An alternate title for this essay could be
    a. "Once an Ex-Convict, Always an Ex-Convict."
    b. "Paying a Debt to Society."
    c. "Rehabilitation Rights."
    (d.) "Employment Discrimination against Ex-Convicts."

---

[4] **kudos:** credit, praise

[5] **supersede:** replace

2. The main idea of this essay is that
   a. alcohol and drug use can lead to crime and time in prison.
   b. ex-convicts should not have to reveal their status on job applications.
   c. ex-convicts can be rehabilitated.
   d. ex-convicts make good employees.

3. What does Scanlon mean when he writes that "our failings should not supersede decades of personal growth and responsible citizenship"?
   a. Ex-convicts who have worked hard to enter society should not be held back by their past mistakes.
   b. Ex-convicts need to grow more and prove that they are responsible citizens before they are forgiven for their mistakes.
   c. Mistakes of ex-convicts should always be remembered.
   d. Ex-convicts need to learn from their mistakes.

4. If you are unfamiliar with the following words, use a dictionary to check their meanings: *drastically, bellowed* (para. 1); *incarceration* (5); *transgression* (8); *misdemeanor, exclusionary, undermines* (9).

READ CRITICALLY

1. What is Scanlon's tone in this essay?

2. In paragraph 6, according to Scanlon what could be done to begin to change the image of ex-convicts? What reinforces the image most people have of ex-convicts?

3. In paragraph 8, what does Scanlon feel should be the basis of employment? Do you agree with him?

4. In paragraph 9, Scanlon writes that asking a question about conviction "without exclusionary criteria . . . serves no one's interest." Why do you think he added the term "exclusionary criteria" to his statement?

5. What are some of Scanlon's accomplishments after he served his time? Do these help to support his main point? Why or why not?

WRITE

■ **TIP:** For a sample narration paragraph, see page 107.

WRITE A PARAGRAPH: Write a paragraph that tells about a time when you did something wrong and tried to make up for it, but still had it held against you.

WRITE AN ESSAY: Scanlon uses personal experience in this essay to make a point about discrimination of ex-convicts. To support his thesis, he uses many specific details. In your essay, write about a time when you felt discriminated against in some way. Like Scanlon, share your personal experience and include details and examples that allow the reader to understand your point of view.

Pat Conroy

Chili Cheese Dogs, My Father, and Me

The writing of Pat Conroy (b. 1945) draws heavily on his life experiences. *The Water Is Wide* (1972) recounts his days teaching at a one-room school in South Carolina. *The Great Santini* (1976) describes the difficulty of growing up with a strict military father. Several of Conroy's books have been made into movies. The most famous of these films is *The Prince of Tides* (1991), which was based on Conroy's 1986 novel of the same name. His most recent books are *My Losing Season* (2002), about a year on the high school basketball team at the Citadel, and *The Pat Conroy Cookbook: Recipes of My Life* (2005), a mix of food writing and memoir.

In the following essay Conroy uses narration to tell a story about two important relationships—with food and with his father—and how they came together.

■ **TEACHING TIP:** Students should see that this essay has three parts: (1) the story of the author's sixth birthday, (2) the story of his first visit to Chicago, and (3) the story of his final days with his father.

GUIDING QUESTION

What is the significance of chili cheese dogs in the narrator's relationship with his father?

■ **IDEA JOURNAL:** Describe a relationship of yours that's changed over time.

When I was growing up and lived at my grandmother's house in Atlanta, 1 my mother would take us after church to The Varsity, an institution with more religious significance to me than any cathedral in the city. Its food was celebratory, fresh, and cleansing to the soul. It still remains one of my favorite restaurants in the world.

I had then what I order now—a habit that has not deviated[1] since my 2 sixth birthday in 1951, when my grandmother, Stanny, ordered for me what she considered the picture-perfect Varsity meal: a chili cheese hot dog, onion rings, and a soft drink called "The Big Orange."

On that occasion, when my family had finished the meal, my mother lit 3 six candles on a cupcake she had made, and Stanny, Papa Jack, my mother, and my sister Carol sang "Happy Birthday" as I blushed with pleasure and surprise. I put together for the first time that the consumption of food and celebration was a natural and fitting combination. It was also the first time I realized that no one in my family could carry a tune.

When my father returned home from the Korean War, he refused to be- 4 lieve that The Varsity—or the American South, for that matter—could produce a hot dog worthy of consumption. My Chicago-born father was a fierce partisan[2] of his hometown, and he promised me that he would take me to eat a real "red hot" after we attended my first White Sox game.

That summer, we stayed with my dad's parents on the South Side of 5 Chicago. There, I met the South Side Irish for the first time on their own turf. My uncles spent the summer teasing me about being a southern hick as they played endless games of pinochle[3] with my father. Then, my father

REFLECT: Based on paragraph 4, how would you describe the father's personality?

_____

_____

_____

[1] **deviated:** changed

[2] **partisan:** one who takes sides

[3] **pinochle:** card game popular in the mid-1900s

took me for the sacramental[4] rite of passage: my first major league baseball game. We watched the White Sox beat the despised Yankees.

After the game, my father drove my Uncle Willie and me to a place 6
called Superdawg to get a red hot. He insisted that the Superdawg sold the best red hots in the city. When my father handed me the first red hot I had ever eaten, he said, "This will make you forget The Varsity for all time." That summer, I learned that geography itself was one of the great formative[5] shapers of identity. The red hot was delicious, but in my lifetime I will never forsake[6] the pleasure of The Varsity chili cheese dog.

When my father was dying of colon cancer in 1998, he would spend his 7
days with me at home on Fripp Island, South Carolina, then go back to Beaufort at night to stay with my sister Kathy, who is a nurse and was in charge of his medications. Since I was responsible for his daily lunch, I told him I would cook him anything he wanted as long as I could find it in a South Carolina supermarket.

"Anything, pal?" my father asked.   8

"Anything," I said.   9

Thus, the last days between a hard-core Marine and his edgy son, who 10
had spent his career writing about horrific father-son relationships, became our best days as we found ourselves united by the glorious subject of food.

My father was a simple man with simple tastes, but he was well-traveled, 11
and he began telling me his life story as we spent our long hours together. The first meal he ordered was an egg sandwich, a meal I had never heard of but one that kept him alive during the Depression.[7] He told me, "You put a fried egg on two slices of white bread which has been spread with ketchup."

"It sounds repulsive,[8]" I said.   12

"It's delicious," he replied.   13

When Dad spoke of his service in Korea, I fixed him kimchi (spicy pick- 14
led vegetables), and when he talked about his yearlong duty on an aircraft carrier on the Mediterranean, I made spaghetti carbonara[9] or gazpacho.[10] But most of the time, I made him elaborate sandwiches: salami or baloney tiered high with lettuce, tomatoes, and red onions. The more elaborate I made them, the more my father loved them.

He surprised me one day by asking me to make him some red hots, done 15
"the Chicago way, pal." That day, I called Superdawg and was surprised that it was still in business. A very pleasant woman told me to dress the red hots with relish, mustard, onion, and hot peppers with a pickle on the side. "If you put ketchup on it, just throw it in the trash," she added.

The following week, he surprised me again by ordering up some chili 16
cheese dogs, "just like they make at The Varsity in Atlanta." So I called The Varsity and learned step by step how to make one of their scrumptious chili cheese dogs.

PREDICT: What do you think will happen next?

_____

_____

[4] **sacramental:** sacred

[5] **formative:** giving form to

[6] **forsake:** give up

[7] **Depression:** a serious economic downturn lasting from 1929 until the late 1930s

[8] **repulsive:** disgusting

[9] **spaghetti carbonara:** pasta with a sauce of cream, eggs, and bacon

[10] **gazpacho:** a cold vegetable soup from Spain

When my father began his quick, slippery descent into death, my brothers and sisters drove from all directions to sit six-hour shifts at his bedside. We learned that watching a fighter pilot die is not an easy thing. One morning, I arrived for my shift and heard screaming coming from the house. I raced inside and found Carol yelling at Dad: "Dad, you've got to tell me you're proud of me. You've got to do it before you die."

17 REFLECT: Why does Carol act as she does here?

_____

_____

I walked Carol out of the bedroom and sat her down on the sofa. "That's Don Conroy in there, Carol—not Bill Cosby,[11]" I said. "You've got to learn how to translate Dad. He says it, but in his own way."

18

Two weeks before my father died, he presented me with a gift of infinite price. I made him the last chili cheese dog from The Varsity's recipe that he would ever eat. When he finished, I took the plate back to the kitchen and was shocked to hear him say, "I think the chili cheese dog is the best red hot I've ever eaten."

19

There is a translation to all of this, and here is how it reads: In the last days of his life, my father was telling me how much he loved me, his oldest son, and he was doing it with food.

20 SUMMARIZE: How do the father's words show that he loves his son?

_____

_____

■ SUMMARIZE AND RESPOND . . . .

In your reading journal or elsewhere, summarize the main point of "Chili Cheese Dogs, My Father, and Me." Then, go back and check off the support for this main point. Next, write a brief summary of the essay. Finally, write a brief response to the reading. What impression does Conroy create of his changing relationship with his father?

■ CHECK YOUR COMPREHENSION . . . .

1. An alternate title for this essay could be
    a. "My Father, the Fighter Pilot."
    (b.) "How My Father Told Me He Loved Me."
    c. "How I Learned to Love Chili Cheese Dogs."
    d. "The Varsity vs. Superdawg."

2. The main point of this essay is that
    a. chili cheese dogs are better tasting than red hots.
    b. men can learn to be excellent and creative cooks.
    (c.) people can communicate their affection for others in indirect ways.
    d. only when a parent is dying does a child learn what that parent is really like.

---

[11] **Bill Cosby:** actor who played a wise, kind father in a 1980s TV comedy

3. What is Conroy's point in telling the story of his sister Carol's angry outburst toward their father (para. 17)?

    a. He wants readers to understand that he comes from a family in which yelling is common.

    b. He wants to show the kind of relationship he has with his sister.

    c. He wants readers to see that anger is not useful in dealing with parents.

    (d.) He wants to show how difficult it is for his father to express feelings for his children.

4. If you are unfamiliar with the following words, use a dictionary to check their meanings: *cathedral* (para. 1); *consumption* (3); *hick, rite of passage* (5); *geography* (6); *edgy, horrific, glorious* (10); *elaborate, tiered* (14); *scrumptious* (16); *infinite* (19).

■   **READ CRITICALLY** . . . .

1. What details show Conroy's father's change in attitude toward The Varsity's chili cheese dogs? What is the significance of this change?

2. What three stories does Conroy narrate in this essay? When does he shift to telling about his father's last days? How do you know?

3. Based on details from the essay, describe the ways in which father and son are "united by the glorious subject of food"?

4. Beginning in paragraph 8, Conroy includes a number of direct quotations from himself and his father. What is the effect of Conroy's presenting this dialogue?

5. Though this essay tells a sad story overall, it has some humorous moments. What are they, and how did they affect you?

■   **WRITE** . . . .

    WRITE A PARAGRAPH: Write a paragraph that tells about a time when a particular food played a special role during a family celebration, such as a birthday or a holiday. Like Conroy, include details about family members and your own response to the occasion.

    WRITE AN ESSAY: In an essay, trace the history of your relationship with an older family member or someone else who has played a significant role in your life. As Conroy does in writing about his relationship with his father, tell specific stories about your times with this person, and suggest ways in which your relationship changed over time.

. . . .

43

Illustration

Each essay in this chapter uses illustration to get its main point across to the reader. As you read these essays, consider how they achieve the four basics of good illustration that are listed below and discussed in Chapter 10 of this book.

 FOUR BASICS OF GOOD ILLUSTRATION

1. It has a point to illustrate.
2. It gives specific examples that show, explain, or prove the point.
3. It gives details to support these examples.
4. It uses enough examples to get the writer's point across.

Dianne Hales

Why Are We So Angry?

PREDICT: After reading the title, what do you expect this essay to do?

Dianne Hales specializes in writing about mental health, fitness, and other issues related to the body and mind. She contributes regularly to *Parade* magazine and *Ladies Home Journal,* and she has written several college-level health textbooks. In her critically acclaimed book *Just Like a Woman* (2000), she examined assumptions about the biological differences between women and men. Most recently, she coauthored *Think to Be Thin. 101 Psychological Ways to Lose Weight* (2005). Both the American Psychiatric Association and the American Psychological Association have presented Hales with awards for excellence in writing. In addition, she has earned an Exceptional Media Merit Award (EMMA) from the National Women's Political Caucus for health reporting. She lives in Marin County, California.

In the following article, Hales uses vivid examples to illustrate the "rage" phenomenon. She reports on the causes and results of the apparent increase in out-of-control anger—and explains what can be done to relieve the problem.

GUIDING QUESTION
Does the author present specific and plentiful examples to answer the question that she poses in her title?

■ **IDEA JOURNAL:** List some examples of publicly displayed anger that you have experienced.

Something snapped inside Jerry Sola during his evening commute through the Chicago suburbs two years ago. When the driver in front of the fifty-one-year-old salesman suddenly slammed on his brakes, Sola got so incensed[1] that he gunned his engine to cut in front of the man. Still steaming when both cars stopped at a red light. Sola grabbed a golf club from the backseat and got out.   1

"I was just about to smash his windshield or do him some damage," the brawny, 6-foot-1 former police officer recalls. "Then it hit me: 'What in God's name am I doing? I'm really a nice, helpful guy. What if I killed a man, went to jail and destroyed two families over a crazy, trivial thing?' I got back into my car and drove away."   2

REFLECT: Do you feel that you are one of the many Americans who are pushed to the breaking point?

Like Sola, more and more Americans are feeling pushed to the breaking point. The American Automobile Association's Foundation for Traffic Safety says incidents of violently aggressive driving—which some dub "mad driver disease"—rose 7 percent a year in the 1990s. Airlines are reporting more outbursts of sky rage. And sideline rage has become widespread: A Pennsylvania kids' football game ended in a brawl involving more than one hundred coaches, players, parents, and fans. In a particularly tragic incident captured national attention, a Massachusetts father—angered over rough play during his son's hockey practice—beat another father to death as their children watched.   3

IDENTIFY: Underline the main point in this paragraph.

No one seems immune to the anger epidemic. Women fly off the handle just as often as men, though they're less likely to get physical. The young and the infamous, such as musicians Sean "Puffy" Combs and Courtney Love—both sentenced to anger-management classes for violent outbursts—may seem more volatile,[2] but even senior citizens have erupted into "line rage" and pushed ahead of others simply because they felt they had "waited long enough" in their lives.   4

"People no longer hold themselves accountable for their bad behavior," says Doris Wilde Helmering, a therapist and author of *Sense Ability.* "They blame anyone and everything for their anger."   5

PREDICT: Pick one of the culprits; how do you think Hales in subsequent paragraphs will show it to be a cause of anger?

It's a mad, mad, world. Violent outbursts are just as likely to occur in leafy suburbs as in crowded cities, and even idyllic[3] vacation spots are not immune. "Everyone everywhere seems to be hotter under the collar these days," observes Sybil Evans, a conflict-resolution expert in New York City, who singles out three primary culprits: time, technology, and tension. "Americans are working longer hours than anyone else in the world. The cell phones and pagers that were supposed to make our lives easier have put us on call 24/7/365. Since we're always running, we're tense and low on patience. And the less patience we have, the less we monitor what we say to people and how we treat them."   6

---

[1] **incensed:** angered

[2] **volatile:** explosive

[3] **idyllic:** peaceful

Ironically,[4] the recent boom times may have brought out the worst in   7
some people. "Never have so many with so much been so unhappy," observes Leslie Charles, author of *Why Is Everyone So Cranky?* "There are
more of us than ever, all wanting the same space, goods, services, or attention. Everyone thinks, 'Me first. I don't have time to be polite.' We've lost
not only our civility but our tolerance for inconvenience."

The sheer complexity of our lives also has shortened our collective fuse.   8
We rely on computers that crash, drive on roads that gridlock, place calls to
machines that put us on endless hold. "It's not any one thing but lots of little
things that make people feel like they don't have control of their lives," says
Jane Middleton-Moz, a therapist and author. "A sense of helplessness is
what triggers rage. It's why people end up kicking ATM machines."

Getting a grip. When his lawn mower wouldn't start, a St. Louis man   9
got so angry that he picked it up by the handle, smashed it against the patio
and tore off each of its wheels. Playing golf, he sometimes became so en-
raged that he threw his clubs 50 feet up the fairway and into the trees and
had to get someone to retrieve them. In anger-therapy sessions with Doris
Wilde Helmering, he learned that such outbursts accomplish nothing.
"Venting" may make you feel better—but only for a moment.

"Catharsis[5] is worse than useless," says Brad Bushman, a psychology   10
professor at Iowa State University whose research has shown that letting
anger out makes people more aggressive, not less. "Many people think of
anger as the psychological equivalent of the steam in a pressure cooker: It
has to be released, or it will explode. That's not true. The people who react
by hitting, kicking, screaming, and swearing just feel more angry."

Over time, temper tantrums sabotage physical health as well as psycho-   11
logical equanimity. By churning out stress hormones like adrenaline,
chronic anger revs the body into a state of combat readiness, multiplying the
risk for stroke and heart attack—even in healthy individuals. In one study
by Duke University researchers, young women with "*Jerry Springer Show*-
type anger," who tended to slam doors, curse and throw things in a fury, had
higher cholesterol levels than those who reacted more calmly.

How do you tame a toxic temper? The first step is to figure out   12
what's really making you angry. Usually the rude sales clerk is the final straw
that unleashes bottled-up fury over a more difficult issue, such as a divorce
or a domineering boss. Next, monitor yourself for early signs of exhaustion
or overload. While stress alone doesn't cause a blow-up, it makes you more
vulnerable to overreacting.

When you feel yourself getting angry, control your tongue and your   13
brain. "Like any feeling, anger lasts only about three seconds," says Doris
Wilde Helmering. "What keeps it going is your negative thinking." As long
as you focus on who or what irritated you—like the oaf who rammed that
grocery cart into your heels—you'll stay angry. "Once you come to understand that you're driving your own anger with your thoughts," adds Helmering, "you can stop it."

Since his roadside epiphany, Jerry Sola has conscientiously worked to   14
rein in his rage. "I am a changed person," he says, "especially behind the

---

[4] **ironically:** opposite to what is or might be expected

[5] **catharsis:** release of emotional tension

Sidebar notes:

IDENTIFY: According to this paragraph, what triggers rage?

_____

_____

SUMMARIZE: In your own words, summarize how letting anger out creates problems.

_____

_____

IDENTIFY: Underline the sentence that presents a solution to releasing anger.

■ **TEACHING TIP:** In addition to providing vivid examples, this article traces the causes and effects of what appears to be an increase in angry outbursts. If you are also teaching the cause-and-effect chapters (16 and 49), you might want to point to this essay as an example of how these (and other) writing strategies can be mixed.

wheel. I don't listen to the news on the car radio. Instead, I put on nice, soothing music. I force myself to smile at rude drivers. And if I feel myself getting angry, I ask a simple question: 'Why should I let a person I'm never going to see again control my mood and ruin my whole day?'"

▮ SUMMARIZE AND RESPOND . . . .

In your reading journal or elsewhere, summarize the main point of "Why Are We So Angry?" Then, go back and check off support for this main idea. Next, write a brief summary of the essay. Finally, write a brief response to the reading. Can you identify with the angry people Hales writes about in this essay? Have you ever been one of them?

▮ CHECK YOUR COMPREHENSION . . . .

1. An alternate title for this essay could be
   a. "Anger Management."
   b. "Road Rage."
   c. "Investigating the Anger Epidemic."
   d. "The Breaking Point."

2. The main point of this essay is that
   a. anger is a widespread occurrence in today's society.
   b. anger is most common in sports.
   c. people should enroll in anger management courses.
   d. road rage must stop.

3. What do experts say about releasing anger?
   a. Releasing anger reduces frustration.
   b. Hitting a pillow is a simple way to release anger.
   c. Releasing anger is not productive.
   d. People in the suburbs are most likely to release anger.

4. If you are unfamiliar with the following words, use a dictionary to check their meanings: *brawl* (para. 3); *immune, epidemic, erupted* (4); *culprits* (6); *gridlock* (8).

▮ READ CRITICALLY . . . .

1. Based on your personal experience and observations, do the examples presented in this essay seem realistic?

2. Throughout the essay, Hales presents information gained from therapists and experts. Does this information strengthen Hales's main point? Would the essay be just as effective without it?

3. What role does technology play in creating anger?

4. Do the steps presented under "How do you tame a toxic temper?" (paras. 12 and 13) seem like a workable solution? Why or why not?

5. Hales begins her essay with the example of Jerry Sola and ends with it. Why do you suppose she uses this technique?

■ **WRITE** . . . .

WRITE A PARAGRAPH: Write a paragraph about a location where you have seen people exhibit their anger. Identify the location, and provide concrete examples of the way people show their anger.

WRITE AN ESSAY: Write an essay about a time when either you or someone you knew lost control. What happened? Give concrete examples of the loss of control. What were the consequences? Did you learn anything from the experience about expressing anger? Feel free to include the ideas you wrote about in your reading journal for Summarize and Respond.

■ **TIP:** For a sample illustration paragraph, see page 121.

. . . .

James Verini

Supersize It

James Verini writes for the *Los Angeles Times,* the *New York Times,* and other publications. He lives in Los Angeles.

In this essay, originally published in the online magazine *Slate,* Verini gives examples of how spaces, clothing, and even caskets are being "supersized" to accommodate ever larger Americans.

GUIDING QUESTION

How would you describe the examples the author presents to illustrate the trend he describes? Do you think he intends any of them to be funny?

■ **IDEA JOURNAL:** What do you think are some of the causes of increasing obesity in the United States?

George Farquhar[1] once said that necessity was the mother of invention, but we know that to be nonsense, really: Who needs an iPod that holds 10,000 songs? There is, however, one area of life in which technology keeps step with nature—the size of things. As we Americans are getting bigger (the Centers for Disease Control and Prevention in Atlanta estimates that roughly a third of Americans are overweight, with 20 percent of us qualifying as obese), so, too, is our stuff.

1

PREDICT: At this point, what kinds of examples do you think the author will provide?

Take our seats, for instance. Irwin Seating, a Michigan company that supplies the AMC and Regal cinema chains, has found that the movie theater industry now demands increasingly wide seats: The standard width used to be 19 inches, but now, according to Irwin, the benchmark[2] is 23 inches. A popular Irwin model, "the Ambassador," is 23 inches wide,

2

---

[1] **George Farquhar:** Irish playwright (1678–1707)

[2] **benchmark:** standard

includes flip-up arms for easy access, and a drink holder wide enough to hold a 44-ounce soda.

IDENTIFY: List one example of how manufacturers are making seating bigger.

The trend continues into every corner of our sitting lives. Cars are get- 3
ting larger, of course—the 2004 Ford Excursion fits eight average-size passengers (or roughly six obese ones). And apparently so are the people driving them—the Excursion's driver's seat is 40 inches wide. The same goes for our places of worship. Thomas McElheny, the CEO of Church Plaza, a manufacturer of "worship furniture" based in Florida, says that whereas 18 inches per worshipper used to be the allotment[3] when fitting for pews, most churches now require 21 inches. Church Plaza's pews have been made to support an almost miraculous 1,700 pounds per seat. "The last thing you want is the tragedy of a chair collapsing in church," McElheny says.

But it's not only more sitting space we require. We also need more room 4
to get into and out of the places where we're sitting, or working, or shopping, as the case may be. Revolving doors are thus getting wider. The average width for revolving doors used to be about 6 feet, or 3 feet per compartment. But these days, says Tim Mohl, of Horton Automatics, a revolving-door maker in Corpus Christi, Texas, he rarely installs anything narrower than 8 feet. "We're just figuring that people are a little larger now." Horton has models that stretch up to 18 feet, particularly popular with Las Vegas casinos.

Horton also makes those extra-large automatic sliding doors you find in 5
the new breed of superbig supermarkets—where, not surprisingly, the aisles have also widened. Supermarket aisles used to be about 5 feet wide; they are now 7 to 7½ feet. This trend is not meant to accommodate larger shoppers, according to industry insiders, but rather to allow for larger carts, which range in size from pretty big (over 3 feet in width) to, in stores such as Costco, platform-on-wheels big (designed to carry several hundred pounds of food). The larger carts allow for larger products—the 4-gallon drum of mayonnaise, the jumbo pack of pork chops—which are made for bargain shoppers with larger appetites.

So are the huge stores making us huge? Or are they huge because we 6
are? Is it even possible to say? Trying to determine cause and effect, one inevitably[4] finds oneself in a kind of What Came First conundrum,[5] the Fried Chicken or the Extra-Large Egg?

SUMMARIZE: In your own words, what is the author saying in this paragraph?

Unfortunately, none of the designers or executives I spoke to was able 7
to answer these questions. Nor did the federal government have much to offer. While it's true that certain things in America (elevators, wheelchair ramps) are more plentiful and bigger these days thanks to the Americans with Disabilities Act, when it comes to larger people, the ADA is not very helpful. The only place where obesity seems to be addressed on the ADA Web site is in the "Myths and Facts" section—"MYTH: The ADA protects people who are overweight. FACT: Just being overweight is not enough. . . . The Department has received only a handful of complaints about obesity."

---

[3] **allotment:** assigned share
[4] **inevitably:** eventually
[5] **conundrum:** difficult problem

But let's get to the important question: What to wear while you're shopping in the 7½-foot-wide supermarket aisle or watching a movie in the 23-inch Irwin Ambassador?   8

For football enthusiasts, Russell Athletic now makes an XXXXXL (that's five X's) team jersey. This fits a 62-inch-wide chest and an even larger belly, if the jersey's mesh-blend stretchiness is put to full use. But high-end clothiers[6] have also come to recognize the value of getting into plus sizes, which now account for about 5 percent to 10 percent of the male clothing market and, by some estimates, as much as 20 percent of the female market. At Rochester Big & Tall, the country's largest clothing store chain for the plus-size male, you can now purchase clothing made by Ralph Lauren, Burberry, and even suits by Ermenegildo Zegna (whose advertisements feature the wafer-thin actor Adrien Brody).   9

There's no question the market for products custom-made for the heavy set is burgeoning. If Tiffany can't supply you with a suitable plus-size band, you can find one at Winged Elephant, a Kent, Washington, jewelry designer that offers rings, necklaces, bracelets, and "hair-sticks" for the "style-conscious BBW"—that's Big, Beautiful Woman. A Bearville, New York, company called Amplestuff offers XL umbrellas, XL bicycle helmets, seat-belt extenders for car and airplane seats, leg lifters (for those who can't lift their own), and the Ample-Sponge, a brick-sized sponge attached to a bendable plastic handle specially designed for reaching between folds of flesh. Amplestuff's motto: "Make your world fit you!"   10

Finally, in the event that you should succumb to[7] the heart disease, diabetes, or risk of stroke that the CDC warns are several times more likely to occur with obesity, you can take solace[8] that even death can be made to fit. At Goliath Casket Inc., in Indiana, orders for specially made double-wide caskets have skyrocketed, says a spokesperson for the company. Goliath introduced a 52-inch model in July (a standard casket is 24 inches wide), and it is already on back order, despite the casket's own weight—200 pounds—the $1,000-plus cost of shipping it out of state, and the fact that it can only be towed on the back of a flatbed truck. (Goliath admits that, as yet, no known hearses can carry its double-wide model.)   11

If we reduced the size of our stuff, would we shrink accordingly[9]? Maybe, maybe not. But in the meantime, there's one thing we can be sure of: We're more comfortable. Who wants to return to the days when you had to squeeze by other patrons in the supermarket? Commodiousness[10] means comfort. Roominess is happiness. Bigger is better.   12

DISCUSSION: You might ask students about Verini's purpose and intended audience. Also, how does he use humor to make his point?

REFLECT: Which example in paragraphs 10 and 11 do you find most surprising?

---

[6] **clothiers:** clothing sellers

[7] **succumb to:** die from

[8] **solace:** comfort

[9] **accordingly:** in the same way

[10] **commodiousness:** spaciousness

■ SUMMARIZE AND RESPOND . . . .

In your reading journal or elsewhere, summarize the main point of "Supersize It." Then, go back and check off support for this main idea. Next, write a brief summary of the essay. Finally, write a brief response to the reading. Do you think that the number of overweight Americans should be a matter of concern? Are manufacturers right to make bigger products to suit the obese?

■ CHECK YOUR COMPREHENSION . . . .

1. An alternate title for this essay could be
    (a.) "Bigger People, Bigger Products."
    b. "The Many Inconveniences Faced by a Heavier Population."
    c. "The Risks of Obesity."
    d. "How Marketers Respond to Consumer Demand."

2. The main point of this essay is that
    a. manufacturers must always meet the needs of consumers, no matter what the consequences are.
    b. Americans today are able to be more comfortable than they were in years past.
    (c.) the fact that Americans are getting larger is reflected in the size of the goods that are being manufactured.
    d. the fact that stores are getting larger is one clear cause of many Americans gaining weight.

3. Which of the following points does Verini *not* make in the essay?
    a. Some businesses market their products exclusively to larger-sized Americans.
    (b.) In general, it is increasingly difficult for overweight people to find fashionable clothing.
    c. It is estimated that 20 percent of Americans weigh more than is good for their health.
    d. Many movie theaters and churches are providing attendees with more ample seat room.

4. If you are unfamiliar with the following words, use a dictionary to check their meanings: *obese* (para. 1); *pews, miraculous* (3); *compartment* (4); *accommodate* (5); *disabilities* (7); *burgeoning, extenders* (10); *diabetes, stroke* (11).

■ READ CRITICALLY . . . .

1. How would you describe Verini's tone here? What is his attitude toward the trend he describes?

2. What transitional words and phrases does Verini use to signal shifts from one example to another? How do these transitions help him to focus his paragraphs?

3. In paragraphs 6 and 12, Verini poses several questions. What is the purpose of these questions? What do they suggest about the author's larger purpose in writing the essay?

4. In paragraphs 2, 3, and 10, Verini puts phrases in quotation marks and offers direct quotations from one manufacturer and from two other manufacturers' Web sites. What is the effect of these uses of quotation?

5. Does Verini provide an effective introduction for his essay? Does his closing provide a satisfying conclusion? Why or why not?

■ WRITE . . . .

WRITE A PARAGRAPH: Write a paragraph about a trend you've observed among people in your peer group. The trend could involve something physical—such as clothing or a type of hairstyle—or it might involve an attitude, a belief, or a common problem. In developing your paragraph, be sure to provide specific examples from your experience and observations.

WRITE AN ESSAY: Write an essay about a national trend in sports, in television programming, or in human behavior, such as the way people relate to one another in public. Like Verini, give specific examples of this trend and provide clear transitions from one example to the next.

. . . .

44

Description

Each essay in this chapter uses description to get its main point across to the reader. As you read these essays, consider how they achieve the four basics of good description that are listed below and discussed in Chapter 11 of this book.

■■ FOUR BASICS OF GOOD DESCRIPTION

1. It creates a main impression—an overall effect, feeling, or image—about the topic.
2. It uses specific details to support the main impression.
3. It supports those examples with details that appeal to the five senses: sight, hearing, smell, taste, and touch.
4. It brings a person, place, or physical object to life for the reader.

Liann Sumner

Discovery

Liann Sumner teaches third grade at Hoover Magnet School in Redwood City, California.

This essay, written while Sumner was a student, describes a trip she made to India, where she learned how to "look below the surface of things." Sumner pays close attention to the details—both startling and beautiful—of her unfamiliar surroundings.

■ **IDEA JOURNAL:** Write about a time you visited a new place.

GUIDING QUESTION
As you read, think about Sumner's purpose in writing this essay. What do you think she wants to communicate to her readers?

From San Francisco to Rishikesh[1] was one long nightmarish haul: thirty-   1
two hours of nonstop, mind-numbing stimulus[2] and nerve-jangling noise
that we couldn't escape, wedged as we were into our narrow airplane seats.
We left before dawn and flew into the next night, following the sun in its
path around the globe. The darkness lasted for only a few hours before the
harsh light again glinted off the metal wings of the plane into my tired eyes.
We reached Delhi at 1:00 in the morning—I'd lost track of what day it
was—and the air was thick and moist and unbreathable. Holding onto my
husband's and son's hands for dear life, I wondered what I was doing here.
I didn't know then that I was beginning an odyssey[3] into India which would
change the way I approached life and which would teach me to look below
the surface of things and give me a new perception of my own world when
I returned to it.

Standing on the bus platform at Delhi, I was surrounded by a sea of   2
haunting, hungry brown faces. So many people! They were sleeping on the
ground everywhere we turned, cooking over small outdoor fires, even relieving themselves by the side of the road. Many lived out their lives un-
sheltered except for some corrugated[4] tin for a wall, or a thin blanket or
sacking[5] for a bed. I felt overwhelmed by culture shock. Maybe if I could get
to our room and wash my face under a spigot of cold water I would feel better, I thought.

By late morning it felt like the end of a long, exhausting week. We were   3
only on the first leg of our journey, and already I saw things that I had never
even imagined before. There was a dead Brahma[6] bull by the side of the
road, with blackbirds tearing at its insides. The water buffaloes that shared
a dirt path with us were huge beasts pulling teetering[7] loads of sugar cane.
They wove their way around careening,[8] honking buses and pony rickshaws.[9] There was no pattern to the traffic that I could discern: drivers
would head straight for an oncoming vehicle or pedestrians (us!), blasting
their horns and veering away at the last second! It seemed like one big free-
for-all with no one in charge.

As the day progressed, I sank into a deep depression. We walked through   4
the village we were staying in, and everything around us was broken or used
up, torn or wrecked. We took our grimy clothes to the Dhobi[10] for washing,
but when the women scrubbed them on the river rocks and laid them on the
banks, I felt uncomfortable. Later, at a little roadside restaurant, I couldn't
eat, although I had been ravenous[11] earlier. The smell of burning wood

IDENTIFY: What specific details does Sumner use in the
final sentence of this paragraph?

_____

_____

---

[1] **Rishikesh:** a city in northern India, holy to those who practice the Hindu religion

[2] **stimulus:** something that gets one's attention

[3] **odyssey:** a long or important journey

[4] **corrugated:** ridged

[5] **sacking:** coarse fabric

[6] **Brahma:** Indian

[7] **teetering:** moving unstably; about to fall

[8] **careening:** moving from side to side

[9] **rickshaws:** small carts that carry passengers

[10] **Dhobi:** Indian washwomen

[11] **ravenous:** very hungry

REFLECT: Do Sumner's tears seem justified?

mixed with the odor of open sewers. The restaurant had a dirt floor and a young boy was sweeping a pile of trash in front of our table with a palm frond. Even in the shade, it must have been over 90 degrees. Sitting there drinking a bottle of warm Limca,[12] I felt lost and stranded. Tears filled my eyes, and I couldn't stop them. The familiar world I had known had vanished, replaced by a nightmare. All I could do was sob.

The devastating images kept coming at me. We passed beggars squatting along the roadside: old men whose skin clung to their bones, mothers surrounded by children, thin hands outstretched. Small boys selling trinkets[13] or shining shoes assaulted us for rupees.[14] They would shove their goods into our hands or tug at our clothing, and if we didn't buy what they were selling, they would cry. If we did buy something, a hundred others would swarm around us until we had to break into a run to escape. Soon we had to learn to harden our hearts and ignore them: their need was so huge that we couldn't solve it by ourselves.

PREDICT: Based on paragraph 6 and the first sentence of paragraph 7, how might Sumner's view of India begin to change?

As we traveled by bus up the Himalayas[15] to Rishikesh and back, I began to notice a few other things. Once we got used to the pushing and shoving for space, and the crazy way in which the bus drivers swerved along the narrow mountain curves bordered by sheer cliffs, we started to observe the world outside our windows. And it was a fascinating world, with its own fierce beauty. I saw huge monkeys with black faces, cows wearing colorful headdresses, fields of lush green sugar cane, fragrant flowering trees unlike any I'd seen before, mud huts with elaborate patterns painted onto the doorsteps, terraced rice paddies[16] stretching for miles, and anthills more than 3 feet high.

When we stopped in the mountain villages, I was still aware of the squalor[17] and poverty, but I also noticed how resourceful the people were, how they made use of every scrap of whatever was available to them and used it for survival. Even the skinny children frying bread or making chai[18] at the roadside tea stalls—they were survivors, tough as gristle. And how little it took to make them happy! We'd often see them playing, engrossed,[19] with bottle caps or potsherds,[20] or swinging on a gate chanting rhymes. A few times we handed pencils to the children who followed us around, and watched their big eyes light up with surprise and pleasure. And we were impressed by how helpful the people were, how willing to share what little they had. Once there were two little boys traveling by themselves on the bus with us. The other passengers made sure they had enough to eat. When they got roadsick and vomited all over the bus, no one got upset with them. Instead, everyone comforted them and helped clean them up, and when it was time for them to get down, the ticket conductor made sure they were met by relatives.

[12] **Limca:** a lemon-lime soft drink

[13] **trinkets:** cheap jewelry or other small items

[14] **rupees:** coins

[15] **Himalayas:** an Asian mountain range

[16] **paddies:** flooded fields

[17] **squalor:** filthiness; poverty

[18] **chai:** spiced tea

[19] **engrossed:** fascinated

[20] **potsherds:** broken pieces of pottery

When we landed in San Francisco a few weeks later, I gazed almost un-   8
believingly at the neatly laid-out highway, the orderly traffic, and the clean,
unlittered suburban streets. Although I'd lived here all my life, it was as
though I'd never really seen it before. For the first time I appreciated the
amount of thought and foresight that went into the grand organization of
civic codes that ensure building safety, sewer treatment, and safe water supplies. I appreciated the health regulations that protected us from diseases
like the ones I'd seen. For the first time I felt a tangible²¹ pride in belonging
to a nation that took such good care of me and ran things so efficiently. All
my life, I had been blind to luxuries that I had taken for granted. Now I
wanted to rush home and pay my taxes and give a loud, joyful cry of "Thank
you! Thank you!" And for months afterwards, every time I turned on a warm
shower or flushed my toilet or drove a car down a road with signal lights that
people obeyed, I marveled at the cooperative human spirit that was responsible for it all and felt a deep comfort, a sense of belonging.

At the same time, I looked at individuals with more perception than be-   9
fore. Perhaps I had learned this in India, where people scrutinized²² us with
a frank and artless²³ curiosity, where everyone was interested in what we did
and who we were. But as I looked around me at the people who shared my
ordered world, I noticed—again for the first time—a distracted, empty look
in their eyes and the stamp of stress on their faces. I saw how they rushed
along on their everyday activities with little time for others, how the least
breakdown in the system they were used to would annoy them. We were paying a high price for civilization! Although just about all the people I knew
had all the food, clothing, and shelter they could want, although they were
surrounded by an affluence²⁴ that would have astounded most Indians, all
of this had failed to bring satisfaction or peace to their souls. I thought back
to the gentle, caring faces of the Indian people which reflected the serenity²⁵
of their spirit. In the midst of chaos, they had possessed a tranquillity²⁶ that
eluded us in our perfectly ordered world.

What I discovered on my trip to India has changed the way I view my   10
surroundings. It has brought my life, hitherto²⁷ a blur of rushing days, into
focus. Ironic,²⁸ isn't it, that I had to go halfway around the world for it!

> **SUMMARIZE:** In your own words, restate the discovery Sumner describes in paragraph 9.

> ■ **ESL:** If your class has many immigrant students—especially students from developing countries—you might ask them whether they share Sumner's feelings about the "luxuries" of living in the United States and whether they think such luxuries cause greater stress.

■ **SUMMARIZE AND RESPOND** . . . .

In your reading journal or elsewhere, summarize the main point of "Discovery." Then, go back and check off support for this main idea. Next, write
a brief summary of the essay. Finally, write a brief response to the reading.
What do you think of Sumner's description of rural India and the "discovery" she writes about at the end of her essay?

²¹ **tangible:** real and identifiable
²² **scrutinized:** examined closely
²³ **artless:** open
²⁴ **affluence:** wealth
²⁵ **serenity:** peacefulness
²⁶ **tranquillity:** calmness
²⁷ **hitherto:** before a certain time
²⁸ **ironic:** opposite from what might be expected

■ **CHECK YOUR COMPREHENSION** . . . .

1. An alternate title for this essay could be
   a. "Seeing through New Eyes." ⟨circled⟩
   b. "The People of India."
   c. "A Trip I Wish I Had Never Taken."
   d. "Heat and Squalor: The World of India."

2. The main point of this essay is that
   a. the author learned that many Indian people live in poverty but are generous and resourceful.
   b. the author realized that most Americans lead lives full of stress and personal dissatisfaction.
   c. the author's visit to India led her to see her own life and those of other Americans in a different light. ⟨circled⟩
   d. the author was so overwhelmed by the heat and squalor of India that she could only sob in despair.

3. Sumner's view of India first began to turn more positive when
   a. she and her family bought trinkets that small boys were selling.
   b. she began to notice the fascinating beauty of the landscape. ⟨circled⟩
   c. she sat in a restaurant sipping a bottle of Limca.
   d. she returned to the United States and realized the high price we pay for civilization.

4. If you are unfamiliar with the following words, use a dictionary to check their meanings: *wedged, glinted* (para. 1); *spigot* (2); *discern, veering* (3); *devastating, tug, swarm* (5); *sheer, terraced* (6); *resourceful, gristle* (7); *unlittered, foresight, civic, marveled, cooperative* (8); *eluded* (9).

■ **READ CRITICALLY** . . . .

1. Reread paragraphs 2 through 5, underlining the details that appeal to the senses. What general impression do these details create of Sumner's initial reaction to India?

2. Reread paragraphs 6 and 7. What impression do these paragraphs create? How does this impression compare with the impression of India created in paragraphs 2 through 5?

3. What two opposing points does Sumner make in paragraphs 8 and 9? What do these two paragraphs contribute to her essay as a whole?

4. At what two places in the essay does Sumner state her main point? Do you think she positions these statements effectively? Why or why not?

5. Summarize Sumner's "discovery" in your own words. Why do you suppose this discovery affected her so deeply? What do you, personally, take from this essay?

■ **WRITE** . . . .

WRITE A PARAGRAPH: Write a paragraph that describes a first impression you had of a new environment: a place you visited for the first time, a new school, a new job, or anything that interests you. The impression you describe may be positive, negative, or a mixture of both. Use physical details that appeal to at least two of the five senses: sight, hearing, smell, taste, and touch.

WRITE AN ESSAY: Write an essay that uses vivid details to describe an experience that had a strong impact on you, an experience that you recall mainly because of what you saw, heard, smelled, tasted, or touched. Like Sumner, be sure to communicate what the experience meant to you. If the experience caused you to look differently at where you live, you could conclude with that, as Sumner does.

■ **TIP:** For a sample description paragraph, see page 134.

. . . .

Barbara Kingsolver
Creation Stories

Barbara Kingsolver (b. 1955) was trained as a biologist and began her career as a science writer. Meanwhile, she was writing novels at night. Kingsolver published her first novel, *The Bean Trees,* in 1988, and it was well received by critics. She continued to publish novels, including *The Poisonwood Bible* (1998), which was nominated for a Pulitzer Prize. In 2000, she was awarded a National Humanities Medal for her writing. Her most recent book, *Small Wonder* (2002), is a collection of essays about both personal joys and political struggles.

In this excerpt from Kingsolver's *High Tide in Tucson* (1995), she describes the tense wait for the first big rain of the year and the release that comes with it.

GUIDING QUESTION
What types of weather does Kingsolver describe in this essay?

June is the cruelest month in Tucson,[1] especially when it lasts till the end of July. This is the season when every living thing in the desert swoons[2] south toward some faint salt dream of the Gulf of Mexico: tasting the horizon, waiting for the summer storms. This year they are late. The birds are pacing the ground stiff-legged, panting, and so am I. Waiting. In this blind, bright still-June weather the shrill[3] of the cicadas[4] hurts your eyes. Every plant   1

■ **IDEA JOURNAL:** Write about your favorite kind of weather.

[1] **Tucson:** a city in southern Arizona (pronounced "too-sawn")
[2] **swoons:** faints
[3] **shrill:** a high-pitched cry
[4] **cicadas:** large, noisy insects

IDENTIFY: Underline the two important definitions that Kingsolver provides in this paragraph.

looks pitiful and, when you walk past it, moans a little, envious because you can walk yourself to a drink and it can't.

The water that came last winter is long gone. "Female rain," it's called 2 in Navajo:[5] the gentle, furtive[6] rains that fall from overcast skies between November and March. That was weather to drink and to grow on. But not to remember, anymore than a child remembers last birthday's ice cream, once the months have passed without another drop. In June there is no vital sign, not so much as a humid breath against a pane of glass, till the summer storms arrive. What we're waiting for now is male rain. Big, booming wait-till-your-father-gets-home cloudbursts that bully up from Mexico and threaten to rip the sky.

The Tohono O'odham[7] have lived in the Sonoran Desert longer than 3 anyone else who's still living; their answer to this season is to make frothy wine from the ripe saguaro[8] fruits, and drink it all day and all night in a do-or-die ceremony to bring down the first storm. When it comes, the answer to a desert's one permanent question, that first storm defines the beginning of the Tohono O'odham new year. The storms themselves are enough to get drunk on: ferocious thunder and raindrops splatting so hard on the cooked ground you hear the thing approaching like mortar[9] fire.

PREDICT: What do you suppose Kingsolver will go on to do in paragraph 5?

I saw my first of these summer storms in 1978. I hadn't been in Arizona 4 long enough to see the calendar open and close, so I spent the early summer in a state of near panic, as the earliest people in any place must have done when they touched falling snow or the dry season's dust and asked each time: This burning cold, these dying plants — is this, then, the end of the world?

REFLECT: What do you think of Kingsolver's response to the rainstorm? What does it tell you about her?

I lived in a little stuccoed[10] house in a neighborhood of barking dogs and 5 front-yard shrines to the Virgin of Guadalupe.[11] One sweltering[12] afternoon I heard what I believed must be kids throwing gravel at the houses, relentlessly and with feeling. It was hot enough so that the neighborhood, all of it, dogs and broken glass on the sidewalks included, had murder in mind. I knew I was risking my neck to go outside and scold kids for throwing rocks, but I went anyway. What I saw from the front stoop[13] arrested me in my footprints: not a troop of juvenile delinquents,[14] but a black sky and a wall of water as high as heaven, moving up the block. I ran into the street barefoot and danced with my mouth open. So did half my neighbors. Armistice Day.[15]

[5] **Navajo:** language of a Native American tribe in the Southwest

[6] **furtive:** secretive; barely noticed

[7] **Tohono O'odham:** Native American natives whose name means "desert people"

[8] **saguaro:** a type of cactus

[9] **mortar:** cannon

[10] **stuccoed:** covered in plaster

[11] **Virgin of Guadalupe:** an important religious icon for Mexican Catholics

[12] **sweltering:** very hot

[13] **stoop:** steps

[14] **juvenile delinquents:** young people who get into trouble

[15] **Armistice Day:** anniversary of the end of World War I

Now I live on the outskirts of town, in the desert at the foot of the Tucson Mountains, where waiting for the end of the drought becomes an obsession. It's literally 110 degrees in the shade today, the kind of weather real southwesterners love to talk about. We have our own kind of Jack London[16] thing, in reverse: Remember that year (swagger,[17] thumbs in the belt) when it was 122 degrees and planes couldn't land at the airport?

This is actually true. For years I held the colorful impression that the tarmac[18] had liquefied, so that aircraft would have plowed into it like mammoth[19] flies bellying into ointment. Eventually an engineer gave me a pedestrian,[20] probably accurate, explanation about heat interfering with the generation of lift above the wings. Either way, weather that stops modern air traffic is high drama in America.

We revel in[21] our misery only because we know the end, when it comes, is so good. One day there will be a crackling, clean, creosote[22] smell in the air and the ground will be charged and the hair on your arms will stand on end and then BOOM, you are thrillingly drenched. All the desert toads crawl out of their burrows, swell out their throats, and scream for sex while the puddles last. The ocotillos[23] leaf out before your eyes, like a nature show on fast forward. There is so little time before the water sizzles back to thin air again. So little time to live a whole life in the desert. This is elemental mortality, the root of all passion.

Since I moved to this neighborhood of desert, I've learned I have other writers for neighbors. Unlike the toads, we're shy—we don't advertise our presence to each other quite so ostentatiously.[24] In fact, I only found out I'd joined a literary commune[25] when my UPS man—I fancy him a sort of manly Dorothy Parker[26] in uniform—began giving me weekly updates. Visitors up at Silko's had been out looking for wild pigs, and Mr. Abbey had gone out in his backyard and shot the TV, again. (Sad to say, that doesn't happen anymore. We all miss Ed.)

I imagine other neighbors: that Georgia O'Keeffe,[27] for example, is out there walking the hills in sturdy shoes, staring down the UPS man with such a fierce eye that he will never dare tell.

What is it that draws creators to this place? Low rent, I tell my friends who

6

7

8   IDENTIFY: Underline the details that you find most vivid in this paragraph.

9   ■ **TEACHING TIP:** Kingsolver uses a number of deliberate sentence fragments in this selection. You may need to explain that in literary writing such as this, authors can take liberties with their prose—usually to create rhythm—but that such liberties are not generally acceptable in academic and professional writing.

10

11

[16] **Jack London:** American writer (1876–1916) whose famous short story "To Build a Fire" told of an outdoorsman's unsuccessful attempt to stay alive in a frozen wilderness

[17] **swagger:** to move in an overly self-confident way

[18] **tarmac:** runway

[19] **mammoth:** huge

[20] **pedestrian:** plain

[21] **revel in:** celebrate

[22] **creosote:** a desert bush that produces a sharp-smelling resin

[23] **ocotillos:** flowering desert plants

[24] **ostentatiously:** openly; extravagantly

[25] **commune:** group of people who live together for some purpose

[26] **Dorothy Parker:** witty American writer (1893–1967)

[27] **Georgia O'Keeffe:** American painter (1887–1986) who did much of her greatest work in the Southwest

SUMMARIZE: Put the writer's point in this paragraph in your own words.

ask, but it's more than that. It's the Southwest: a prickly land where mountain lions make bets with rabbits, and rabbits can win. Where nature rubs belly to belly with subdivision and barrio,[28] and coyotes take shortcuts through the back alleys. Here even the rain has gender, the frogs sing *carpe diem,*[29] and fast teenage girls genuflect[30] quickly toward the door of the church, hedging their bets, as they walk to school in tight skirts and shiny high heels.

When I drive to the post office every few days to pick up my mail, it's only   12 about twelve miles round trip, but I pass through at least half-a-dozen neighborhoods that distinguish themselves one from the other by architecture and language and even, especially, creation myth. First among them is the neighborhood of jackrabbits and saguaros, who imperiously[31] tolerate my home, though I can't speak their language or quite understand their myths.

Then, just inside the city limits, a red cobble[32] of just-alike roofs—paved   13 air—where long strands of exurban[33] condominiums shelter immigrants from Wisconsin, maybe, or Kansas, who dream in green and hug small irrigated lawns to their front doors.

Next I cross the bridge over the Santa Cruz, whose creation story bub-   14 bles from ephemeral[34] springs in the mountains of southern Arizona and Mexico. In these lean days she's a great blank channel of sand, but we call her a river anyway, and say it with a straight face too, because in her moods this saint has taken out bridges and houses and people who loved their lives.

Then I pass under the artery of Interstate 10, which originates in Los   15 Angeles or Jacksonville, Florida, depending on your view of destiny; and the railroad track, whose legend is a tale tasting of dynamite, the lives and deaths of immigrants who united a continent and divided in twain the one great original herd of American bison.[35]

IDENTIFY: In two places in this paragraph, Kingsolver says that something is like something else. Put a check mark by these places.

Then without warning I am smack in the middle of a Yaqui[36] village that   16 is fringe-edged and small like ✓a postage stamp, and every bit alive. Despite its size, Pascua Yaqui is a sovereign world; I come here every Easter to watch an irresistible pageant[37] combining deer dances with crucifixion. Like the Tohono O'odham singing down the rain, the masked Yaqui dancers listen for the heartbeat of creation, and keep a promise with every vernal equinox[38] to hold the world to its rightful position. On this small patch of dusty ground, the religion of personal salvation is eclipsed[39] by a faith whose question and answer are matters of order in the universe. Religion of that kind can crack your mind open the ✓way lightning splits a pine, leaving the wind to howl through the scorched divide. I can hardly ever even drive through

---

[28] **barrio:** neighborhood

[29] *carpe diem*: Latin for "seize the day"

[30] **genuflect:** to bend one's knee in worship

[31] **imperiously:** in an imperial or royal way

[32] **cobble:** mixture

[33] **exurban:** outside of a suburban area

[34] **ephemeral:** temporary

[35] **bison:** buffalo

[36] **Yaqui:** a tribe living in Arizona and northern Mexico

[37] **pageant:** show

[38] **vernal equinox:** the beginning of spring

[39] **eclipsed:** reduced in importance

here, in my serviceable old Toyota, without biting my lip and considering immensity.

Calle Ventura[40] marks the entrance to another state, where on a fine, still 17
day your nose can compare the goods from three tortilla factories. From here the sidewalks roll, the walls crumble and shout with territorial inscription, brown dogs lie under cherry Camaros and the Virgin of Guadalupe holds court in the parking lot of the Casa Rey apartments.

Across the street stands the post office, neutral territory: mailboxes all 18
identical, regardless of the keyholder's surname, as physically uniform as a table of contents. We are all equals in the eyes of the USPO, containing our secrets. I grab mine and scuttle[41] away. The trip home takes me right back through all these lands again, all these creation stories, and that's enough culture for one day, usually.

I close the door, breathless, and stare out my window at a landscape of 19
wonders thrown together with no more thought than a rainstorm or a volcano can invoke on its own behalf. It's exactly as John Muir[42] said, as if "nature in wildest extravagance held her bravest structures as common as gravel-piles."

From here I begin my story. I can't think of another place like it. 20

■ **SUMMARIZE AND RESPOND** . . . .

In your reading journal or elsewhere, summarize the main point of "Creation Stories." Then, go back and check off support for this main idea. Next, write a brief summary of the essay. Finally, write a brief response to the reading. How effectively does Kingsolver describe the natural environment? Do any of the details she presents strike you as particularly vivid?

■ **CHECK YOUR COMPREHENSION** . . . .

1. An alternate title for this piece could be
   a. "My First Summer Living in Tucson."
   b. "So Little Time."
   c. "The Dry Heat of June in the Desert."
   d. "Waiting for the Desert Rain."

2. The main point of this essay is that
   a. in the Sonoran Desert there is a difference between "female" rain and "male" rain.
   b. Sonoran Desert dwellers look forward to the first rainstorms of the dry early summer and cherish the diversity of desert life.
   c. when rain comes in the Sonoran Desert, it is always as a sudden, great downpour.
   d. no plants can grow in the Sonoran Desert until the rainstorms finally come in early summer.

[40] **Calle Ventura:** name of a road in Arizona
[41] **scuttle:** move quickly
[42] **John Muir:** Scottish American environmentalist (1838–1914)

3. According to Kingsolver, the one good thing about the dry early summers of the Sonoran Desert is that

   a. the native Tohono O'odham make saguaro wine.

   b. everyone remembers the gentle rains that fall during the wintertime.

   c. everyone knows the rainstorms will finally come with a thrilling *boom.*

   d. real southwesterners love to talk about how high the temperature will get.

4. If you are unfamiliar with the following words, use a dictionary to check their meanings: *vital* (para. 2); *frothy, ferocious, splatting* (3); *shrines, relentlessly, scold, arrested* (5); *outskirts, drought, obsession* (6); *drenched, burrows, sizzles, mortality* (8); *subdivision* (11); *irrigated* (13); *destiny, twain* (15); *sovereign, irresistible, crucifixion, scorched, serviceable, immensity* (16); *surname* (18); *invoke, extravagance* (19).

■   **READ CRITICALLY** . . . .

1. Locate examples of language in the essay that appeals to each of the five senses: sight, hearing, smell, taste, and touch. What, for you, are the most memorable descriptive details Kingsolver offers?

2. What contrast does Kingsolver set up in paragraph 2? What is the purpose of this contrast?

3. What is Kingsolver's point in paragraph 4? How does paragraph 4 prepare us for paragraph 5?

4. Locate places in the essay where Kingsolver refers to aspects of the natural world as if they had human qualities. What is the effect of such references?

5. What, in your own words, is the meaning of Kingsolver's final sentence?

■   **WRITE** . . . .

   WRITE A PARAGRAPH: Write a paragraph about a time when you experienced an unexpected change in the weather, as Kingsolver does in paragraph 5, or about a weather condition that makes you very uncomfortable. Be sure to include details that will show readers what your surroundings or feelings were like before and after the change. Try to appeal to at least three of the five senses.

   WRITE AN ESSAY: Write an essay describing your responses to a physical environment. You might consider the changing of the seasons, as Kingsolver does, or you might focus on a place that you enjoy or that you spend a lot of time in. Be sure to include as many physical sensations as you can.

45

Process Analysis

Each essay in this chapter uses process analysis to get its main point across to the reader. As you read these essays, consider how they achieve the four basics of good process analysis that are listed below and discussed in Chapter 12 of this book.

■■ FOUR BASICS OF GOOD PROCESS ANALYSIS
■■

1. It tells readers what process the writer wants them to know about and makes a point about it.
2. It presents the essential steps in the process.
3. It explains the steps in detail.
4. It presents the steps in a logical order (usually time order).

Malcolm X

A Homemade Education

Malcolm X (1925–1965) was one of the best-known African American activists of the 1960s. Born Malcolm Little in Omaha, Nebraska, he first gained fame in the 1950s as a minister for Elijah Muhammad's Nation of Islam. Malcolm X gave fiery speeches in support of black separatism, attracting many followers to the organization. After learning about the extramarital affairs of his mentor, Elijah Muhammad, Malcolm X broke with the Nation of Islam in 1964. He made a pilgrimage to the Islamic holy city of Mecca in Saudi Arabia that year and met "blond-haired, blue-eyed men I could call my brothers." Upon his return to the United States, his new openness toward working with people of all races did not improve his relationship with those in the Nation of Islam who still resented his leaving the organization and renouncing its leader. On February 21, 1965, he was killed by three gunmen as he spoke at the Audubon Ballroom in New York.

■ **TEACHING TIP:** In his second paragraph, Malcolm X refers to the problems of writing in slang, but he doesn't go into detail about them. Ask students to comment on what these problems might be. If you want to cover this issue in more detail, see Chapter 33.

In his speeches and writings, Malcolm X urged his followers to educate themselves. A high-school dropout who had turned to petty crime as a teenager, he realized the importance of a good education after being sentenced to seven years in prison when he was twenty-one. The following selection from *The Autobiography of Malcolm X* (1965) explains the learning process that he put himself through during his years behind bars.

GUIDING QUESTION
What does Malcolm X mean by a "homemade education," and how does he get it?

■ **IDEA JOURNAL:** Have you experienced similar frustrations about your ability to communicate with others?

PREDICT: Pause after the third paragraph. What role do you think the prison system played in Malcolm X's education?

IDENTIFY: Read paragraphs 5–10 carefully and put an X by the steps Malcolm X took to educate himself.

It was because of my letters that I happened to stumble upon starting to acquire some kind of homemade education. 1

I became increasingly frustrated at not being able to express what I wanted to convey in letters that I wrote, especially those to Mr. Elijah Muhammad. In the street, I had been the most articulate[1] hustler out there—I had commanded attention when I said something. But now, trying to write simple English, I not only wasn't articulate, I wasn't even functional. How would I sound writing in slang, the way I would *say* it, something such as "Look, daddy, let me pull your coat about a cat, Elijah Muhammad—" 2

Many who today hear me somewhere in person, or on television, or those who read something I've said, will think I went to school far beyond the eighth grade. This impression is due entirely to my prison studies. 3

It had really begun back in Charlestown Prison, when Bimbi first made me feel envy of his stock of knowledge. Bimbi had always taken charge of any conversation he was in, and I had tried to emulate[2] him. But every book I picked up had few sentences which didn't contain anywhere from one to nearly all the words that might as well have been in Chinese. When I just skipped those words, of course, I really ended up with little idea of what the book said. So I had come to Norfolk Prison Colony still going through only book-reading motions. Pretty soon, I would have quit even these motions unless I had received the motivation that I did. 4

I saw that the best thing I could do was to get hold of a dictionary—to study to learn some words. I was lucky enough to reason also that I should try to improve my penmanship. It was sad. I couldn't even write in a straight X line. It was both ideas together that moved me to request a dictionary along with some tablets and pencils from the Norfolk Prison Colony school. 5

X   I spent two days just riffling[3] uncertainly through the dictionary's pages. I'd never realized so many words existed! I didn't know *which* words I X needed to learn. Finally, just to start some kind of action, I began copying. 6 7

X   In my slow, painstaking, ragged handwriting, I copied into my tablet everything printed on that first page, down to the punctuation marks.

[1] **articulate:** well-spoken

[2] **emulate:** imitate

[3] **riffling:** leafing through (a book)

X   I believe it took me a day. Then, aloud, I read back, to myself, everything   8
I'd written on the tablet. Over and over, aloud, to myself, I read my own
handwriting.

X   I woke up the next morning, thinking about those words—immensely   9
proud to realize that not only had I written so much at one time, but I'd
written words that I never knew were in the world. Moreover, with a little
X effort, I also could remember what many of these words meant. I reviewed
the words whose meanings I didn't remember. Funny thing, from the dictionary first page right now, that "aardvark" springs to my mind. The dictionary had a picture of it, a long-tailed, long-eared, burrowing African
mammal, which lives off termites caught by sticking out its tongue as an
anteater does for ants.

X   I was so fascinated that I went on—I copied the dictionary's next page.   10
And the same experience came when I studied that. With every succeeding
X page, I also learned of people and places and events form history. Actually
the dictionary is like a miniature encyclopedia. Finally the dictionary's A
X section had filled a whole tablet—and I went on into the B's. That was the
way I started copying what eventually became the entire dictionary. It went
a lot faster after so much practice helped me to pick up handwriting speed.
Between what I wrote in my tablet, and writing letters, during the rest of my
time in prison I would guess I wrote a million words.

I suppose it was inevitable that my word-base broadened, I could for the   11   IDENTIFY: Underline the sen-
first time pick up a book and read and now begin to understand what the   tence that states the result
book was saying. Anyone who has read a great deal can imagine the new   of all his work.
world that opened. Let me tell you something: from then until I left that
prison, in every free moment I had, if I was not reading in the library, I was
reading on my bunk. You couldn't have gotten me out of books with a
wedge. Between Mr. Muhammad's teachings, my correspondence, my visitors—usually Ella and Reginald—and my reading books, months passed
without my even thinking about being imprisoned. In fact, up to then, I had
never been so truly free in my life.

■ **SUMMARIZE AND RESPOND** . . . .

In your reading journal or elsewhere, summarize the main point of "A
Homemade Education." Then, go back and check off the support for this
main idea. Next, write a brief summary of the essay. Finally, write a brief response to the reading. How is it that Malcolm X is able to obtain knowledge? Consider his skill level before and after his self-education process.

■ **CHECK YOUR COMPREHENSION** . . . .

1. An alternate title for this essay could be
    a. "An Open Book."
    b. "Freeing the Mind."
    c. "The dictionary: One Man's Door to Knowledge."
    d. "No More Slang."

2. The main point of this essay is that
   a. reading makes time go by fast for prisoners.
   (b.) anyone with desire and commitment can obtain knowledge.
   c. there is a connection between reading and writing.
   d. education is best obtained in steps.

3. To what or whom does Malcolm X attribute his ability to speak, read, and write?
   (a.) A dictionary
   b. Bimbi
   c. Elijah Muhammad
   d. The prison educational system

4. If you are unfamiliar with the following words, use a dictionary to check their meanings: *hustler* (para. 2); *immensely, burrowing* (9); *inevitable* (11).

■ READ CRITICALLY ....

1. What is Malcolm X's purpose in this essay?

2. In what order did Malcolm X write about the steps he took to increase his word base?

3. Details are important to understanding the steps in a process. In this essay, what details stand out for you?

4. In paragraph 10, what do you think Malcolm X means when he writes that "the dictionary is like a miniature encyclopedia"?

5. What is significant about the last line? What point is Malcolm X making about reading specifically and education in general?

■ WRITE ....

■ **TIP:** For a sample process analysis paragraph, see page 149.

WRITE A PARAGRAPH: Write a paragraph about how you have improved or might improve your academic performance in an area.

WRITE AN ESSAY: Write an essay that traces the steps you took to learn a particular skill or accomplish a particular goal. As Malcolm X does in this essay, be sure to include what you were like before and after you developed your skill or reached your goal.

Joey Green

Beauty and the Beef

A humorist and observer of American culture, Joey Green is the author of more than a dozen books, among them the best-selling *Polish Your Furniture with Panty Hose* series, detailing hundreds of alternative uses for brand-name household products. To demonstrate some of these "wacky uses," he has appeared on numerous national and regional radio and television shows. Some of his ideas are at <**www.wackyuses.com**>.

Previously, Green worked at the J. Walter Thompson advertising agency, where he wrote television commercials for Burger King and Walt Disney World.

In "Beauty and the Beef," originally published in *Spy* magazine (1987), Green provides many colorful details as he shows, step-by-step, how a hamburger is made into a television star.

GUIDING QUESTION
How does the title of the essay relate to the process being analyzed?

When was the last time you opened a carton in a fast-food restaurant to find a hamburger as appetizing as the ones in the TV commercials? Did you ever look past the counter help to catch a glimpse of a juicy hamburger patty, handsomely branded by the grill, sizzling and crackling as it glides over roaring flames, with tender juices sputtering into the fire? On television the burger is a magnificent slab of flame-broiled beef—majestically topped with crisp iceberg lettuce, succulent red tomatoes, tangy onions, and plump pickles, all between two halves of a towering sesame-seed bun. But, of course, the real-life Whoppers don't quite measure up. [1]

PREDICT: Stop after paragraph 2. What kind of "makeup" might be used?

The ingredients of a TV Whopper are, unbelievably, the same as those used in real Whoppers sold to average customers. But like other screen personalities, the Whopper needs a little help from makeup. [2]

When making a Burger King commercial, J. Walter Thompson, the company's advertising agency, usually devotes at least one full day to filming "beauty shots" of the food. Burger King supplies the agency with several large boxes of frozen beef patties. But before a patty is sent over the flame broiler, a professionally trained food stylist earning between $500 and $700 a day prepares it for the camera. [3]

The crew typically arrives at 7:00 A.M. and spends two hours setting up lights that will flatter the burger. Then the stylist, aided by two assistants, begins by burning "flame-broiling stripes" into the thawed hamburger patties with a special Madison Avenue[1] branding iron. Because the tool doesn't always leave a rich, charcoal-black impression on the patty, the stylist uses a fine paintbrush to darken the singed crevices[2] with a sauce the color of used [4]

IDENTIFY: Check off the steps in the process described in paragraph 4.

---

[1] **Madison Avenue:** street in New York City where many big advertising companies are located

[2] **crevices:** narrow openings

REFLECT: Did you know that food is "made up" this way for ads? Does the process surprise you?

motor oil. The stylist also sprinkles salt on the patty so when it passes over the flames, natural juices will be encouraged to rise to the meat's surface.

Thus branded, retouched, and juiced, the patties are run back and forth 5 over a conveyor-belt broiler while the director films the little spectacle from a variety of angles. Two dozen people watch from the wings: lighting assistants, prop people, camera assistants, gas specialists, the client, and agency people — producers, writers, art directors. Of course, as the meat is broiled, blood rises to the surface in small pools. Since, for the purpose of advertising, bubbling blood is not a desirable effect, the stylist, like a prissy[3] microsurgical nurse, continually dabs at the burger with a Q-Tip.

Before the patty passes over the flame a second time, the food stylist ma- 6 neuvers a small electric heater an inch or so above the burger to heat up the natural fatty juices until they begin to steam and sizzle. Otherwise puddles of grease will cover the meat. Sometimes patties are dried out on a bed of paper towels. Before they're sent over the flame broiler again, the stylist relubricates them with a drop of corn oil to guarantee picturesque crackling and sizzling.

If you examine any real Whopper at any Burger King closely, you'll dis- 7 cover flame-broiling stripes only on the top side of the beef patty. Hamburgers are sent through the flame broilers once; they're never flipped over. The commercials imply otherwise. On television a beef patty, fetchingly covered with flame-broiling stripes, travels over the broiler, indicating that the burger has been flipped to sear stripes into the other side.

■ **DISCUSSION:** Ask students to describe other processes intended to make things look better than they really do.

In any case, the camera crew has just five or ten seconds in the life cycle 8 of a TV Whopper to capture good, sizzling, brown beef on film. After that the hamburger starts to shrink rapidly as the water and grease are cooked from it. Filming lasts anywhere from three to eight hours, depending upon the occurrence of a variety of technical problems — heavy smoke, grease accumulating on the camera equipment, the gas specialist's failure to achieve a perfect, preternaturally[4] orange glowing flame. Out of one day's work, and anywhere between fifty and seventy-five hamburgers, the agency hopes to get five seconds of usable footage. Most of the time the patties are either too raw, bloody, greasy, or small.

Of course, the cooked hamburger patty depicted sitting on a sesame- 9 seed bun in the commercial is a different hamburger from those towel-dried, steak-sauce-dabbed, corn-oiled specimens that were filmed sliding over the flames. This presentation patty hasn't been flame-broiled at all. It's been branded with the phony flame-broiling marks, retouched with the steak sauce — and then microwaved.

■ **IDEA JOURNAL:** Think of a common process (such as an ATM withdrawal or filling out an application), and write a how-to process analysis of it.

Truth in advertising, however, is maintained, sort of: When you're 10 shown the final product — a completely built hamburger topped with sliced vegetables and condiments — you are seeing the actual quantities of ingredients found on the average real Whopper. On television, though, you're only seeing half of the hamburger — the front half. The lettuce, tomatoes, onions, and pickles have all been shoved to the front of the burger. The stylist has carefully nudged and manicured the ingredients so that they sit just right. The red, ripe tomatoes are flown in fresh from California the morning

---

[3] **prissy:** extremely proper

[4] **preternaturally:** extraordinarily, beyond what is natural

of the shoot. You might find such tomatoes on your hamburger—if you ordered several hundred Whoppers early in the morning, in Fresno. The lettuce and tomatoes are cut, trimmed, and then piled on top of a cold cooked hamburger patty, and the whole construction is sprayed with a fine mist of glycerine⁵ to glisten and shimmer seductively. Finally the hamburger is capped with a painstakingly handcrafted sesame-seed bun. For at least an hour the stylist has been kneeling over the bun like a lens grinder, positioning each sesame seed. He dips a toothpick in Elmer's glue and, using a pair of tweezers, places as many as 300 seeds, one by one, onto a formerly bald bun.

When it's all over, the crew packs up the equipment, and seventy-five   11
gorgeous-looking hamburgers are dumped in the garbage.

▪ SUMMARIZE AND RESPOND . . . .

In your reading journal or elsewhere, summarize the main point of "Beauty and the Beef." Then, go back and check off the support for this main idea. Next, write a brief summary of the essay. Finally, write a brief response to the reading. Were you surprised by how much is done to a hamburger to make it look appetizing? What other products have you seen advertised that probably go through a similar process?

▪ CHECK YOUR COMPREHENSION . . . .

1. An alternate title for this essay could be
   a. " 'Truth' in Advertising."
   b. "Fast Foods in America."
   c. "Why Hamburgers Are Good to Eat."
   d. "J. Walter Thompson: King of Madison Avenue."

2. The main point of this essay is that
   a. food stylists make a lot of money.
   b. advertising agencies are totally unethical.
   c. advertisements present better-than-real-life products.
   d. Burger King spends a lot of money on advertising.

3. What does the author say about truth in advertising?
   a. It doesn't exist.
   b. It is stretched.
   c. It is always the primary concern of advertisers.
   d. It is easy to find.

4. If you are unfamiliar with the following words, use a dictionary to check their meanings: *succulent* (para. 1); *flatter, singed* (4); *maneuvers, relubricates* (6); *sear* (7); *depicted* (9).

---

⁵**glycerine:** colorless liquid

■ READ CRITICALLY . . . .

1. What do you think is the author's purpose in writing this essay?

2. The essay opens with a question. Why is this question more effective than a simple statement such as "Hamburgers never look as good as they do in TV commercials"?

3. What, to you, was the most interesting step in the process of beautifying a burger? Why? What details made it stand out?

4. How does the author organize his ideas? Would another order of organization work well? Why or why not?

5. How would you describe the author's attitude about the beautifying of beef? Find three examples in the essay that reveal this attitude.

■ WRITE . . . .

WRITE A PARAGRAPH: Write a paragraph that explains how to beautify something or someone (for example, how to put on makeup or how to make something look good to sell it). Feel free to exaggerate and use humor.

WRITE AN ESSAY: Look through some magazines or watch a few TV commercials to find an advertisement that you think makes something look better than it really is. You may want to look at the ideas you wrote in your reading journal for Summarize and Response. Then, write an essay that explains what steps the advertiser might have taken to create the better-than-real image.

46
Classification

Each essay in this chapter uses classification to get its main point across to the reader. As you read these essays, consider how they achieve the four basics of good classification that are listed below and discussed in Chapter 13 of this book.

■■ FOUR BASICS OF GOOD CLASSIFICATION

1. It makes sense of a group of people or items by organizing them into categories.
2. It has a purpose for sorting the people or items.
3. It categorizes using a single organizing principle.
4. It gives detailed examples or explanations of what fits into each category.

Stephanie Ericsson
The Ways We Lie

Stephanie Ericsson was born in 1953 and raised in San Francisco. She has lived in a variety of places, including New York, Los Angeles, London, Mexico, the Spanish island of Ibiza, and Minnesota, where she currently resides. Ericsson's life took a major turn when her husband died suddenly, leaving her two months pregnant. She began a journal to help her cope with the grief and loss and later used her writing to help others with similar struggles. An excerpt from her journal appeared in the *Utne Reader,* and her writings were later published in a book entitled *Companion through the Darkness: Inner Dialogues on Grief* (1993). About her book, Ericsson writes, "It belongs to those who have had the blinders ripped from their eyes, who suddenly see the lies of our lives and the truths of existence for what they are."

In "The Ways We Lie," which also appeared in the *Utne Reader* and is taken from her follow-up work, *Companion into the Dawn: Inner Dialogues on Loving* (1994), Ericsson continues her search for truth by examining and classifying our daily lies.

GUIDING QUESTION
As you read this essay, pay attention to the examples Ericsson provides. What examples of lying can you think of from your own experience?

X The bank called today, and I told them my deposit was in the mail, even though I hadn't written a check yet. It'd been a rough day. The baby I'm pregnant with decided to do aerobics on my lungs for two hours, our three-year-old daughter painted the living-room couch with lipstick, the IRS put me on hold for an hour, and I was late to a business meeting because I was tired. 1

X   I told my client that the traffic had been bad. When my partner came home, his haggard face told me his day hadn't gone any better than mine, X so when he asked, "How was your day?" I said, "Oh, fine," knowing that one more straw might break his back. A friend called and wanted to take me to X lunch. I said I was busy. Four lies in the course of a day, none of which I felt the least bit guilty about. 2

We lie. We all do. We exaggerate, we minimize, we avoid confrontation, 3 we spare people's feelings, we conveniently forget, we keep secrets, we justify lying to the big-guy institutions. Like most people, I indulge in small falsehoods and still think of myself as an honest person. Sure I lie, but it doesn't hurt anything. Or does it?

I once tried going a whole week without telling a lie, and it was paralyzing. 4 I discovered that telling the truth all the time is nearly impossible. It means living with some serious consequences: The bank charges me $60 in overdraft fees, my partner keels over when I tell him about my travails, my client fires me for telling her I didn't feel like being on time, and my friend takes it personally when I say I'm not hungry. There must be some merit to lying.

But if I justify lying, what makes me any different from slick politicians 5 or the corporate robbers who raided the S&L industry? Saying it's OK to lie one way and not another is hedging.[1] I cannot seem to escape the voice deep inside me that tells me: When someone lies, someone loses.

What far-reaching consequences will I, or others, pay as a result of my 6 lie? Will someone's trust be destroyed? Will someone else pay *my* penance because I ducked out? We must consider the *meaning of our actions*. Deception, lies, capital crimes, and misdemeanors[2] all carry meanings. *Webster's* definition of *lie* is specific:

1. a false statement or action especially made with the intent to deceive;

2. anything that gives or is meant to give a false impression.

A definition like this implies that there are many, many ways to tell a lie. 7 Here are just a few.

---

[1] **hedging:** avoiding the question

[2] **misdemeanors:** minor violations of rules

IDENTIFY: In the first two paragraphs, the author provides four examples of lies she's told. Put an X by these examples.

REFLECT: Do you agree that there "must be some merit to lying"? Why or why not?

■ TEACHING TIP: Have small groups diagram the essay. Discuss whether all the categories in the essay are really lies (for example, is stereotyping really a lie?). What other categories should the author have included? Have students record the ways they lie and share their responses at the next class meeting (anonymously, if necessary). Classify the responses according to category.

The White Lie

The white lie assumes that the truth will cause more damage than a simple,   8
harmless untruth. Telling a friend he looks great when he looks like hell can
be based on a decision that the friend needs a compliment more than a frank
opinion. But, in effect, it is the liar deciding what is best for the lied to. Ultimately, it is a vote of no confidence. It is an act of subtle arrogance[3] for
anyone to decide what is best for someone else.

Yet not all circumstances are quite so cut and dried. Take, for instance,   9
the sergeant in Vietnam who knew one of his men was killed in action but
listed him as missing so that the man's family would receive indefinite com-
pensation instead of the lump-sum pittance[4] the military gives widows and
children. His intent was honorable. Yet for twenty years this family kept their
hopes alive, unable to move on to a new life.

Facades

We all put up facades[5] to one degree or another. When I put on a suit to go   10
to see a client, I feel as though I am putting on another face, obeying the expectation that serious businesspeople wear suits rather than sweatpants. But
I'm a writer. Normally, I get up, get the kid off to school, and sit at my computer in my pajamas until four in the afternoon. When I answer the phone,
the caller thinks I'm wearing a suit (although the UPS man knows better).

But facades can be destructive because they are used to seduce others   11   IDENTIFY: Underline the
into an illusion. For instance, I recently realized that a former friend was a   main point of this para-
liar. He presented himself with all the right looks and the right words and   graph. What example does
offered lots of new consciousness theories, fabulous books to read, and fas-   Ericsson use to support it?
cinating insights. Then I did some business with him, and the time came for
him to pay me. He turned out to be all talk and no walk. I heard a plethora[6]   _____
of reasonable excuses, including in-depth descriptions of the big break
around the corner. In six months of work, I saw less than a hundred bucks.   _____
When I confronted him, he raised both eyebrows and tried to convince me
that I'd heard him wrong, that he'd made no commitment to me. A simple   _____
investigation into his past revealed a crowded graveyard of disenchanted former friends.

Ignoring the Plain Facts

In the sixties, the Catholic Church in Massachusetts began hearing com-   12   SUMMARIZE: In your own
plaints that Father James Porter was sexually molesting children. Rather   words, summarize the
than relieving him of his duties, the ecclesiastical authorities simply moved   example in this paragraph
him from one parish to another between 1960 and 1967, actually providing   in one or two sentences.
him with a fresh supply of unsuspecting families and innocent children to
abuse. After treatment in 1967 for pedophilia,[7] he went back to work, this   _____
time in Minnesota. The new diocese[8] was aware of Father Porter's obsession
with children, but they needed priests and recklessly believed treatment had

[3] **arrogance:** belief in one's superiority

[4] **pittance:** small amount

[5] **facades:** masks

[6] **plethora:** excess

[7] **pedophilia:** sexual abuse of children

[8] **diocese:** district or churches under the guidance of a bishop

cured him. More children were abused until he was relieved of his duties a year later. By his own admission, Porter may have abused as many as a hundred children.

Ignoring the facts may not in and of itself be a form of lying, but consider the context of this situation. If a lie is *a false action done with the intent to deceive,* then the Catholic Church's conscious covering for Porter created irreparable consequences. The church became a coperpetrator with Porter.

Stereotypes and Clichés

Stereotype and cliché serve a purpose as a form of shorthand. Our need for vast amounts of information in nanoseconds[9] has made the stereotype vital to modern communication. Unfortunately, it often shuts down original thinking, giving those hungry for truth a candy bar of misinformation instead of a balanced meal. The stereotype explains a situation with just enough truth to seem unquestionable.

All the *isms*—racism, sexism, ageism, et al.—are founded on and fueled by the stereotype and the cliché, which are lies of exaggeration, omission, and ignorance. They are always dangerous. They take a single tree and make it a landscape. They destroy curiosity. They close minds and separate people. The single mother on welfare is assumed to be cheating. Any black male could tell you how much of his identity is obliterated[10] daily by stereotypes. Fat people, ugly people, beautiful people, old people, large-breasted women, short men, the mentally ill, and the homeless all could tell you how much more they are like us than we want to think. I once admitted to a group of people that I had a mouth like a truck driver. Much to my surprise, a man stood up and said, "I'm a truck driver, and I never cuss." Needless to say, I was humbled.

Out-and-Out Lies

Of all the ways to lie, I like this one the best, probably because I get tired of trying to figure out the real meanings behind things. At least I can trust the bald-faced lie. I once asked my five-year-old nephew, "Who broke the fence?" (I had seen him do it.) He answered, "The murderers." Who could argue?

At least when this sort of lie is told it can be easily confronted. As the person who is lied to, I know where I stand. The bald-faced lie doesn't toy with my perceptions—it argues with them. It doesn't try to refashion reality, it tries to refute[11] it. *Read my lips* . . . No sleight[12] of hand. No guessing. If this were the only form of lying, there would be no such thing as floating anxiety or the adult-children of alcoholics movement.

These are only a few of the ways we lie. Or are lied to. As I said earlier, it's not easy to entirely eliminate lies from our lives. No matter how pious[13] we may try to be, we will still embellish, hedge, and omit to lubricate[14] the daily machinery of living. But there is a world of difference between telling

13

14

15

16

17

18

■ **IDEA JOURNAL:** Think of another common human behavior. Break it into categories, and give examples for each category.

PREDICT: Pause just as you start the "Out-and-Out Lies" section. How do you think Ericsson might define such lies?

[9] **nanoseconds:** billionths of a second

[10] **obliterated:** wiped out

[11] **refute:** deny

[12] **sleight:** skillful trick

[13] **pious:** religious

[14] **lubricate:** oil

functional lies and living a lie. Martin Buber once said, "The lie is the spirit committing treason against itself." Our acceptance of lies becomes a cultural cancer that eventually shrouds[15] and reorders reality until moral garbage becomes as invisible to us as water is to a fish.

How much do we tolerate before we become sick and tired of being sick and tired? When will we stand up and declare our *right* to trust? When do we stop accepting that the real truth is in the fine print? Whose lips do we read this year when we vote for president? When will we stop being so reticent about making judgments? When do we stop turning over our personal power and responsibility to liars?

Maybe if I don't tell the bank the check's in the mail I'll be less tolerant of the lies told to me every day. A country song I once heard said it all for me: "You've got to stand for something or you'll fall for anything."

19

20

REFLECT: Think back on your answer to the question on page 634 about whether lying ever has any merit. Have your views on this issue changed? Why or why not?

_____

_____

▪ SUMMARIZE AND RESPOND . . . .

In your reading journal or elsewhere, summarize the main point of "The Ways We Lie." Then, go back and check off the support for this main idea. Next, write a brief summary of the essay. Finally, write a brief response to the reading. What did it make you think about or feel? Do you agree with Ericsson's claim that we all tell lies every day? Provide examples from your own experience that support this idea.

▪ CHECK YOUR COMPREHENSION . . . .

1. An alternate title for this essay could be
   a. "Lying Never Hurt Anyone."
   b. "The Check's in the Mail: The Greatest Lie of All."
   c. "Justification for Lying."
   d. "Lies in Our Lives." ⓓ

2. The main point of this essay is that
   a. small lies are OK because everyone lies.
   b. we should reevaluate the role that lies play in our lives. ⓑ
   c. lies told by someone you trust are the worst.
   d. to trust and be trusted, we must refuse to lie.

3. What distinction does Ericsson make between telling a functional lie and living a lie?
   a. Telling a functional lie makes someone feel bad, and living a lie cheats big institutions.
   b. Telling a functional lie is relatively harmless, but living a lie can have serious consequences. ⓑ
   c. Telling a functional lie has no merit, and living a lie is a good idea.
   d. Telling a functional lie is honest, and living a lie is dishonest.

[15] **shrouds:** covers

4. If you are unfamiliar with the following words, use a dictionary to check their meanings: *confrontation* (para. 3); *merit* (4); *penance* (6); *irreparable* (13); *cliché, vital* (14); *refashion* (17); *tolerant* (20).

READ CRITICALLY

1. Describe Ericsson's tone in this essay. For example, what is her tone in paragraph 1 when she tells us that "the baby I'm pregnant with decided to do aerobics on my lungs for two hours"?

2. How does Ericsson organize her essay? How does she classify the ways we tell lies?

3. What images does Ericsson associate with telling lies? Select one that you like, and explain why.

4. What is Ericsson's attitude toward lying? What examples in the essay support your answer?

5. In paragraph 16 Ericsson writes, "At least I can trust the bald-faced lie." What do you think she means by trusting a lie?

WRITE

■ **TIP:** For a sample classification paragraph, see page 162.

WRITE A PARAGRAPH: Write a paragraph that describes another category of lies. Be sure to provide examples for your readers.

WRITE AN ESSAY: Write an essay that continues Ericsson's classification of the ways we lie. Provide detailed examples from your experiences—or the experiences of people you know—for at least two of the categories she provides. Develop two new categories of your own. Feel free to include the ideas you wrote about in your reading journal for Summarize and Respond.

Damon Darlin

Some Ways to Prepare
for the Absolute Worst

Damon Darlin writes for the *New York Times,* in which the following essay was published. Before that, he was a senior editor at *Business 2.0,* where he wrote pieces for the magazine's Web log. He has also reported for *Forbes* and the *Wall Street Journal* and served as managing editor for *U.S. News & World Report.*

In "Some Ways to Prepare for the Absolute Worst," Darlin draws on advice from survivalists and disaster experts to provide some basic tips for emergency preparation. By sorting the advice into a few broad categories, Darlin makes sure to cover all of the necessities.

GUIDING QUESTION
How easy do you think it is to take the advice Darlin offers here? Would reading this essay change people's behavior?

Pam Stegner knows a lot about preparing for an emergency. After all, Mrs. Stegner, a former emergency medical technician in Collins, Missouri, has been stockpiling for years now.

To take care of her family of five during a catastrophe,[1] she has a gravity-fed water purifier able to process 30 gallons of water a day, as well as 600 pounds of rice and beans, 18,000 dried eggs, and 16 tons of organically grown hard winter wheat stored in a semi-tractor trailer and a temperature-controlled storehouse.

Mrs. Stegner is the first to admit that she may take preparedness to an extreme, but her reasons for doing it may not sound so odd after watching victims of Hurricane Katrina languish for days without aid. "You can't wait for the government to get there," she said. "You will die before they get there."

Indeed, the Federal Emergency Management Agency advises that Americans prepare a two-week supply cache[2] because it could take that long for help to arrive. FEMA says on its Web site, "A two-week supply can relieve a great deal of inconvenience and uncertainty until services are restored."

Getting ready for the next disaster doesn't seem so crazy anymore. Mrs. Stegner, who is the host of a radio show on preparedness and sells survival products from a store in nearby Humansville, says it has been easy to "get labeled a nutcase" for worrying about catastrophes. But she and other survivalist outfitters are noticing how, at least right now, the general public is a bit more receptive.

John Maniatty, who runs the FrugalSquirrels.com Web site out of Morrisville, Vermont, says he is getting six times the traffic he had in early August and considerably more than after the terrorist attacks of September 11, 2001. "So many more normal people—I use that term because I get wackos, too—are taking a look," he said.

You don't have to go as far as a survivalist, but you can certainly learn from them. Here is a distillation[3] of advice from emergency preparedness experts from across the spectrum:[4]

Water

If you take nothing else away from this article, at least heed[5] this advice: stock up on water. It is cheap, it has a long shelf-life, and, most important, you cannot live without it. Most of us can do without food—not to mention e-mail and *Desperate Housewives*—for several weeks.

But dehydration is a very real and life-threatening danger after a calamity. Though you drink half a gallon of water a day, you should store one gallon of water per person per day. Assume you will be cut off for at least three days and store as much extra as you have room for in a cool, dark

1   **IDEA JOURNAL:** What sort of disaster can you imagine living through in the future? What would you do to survive such a disaster?

2

3

4

5   IDENTIFY: Underline the sentence in paragraph 5 that summarizes the main point of this and the following paragraph.

6

7   PREDICT: Based on paragraph 7, what do you expect Darlin to do in the rest of the essay?

8   _____

9

---

[1] **catastrophe:** disaster

[2] **cache:** supply

[3] **distillation:** summary

[4] **spectrum:** range

[5] **heed:** follow

space. The International Bottled Water Association says jugs of water can be kept indefinitely, though they may pick up an off-flavor from the plastic after a year or so. But it is pretty easy to rotate the stock every couple of months since many people drink bottled water.

If you have the room, store some of the water in the freezer. When the 10 electricity goes, you'll have more ice to preserve the food in the refrigerator for a day or two longer.

If worse comes to worst and you run out of water while your commu- 11 nity's water supply is contaminated, turn off the water supply to your house and drain water from your water heater or scoop it from the toilet tank. It must be purified by boiling it for several minutes or by mixing in two drops of old-fashioned bleach—not the "mountain fresh" scented varieties—to each quart of water.

Food

The odds of anything calamitous[6] happening are slim, so you don't want to 12 spend several thousand dollars buying and storing food. You have better things to do with your money than investing in creamed corn and sardines. If you have a pantry or basement with a decent supply of canned foods and bottled juices, you should do just fine for several weeks. "You could survive for two weeks just on Tang," said Eric Zaltas, nutritionist with PowerBar Inc., a maker of nutrition bars.

Given that in most emergencies—floods, earthquake, or fire—you may 13 have to flee, it is smart to keep a 72-hour bug-out kit. That's a three-day sup- ply that you can easily carry out to the car at a moment's notice. The cru- cial concept here is high nutrition in a small amount of space. Freeze-dried foods would be perfect, except you'll need clean and heated water to recon- stitute[7] those products.

Some people buy the military's Meals Ready to Eat. A case of twelve 14 meals costs about $73 and they are currently in short supply. Nutrition bars are another good choice. The rap[8] against them—loads of fat, carbohy- drates, and calories—is actually a plus during a disaster. Something like the PowerBar Performance Bar also contains electrolytes, which when taken with water, will help keep your body chemistry in order. Avoid the choco- late-coated varieties because they will just get messy when it gets hot and water for cleanup is at a premium.

High-protein diet shakes are a bit expensive, but have the added advan- 15 tage of supplying you with liquid, as would high-fiber potassium-packed vegetable juice. Throw in some dried fruit and you have enough calories to get by for three days.

SUMMARIZE: What is Darlin's basic advice about food in times of emergency?

Don't forget ready-to-feed baby formula if you have an infant. People 16 with medical conditions like diabetes or kidney disease will have to pay more attention to what they store and what they eat. As for pets, buy the dried pet food your pets don't really like and they won't eat as much.

For the truly serious food hoarder,[9] FrugalSquirrels.com, the survivalist 17

---

[6] **calamitous:** relating to a disaster

[7] **reconstitute:** to add moisture back into something that has been dried

[8] **rap:** complaint

[9] **hoarder:** one who gets and keeps things

outfitter, sells an $18 software package called Food Storage Planner that will compute exactly how much you need and alert you when to replace it.

Cash

If you get a warning, head to the nearest cash machine ASAP. (You'll already have all the food and water you need, right?) The time to raid the A.T.M. is before the disaster because when the electricity fails, you won't find one that works. Take out as much as you can because you may need it to buy supplies at post-disaster inflated prices and credit cards won't work if there is no electricity or computer networks are down. When the disaster has passed put the money back in the bank.   18

Communications

In almost every disaster, cell phones have proved remarkably useless. (Old-fashioned landline phones hold up much better.) Without electricity, desktop computers become expensive paperweights and laptops follow in short order as their batteries drain. Short of a $1,000 satellite phone, there is precious little you can do to reach out to the world in an emergency. Face it. When a disaster strikes, you can't think like Steven P. Jobs.[10] Abraham Lincoln must be your role model because when the electricity goes, all you have at your disposal are the things people of the nineteenth century got by on.   19

Two things that might help: get an e-mail account from Google or Yahoo that allows you access to e-mail from any computer you happen to find and buy a hand-crank cell phone charger.   20

■ **TEAMWORK:** This essay was written for a newspaper and so, according to newspaper style, is made up of several brief paragraphs. You might point this out to students, and then have them work in small groups to combine some of the paragraphs into longer ones. Next, the groups could share their revisions and discuss which seem to be most effective.

Extras

You cannot do without a first-aid kit, a radio, and lots of batteries. The new flashlights that use light-emitting diodes will help you conserve juice.[11] Camping gear—butane stoves, coolers, and lightweight tents—easily doubles as survival gear. What else? An adapter that turns your car's cigarette lighter into an electrical outlet for any appliance could be a lifesaver. Consider sticking a can of fluorescent spray paint among your other supplies and then stash[12] all this stuff in a plastic box that can serve to float things out to safety.   21

Medicines

Thanks to health insurance companies' rules, it is often not easy to get extra medicine without paying full price. But with a little planning it can be done. Ask your doctor for help. Or for several months in a row, start refilling prescriptions a week or so before they run out until you have accumulated several weeks' supply.   22

Documents

Pulling together documents you need on the run may be the hardest thing to do. Financial planners have been after people for years to make a "beneficiary book" to help their heirs or executors more easily sort through affairs. It should hold copies of birth and marriage certificates, adoption papers, key identification numbers, copies of bank statements, deeds, titles, credit cards,   23

REFLECT: Based on this essay, what do you think are the most important things one can do to "prepare for the absolute worst"?

---

[10] **Steven P. Jobs:** cofounder of Apple Computer

[11] **juice:** power; electricity

[12] **stash:** store

and insurance policies as well as passwords to online accounts. The same information would be useful to you in case you lose access to your primary records in a disaster. Just keep it in a secure place and grab it on the way out of the house.

Guns

Some survivalists recommend a gun for protection. But if you haven't used   24
one regularly, don't know how to store it safely, and haven't made the moral decision that you could kill a person, forget it. Someone is just going to get hurt and it will probably be you. Your best protection is banding together with neighbors—and sharing that food all of you stashed.

■ SUMMARIZE AND RESPOND . . . .

In your reading journal or elsewhere, summarize the main point of "Some Ways to Prepare for the Absolute Worst." Then, go back and check off support for this main idea. Next, write a brief summary of the essay. Finally, write a brief response to the reading. Does Darlin's advice seem practical and necessary? Did he persuade you to take this advice? Why, or why not?

■ CHECK YOUR COMPREHENSION . . . .

1. An alternate title for this essay could be
    a. "Stocking Up for a Disaster."
    b. "The Failure of the Government to Aid People during Emergencies."
    c. "Why More People Are Worrying about Catastrophes."
    d. "Taking Disaster Preparedness to an Extreme."

2. The main point of this essay is that
    a. preparing to survive a disaster takes more time and effort than most people are willing to spend.
    b. in case of a disaster, there are some crucial items one should have on hand.
    c. survivalists have exactly the right idea when it comes to preparing for a disaster.
    d. disasters may cause people to flee their homes, so they should prepare to take food and water with them.

3. According to Darlin, the one thing we cannot live without in the aftermath of a disaster is
    a. a three-day supply of food.
    b. nutrition bars and high-protein diet shakes.
    c. a first-aid kit.
    d. water.

4. If you are unfamiliar with the following words, use a dictionary to check their meanings: *stockpiling* (para. 1); *receptive* (5); *dehydration, indefinitely* (9); *contaminated, purified* (11); *crucial* (13); *electrolytes, premium* (14); *potassium* (15); *inflated* (18); *emitting, diodes, butane, fluorescent* (21); *accumulated* (22); *beneficiary, executors* (23).

READ CRITICALLY

1. Why do you suppose Darlin begins by writing about Pam Stegner, someone who takes disaster preparedness to an extreme? What does he seem to expect readers to learn from her?

2. Do you find the order in which Darlin presents his categories to be effective? Why or why not?

3. Are the eight categories adequately developed? Why or why not? Can you think of any other categories he might have included?

4. How does Darlin's discussion of his fourth category, "communications," and his final category, "guns," differ from his discussion of his other six categories? Why do you think he included these two categories?

5. Darlin's essay lacks a conclusion. Do you think one is needed? If you were to add a conclusion, what would it say?

WRITE

WRITE A PARAGRAPH: Imagine that you have to move into a shelter because of a disaster. In addition to the essentials that Darlin writes about, what kinds of things would you want to take for yourself and other family members? Write a paragraph listing and describing at least three categories of things you would take to the shelter.

WRITE AN ESSAY: Darlin writes about the essentials for mere survival, but what would you say are the essentials for living a comfortable and happy life? Into what categories can you group these essentials? In an essay, discuss the categories of things that you require for a comfortable and happy life, and develop your categories, as Darlin does, with specific examples.

47
Definition

Each essay in this chapter uses definition to get its main point across to the reader. As you read these essays, consider how they achieve the four basics of good definition that are listed below and discussed in Chapter 14 of this book.

▪▪ FOUR BASICS OF GOOD DEFINITION
1. It tells readers what is being defined.
2. It presents a clear basic definition.
3. It uses examples to show what the writer means.
4. It gives details about the examples that readers will understand.

Michael Thompson
Passage into Manhood

Michael Thompson is a consultant, child psychologist, and author. His 1999 book *Raising Cain: Protecting the Emotional Life of Boys,* cowritten with Dan Kindlon, was the inspiration for a PBS documentary of the same name. Both the book and documentary, which was hosted by Thompson, explore boys' emotional development and the negative consequences of common misunderstandings about them. Thompson's other books include *Speaking of Boys: Answers to the Most-Asked Questions about Raising Sons* (2000), *Best Friends/ Worst Enemies: Understanding the Social Worlds of Children* (with Catherine O'Neill Grace and Larry Cohen, 2001), *Mom, They're Teasing Me: Helping Your Child Solve Social Problems* (2002), and *The Pressured Child: Helping Your Child Achieve Success in School and in Life* (with Teresa Barker, 2004).

In "Passage into Manhood," which appeared in the *Boston Globe* in 2005, Thompson gets one young man's definition of manhood, raising questions about what our society does—and, more important, doesn't do—to prepare boys to become men.

GUIDING QUESTION
What is necessary for the passage into manhood, according to the author?

The boy sitting next to me on the plane from Toronto to North Bay was seventeen years old, a rising high school senior with a slight beard. He had the misfortune[1] to sit next to a child psychologist, a so-called expert on boys, who would pester him with questions for the entire trip about how he was spending his summer, and why. "This is kind of like a final exam," he observed, trying to get me to relent,[2] but I wouldn't let go.

After he had gamely[3] answered a number of my questions about the summer camp to which he was headed, I sprang the big one on him, the question I have asked many boys his age. "Do you consider yourself to be a man?"

"Yes," he replied immediately. Then he caught himself, hesitating momentarily before declaring with conviction:[4] "Well, no. But I will be in August!"

REFLECT: In paragraph 3, why do you suppose the boy answered "yes" and then changed his mind?

What could a seventeen-year-old boy do between the last week of June and August that he could anticipate would make him a man? American culture doesn't have any universal ritual[5] that sees a boy through that psychologically difficult passage from boyhood to manhood. Many boys, actually, almost every boy, struggles with what it means to become a man. Boys (or young men, if you prefer) of seventeen, nineteen, and into their early twenties wrestle with the riddle: What test do I have to pass to become a man, and who will be able to recognize that I have reached that point? My young companion thought he had found an answer.

It turned out that he was going to embark[6] the next morning on a fifty-day canoeing trip that would take him and nine companions through lakes, rivers, rapids, mud, and ferocious[7] mosquitoes, all the way up to Hudson's Bay, a distance of six hundred miles. He and his friends had been preparing for this by developing wilderness skills for the last four years at their camp. They would carry all of their own food, they would take risks, and they would suffer. Toward the end of their journey they would see the Northern lights[8] and would visit an Inuit[9] settlement. They might see moose and wolves, but, he told me, they were not going to be tourists. "This isn't about seeing wild animals," he asserted.

IDENTIFY: Paragraph 5 provides several examples. Check off the experiences that the boy expects to have.

What was his definition of manhood? "It's taking responsibility," he said. "At the end of the day, it's taking responsibility and taking things you've learned from others and creating your own self."

"It's about finishing a grueling portage,"[10] he said, "It's about doing work and getting a result."

IDENTIFY: In paragraphs 6 and 7, underline the boy's definitions of manhood.

[1] **misfortune:** bad luck

[2] **relent:** to give up; to stop

[3] **gamely:** enthusiastically

[4] **conviction:** a strong belief or feeling

[5] **ritual:** a ceremony or rite of passage

[6] **embark:** to go away

[7] **ferocious:** fierce; menacing

[8] **Northern lights:** a colorful display of lights in the sky, caused by solar winds

[9] **Inuit:** native people of North America

[10] **grueling portage:** a difficult journey that requires the carrying of supplies

Didn't he get that from school and varsity athletics? No. Though he did   8
well in school and had bright college prospects, school didn't address his
hunger to be a man, not even playing sports. "After sports you go home, take
a shower, and watch TV." When he was canoe tripping, he felt as if he made
a sustained[11] effort that connected him to all the men who had canoed before him at that camp for more than one hundred years.

Could he find the experience he sought among his friends back home?   9
What were they doing this summer? "Hanging out. They're playing video
games," he said. They didn't get it. "It's frustrating. You try to explain to
them how great it is. You tell them about paddling all day, and cooking your
own food, about the mosquitoes, and carrying a wood canoe, and they say,
'What, are you crazy?'"

SUMMARIZE: In a sentence
or two (in your own words)
sum up the point that
the author makes in para-
graph 10.

This young about-to-be man described his father as a "good guy," his   10
mother as a hardworking professional, and his step-father as financially successful, but none of them seemed to hold the key to helping him become a
man. American culture has no universal ritual for helping boys move from
boyhood to manhood. Jewish boys have their bar mitzvahs,[12] Mormon boys
have their year of missionary service, other boys sign up for the military. Yet
every boy yearns to be a man, and traditional societies always took boys
away from their parents to pass an initiation rite. We no longer have such rituals, but boys still wonder: What is the test, where do I find it, how do I pass
it, and who will recognize that moment when I pass from boyhood to manhood? We fail to provide a meaningful, challenging path that speaks to the
souls of a majority of boys.

■ TEACHING TIP: Write
"man" on one side of the
board and "woman" on the
other. Then, ask students to call
out the names of people (famous or otherwise) that they
consider to be ideal men and
women, and write the names
down. Students should give at
least one reason for their
choices; write the reasons down
as well. Next, discuss the similarities and differences among
the people and reasons listed.
Did students give different reasons for the different genders?
If so, what do the differences
suggest about what society values in men versus women?

The key to his manhood lay with the counselors who accompany him on   11
the journey and with his companions whose lives he would protect and who
would, in turn, look out for him. Past the rain, the bugs, the smelling bad,
he would discover his manhood in community and in the kind of challenge
that only nature offers up.

Our plane journey over, I wished him luck. And then I couldn't get our   12
conversation out of my mind. While a demanding canoe trip is not for every
boy, I'm certain that every boy is searching for a test. You can find the test
by taking on anything that requires commitment and courage. However,
there is something that happens out-of-doors that strips you down to the essentials: safety, companionship, a shared sense of mission. You set aside the
busyness and crap of daily life, and then you can think about what it actually means to be a man.

■ IDEA JOURNAL: Write
about a personal experience
that you felt marked a passage from youth to adulthood.
What happened, and how did
the experience change you?

■   **SUMMARIZE AND RESPOND** . . . .

In your reading journal or elsewhere, summarize the main point of "Passage into Manhood." Then, go back and check off support for this main
idea. Next, write a brief summary of the essay. Finally, write a brief response
to the reading. Do you agree with the author about what is needed for boys
to make the passage into manhood?

[11]**sustained:** continuous; ongoing

[12]**bar mitzvahs:** ceremonies marking Jewish boys' thirteenth birthdays and the beginning
of their religious responsibilities

■ CHECK YOUR COMPREHENSION . . . .

1. An alternate title for this essay could be
   a. "American Boys Overwhelmed by Adult Responsibilities."
   b. "One Teen's Story of His Passage into Manhood."
   c. "The Path to Manhood: A Difficult Journey for Most Boys."
   d. "American Boys Need a Meaningful Path to Manhood."

2. The main point of this essay is that
   a. undergoing a wilderness challenge is the only real way to become a man.
   b. young men should be able to define for themselves what it means to be a man, even if most people would disagree.
   c. going through a significant ritual or test makes boys feel like men, but American culture fails to provide such paths.
   d. American boys should be given a bar mitzvah or be required to perform missionary service.

3. What challenge was the boy Thompson spoke with about to take on?
   a. A boating competition
   b. A fifty-day canoeing trip
   c. A hiking and biking tour
   d. A Canadian triathalon

4. If you are unfamiliar with the following words, use a dictionary to check their meanings: *pester* (para. 1); *momentarily* (3); *anticipate* (4); *prospects* (8); *missionary, yearns, initiation, rite, majority* (10).

■ READ CRITICALLY . . . .

1. In paragraph 2, the author asks the boy what he considers to be a "big" question: Does the boy consider himself to be a man? Why does the author consider this to be a big question, and do you agree? Why or why not?

2. How do you define manhood or womanhood? How is your definition similar to or different from that provided by the boy Thompson speaks to?

3. In paragraph 10, Thompson argues, "We fail to provide a meaningful, challenging path [to adulthood] that speaks to the souls of a majority of boys." Do you agree? Why or why not? What other possible paths to manhood are not mentioned by Thompson?

4. Why, according to Thompson, are outdoor challenges especially useful for boys making the passage toward manhood? Do you share his view?

5. Why do you suppose Thompson is interested in the opinions of one young person he meets on a plane? How do the quotations from the boy contribute to the point of Thompson's essay?

■ **WRITE** . . . .

■ **TIP:** For a sample definition paragraph, see page 177.

WRITE A PARAGRAPH: Write a paragraph that gives at least two pieces of advice to a boy who is about to become a man or to a girl who is about to become a woman. The person could be a brother or sister, a son or daughter, or a friend. Or you could imagine a boy or girl to address the advice to. Be sure to explain why each piece of advice is important, and give examples to show what you mean.

WRITE AN ESSAY: Write an essay that defines what it is to be a man or woman. Use examples from your personal experience to help define the concept. If you answered question 2 under Read Critically, you might want to use some of the insights from that question to develop your essay. Explain why you think Thompson, or the boy he interviewed, might agree or disagree with your definition.

*Janice E. Castro with
Dan Cook and Cristina Garcia*

Spanglish

Janice E. Castro is an assistant professor in the Medill New Media Program at Northwestern University. She worked as a reporter for *Time* for more than twenty years and started the magazine's health policy beat. After the publication of her book, *The American Way of Health: How Medicine Is Changing, and What It Means to You* (1994), she became the managing editor of *Time's* online division.

Castro wrote "Spanglish" while at *Time* with the help of Dan Cook and Cristina Garcia. In the essay, she defines the language created when Spanish and English speakers come together in our blended culture.

GUIDING QUESTION
What are some of the reasons the authors provide for the rise of the use of Spanglish?

REFLECT: The authors in-
clude several Spanish terms
in the first paragraph. What
do you think they mean?

In Manhattan a first-grader greets her visiting grandparents, happily ex-   1
claiming, "Come here, *siéntate!*" Her bemused[1] grandfather, who does not speak Spanish, nevertheless knows she is asking him to sit down. A Miami personnel officer understands what a job applicant means when he says,

[1] **bemused:** surprised and a bit confused

"*Quiero un* part time." Nor do drivers miss a beat reading a billboard alongside a Los Angeles street advertising CERVEZA — SIX-PACK!

This free-form blend of Spanish and English, known as Spanglish, is common linguistic currency[2] wherever concentrations of Hispanic Americans are found in the U.S. In Los Angeles, where 55 percent of the city's 3 million inhabitants speak Spanish, Spanglish is as much a part of daily life as sunglasses. Unlike the broken-English efforts of earlier immigrants from Europe, Asia, and other regions, Spanglish has become a widely accepted conversational mode used casually — even playfully — by Spanish-speaking immigrants and native-born Americans alike.

SUMMARIZE: In your own words, describe how Spanglish differs from the broken English of earlier immigrants to the United States.

Consisting of one part Hispanicized English, one part Americanized Spanish, and more than a little fractured syntax,[3] Spanglish is a bit like a Robin Williams comedy routine: a crackling line of cross-cultural patter[4] straight from the melting pot.[5] Often it enters Anglo[6] homes and families through the children, who pick it up at school or at play with their young Hispanic contemporaries.[7] In other cases, it comes from watching TV; many an Anglo child watching *Sesame Street* has learned *uno dos tres* almost as quickly as one two three.

Spanglish takes a variety of forms, from the Southern California Anglos who bid farewell with the utterly silly "*hasta la* bye-bye" to the Cuban American drivers in Miami who *parquean* their *carros*. Some Spanglish sentences are mostly Spanish, with a quick detour for an English word or two. A Latino friend may cut short a conversation by glancing at his watch and excusing himself with the explanation that he must "*ir al* supermarket."

PREDICT: Based on the first part of the first sentence of paragraph 4, how do you suppose the authors will go on to develop this paragraph?

Many of the English words transplanted in this way are simply hardier than their Spanish counterparts. No matter how distasteful the subject, for example, it is still easier to say "income tax" than *impuesto sobre la renta*. At the same time, many Spanish-speaking immigrants have adopted such terms as *VCR, microwave,* and *dishwasher* for what they view as largely American phenomena. Still other English words convey a cultural context that is not implicit[8] in the Spanish. A friend who invites you to *lonche* most likely has in mind the brisk American custom of "doing lunch" rather than the languorous[9] afternoon break traditionally implied by *almuerzo*.

Mainstream Americans exposed to similar hybrids of German, Chinese, or Hindi might be mystified. But even Anglos who speak little or no Spanish are somewhat familiar with Spanglish. Living among them, for one thing, are 19 million Hispanics. In addition, more American high school and university students sign up for Spanish than for any other foreign language.

Only in the past ten years, though, has Spanglish begun to turn into a national slang. Its popularity has grown with the explosive increases in U.S.

[2] **linguistic currency:** typical speech

[3] **fractured syntax:** language that breaks grammatical rules

[4] **patter:** quick speech

[5] **melting pot:** a blending of people from different cultures

[6] **Anglo:** white, English-speaking person

[7] **contemporaries:** peers

[8] **implicit:** understood but not expressed directly

[9] **languorous:** long and relaxing

■ **IDEA JOURNAL:** How important do you think it is for non-Hispanics in the United States to understand at least some Spanish?

■ **ESL:** If your class includes a number of Hispanic students, you might ask them to discuss whether Spanglish is as common in their conversation as the authors suggest. If they are willing, you might also have them give some examples of Spanglish in conversation. If you have ESL students whose native language is something other than Spanish, you might have them discuss the extent to which they use English terms when speaking in their native language.

immigration from Latin American countries. English has increasingly collided with Spanish in retail stores, offices and classrooms, in pop music, and on street corners. Anglos whose ancestors picked up such Spanish words as *rancho, bronco, tornado,* and *incommunicado,* for instance, now freely use such Spanish words as *gracias, bueno, amigo,* and *por favor.*

Among Latinos, Spanglish conversations often flow easily from Spanish 8 into several sentences of English and back.

Spanglish is a sort of code for Latinos: the speakers know Spanish, but 9 their hybrid[10] language reflects the American culture in which they live. Many lean to shorter, clipped phrases in place of the longer, more graceful expressions their parents used. Says Leonel de la Cuesta, an assistant professor of modern languages at Florida International University in Miami: "In the U.S., time is money, and that is showing up in Spanglish as an economy of language." Conversational examples: *taipiar* (type) and *winshi-wiper* (windshield wiper) replace *escribir a màquina* and *limpiaparabrisas.*

Major advertisers, eager to tap the estimated $134 billion in spending 10 power wielded[11] by Spanish-speaking Americans, have ventured into Spanglish to promote their products. In some cases, attempts to sprinkle Spanish through commercials have produced embarrassing gaffes.[12] A Braniff Airlines ad that sought to tell Spanish-speaking audiences they could settle back *en* (in) luxuriant *cuero* (leather) seats, for example, inadvertently said they could fly without clothes (*encuero*). A fractured translation of the Miller Lite slogan told readers the beer was "Filling, and less delicious." Similar blunders[13] are often made by Anglos trying to impress Spanish-speaking pals. But if Latinos are amused by mangled Spanglish, they also recognize these goofs as a sort of friendly acceptance. As they might put it, *no problema.*

■ SUMMARIZE AND RESPOND . . . .

In your reading journal or elsewhere, summarize the main point of "Spanglish." Then, go back and check off support for this main idea. Next, write a brief summary of the essay. Finally, write a brief response to the reading. Was the term *Spanglish* new to you, or were you already familiar with it? What did you find most interesting about the essay? Did you find any of it amusing?

■ CHECK YOUR COMPREHENSION . . . .

1. An alternate title for this essay could be
   a. "The Influence of Hispanic Americans on U.S. Culture."
   b. "The Economic Power of Hispanic Americans."
   c. "How Language Changes over the Course of Time."
   d. "A New Cross-Cultural 'Language.'"

[10] **hybrid:** a combination of two things
[11] **wielded:** held
[12] **gaffes:** mistakes
[13] **blunders:** mistakes

2. The main point of this essay is that

   a. most Hispanic American children find it easy to learn English.

   (b.) Spanglish is becoming common wherever speakers of Spanish and English come together.

   c. many Hispanic Americans prefer to speak to one another in Spanish than in English.

   d. Spanglish is a kind of code for Hispanic Americans that distinguishes them from other English speakers.

3. Which of the following is *not* a reason cited in the essay for the rise of Spanglish?

   a. Some English terms refer to things that Hispanic Americans regard as essentially American.

   b. In many cases, an English term is shorter than its Spanish counterpart.

   c. The mixture of English and Spanish reflects the hybrid culture in which Hispanic Americans live.

   (d.) People who speak both English and Spanish are naturally going to switch back and forth.

4. If you are unfamiliar with the following words, use a dictionary to check their meanings: *personnel* (para. 1); *concentrations* (2); *utterly, detour* (4); *transplanted, counterparts, distasteful, phenomena, convey, context, brisk* (5); *mainstream, mystified* (6); *collided* (7); *clipped* (9); *ventured, inadvertently, mangled* (10).

■ READ CRITICALLY . . . .

1. Do the authors give enough examples of what they mean by *Spanglish*? Do they provide enough details about the examples to help readers understand their definition? Why or why not?

2. Whom would you say the authors see as the primary audience for this essay? What makes you think so?

3. The authors suggest that many Anglos can understand Spanglish and even speak it themselves. To what extent do you believe that this is the case?

4. How would you evaluate the authors' final paragraph? Why do you suppose they chose to conclude as they do?

5. This essay was first published in 1988. Since then, the Hispanic population of the United States has grown even larger. What would you point to as some further ways that Hispanic culture has influenced mainstream American culture?

■ WRITE . . . .

WRITE A PARAGRAPH: Write a paragraph that defines an expression common to your group of friends, your workplace, your region, or some other group to which you belong. As you draft, assume that your readers are not familiar with the expression or its special use within your group. In developing your paragraph, consider using contrast, as the authors of "Spanglish" do in paragraph 2, and choose clear examples to communicate your meaning.

WRITE AN ESSAY: In an essay, define a concept that is important to a culture to which you belong. You might, for example, choose to define *success, diversity,* or some other concept in terms of U.S. culture. Or you might choose to define a concept that has a special significance at your job, in a hobby you have, or in your ethnic culture. Before you begin to draft, be sure to define your audience. If your readers will already be somewhat familiar with the concept, you will need to bring your own particular slant to the definition to maintain their interest. If readers will be unfamiliar with the concept, you will need to give enough background for your definition.

48
Comparison and Contrast

Each essay in this chapter uses comparison and contrast to get its main point across to the reader. As you read these essays, consider how they achieve the four basics of good comparison and contrast that are listed below and discussed in Chapter 15 of this book.

■■ FOUR BASICS OF GOOD COMPARISON AND CONTRAST
■■

1. It uses subjects that have enough in common to be compared or contrasted in a useful way.

2. It serves a purpose — either to help readers make a decision or to understand the subjects.

3. It presents several important, parallel points of comparison or contrast.

4. It arranges points in a logical order.

Adora Houghton
My Indian

Adora Houghton wrote this essay while she was a student at Foothill College in Los Altos Hills, California. In her piece, she compares and contrasts the view of American Indians she learned from books as a child and the reality she later came to understand. The essay was originally published in the anthology *Multitude: Cross-Cultural Readings for Writers* (1993).

GUIDING QUESTION
How does a young girl's image of the Native American change? Does the author's story effectively capture her disappointment and eventual acceptance?

■ **IDEA JOURNAL:** Think of a time when your expectations about someone, or a group of people, were inaccurate.

IDENTIFY: Put an X by the details Houghton uses to describe her image of Native Americans.

I've always been fascinated by Native Americans—or, as we said when I was growing up, American Indians. Even as far back as first grade, my favorite game was to pretend I was an Indian. I remember how after school I would transform myself into a brave by donning[1] my cloth "buckskin," complete with the headdress I had fashioned out of construction paper and feathers which I had found in our backyard. In times of war I would use my mother's makeup for war paint! Then, with war paint on and headdress in place, I would hop onto my sawhorse, and off we'd go to imaginary lands of mountains with perilous passes and plains filled with wild buffalo. As I rode my trusty steed,[2] I sometimes dreamed of what it would be like to come face to face with an authentic Indian. But when that dream finally came true, my Indian turned out to be quite different from what I had expected.

I was six years old at that time, or, as I would have described it in the Indian way (according to me), entering my sixth harvest moon. I read everything I could find about Indians—the *Encyclopaedia Britannica* and the book club selections that arrived each month at our house. Actually, since I couldn't read most of those big words, I'd just look at the pretty pictures. They told me all I needed to know. How glamorous the Indians were! How noble! Their long braided hair gleamed in the sun, and their feathers waved *X* gently in the breeze that blew across their weathered faces as they rode their *X* painted ponies through the desert. Some Indians had short spiky hair *X* painted in bright colors. Others wore buckskin clothes with fringes and *X* moccasins on their feet. But what I liked most of all was their jewelry, the carved beads that were sewn onto the edges of their leather coats and the *X* porcupine-quill chokers that adorned their necks. My favorites, of course, *X* were the turquoise and silver combinations that I would study carefully, *X* peering as closely at the picture as possible.

As I grew, so did my fascination. I named myself Wa-bish-kee-pe-nas, which I had found out was Chippewa for One White Pigeon, and to it I added "with blue eyes." I fashioned a backyard camp, making it look as much like the picture in my schoolbook as I could. It consisted of a tepee made from local resources such as branches from our pine trees and my bed linen, and a pole to tie intruders to (which was actually one end of my mother's clothesline). I even had a campfire, just like the ones built when we went camping, only Mother wouldn't let me light it. That year on my birthday, I asked for and received a peace pipe. I attempted to use it one night by stealing one of my dad's cigarettes, emptying the tobacco into it, and trying to smoke it. It didn't work too well, and when Dad found out, he made sure that it would be my last attempt!

■ **TEACHING TIP:** You might want to point out to students that this essay is also a good example of narration. Ask them why it is an effective narrative, referring to the "four basics" in Chapter 9 if that's helpful.

One day as I was sitting by my campfire chanting, Dad came out to join me. He told me that a friend of his was in town and asked me if I would like to go meet him the next day. Imagine my excitement when he added that his friend was an Indian!

"An Indian!" I shouted, and my heart beat as hard as a tom-tom. "Of course I'll go!"

All that night I couldn't sleep. I lay in bed, wide awake, thinking that my biggest dream was about to come true. I was going to meet a real, true, live

---

[1] **donning:** putting on

[2] **steed:** stallion

Indian. Perhaps he would take me to his tribe and introduce me to the elders. They would give me a pair of moccasins and my own buckskin coat and call me by my Indian name. Then we would go through a ceremony to make me part of the tribe. I couldn't wait!

Morning finally arrived. I could hardly eat any breakfast. At last Father   7
was ready, and we climbed into the car and took off for our exciting adventure. Pretty soon we stopped in front of a small store. I was a bit perplexed.[3] It seemed like a strange place to meet an Indian. But when I entered I noticed that the store was filled with Indian artifacts.[4] There were medicine wheels and tomahawks, bows and arrows and Kachina dolls. And in the corner, inside a glass case, was the jewelry: bracelets, necklaces, rings, and earrings — all in silver and turquoise, all more exquisite[5] than the pictures I'd seen. I'd never imagined there could be so much Indian jewelry in one place.

As I stood mesmerized[6] by the shiny pieces, a man walked up to my fa-   8
ther. I turned to watch the two of them greet each other. The man was slender, dressed in regular street clothes, with short hair framing his thin face. There was something vaguely familiar about his face, with its dark skin and high cheekbones and brown eyes, but before I could quite figure out what it was, he looked at me and smiled.

"Hello!" he said. "You must be Adora. My name's Ed Kee."   9

"Hello!" I replied. He seemed like a nice guy, but I didn't want to waste   10
any time, so I quickly added, "Are you going to take me to meet Dad's Indian friend?"

The man had an understanding look in his eyes, as if he'd heard that line   11
before.

"I am your Dad's Indian friend."   12

"You!" My voice went high with shock. "You're an Indian?"   13

Ed nodded and smiled, and as though he sensed my dismay, he began   14
to tell me about the tribe he came from and some of their myths.[7] They were good stories, but although I tried to listen, I couldn't pay much attention to them because I was so disappointed inside.

He didn't look anything like the Indians I had grown up with and loved,   15
the Indians in my picture-books. He didn't have long braided hair, or even short colored hair. His hair was cut in the latest style, and its color looked almost like my dad's. He didn't wear a buckskin or moccasins or even a shawl. He was attired in blue jeans and a T-shirt that said "Hawaii," and on his feet, of all things, he wore cowboy boots. Worst of all, his name wasn't Running Red Bear or He Who Kills Three Sioux. It was Ed. I had two Eds in my class at school.

In a last effort to salvage[8] the situation, I asked Ed where he lived. I was   16
hoping he'd say it was in a tepee on the top of the hills I could see from my house, or at least in an adobe[9] hut.

REFLECT: What does Houghton mean when she writes "as if he'd heard that line before"?

_____

_____

_____

IDENTIFY: Underline the topic sentence of this paragraph.

---

[3] **perplexed:** confused

[4] **artifacts:** objects

[5] **exquisite:** beautiful

[6] **mesmerized:** fascinated

[7] **myths:** traditional stories; can also mean false stories

[8] **salvage:** save

[9] **adobe:** clay

REFLECT: Interpret the line "Everything I envisioned had turned out to be just that, a vision."

_____

_____

_____

REFLECT: Why does Houghton state that "for a long time I didn't go into the backyard"?

_____

But he simply said, "In a house, just like you do."   17

I was crushed. Everything I envisioned had turned out to be just that, a   18
vision.

Finally, it was time to leave. We said goodbye to Ed, climbed into the car,   19
and drove off. All the way home, I didn't say a word, and my dad knew why.
He tried to explain to me that even though Ed didn't look like my idea of
an Indian, it didn't mean he was any less one. It only meant that Indians,
like all living beings, change with time and circumstance, and I needed to
understand that. He added that what was important was that I should keep
my respect for the heritage and the spirit of the Indians, because that would
never die. What he said made sense, but I still struggled for days with my
disillusionment, and for a long time I didn't go into the backyard.

Then one day, quite some time later, I received a package in the mail.   20
What could it be? I wasn't expecting anything. I opened it with all the excitement of a child on Christmas morning. There was no note and no return
address, but inside the box was a beautiful turquoise and silver bracelet. It
was simple and elegant and just my size, and I instantly fell in love with it.
I started to put it on, and then I noticed an engraving on the back. It read:
Ed Kee, Navajo. My Indian! He had kept in mind the disappointment of a
little girl and had taken the time to make and send her something special,
something that showed he cared, something that was part of who he was.

I ran to my father to show him my bracelet and to tell him that I had   21
finally understood what he had been trying to tell me the day we met my
Indian.

■ SUMMARIZE AND RESPOND . . . .

In your reading journal or elsewhere, summarize the main point of "My
Indian." Then, go back and check off the support for this main idea. Next,
write a brief summary of the essay. Finally, write a brief response to the
reading. What is Houghton's image of Native Americans before she meets
her father's friend? What is it after?

■ CHECK YOUR COMPREHENSION . . . .

1. An alternate title for this essay could be
    a. "An Unexpected Lesson."
    b. "The Ideal Native American."
    c. "A Turquoise Treasure."
    d. "A Childhood Adventure."

2. The main point of this essay is that
    a. young children are easily disappointed but quickly recover.
    b. impressions of people that are formed based on how others see
        them often conflict with reality.
    c. stereotyping people is dangerous.
    d. Native Americans are misunderstood largely because of television
        and books.

3. The word *myths* in paragraph 14 is generally significant to the entire essay because

    a. Native Americans have many myths in their culture.

    (b.) the young girl Adora had accepted myths about Native Americans.

    c. myths, an essential part of all heritages, should be cherished.

    d. myths are an important part of growing up.

4. If you are unfamiliar with the following words, use a dictionary to check their meanings: *peering* (para. 2); *chanting* (4); *vaguely* (8); *dismay* (14); *heritage, disillusionment* (19).

■ **READ CRITICALLY** . . . .

1. What sentence in the first paragraph could function as the thesis statement for this essay?

2. What details give you a clear picture of what Houghton expected a Native American to look and act like?

3. How does Houghton arrange her details in paragraph 15? What is the effect of this technique?

4. What is meaningful about the turquoise and silver bracelet that she receives from Ed Kee (para. 20)?

5. In paragraph 1, Houghton uses the term "my Indian." She uses the term again at the end of her essay in paragraphs 20 and 21. What is significant about the absence of the term in the rest of the essay and its repetition at the end?

■ **WRITE** . . . .

    WRITE A PARAGRAPH: Pick a person that you knew at a different point in your life, such as when you were a child, and compare that person with how you see him or her today.

    WRITE AN ESSAY: In this essay, Houghton learns the lesson that people aren't always as we imagine them to be. In your essay, select a person, place, event, or item that turned out to be different from what you had imagined or expected. As Houghton does, use contrast to point out the differences.

■ **TIP:** For a sample comparison/contrast paragraph, see page 189.

Deborah Tannen

Gender Patterns Begin at the Beginning

Deborah Tannen (b. 1945) earned a doctorate in linguistics from the University of California, Berkeley, in 1979, and she now teaches linguistics at Georgetown University. She has written on communication in doctor-patient relationships and across cultures, but her most popular books have focused on communication and gender. *You Just Don't Understand: Men and Women in Conversation* (1990) was number one on the *New York Times* bestseller list for eight months. She has also published, among many other books, *Talking from 9 to 5* (1994), in which she discusses how different communication styles affect men and women in the workplace. Her most recent book is *You're Wearing* That? *Understanding Mothers and Daughters in Conversation* (2006).

Following is an excerpt from Tannen's book *I Only Say This Because I Love You* (2001). Comparing the communication styles of men and women, she shows how patterns learned at an early age can affect not only how adults interact but also how parents relate to their opposite-sex children.

GUIDING QUESTION

What does Tannen see here as the main difference between the way women and girls communicate with one another and the way men and boys do?

PREDICT: Based on the first two sentences of this paragraph, what do you think Tannen will do in the paragraphs that follow?

IDENTIFY: What pattern of comparison and contrast does Tannen use to organize paragraphs 2 and 3?

1   Genderspeak[1] creates confusion between parents and children of the opposite sex just as surely as it does between parents themselves. For mothers, having sons can be a mystery, just as having daughters can be a mystery for fathers. The seeds of these confusions are planted in the different ways boys and girls relate to their friends while growing up. So adults who were girls and adults who were boys often have greater automatic understanding of the children who were the same kind of children they were.

2   Some years ago, I conducted a research project in which I asked pairs of best friends, boys and girls, to take chairs into a room and talk. When I show clips from these tapes to audiences, they always laugh at the contrast. In the first clip, two five-year-old girls sit directly facing each other. They lean in toward each other; one reaches out to adjust the other's headband; and both talk intently[2] while keeping their gazes fixed steadily on each other's faces.

3   Then come the five-year-old boys, who look lost and antsy[3] in their little chairs. Sitting side by side, they never look directly at each other—never turn toward each other at all. They bounce in their seats as they talk about what they'd rather be doing—activities like blowing up the house (but only the upstairs, where I have forced them to sit and talk, not the downstairs, where the Nintendo is). A few moments after this sequence, the boys were up out of their chairs, running around the room. I quickly called a halt to the taping when I saw, from my seat beside the camera operator outside the room, that one of the boys had lifted his small plastic chair above his head and was running with it straight toward the camera.

[1] **Genderspeak:** Tannen's word for the differing communication styles of women and men
[2] **intently:** with great interest or attention
[3] **antsy:** restless

Then come the ten-year-olds. The girls sit and face each other, talking in-   4
tently; they never take their eyes off each other's faces. The boys sit side by
side, awkwardly shifting and squirming, and their eyes never meet: When one
turns his head slightly toward the other, the other is always looking away.

The fifteen-year-olds always spark laughter. The girls sit directly facing   5
each other, their gazes fixed unswervingly[4] on each other's faces as one describes to the other a gift she bought for a friend. Then come the boys, sitting
side by side, leaning forward. One boy rests his elbows on his knees and looks
at the floor; the other rests his right foot on his left knee as he plays with his
shoelace, keeping his eyes firmly fixed on his foot rather than on his friend.

You can observe similar patterns on a sunny day when pairs of women   6
and men are sitting outside having lunch, or just about anywhere friends are
lounging in a casual setting: The women sit face-to-face and keep their eyes
focused on each other's faces as they talk incessantly;[5] the men sit at angles
or side by side and look around them while talking intermittently.[6]

REFLECT: What do you think
of Tannen's characterization
of the behavior of men and
women? How accurate do
you think it is?

These different patterns often lead to confusion and frustration between   7
women and men: The woman complains, "You're not listening to me," to a
man who is not looking at her, and the man feels wrongly accused. He
would be uncomfortable if the person he was talking to looked too intently
at him. If it's a man, the direct gaze feels like a challenge; if it's a woman, it
feels like flirting. But many women perceive the lack of direct gaze as a failure of listening—which to them is the most important gift a person can
give. A letter published by *Newsweek* following an article regarding women's
sexuality reflected this value: "Now, if only the pharmaceutical companies
could develop a drug to increase blood flow to men's ears," wrote Julie
Wash, "*that* would be the women's Viagra."

IDENTIFY: Underline the
main point of paragraph 7.

Imagine a scene in a kitchen when the kids come home from school.   8
Mother and daughter sit at the kitchen table facing each other. The mother
asks what happened at school, and the daughter tells her. She talks about
the teacher, her friends, and the conversations they had. In another kitchen
a mother asks the same question of her little boy and gets in reply the equivalent of the 1950s popular book title: *"Where did you go?" "Out." "What did
you do?" "Nothing."* But there is hope: Instead of expecting their sons to sit
opposite them and talk, many mothers find they are more likely to hear information they are interested in while doing something with their sons, like
driving in the car or weeding the garden. One mother on hearing me say this
exclaimed, "That's true! And my son is only four!"

SUMMARIZE: What, accord-
ing to Tannen, should
mothers do to get their
sons to communicate with
them?

Many fathers understand this automatically. David Reimer, a man who   9
was raised as a girl following a surgical accident that destroyed his genital
organ, tells of the moment when he was nearly fifteen and his parents revealed to him the truth of his birth. The teenager, who up until then knew
herself as a girl named Brenda, suspected something was up when her father picked her up and suggested they get some ice cream instead of going
straight home. Looking back, David recalls that his first thought was that
something dreadful had happened to his parents or his brother: "Usually
when there was some kind of disaster in the family, good old dad takes you
out in the family car for a cone or something. So I was thinking, 'Is Mother

■ IDEA JOURNAL: What
other differences have you observed between women and
men in terms of how they
communicate?

■ DISCUSSION: Ask students
whether Tannen's points about
mother-daughter, mother-son,
father-daughter, and father-son
relationships ring true. In terms
of communicating with spouses
or significant others, do they
encounter the same kinds of
confusion and frustration Tannen mentions? Have they, perhaps, learned anything from
this essay?

[4] **unswervingly:** without moving

[5] **incessantly:** without stopping

[6] **intermittently:** not continuously; occasionally

dying? Are you guys getting a divorce? Is everything OK with Brian?'" In other words, the teenager immediately sensed that the father was setting the stage for a momentous[7] revelation—probably involving a family member—by arranging for them to sit side by side, with eyes fixed straight ahead.

■ **SUMMARIZE AND RESPOND** . . . .

In your reading journal or elsewhere, summarize the main point of Tannen's essay. Then, go back and check off support for this main idea. Next, write a brief summary of the essay. Finally, write a brief response to the reading. To what extent does your own experience match with Tannen's observations? In your opinion, how significant are the differences she describes?

■ **CHECK YOUR COMPREHENSION** . . . .

1. An alternate title for this essay could be
    a. "As Boys and Girls Communicate, So Do Men and Women." ✓
    b. "Gender as a Force in the Development of One's Personality."
    c. "Why Mothers and Daughters Communicate Better than Fathers and Sons."
    d. "The Hardest Thing about Communicating with Adolescents."

2. The main point of this essay is that
    a. little boys have short attention spans, while little girls generally have better concentration.
    b. differences in communication styles between men and women can be traced back to childhood. ✓
    c. a woman may think a man is not listening to her because the man is not looking at her directly.
    d. as people get older they learn to communicate more effectively with the opposite sex.

3. Tannen describes the tapes of the five-year-old, ten-year-old, and fifteen-year old boys and girls to
    a. show why her audiences always laugh at the contrast between the boys and the girls.
    b. show how the communication styles of boys and girls change over time.
    c. show the consistency of differences in communication styles between boys and girls. ✓
    d. show how she uses videotape in her research about communication differences.

---

[7]**momentous:** of great importance

4. If you are unfamiliar with the following words, use a dictionary to check their meanings: *automatic* (para. 1); *gazes* (2); *awkwardly, squirming* (4); *lounging* (6); *perceive* (7); *dreadful* (9).

READ CRITICALLY

1. Who do you suppose is Tannen's intended audience for this essay? Why?

2. How effective do you find Tannen's descriptions of the children she videotaped (paras. 3–5)? Pick out some passages that you think work well, and explain why you think they do.

3. Tannen writes that their different communication patterns "often lead to confusion and frustration between women and men" (para. 7). How accurate do you find this observation? Think, perhaps, about how men and women communicate when they are not with one another physically—when using the telephone or e-mail, for example. How similarly or differently do they communicate then?

4. In paragraph 8, Tannen contrasts the way a daughter communicates with a mother with the way a son does. Do you agree that the contrast in communication styles is as sharp as she describes?

5. Evaluate Tannen's final paragraph. How effective is it as a conclusion to the essay? What purpose is served by the extended example she offers here?

WRITE

WRITE A PARAGRAPH: Write a paragraph describing some other difference in behavior between boys and girls of the same age. Be sure to describe this differing behavior clearly and in detail.

WRITE AN ESSAY: Tannen focuses exclusively on differences between girls and boys, and women and men. Write an essay on the behavior of males and females in a particular situation (or in various situations), but try not to limit yourself to contrasts; consider similarities as well. Be sure to develop a clear thesis that makes a general point about the behavior of women and men, and support this point using specific examples from your own observations and experiences.

49

Cause and Effect

Each essay in this chapter uses cause and effect to get its main point across to the reader. As you read these essays, consider how they achieve the four basics of good cause and effect that are listed below and discussed in Chapter 16 of this book.

▐▐ FOUR BASICS OF GOOD CAUSE AND EFFECT

1. The main point reflects the writer's purpose: to explain causes, effects, or both.
2. If the purpose is to explain causes, the writing presents real causes.
3. If the purpose is to explain effects, it presents real effects.
4. It gives readers detailed examples or explanations of the causes or effects.

Pat Wingert

Uniforms Rule

Pat Wingert earned a B.S. in journalism from the University of Illinois, Champaign–Urbana, and learned her craft working for the Pulitzer Prize–winning columnist Mike Royko at the *Sun-Times.* She became a reporter at the paper herself and later worked for the *Chicago Tribune.* After nine years at the two Chicago newspapers, she left her native city for the Washington bureau of *Newsweek* in 1986 and has worked there ever since. Wingert has cowritten many cover stories over the years on issues related to children, families, and education.

In "Uniforms Rule," originally from *Newsweek* (October 1999), Wingert examines how and why uniforms and other dress codes affect public-school safety and student behavior.

GUIDING QUESTION
Why would wearing a uniform influence students' behavior?

Kiara Newsome's spotless navy jumper and demure white blouse won't win raves on the runways. But to school reformers, the six-year-old is a real trendsetter. This fall, Kiara and her classmates at P.S. 15 on Manhattan's Lower East Side joined hundreds of thousands of students in the nation's largest school system and donned[1] uniforms for the first time.

Kiara likes her new duds "'cause they're pretty." Her mother, Alelia, is happy because "it's much easier to find the clothes in the morning." Educators in New York and around the country believe uniforms could also solve some of the toughest problems facing schools today. In the aftermath of the Littleton, Colorado, shootings, many see dress codes as a cheap and simple way to make schools safer. This fall, Los Angeles, Chicago, Miami, Boston, Houston, Cleveland, and Washington, D.C., all have a majority of their students in uniforms. "It's spreading to the suburbs now," says Vince Ferrandino, president of the National Association of Elementary School Principals. "It's become a national phenomenon."[2]

Proponents say clothing rules eliminate the baggy gang-inspired look that makes it easy for students to smuggle in weapons, drugs, and other banned items. Dress codes also make it easier to spot intruders. "Last week this boy walked into our cafeteria in jeans, and we knew right away he wasn't one of ours," says Ramond Rivera, an elementary-school principal in El Paso, Texas, whose students wear uniforms. "We immediately escorted him out."

Researchers say there's very little hard evidence that uniforms improve students' behavior or academic success. They do, however, affect student attitudes. One of the best studies compared two middle schools in Charleston County, South Carolina, one with a uniform policy, the other without. A survey of more than 300 sixth to eighth graders revealed that uniformed students gave their schools higher scores. "Although school uniforms do not represent a panacea[3] for all society's problems," says the lead researcher, Richard K. Murray, a principal in Dorchester, South Carolina, "research now shows that school uniforms do significantly affect student perceptions of school climate."

Keith King of the University of Cincinnati recently published a review of research on the effectiveness of dress codes. He says that overall, students in uniforms "felt more like a team." That's important, King says, because "the No. 1 protective factor against school violence is having a student feel connected to his school and that he fits in."

Uniforms are getting the most attention at middle and high schools, where security and school unity are big issues, along with the extremes of current teen fashion: spaghetti-strap tanks, face painting, body piercing. "You'd be amazed at the amount of time administrators have been spending on what kids are wearing to school," says Susan Galletti, a middle-school specialist at the National Association of Secondary School Principals [NASSP]. "With uniforms, all that is eliminated, and they can spend more time on teaching and learning."

---

[1] **donned:** put on

[2] **phenomenon:** occurrence or circumstance

[3] **panacea:** remedy for all problems or diseases; cure-all

---

SUMMARIZE: Summarize the reasons in paragraphs 2 and 3 in favor of school uniforms.

■ **TEACHING TIP:** Have students circle the effects of the trend toward requiring schoolchildren to wear uniforms. Then ask them to double-underline the causes of the trend. Have them list at least two additional causes or effects that Wingert has not mentioned and then prepare a response to Wingert's essay in which they either support the trend or oppose it.

IDENTIFY: Underline the sentences that identify a positive effect of uniforms in middle schools and high schools.

IDENTIFY: Underline the sentence that presents the courts' decision about uniforms in schools.

While some schools stick to traditional plaids and navy blue, others   7 allow polo shirts, chinos, and even capri pants. Still, teens in the throes[4] of adolescent rebellion often object and in a few cases, they've even sued for the freedom to choose their own clothes. "The older kids get, the more aware they are of their rights," says Stephen Yurek, general counsel of the NASSP. "If you try to restrict what they can say or wear, you'll start hearing that their rights are being violated." Yurek says the courts have made it clear that students don't have the same rights inside school as they do outside; clothing requirements are not considered a violation of their freedom of expression if there's a valid educational reason for imposing them. To avoid legal hassles, though, most schools will provide uniforms to poor students who can't afford to buy them, and many allow parents to opt out if they have religious objections.

■ **IDEA JOURNAL:** If you have never worn a uniform, how would you feel if you were required to wear one? If you have worn a uniform, did you like doing so?

Educators say the best way to get kids to accept uniforms is to start in   8 the early grades. Noelle Ebright, sixteen, a student at Wilson High School in Long Beach, California, has been wearing a uniform for eight years. "I've slowly adapted to it," she says. This year, she says, "all I have to do is grab some khaki bottoms and a white shirt with a collar and I'm out of the house." Still, she admits, "if I had my personal preference, of course I would prefer not to wear one. Any kid would."

Some adults sympathize. Norman Isaacs, principal of Millikan Middle   9 School in Sherman Oaks, California, has resisted uniforms. He believes clothing gives teachers insights into what's happening with individual students. "Our counselors and teachers monitor the way kids are dressed," he says. "If we see a big change in the way a student dresses, that sends up a signal and tells us we need to address that person."

REFLECT: Wingert offers an example of a creative loophole. Based on your experience, what other loopholes might students create?

Other critics say they fear the spread of uniforms will smother student   10 creativity. But experienced educators have learned that kids often dream up truly inspired loopholes.[5] El Paso's Rivera remembers the girl who came to school wearing contact lenses that gave her the appearance of having yellow cat eyes. It wasn't a strict violation; no one had thought to include contacts in the dress code. Still, he says, "We had to put a stop to that. . . . It was a distraction to every kid in her class." And a real eye-opener for the principal.

■   **SUMMARIZE AND RESPOND** . . . .

In your reading journal or elsewhere, summarize the main point of "Uniforms Rule." Then, go back and check off support for this main idea. Next, write a brief summary of the essay. Finally, write a brief response to the reading. What did it make you think or feel? Do you have an opinion on the subject? Do you think wearing uniforms could result in better student behavior?

. . . .

---

[4] **throes:** painful struggle

[5] **loopholes:** ways to get around a rule

■ **CHECK YOUR COMPREHENSION** . . . .

1. An alternate title for this essay could be
   a. "School Uniforms Kill Student Creativity."
   b. "Dress Codes and Public Schools."
   c. "School Uniforms and Student Behavior."
   d. "School Uniforms and Freedom of Expression."

2. The main point of this essay is that
   a. teenagers do not care what they wear to school.
   b. school uniforms have a positive effect on student attitudes.
   c. schools that require uniforms are stricter than schools that do not.
   d. wearing a school uniform cuts down on the time required to get ready for school in the morning.

3. According to research, what is one effect of wearing school uniforms?
   a. Uniforms make students feel as if they are part of a team and fit in.
   b. Uniforms make students feel like they are in grade school.
   c. Students will always find loopholes in the dress code.
   d. Uniforms will cause an increase in body piercing.

4. If you are not familiar with the following words, use a dictionary to check their meanings: *demure, trendsetter* (para. 1); *proponents* (3); *valid, hassles* (7).

■ **READ CRITICALLY** . . . .

1. According to Wingert, what are the effects of wearing school uniforms? What has caused schools to adopt school uniform policies?

2. Why don't the courts consider requiring school uniforms a violation of students' freedom of expression? Do you agree or disagree with this view?

3. How can wearing school uniforms improve school safety?

4. Can you tell from the essay what Wingert's attitude toward school uniforms is? How would you describe the tone of the essay?

5. As a parent, how would you react if your child were required to wear a uniform to school? How would you react if you were required to wear a uniform to class? Is your response different, and if so, why?

. . . .

■ **WRITE** . . . .

■ **TIP:** For a sample cause/
effect paragraph, see
page 206.

WRITE A PARAGRAPH: Write a paragraph about what causes students at a particular grade level to feel alienated from their schools or classmates.

WRITE AN ESSAY: Write an essay that explores the possible effects of a high school dropping its uniform policy and allowing students to wear whatever they choose. If you addressed this issue in Summarize and Respond, feel free to use those ideas.

Daryn Eller

Move Your Body, Free Your Mind

Daryn Eller graduated from the University of California, Berkeley, and then spent fifteen years living and working in New York, where she gained the experience and connections that enable her to work as a freelance writer today. Eller began writing professionally when she was promoted from an assistant at *Mademoiselle* magazine to a copywriter responsible for covering topics like fashion, beauty, and health. "The health was what stuck," she says. She later took a position writing about food and nutrition for *Self* magazine before turning to freelance writing—mainly about nutrition and fitness—in 1990.

The essay that follows is a favorite of Eller's because it came from her personal conviction that exercise could inspire creativity. After finding that scientific research backed up her gut feeling, she got an assignment to write the piece, which first appeared in *Health* magazine (May 2002). Eller notes, "I continue to use the technique to get my brain working. When I don't have the time to fit in exercise, I take a shower—that seems to work too!" (A sidebar that accompanied this essay appears on page 155. It describes a process.)

GUIDING QUESTION
What are the mental effects of exercise?

■ **IDEA JOURNAL:** Has
exercise, or any other technique, ever helped you "free
your mind"?

This is a true story: I was sitting at my desk, facing the challenge of how to   1
begin a piece about the power of exercise to enhance creative thinking. Naturally, I wanted this beginning to engage you, but nothing all that engaging was coming to mind. Zilch,[1] in fact. So I did what I often do: I went to the pool and swam for an hour. Now here I am, back at my desk typing away, my writer's block well behind me.

Exercise can do that for you. "It helps me get a fresh perspective on   2
things," says Katlin Kirker, a forty-five-year-old painter who takes work-break walks on the beach near her home in Venice, California, whenever she feels the need to clear her mind. One writer I know generates so many ideas when running that he tucks a pad of paper and pen into his pocket before leaving the house.

[1] **Zilch:** zero; nothing

It's all too easy to shrug off exercise, especially when you've got a lot of work to do. Why spend the time sweating when you could be pushing some of that paper off your desk? But research suggests that exercise can get the creative juices flowing and may even make you more productive. And it doesn't just apply to "creative types" like writers, musicians, and artists; anyone who needs to solve problems and generate ideas can get a mental boost from a good workout.

REFLECT: Can you identify with the desire to "shrug off" exercise when you are busy?

The best measure so far of the exercise-creativity connection is a 1997 study at Middlesex University in Middlesex, England, involving men and women ages nineteen to fifty-nine. On the first day of the study, the researchers had the group do aerobic[2] exercise for twenty-five minutes and then asked them to think of as many uses for empty cardboard boxes and tin cans as they could. On the second day, the group watched an "emotionally neutral" video on rock formations and were given the same creativity test. As you probably guessed, after working out, the volunteers came up with more solutions to the box/tin can dilemma than they did after watching the video.

PREDICT: Read most of paragraph 4 but pause when you reach the sentence beginning "As you probably guessed . . ." What do you predict the study proved?

What is it about exercise that can make people more inventive thinkers? Robert Thayer, Ph.D., a professor of psychology at California State University–Long Beach and author of *Calm Energy: How People Regulate Mood with Food and Exercise,* believes it may have to do with the ability of physical activity to alter ~~some f~~ ~~~~ ~~~~ ~~~~ ~~~~ One is a lack of energy. "When you exercise, you experience a host of physiological changes, such as an increase in metabolism,[3] more cardiac activity, and the release of neurotransmitters[4] that affect alertness," Thayer says. "These all add to a state of general bodily arousal, and that increases energy."

Another factor could be mood, says Eric Maisel, Ph.D., a California psychotherapist and author of *Write Mind: 299 Things Writers Should Never Say to Themselves (and What They Should Say Instead).* "What often stops people from creating is that they're depressed, so it's perfectly logical that if exercise reduces your experience of depression, you're more likely to create," he says. "Same with anxiety. Creative blocks can be a form of performance anxiety, so anything that reduces anxiety can help."

Another theory of Maisel's—and the one I relate to the most—is that exercise produces a state Zen Buddhists call the "empty mind." When the mind empties, preoccupations slip away and that nagging little voice inside your head that says "Maybe I'm just not smart enough to figure this out" or "I used to be a good writer but not anymore" shuts up. During those moments of silence, creative thoughts have a chance to develop. "If we're always worried about something or concerned about our to-do list, there is no way for ideas to enter our brain," Maisel says. "But with the emptying of the mind, worries fade away, and when that happens, ideas come."

REFLECT: Based on your personal experience, does this explanation seem logical to you?

While you can't exactly prescribe a workout to build creativity like you would to build biceps, the twenty-five minutes of aerobic exercise employed in the Middlesex study is a good place to start. (By the way, in the study, volunteers did instructor-led aerobic exercise, but the researchers speculate that

SUMMARIZE: In your own words, summarize the effects of exercising heavily.

[2] **aerobic:** exercise that conditions the heart and lungs

[3] **metabolism:** the process of converting food into energy

[4] **neurotransmitters:** chemicals that transmit nerve impulses from one nerve cell to another

running and walking may be equally, and possibly even more beneficial.) And a longer, harder session may make you even more creative, depending on the reason for your imaginative angst.[5] For instance, if stress is hindering[6] your thought process, an hour of vigorous aerobic exercise could spark a breakthrough. "Heavy exercise, like working out hard at the gym for an hour, has been shown to significantly decrease tension," Thayer says. "But it can also make you very tired afterward, and you may not get a resurgence[7] of energy for a while." Sometimes, though, less is better: If you need more energy, Thayer's studies have shown that a fast-paced walk as brief as ten minutes can help. "We've found that short, brisk walks can raise energy for up to two hours afterward," he reports.

You may have to experiment a little to find out what works for you. For 9 me, a moderate workout is best—that is, one long enough to help me get an "empty mind," but not so hard that it tires me out. Once I get to that quiet state, so many ideas start percolating[8] in my head that when I get home I often go straight to my desk to capitalize[9] on the momentum. Need proof that it works? I finished this article, didn't I?

■ **TEACHING TIP:** Ask students if they would consider trying exercise as a way of "freeing their minds" for school work and other work. You might also remind them that the prewriting techniques described in Chapter 3 can help them with writing tasks specifically.

■ SUMMARIZE AND RESPOND . . . .

In your reading journal or elsewhere, summarize the main point of "Move Your Body, Free Your Mind." Then, go back and check off support for this main idea. Next, write a brief summary of the essay. Finally, write a brief response to the reading. Do the examples, details, and research presented illustrate the psychological benefits of exercise? Does your personal experience verify those benefits?

■ CHECK YOUR COMPREHENSION . . . .

1. An alternate title for this essay could be
    a. "Move It or Lose It."
    b. "Add Exercise to Your Life."
    c. "Jump-Start Your Mind by Exercising."
    d. "The Benefits of Exercise."

2. The main point of this essay is that
    a. weightlifting decreases tension and makes people tired.
    b. certain types of exercises can make people creative and productive.
    c. certain types of exercise are more beneficial than others.
    d. certain exercise programs should be monitored by professionals.

[5] **angst:** worry

[6] **hindering:** interfering with

[7] **resurgence:** reappearance

[8] **percolating:** bubbling

[9] **capitalize (on):** make the most of

3. According to research,
   a. exercise alters factors that inhibit creativity.
   b. exercise most frequently helps writers, musicians, and artists to generate ideas.
   c. because exercise decreases bodily arousal, it increases mental ability.
   d. exercise is addictive.

4. If you are unfamiliar with the following words, use a dictionary to check their meanings: *generates* (para. 2); *alter, inhibit, physiological* (5); *preoccupation* (7); *speculate, vigorous* (8).

READ CRITICALLY

1. Notice that Eller uses the "I" point of view in the first paragraph. Is this approach effective? Why or why not?

2. What are some of the factors (see paras. 5–7) that inhibit creativity?

3. Does Eller create logical links between causes (exercise) and effects (mental changes)? Based on the information presented, how does physical activity create changes in the mind?

4. To experience the mental rewards of physical activity, what type of exercise session is recommended? Not recommended?

5. What technique does the author use in the last two lines? Is it effective?

WRITE

WRITE A PARAGRAPH: Write a paragraph about how you have used exercise or some other activity to achieve a particular state of mind. What did you do? What were the specific effects of those actions?

WRITE AN ESSAY: At the end of her essay, Eller notes the effects that a moderate workout has on her mental state. In your essay, discuss the effects of your involvement in a particular sport, exercise program, or other activity. These effects might be mental, social, or physical. If you wish, include any ideas you developed for Summarize and Respond.

50
Argument

The essays in this chapter use argument to get their main point across. We have provided a pro and con essay for each of two topics—racial and ethnic profiling, and junk food in schools. This will allow you to compare and contrast the argumentative strategies used. As you read the essays in each pair, decide which one you find stronger and why.

As you read these essays, consider how they achieve the four basics of good argument that are listed below and discussed in Chapter 17 of this book.

■■ FOUR BASICS OF GOOD ARGUMENT

1. It takes a strong and definite position.
2. It gives good reasons and supporting evidence to defend the position.
3. It considers opposing views.
4. It has enthusiasm and energy from start to finish.

Profiling

William Raspberry
Why Profiling Won't Work

William Raspberry (b. 1935) is a columnist for the *Washington Post*. He grew up in a segregated Mississippi town and later attended Indiana Central College. In 1962, he joined the *Post* as a teletype operator and was quickly promoted to reporter, copyeditor, and then assistant city editor. In 1994, he won a Pulitzer Prize for his commentary on social and political issues. His column is now syndicated in more than one hundred newspapers across the country.

In this 2005 essay from the *Washington Post*, Raspberry argues that ethnic profiling is not the answer to airline security problems.

GUIDING QUESTION
Why does the author think that profiling is wrong?

The Transportation Security Administration,[1] having rendered[2] cockpit crews less vulnerable[3] to hijackers by strengthening the cockpit doors, is now (1) reviewing its list of items passengers may not bring aboard, (2) proposing to minimize the number of passengers who have to be patted down at checkpoints, and (3) taking another look at the rule that requires most passengers to remove their shoes.   1

These are encouraging moves toward common sense.   2

This isn't: A gaggle[4] of voices is proposing—almost as though responding   3 to the same memo from some malign[5] Mr. Big—that the TSA replace its present policy of random searches with massive racial and ethnic profiling.[6]

After all, they argue, weren't the September 11 terrorists all young Mus-   4 lim men? Isn't it likely that the next terrorist attack will be carried out by young Muslim men? So why waste time screening white-haired grandmothers and blue-suited white guys? Much more efficient to tap the shoulder of any young man who looks Muslim—a category that covers not just Arabs but also Asians, Africans, and, increasingly, African Americans.

It must have been just such sweet reason that led to the internment[7] of   5 thousands of Japanese Americans during World War II. Even Andrew C. Mc-Carthy of the Foundation for the Defense of Democracies—and one of the advocates[8] of profiling—acknowledges that the Japanese internments were excessive. But only, he says in the current issue of *National Review*, because "they included American citizens of Japanese descent; there was nothing objectionable in principle about holding Japanese, German, or Italian nationals."

That distinction doesn't hold up in the case of airport profiling, since   6 there's no way visually to distinguish between a Saudi citizen and an Arab American. The profilers wouldn't even try.

Actually, anyone who's ever been inconvenienced by security checks—   7 whether as trivial[9] as having to give up a fingernail clipper or as serious as having to take a later flight—will see some merit in the case for profiling. Can't they see that I'm just a guy trying to get from here to there, while that fellow over there looks like he could be a hijacker?

One trouble with that line is that the obviously innocent tend to look a lot   8 like ourselves, while the clearly suspect tend to look like the other fellow. Which is why so many Middle Eastern-looking men (and Sikhs[10]) were

---

[1] **Transportation Security Administration:** U.S. government agency responsible for protecting airlines and other transportation from security threats

[2] **rendered:** made

[3] **vulnerable:** open to attack

[4] **gaggle:** group

[5] **malign:** evil

[6] **profiling:** singling out a particular group for attention

[7] **internment:** imprisonment

[8] **advocates:** supporters

[9] **trivial:** minor; small

[10] **Sikhs:** followers of an Asian Indian religion

■ **IDEA JOURNAL:** Have you ever been treated with suspicion or singled out for negative attention because of the way you look or dress? How did it make you feel?

SUMMARIZE: What contrast does McCarthy make here, and why in the next paragraph does Raspberry say the distinction "doesn't hold up in the case of airport profiling"?

_____

_____

REFLECT: What, in terms of argument strategy, is the purpose of this paragraph?

_____

_____

stopped and frisked in the days just after September 11 — and why at least one member of President Bush's Secret Service detail was thrown off an airliner.

The other, more serious problem is that the pro-profilers are fighting the last war. If someone had stopped nineteen young Muslim men from boarding four jetliners four years ago, September 11 wouldn't have happened. Therefore, security requires that we make it difficult for young Muslim men to board jetliners. It's as though white people come in all sizes, ages, and predispositions,[11] while young Arab men are fungible.[12]   9

Random checks at least have the virtue of rendering us all equal. I can talk with any fellow passenger about the absurdity of having to remove my loafers, because that fellow passenger has been similarly inconvenienced. But with whom does a young Arab (or Turk or dreadlocked[13] college student) share his humiliation?   10

And make no mistake, it is humiliating. Stop me once because someone fitting my description or driving a car like mine is a suspect in a crime and I shrug and comply. Stop me repeatedly because of how I look and I respond with less and less grace.   11

Am I arguing against all efforts to protect America from terrorism? Of course not. But since Americans look all sorts of ways, a more sensible way of deciding who gets extra attention is behavior.   12

The profilers say this is just political correctness[14] gone mad. McCarthy puts it bluntly: "Until we stop pretending not to see what the terrorists who are attacking us look like, we may as well give them an engraved invitation to strike again."   13

Well, we do know what they look like. They look like the nineteen hijackers of September 11, but they also look like Richard "Shoe Bomber" Reid, John Walker Lindh, Jose Padilla, and — don't forget — Timothy McVeigh.   14

Profile that.   15

■ DISCUSSION: You might point out that Raspberry is an African American whose looks make it unlikely that he would fit the profile of a potential Arab terrorist. However, police have been accused of stopping African American drivers on suspicion of crime simply because of the color of their skin. This "crime" has been referred to as "DWB," or "driving while black."

IDENTIFY: Underline the main point of paragraph 11.

■ TEACHING TIP: Students may not know who the people mentioned in paragraph 14 are or what they look like. As a short research assignment, have students find out who the people are and what they have been accused or convicted of. Students could write about or discuss how racial profiling would or would not have helped identify these people. (Reid and Lindh are convicted terrorists. Padilla is a Puerto Rican American detained for suspected terrorist activities, and McVeigh, who looked like a typical white American, was executed for the 1995 bombing of a government building that killed 168 people.)

■   **SUMMARIZE AND RESPOND** . . . .

In your reading journal or elsewhere, summarize the main point of "Why Profiling Won't Work." Then, go back and check off support for this main idea. Next, write a brief summary of the essay. Finally, write a brief response to the reading. Do you think racial and ethnic profiling should be used in efforts to find criminals?

■   **CHECK YOUR COMPREHENSION** . . . .

1. An alternate title for this essay could be
    a. "Protecting Innocent People from Terrorists."
    b. "The Best Way to Identify Potential Terrorists."

---

[11] **predispositions:** inclinations; interests

[12] **fungible:** interchangeable

[13] **dreadlocked:** wearing locks of twisted hair

[14] **political correctness:** avoidance of anything that might offend ethnic, racial, or other societal groups

c. "The Problems of Using Profiling to Identify Potential Terrorists."

d. "The Humiliation of Being Subjected to Racial or Ethnic Profiling."

2. The main point of this essay is that

a. profiling is neither a fair nor an effective way of identifying potential terrorists.

b. profiling presents a serious inconvenience to most airline passengers at security checkpoints.

c. the best way to identify potential terrorists is through the use of profiling.

d. terrorists are just as likely to be elderly grandmothers and business executives as they are to be young Muslim men.

3. One important point Raspberry makes to further his argument is that

a. people who are against profiling are simply giving in to political correctness.

b. not all terrorist attacks or attempts at terrorism have been committed by young Muslim men.

c. profiling is not the equivalent of the internment of Japanese Americans during World War II.

d. many people believe that any future terrorist attack will be carried out by young Muslim men.

4. If you are unfamiliar with the following words, use a dictionary to check their meanings: *cockpit, checkpoints* (para. 1); *random, massive* (3); *efficient* (4); *excessive, descent, objectionable* (5); *distinction, distinguish* (6); *inconvenienced, merit* (7); *frisked* (8); *virtue, absurdity, humiliation* (10); *engraved* (13).

■ **READ CRITICALLY** . . . .

1. Why do you think Raspberry opens his essay as he does? What is the purpose of his shift at the beginning of paragraph 3?

2. Why might Raspberry have chosen to present the arguments of profiling supporters as questions (para. 4)? What would have been the difference if he had presented these sentences as direct statements?

3. How effective do you find Raspberry's argument in paragraphs 8–11? Do you agree that the fact that profiling might be "humiliating" is a strong argument against profiling? Why, or why not?

4. How might Raspberry have further developed his point in paragraph 12 about identifying potential terrorists based on behavior rather than on appearance?

5. Raspberry ends his essay with a two-word sentence. How effective do you find this conclusion? Why?

■ **TIP:** For a sample
argument paragraph, see
page 220.

■ WRITE . . . .

WRITE A PARAGRAPH: In a paragraph, respond to Raspberry's argument. You may wish to defend his position, challenge it, or take a stance somewhere in between. If you wish, include any ideas you developed for Summarize and Respond.

WRITE AN ESSAY: Think of a controversial issue that you feel strongly about—political or social, national or local, relating to people generally or to your own peer group. Be sure that it is an issue about which people have differing views and one about which you understand—or can research—the views of those who disagree with you. Then, like Raspberry, write an editorial for your local paper that argues against the opposing position and for your own position on the issue. Before you begin to write, think carefully about your readers. Will you need to explain the controversy to them, or will they already be familiar with it? While drafting, you might use personal experience and observations, the experiences of others you know, and any reading you have done on the subject to support your position. If you quote from published sources, be aware that you need to acknowledge them clearly. (See Chapter 19 for advice.)

Linda Chavez

Everything Isn't Racial Profiling

Linda Chavez (b. 1947) is a columnist, radio commentator, and author. Her weekly columns are syndicated in newspapers across the country, and she hosts a daily radio show on WMET in Washington, D.C., and appears as a political analyst on Fox News. Chavez is president of the Center for Equal Opportunity, a policy research organization. Additionally, she has held several government positions, including chair of the National Commission on Migrant Education and White House director of public liaison. Her most recent book is *Betrayal: How Union Bosses Shake Down Their Members and Corrupt American Politics* (2004).

In the following essay, from Townhall.com, Chavez argues that it sometimes makes sense to focus on people of certain ethnicities or nationalities, in spite of possibly unfortunate consequences.

GUIDING QUESTION
In what way does Chavez think racial profiling is different from profiling those who might resemble Arab terrorists?

■ **IDEA JOURNAL:** How did
the terrorist attacks of September 11, 2001, change your
views about the world, your
personal safety, and the responsibility of government?

R‍acial profiling is an ugly business—and I have been on record opposing 1
it for years. But I'm not opposed to allowing—no, requiring—airlines to pay closer attention to passengers that fit a terrorist profile, which includes national origin. The problem is distinguishing between what is permissible,

indeed prudent,[1] behavior and what is merely bigotry.[2] As the Christmas day incident involving an Arab American Secret Service agent who was denied passage on an American Airlines flight makes clear, it's not always easy to tell the difference.

Racial profiling entails[3] picking someone out for special scrutiny[4] simply because of his race. It happens when highway patrolmen pull over blacks who've committed no traffic violations for spot checks but ignore other drivers who share similar characteristics, say out-of-state plates or expensive cars. It happens when security guards at a mall tail black customers in stores or insist on inspecting only their bags, ignoring whites. The underlying presumption in these cases is that blacks are more likely to be involved in criminal acts because of the color of their skin.

This kind of racial profiling is both morally wrong and ineffective. But there are times when it makes sense to include race or national origin in a larger, criminal profile, particularly if you're dealing with a crime that has already been committed or is ongoing and the participants all come from a single ethnic or racial group.

It would make no sense if witnesses identified a six-feet-tall, blond male fleeing a homicide but police stopped females, short men, or blacks or Latinos for questioning. Likewise, if you stopped every tall, blond man, a lot of innocent people would be inconvenienced, if only temporarily. Which brings us to the case of the Arab American Secret Service agent.

Walid Shater was allowed initially to board an American Airlines plane in Baltimore headed for Texas, carrying a loaded gun, but then was pulled off the plane, along with a handful of other passengers, for questioning. In the intervening[5] ninety minutes, Shater's lawyers allege[6] that he was mistreated and denied the right to fly because he was an Arab American, while the pilot claims that the agent became loud and abusive, leading him to keep Shater off the flight.

I can fully sympathize with the agent's anger—but I don't think the airline acted improperly. I've had encounters similar to Shater's, largely because of my appearance. When I used to travel frequently in Europe from the mid-'80s to the mid-'90s, I was routinely questioned more than other passengers, I suspect because I look vaguely Middle Eastern—or as one airline agent put it, "Your passport's American, but you don't look American."

On a trip from Israel[7] in 1985, where I was an official government guest of the Israelis, security agents at Tel Aviv Airport questioned me for almost an hour. "But you can't keep me from leaving Israel," I protested. "No, but we can keep you from doing so on an airplane," the guard responded. They

2

3

4

5

6

7

REFLECT: What point does Chavez intend to illustrate through the use of the invented example in paragraph 4?

_____

_____

PREDICT: Based on this paragraph, what do you think Chavez might go on to do in the following paragraph or two?

_____

_____

■ **DISCUSSION:** A major element of Chavez's argument is that she herself was subjected to terrorist profiling, but she never felt discriminated against because she felt the authorities were only doing what was necessary to ensure passenger safety. Ask students to consider how strong an argument they find this. You might tie this discussion to question 5 under Read Critically.

[1] **prudent:** wise; cautious

[2] **bigotry:** prejudice

[3] **entails:** involves

[4] **scrutiny:** close examination

[5] **intervening:** following (in this usage)

[6] **allege:** claim

[7] **Israel:** the Jewish state in the Middle East that has been the target of Arab terrorist attacks for years

finally let me go when another passenger, who recognized me from the newspapers, vouched for[8] me.

On another flight, this time from Switzerland, I was asked to de-board   8
the plane after the passengers were in their seats and questioned about items in my checked luggage. It was humiliating to be called off the plane and to have the passengers told the flight would be delayed because of concerns about one of the passenger's bags.

IDENTIFY: In paragraph 9, underline the reasons that Chavez thought airlines were justified in looking more closely at her than at other passengers.

But I didn't rush to file a discrimination complaint. I didn't like being   9
singled out, but I understood why I was being subjected to more scrutiny. At the time I was hassled, <u>Middle Eastern terrorism was very prevalent[9] in Europe</u>, and <u>female terrorists were operating as well as men, usually on stolen or phony passports</u>. It wasn't unreasonable for airlines to look at me a little more closely than other passengers given these facts.

In Shater's case, nineteen Arab terrorists killed more than three thou-   10
sand Americans on September 11, and several of the hijackers possessed stolen identification cards and pilots' uniforms. It wasn't unreasonable for the American Airlines pilot to be extra cautious with Shater under the circumstances, despite his official ID. As a law enforcement officer himself, Shater might have cut these guys a little more slack.[10]

REFLECT: What do you think Chavez means here by "their pertinent characteristics"?

Sure it's unpleasant to be a suspect when you're innocent. But it's worse   11
to overlook terrorists because we ignored their pertinent[11] characteristics. I sometimes felt annoyed when I was singled out, but I also felt safer because the airlines were doing their job.

■ SUMMARIZE AND RESPOND ·

In your reading journal or elsewhere, summarize the main point of "Everything Isn't Racial Profiling." Then, go back and check off support for this main idea. Next, write a brief summary of the essay. Finally, write a brief response to the reading. Do you think that Chavez argues effectively for the point she makes in her title? Why, or why not?

■ CHECK YOUR COMPREHENSION ·

1. An alternate title for this essay could be
   a. "The Ugly Business of Racial Profiling."
   b. "Profiling for Terrorists Is Justified."
   c. "My Personal Experiences with Racial Profiling."
   d. "What Does a Terrorist Look Like?"

---

[8] **vouched for:** said someone or something is okay

[9] **prevalent:** common

[10] **cut [someone] slack:** to be more forgiving

[11] **pertinent:** relevant; meaningful

2. The main point of this essay is that

   a. racial profiling of blacks by police and other authorities is morally wrong and doesn't achieve its intended goals.

   (b.) to fight terrorism, special attention should be paid to airline passengers who appear to be from the Middle East.

   c. we will all feel safer when people who look like possible terrorists are no longer allowed to fly.

   d. it is always annoying and unpleasant for a person to be considered a suspect when he or she is innocent.

3. Chavez writes that she herself has been singled out for questioning when traveling by air because

   a. she is American but does not carry an American passport or other relevant identification.

   b. she was born in the Middle East.

   c. she has frequently flown to and from Israel.

   (d.) she looks like she might be from an ethnic group associated with terrorism.

4. If you are unfamiliar with the following words, use a dictionary to check their meanings: *permissible, merely, incident* (para. 1); *presumption* (2); *homicide, inconvenienced* (4); *abusive* (5); *encounters, vaguely* (6); *de-board, humiliating* (8); *subjected, hassled* (9).

█ **READ CRITICALLY** . . . .

1. Why do you think Chavez defines racial profiling in such detail in paragraph 2? What purpose does this definition serve in her argument?

2. What is Chavez's point in paragraphs 3–4? Do you think her invented example in paragraph 4 illustrates this point effectively? Why or why not?

3. In paragraphs 6–9, Chavez describes her own experiences of being singled out for questioning when traveling by air. Why do you suppose she does this? What does she hope her experiences will help convince readers to believe?

4. How do you respond to Chavez's tone in this essay? What kind of response does she seem to expect? What makes you think so?

5. For you, does the fact that Chavez is *not* Middle Eastern have any bearing on the effectiveness of her argument? Might, for example, Arab Americans singled out for special attention when flying respond differently than Chavez? How convincing do you think someone like Walid Shater would find her argument?

■ **WRITE** ·

WRITE A PARAGRAPH: An important part of Chavez's argument is her point that the racial profiling of blacks suspected of no particular crime is not the same as profiling those who appear to be from the Middle East as suspected terrorists. The first she sees as wrong, the second as legitimate. In a paragraph, respond to this point. Do you agree that there is a clear difference, or do you find the distinction less than convincing? Be sure to explain why you think as you do. If you wish, include any ideas you developed for Summarize and Respond.

WRITE AN ESSAY: How do you believe that the United States (and, perhaps, other countries) should respond to the threat of terrorism? To what extent should the government have enhanced powers to spy on citizens, to detain suspects without making charges, to limit personal freedoms, or even to kill airline passengers whose behavior seems odd even if not clearly dangerous? In an essay, explain what you see as the proper balance between the traditional freedoms Americans have enjoyed and the need to keep its citizens safe in an increasingly dangerous world.

Junk Food in Schools

Nancy Huehnergarth

Sugar High

Nancy Huehnergarth is a freelance writer living in Chappaqua, New York. When she moved there from New York City, she was disappointed to see how much junk food was available in her daughters' schools. To promote more healthy food, she became the Parent Teacher Association nutrition coordinator for the Chappaqua school district. Later, she was appointed to a nutrition task force started by a New York State Assembly member. Huehnergarth is also a member of the Westchester [New York] Coalition for Better School Food.

"Sugar High," originally published in the *New York Times,* is a response to legislation that will require New Jersey schools to eliminate junk food by September 2007. In the essay, Huehnergarth urges New York to make similar changes.

GUIDING QUESTION
What problem does Huehnergarth describe in this essay? How well would the solution she offers address this problem?

■ **IDEA JOURNAL:** Do you think most students would support Huehnergarth's proposal? Why or why not?

Soda and junk food will be all but outlawed in New Jersey public schools   1
and private schools that take part in the federal school lunch program by
September 2007. New York would be wise to follow suit.[1]

In the face of alarming trends in childhood obesity and health, Gover-   2

---

[1] **follow suit:** do the same thing

nor Richard J. Codey and New Jersey's Department of Agriculture have responded boldly with amended[2] nutrition rules that restrict the types of foods that may be sold in New Jersey schools during school hours. The new rules will limit beverages to choices like milk, bottled water, and 100 percent fruit or vegetable juice in elementary schools, with some flavored iced teas and sports drinks allowed in middle and high schools. In addition, schools will be asked to cut back on foods containing trans fats,[3] like cookies and crackers, as well as foods that are high in fat and sugar. The New Jersey rule also specifies that classes on nutrition must be taught in every school district.

Why has New Jersey taken such a proactive[4] stance? The facts tell it all. Obesity and poor eating habits are at epidemic[5] proportions. Some studies suggest that in New Jersey as well as in New York, as many as one in five children are obese. According to the Center for Science in the Public Interest, the average child eats 80 to 230 calories per day more than he needs. Snack foods and soft drinks are major contributors to the excess.   3

Even worse, doctors are now having to treat weight and nutrition-related illnesses in children that used to be seen only in adults. New York's Department of Health reports that approximately 180 cases of Type 2 diabetes[6] are being diagnosed in our state's children every year.   4

Few New York school districts have taken steps to improve what is available in their cafeterias even though nutrition experts say that 75 percent of drinks and 85 percent of snacks in middle and high school vending machines are of poor nutritional quality. With more than 2.8 million public school students in New York, it's time we ensure that our children are offered nutritious foods at school, even if we have to legislate change.   5

Legislation is necessary because so many school districts have grown so dependent on money raised through selling junk food and soda that they're unwilling or unable to stop. Districts like Greenburgh in Westchester County, Mahopac in Putnam and Cicero-North Syracuse, Fulton, Niskayuna and Liverpool upstate have entered into exclusive "pouring rights" contracts—where some of them can earn more than $100,000 per year—with corporations like PepsiCo, Coca-Cola Company, or local distributors. The money is often used to pay for after-school programs and sports, but should we really be financing these programs at the expense of our children's health?   6

Legislating what foods our children can and can't purchase in school is bound to be unpopular with food companies and even some students and parents. But the benefits would be enormous. Studies show that <u>schools that model good nutritional habits on campus have more attentive students with fewer behavioral problems.</u>   7

And healthier food does sell. When the Lakeland Central School District in Westchester voluntarily switched from soda and candy vending machines to those selling healthy food and drinks, the district increased its profits. Dutchess County's Red Hook Central School District switched to healthier cafeteria and vending-machine fare six years ago and saw participation in the lunch program grow by nearly a quarter.   8

---

[2] **amended:** changed or updated

[3] **trans fats:** unhealthy fats common in manufactured foods

[4] **proactive:** acting in expectation of future problems

[5] **epidemic:** affecting a large number of people

[6] **Type 2 diabetes:** a lifelong disease often brought on by obesity and lack of exercise

---

SUMMARIZE: What is the main point of paragraphs 3 and 4?

■ **DISCUSSION:** If you are also teaching the other reading in this pair, "Obesity Is Not Just about Food" by Carol Glazer, you might have students consider the point Huehnergarth makes at the end of paragraph 6 in relation to Glazer's argument. Glazer calls for more after-school programs that encourage physical activity. Huehnergarth likely would agree with this. What, however, would she likely say to school districts that claim they can't afford such programs without entering into lucrative contracts with junk food and soda manufacturers?

IDENTIFY: Underline the additional benefits of her proposal that Huehnergarth suggests in paragraph 7.

REFLECT: Based on her final paragraph, to what audience do you think Huehnergarth is addressing this essay?

Who says children don't want healthier choices? In April, students at 9 East Hampton Middle School in Suffolk County boycotted[7] their cafeteria food, demanding less junk and more salads and vegetables.

Assemblywoman Sandra Galef, a Democrat from Westchester County, 10 and Senator Mary Lou Rath, a Buffalo Republican, have sponsored a bill that would require the removal of nonnutritious foods and beverages like soda and candy from public school vending machines during school hours. If this bill becomes law, New York would be taking a good step toward making our children and our schools healthier.

■ SUMMARIZE AND RESPOND . . . .

In your reading journal or elsewhere, summarize the main point of "Sugar High." Then, go back and check off support for this main idea. Next, write a brief summary of the essay. Finally, write a brief response to the reading. Do you agree with Huehnergarth's views on getting rid of high-calorie snacks and sodas in public schools? Why or why not?

■ CHECK YOUR COMPREHENSION . . . .

1. An alternate title for this essay could be
   a. "The Problem of Obesity among Children."
   b. "Why Public Schools Promote Junk Food."
   c. "The Dangers of High-Calorie Snacks and Sodas."
   (d.) "Get Junk Food Out of Our Schools."

2. The main point of this essay is that
   (a.) lawmakers should require that schools not make high-calorie snacks and sodas available to students.
   b. obesity among children and its related health problems must be addressed immediately.
   c. the state of New Jersey has taken important steps to remove high-calorie snacks and sodas from its schools.
   d. given the option at school, many children would actually choose healthy food over junk food.

3. According to Huehnergarth, why are school districts unlikely to ban junk food from schools on their own?
   a. Doing so would be unpopular with food companies and with some students and parents.
   (b.) Many school districts depend on the money raised by the sale of junk food.
   c. Most school districts believe that offering courses in nutrition is more important than banning junk food.
   d. School districts often do not realize what is healthiest for their students.

[7] **boycotted:** refused

4. If you are unfamiliar with the following words, use a dictionary to check their meanings: *outlawed* (para. 1); *obesity, restrict* (2); *stance, proportions, excess* (3); *legislate* (5); *attentive* (7); *voluntarily* (8).

READ CRITICALLY

1. Why does Huehnergarth open her essay by describing in detail how the state of New Jersey has responded to "alarming trends in childhood obesity and health" (para. 2)? Do you find this an effective opening? Why or why not?

2. Who is Huehnergarth's audience for this essay? Whose opinion is she trying to influence? How can you tell?

3. Do you think that Huehnergarth adequately establishes her point that childhood obesity is a problem? That removing junk food from schools would help lessen the number of overweight children? Why do you think as you do?

4. Why do you suppose that Huehnergarth chose not to develop the case for the additional benefits she mentions in paragraph 7? In what ways might doing so have strengthened her argument?

5. In her sixth and seventh paragraphs, Huehnergarth introduces two arguments against her proposal. What are these arguments? How does she deal with them? Do you think she does so effectively? Are you ultimately convinced by her proposal? Why or why not?

WRITE

WRITE A PARAGRAPH: In a paragraph, argue from a student's perspective whether junk food should be banned from schools. Do you think it is right that students not have the option of purchasing snack foods and sodas in their schools? Or do you find this an unfair limitation? What kinds of foods do you think students should be able to purchase at school? Like Huehnergarth, direct your argument to a specific audience. If you wish, refer to thoughts you developed for your Idea Journal.

WRITE AN ESSAY: Think of a school-related problem that affects you and other students at your college. If you have children in elementary, middle, or high school, you might instead think of a problem that affects them and their classmates. Write an essay, directed to your college's administration or to those in charge of your children's school or school district, in which you argue for a particular solution to this problem. As Huehnergarth does, be sure to establish that the problem exists. You should also offer convincing evidence that your solution would be effective.

Carol Glazer

Obesity Is Not Just about Food

Carol Glazer has been a program development consultant for a number of foundations and is currently director of the Robert Wood Johnson Foundation's After School Project. She earned a master's degree in public policy from Harvard's John F. Kennedy School of Government.

In this opinion piece from the *Boston Globe,* Glazer argues that junk food alone doesn't cause childhood obesity and that after-school programs could help keep students healthy.

IDEA JOURNAL: What do you think are the causes of increased obesity among young people in the United States today?

GUIDING QUESTION
What specific examples does Glazer use to develop her argument?

Pundits[1] and politicians have homed[2] in on one culprit[3] in the childhood obesity epidemic: fattening food. Despite its obvious sizzle,[4] scapegoating[5] junk food isn't the answer; better school nutrition and less fast food is not the panacea[6] for this public health crisis. A big part of the problem is that many children have very few options after school to do anything other than sit in front of television or computer screens or hang out on their neighborhood streets.

REFLECT: What is Glazer's point in presenting the statistics in paragraph 2?

Approximately 5 million children under the age of twelve, most of them African American or Latino, living in poor neighborhoods, spend their time after school home alone. The result is a host of potential problems that compromise[7] their healthy development—social, intellectual, and physical—into adulthood. Among these problems in childhood obesity, which is of epidemic proportions among America's African American and Latino children, 9 million of whom are now obese.

The effort to ensure that our children live longer and avoid obesity has many voices, including former President Bill Clinton, who recently teamed up with the American Heart Association—and now Nickelodeon[8]—to get the message straight to our youth about the importance of developing healthy eating habits. But if this nation wants to effectively battle the obesity epidemic, we need to look beyond what kids are eating and start considering what happens after the school bell rings. Can we offer them choices that will help them stay safe and physically active, as well as learn social skills and build self-confidence?

The very same after-school programs that provide academic help and cultural enrichment can also counter obesity by encouraging physical activ-

---

[1] **pundits:** experts; commentators

[2] **homed:** focused

[3] **culprit:** guilty party; villain

[4] **sizzle:** appeal

[5] **scapegoating:** blaming

[6] **panacea:** total cure

[7] **compromise:** interfere with

[8] **Nickelodeon:** a children's network on cable television

ity in a supportive and secure environment. And their impact can be long term: after-school programs teach young people healthy habits that extend beyond the immediate, habits that they will carry with them into the future for a longer, healthier life.

One example of such a program is G-ROW Boston, which provides girls in Boston Public Schools two life-changing opportunities: to learn how to competitively row on the Charles River and apply to colleges. Launched in 1998, G-ROW aims to diversify the traditionally exclusive sport of rowing and introduce girls to higher education opportunities many never knew were available to them. The staff and coaches build girls' strength and confidence by working with them in the out-of-school hours on the water, in the gym, and in conversations about their future.

5

In Chicago, there is After School Matters, an apprenticeship[9]-based program that offers teens the chance to learn a sport and work within it, such as coaching for soccer and football, swimming well enough to be a lifeguard at the city's public pools in the summer, and other athletic positions. Another program is ABADÁ-Capoeira San Francisco, located in the city's Mission District. The program offers professional instruction of Capoeira, a dynamic Afro-Brazilian art form that combines ritual,[10] self-defense, acrobatics, and music. Using Capoeira as its medium,[11] the program seeks to inspire and empower students, especially youth from disadvantaged backgrounds, to realize their full potential as responsible, confident, productive citizens.

6

All three programs not only promote health and athleticism but foster healthy relationships between kids and caring adults, helping the kids to gain a sense of belonging and a higher self-esteem.

7

Of course, these programs, and others like them, cannot exist without support. Unfortunately, too often a lack of financial, technical, and other support hinders after-school programs' ability to do more than scratch the surface in the battle against obesity. It is up to leaders and creative thinkers from the realms[12] of education, government, philanthropy,[13] or business to demand or create solutions.

8

We must resist the urge to look for just one solution for obesity and consider the very urgent need to provide our children with healthy activities that rev up their brains and bodies after the school bell rings. Let's use the opportunities that after-school programs offer for a brighter, healthier future for all of our kids.

9

■ **SUMMARIZE AND RESPOND** . . . .

In your reading journal or elsewhere, summarize the main point of "Obesity Is Not Just about Food." Then, go back and check off support for this main idea. Next, write a brief summary of the essay. Finally, write a brief response to the reading. Do you think Glazer's suggestions would help decrease obesity in children? What do you think of the other benefits she

---

[9] **apprenticeship:** learning by doing under the guidance of an expert

[10] **ritual:** something that is done regularly, often for spiritual purposes

[11] **medium:** means of doing or creating something

[12] **realms:** fields or areas

[13] **philanthropy:** charitable giving

PREDICT: Based on the first part of the first sentence of paragraph 5, what do you expect Glazer will do in the rest of the paragraph?

IDENTIFY: Underline the benefits Glazer describes that result from the two programs she discusses here.

■ **TEACHING TIP:** If you plan to have students read both this essay and the previous one by Nancy Huehnergarth, ask them whether they find one writer more convincing than the other. The two proposals are not, in fact, mutually exclusive—that is, schools could both limit sales of junk food and develop after-school programs that encourage physical activity. Nevertheless, which action do they think would have the greater impact? Or is this an issue where reaching common ground would have the greatest impact?

mentions? How likely do you think it is that money could be found to fund the kinds of programs she writes about?

■   CHECK YOUR COMPREHENSION . . . .

1. An alternate title for this essay could be
    a. "The Dangers of Childhood Obesity."
    (b.) "Create After-School Programs to Combat Childhood Obesity."
    c. "Banning Junk Food Will Not Cause a Decrease in Childhood Obesity."
    d. "Creating a Brighter Future for All Our Children."

2. The main point of this essay is that
    (a.) after-school programs that encourage physical activity and promote self-esteem are the best way to decrease obesity among children.
    b. politicians and others are wrong to argue that limiting children's access to junk food is a cure-all for the increasing obesity among the young.
    c. it will require creative leadership to develop and find funding for after-school programs that can provide a brighter future for all our children.
    d. childhood obesity is a dangerous problem that can be solved only when children are required to be more physically active.

3. One reason Glazer supports the after-school programs she describes is that
    a. they require significant financial, technical, and other support.
    b. they offer disadvantaged students access to traditionally exclusive sports like rowing.
    c. they have already been developed at schools in Boston, Chicago, and San Francisco.
    (d.) they can have long-term effects that result in a healthier life in the future.

4. If you are unfamiliar with the following words, use a dictionary to check their meanings: *obesity, epidemic* (para. 1); *proportions* (2); *enrichment, counter, supportive* (4); *diversify, exclusive* (5); *acrobatics, inspire, empower, disadvantaged, productive* (6); *foster* (7); *lack, hinders,* (8); *resist, urge, urgent* (9).

■   READ CRITICALLY . . . .

1. Why do you suppose Glazer felt she needed to open her argument by denying the claim that junk food is the primary culprit behind childhood obesity?

2. In paragraph 2, Glazer points out that disadvantaged children face many problems in addition to increased obesity. Why might she make this point? What does it contribute to her argument?

3. Glazer ends paragraph 3 with a question. What is the effect of this question? How does it relate to her next-to-last paragraph?

4. Evaluate Glazer's description of the three model programs she writes about in paragraphs 5 and 6. Does she provide enough detail so that you can understand how each program operates? To what extent do you agree with her that each seems to "not only promote health and athleticism but foster healthy relationships between kids and caring adults, helping the kids to gain a sense of belonging and a higher self-esteem" (para. 7)? Would you have benefited—or might your children benefit—from programs like these? What might be the relationship between low self-esteem and obesity?

5. How likely do you think it is that "leaders and creative thinkers" will be able to "demand or create solutions" to find support for programs that fight childhood obesity (para. 8)? Should Glazer have developed this idea in more detail? How might she have done so?

WRITE . . . .

WRITE A PARAGRAPH: In a paragraph directed at administrators in your community, make a case for creating an after-school program like one of those Glazer describes in paragraphs 5 and 6. You might adapt one of these to suit your particular community or come up with a program of your own. (As an alternative, if you participated—or if your children participate—in some sort of after-school program, imagine that there is talk of funding being cut for that program, and make a case for why the program should be continued.) Like Glazer, be sure to describe both the program and its benefits.

WRITE AN ESSAY: What do you think can be done to solve the problem of increasing obesity among Americans of all ages? In an essay, lay out several proposals that you believe would be both possible and effective. You might want to do some research to establish the existence of the problem, as Glazer and the author of the previous essay did to establish the existence of obesity among children. You might also want to specify what you see as the main causes of the problem to argue that your proposed solutions would deal with these causes directly.

51

Mini-Casebook of Readings: Stereotypes

This chapter presents readings (and refers to earlier readings) on the theme of stereotypes: often false, and potentially damaging, generalizations about people. The readings are followed by a set of assignments that ask you to draw on multiple selections while using the writing strategies covered in Part Two of this book.

As you read the essays, you might want to annotate them or use other reading strategies discussed in Chapter 1. The first selection is typical of a blog posted to a Web site. The author is a college student.

We're Not All Drunken Party Animals

Our professors tell us we shouldn't stereotype others, but what about the stereotypes of college students that many people seem to believe? The media portrays us as useless individuals who spend all of our time going to bars or parties, having sex, and—of course—drinking until we pass out or do something destructive, rowdy, humiliating, or illegal. I don't doubt that the college students we see in the media do these things, but let me tell you, I'm a college student, and I don't have the time, money, or inclination to do what the media says I do.

The newspapers love to report on college students who party hearty. When a beautiful and promising student at Colorado State died from drinking too much at a fraternity party, the papers just couldn't seem to get enough of the story. When a young woman who had just graduated from high school went to Aruba and disappeared, all the stories focused as much on her being at a bar drinking as on the fact that she was probably murdered. Just recently, a graduate student was murdered in New York City after being in a bar until 4 A.M., and all the reports were about how drunk she was and how many college students just hang out at bars every night, all night.

MTV just adds to the stereotype with shows like *Undressed,* where the college student characters have nothing better to do than think about when they'll have sex next and how many parties they can go to. The MTV spring break specials might as well be called "College Students Behaving Badly."

Everyone's running around at the beach doing stupid things and, of course, drinking.

Because people are bombarded with images of college students as drunken party animals with lots of time and money to waste, I don't exactly blame them for forming negative stereotypes. But those stereotypes don't fit me, no way. Here's what one college student's life is like.　4

I get up at 5 every morning, sometimes earlier, to do a few fun things—like laundry—before the rest of my family starts making demands of me. Then, I'm getting my kids up, making sure they get dressed and eat something, and getting them off to school with all the stuff they need. Nothing ever goes very smoothly in the morning.　5

Then, I go to work, from 8:30 to 4:30. Working is the easiest part of my day. During lunch, I run errands, make appointments, or check on my mother. After work, I catch up with the kids, get something going for dinner, and nag them about homework. Two nights a week, I have classes from 7 to 10. On those nights, I come home tired but a long way from being able to go to bed. There's laundry to be put away and maybe more to do. There's homework, if I can stay awake. There's studying if there's a test coming up. And, oh yes, there are the bills to pay. That takes a long time. One night a week, I go to my mother's house, bringing her groceries, cleaning her place, and doing laundry. And so it goes . . .　6

I know, this is getting boring, but my life just couldn't be more different from the stereotypes of the "typical" college student. Even if I had the time, I couldn't afford to drink and party. And even if I had the money, I'd be too tired. What about the rest of you? Are you as sick as I am of being stereotyped?　7

Firoozeh Dumas
Bernice

In the early 1970s, when she was seven, Firoozeh Dumas moved with her family from Iran to Southern California, where they lived for two years before returning to Iran. Soon, the family came back to California, and Dumas eventually graduated from the University of California at Berkeley. The following is an excerpt from Dumas's book *Funny in Farsi: A Memoir of Growing Up Iranian in America* (2003), in which she humorously describes her family's reactions to a new country—and Americans' reactions to the recent immigrants. The book was selected as a finalist for the PEN award for creative nonfiction.

A "rule of thumb" from Dumas's California childhood was, "If not blond, then Mexican"—or Alaskan, as she describes in a story involving the Bernice of this essay's title. Political events during Dumas's childhood also shaped many Americans' views about Iranians. In 1979, during a revolution in Iran, militants invaded the U.S. Embassy there, taking about seventy Americans hostage in a standoff that lasted 444 days. As she notes, "People see me and think of hostages."

In America, I have an "ethnic" face, a certain immigrant look that says, "I'm 1
not Scandinavian." When I lived in Abadan,[1] my mother and I stood out because we looked foreign. Abadan's desert climate, which resembles that of
Palm Springs,[2] produces olive-skinned inhabitants. My mother and I, because of her Turkish ancestry, possess a skin color that on Nicole Kidman is
described as "porcelain" and on others as "fish-belly white." In Abadan,
people always asked my mother whether she was European. "Well," she'd
always gush,[3] "my aunt lives in Germany."

When we moved to California, we no longer looked foreign. With its 2
large Mexican population, Whittier could have passed as our hometown. As
long as we didn't open our mouths, we looked as if we belonged. But just
one of my mother's signature rambling[4] sentences without a verb ("Shop so
good very happy at Sears"), and our cover was blown. Inevitably,[5] people
would ask us where we were from, but our answer didn't really matter. One
mention of our homeland and people would get that uncomfortable smile
on their face that says, "How nice. Where the heck is that?"

In 1976, my father's new job took us to Newport Beach, a coastal town 3
where everyone is blond and sails. There, we stood out like a bunch of
Middle Eastern immigrants in a town where everyone is blond and sails.
People rarely asked us where we were from, because in Newport Beach, the
rule of thumb was "If not blond, then Mexican." People would ask me
things like "Could you please tell Lupe that she doesn't have to clean our
house next week, since we're going to be on vacation."

One would think that the inhabitants of Newport Beach, a town two 4
hours from the Mexican border, would speak at least a few words of Spanish. But in a place where one's tan is a legitimate topic of conversation ("Is
that from last weekend at the beach?" "No, I got this playing tennis yesterday"), learning the language of the domestic help is not a priority.

During my first year in Newport Beach, my junior high was conducting 5
mandatory[6] scoliosis[7] checks. All the sixth-graders were herded into the gym
where we waited for the nurses to check the curvature in our backs. When
it came my turn, the nurse took a long look at my face and said, "Oh my
God! Are you Alaskan?"

"No, I'm Iranian," I replied. 6

"No way!" she shrieked. "Bernice, doesn't this one look Alaskan?" 7

As Bernice waddled across the gym, I wanted to make her an offer. 8
"How about I tell Lupe not to come next week since you're going to be on
vacation, and we just call it a day?"

During that same year, I was asked to speak about my homeland to a 9
seventh-grade class at my school. The girl who had asked me was a neighbor who needed some extra credit in social studies. I showed up complete

---

[1] **Abadan:** city in southwestern Iran

[2] **Palm Springs:** a resort town in southern California

[3] **gush:** to speak enthusiastically

[4] **rambling:** long; wandering

[5] **inevitably:** eventually

[6] **mandatory:** required

[7] **scoliosis:** a curve in the spine that may require treatment

with my books in Farsi, a doll depicting a villager weaving a Persian rug, several Persian miniatures, and some stuffed grape leaves, courtesy of my mother. I stood in front of the class and said, "Hello, my name is Firoozeh and I'm from Iran." Before I could say anything else, the teacher stood up and said, "Laura, you said she's from Peru!" If my life were a Hollywood musical, this would have been the beginning of the big dance number.

> *You say tomato,*
> *I say tomahto.*
> *You say Persia,*
> *I say Peru.*
> *Let's call the whole thing off.*

So home I went with my Persian miniatures, my doll depicting a villager   10
weaving a Persian rug, and my books. At least my mother didn't have to cook dinner that night, since the thirty grape leaves were enough for all of us.

During our stay in Newport Beach, the Iranian Revolution took place   11
and a group of Americans were taken hostage in the American embassy in Tehran. Overnight, Iranians living in America became, to say the least, very unpopular. For some reason, many Americans began to think that all Iranians, despite outward appearances to the contrary,[8] could at any given moment get angry and take prisoners. People always asked us what we thought of the hostage situation. "It's awful," we always said. This reply was generally met with surprise. We were asked our opinion on the hostages so often that I started reminded people that they weren't in our garage. My mother solved the problem by claiming to be from Russia or "Torekey." Sometimes I'd just say, "Have you noticed how all the recent serial killers have been Americans? I won't hold it against you."

From Newport Beach, I moved to Berkeley, a town once described as   12
the armpit of California. But Berkeley wasn't just any armpit, it was an armpit in need of a shave and a shower, an armpit full of well-read people who had not only heard of Iran but knew something about it. In Berkeley, people were either thrilled or horrified to meet an Iranian. Reactions included "So what do you think of the fascist[9] American CIA[10] pigs who supported the Shah's[11] dictatorship only to use him as a puppet in their endless thirst for power in the Middle East and other areas like Nicaragua?" Sometimes, mentioning that I was from Iran completely ended the conversation. I never knew why, but I assume some feared that I might really be yet another female terrorist masquerading[12] as a history of art major at UC–Berkeley. My favorite category of question, however, assumed that all Iranians were really just one big family: "Do you know Ali Akbari in Cincinnati?" people would ask. "He's so nice."

[8] **contrary:** opposite

[9] **fascist:** referring to fascism, an authoritarian form of government

[10] **CIA:** Central Intelligence Agency, the U.S. agency concerned with gathering information about possible threats to U.S. security

[11] **Shah:** U.S.-backed leader of Iran who fled the country in 1979 as a revolution took hold there

[12] **masquerading as:** pretending to be

During my years at Berkeley, I met François, a Frenchman who later be- 13
came my husband. It was during our friendship that I realized how unfair
my life had truly been. Being French in America is like having your hand
stamped with one of those passes that allows you to get into everything. All
François has to do is mention his obviously French name and people find
him intriguing. It is assumed that he's a sensitive, well-read intellectual,
someone who, when not reciting Baudelaire,[13] spends his days creating Impressionist[14] paintings.

Every American seems to have a favorite France story. "It was the loveli- 14
est café and I can still taste the *tarte tatin!*"[15] As far as I know, François had
not made that *tarte tatin*, although people are more than happy to give him
credit. "You know," I always add, "France has an ugly colonial[16] past." But
it doesn't matter. People see my husband and think of Gene Kelly dancing
with Leslie Caron.[17] People see me and think of hostages.

This is why, in my next life, I am applying to come back as a Swede. I 15
assume that as a Swede, I will be a leggy blonde. Should God get things confused and send me back as a Swede trapped in the body of a Middle Eastern woman, I'll just pretend I'm French.

[13] **Baudelaire:** nineteenth-century French poet

[14] **Impressionist:** style of painting, first popular in the nineteenth century, in which
touches of pure color are used to produce "impressions" of light and form

[15] *tarte tatin*: a French apple tart

[16] **colonial:** a system in which one society has political and/or economic control over
another

[17] **Gene Kelly and Leslie Caron:** both actors and graceful dancers who appeared
together in the movie *An American in Paris* (1951).

Brent Staples

Just Walk on By:
Black Men and Public Space

Brent Staples (b. 1951) attended Widener University in Chester, Pennsylvania,
and then went on to earn a doctorate in psychology from the University of
Chicago. He has been an editorial writer for the *New York Times* since 1990
and has written for many other publications. His memoir, *Parallel Time: Growing Up in Black and White,* was published in 1994.

In "Just Walk on By," which originally appeared in *Ms.* magazine, Staples
describes how he, as a black man, has tried to make himself less threatening to
strangers on his evening walks, and how this has affected him over the years.

My first victim was a woman—white, well dressed, probably in her early 1
twenties. I came upon her late one evening on a deserted street in Hyde
Park, a relatively affluent[1] neighborhood in an otherwise mean, impoverished section of Chicago. As I swung onto the avenue behind her, there

[1] **affluent:** wealthy

seemed to be a discreet,[2] uninflammatory[3] distance between us. Not so. She cast back a worried glance. To her, the youngish black man—a broad six feet two inches with a beard and billowing[4] hair, both hands shoved into the pockets of a bulky military jacket—seemed menacingly[5] close. After a few more quick glimpses, she picked up her pace and was soon running in earnest.[6] Within seconds she disappeared into a cross street.

That was more than a decade ago, I was twenty-two years old, a gradu-   2
ate student newly arrived at the University of Chicago. It was in the echo of that terrified woman's footfalls[7] that I first began to know the unwieldy[8] inheritance I'd come into—the ability to alter public space in ugly ways. It was clear that she thought herself the quarry[9] of a mugger, a rapist, or worse. Suffering a bout of insomnia, however, I was stalking sleep, not defenseless wayfarers.[10] As a softy who is scarcely able to take a knife to a raw chicken— let alone hold one to a person's throat—I was surprised, embarrassed, and dismayed all at once. Her flight made me feel like an accomplice[11] in tyranny.[12] It also made it clear that I was indistinguishable from the muggers who occasionally seeped into the area from the surrounding ghetto. That first encounter, and those that followed, signified that a vast, unnerving gulf lay between nighttime pedestrians—particularly women—and me. And I soon gathered that being perceived as dangerous is a hazard in itself. I only needed to turn a corner into a dicey[13] situation, or crowd some frightened, armed person in a foyer somewhere, or make an errant[14] move after being pulled over by a policeman. Where fear and weapons meet—and they often do in urban America—there is always the possibility of death.

In that first year, my first away from my hometown, I was to become thor-   3
oughly familiar with the language of fear. At dark, shadowy intersections, I could cross in front of a car stopped at a traffic light and elicit the *thunk, thunk, thunk, thunk* of the driver—black, white, male, or female—hammering down the door locks. On less traveled streets after dark, I grew accustomed to but never comfortable with people crossing to the other side of the street rather than pass me. Then there were the standard unpleasantries with policemen, doormen, bouncers, cabdrivers, and others whose business it is to screen out troublesome individuals *before* there is any nastiness.

I moved to New York nearly two years ago and I have remained an avid   4
night walker. In central Manhattan, the near-constant crowd cover minimizes

[2] **discreet:** polite

[3] **uninflammatory:** nonthreatening

[4] **billowing:** floating out, as if on a wind

[5] **menacingly:** threateningly

[6] **in earnest:** flat out; intensely

[7] **footfalls:** footsteps

[8] **unwieldy:** hard to handle

[9] **quarry:** victim

[10] **wayfarers:** wanderers or travelers

[11] **accomplice:** helper

[12] **tyranny:** oppression

[13] **dicey:** uncertain or unstable

[14] **errant:** wrong or mistaken

tense one-on-one street encounters. Elsewhere — in SoHo,[15] for example, where sidewalks are narrow and tightly spaced buildings shut out the sky — things can get very taut[16] indeed.

After dark, on the warrenlike[17] streets of Brooklyn where I live, I often see women who fear the worst from me. They seem to have set their faces on neutral, and with their purse straps strung across their chests bandolier[18]-style, they forge ahead as though bracing themselves against being tackled. I understand, of course, that the danger they perceive is not a hallucination. Women are particularly vulnerable[19] to street violence, and young black males are drastically overrepresented among the perpetrators[20] of that violence. Yet these truths are no solace[21] against the kind of alienation that comes of being ever the suspect, a fearsome entity with whom pedestrians avoid making eye contact.   5

It is not altogether clear to me how I reached the ripe old age of twenty-two without being conscious of the lethality[22] nighttime pedestrians attributed to me. Perhaps it was because in Chester, Pennsylvania, the small, angry industrial town where I came of age in the 1960s, I was scarcely noticeable against a backdrop of gang warfare, street knifings, and murders. I grew up one of the good boys, had perhaps a half-dozen fistfights. In retrospect,[23] my shyness of combat has clear sources.   6

As a boy, I saw countless tough guys locked away; I have since buried several, too. They were babies, really — a teenage cousin, a brother of twenty-two, a childhood friend in his mid-twenties — all gone down in episodes of bravado[24] played out in the streets. I came to doubt the virtues of intimidation early on. I chose, perhaps unconsciously, to remain a shadow — timid, but a survivor.   7

The fearsomeness mistakenly attributed to me in public places often has a perilous[25] flavor. The most frightening of these confusions occurred in the late 1970s and early 1980s, when I worked as a journalist in Chicago. One day, rushing into the office of a magazine I was writing for with a deadline story in hand, I was mistaken for a burglar. The office manager called security and, with an ad hoc posse,[26] pursued me through the labyrinthine[27] halls, nearly to my editor's door. I had no way of proving who I was. I could only move briskly toward the company of someone who knew me.   8

Another time I was on assignment for a local paper and killing time before an interview. I entered a jewelry store on the city's affluent Near North   9

[15] **SoHo:** fashionable Manhattan neighborhood

[16] **taut:** tight

[17] **warrenlike:** mazelike

[18] **bandolier:** a band worn around the body, crossing from one shoulder to the opposite hip

[19] **vulnerable:** open (to danger or attack)

[20] **perpetrators:** those who commit crimes

[21] **solace:** comfort

[22] **lethality:** deadliness

[23] **in retrospect:** looking back

[24] **bravado:** an arrogant (and perhaps foolish) display of bravery

[25] **perilous:** dangerous

[26] **ad hoc posse:** quickly assembled group

[27] **labyrinthine:** winding or mazelike

Side. The proprietor excused herself and returned with an enormous red Doberman pinscher straining at the end of a leash. She stood, the dog extended toward me, silent to my questions, her eyes bulging nearly out of her head. I took a cursory[28] look around, nodded, and bade her good night.

Relatively speaking, however, I never fared as badly as another black male journalist. He went to nearby Waukegan, Illinois, a couple of summers ago to work on a story about a murderer who was born there. Mistaking the reporter for the killer, police officers hauled him from his car at gunpoint and but for his press credentials would probably have tried to book him. Such episodes are not uncommon. Black men trade tales like this all the time.   10

Over the years, I learned to smother the rage I felt at so often being taken for a criminal. Not to do so would surely have led to madness. I now take precautions to make myself less threatening. I move about with care, particularly late in the evening. I give a wide berth[29] to nervous people on subway platforms during the wee hours, particularly when I have exchanged business clothes for jeans. If I happen to be entering a building behind some people who appear skittish,[30] I may walk by, letting them clear the lobby before I return, so as not to seem to be following them. I have been calm and extremely congenial[31] on those rare occasions when I've been pulled over by the police.   11

And on late-evening constitutionals[32] I employ what has proved to be an excellent tension-reducing measure: I whistle melodies from Beethoven and Vivaldi and the more popular classical composers. Even steely New Yorkers hunching toward nighttime destinations seem to relax, and occasionally they even join in the tune. Virtually everybody seems to sense that a mugger wouldn't be warbling bright, sunny selections from Vivaldi's *Four Seasons*. It is my equivalent of the cowbell that hikers wear when they know they are in bear country.   12

[28] **cursory:** quick

[29] **a wide berth:** plenty of room

[30] **skittish:** nervous

[31] **congenial:** friendly

[32] **constitutionals:** walks

Austin Silver

Why Does the Media Make Men Look Stupid?

Austin Silver is a fashion commentator for AskMen.com, an online advice and entertainment magazine for men. The following is one of his columns.

People picket everything. If someone kills a rat in a movie, members of PETA[1] will be outside ready to bark. If a TV ad depicts a woman as helpless, feminists worldwide will gather and boycott the product the ad is endorsing.   1

[1] **PETA:** People for the Ethical Treatment of Animals, an animal-rights organization

If any visible minority is stereotyped, you know that the community will take issue. And don't even get me started on what happens if you crack a gay joke—but who defends the heterosexual guy that constantly gets depicted as a hormonal reject?

Burping, farting, ignorant, and virtually useless—that's how the average   2
man is depicted nowadays. Why? Well, that's easy—because they won't raise Cain[2] about it. Advertisers put their money on the men because they're pretty sure that a lawsuit won't follow; we just don't get offended. But should we?

More and more it seems that women are being depicted as the intelligent,   3
all-knowing beings, minorities are being portrayed like the wise and stylish ones, and guys are, well, the morons of the operation. What's going on?

Feel the Sting

Why is it acceptable that guys are portrayed as though they can't fend for   4
themselves and need a woman to point out how useless they are? After all, stereotypes do stem from somewhere, so maybe most guys are virtually useless in certain aspects of their lives and need women to come in and rescue them. Yeah right.

Granted, guys have been running the corporate world since the dawn of   5
time; nevertheless, in matters of pop culture, guys are never depicted in the most glamorous fashion. In every TV commercial I see nowadays, men are controlled by either their cars, their hormones, their need for a brewskie, their appetites, or all of the above. Do we really have no depth to speak of? Oh wait, big breasts, 12 o'clock . . . hey, I'm kidding.

Everywhere I turn, men are being belittled[3] and no one is saying a word   6
about it. Maybe we should start protesting every time a woman in a movie says that "all men are pigs," or that "men always think with the wrong head . . ." Those things just aren't true. But instead of tripping out, we just shrug our shoulders and move on. Well, I'm taking a stand, dammit.

Considering that not many men are willing to draw up picket signs that   7
say things like "Men aren't swine!" and "We're human too!" and walk in circles in front of movie debuts and corporate buildings, mass media will continue to portray us as though we're Neanderthals. Anyone can make fun of us because there's a certain safety in doing so.

You're So Insensitive

There are commercials that portray girlfriends fantasizing that their boy-   8
friends are perfect when in reality they're fat couch potatoes. But let's say we turned the tables and showed a commercial where there was a fat woman whose boyfriend was imagining that she was perfect? Man, I could just imagine the drama. It would be the hot topic on Entertainment Tonight and you'd have Camryn Manheim[4] speaking out about the injustices regarding big women.

---

[2] **raise Cain:** to protest or become angry; a biblical reference

[3] **belittled:** criticized

[4] **Camryn Manheim:** Overweight actress who played an attorney on a popular TV show, *The Practice*

Would fat guys start tripping on a company because they're depicted as 9
undesirable? No, they face the facts and don't cry out to anyone who will
give them airtime. They suck in their guts (as best they can) and take it on
the chins. Why? Because they're men — they're not going to get all "girlie"
about it.

It seems that the media has to walk on eggshells when it comes to hurt- 10
ing women's feelings or taking a stab at a gay guy, or worse, mimicking
stereotypes regarding any minority. But when it comes to men, hey, that's
fair play — take your best shot, it's a free-for-all.

Oh My God, That's Me

So perhaps I'm contradicting myself right now considering I'm complaining 11
about the way men are depicted through the media, but perhaps I can open
a door that will either make the media more sensitive toward men (which is
not my intended goal), or rather, encourage everyone else that walks this
Earth to chill out and stop taking everything so damn personally (bingo!).

Yes, platinum blonde, breastily enhanced women are typically repre- 12
sented as dizzy chicks, but that's because they usually use their looks and
not their brains to get what they want; homosexual men are portrayed as
fashionable because the majority of them dress like stars; and African Americans are shown rapping or playing basketball because they dominate the in-
dustries. There's no need to get all emotional about it.

I'm sure that now that I've brought this issue to your attention, you'll 13
start watching TV, movies, and even look at ads differently. And although I
recommend bringing it to people's attention, please don't gather up your
buddies and have a bitch-fest in front of NBC. Then again, maybe we should
start mocking all these "sensitive" people.

WRITING ASSIGNMENTS EXPLORING STEREOTYPES . . . .

1. The selections in this chapter as well as the definition of stereotypes
   on page 728, "It's Time I Shed My Ex-Convict Status (p. 597), "My
   Indian" (p. 653), "Gender Patterns Begin at the Beginning" (p. 658),
   and "Why Profiling Won't Work" (p. 670) consider the potentially negative consequences of stereotypes. Choose at least two of these pieces
   and refer to them as you write an essay that does one of the following:

   - Tells a story of a time when you stereotyped someone (or a group)
     or had a stereotype applied to yourself; relate your story to the sto-
     ries of other writers from this book

   - Gives examples of stereotyping based on this chapter's essays and, if
     relevant, your own experience

   - Describes the process through which we learn stereotypes or how
     we might teach our children to avoid them

   - Classifies different stereotypes

   - Defines *stereotype* and gives examples of stereotypes from the essays
     in this chapter or from your own experience

   - Compares or contrasts different types of stereotypes (for example,
     ethnic or racial versus regional)

- Discusses the causes or effects of stereotypes
- Argues that stereotyping can sometimes be a good thing or argues for actions to reduce stereotyping

■ **TIP:** You should properly cite outside sources that you use in your essay. For advice, see Chapter 19.

2. Write an essay about ways in which you might have been stereotyped (based on where you live, how you speak, what you look like, and so on) and how you are or are not like that stereotype. Has your response to the stereotyping been at all similar to (or different from) that of the other writers in this chapter?

3. Write an essay about how any stereotype about college students is wrong because students are so diverse. Include specific examples about students at your college. Also, you might draw on the college student's blog on page 686.

■ **TEACHING TIP:** This activity takes about twenty minutes. Give students eight to ten minutes for steps 1 to 3, giving them a two-minute warning for filling in the sentence in step 3. The rest of the time should be devoted to sharing responses to the activity.

COLLABORATIVE ACTIVITY EXPLORING STEREOTYPES . . . .

The following activity is based on one posted on the Multicultural Pavilion at EdChange, **<edchange.org>**.

Pair up with another student whom you don't know very well, and follow these steps:

1. Each of you should take out a sheet of paper and draw a circle in the center of it. Then, write your name in the center circle, and draw other circles coming out from the center circle. In each of the outer circles, write important parts of your identity. For example, the outer circles could say, *female, athlete, Jewish, middle class,* and so on.

2. Share two stories with each other. First, talk about a time when you felt especially proud to be associated with one of the parts of your identity. Next, share a story about a time when it was particularly painful to be associated with one of the parts of your identity.

3. Each of you should then share a stereotype you have heard about a part of your identity, a stereotype that fails to describe you accurately. You can fill in the blanks in this sentence: "I am (a/an) _____, but I am NOT (a/an) _____." For instance, you might say, "I am a Christian, but I am NOT a radical Republican."

4. Break out of the groups, and share stories from step 2.

5. Take turns reading your stereotype statements from step 3 to the class. Then, you might talk about how parts of your identity that are important to you differ from the judgments that others make. Or, you might talk about how others' statements challenged stereotypes you had about other groups.

Appendix A

Succeeding on Tests

Adam Moss
DeVry, South Florida

This appendix will help you prepare for any testing situation, increasing your confidence and your chances of success.

Understand Testing Myths and Facts

Test makers do not set out to create test questions that will trip you up or confuse you. That's one of many common myths about tests. Here are some others.

> **MYTH:** Test makers pick obscure topics for reading passages to confuse you.

> **FACT:** Test makers often avoid very common topics because they don't want students who are familiar with those topics to have an unfair advantage.

> **MYTH:** Tests often have hidden patterns, and if you can just figure out these patterns, you'll get a good score.

> **FACT:** Tests answers rarely follow a pattern, and if they do, the pattern is often hard to figure out, and you'll waste time trying. The best strategy is good preparation.

> **MYTH:** Some people are just good at taking tests, but I'm not one of them.

> **FACT:** Students who are good at tests are usually those who have learned to manage their anxiety and to be "test wise": They know what to find out about the test, they know how to study, and they know how to read and answer test questions. In other words, they are informed about and prepared for tests. You, too, can be a good test taker if you learn the strategies that are discussed in the pages that follow.

Understand What to Do Before and During Tests

Before the Test

To do well on a test, take the time to gather information that will help you study effectively.

Ask Questions

Although your instructors won't give you the test questions in advance, most will give you general information that will help you prepare. Ask a few key questions, and write down the answers.

- What subjects are on the test or what chapters are covered? If the test has more than one part, do you have to take all the parts or just some?
- What kinds of questions appear on the test? Question types include multiple choice, true/false, matching, short answer, and essay. Many tests combine several types of questions.
- How much time do you have for the entire test? How much time do you have for each section? Are there breaks between sections?
- What should you review? The text? Handouts? Lecture notes? Something else?
- Is the test paper-and-pencil or computerized? If it will be paper-and-pencil, practice that format. If it will be computerized, practice that. In some cases, your teacher may be able to provide or refer you to sample tests on paper or on computer. See also the suggestions in the next section.
- What materials are you required or allowed to bring? Do you need pens, pencils, or both? Can you use notes or the textbook? Are you allowed to use a calculator? Do you need to bring an ID? Are you required to provide your own scratch paper?
- What score do you need to achieve to pass, and are you allowed to retake the test?
- For objective tests, will you be penalized for guessing answers?

Study Effectively

Once you have collected information about the test you are about to take, write out a plan of what you need to study and follow it. The following tips will also help you study effectively.

- Choose a good place to study. Find a straight-backed chair and table in the dining room or kitchen and study there, or study in the library or another quiet place with similar conditions. Be careful about studying in bed or on the sofa; you may fall asleep or lose concentration.
- Use test-specific study materials like "prep" books and software, if they are available. These materials often include old, real test questions and

usually have full practice tests. Be sure to get an up-to-date book to ensure that any recent changes to the test are covered. Also, your instructor may have practice tests. Note that this textbook has sample tests at the end of each grammar chapter and part. Additionally, grammar practices are available at **bedfordstmartins.com/realwriting** and on a CD-ROM available with this book, *Exercise Central to Go*.

- Visit Web sites with practice tests. Following are some sites that have samples of tests required in certain states: the CUNY/ACT Basic Skills Test, <**www.lehman.cuny.edu/provost/enrollmentmgmt/ testing/act.html**>; the Florida College Basic Skills Exit Test, <**net2 .valenciacc.edu/mwhissel/Grammar/FCBSET/fcbset_wr_01c.htm**>; Florida's College Level Academic Skills Test (CLAST), <**www .dianahacker.com/writersref/add_clast.html**>; the Georgia Regents' Test, <**www2.gsu.edu/~wwwrtp/index94.htm**>; and the Texas Higher Education Assessment (THEA), <**www.thea.nesinc.com**>.

- Make up and answer your own test questions. Try to think like your instructor or the test writer.

- Take a test-preparation class if one is available. Many schools offer free or reduced-cost classes to students preparing for entrance or exit tests.

- If your test is going to be timed, try to do a sample test within a time limit. Grab an egg timer from the kitchen and set it for a time similar to that of the test.

- Use all the study aids available to you: chapter reviews, summaries, or highlighted terms in your textbook; handouts from your instructor; study guides; and so on. Also, many schools have writing centers that offer tutoring or study-skills worksheets. Check out your school's resources. Your tuition pays for these services, so you should take advantage of them.

- Learn what study strategies work best for you. Some students find that copying over their notes is effective because they are doing something active (writing) as they review the material. Other students find that reading their notes aloud helps them to remember the ideas. Still others find that drawing a concept helps them remember it.

- Study with other students in your class. By forming a study group, you can share each other's notes and ideas.

- Don't give up! The key to studying well is often to study until you are "sick" of the material. Whatever pain you feel in studying hard will be offset by the happiness of doing well on the test.

■ **RESOURCES:** To give your students lots of testing practice, use the *Testing Tool Kit* CD-ROM available with this book. Still more tests are available in *Additional Resources*. Also, if you need to prepare students for the Florida College Basic Skills Exit Test, have students use *From Practice to Mastery*, a test-preparation workbook available with *Real Writing*.

Reduce Test Anxiety

Everyone gets test anxiety. The trick is to manage your nerves instead of letting them control you. Turn your nervousness into positive energy, which can sharpen your concentration. Also, the following tips can help.

- Study! Study! Study! No test-taking strategies or anxiety-reducing techniques can help if you do not know the material. Think about a job you do well. Why don't you get nervous when you do it, even under pressure? The answer is that you know how to do it. Similarly, if you have studied well, you will be more relaxed as you approach a test.

- Eat a light meal before the test; overeating can make you uncomfortable or sleepy. Consider including protein, which can help your brain work better. Do not consume too much caffeine or sugar, however. Be especially wary of soft drinks, because they contain both. Take a bottle of water with you if you are allowed to. Sipping water as you work will help you stay hydrated, especially during long testing periods.

- Take the test at a time that is good for you, if possible. For example, if you are a "morning person," take the test early in the day. With computerized testing, more and more schools offer flexible test schedules or individual appointments. If you can choose your testing time, do not take the test after a long day of work or if you are very tired.

- Get to the test early. Nothing is more stress-inducing than arriving late, and you might miss the valuable pretest instructions. Also, you may not be allowed to take the test at all if you arrive too late.

- Resist the urge to discuss the test with others before you begin. Anxiety can be contagious, and others who are less prepared can make you needlessly nervous.

- Be sure to breathe deeply, in through your nose and out through your mouth. When you get nervous, your breathing becomes rapid and shallow. By controlling your breathing, you can reduce your nervousness.

- Think positive thoughts. Don't think about how terrible it will be if poor test scores keep you from getting accepted into school, advancing to the next class, or getting a new job. Instead, remind yourself of how much you know and how well prepared you are. Harness your energy and believe in yourself.

During the Test

■ **TIP:** For more tips on understanding test directions, see Chapter 1.

As the test begins, it's important to listen to any directions your instructor or test monitor gives. Resist the temptation to start flipping through the test as soon as you get it; if you're not paying attention, you might miss important instructions that aren't included in the written directions.

Also, it's important to monitor your time. Many test takers lose track of time and then complain, "I didn't have time to finish." Don't let that happen to you. After you have listened to the directions, survey the whole test, unless you are told not to do so. This way, you will know how many parts the test has, what kinds of questions are asked, and, in some cases, how many points each part or question is worth. Then, make a time budget.

Look at one student's time budget.

	MINUTES (55 TOTAL)
Part 1: 10 multiple-choice questions (2 point each)	5
Part 2: 10 fill-ins (3 points each)	10
Part 3: 2 paragraphs to edit (10 points each)	15
Part 4: 1 paragraph to write (30 points)	20
Final check of work	5

Here is a good strategy for taking this test:

1. Do items in Parts 1 and 2 that you know the answers to; don't spend time on items for which you don't know the answer immediately. (However, if you are not penalized for guessing, you may want to fill in answers; you can always change them later.)

2. Move on to Part 3, making all the edits you can and leaving at least twenty minutes for Part 4.

3. Write the paragraph for Part 4. Reread it to fix any problems you see.

4. Go back and try to answer questions from Parts 1 and 2 that you were unsure of.

5. If you have time, do a final check of your work.

Do not work too slowly or too quickly. Spending too much time on questions can lead to "overthinking" and a loss of attention. You have only so much energy, so use it wisely. However, rushing is as big a problem as overthinking. Test designers sometimes make the first choice in a multiple-choice question appear correct, while the truly correct answer is presented later. This approach trips up students who don't take the time to read each question and answer carefully.

Understand How to Answer Different Types of Test Questions

The general strategies just described will help you on any test. However, it is equally important to develop strategies to attack specific types of questions. Following are some ways to approach typical kinds of questions.

Multiple Choice

- Read the directions carefully. Most tests allow only one answer choice per question, but some tests allow multiple responses.

- For each question, see if you can come up with an answer before looking at the answer choices.

- Be sure to read all answer choices. Answer A may seem correct, but B, C, or D may be a better answer.

- Use the process of elimination, ruling out those answers that you know are incorrect first. Your odds of guessing correctly will increase with every answer eliminated.

- Stick with your first choice unless you're sure it is wrong. Your initial thinking will often be correct.

- If there is no penalty for guessing, try to answer even those questions for which you are unsure of the answer. If there is a penalty, make an educated guess, a guess based on having narrowed the choices to one or two.

- Many students fear "all of the above" and "none of the above" questions, but you can actually use them to your advantage. If you know that any single answer is correct, you can eliminate "none of the above"; likewise, if you know that any single answer is incorrect, you can eliminate "all of the above." If you know that more than one answer is correct, you can safely choose "all of the above."

- Be sure to interpret questions correctly. A question that asks "Which of the following is not true?" is actually asking "Which of the following is false?" Consider the following example.

EXAMPLE

Which of the following instruments does not belong in an orchestra?

a. tympani drum

b. cello

c. electric guitar

d. oboe

The question is asking which instrument is *not* in an orchestra, but students who do not read carefully may miss the word *not* and choose incorrectly. The correct answer is C.

- Pay attention when there are two similar but opposite answers. The following question is based on a reading passage not shown here.

EXAMPLE

Which of the following is true based on the passage you have read?

a. Drug abusers who enter treatment under legal pressure are as likely to benefit from it as those who enter treatment voluntarily.

b. Drug abusers who enter treatment under legal pressure are less likely to benefit from it than are those who enter treatment voluntarily.

c. Drug abusers who have committed crimes should be treated only in high-security facilities.

d. Drug abusers can overcome their addictions more easily if they get treatment in isolated facilities.

Answer options A and B say the opposite things, so one of them must be eliminated as incorrect. In this case, A happens to be the correct answer.

- Usually, you can eliminate two answers that say the same thing in different words. If one is true, the other must be too. Therefore, you cannot choose both of them, unless the test allows you to select more than one answer.

EXAMPLE

Upton Sinclair's novel *The Jungle* was famous for its stark view of what?

a. unsafe and filthy working conditions in the American meat-packing industry

   b. the situation of poor and jobless Americans during the Great
       Depression

   c. the events of the last days of the Vietnam War

   d. working-class Americans and their plight during the Depres-
       sion era

Answers B and D can clearly be eliminated because they contain
the same idea. If one were to be correct, the other would automatically be correct as well. Eliminate these two choices. The correct
answer is A.

- Keep in mind that longer and more detailed answers are often the correct ones. Test makers may put less time and effort into creating the
  wrong answer choices.

EXAMPLE

   One role of hemoglobin in the bloodstream is to

   a. fight disease.
   b. bind to oxygen molecules and carry them to cells.
   c. help form blood clots.
   d. carry proteins to cells.

Answer choice B is the longest and most detailed answer, and it is the
correct choice. Always be sure, however, to read every answer option,
for it is not always the case that the longest one is correct.

- Be aware of absolute statements that include words like *all, always,
  every, everyone, never, none,* and *only*. They are rarely the correct
  answer. The following question is based on a reading passage not
  shown here.

EXAMPLE

   Which of the following statements is true based on the reading
   passage?

   a. Catheter-based infections are less treatable than other hospital
       infections.

   b. Meticillin-resistant *Staphylococcus aureus* is always more serious
       than regular *Staphylococcus aureus*.

   c. Meticillin-resistant *Staphylococcus aureus* is treatable, but
       fewer antibiotics work against it than against other staph
       infections.

   d. Hand-washing plays a small role in preventing the spread of
       staph infections.

B contains the word "always," suggesting that there are no exceptions.
This is not true; therefore, B can be eliminated. C happens to be the
correct answer.

True-False

- You have a 50 percent chance of guessing correctly, so it is usually wise to guess on true-false questions.
- There are usually more true answers than false answers on a test. Start with the presumption that an item is true, and then look for information that may make it false.
- If any part of a question is false, the whole question is false. Students tend to focus on just the true section.

EXAMPLE

True or false? In 1492, Christopher Columbus reached the New World with three ships: the *Niña,* the *Pinta,* and the *Santa Dominga.*

Even though most of this statement is correct, the mistake in the third name, which should read "*Santa Maria,*" is enough to make the whole statement false.

- Be aware that statements with absolute words like *all, always, never,* and *none* are usually false (see p. A–7).
- However, "possibility" words like *most, often, probably, some, sometimes,* and *usually* often indicate true answers.

EXAMPLE

True or false? Penguins usually live in cold climates.

Penguins do not always live in cold climates, and the word *usually* allows for these exceptions. This statement is true.

- Beware of cause-and-effect statements that may seem true at first but that show a false cause.

EXAMPLE

True or false? A koala bear is a marsupial because it eats eucalyptus leaves.

It is true that a koala is both a marsupial and eats eucalyptus leaves, but it not a marsupial *because* it eats eucalyptus leaves.

Reading Comprehension Questions

These questions are usually based on a paragraph (or paragraphs) that you have to read. Follow these tips for success:

- Read all the questions before reading the passage. This will help you pay attention to important points as you read.
- Understand that you must "read for speed." Reading passages are the number one time killer on tests. If you take too long to read, you will use up much of your time.

- On a related point, try to absorb whatever you can, and do not stop on any one word or idea. Chances are that the questions will not require a perfect understanding of the word(s) you are finding difficult.

- Take a "leap of faith" when answering reading comprehension questions. Sometimes, students will agonize over a question even if they are fairly sure they know the right answer. In this case, take an educated guess and move on.

Essay Questions and Timed Writing Assignments

Many students think essay questions are harder than other types of questions, but they actually offer a little more flexibility because there is not just one limited answer. There are, however, certain standards you need to follow. These are described in the following sections.

Understand the Essay Rubric

Most standardized or departmental essay tests have their own scales, called *rubrics*. Rubrics show what elements graders look for and rate in an essay answer or timed writing, and they often present the number of possible points for each element. Rubrics are often available from a college's testing center, writing center, or learning lab. Also, instructors often include scoring rubrics as part of the course syllabus.

Regardless of the particular rubric used, every essay test is graded based on similar fundamentals, described in the chart on page A–10.

■ **RESOURCES:** Sample rubrics and detailed advice on assessment—including how to mark seriously flawed papers—are included in *Practical Suggestions*.

■ **TIP:** When considering the length of your answer, be especially careful with paragraphs. Some test graders penalize short paragraphs, even if they are well written.

Understand the Question

Every writing test comes with a topic or set of topics from which you must choose one. Read the topic(s) and directions carefully, and make sure you understand whether a single paragraph or a whole essay is required. Is there a minimum or maximum length for the paragraph or essay? How many words should it be? How much time do you have, and does that include "prewriting" time?

Then, read the question/topic carefully, looking for **key words** that tell you

- what subject to write on
- how to write about it
- how many parts your answer should have

See page 20 for a list of common key words in essay exam questions.

Follow Key Writing Steps Using Standard Essay Structure

Once you understand the question or topic, plan your answer, using prewriting to get ideas and at least three major support points. (See Chapter 5.)

As you begin to write, bear in mind that your test essay, just like other essays you write, should have the parts shown in the chart at the right.

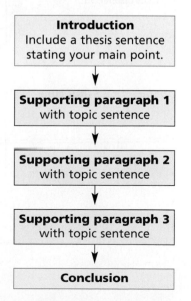

Introduction
Include a thesis sentence stating your main point.

↓

Supporting paragraph 1
with topic sentence

↓

Supporting paragraph 2
with topic sentence

↓

Supporting paragraph 3
with topic sentence

↓

Conclusion

Typical Rubric for an Essay Exam Answer
(what elements it may be graded on)

ELEMENT	CRITERIA FOR EVALUATION	SCORE/COMMENTS
RELEVANCE	The essay should address the question completely and thoroughly. If there is more than one part to the question, the answer should address all parts.	Total points possible: [will vary] This essay's score:
ORGANIZATION	The essay should follow standard essay structure, with the following items: —an introduction with a clear and definite thesis statement —body paragraphs, each of which starts with a topic sentence that supports the thesis —a conclusion If a paragraph, as opposed to an essay, is called for, the paragraph should include a topic sentence followed by enough supporting sentences to back up the main point.	Total points possible: [will vary] This essay's score:
SUPPORT	The body paragraphs contain sufficient, detailed examples to support the thesis statement.	Total points possible: [will vary] This essay's score:
COHERENCE	The essay sticks to the thesis, with all support related to it. There are no "detours." The writer uses transitions to move the reader smoothly from one idea to the next.	Total points possible: [will vary] This essay's score:
CONCISENESS	The essay does not repeat the same points.	Total points possible: [will vary] This essay's score:
SENTENCE STRUCTURE	The sentences are varied in length and structure (they are not all short and choppy).	Total points possible: [will vary] This essay's score:

ELEMENT	CRITERIA FOR EVALUATION	SCORE/COMMENTS
SENTENCE GRAMMAR	The essay should not have any of the following: —fragments —run-ons or comma splices —errors in subject-verb agreement —errors in verb tense	Total points possible: [will vary] This essay's score:
CONSISTENCY	The essay should use consistent point of view and verb tense.	Total points possible: [will vary] This essay's score:
WORD CHOICE	The essay should use the right words for the intended meaning and demonstrate an understanding of formal, academic English, especially avoiding slang.	Total points possible: [will vary] This essay's score:
PUNCTUATION	The essay should use commas, periods, semicolons, question marks, and other punctuation correctly.	Total points possible: [will vary] This essay's score:
SPELLING	Most words should be spelled correctly.	Total points possible: [will vary] This essay's score:
LEGIBILITY	The essay should be readable (if it's handwritten, the cross-outs should be neat).	Total points possible: [will vary] This essay's score:
TOTAL SCORE:		

Follow this process to complete the essay:

1. Try to write a scratch outline based on your prewriting. This should include your thesis statement and at least three support points. The outline doesn't have to be in complete sentences.

2. Write an introduction, concluding with your thesis statement.

3. Write your body paragraphs. Each paragraph should begin with a topic sentence based on the support points you wrote for step 1. You should include at least three minor supporting details in each body paragraph.

4. Finish with a short concluding paragraph. It should refer back to your main point and make an observation.

5. If you have time, revise and proofread your essay, looking for any grammar errors and other issues from the rubric on page A–10. Usually, it is acceptable to make corrections by crossing out words and neatly writing the correction above.

Sample Student Essays

Following are some sample essays written in response to a single exam topic. After each sample is an analysis of the student's work.

Here is the topic that the essays were written in response to:

TOPIC: As we mature, our hobbies and interests are likely to change. In an essay of no more than 500 words, describe how your interests have changed as you have gotten older.

A LOW-LEVEL ESSAY

I had many hobbies over the years. I use to play T-ball but I moved on to playing real Baseball. I played baseball for more than ten years finaly I became a pitcher for my High School varsity squad. The one hobby that I can think of that I use to have that I don't do anymore is riding bicycles. My friends and I cruised all over our neighborhood on our bicycles looking for trouble to get into all the time and once even running from the cops, who caught my friend Jimmy, who was the leader of our so called gang. When I got in high school, though I got another hobby which took all my time and money, my car was my new love. I got it when I was 17 and I put everything I had into it and I loved it almost as much as my girlfriend Kate. As you can see, by my senior year, my only hobbies were playing baseball for my school team and taking care of my sweet car.

ANALYSIS

This response likely will not pass. To begin with, it is a single paragraph, which is unacceptable given that the question requires an essay. It begins with a general thesis and has no real conclusion at the end. The essay offers examples of hobbies but gives no supporting details about them, and it fails to clearly show the changes in interests over the years. The writer strays from the topic when discussing his "gang" and follows no real pattern of organization. In addition, the writing lacks varied sentence structure and contains few transition words. There are a number of grammar and spelling errors, and the language is too informal for an essay.

A MID-LEVEL ESSAY

Everybody has some kind of hobby, whether it is playing piano, or skiing. People's hobbies change sometimes over the years as they change too. This is certainly true for me. I have had many hobbies over the years, and they have certainly changed.

As a child, I played T-ball, and I eventually moved on to playing real baseball. I played baseball for more than ten years; finally, I became a

■ TIP: Ask if you will be penalized for using contractions in writing for tests. Some graders won't care, but others might mark you down for this.

■ TEACHING TIP: Ask students to read and discuss these answers and why they received the ratings they did.

pitcher for my High School varsity squad, and I played during my junior and senior years. I am looking forward to pitching in the college ranks.

The one favorite hobby I used to have that I don't have anymore is riding bicycles. My friends and I cruised all over our neighborhood on our bicycles looking for trouble to get into all the time and once even running from the cops, who caught my friend Jimmy, who was the leader of our so called gang. I eventually outgrew this hobby, as it was replaced by a new more exciting vehicle.

When I got in high school, though I got another hobby which took all my time and money, my car was my new love. It is a Nissan 300 ZX, and it is black with a black interior. It had 16" rims and a sweet body kit. I got it when I was 17 and I put everything I had into it and I loved it almost as much as my girlfriend Kate.

As you can see, by my senior year, my only hobbies were playing baseball for my school team and taking care of my car. I once spent all my time riding my bicycle with my friends but I guess I've outgrown that. The one hobby that has lasted throughout my life is my love for baseball. I will probably play that until I am an old man.

ANALYSIS

This essay is better, showing a clearly identifiable introduction, body, and conclusion. There is a thesis statement that addresses the topic, but it could be more specific. The body paragraphs are generally cohesive, and the essay shows chronological (time order) development. However, the writing still strays from the topic in a few areas and could use several more transitions to help readers move smoothly from one paragraph to the next. This essay has fewer grammar and punctuation errors than the previous one, but the language is still too informal in spots. The essay's biggest problem remains a lack of supporting details about the hobbies and the changes in them over the years.

A HIGH-LEVEL ESSAY

Everybody has some kind of hobby, whether it is a craft, a musical instrument, or a sport. While some hobbies last a lifetime, many fade or appear at different times during our lives. Some people play sports as youngsters that they cannot play later in life, and some people adopt new hobbies as adults that they would never have enjoyed as a young person. This is certainly true for me. I have had many hobbies over the years, and as I have gotten older, they have changed. As I have grown, I have lost my interest in riding bicycles, gained a love for cars, and undergone some changes in the way I play baseball, the one hobby I have always enjoyed.

My earliest hobby was one that I outgrew some time during junior high school: riding bicycles with my friends. As a child, my bicycle was my only real means of independence. My friends and I rode all over our neighborhood, looking for trouble to get into and even tangling with the police on one occasion. As I got older and my friends began to get cars, this hobby faded and a new one emerged, featuring a new type of vehicle.

Working on my car is my new interest, and it is a hobby that grew from my love for my bicycle. The car is a Nissan 300 ZX, and it is black with a black interior, sixteen-inch rims, and a beautiful body kit. I got it when I was seventeen, and for the past two years, I have put all of my time and money into it. My high school friends joked that I loved it almost as much as my girlfriend, Kate. It offers me the same sense of freedom as the bicycle, and I feel the same pride in keeping in it perfect shape.

My one love that has remained throughout my life is baseball, but even that hobby has undergone some changes as I have matured. As a young child, I played T-ball and quickly grew to love it. I eventually moved on to playing real baseball and played second base and shortstop in little league for more than ten years. After years of hard work, I became a pitcher for my high school varsity squad, and I pitched in the starting rotation for both my junior and senior years. I am looking forward to pitching in college and beginning a new stage in my baseball "career."

My hobbies have changed as I've matured, but in many ways, they have stayed the same. My first hobby, riding my bicycle, grew into my love for my car, and in many ways, the change from two wheels to four wheels reflects my growing maturity. My one lifetime hobby, baseball, has evolved as well, as I've lost the "T" and changed positions. One day, I may play another position or even another sport. However, like my love for speed, my love for competition will always define my hobbies.

ANALYSIS

This essay is clear, effective, and well-supported. All the essential elements are present, and the thesis is specific, clearly setting up the rest of the essay. The writer has described the hobbies in a clear chronological order, and he uses transitions effectively. The introduction and conclusion are reflective, and descriptions of the hobbies are detailed, using more varied and exciting language and sentence structure than the previous examples. The writing stays on topic throughout and answers the essay question thoughtfully and thoroughly.

Use *Real Writing* to Succeed on Standardized Tests

■ **TEACHING TIP:** Pass out the rubric for your departmental, school, or state exam so that students can annotate it with the relevant chapters of *Real Writing*. They can use this as a study guide.

Many standardized, departmental, and state exams (like those listed on p. A–3) test for the same basic skills, whether through multiple-choice questions, essay questions, or other items. Following is a list of typical skills tested and where you can get help in *Real Writing*.

SKILL	CHAPTER IN *REAL WRITING*
Writing/Essay Questions	
Using thesis statements and topic sentences (main ideas)	4
Using adequate and relevant support	5
Arranging ideas in a logical order	6
Writing unified sentences/paragraphs	8
Using effective transitions	8
Choosing appropriate words	33
Avoiding confused or misused words	34
Taking a position on an issue (typical in essay exams)	17
Reading	
Understanding readings	1 (and the "Readings for Writers" section of *Real Writing with Readings*)
Understanding purpose/audience	2
Identifying thesis statements and topic sentences (main ideas)	1, 4
Identifying adequate and relevant support	1, 5
Understanding word meaning	Appendix B
Grammar/Mechanics	
Using modifiers correctly	27
Using coordination and subordination correctly	28, 29
Understanding parallel structure	30
Avoiding fragments	21
Avoiding run-ons and comma splices	22
Using standard verb forms/tenses	24
Avoiding inappropriate shifts in verb tense	24
Making subjects and verbs agree	23
Making pronouns and antecedents agree	25
Avoiding pronoun shifts in person	25
Maintaining clear pronoun references	25
Using proper case forms of pronouns	25
Using adjectives and adverbs correctly	26
Using standard spelling	35
Using standard punctuation	36–39
Using standard capitalization	40

Appendix B

Building Your Vocabulary

Patti Levine-Brown
Florida Community College, Jacksonville

Building a good vocabulary helps you to understand everything you read; to write better papers and tests in college; to communicate better with coworkers, bosses, and customers at work; and to get people to see things your way in your everyday life. Students who are able to speak, write, and read more ⌐ctively are more successful in both their college and work careers, and even in their personal lives.

The⌐ are several strategies you can use to build your vocabulary and increase your understanding of what you read.

Use Context Clues

Context clues are clues in a sentence or paragraph that suggest the meaning of a word you don't know. While reading, use the information you get from context clues to help you understand what a word means. Several of the most common context clues are described in the chart that follows.

In the following chart, the words that you may not know are underlined in the "Examples" column. Read the "What It Is" column and the example, and, using the context clues, guess the meaning of the words. The meaning is already provided for the first word. Many times, readings will have a variety of context clues that help the reader understand the author's point. While reading, make a note of any unfamiliar words. Then, see if you can figure out their meaning by using context clues. If you can't, look up the word's meaning in a dictionary. *Answers will vary somewhat. Possible answers shown.*

TYPE OF CONTEXT CLUE	WHAT IT IS	EXAMPLES
DEFINITION/RESTATEMENT	A definition of the word is actually given. Definition/restatement is often used in textbooks, particularly after a **boldfaced** or *italicized* word. Or the definition may be in parentheses. **Words that signal a definition/restatement:** *are, defined as, is*	• Students must avoid plagiarism, using someone else's work as your own. *Using someone else's work as your own* is a definition/restatement of *plagiarism*.
EXAMPLE	Giving illustrations, details, or other kinds of examples that make the meaning of a word clear. **Words that signal examples:** *for example, for instance, like, such as*	• Misdemeanors, such as petty theft, trespassing, and vandalism, go on a person's record. The phrase *such as petty theft, trespassing, and vandalism* provides examples of *misdemeanors*. I think *misdemeanors* means <u>minor crimes</u>.
COMPARISON	Comparing something (finding similarities) to something else. **Words that signal comparisons:** *alike, as, like, similar*	• She was as conspicuous as a bear in a church. *As* signals that the subject of the sentence, *she*, was like something: *a bear in a church*. I think *conspicuous* means <u>standing out, noticeable</u>.
CONTRAST	Contrasting something (finding differences) with something else: The things being contrasted are opposites. **Words that signal contrasts:** *although, but, however, in contrast, not, unlike*	• The house was once very well maintained, but now it is decrepit. The word *but* signals a contrast: The house is no longer well maintained. I think *decrepit* means <u>in poor condition</u>.
RELATED WORDS	Finding words related to the one you don't know. If you know the meaning of the related words, you can guess the meaning of the word you don't know. **Words to look for:** *and* = similar, *because* = cause or reason, *but* = contrast, *however* = contrast	• The teacher said my son's behavior was incorrigible and impossible. *And* signals that *incorrigible* is similar to *impossible*. I think *incorrigible* means <u>not acceptable</u>. • Her expression is dour, but she is actually very funny.

continued

TYPE OF CONTEXT CLUE	WHAT IT IS	EXAMPLES
		But signals that *dour* is unlike *funny*.
		I think *dour* means <u>sour, humorless</u>.
		• Geri's voice sounds <u>rasping</u> because she has strep throat.
		Because signals that strep throat caused Geri's voice to sound this way.
		I think *rasping* means <u>rough</u>.

Read the paragraph that follows, which is from an organizational communication textbook. Try to figure out the meaning of the underlined words using context cues, and write their meanings in the blanks that follow the reading. If you can't figure out the meanings of certain words, look them up in a dictionary.

The Meaning of Work

Some of the values being <u>espoused</u> today about work signal not a retreat from it but a transformation of its meaning—from <u>drudgery</u> to a source of personal significance and fulfillment. Employees want to feel that the work they do is worthwhile, not just a way to draw a paycheck. This trend is increasingly <u>pervasive</u>. For example, while white-collar workers and college students tend to view blue-collar workers as being motivated primarily by money, job security, and benefits, the most important <u>incentives</u> for workers at all levels include positive relationships with co-workers and managers. Also important are opportunities to participate in organizational decision-making. Without these major <u>determinants</u> of job satisfaction, worker stress and burnout may occur. Work has considerable social significance for Americans, who, despite increased concerns for balance, as a rule spend more time on the job than they do with their families.

> —Eric M. Eisenberg and H. L. Goodall, *Organizational Communication: Balancing Creativity and Constraint*

Answers will vary. Possible answers shown.

espoused: *talked about, recommended*

drudgery: *boring or unimportant work*

pervasive: *widespread*

incentives: *benefits, rewards, motivators*

determinants: *factors, influencers*

Understand Word Parts

Knowing word parts—prefixes, suffixes, and roots—can help you break words down into smaller parts so that you can understand them.

A **prefix** is used at the beginning of a word to give the word a certain meaning.

DEFINITION: The prefix *sub-* means under or below.

EXAMPLE: The patient's temperature was *subnormal*.   [This means the temperature was lower than normal.]

DEFINITION: The prefix *hyper-* means excessive or above normal.

EXAMPLE: He was in shock from the accident and began to *hyperventilate*.   [This means he began to breathe unusually fast.]

A **suffix** is a word part at the end of a word.

DEFINITION: The suffix *-ment* at the end of a word describes the state or quality something.

EXAMPLE: As the drum roll started, the crowd's *excitement* was obvious. [*Excitement* is the state of being excited.]

DEFINITION: The suffix *-ize* means to become a certain way.

EXAMPLE: Christmas has become very *commercialized*.   [*Commercialize* means to become commercial.]

The **root** of a word is its base form.

DEFINITION: The root *wise* means informed or intelligent. Prefixes and suffixes added to this word change its meaning.

EXAMPLES:

wise + dom (suffix) = wisdom   [The state of being wise]
un (prefix) + wise = unwise   [Not wise]

DEFINITION: The root *ped* means foot (and sometimes leg).

EXAMPLES:

ped + al (suffix) = pedal   [Something pushed with the foot]
centi (prefix) + pede (root with *e* ending) = centipede   [Bug with many legs]

The following tables contain some common prefixes, suffixes, and roots. If you can't figure out the meanings of the words in the "Examples" column, look them up in a dictionary.

Prefixes

PREFIX	MEANING	EXAMPLES
a-	not	amoral
ad-	to; toward	admit
ante-	before	anteroom
anti-	against	anti-aircraft
bi-	twice; two	biweekly; bipartisan
co-	together	cohabitate
de-	to decrease or go down	de-escalate
dis-	not; to undo	dissatisfied; dissemble
ex-	beyond; former	extend; ex-husband
hyper-	excessive	hyperactive
il-, in-, ir-	not	illiterate, insensitive, irrelevant
inter-	among; between	interstate
intra-	within, inside	intramural
mis-	not; mistaken or wrong	misinformed; mistrial
mono-	one	monotone
multi-	many; much	multiply
non-	not	nonsensical
per-	throughout	pervasive
poly-	many	polymorphic
post-	after; behind	posterior
pre-	before	preview
re-	again; back	refinish; return
sub-	under; below	subordinate
super-	over; above	supersonic
tri-	three	triumvirate
un-	not	unable

Choose five prefixes and use them to make new words (not those given in the examples in the chart)   *Answers will vary.*

Suffixes

SUFFIX	MEANING	EXAMPLES
-able, -ible	capable of being or happening	achievable
-al	relating to	physical
-an	belonging to; from	Canadian
-ance, -ancy, -ence	state of being	dependence
-ant	state of being	defiant
-ard	one who is a certain way	coward
-dom	state of being or realm	kingdom
-ee	one who plays a certain role	trustee
-er	one who does a certain thing	speaker
-ful	full of	helpful
-fy	to make; to do	beautify; classify
-hood	a certain group or state of being	sisterhood
-ic	pertaining to; having a quality	mystic
-ier; -yer	one who does a certain thing	lawyer
-ion, -sion, -tion	a certain thing or quality	emotion
-ism	a certain thing or quality	capitalism
-ist	one who does a certain thing	physicist
-ity	a certain thing or quality	minority
-ive	a certain thing or quality	captive; restive
-ize	to make something a certain way	sensitize
-less	without	helpless
-ment	a certain thing or quality	content-ment
-ness	state of being	loneliness
-ology	study of	pathology
-or	one who plays a certain role	mayor
-ous	full of	famous
-phobia	fear of	claustro-phobia
-ship	a certain thing or quality	seamanship
-tude	a certain thing or quality	attitude
-ward	in the direction of	eastward

Choose five suffixes and use them to make new words (not those given in the examples in the chart)   *Answers will vary.*

Roots

ROOT WORD	MEANING	EXAMPLES
act	do	activate
alter	other	alternative
amor	love	amorous
ann	year	anniversary
anthrop	human	anthropological
aqua	water	aquamarine
audio	hear	auditorium
auto	self	automobile
belli; bellum	war	bellicose; antibellum
biblio	book	bibliomania
bio	life	biology
cap; capit	head	captain; capital
cardi	heart	echocardiogram
chrome	color	monochrome
cred	belief	credible
cycl	circle; cycle	cyclical
derm	skin	hypodermic
dict	speak	dictation
frater	brother	fraternize
geo	earth	geographical
gram; graph	write	grammar; graphic
hetero	different	heterogeneous
homo	same	homogenize
junct	join	junction
loc	place	locate
log; logue	speak; word	dialogue
mater	mother	maternal
micro	small	microcosm
mot; mov	move	motivate; moveable

ROOT WORD	MEANING	EXAMPLES
neo	new	neonatal
nym	name	synonym
orig	beginning	original
pater	father	paternity
path	feeling	empathy
ped; pod	foot; leg	pedestrian
photo	light	photograph
port	carry	portable
quer; ques; quiz	to ask	query; question; quizzical
rupt	break	disrupt
scope	view	microscope
scrib; script	write	scribble; manuscript
spect	look	inspect
tact	touch	tactile
terra	earth	terrarium
vac	empty	vacuum
ver	truth	verdict
voc	voice	vocal

Choose five roots and use them to make new words (not those given in the examples in the chart)   *Answers will vary.*

Use Vocabulary Resources

Another way to improve your vocabulary is to use a dictionary, a thesaurus, and glossaries to expand your knowledge of words.

A Dictionary

A dictionary includes word meanings, pronunciations, and more. Here is a sample entry.

Spelling and syllabication   Pronunciation   Part of speech   Definitions

pla • ce • bo (pluh – SEE – bo) *n.* **1a**. A substance containing no medication that is given to reinforce a patient's expectation to get well. **1b**. An inactive substance used as a control in an experiment. **2**. Something of no medical value that is used to reassure.

■ **TIP:** For more on dictionaries, see page 503.

When using a dictionary to look up a word, whether you find the word in your reading or want to use it in your writing, carefully consider the context: the general meaning of the sentence or passage. The same word can have quite a different meaning depending on the context.

Glossaries

A **glossary** is a list of difficult or technical terms with definitions. Not all books have glossaries, but textbooks and technical manuals often do. Usually, glossaries appear at the end of books or at the end of chapters or units.

A Thesaurus

While trying to express your thoughts or feelings in writing, have you ever felt you were using the same words over and over? Next time this happens, try using a **thesaurus**, a book of synonyms, words that have the same or similar meanings. For example, the word *efficient* has several synonyms: *proficient, professional, competent, resourceful, able, well-organized, economical, cost-effective, useful,* and *helpful.*

However, make sure you choose the right synonyms for the context of your writing, and avoid using a thesaurus just for the sake of picking out big or fancy words. Such words can make your writing sound odd or overly complicated.

Use Vocabulary Study Tools

To continue building your vocabulary, consider using a few study tools either alone or in a group.

Vocabulary Cards

Making your own vocabulary cards can help you learn and remember new words.

Image Cards

To make vocabulary cards with images, follow these steps.

- Print the word you do not know on the front of an index card (use one card for each word).
- Next, turn the card over and write the definition of that word on the back.
- Then, write a sentence using the word.
- Finally, think of an image or symbol you can draw that will help you connect the word and its definition. Draw this next to the definition,

using colored markers if you like. The idea is to come up with an image that will trigger your memory in terms of the word's definition.

Mnemonic Cards

A **mnemonic** is a system of remembering things. For example, a common mnemonic for remembering how many days each month has is the saying, "Thirty days hath September, April, June, and November. . . ." Another example is the spelling rhyme, "*I* before *e* except after *c* or when sounded like *a* as in *neighbor* or *weigh*." To make mnemonic cards, follow these steps.

- Print the word you do not know on the front of an index card (use one card for each word).
- Next, turn the card over and write the definition of that word on the back.
- Then, write a sentence using the word.
- Now, carefully examine the word and definition and try to come up with an acronym (letters that stand for a group of words) that will help you remember the word and its definition. For example, an acronym used to remember the names of the Great Lakes is the acronym HOMES (Huron, Ontario, Michigan, Erie, Superior). An acronym used in this book to help you remember the coordinating conjunctions is FANBOYS (*for, and, nor, but, or, yet, so*). The idea is to come up with an mnemonic that will trigger your memory in terms of the word's definition.

Whether you use image or mnemonic cards, keep the cards with you and refer to them between classes or at other free times. The more you refer to the cards, the better your chances of really learning and understanding the words and their definitions.

Vocabulary Games

Word games are a fun way to build your vocabulary. Here is one game you might try.

TEAMWORDS

- Your teacher will have created index cards with vocabulary words. These should be stacked and placed at the front of the room.
- Pick a student monitor.
- The rest of you should break into two teams, perhaps by counting off by twos.
- Each team should pick a captain.
- The monitor should take the index cards, pick one, and call the word out to the first team.
- The team will confer and give the team captain the answer.
- The team captain will then give the answer to the monitor, who will determine whether the answer is correct, checking a dictionary if necessary.

■ **TEACHING TIP:** For this game, you will need to have as many index cards as there are students in your class. Write a different vocabulary word on each card. Pick reasonably challenging words, perhaps from readings assigned for this course. You may need to help the monitor determine whether certain definitions are acceptable.

■ **TEACHING TIP:** Give students one or more words for which they are responsible for knowing the meaning. Try to use these words in class as often as possible, and encourage students to use them as well, in context. Give students a point each time they use the word correctly. At the end of the class, week, or whatever time period you choose, give a prize to the student who has used the word correctly the most.

- If the answer is correct, the team receives a point.
- The monitor will then select a word to give to the second team, and that team will go through the same procedure as the first team.
- If at any time a team does not know the definition of a word given to them, or if they give an incorrect answer, the opposing team is given a chance to answer.
- If the opposing team gives the correct answer, this team gets the point.
- Keep playing until the monitor has used the whole stack of cards.

Look and Listen

Finally, be aware of words outside of the college classroom. When you're listening to the radio, watching television, or reading newspapers or online Web sites, make a note of words you don't know. If you can't understand them from the context in which they're used, look them up in a dictionary. Even if you do understand the general meaning from the context, add the word to a personal vocabulary list and try to use it in speech or in writing.

Appendix C
Getting a Job

This appendix will lead you through the steps of getting a good job—one that uses your skills and leads to a satisfying career.

Do Some Research

Before applying for specific jobs, find out about various kinds of jobs that are suited to your interests and skills. Many Web sites describe jobs, the skills they require, and typical salary ranges. For example, you can go to Monster.com or JobSearch.com and browse for kinds of jobs you might be interested in.

Look for Internships

Many students find that an internship gives them good experience in a particular kind of job as well as connections within a company they might be interested in working in after graduation. Some internships are paid, while others are not; make sure you know whether an internship you are interested in is paying or nonpaying. Quite often, internships can lead to job offers, so even if an internship doesn't pay, or pay much, it may be worth taking. Many Web sites provide information about internships, including InternJobs.com and CollegeBoard.com. (When you get to the College Board site, type "internships" into the search box.)

Find Out about Specific Companies

If you are interested in working for a specific company or have an interview there, get as much information as you can about the company by visiting its Web site or by calling and asking for an annual report or other information that is available to the public.

Prepare a Résumé

To apply for a job, you will need a good résumé. A model is included here, but you can also get help from two other sources: your college's placement office and a variety of Web sites. Do a Web search using the words "how to write a résumé," and many sites will appear. Your résumé should be simple and professional: Its purpose is to provide information, not to entertain the person to whom you send it. Try to keep your résumé to one page.

Following is an example of a résumé, with annotations indicating what each section is and what it should do. When you have prepared a résumé, make sure that you proofread it carefully; it is important that your résumé be error-free.

PAT GEMELLI
12856 Glover Street
Manchester, NH 03110
603-441-2248
pgemelli@hotmail.com

List full name and current contact information, centered.

OBJECTIVE   To work as a city probation officer in New Hampshire

Describe what job you are seeking and/or what skills you want to use. You can tailor the objective to different jobs you are applying for.

EDUCATION   Mill City College
Manchester, NH
Major: Criminal justice
B.S. degree to be granted in May 2006
Grade point average: 3.4
Courses taken included
    Criminal Law
    Criminal Investigation
    Technology in Criminal Justice
    Evidence and Court Procedures
    Abnormal Psychology
    Sociology of the Family

Include college, major, degree, graduation date, and courses related to the position sought. You may also wish to include your grade point average.

EXPERIENCE   **Youth Leader**
September 1996 to present
Grace Unity Church, Manchester, NH
- Teach a variety of courses to high school students
- Lead regional seminars for students
- Perform outreach activities
- Counsel teens
- Work with families of teens to understand issues
- Designed a community service program

List relevant jobs and internships with dates and skills, putting the most recent experience first.

Internship
September 2005 to April 2006
New Hampshire Corrections Institution, Nashua, NH
- Worked in the warden's office, providing administrative assistance to warden
- Attended meetings with warden and prison guards
- Attended and took minutes for meetings with assistant warden and county parole officers
- Observed meetings between parole officer and one of his assigned parolees
- Worked as ad hoc member of prisoners' rights committee

SPECIAL SKILLS   Fluent in Spanish and Portuguese. Experienced with most PC and Macintosh computer programs and applications.

Include any skills that are a plus, especially for specific position.

OTHER ACTIVITIES   Volunteer, King City Soup Kitchen
Player, Gael's Adult Soccer League
Soccer coach, middle school intramural program

List anything that shows you are an active and involved person. Activities can distinguish you from other applicants, so do not be falsely modest.

REFERENCES   Available on request

References are people who can speak favorably about your suitability for the job. Before you give anyone's name as a reference, be sure to ask the person if you may do so.

CHECKLIST: HOW TO WRITE A RÉSUMÉ

STEPS	HOW TO DO THE STEPS
☐ **Include your name and contact information.**	• Write your full name (no nicknames), address, telephone number, and e-mail address, centered, at the top of the page.
☐ **State your career objective, briefly and specifically.**	• Write an objective that is concrete (not, for instance, "to find an interesting position"). • Be prepared to modify your objective slightly to fit various positions you apply for or are interested in.
☐ **Describe your education.**	• List college(s), degree(s) received, and graduation date(s) (or date(s) when degrees will be awarded). • List any college honors (dean's list and so on). • If you have a good grade point average, include it. • List courses that are relevant to the position you are interested in.
☐ **Describe your experience.**	• Start with your most recent position. • List your title, the company name and location, and the dates of employment. • List your responsibilities and achievements, using active verbs (for example, *organized* *a youth retreat*). • Include both paid and unpaid positions, including internships.
☐ **Describe your special skills.**	• Include languages, computer skills, and other skills that could be relevant to the position and that can be demonstrated (for example, *Strong organizational skills: developed a mentoring program; Strong teamwork skills: served as part of team that . . .*).
☐ **Describe other activities or awards.**	• Include any activities that show you are an involved person, such as volunteer or community service activities, sports, and relevant hobbies.
☐ **Provide a list of references or state "References available on request."**	• Select people who can speak favorably about your qualifications. • Contact references before listing them.
☐ **Revise and edit your résumé.**	• Add other skills and experiences that will distinguish you from others. • Make sure there are no errors in spelling, grammar, or punctuation. • Ask someone else to read the résumé.

STEPS	HOW TO DO THE STEPS
☐ **Format and print your résumé.**	• Use a typeface that is simple and easy to read (not fancy), like Times New Roman. • Leave enough space between items so that the information is easy to read, not cramped. • Use **bold** to highlight key information. • Use a high-quality printer to print your résumé, and use high-quality paper that is white or a light, neutral color. The résumé must look professional.

A FINAL WORD: Never make up information for a résumé. More and more employers are checking facts on résumés, and being caught in a lie will automatically eliminate you from consideration for a job.

Write a Cover Letter

When you send your résumé, include a cover letter. Although your résumé provides crucial information about your experience and skills, your cover letter is the first item a prospective employer sees, so it is an important piece of writing. It should be direct, telling the reader why you are interested in the job and what you have to offer. It should also be confident and enthusiastic, but professional, and written in formal English. For example, express your strong interest in the position and the organization, but avoid informal language such as, "Working for your company would be awesome."

Following is an example of a cover letter, with annotations indicating what each section does. When possible, try to address your letter to a specific person. You may have to call the company to get the appropriate contact name. Verify that you have the correct spelling.

SAMPLE COVER LETTER

Full name and current contact information, centered, using same format as for résumé

PAT GEMELLI
12856 Glover Street
Manchester, NH 03110
603-441-2248
pgemelli@hotmail.com

Date of letter

May 4, 2006

Full name, position, department, and address of person being contacted

Richard Willey, Director
Human Resources
New Hampshire Department of Corrections
State Office Park West
8900 River Street
Concord, NH 03665

Dear Mr./Ms. and last name followed by a colon (:)

Dear Mr. Willey:

States position writer is interested in

I am interested in a position as a probation officer in New Hampshire, specifically in Nashua, Manchester, or Concord, our major cities.

Shows knowledge of organization

Has confident and enthusiastic tone

Having grown up in Manchester, I am committed to contributing to our state, specifically in efforts to both ensure the protection and safety of our residents and to rehabilitate convicts. My internship at the New Hampshire Corrections Institution in Nashua allowed me to participate in some of the very innovative and successful initiatives launched by the Department of Corrections. I believe strongly that my experience and education make me uniquely qualified for the position of New Hampshire probation officer, and I would be proud to serve in such a forward-looking organization.

Summarizes education and shows extra effort

This month, I will receive a bachelor of science degree from Mill City College, having maintained a 3.4 grade point average. I took advantage of the many courses offered by the college by taking an extra course load each semester. Doing so allowed me to fulfill all the criminal justice requirements and also to learn about areas that could benefit my work as a probation officer, such as psychology and sociology.

Cites specific skills; expresses enthusiasm

My experiences as a youth counselor and as an intern at NHCI, Nashua, have developed my abilities to communicate with others; to observe the blend of authority, objectivity, and compassion that make a good law enforcement officer; and to understand the role of sound teamwork in criminal justice. I am eager to further advance these skills and learn from others by working with professionals at the New Hampshire Department of Corrections.

Ends confidently and thanks the addressee

I have enclosed a résumé that provides more details about my education and experience. I believe I will be a good probation officer because I am motivated and certain of my career choice. I hope you will consider me as a candidate and look forward to speaking with you. Thank you for your consideration.

Sincerely,

Pat Gemelli

Pat Gemelli

CHECKLIST: HOW TO WRITE A COVER LETTER

STEPS	HOW TO DO THE STEPS
☐ **Include your identifying information.**	• Put your name, address, telephone number, and e-mail address in a letterhead that is centered at the top of the page.
☐ **Write the date and address of your letter.**	• Write the date and skip two spaces. • Write the name, title, and address of the person you are writing to. Skip two more spaces.
☐ **Write your salutation.**	• Write Dear Mr./Ms./Mrs./Dr. and the person's last name. Put a colon (:) after the name. Skip two spaces.
☐ **Write the body of your letter.**	• In the first paragraph, state the position you are interested in. • In the body paragraphs, briefly, but specifically, state your qualifications, skills, and strengths. • In your final paragraph(s), restate your interest in the position, your enthusiasm, and your confidence in your ability to succeed in the position; indicate how the prospective employer can contact you; and thank him or her for considering you. Skip two spaces.
☐ **Write your closing.**	• Write *Sincerely* followed by a comma (,). Skip four spaces. • Type your name. • Sign your name, neatly, above your typed name.
☐ **Revise your letter.**	• Reread what you have written, and add anything that would strengthen your appeal to the prospective employer.
☐ **Edit your letter.**	• Carefully edit your letter, making sure that it has no errors in spelling, grammar, or punctuation.
☐ **Format and print your letter.**	• Make sure that the letter follows the standard format for a letter of application and includes all of the elements. • Use a high-quality printer and paper, or go to a copy shop to print your letter. It is important that it look clean, crisp, and professional. • Make a copy of your letter for your files.

Prepare for an Interview

When you are called in for an interview, be prepared. If you haven't already gone to the company's Web site, do so now, and learn as much as you can about the organization, its products and services, and its "culture." Search your library's holdings to see if the company has been written about in magazines or professional journals.

Rehearse Interview Questions

As confident as you may feel about your qualifications for a position, you should practice your answers to some typical interview questions so that you will respond to them well. As you form answers, always keep an interviewer in mind, remembering that he or she is looking for qualities that will benefit the company and fit the position for which you are applying. Here are ten common interview questions to which you should have answers.

1. ***How would you describe yourself?***
   The interviewer wants to know about traits that would make you a valuable employee. Consider adjectives that describe positive traits, such as *honest, hardworking, intelligent, flexible, creative, motivated, good listener,* and so on.

2. ***How would a friend describe you?***
   This question tries to get at your character. It gives you an opportunity to say lots of good things about yourself without feeling as if you're bragging. Take advantage of the opportunity, and use positive descriptions, like *born leader, great sense of humor, dedicated,* and so on.

3. ***What are your greatest strengths/weaknesses?***
   When asked this question, you really want to describe your weaknesses as the flip side of a strength. So, for example, if you give "hardworking" as a strength, you might then give "sometimes a little driven" as a weakness. It's not really a weakness because it tells the interviewer that you push yourself.

   Here are some other examples of strengths that can also be (good) weaknesses:

STRENGTH		WEAKNESS
Motivated	→	Sometimes impatient when others are negative about everything
Organized	→	Sometimes spend too much time helping others who are not organized
Hardworking	→	Impatient with slackers
Creative	→	Sometimes impatient with those who hold onto old ways of doing things for no good reason
Good communicator	→	Sometimes spend too much time trying to understand those who are poor communicators

4. ***Describe a problem that you solved.***
The problem doesn't have to be a huge one, just one where you looked at a challenging situation and figured out how to deal with it. If you can think of a situation that involved other people, all the better. An example could be consulting with coworkers to figure out a better filing system for a disorganized office.

5. ***Name someone you admire and tell why.***
Because you are in a business interview, avoid controversial political or religious figures. You might choose someone who has helped others, showed bravery, or changed the world in some way. If there is a member of your family you particularly admire, you can name that person, but make sure to describe concretely what that person did to make you admire him or her.

6. ***Name an accomplishment that you are proud of.***
This doesn't have to be a minor miracle, just something you did that made you stand out. It could be achieving an athletic or academic success, committing to and sticking with something (like learning to play an instrument), or helping someone else in need. The point is to prove that you have traits that will be valuable in the workplace (stamina, commitment, ability to work well with others, and so on).

7. ***Describe your ideal job.***
Obviously, you want to describe some elements of the job you're applying for. If you have particular skills that fit the job, mention how you would welcome an opportunity to use those skills. Also, you might say you're looking for a job that presents a challenge, an opportunity to learn, and an opportunity for advancement. Avoid mentioning things like a good salary, a nice office, good vacation benefits, and the ability to dress casually. Instead, stick to things that demonstrate your interest in doing a good job.

8. ***Why do you want to work here?***
Mention some of the positive things you have learned about the company from your research. For example, you might point to the company's high-quality products, involvement in the community, or size (small enough or large enough to allow employees to learn and grow). Be as specific as you can, but keep your comments at a professional level, and avoid saying things like, "It's close to my house."

9. ***Why should we hire you?***
Many people have trouble with this question, but it's an important one, and it gives you a wonderful opportunity to sell yourself. Telling a prospective employer why you would be an asset to the company isn't bragging; it's a good way to reinforce your earlier descriptions of your strengths. Be as specific as possible, listing specific skills you have that will benefit the company. Also, reemphasize your good qualities—for instance, your motivation, your willingness to work hard and solve problems, and so on. Know in advance what you will say to sell yourself.

10. ***Where do you want to be in five years?***
If you have researched the company, state a job that is a level or two above the one you're applying for. Be reasonable but optimistic. If

you're applying for an entry-level job, it would be unrealistic to say, "I'd like to be president of the company." However, it would be realistic to say, "I'd like to be entering a management position." Then, say you hope that in five years you will have learned a good deal and will be able to apply your skills in a job that will challenge you and benefit the company. Again, avoid mentioning salary.

Have a Few Questions to Ask

At some point toward the end of the interview, the interviewer will probably ask if you have any questions. Based on what you know about the company or the general industry, have one or two questions to ask, such as, "I read on the Web site that the company is planning to expand overseas. That's exciting. Can you tell me a little more about that?" or "What do you like best about working here?" Asking a couple of questions shows your interest and initiative.

As important as money is, salary isn't usually discussed in a first interview. The interviewer might ask you to specify an ideal salary range, and if you've done your homework about the job and comparable positions, you should be able to answer this question. If the interviewer doesn't mention salary and you haven't been able to determine a salary range for the position, you might ask what a general range for the position is.

Some Interview Tips

- Leave plenty of time to get to the interview, and try to arrive a few minutes early. If you have a morning interview, and you have trouble getting up early, ask a friend to call you. Do whatever you need to do to get to an interview on time; if you arrive late, you have already created a bad impression.

- Dress simply and professionally: no flip-flops, T-shirts, shorts, jeans, or too-short skirts. As a general rule, men should wear a light-colored, unwrinkled shirt, unwrinkled dress pants, and dress shoes with socks. If people in the type of job you're interested tend to dress conservatively, you should wear a jacket and tie as well. When in doubt, it's better to dress up than dress down. Women should wear an unwrinkled blouse, dress pants or a skirt, hose, and either flat shoes or shoes with modest heels. Avoid overly bright colors, elaborate hairdos, and lots of big jewelry. Both men and women should avoid heavy colognes. *Neat* and *conservative* are the code words for interview attire: You want to be remembered for your qualifications, not your unique look.

- Do not drink, eat, or chew gum while waiting for, or taking part in, an interview.

- When you meet the interviewer, stand up straight, walk toward him or her, and shake his or her hand. Your handshake should be firm, not wimpy, but not so firm that the person's hand is crushed.

- Look the interviewer in the eye, both during the greeting and as you respond to questions.

- During the interview, sit up straight; slouching is often perceived as sloppy—a characteristic that will turn off prospective employers. Try to create an impression of confidence and interest.

- When you speak, speak clearly while looking at the interviewer. Mumbling and avoiding eye contact give negative impressions that can wipe out all of your good qualifications.

- When the interview is at an end, thank the interviewer for his or her time, express your interest, and ask what the time frame for making a decision is. Ask whether there is any additional information that would help bolster your candidacy.

- Shake the interviewer's hand again, and walk away with good posture.

Follow Up After the Interview

Within twenty-four hours of your interview, write a thank-you note to the person or people with whom you spoke. Your sending such a note shows the interviewer(s) that you have the ability to follow up, a characteristic that is essential in business.

In the thank-you note, restate your interest and enthusiasm, mention your good fit with the position, and say that you hope to have an opportunity to join the company. Depending on the culture of the organization, a typed letter, handwritten note, or an e-mail can be appropriate. In any case, use formal English, and proofread what you write carefully. Make sure you spell the name of the interviewer(s) correctly.

An example of a thank-you note follows.

PAT GEMELLI
12856 Glover Street
Manchester, NH 03110
603-441-2248
pgemelli@hotmail.com

May 19, 2006

Richard Willey, Director
Human Resources
New Hampshire Department of Corrections
State Office Park West
8900 River Street
Concord, NH 03665

Dear Mr. Willey:

Thank you for taking the time to talk with me about the position of probation officer for the New Hampshire Department of Corrections. Our interview confirmed my strong interest in the position, where I believe I could both learn and contribute a great deal.

I realize you have many responsibilities, and I do appreciate your time. If I can provide any further information, please contact me. I look forward to the opportunity to join the organization.

Sincerely,

Pat Gemelli

Pat Gemelli

If you have not heard from the company by the time a decision about the position was expected, write another note or e-mail, again stating your interest in the position and inquiring about the status of the decision. Once again, thank the interviewer for his or her time, and express your hope that you will become part of the organization.

Appendix D

Solving Problems

Writing in the Real World/Solving a Problem (Writing Assignment 3 in Chapters 9–17) offers you the opportunity to solve real-world problems by working alone or as a part of a team. Your instructor will probably decide whether you will do these assignments independently or in groups.

Problem solving and teamwork are important in today's workplace as well as in your college courses and in everyday life, so this is great real-world practice.

This section will explain both what skills are and how to use them effectively.

Problem Solving

Problem solving is the process of identifying a problem and figuring out a reasonable solution.

Problems range from minor inconveniences like finding a rip in the last clean shirt you have when you're running late to more serious problems such as being laid off from your job. While such problems disrupt our lives, they also give us opportunities to tackle difficult situations with confidence.

Too often people are paralyzed by problems because they don't have strategies for attacking them. However, backing away from a problem rarely helps solve it. When you know how to approach a challenging situation, you are better able to take charge of your life.

Problem solving consists of five basic steps, which can be used effectively by both individuals and groups of people.

The Problem-Solving Process

Understand the problem.

You should be able to say or write it in a brief statement or question.

EXAMPLE:

Your ten-year-old car needs a new transmission, which will cost at least $750. Do you keep the car or buy a new one?

Identify people or information that can help you solve the problem (resources).

EXAMPLES:

- Your mechanic
- Friends who have had similar car problems
- Car advice from print or Web sources

List the possible solutions.

EXAMPLES:

- Pay for the transmission repair.
- Buy a new car.

Evaluate the possible solutions.

1. Identify the steps each solution would require.
2. List possible obstacles for each solution (like money or time constraints).
3. List the advantages and disadvantages of the solutions.

EXAMPLES (considering only advantages and disadvantages):

- Pay for the transmission repair.

Advantage: This would be cheaper than buying a new car.

Disadvantage: The car may not last much longer, even with the new transmission.

- Buy a new car.

Advantage: You'll have a reliable car.

Disadvantage: This option is much more expensive.

↓

> **Choose the most reasonable solution, one that is realistic—the simpler the better. Be able to give reasons for your choice.**
>
> **SOLUTION:** Pay for the transmission repair.
>
> **REASONS:** You do not have money for a new car, and you don't want to assume more debt. Opinions from two mechanics indicate that your car should run for three to five more years with the new transmission. At that point, you'll be in a better position to buy a new car.

Teamwork

Teamwork is working with others to achieve a common goal. Working with others to solve a problem has many benefits: more possible solutions, more people to share the work, more ideas and perspectives. But effective teamwork involves more than simply meeting with people: You need to understand and apply good teamwork skills. For example, sports teams don't win merely because the individual players are talented; they win because the individual players pool their individual talents into a coordinated whole. Each player on the team works hard, but each player also supports and cooperates with other players. Players may also discuss strategies together to help ensure the team's success. The same is true of teamwork in other arenas as well.

Following are some basics to keep in mind when you are part of a team.

BASICS OF EFFECTIVE TEAMWORK

- The team establishes ground rules that ensure each person on the team can contribute.
- Members listen to each other and respect different points of view.
- Although one person may function as team leader, all individuals play an equal role and are equally appreciated.
- Members recognize that they must depend on one another.
- All members contribute and feel responsible for their own work because it affects the outcomes of the team's efforts.

Answers to Odd-Numbered Editing Exercises

Chapter 20

Practice 20-1, page 276
Possible answers: **1.** rare, nest, of **3.** complained, but, across, them **5.** of, return, nest

Practice 20-2, page 279
Answers: **1.** Subject: company; prepositional phrase: without a chief executive officer **3.** Subject: people; prepositional phrase: on the short list of candidates **5.** Subject: man; prepositional phrase: from a bankrupt firm **7.** Subject: appearance; prepositional phrase: before the members of the board **9.** Subject: workforce; prepositional phrase: within the company

Practice 20-3, page 283
Answers: **1.** Subject: Egyptians; verb: invented (action verb) **3.** Subject: they; verb: bowled (action verb) **5.** Subject: alley; verb: opened (action verb) **7.** Subject: alley; verb: offers (action verb) **9.** Subject: people; verb: would think (helping verb + main verb)

Practice 20-4, page 284
Answers and possible edits: **1.** I (incomplete thought); I will wait until the store closes at midnight. **3.** Correct **5.** Correct **7.** Correct **9.** I (incomplete thought); Mary joined a book club because she likes novels.

Chapter 21

Practice 21-2, page 290
Answers and possible edits: **1.** Preposition: about. Some parents worry about their children's imaginary companions. **3.** Preposition: of. Some parents think imaginary companions are a waste of time and energy. **5.** Preposition: between. Children should be taught the difference between lies and imagination. **7.** Preposition: of. A child might not want to admit to being afraid of the dark. **9.** Preposition: after. Children usually give up their imaginary companions after grade school.

Practice 21-3, page 292
Answers: **1.** Dependent word: because. Going to a gym does not work for some people because their schedules do not allow it. **3.** Dependent word: since. Since online trainers usually charge less than in-person trainers, some people train online for the savings. **5.** Dependent word: unless. People who use online training say they will not exercise unless someone holds them accountable for it. **7.** Dependent word: while. While online trainers push clients to exercise, many people believe this is not as intimidating as having an in-person trainer. **9.** Dependent word: before. Before anyone selects an online trainer, he or she must be serious about exercising.

Practice 21-4, page 294
Answers and possible edits: **1.** *-ing* verb: walking. In 1931, Plennie Wingo set out on an ambitious journey, walking backward around the world. **3.** *-ing* verb: halting. After eight thousand miles, Wingo's journey was interrupted by a war, halting his progress in Pakistan. **5.** *-ing* verb: taking. Mullikin's trip took so long because he lingered, taking time out to earn money as a logger and a Baptist minister. **7.** *-ing* verb: driving. Farmers hoping for government help traveled from the Great Plains to Washington. They were driving large, slow-moving harvesting machines. **9.** *-ing* verb: looking. Americans may also have heard the story of Alvin Straight, looking for his long-lost brother as he traveled across the Midwest.

Practice 21-5, page 297
Answers: **1.** *to* + verb: to put. Now it is easy to put just about any face or object on a stamp. **3.** *to* + verb: to use. It is not necessary to use a photo of a face. **5.** *to* + verb: to choose. It is not acceptable to choose a photo of a famous person or to show anything offensive. **7.** *to* + verb: to personalize. Some people use the stamps to personalize invitations to weddings and other events. **9.** *to* + verb: to get. To get the personalized stamps, one has to pay a price.

Practice 21-6, page 299
Answers and possible edits: **1.** Example or explanation: Like financing charges. At car dealerships, important information, like financing charges, is often in small type. **3.** Example or explanation: For instance, the cost of printing each page for an inkjet printer. Sometimes, the costs that are really important are not widely known. For instance, the cost of printing each page for an inkjet printer is not often considered by consumers. **5.** Example or explanation: Like groceries or car maintenance. A consumer must be careful with everyday purchases, like groceries or car maintenance. **7.** Example or explanation: Especially if you have a trusted mechanic. Car maintenance might be cheaper elsewhere, especially if you have a trusted mechanic. **9.** Example or explanation: Essentially, a free loan. Those who pay their entire credit card balance every month get a great deal. Essentially, they get a free loan.

Practice 21-7, page 300
Answers and possible edits: **1.** Fragment: To add to their income. To add to their income, publishers are placing advertisements in their games. **3.** Fragment: Across the finish line. One character, a race-car driver, drove his ad-covered car across the finish line. **5.** Fragment: Worrying that ads are distracting. Worrying that ads are distracting, some publishers are trying to limit the number of ads per game. **7.** Fragment: Like grocery carts and restroom walls. These players are used to seeing ads in all kinds of places, like grocery carts and restroom walls. **9.** Fragment: To strike a balance between profitable advertising and high game quality. To strike a balance between profitable advertising and high game quality is what publishers want.

Practice 21-8, page 301
Possible edits: **1.** (1) Correct (3) She was so sick that everyone thought she would die. (5) Correct (7) After years of treatment,

braces, and hard work, she started running for exercise. (9) Correct
2. (1) Correct (3) Correct (5) It was a very complicated and difficult system. (7) Correct; combined with (6): Becoming interested in the idea of inventing a writing system the blind could read, Braille worked for two years on his own idea.   **3.** (1) Combined with (2): Most people think of Thomas Edison as a famous inventor who invented the lightbulb. (3) Correct (5) Combined with (4): His parents took him out of school because they did not believe the teachers. (7) Combined with (8): He was then homeschooled by his very determined mother. (9) Correct

Practice 21-9, page 302

Possible edits: (1) Thank you so much for taking the time to meet with me this past Wednesday. (3) I am more excited than ever about the administrative assistant position at Fields Corporation. (5) Correct (7) Combined with (6): With my strong organizational skills, professional experience, and friendly personality, I'm sure that I would be an asset to the company. (9) Combined with (10): Please let me know if you need any other information, like references or a writing sample. (11) Thanks again for your time.

Chapter 22

Practice 22-2, page 308

Answers and possible edits: **1.** RO (run-on); The holiday we now call Valentine's Day was celebrated in the Roman Empire on February 15; it was called Lupercalia.   **3.** CS (comma splice); The Romans held a festival to honor Lupercus; this was the feast of Lupercalia.   **5.** RO (run-on); The night before the feast, all of the young women wrote their names on pieces of paper. They put the names in a jar.   **7.** RO (run-on); The emperor ordered his soldiers not to get married. He was afraid they would want to stay home instead of going to war.   **9.** CS (comma splice); The emperor had Valentine killed on February 14. Later the priest was declared a saint.

Practice 22-3, page 312

Possible edits: **1.** In most cultures, popular foods depend greatly on availability and tradition, so people tend to eat old familiar favorites.   **3.** In many societies, certain foods are allowed to age, for this process adds flavor.   **5.** As an American, you might not like such eggs, or the thought of eating them might even revolt you.   **7.** Many Koreans love to eat kimchee, a spicy aged cabbage, but Americans often find the taste odd and the smell overpowering.   **9.** Americans on a visit to Kyrgyzstan consider themselves brave for tasting kumiss, but local children drink it regularly.

Practice 22-4, page 315

Possible edits: **1.** Although many spring wildflowers once grew in these woods, many fewer are appearing now.   **3.** When Japanese honeysuckle and other invasive plants quickly cover large areas of forest, many native wildflowers cannot survive.   **5.** The number of native wildflowers in an area usually decreases after the number of deer goes up.   **7.** Pollution and nonnative worms can also harm woods where wildflowers are already struggling to survive.   **9.** Other wildflowers will not bloom until invasive plants or other threats are removed.

Practice 22-5, page 317

Possible edits: **1.** Even though jumbo-sized airplanes can hold up to 900 people, they are now being designed with only 500 seats.   **3.** Another way to add room is to eliminate the phones on the seatbacks since hardly anyone uses those phones anyway.   **5.** New design features will also make passengers feel more comfortable. These include softer lighting and larger overhead luggage bins.   **7.** The most noticeable difference in the new planes will be the large windows. They will be 19 inches high and 11 inches wide.   **9.** There is

something about being able to see more of our surroundings that puts us at ease; at least that is what the airlines hope.

Practice 22-6, page 318

Possible edits: **1.** (1) Few people like talking about saliva; in fact, many think it's disgusting. (3) Nine laboratories across the United States are now attempting to create tools to detect the molecular components of saliva. They are part of a program funded by the National Institute of Dental and Craniofacial Research. (5) Correct (7) Although this problem has been challenging to overcome, engineers recently developed extremely precise detectors for tiny amounts of molecules. **2.** (1) Having a blood test is an experience nobody enjoys. The use of needles can also transmit infections. (3) Furthermore, saliva could be checked often to quickly detect changes. A person could easily take a saliva test a dozen times during a day. (5) Some saliva tests are already in use; they check for HIV and substance abuse. (7) Correct (9) This will be inserted into a machine so that the saliva's components can be detected.

Practice 22-7, page 319

Possible edits: (1) I'm writing to you because I was seriously overcharged for the Star 3 MP3 player I ordered from your Web site last week. (3) If you check out any competitors' sites, you will see that no one expects people to pay that much money for the Star model.
(5) Sincerely,
Chris Langley

Chapter 23

Practice 23-2, page 326

Answers: **1.** Subject: sleep; verb: is   **3.** Subject: lights; verb: were   **5.** Subject: home; verb: has   **7.** Subject: student; verb: doesn't   **9.** Subject: you; verb: are

Practice 23-3, page 327

Answers: **1.** Subject: stars; verb: are   **3.** Subject: I; verb: do   **5.** Subject: you; verb: have   **7.** Subject: one; verb: is   **9.** Subject: Orion; verb: is

Practice 23-4, page 328

Answers: **1.** Prepositional phrase: from a job or family commitments; verb: makes   **3.** Prepositional phrase: with cable television; verb: want   **5.** Prepositional phrase: from all parts of our society; verb: are   **7.** Prepositional phrase: across America; verb: sleep   **9.** Prepositional phrase: of us; verb: need

Practice 23-5, page 330

Answers: **1.** Dependent clause: that hired my cousins. The restaurant that hired my cousins is not treating them fairly.   **3.** Dependent clause: who supervises the morning shift. Correct   **5.** Dependent clause: whose hand was injured slicing potatoes. Ramón, whose hand was injured slicing potatoes, needs to have physical therapy.   **7.** Dependent clause: who cleaned his wound and put in his stitches at the hospital. The doctors who cleaned his wound and put in his stitches at the hospital expect him to pay for the medical treatment.   **9.** Dependent clause: whose English is not yet perfect. My cousins, whose English is not yet perfect, feel unable to leave their jobs.

Practice 23-6, page 332

Answers: **1.** Subject joined by: and; verb: share   **3.** Subject joined by: and; verb: are   **5.** Subject joined by: or; verb: provides   **7.** Subject joined by: or; verb: finds   **9.** Subject joined by: or; verb: costs

Practice 23-7, page 334

Answers: **1.** Subject: everyone; verb: remembers; prepositional phrase: none   **3.** Subject: one; verb: realizes; prepositional phrase: of you   **5.** Subject: someone; verb: knows; prepositional phrase: in your family   **7.** Subject: one; verb: plans; prepositional phrase: of your relatives   **9.** Subject: someone; verb: connects; prepositional phrase: in this class

Practice 23-8, page 337
Edits: **1.** What is the best reason to study music? **3.** Correct **5.** Here are a guitar, a saxophone, and a piano. **7.** What time of day do you usually practice? **9.** What musician do you admire most?

Practice 23-9, page 337
Answers: **1.** The shoppers who take on this work earn money for checking on a store's quality of service. **3.** Chain stores across the nation hire mystery shoppers. **5.** What reasons motivate a person to become a mystery shopper? **7.** Others say they have only one reason: the money they are paid. **9.** One does not have to pay a fee to become a mystery shopper.

Practice 23-10, page 338
Answers: **1.** (1) A study I came across while doing research for my sociology class rates U.S. cities by "most things to do." (3) Each of the cities was assigned a total from 0 to 100 points in each category. (5) Correct (7) Correct **2.** (1) Correct (3) Correct (5) There are also fast talkers in Boston and Bakersfield, California. (7) Other postal workers who speak very slowly live in Los Angeles; Shreveport, Louisiana; and Chattanooga, Tennessee.

Practice 23-11, page 339
Possible edits: (1) Dear Professor Harper, (3) Correct (5) Students I know who are taking your class now say it's really great, and the idea of learning about how humans grow and develop interests me greatly. (7) Are you able to accommodate me?

Chapter 24

Practice 24-2, page 345
Answers: **1.** Subject: classes; verb: require **3.** Subject: employees; verb: agree **5.** Subject: job; verb: pays **7.** Subject: he; verb: wonders **9.** Subject: bicycle; verb: allows

Practice 24-3, page 346
Answers: **1.** displayed **3.** annoyed, seemed **5.** assumed **7.** learned, remained **9.** disappeared, passed

Practice 24-4, page 347
Answers: **1.** received **3.** climbed **5.** handed **7.** purchased **9.** saved

Practice 24-5, page 351
Answers: **1.** have **3.** is **5.** are **7.** has **9.** have

Practice 24-6, page 351
Answers: **1.** was **3.** was **5.** was **7.** were

Practice 24-7, page 352
Answers: **1.** began **3.** gave **5.** knew **7.** left **9.** shut

Practice 24-8, page 353
Edits: **1.** In 1900, my great-grandfather grew wheat and raised a few cattle on his farm in Wyoming. **3.** The family did not have much money, and they hoped for good weather every year. **5.** One year, high winds blew down the barn, and hailstones broke their windows. **7.** Somehow, they kept going in spite of their difficulties.

Practice 24-9, page 354
Answers: **1.** had become **3.** had begun **5.** had grown **7.** have put **9.** has run

Practice 24-10, page 356
Answers: **1.** have begun **3.** needed **5.** have spent **7.** have expressed **9.** have kept

Practice 24-11, page 357
Answers: **1.** had been **3.** had become **5.** encouraged **7.** spent **9.** refined

Practice 24-12, page 359
Possible edits: **1.** The Civil War was fought from 1861 to 1865. **3.** Paint was smeared on the statues in the park. **5.** The winner has been announced.

Practice 24-13, page 360
Answers: **1.** Verbs: take, wanted; correct verb: wants **3.** Verbs: feel, were blinking, making; correct verb: felt **5.** Verbs: included, offers; correct verb: offered **7.** Verbs: provide, advised, to wear, to take; correct verb: advise **9.** Verbs: use, liked; correct verb: like

Practice 24-14, page 361
Edits: **1.** Many of Sheena's friends were getting tattoos ten years ago. **3.** Sheena was twenty-two when she went to the tattoo parlor. **5.** Her sister liked the tattoo, but her mother fainted. **7.** Today, however, a typical person with a ten-year-old tattoo expresses some regret about following that 1990s trend. **9.** Dermatologists have seen the development of a new trend toward tattoo removal. **11.** That technique left scars. **13.** Six months ago, Sheena started to have treatments to remove her tattoo. **15.** Purple ink has longer staying power than black, blue, and red, so Sheena's treatments will continue for more than two years.

Practice 24-15, page 362
Edits: **1.** (1) When Teresa saw her friend Jan drop makeup into her bag, she frowned. (3) She also knew that Jan would be mad if Teresa said anything. (5) As they left the store, Teresa's heart beat hard. (7) Still, she felt bad, so she spoke to Jan. (9) Teresa felt much better. **2.** (1) George Crum, a Native American chef, invented potato chips in 1853. (3) Crum decided to make superthin fries to get even. (5) In the 1920s, Herman Lay brought the potato chip to grocery stores. (7) Since then, people have eaten millions of chips. **3.** (1) Many people in the world are consumers of the same energy-boosting drug. (3) Caffeine has the power to increase both physical and mental alertness. (5) It was only about 150 years ago that chemists discovered that coffee and tea contain the same effective ingredient. (7) The caffeine also kept workers awake at their machinery. (9) Scientists have found that consuming caffeine at moderate levels is not dangerous.

Practice 24-16, page 363
Possible edits: **1.** Dear Dr. Kerrigan, (3) I became sick about a day ago. (5) Also, I have a very high fever, and I am very tired. (7) I look forward to seeing you during my appointment.

Chapter 25

Practice 25-1, page 376
Answers: **1.** Pronoun: they; noun: coins **3.** Pronoun: he; noun: President Franklin Roosevelt **5.** Pronoun: they; noun: delegates **7.** Pronoun: he; noun: King Farouk **9.** Pronoun: he; noun: Stephen Fenton

Practice 25-2, page 378
Answers: **1.** his or her **3.** its **5.** he or she no longer works **7.** himself or herself **9.** he or she

Practice 25-3, page 380
Answers: **1.** their **3.** its **5.** its **7.** their **9.** its

Practice 25-4, page 382
Possible edits: **1.** My doctor referred me to a physical therapist, who said I needed to exercise more. **3.** I tried a lower fat diet along with the exercising, but this combination did not really work either.

5. Therefore, I started eating fats again and stopped consuming carbs, but these methods were not a permanent solution.   7. Last week, I overheard my Uncle Kevin talking to my brother, and my uncle explained how he stayed slender even while traveling a lot.   9. He says it's not hard to pack carrots or apples for a trip, so anyone can plan in advance.

Practice 25-5, page 384
Edits: 1. Young people sometimes take advertisements too literally.   3. People who see or hear an advertisement have to think about the message.   5. A recent study said that parents can help kids overcome the influence of advertising.

Practice 25-6, page 387
Edits: 1. In 1974, George Foreman was the heavyweight boxing champion, and he and Muhammad Ali agreed to a fight for the title.   3. Because American officials considered Mobutu a strong anticommunist, they and he were allies, but Mobutu was a dictator who stole money intended for his impoverished country.   5. Foreman angered the people of Zaire immediately when he and his German shepherd dog were seen getting off the airplane.   7. The people loved Muhammad Ali, and pictures of him and his group in Zaire showed adoring crowds everywhere.   9. Ali may have feared losing the fight, but when he and Foreman finally got in the ring, Ali took punch after punch.

Practice 25-7, page 389
Edits: 1. In addition, I was nowhere near as well equipped for camping as she.   3. Correct   5. He seemed to believe that we were more experienced than they.   7. They all hurried past us, but Hannah kept hiking just as slowly as I.   9. When Hannah and I saw the group running back toward us, I was more alarmed than she.

Practice 25-8, page 391
Answers: 1. whom   3. who   5. who

Practice 25-9, page 392
Possible edits: 1. A writing tutor must know his or her way around college writing assignments.   3. Students signing up for tutoring at the writing center may not be in their first semester of college.   5. The writing-center tutor is very careful not to correct his or her students' papers.   7. Every student has to learn to catch his or her own mistakes.   9. No student gets his or her grade on a paper from a writing tutor.

Practice 25-10, page 393
Possible edits: 1. My class received their term paper grades yesterday.   3. I usually get better grades than he, but he doesn't usually fail.   5. When Gene went to the department office, the office assistant told him where to find Mr. Padilla.   7. The paper contained language that was unusual for Gene.   9. Mr. Padilla, who had typed some passages from Gene's paper into a search engine, found two online papers containing sentences that were also in Gene's paper.   11. Gene told my girlfriend and me later that he did not realize that borrowing sentences from online sources was plagiarism.   13. Anyone doing Internet research must be especially careful to document the sources, as Gene now knows.   15. Mr. Padilla will let Gene take his class again and will help him avoid accidental plagiarism, and Gene said that no one had ever been more relieved than he to hear that news.

Practice 25-11, page 394
Possible edits: 1. (1) Can a person make his or her own luck? (3) If you and I feel optimistic and in control of the future, we are more likely to have good luck. (5) Rabbit feet are common charms, but people say the feet didn't bring the rabbit any luck! (7) "Lucky" rituals are also common among students; for example, they might wear the same shirt for every test.   2. (1) In the early 1980s, a group of young Canadians who walked on stilts started a street theater group. (3) The theater group's big opportunity came in 1984, when Canada

was celebrating the 450th anniversary of its discovery. (5) The show was a big success, and today almost everyone has heard of the group, now called *Cirque du Soleil*. (7) Fans enjoy the show so much that they have to tell everyone about it. (9) No one likes this performing group more than I.

Chapter 26

Practice 26-1, page 400
Answers: 1. *Stubborn* modifies *smokers*.   3. *Typical* modifies *smoker*.   5. *Terrible* modifies *effect*.   7. *Strongly* modifies *smell*.   9. *Large* modifies *dose*.

Practice 26-2, page 402
Answers: 1. more relaxed   3. easiest   5. harder   7. closer   9. Calmer

Practice 26-3, page 404
Answers: 1. *Well* modifies *communicate*.   3. *Well* modifies *feel*.   5. *Well* modifies *see*.   7. *Well* modifies *hear*.   9. *Good* modifies *solution*.

Practice 26-4, page 404
Answers: 1. worst   3. better   5. better   7. worse   9. worse

Practice 26-5, page 406
Edits: 1. (1) One of the jobs most commonly held by teenagers is a position in a fast-food restaurant. (3) Teens will work for lower pay than many other workers, so the restaurant can keep its prices down. (5) Jobs in fast food are not glamorous, but they are plentiful; a teenager who wants to work in a fast-food restaurant can usually find a job quickly. (7) Fast-food restaurants keep large amounts of cash on hand, and this fact is known well by people who want to commit a robbery. (9) Many teenagers think that a fast-food job is a boring but harmless way to spend a summer.   2. (1) One of the most important things I've learned since starting college is to avoid waiting until the last minute to begin my work. (3) This technique worked well for me in high school. (5) I promised myself that I would do better than that in the future. (7) If a task is harder than I expected, I will arrange to ask the professor or a tutor for help. (9) If no outside help is available, I will usually put the work away for a few hours, or overnight, and start again when I feel better about my ability to concentrate.

Chapter 27

Practice 27-1, page 411
Edits: 1. I still write in a diary about all kinds of personal things and private observations.   3. Any story that is entertaining might show up in my blog.   5. Wanting the video to be funny, I had invited to the birthday party my loudest, wildest friends.   7. Unfortunately, the battery in the video recorder that Tim loaned me died.   9. I explained how I would include in the blog the funny story about the failed videotaping.

Practice 27-2, page 412
Possible edits: 1. While I was preparing a big family dinner, the oven suddenly stopped working.   3. With everyone trying to help, the kitchen was crowded.   5. Discouraged, we almost cancelled dinner.   7. Correct   9. When I returned to the crowd in the kitchen, family members still surrounded the oven.

Practice 27-3, page 413
Possible edits: 1. (1) Believing they can do nothing to make a difference in the environment, people often waste energy. (3) Bad choices, such as buying a gas-guzzling car or SUV, can have an effect too.

(5) Some products that cost more up front will save people money for many years. (7) Correct   **2.** (1) Correct (3) I am currently working on a bachelor's degree in political science and have taken nearly fifty credit hours of courses, including classes in jurisprudence, law and public policy, and business law. (5) Sometimes, while sitting in class, I dream of becoming a corporate attorney. (7) I am already planning to go on to law school, and my grade point average is in the top 10 percent of my class. (9) However, I am confident that someday I will be able to find a good-paying job.

Chapter 28

Practice 28-1, page 418
Possible answers: **1.** or   **3.** so   **5.** and   **7.** but   **9.** so

Practice 28-2, page 419
Possible edits: **1.** Many professionals use e-mail to keep in touch with clients and contacts, so businesspeople must be especially careful not to offend anyone with their e-mail messages.   **3.** Employees may have time to send personal messages from work, but they should remember that employers often have the ability to read their workers' messages.   **5.** No message should be forwarded to everyone in a sender's address book, and senders should ask permission before adding someone to a mass-mailing list.   **7.** Typographical errors and misspellings in e-mail make the message appear less professional, yet using all capital letters—a practice known as *shouting*—is usually considered even worse.   **9.** Viruses are a major problem with attachments, but no one wants to receive even a harmless attachment if it takes a long time to download.

Practice 28-3, page 421
Answers: **1.** Too much exposure to the sun can cause skin cancer; using tanning booths has similar risks.   **3.** It's easy to ignore long-term health dangers; the desire to look good is tempting.   **5.** Ultraviolet light can injure the eyes; tanning-salon patrons should always wear protective goggles.

Practice 28-4, page 422
Possible edits: **1.** Only 40 percent of mothers worked outside the home in 1970; then, the American workforce changed.   **3.** A new study shows that children of working parents don't necessarily feel neglected; in fact, they think they get to spend enough time with their mothers and fathers.   **5.** Compared with earlier generations, parents today generally have fewer children; in addition, fathers today may spend more time parenting.   **7.** For most children, their parents' jobs are not the problem; however, they want their time with their parents to be more relaxed.   **9.** Most working parents try not to give up time with their families; instead, they cut out personal time and hobbies.

Practice 28-5, page 423
Possible answers: **1.** and   **3.** ; however,   **5.** , nor   **7.** ; then,   **9.** , so

Practice 28-6, page 424
Possible edits: **1.** (1/2) Candies, hamburgers, and soft drinks all used to come in familiar, standard sizes, but now snack and fast-food companies offer many extra-large products. (3) Some nutritionists say that this trend is worrisome. (4/5) They point out that when people are offered more, they eat more; bigger portions make bigger consumers. (7/8) The company recently offered consumers a trial of super-sized pieces of a popular chocolate candy; as a result, one out of every three callers to the company asked if the candy could be made into a regular product.   **2.** (1/2) In recent years, encounters between hikers and black bears have increased, and several people have been seriously injured. (3) A few hikers have even been killed by out-of-control bears. (4/5) Bears usually try to avoid any contact with people; however, bears that associate people with food can become aggressive. (7/8) The most important tip seems obvious; it is to never feed bears or any other wild animals. (9) In addition, don't keep food in tents or leave it lying around in easy reach. (10/11) Do not burn or bury garbage, for bears will smell it and dig it up. (13/14) Coolers are not airtight, and bears often associate them with food. (15) Keep your campsite and tools clean, especially cooking and eating utensils. (16/17) Finally, report any bear damage to wildlife officials, so they can keep an eye on any bears that might be dangerous.

Chapter 29

Practice 29-1, page 430
Possible answers: **1.** because   **3.** so that   **5.** While   **7.** When   **9.** because

Practice 29-2, page 430
Possible edits: **1.** Almost all college students used typewriters until the 1980s when computers became more affordable.   **3.** Computers offer many advantages, although there are also some drawbacks.   **5.** When computers became widely used in the 1980s, professors were surprised to hear students say, "The computer ate my paper."   **7.** Some people like to print out a document to proofread it because they fail to catch all their mistakes on the screen.   **9.** Even though spell-checking programs prevent many errors, only a person is able to recognize sound-alikes such as *their* and *there*.

Practice 29-3, page 431
Completed sentences might read as follows: **1.** We have all heard stories of people who lived long lives even though they smoked, ate meat every day, and drank alcohol regularly.   **3.** Because very elderly people are unusual, scientists are studying them to learn their secrets.   **5.** While some say it may be possible to develop drugs that greatly extend our lives, many others are skeptical.   **7.** You will hear a lot of different stories if you ask very old people what they do every day to stay happy and healthy.   **9.** Before she goes to bed, she watches her favorite TV shows and has a beer.

Practice 29-4, page 432
Possible edits: **1.** (1) Correct (2/3) for example, not all manufacturers of sunscreen give expiration dates because there are no federal regulations requiring these dates on sunscreen. (5/6) Although most professionals believe it's not necessary to regularly replace a bike helmet, it's best to get a new helmet if the wearer has fallen on his or her head. (7) According to industry experts, bottled water is safe to use indefinitely when it is stored properly; but bottled water always has an expiration date because of state laws. (8/9) Car tires, which eventually start disintegrating, should be replaced within five years even though tires never have expiration dates.   **2.** (1) Most people don't expect to get a stunning view of Jupiter while they are out for a walk. (3/4) When a volunteer sidewalk astronomer sets up a telescope on a city sidewalk, anybody who comes by is invited to take a look. (5) Correct (6/7) As her grandsons gazed through the telescope, other people lined up to see for themselves. (9/10) After he sanded down a 12-inch piece of porthole glass into a reflecting telescope mirror, he made a mount for the scope out of a plywood box, some pieces of cardboard, and roof shingles. (11) Correct (12/13) When he pointed the telescope at the moon, he found that the scope made the moon's craters, mountains, and ridges appear to be right in front of him. (15/16) He wheeled the telescope around the streets of San Francisco, where he loaned it to kids and taught them how to make their own telescopes. (17) Correct

Chapter 30

Practice 30-1, page 437
Answers and possible edits: **1.** Parts that should be parallel: hunt/are taking over. Wild predators, such as wolves, are vanishing because people hunt them and take over their land.   **3.** Parts that should be parallel: varied diet/adapting easily. The success of the coyote is due to its varied diet and adaptability.   **5.** Parts that should be parallel: spreading/populate. Today, they are spreading and populating the East Coast for the first time.   **7.** Parts that should be parallel: more populated/it's not as wild as. The animals have chosen an area more populated and less wild than their traditional home.   **9.** Parts that should be parallel: identified/tracked/they captured him. One coyote was identified, tracked, and captured in Central Park in New York City.

Practice 30-2, page 438
Answers and possible edits: **1.** Parts that should be parallel: for leasing/for the purchase of one. Car dealers often require less money down for leasing a car than for purchasing one.   **3.** Parts that should be parallel: the terms of leasing/to buy. You should check the terms of leasing to make sure they are as favorable as the terms of buying.   **5.** Parts that should be parallel: by leasing/to own. You will be making less of a financial commitment by leasing a car than by owning it.   **7.** Parts that should be parallel: used car/getting a new one. A used car can be more economical than a new one.   **9.** Parts that should be parallel: a used car/buying a brand-new vehicle. A used car may not be as impressive as a brand-new vehicle.

Practice 30-3, page 439
Answers and possible edits: **1.** Paired words: neither/nor. Parts that should be parallel: had cell phones/did they want them. Fifteen years ago, most people neither had cellular telephones nor wanted them.   **3.** Paired words: rather/than. Parts that should be parallel: ban cell phones on buses and trains/being forced to listen to other people's conversations. Cell phones are not universally popular: Some commuters would rather ban cell phones on buses and trains than be forced to listen to other people's conversations.   **5.** Paired words: rather/than. Parts that should be parallel: have a cell phone/to walk to the nearest gas station. A motorist stranded on a deserted road would rather have a cell phone than be forced to walk to the nearest gas station.   **7.** Paired words: neither/nor. Parts that should be parallel: worry about radiation from cell phones/other injuries. Most Americans today neither worry about radiation from cell phones nor fear other injuries.   **9.** Paired words: both/and. Parts that should be parallel: affect people's reflexes/it might alter the brain's blood vessels. Cell phones probably do not cause brain tumors, but some experiments on human cells have shown that energy from the phones may both affect people's reflexes and alter the brain's blood vessels.

Practice 30-4, page 440
Possible edits: **1.** I could bring to this job not only youthful enthusiasm but also relevant experience.   **3.** My current job neither encourages initiative nor allows flexibility.   **5.** In college, I learned a lot both from my classes and from other students.

Practice 30-5, page 441
Possible edits: **1.** (1) Karaoke started about thirty years ago in Japan, found many fans in that country, and became a popular form of entertainment around the world. (3) Correct (5) Karaoke rooms allow customers to sing, relax, and enjoy being the center of attention for a little while. (7) Japanese karaoke singers know that they can entertain either by singing well or by singing badly.   **2.** (1) Correct (3) In the 1890s, Freud, a medical doctor by training, began studying and documenting causes of hysteria, and he discovered that many of his female patients had been sexually abused by their fathers. (5) Correct (7) But it was deeply rewarding as well, not only to Freud as a scientist but also to Freud as an individual. (9) Correct (11) Correct

Chapter 31

Practice 31-1, page 446
Edits: **1.** Once, rabies was a major threat to domestic pets in this country.   **3.** Frequently, people fail to have their pets vaccinated against rabies.   **5.** Worriedly, veterinarians note that wildlife with rabies can infect pets and people.

Practice 31-2, page 447
Possible answers: **1.** Recently   **3.** Thankfully   **5.** Unfortunately

Practice 31-4, page 448
Possible edits: **1.** Testing children's abilities to interpret facial expressions, a recent study made headlines.   **3.** The children told researchers what emotion was most obvious in each face, choosing among fear, anger, sadness, happiness, and other emotions.   **5.** All of the children in the study were equally good at identifying most emotions, responding similarly to happiness or fear.   **7.** Having learned to look for anger, the abused children protect themselves with this early-warning system.   **9.** Tending to run from anger they observe, abused children have difficulty connecting with teachers or friends who exhibit anger.

Practice 31-5, page 449
Possible answers: **1.** delaying   **3.** Striding   **5.** pointing

Practice 31-7, page 451
Possible edits: **1.** Angered by British colonial rule in 1929, the women of southern Nigeria organized a protest.   **3.** Pumped by American and other foreign oil companies, the oil often ends up in wealthy Western economies.   **5.** Polluted by the oil industry, the Nigerian countryside becomes a wasteland.   **7.** Inspired by the 1929 women's protests, local Nigerian women launched a series of protests against the oil industry in the summer of 2002.   **9.** Concerned about the women's threat to take their clothes off, many workers at the oil company told company officials that such a protest would bring a curse on the company and shame to its employees.

Practice 31-8, page 452
Possible answers: **1.** taken   **3.** Regarded   **5.** prescribed

Practice 31-10, page 453
Possible edits: **1.** Jacob Davis, a Russian immigrant working in Reno, Nevada, was the inventor of Levi's jeans.   **3.** Davis bought denim from a wholesaler, Levi Strauss.   **5.** Davis joined the firm in 1873 and supervised the final development of its product, the famous Levi's jeans.   **7.** Another choice Davis made, the curved stitching on the back pockets, also survives in today's Levi's.   **9.** During World War II, Levi Strauss temporarily stopped adding the pocket stitches because they wasted thread, a valuable resource.

Practice 31-11, page 454
Possible answers: **1.** a college freshman   **3.** a quiet, tree-lined neighborhood   **5.** a dark, cramped apartment

Practice 31-12, page 455
Possible edits: **1.** While Erin goes to classes, her baby boy stays at a day-care center, which costs Erin about $100 a week.   **3.** Occasionally, Erin's parents, who live about seventy miles away, come up and watch the baby while Erin is studying.   **5.** She feels that some of her professors who have never been parents themselves aren't very sympathetic.   **7.** Her grades, which were once straight A's, have suffered somewhat since she had her son.   **9.** Her son, who is the most important thing to her, is more important than an A in geology.

Practice 31-13, page 456
Possible answers: **1.** that was probably caused by faulty wiring   **3.** , who has always been a light sleeper,   **5.** , which was the only home I had ever lived in,

Practice 31-14, page 457

Possible edits: **1.** (1) Immunizations, which have saved countless lives in this century, have recently become controversial. (3) A few children, a very small minority, have reactions to the vaccines. (5) Worrying that vaccinations are harmful, some parents are speaking out against routine immunization. (7) Correct **2.** (1) Movies were made possible by Thomas Edison, the inventor of the motion picture camera. (3) One of the first films showed scenes of an on-coming train, which frightened audiences early in the twentieth century. (5) Correct (7) Correct (9) Called "special effects," this magic is not cheap. (11) Hollywood studios, which are corporations trying to earn a profit, spend millions to make blockbusters. (13) Correct (15) There is another kind of magic in moviemaking that makes us remember why we loved movies in the first place. (17) Correct (19) It may be small and personal, capturing our imagination or our hearts. (21) The movies we love may show us the invention of a completely new world, unimagined even by Thomas Edison.

Chapter 32

Practice 32-1, page 462

Answers and possible edits: **1.** Complete subject: the young man. At the age of twelve, the young man entered private school. **3.** Complete subject: three different schools. In fact, three different schools dismissed him. **5.** Complete subject: Albee. At the age of thirty, Albee completed his first major play. **7.** Complete subject: New York theaters. New York theaters refused to stage the play. **9.** Complete subject: *Who's Afraid of Virginia Woolf? Who's Afraid of Virginia Woolf?* is the playwright's most famous play.

Practice 32-2, page 465

Possible answers: **1.** it **3.** He **5.** my **7.** They **9.** their

Practice 32-3, page 468

Answers: **1.** had **3.** returned **5.** ran **7.** made **9.** seems

Practice 32-4, page 469

Answers: **1.** Does Tanya play with the baby? **3.** Did Shelly play her flute in the orchestra? **5.** Did David walk five miles this morning?

Practice 32-5, page 471

Answers: **1.** starting **3.** visiting **5.** sleeping **7.** eating **9.** exercising

Practice 32-6, page 472

Answers: **1.** Is Betsy golfing today? **3.** Are you going to the mall? **5.** Was Meriam eating when you arrived?

Practice 32-7, page 476

Possible answers: **1.** should **3.** might **5.** cannot **7.** should not **9.** can

Practice 32-8, page 477

Answers: **1.** Can you help me? **3.** Should they learn how to cook? **5.** Would Terrell like to join us?

Practice 32-9, page 480

Answers: **1.** have been **3.** had met **5.** had experienced **7.** had come **9.** has provided

Practice 32-10, page 481

Possible answers: **1.** Have [you] seen **3.** will convince **5.** had lost **7.** inherited **9.** would [not] have **11.** turned **13.** was running **15.** was **17.** should have been **19.** could [he] have meant

Practice 32-11, page 482

Possible answers: **1.** strap **3.** reported **5.** are looking **7.** has had **9.** have [often] struck **11.** Correct **13.** made, hiked **15.** fell, had erupted

Practice 32-12, page 485

Possible answers: **1.** to be **3.** to take **5.** Correct **7.** repeating **9.** to try

Practice 32-13, page 487

Answers: **1.** The **3.** no article **5.** the **7.** a **9.** no article

Practice 32-14, page 488

Edits: **1.** Have you ever heard of the author Jhumpa Lahiri? **3.** However, *Interpreter of Maladies* has been translated into twenty-nine different languages and became a bestseller around the world. **5.** Although Lahiri visited India many times, she felt removed from the country's culture as a child. **7.** She identified neither as an American nor as an Indian.

Practice 32-15, page 490

Edits: **1.** Of course, my classmates are aware of this trend. **3.** Correct **5.** "Hello, Seth!" he said. "Did you forget to hand in your paper in class?" **7.** "Oh," said Mr. Johnson thoughtfully. "I'm sorry about that." **9.** "Sure," said Mr. Johnson. "It will make them more responsible for their homework, anyway."

Practice 32-16, page 491

Edits: **1.** She is almost finished with her English paper and will hand it in on Friday. **3.** Correct **5.** Correct **7.** Saturday morning, she plans to sign up for a gym membership. **9.** Lucy was going to check out an event in the park on Sunday, but it has been called off. **11.** Correct

Chapter 33

Practice 33-1, page 505

Answers and possible edits: **1.** Vague or abstract words: local zoo a lot. I visit the Bronx Zoo at least twice a year. **3.** Vague or abstract words: sad; zoo in my city. Living in a cage would be painfully boring and uncomfortable, but the Bronx Zoo doesn't have cages. **5.** Vague or abstract words: some; very pretty. The zoo has two different species of birds with purple and turquoise feathers. **7.** Vague or abstract word: great. Watching the bats is like watching a creepy old movie or a thrilling air show. **9.** Vague or abstract words: a lot; information. The zoo's exhibits teach visitors about wildlife conservation.

Practice 33-2, page 506

Answers and possible edits: **1.** Slang: chew me out. I don't see why it is necessary for you to reprimand me so often. **3.** Slang: jazzed. I was really enthusiastic about the last project I worked on. **5.** Slang: sweet gig; hang around. This is a good job, and I'd like to remain here for at least another year. **7.** Slang: get into it over. Jim Hoffman and I did once have a disagreement about scheduling. **9.** Slang: talking me down. If anyone has been complaining about me, I would like to know about it.

Practice 33-3, page 507

Answers and possible edits: **1.** Wordy/repetitive language: It is a well-known fact that. Television helped Richard Nixon lose the 1960 presidential election. **3.** Wordy/repetitive language: In spite of the fact that. Although technicians encouraged Nixon to wear makeup for the debate, he refused. **5.** Wordy/repetitive language: The fact of the matter is that. Nixon did not look much better on television during his presidency from 1968 to 1974. **7.** Wordy/repetitive language: due to the fact that. He had experience standing in front of cameras because he had been an actor. **9.** Wordy/repetitive language: In this day and age/of the most paramount importance. Some people have pointed out that looking good on television is one of the most important requirements for future presidents.

Practice 33-4, page 509
Answers and possible edits: **1.** Clichés: sweat blood; work like a dog. You have to persuade yourself to devote every bit of your strength to the challenge for up to ten hours.   **3.** Clichés: the bitter end; easier said than done. Staying on your bike until the very last mile, of course, is an enormously difficult task.   **5.** Cliché: better late than never. No matter how long it takes you to cross the finish line, remind yourself that finishing at all is a tremendous achievement.   **7.** Clichés: a will of iron; keep your nose to the grindstone. It may take discipline to make yourself train, but you should continue to work hard.   **9.** Cliché: keep an eye peeled. When you train for road racing, watch carefully for cars.

Practice 33-5, page 510
Possible edits: **1.** (1) Space travel is not available to ordinary citizens now, but that situation may change. (3) Many entrepreneurs are speculating that space tourism will happen soon. (5) Only wealthy people will be able to afford half a million dollars for a cruise around the moon. (7) Correct   **2.** (1) Throughout recorded history, humans have done devastating things to the environment. (3) Because wood has a high carbon-to-hydrogen ratio, the burning of wood is a dirty and inefficient source of fuel. (5) When oil furnaces began to replace coal furnaces, the air in many cities slowly became somewhat cleaner. (7) Each year, thousands of whales were killed, until they were almost extinct. (9) However, our dependence on oil is a significant problem. (11) It is foolish to continue to use fossil fuels when scientists have shown that these fuels contribute to global warming.

Chapter 34

Practice 34-1, page 522
Answers: **1.** accept   **3.** They're; their   **5.** principles   **7.** knows; no   **9.** have; our

Practice 34-2, page 523
Possible edits: **1.** (1) More and more women are purchasing handguns, against the advice of law enforcement officers. (3) They know the risks of guns, and they accept those risks. (5) They don't want to contribute to the violence in our society, but they also realize that women are the victims of violent attacks far too often. (7) Some women have made a conscious decision to arm themselves for protection. (9) Having a gun in your house makes it three times more likely that someone will be killed there—and that someone is just as likely to be you or one of your children as a criminal. (11) Every year, there are tragic examples of children who accidentally shoot and even kill other youngsters while they are playing with guns. (13) Reducing the violence in our society may be a better solution.

Chapter 35

Practice 35-2, page 529
Possible answers: **1.** niece   **3.** believe   **5.** freight

Practice 35-3, page 530
Answers: **1.** peaceful   **3.** believing   **5.** valuable   **7.** purer   **9.** shameful

Practice 35-4, page 531
Answers: **1.** playful   **3.** comedian   **5.** defiant   **7.** burial   **9.** puffiness

Practice 35-5, page 532
Answers: **1.** lifted   **3.** commander   **5.** cheaper   **7.** spotted   **9.** scrapped

Practice 35-6, page 532
Answers: **1.** addresses   **3.** tomatoes   **5.** stretches   **7.** dashes   **9.** discovers

Practice 35-7, page 534
Answers: (1) In today's schools, there is a raging argument about whether to separate children of different abilities into classes with others of similar achievement levels. (3) These same experts state that dividing students will prejudice teachers against the slower students. (5) Basically, the experts claim, students lose all motivation to achieve. (7) They say that grouping by ability allows students to learn at a more natural rate. (9) For example, if students with similar writing skills are together in class, the teacher either can spend a lot of time with grammar if the class needs it or can skip over it if the students have mastered the basic rules. (11) Both sides have interesting, persuasive arguments that they present to local, state, and federal government officials.

Chapter 36

Practice 36-1, page 544
Answers: **1.** Continued expansion depends on our ability to promote novelty beverages such as papaya, mango, and boysenberry juices in grocery stores and restaurants.   **3.** Correct   **5.** In areas where our juice is new, we'd like increases of 10 percent, 20 percent, or 25 percent.   **7.** We want to target New England states such as Connecticut, Massachusetts, and Maine, where attitudes about fruit juice are similar to those in Seattle, Portland, and other Northwest cities.   **9.** We should set up displays, provide free samples of our juice, and sponsor contests.

Practice 36-2, page 546
Answers: **1.** Correct   **3.** She had chosen the college carefully, for it had an excellent program in physical therapy.   **5.** Correct   **7.** Correct   **9.** She didn't want to have to choose between her husband and an education, and she didn't have to.

Practice 36-3, page 547
Answers: **1.** As we all know, AIDS is spread mainly through sexual contact and through drug use that involves the sharing of needles.   **3.** Since basketball star Magic Johnson revealed in 1991 that he is HIV-positive, an NBA player must be removed from a game if he is bleeding.   **5.** Not surprisingly, many college sports follow similar rules.   **7.** According to some student athletes, mandatory HIV testing would violate their civil liberties.   **9.** Correct

Practice 36-4, page 549
Edits: **1.** Gated communities, those fancy neighborhoods with a gate at the entrance, have been part of the American landscape for years.   **3.** The terrorist attacks of 2001, the hijackings and anthrax scares, have left many people feeling insecure.   **5.** The fear of crime may, in fact, be worse than crime itself in most parts of the United States.   **7.** The criminals behind such acts, often neighborhood teenagers, may live inside the gates.   **9.** The gate, a sign of a safe community, is nothing more than that, a sign.

Practice 36-5, page 551
Edits: **1.** My mother, who has always loved music, was not a big fan of Elvis Presley when she was younger.   **3.** Correct   **5.** Correct   **7.** My mother's best friend from high school, who also attended the party, introduced her to a handsome Elvis impersonator.   **9.** My father's stage show, which now emphasizes the King's Las Vegas years, is only a little embarrassing to me.

Practice 36-6, page 553
Answers: **1.** Correct   **3.** Asked if he was losing patience, McGregor replied, "Yes, I sure am."   **5.** His wife said, "Rob, don't go

mouthing off to any reporters." **7.** An official of Value-Safe Insurance of Wrightsville, Ohio, said the company will process claims within the next few months. **9.** Correct

Practice 36-7, page 554

Answers: **1.** (1) According to etiquette experts, e-mail users need to practice good manners. (3) Not everyone appreciates receiving jokes, electronic greeting cards, and bogus virus warnings regularly. (5) E-mail is similar to a telephone call, a quick and informal way to keep in touch. (7) In addition, you should use the subject header to let the recipient know whether or not the message is important. **2.** (1) In April 1990, the book *You Just Don't Understand* was published by William Morrow in New York, New York. (3) It gives examples of how men and women misunderstand each other, and it describes the causes of and possible solutions to the differences in their language expectations. (5) Tannen writes, "Even if they grow up in the same house, girls and boys grow up in different worlds of words. (7) And although some of their play activities are similar, their favorite games are different, and their ways of using language in their games are also different." (9) Girls, on the other hand, play in small groups or pairs. (11) Later in life, these differences can cause disagreements between men and women.

Chapter 37

Practice 37-1, page 559

Answers: **1.** A person's feelings about personal space depend on his or her culture. **3.** Putting your face too close to another's is considered rude. **5.** The expression "Get out of my face!" is a warning meant to prevent the confrontation's violent conclusion. **7.** The hair on dogs' necks may stand on end. **9.** For example, seagulls' positions on a log follow a pattern similar to that of people lined up waiting for a bus.

Practice 37-2, page 561

Answers: **1.** You'll notice right away if a stranger leans over and talks to you so his face is practically touching yours. **3.** There isn't one single acceptable boundary we'd use in all situations. **5.** With coworkers, we're likely to keep a personal space of four to twelve feet. **7.** The last sixteen inches are reserved for people we're most intimate with. **9.** A supervisor who's not aware of the personal space boundaries of his or her employees might make workers uncomfortable.

Practice 37-3, page 562

Answers: **1.** I sorted letters alphabetically, starting with A's. **3.** When I checked my e-mail, the screen flashed 48's to show that I had forty-eight messages. **5.** I needed another week's time just to return all the phone calls.

Practice 37-4, page 562

Answers: **1.** (1) An astronaut goes through extreme adjustments in zero gravity. (3) The brain can't tell up from down. (5) Heartbeats can speed up and then slow down for no apparent reason. (7) The physical effects of a few weeks' space travel can imitate what a body experiences after thirty years' aging. **2.** (1) People's names often have strange stories attached to them. (3) It's actually misspelled. (5) Somehow, *The Orpah Winfrey Show* doesn't sound like a popular television program. (7) Winfrey herself is certainly not upset that she didn't end up with her parents' choice of name; her production company's name is Harpo, which is Oprah spelled backward. (9) If a clerk's a's look like o's, for example, Dana becomes Dona and Jarvis becomes Jorvis. (11) You've probably heard of names such as Candy Cane or Stormy Winters. (13) Think, for example, of a surgeon who's named Carver, or a dentist called Dr. Drill. (15) There's no way to explain any of these names except by attributing them to pure chance.

Chapter 38

Practice 38-1, page 568

Answers: **1.** "If I could quickly answer that question," the nurse replied, "I'd deserve an honorary degree in ethics." **3.** "How would you describe that dilemma?" the reporter asked the nurse. **5.** The reporter asked, "So there are times when you'd favor letting patients die on their own?" **7.** The reporter asked, "Under what circumstances should a patient be allowed to die?" **9.** "Is this a matter of deciding how to allocate scarce resources?" the reporter asked.

Practice 38-2, page 569

Answers: **1.** "Have you complained to the landlord yet?" her friend asked. **3.** Correct **5.** When Jocelyn phoned the landlord after the burglary, she said, "I know this wouldn't have happened if that lock had been installed." **7.** Correct **9.** "If I were you," the person said, "I'd let your landlord know about your plans."

Practice 38-3, page 570

Edits: **1.** In 2002, Bruce Springsteen released his first new album in years, containing songs like "Worlds Apart" that dealt with the terrorist attacks on the United States. **3.** No one made that complaint about "John Walker's Blues," a song by Steve Earle based on the story of the young American captured while fighting for the Taliban in Afghanistan. **5.** As a *Time* magazine article, "Don't Even Tell These Guys About Eminem," pointed out, the controversy was peculiar because it occurred before Earle's song had even been released, and those objecting had apparently neither heard the song nor read its lyrics.

Practice 38-4, page 571

Answers: **1.** (1) When I first read Edgar Allan Poe's "The Tell-Tale Heart," I thought it was the scariest story ever written. (3) The narrator is a murderer who knows that readers will think he's mad. (5) Correct (7) Correct **2.** (1) Correct (3) Ruiz answered, "I've always gotten bad grades, and I don't know how to get any better." (5) "I've just about given up." (7) Correct (9) I said, "There are plenty of programs to help you. (11) "Can you be a little more specific?" he asked. (13) Correct (15) "Take a look at these," I said. (17) And I don't have time." (19) I paused and then added, "Sounds to me like you're wasting the money you spent on tuition. (21) Ruiz thought for a moment, while he looked out the window, and finally told me that he'd try. (23) "I'm glad to hear it."

Chapter 39

Practice 39-1, page 578

Possible edits: **1.** (1) We already know that natural light can improve our mood; now it seems that light from the sun has other positive effects. (3) One study indicates that natural light—even on a cloudy day—can help students learn. (5) The scores improved by up to twenty-six percent, even when other factors affecting scores were taken into account. (7) The sun-filled stores had much higher sales—an average of forty percent higher. **2.** (1) More than fifty thousand domestic adoptions take place in this country each year; despite minor difficulties, most of them go smoothly. (3) Richard was in a good situation: healthy, happy, loved by the couple who had adopted him at birth. (5) They were prepared to spend years battling the case in court; they desperately wanted their son back. (7) Therefore, a few days after the baby's birth, the baby was put up for adoption—his mother didn't want him. (9) Eventually, however, the father discovered that his former girlfriend had lied; his son was still alive. (11) After years of legal arguments, the Illinois Supreme Court reached its verdict: Baby Richard belonged to the parents whose genes he shared.

Chapter 40

Practice 40-1, page 581
Answers: **1.** Correct   **3.** Almost seventy years later, in the midst of the Great Depression, Franklin Roosevelt declared, "We have nothing to fear but fear itself."

Practice 40-2, page 584
Answers: **1.** Unlike most American cities, New York has a great mass transportation system, so visitors don't need a car.   **3.** You can arrive by train at Pennsylvania Station or Grand Central Station.   **5.** There are many internationally known buildings, such as the Empire State Building.   **7.** One of the best things about the city is the restaurants, which serve food from all over the world.   **9.** Famous New Yorkers include Gwyneth Paltrow, Woody Allen, and Al Sharpton.

Practice 40-3, page 585
Answers: **1.** The American West has been a common topic in popular culture since early films like *The Big Trail*.   **3.** Television, too, relied on westerns in its early years, making *Gunsmoke* one of the longest-running shows of all time.   **5.** John Ford movies, including *The Searchers* and *She Wore a Yellow Ribbon,* popularized an image of the West.

Practice 40-4, page 585
Answers: **1.** The names and accomplishments of some presidents of the United States are familiar to almost every American.   **3.** Being president is no guarantee that a person will have lasting fame, however.   **5.** The Millard Fillmore Society celebrates his birthday every year on January 7.   **7.** Nevertheless, the facts about Fillmore are known mainly to students of history.   **9.** The candidate for president was Zachary Taylor, a hero of the Mexican War.   **11.** Taylor, who remained neutral, was elected, but he died in office, so Fillmore became president in 1850.   **13.** The newspaperman H. L. Mencken wrote a column in the *New York Evening Mail* in 1917 claiming that Fillmore had installed the White House's first bathtub.   **15.** Poor Millard Fillmore—when he is remembered at all, it is usually to be given credit for something he didn't really do.

Index

Incomplete thoughts, 284
Indefinite pronouns
    singular versus plural, 334, 378–79
    subject-verb agreement and, 333–35
Independent clauses
    colons with, 576
    definition of, 306
    semicolons to join, 575
Indirect objects, 277
Indirect quotations
    citing, 264
    definition of, 566
    punctuation for, 569–70
    research guidelines for using, 258, 259,
        260, 262–63
Infinitives. *See to* verb forms
-ing verb forms
    adjectives and, 400
    definition of, 293
    ESL concerns with, 483–85
    fragments that start with, 293–95
    misplaced modifiers and, 411
    progressive tense and, 469–72
    sentence variety using, 448–50
Internet
    citing quotations from, 264
    citing sites on, 258, 264, 266
    citing sources on, 266–67
    dictionaries on, 525
    evaluating sources on, 255–57
    exploring topics using, 38
    finding research material on, 253–54
    plagiarism and, 31
Internships, A–27
Interrupters
    commas around, 548–50
    definition of, 548
Interviews
    citing, 265, 267
    job searches and, A–34–A–38
    research using, 255
Introduction to an essay
    basics of, 80
    conclusion and, 83
    drafting, 80–82
    purpose of, 28
Introduction to an essay exam answer, A–9,
    A–11
Introductory word groups, with commas,
    546–48
Invisible writing, 35
Irregular verbs. *See also be; do; have*
    correct form and tense of, 348–55
    definition of, 324–25
    ESL concerns with, 467
    subject-verb agreement and, 324–27
it, 466
Italics, for titles, 570
its/it's, 517, 559
"It's Time I Shed My Ex-Convict Status"
    (Scanlon), 597–99

J

Job searches, A–27–A–38
    cover letters for, A–30–A–33
    interviews and, A–34–A–38
    research and, A–27
    résumés in, A–28–A–31
Journal articles, citing, 258
Journal keeping, to explore a topic,
    38–39

Journals, research using indexes and databases of, 252
just, 410
"Just Walk on By: Black Men and Public
    Space" (Staples), 690–93

K

Kenneally, Joyce, 162–63
Key words
    coherence from repetition of, 97
    essay exam questions with, 19–20, A–9
    online library catalog searches with,
        251–52
    online research with search engines using,
        254, 255–56
Kingsolver, Barbara, 619–23
knew/new/know/no, 517
know/no/knew/new, 517
Koran, 570

L

Labidou, Katilya, 4, 8
Languages, capitalization of names of, 583
Layland, Kelly, 108
Learning journal, 39
Leibov, Brad, 190–91
Lester, Jimmy, 306
Letters, apostrophes with, 562–63
Levine-Brown, Patti, A–16–A–26
Librarians and libraries, and research,
    251–52
light, 528
Linking verbs, 280–81, 282
Listing, to explore a topic, 36
Lists
    colon before, 576
    parallelism in, 436–37
    semicolons with commas in, 575
Logical order
    arranging ideas in, 67–68
    understanding, 65–66
loose/lose, 517
lose/loose, 517
Lycos, 254
-ly words, 446. *See also* Adverbs

M

Magazine articles
    capitalization of titles of, 585
    citing, 258, 266
    quotation marks for titles of, 570
    research using indexes and databases of,
        252
Magazines
    capitalization of titles of, 585
    research using indexes and databases of,
        252
    underlining or italicizing titles of, 570
Main idea. *See* Main point
Main impression, in description, 134,
    136–38
Main point. *See also* Theme statements;
    Topic sentences
    argument with, 223–24
    cause and effect with, 209–11
    checklist for evaluating, 54
    classification with, 165–67
    comparison and contrast with, 191–92
    concluding sentence referring back to, 74

conclusion referring back to, 82
    definition with, 179–80
    definition of, 41
    description with, 136–38
    illustration and, 123–24
    narration with, 109–10
    prewriting techniques for, 42
    process analysis and, 151
    reading for, 10–11
    report with, 245
    single versus multiple, 48–49
    summary with, 240
    supporting. *See* Support
    title and, 84
    thesis statement and, 41, 48–49
    topic sentence and, 27, 41, 48–49
    writing process basics and, 25
Main verb, 280
Major events, in narration, 107, 110,
    111–12
Major support. *See* Primary support
Malcom X, 625–27
Mancuso, Tony, 275
Mapping, 37
may, 474
might, 474
mind/mine, 517–18
mine/mind, 517–18
Misplaced modifiers, 410–12
    Chapter Review for, 414
    correcting, 411–12
    definition of, 410
    editing, 413–14
    understanding, 410–11
Misspelled words, common, 533 *See also*
    Spelling
MLA system, 260, 264–69
Mnemonic vocabulary cards, A–24–A–25
Modal auxiliaries (helping verbs), 472–77,
    480–83
Modern Language Association (MLA) system, 260, 264–69
Modifiers
    dangling. *See* Dangling modifiers
    definition of, 410
    misplaced. *See* Misplaced modifiers
Months
    capitalization of names of, 583
    commas with, in dates, 553
more, with comparatives, 402
Moss, David, A–1–A–15
most, with superlatives, 402
"Move Your Body, Free Your Mind" (Eller),
    80, 83, 666–68
Movies
    capitalization of titles of, 585
    citing, 267
    underlining or italicizing titles of, 570
Multiple choice tests, A–5–A–7
Murillo, Rocio, 150–51
must, 474, 476
"My Indian" (Houghton), 653–56

N

Names
    capitalization of, 582–84
    commas with, 553
Narration, 107–20
    Chapter Review for, 120
    checklist for writing, 119–20
    definition of, 107

Acknowledgments, Continued

Austin Silver. "Why Does the Media Make Men Look Stupid?" From www.AskMen.com, the Leading Men's Destination. Reprinted by permission of AskMen.com

Brent Staples. "Just Walk on By: Black Men and Public Space." Originally published in *Ms. Magazine*. Reprinted by permission of the author.

Liann Summer. "Discovery." Originally published in *Multitude: Cross-Cultural Reading for Writers* (McGraw-Hill, Inc.), edited by Chitra Banerjee Divakaruni. Copyright © Liann Summer. Reprinted by permission of the author.

Deborah Tannen. "Gender Patterns Begin at the Beginning." From *I Only Say This Because I Love You* by Deborah Tannen. Copyright © 2001 by Deborah Tannen. Used by permission of Random House, Inc.

Wallace Terry. "When His Sound Was Silenced." First published in *Parade* magazine. Copyright © 2004 by Wallace Terry. Reprinted by permission of the author and his agents, Scovil Chicak Galen Literary Agency, Inc.

Michael Thompson. "Passage into Manhood." First published in the *Boston Globe*, July 26, 2005. Copyright © 2005 by Michael Thompson. Reprinted by permission of the author. Michael Thompson is the coauthor of *Raising Cain: Protecting the Emotional Life of Boys*.

James Verini. "Supersize It." From *Slate* magazine, March 3, 2004. Copyright © 2004 James Verini. Reprinted by permission of Slate.msn.com, James Verini. This article can be found at www.slate.msn.com

Andrew Weil. "Stop the Federal War on Medical Marijuana." Originally published in the *San Francisco Chronicle*, June 6, 2002. Copyright © 2002 by Andrew Weil. Reprinted by permission of the author. Dr. Andrew Weil is a world-renowned leader and pioneer in the field of integrative medicine and a best-selling author. Dr. Weil's books include *The Natural Mind* and the national bestsellers *Spontaneous Healing, 8 Weeks to Optimum Health, Eating Well for Optimum Health, The Healthy Kitchen*, and *Healthy Aging: A Lifelong Guide to Your Physical and Spiritual Well-Being*.

Pat Wingert. "Uniforms Rule." From *Newsweek*, October 4, 1999, p. 72–74. Copyright © 1999 Newsweek, Inc. Reprinted by permission. All rights reserved.

Malcolm X. "A Homemade Education." Excerpted text from *The Autobiography of Malcolm X* by Malcolm X and Alex Haley. Copyright © 1964 by Alex Haley and Malcolm X. Copyright © 1965 by Alex Haley and Betty Shabazz. Used by permission of Random House, Inc., and John Hawkings and Associates.

Photo/Art Credits

Page 1: Robert Ullmann/Design Conceptions

Page 14: David Young-Wolff/PhotoEdit; © Robert Brenner/PhotoEdit

Page 38: Courtesy of Google. Reprinted by permission.

Page 105: David Young-Wolff/PhotoEdit

Page 118: Michael Newman/PhotoEdit

Page 130: Leadership Conference on Civil Rights Education Fund/Department of Housing and Urban Development

Page 146: Alexandra Boulat/Cosmos/AURORA

Page 159: Randy Glasbergen, randy@glasbergen.com

Page 174: © Image Source Ltd./Index Stock Imagery

Page 186: © David Jennings/The Image Works

Page 202: © Andrew Holbrooke/Corbis

Page 203: © 2005 by Consumers Union of U.S., Inc. Yonkers, NY 10703-1057, a nonprofit organization. Reprinted with permission from the February 2005 issue of CONSUMER REPORTS® for educational purposes only. No commercial use or reproduction permitted. To learn more about Consumers Union, log onto www.ConsumerReports.org.

Page 217: © Mike Thompson/*Detroit Free Press*

Page 233: © Karen Fiorito/Hard Pressed Studios

Page 237: Michael Newman/PhotoEdit

Page 256: Courtesy of Hoodia Maxx

Page 257: Mayo Foundation for Medical Education and Research. All rights reserved. Used with permission.

Page 261: © 2005 by Consumers Union of U.S., Inc. Yonkers, NY 10703-1057, a nonprofit organization. Reprinted with permission from the March 2006 issue of *Consumer Reports Money Advisor*™ for educational purposes only. No commercial use or reproduction permitted. www.ConsumerReports.org.

Page 273: Jeff Greenberg/eStock

Page 373: Michael Newman/PhotoEdit

Page 501: Joel Gordon

Page 541: Joel Gordon

Page 593: David Wells/The Image Works

Correction Symbols

This chart lists typical symbols that instructors use to point out writing problems. The explanation of each symbol includes a step you can take to revise or edit your writing. Included also are suggested chapters to check for more help and information. If your instructor uses different symbols for some errors, write them in the left-hand column for future reference.

YOUR INSTRUCTOR'S SYMBOL	STANDARD SYMBOL	HOW TO REVISE OR EDIT (NUMBERS IN BOLDFACE ARE CHAPTERS WHERE YOU CAN FIND HELP)
	adj	Use correct adjective form **26**
	adv	Use correct adverb form **26**
	agr	Correct subject-verb agreement or pronoun agreement **23; 25**
	awk	Awkward expression: edit for clarity **8**
	cap	Use capital letter correctly **40**
	case	Use correct pronoun case **25**
	cliché	Replace overused phrase with fresh words **33**
	coh	Revise paragraph or essay for coherence **8**
	combine	Combine sentences **28; 29; 31**
	con t	Correct the inconsistent verb tense **24**
	coord	Use coordination correctly **28**
	cs	Comma splice: join the two sentences correctly **22**
	d or dic	Diction: edit word choice **33**
	dev	Develop your paragraph or essay more completely **3; 5**
	dm	Revise to avoid a dangling modifier **27**
	frag	Attach the fragment to a sentence or make it a sentence **21**
	fs	Fused sentence (also known as a *run-on*): join the two sentences correctly **22**
	intro	Add or strengthen your introduction **7**
	ital	Use italics **38**
	lc	Use lowercase **40**
	mm	Revise to avoid a misplaced modifier **27**
	pl	Use the correct plural form of the verb **24**
	ref	Make pronoun reference clear **25**
	ro	Run-on sentence; join the two sentences correctly **22**
	sp	Correct the spelling error **34; 35**
	sub	Use subordination correctly **29**
	sup	Support your point with details, examples, or facts **5**
	tense	Correct the problem with verb tense **24**
	trans	Add a transition **8**
	ts	Add or strengthen your topic sentence or thesis statement **4**
	u	Revise paragraph or essay for unity **8**
	w	Delete unnecessary words **33**
	?	Make your meaning clearer **8**
	,	Use comma correctly **36**
	; : ( ) - --	Use semicolon/colon/parentheses/hyphen/dash correctly **39**
	" "	Use quotation marks correctly **38**

Useful Lists, Checklists, and Charts

Succeeding in College

Prewriting, Drafting, and Revising

Basic Features of Good Writing

Profiles of Success